Handbook of
Personality Disorders

Handbook of
Personality Disorders

Theory and Practice

Edited by

Jeffrey J. Magnavita

WILEY

John Wiley & Sons, Inc.

Library of Congress Cataloging-in-Publication Data:

Handbook of personality disorders : theory and practice / edited by Jeffrey J. Magnavita.
    p. cm.
  Includes bibliographical references and index.
  ISBN 0-471-20116-2 (cloth)
    1. Personality disorders—Handbooks, manuals, etc.   2. Personality disorders—Treatment—Handbooks, manuals, etc.   I. Magnavita, Jeffrey J.

  RC554.H357   2003
  616.85'8—dc21

                                                   2003053826

Printed in the United States of America.

10 9 8 7 6 5 4 3 2 1

*This volume is dedicated to my wife, Anne Gardner Magnavita,
and children, Elizabeth, Emily, and Caroline.*

Foreword

IT IS CRITICAL that mental health professionals have a detailed, working knowledge of the personality of the individual patient, whether the patient is presenting with symptoms, problems in relating to others, or difficulties coping with stressors and life events. The clinical community has a growing awareness of personality, its deviations, and the impact on psychotherapy (see chapter 3).

Over the years, there have been developments in the understanding and specification of the relationship between therapist and patient that fosters or hinders treatment and its outcome. The impact of patient characteristics on psychotherapy process and outcome is considerable. Long-standing patient characteristics related to personality such as attachment style, repetitive interpersonal behavior, reactance, and coping styles all significantly influence the therapeutic endeavor. Every clinician must develop a therapeutic alliance with the patient, and the nature of this alliance depends on the personality of the patient in interaction with the personality of the therapist. Relating to patients with personality difficulties is not a specialty of a few, but a clinical skill needed by all.

In academic psychology, there is a rich history of the study of personality. Enduring issues in that academic tradition that are relevant to the pursuit of such issues in clinical psychology and psychiatry are the conceptualization and definition of personality, the relative influence on personality of nature and nurture, persistence and change in personality features, and emphasis on conscious versus unconscious processes. The mutual contact and fertilization between this academic tradition and clinical work has been variable and sporadic. There is an obvious parallel between the major theories of personality and the dominant theories of personality disorder These theories need further development as the research unfolds.

With the introduction of *DSM-III* in 1980, it has become commonplace in clinical work and psychotherapy research to distinguish between patients with and without personality disorders. This "official" recognition of the difference between symptom conditions and abnormality in the personality itself has given legitimacy to the investigation of personality disorders in their own right, and has alerted clinicians to the need to assess both symptom conditions and personality dysfunction. Armed with this helpful but somewhat arbitrary and oversimplified distinction, clinicians have been aware that they are treating symptomatic patients with and without co-existing personality disorders, and researchers have gathered empirical outcome data on these treatments. It has become evident in the empirical literature that the treatment of symptoms in the context of personality disorders is more complicated, slower, and less effective than the treatment of symptomatic patients without personality disorders (see chapter 23).

Our current diagnostic system—*DSM-IV*—is better at describing the indicators of the presence of a personality disorder than it is in describing the different constellations of personality disorder or dysfunction. In the diagnostic system, the overall description of a personality disorder is the presence of serious and chronic interference in cognition and emotion regulation that affects functioning in the domains of work and interpersonal relationships. Thus, chronic dysfunction in relationships and work is the hallmark and final common pathway of the personality disorders. These deficits must be clear before the clinician considers the specific type or constellation of personality disorder category.

Clinicians are attuned to deficits and dysfunction in work and relationships, but often find the specific types of personality disorder as described currently in *DSM-IV* as a mixture of feelings, attitudes, behaviors and symptoms, insufficient for describing the patients' personalities and for treatment planning. This dissatisfaction and alternative ways of describing personality difficulties for intervention are grappled with in this volume, especially in chapters 2 and 5 in section 1.

The identification of individuals with personality difficulties begins with the assessment of work functioning and the nuances of interpersonal relations. However, that is a somewhat gross indication, and the task for the therapist is to arrive at a conceptualization of the current functional characteristics of the patient that, if changed, would lead to improvement in the individual's life. The conceptualization of mechanisms of personality dysfunction orient the clinician directly to the target of treatment. This is the leading edge of clinical work. How does the therapist assess and conceptualize the active and repetitive functions of the individual that are directly related to dysfunctional personality and personality organization? Does the clinician assess personality traits (chapter 4), the social cultural context (chapters 6 and 7), and/or how the personality itself is organized (chapter 5)? Indeed, without theory we are in a sea of observations and facts that do not adequately guide the clinician (chapter 3), either in assessment or in the choice of focus of treatment. The much touted atheoretical orientation of *DSM-IV* has lead to some of the serious difficulties with *DSM-IV* Axis II.

This volume rightfully assumes that targeted and thorough assessment logically leads to planned interventions (section 2). The treatment of personality disorders specifically is difficult and fraught with problems. Progress on the treatment of symptom conditions depends upon the personality and personality traits of the patient; cooperativeness with the therapist, and focus and persistence on the work of the therapy are major considerations. This therapeutic work becomes even more complex and difficult when the patient has the characteristics of those designated as having a personality disorder. What are the mechanisms of change, and, related to that, what are the foci of the therapists' interventions when treating patients with personality difficulties/disorders?

Should the primary focus be on working models of relationships (chapter 8), automatic thoughts and cognitive distortions (chapter 9), developing skills (chapter 11), and/or problematic relationship patterns (chapter 12)? Of course, these foci of therapeutic intervention are not mutually exclusive, and some of them seem to be touching on the same reality but with different metaphors and terminology. There is a growing consensus toward a focus on the patients' characteristic ways of attending to and processing information on the interaction between self and others. Thus, this volume is informative on the foci of interventions in general (section 2) and with special populations and settings (section 3).

Related to the focus of therapist intervention, is the question of treatment goals. Is the goal of treatment the amelioration of symptoms (e.g., reduction of situational depression in an individual with narcissistic personality disorder) or change in behaviors (e.g., reduction of parasuicidal behavior in borderlines) of those with personality disorders, or is it more directly to change the organization of the personality itself? This is an unresolved issue, and each author in this volume addresses the goal of treatment. The way in which each theoretician and clinician answers this question relates to a whole complex of issues, involving managed care and the clinician's conception of the existence and nature of personality, and whether or not personality can be changed. In a very practical way, the answer to this question relates to the duration of treatment.

There is much written today about evidence based treatment planning, and matching patient diagnosis with treatment packages that have been empirically investigated as compared to treatment as usual. Evidence based approaches to treatment planning are presented as definitive, but leave many details unaccounted for: the uniqueness of the patients who are more than their diagnosis, the aspects of the patients unrelated to diagnosis that affect the therapeutic relationship, the unique relationship qualities of the therapist, the social milieu of the patient, to name a few. The data on the treatment of personality disorders is too meager to approach evidence based treatment planning, which makes the value of this volume of even greater value to the practicing clinician.

The practitioner needs an expert guide through the winding paths and thickets of a new and developing field such as personality disorders. Jeffrey Magnavita is both a theoretician and clinician with many years of experience with this patient population. He has skillfully constructed and edited this volume, bringing together a number of thoughtful experts who highlight the unique aspects of treatment planning with patients with personality disorders. Each of the authors expands our horizon in thinking about personality and personality dysfunction, combining clinical experience with empirical data. These authors are pioneers, as the development of assessment and treatment of personality disorders is in its infancy compared to comparable efforts in the treatment of symptom conditions.

JOHN F. CLARKIN, PhD

Preface

THE INSPIRATION FOR this volume emerged from my work over the past 20 years conducting psychodiagnostic assessments and practicing psychotherapy with children, adolescents, adults, and the elderly, first in an inpatient and then outpatient settings. What struck me was that across the spectrum of individuals and families that I encountered presenting with complex clinical syndromes was how many struggled with self-defeating and self-destructive personality patterns that were so difficult to impact with standard methods and techniques. With most clinicians, as it is with me, the compelling force that drives us is to reduce human suffering, and we often gain an understanding of our own suffering and developmental challenges. During a crisis or a major life transition, many have experienced personality "dysfunction," but for most, this is short lived. Yet, for many others, as addressed in this volume, these patterns or systems are often entrenched, enduring, and chronically dysfunctioning. These dysfunctioning systems cause much disruption to the individual, family, and society. Attempting to understand this complex phenomenon that clinicians are faced with daily is challenging, fascinating, and often daunting. It is my hope that this volume clarifies some of these challenges and adds to our hope. It seems clear that the phenomenon we are dealing with, whether symptoms of clinical syndromes or relational disturbance, rests on the integrity of the personality system. If the personality system is not functioning especially well, trouble looms, symptom complexes emerge, and relationships falter. Clinical syndromes and symptom complexes are expressed sometimes somatically or psychologically but always in the relational matrix. In my diverse clinical work with individuals, couples, families, and groups, it has been clear to me that there is one central system that informs the way in which we conceptualize psychopathology; understand intrapsychic, interpersonal, and family functioning; and formulate our psychotherapeutic strategies. This central organizing system is personality. Although personality has been primarily conceptualized as housed in the individual or *self-system,* theoretical advances over the past century have underscored the necessity of expanding our conceptual field to other domains such as the interpersonal (dyadic), triadic (threesomes), and larger family and social systems that form the entire ecological system or biosphere.

When the personality system is vulnerable or not operating effectively at any of the biopsychosocial domains, the system becomes *dys*functional. When the level of adaptive functioning meets appropriate diagnostic criteria, a personality *disorder* is diagnosed. The diagnostic category and label personality *disorder* is not necessarily the best way to classify what we experience in relationships and observe clinically, as it is necessarily reductionistic. It is, however, what we have at this phase in the development of the field and some consider the state of the art. I prefer the term *personality dysfunction*, but many others represented in this volume may not agree. For some individuals, personality dysfunction is something that affects their lives but that they suffer in silence and may go undetected, except by those in immediate proximity such as spouses, partners, children, and coworkers. These individuals have been termed *neurotic* characters in the past. Yet others show more dramatic signs and may be stuck in chronic maladaptive patterns that cause severe suffering as well as having major impact on the family and society. These patterns are often referred to as the *severe* personality disorders. Couples and families may have faltering personality systems that can result in what I have termed *dysfunctional personologic systems* that can transmit this dysfunction from one generation to another, often downward spiraling, unless intervention takes place.

Personality has been an interest to humankind since we became conscious and able to "observe" ourselves. Over the past century of modern behavioral science, personality and its disorders has been a subject of interest to many disciplines including anthropologists, primatologists, academic psychologists, psychopathologists, clinical psychiatrists, and psychologists, and, more recently, neuroscientists. We are entering a new phase of the field where interdisciplinary collaboration and advances in fields such as neuroscience may help us map human consciousness and develop efficient, effective, and accelerated treatments for even the most refractory of these dysfunctional systems.

Theories, methods, and techniques have been developed to address these faltering or dysfunctioning personality systems. Many of these models presented in this volume offer a rich array of conceptual systems, approaches, and therapeutic stances. In spite of all these remarkable developments, we should not forget about the importance of the therapeutic relationship, which tends to be given a back seat as we head toward an era of *empirically validated treatments* (EVTs) and the concomitant pressure to produce treatment manuals. Although they can be useful, we should not forget that our endeavor is complex and human to human, requiring clinical intuition and a genuine desire to alleviate human suffering.

PURPOSE OF THIS VOLUME

This volume provides the latest information to clinicians who are treating personality dysfunction or disorders of personality, students who are interested in the topic, and others such as theorists and researchers. A goal was for each contributor to provide as much in the way of clinical utility as possible. Therefore, the book focuses primarily on theory, which is essential, and methods and techniques of practice. *The approaches, methods, and techniques presented in this volume are for professional purposes and should be used only by qualified mental health clinicians and, in some cases, require additional training and supervision.* For those primarily interested in research, other excellent volumes are available on the topic and may be used in conjunction with this one. In rapidly advancing fields such as personality, personality disorders, psychotherapy, and psychopathology, it is impossible to present a comprehensive overview of these interrelated areas in a single volume. However, the reader will appreciate the selective and in-depth treatment of the topic with special emphasis on theory and practice. Another goal of this volume is to present the spectrum of approaches that remain contemporaneous in that they continue to evolve and have clinical utility as well as many newer ones that hold promise. There are many similarities in the approaches presented in this volume, yet there are some approaches that remain highly divergent and offer the reader contrasting viewpoints with which to consider the clinical phenomenon. Another goal is to provide a sample of some of the cutting edge applications of treatment approaches using various methods, techniques, and modalities creatively and apply these to other populations not previously considered as a focus of intervention.

OUTLINE OF VOLUME

This volume is divided into five sections. The first section, Etiology, Theory, Psychopathology, and Assessment, begins with some of the fundamental conceptual theoretical bulwark for the topic and exposes the reader to some of the challenges and controversies around conceptualizing, diagnosing-labeling, and assessing personality.

The next section, Contemporary Psychotherapeutic Treatment Models, presents a number of current approaches to treating personality dysfunction. It is interesting that the majority of these models are primarily used individually. The modality of individual psychotherapy has been the mainstay for treatment delivery, but newer models delivered in couples, family, and group treatment modalities are beginning to emerge.

The third section, Broadening the Scope of Treatment: Special Populations and Settings, offers readers a sample of some of the groundbreaking work being done by contemporary workers who are applying technological and theoretical innovations to those populations with co-occurring personality dysfunction who are underserved and difficult to treat, such as substance abusers, medical patients, and the severely disturbed, who often require day treatment and inpatient hospitalization. This cutting edge work represents a growing interest in modifying and discovering methods that can assist clinicians as well as ways of conceptualizing the role of memory and trauma in the development and maintenance of these dysfunctioning personality systems.

The fourth section, Expanding the Range of Treatment: Child, Adolescent, and Elderly Models, presents the extension of treatment paradigms to children and adolescents as well as the elderly. In this section, leading figures explore the edges of diagnostic knowledge and add substantially to our understanding of these often difficult-to-reach developmental phases that have been virtually overlooked in the past. Often because of the controversy surrounding labeling, these phases have not received the consideration of theorists, practitioners, and researchers, although this is beginning to slowly change as these topics are opened for discussion.

The final section, Research Findings and Future Challenges, presents a cogent summary of the extant, albeit limited, research findings on personality disorders and then explores an emerging theoretical movement toward unified treatment. The model for this treatment, which I consider the next wave of development in personality and psychotherapy—beyond integration—should stir some polemics.

FINAL ACKNOWLEDGMENTS

I am very fortunate to have had the opportunity to collaborate on this volume with some of the leading figures in the fields of personality disorders, psychotherapy, research, and pharmacotherapy. The contributors to this volume represent some of the most forward, innovative thinkers and courageous pioneers of approaches developed from their interest in alleviating human suffering and their commitment and passion for clinical work. All contributors toiled on their chapters to bring the material to the readers in a clinically relevant way. I thank them for their devotion to this task.

I would like to express my appreciation to Dr. John Clarkin, one of the leading figures in the field, whose work I have absorbed even though it has become a part of my procedural memory and thus is not adequately cited. Dr. Clarkin graciously agreed to read this volume and write the Foreword. This is a task that no one looks forward to after a tiring day of clinical practice, research, writing, and supervision. For his generosity, I am indebted and very grateful.

I also want to express my appreciation to all those at John Wiley & Sons who have supported this endeavor and for their belief in the value of a volume of this nature. Special thanks are due to Peggy Alexander and Isabel Pratt for shepherding this volume through the stages of development necessary to bring the final product to the reader.

Last, but most important to me, is my tremendous appreciation to my wife, Anne Gardner Magnavita, who edited the final drafts of my chapters and who always seems to understand and support the demands of my work and professional life and seemingly endless writing projects.

JEFFREY J. MAGNAVITA

Contents

About the Editor   xvii

Contributors   xix

SECTION ONE   ETIOLOGY, THEORY, PSYCHOPATHOLOGY, AND ASSESSMENT

1. Classification, Prevalence, and Etiology of Personality Disorders:
   Related Issues and Controversy   3
   Jeffrey J. Magnavita
2. Psychopathologic Assessment Can Usefully Inform Therapy:
   A View from the Study of Personality   24
   Theodore Millon and Seth D. Grossman
3. The Relevance of Theory in Treating Personality Dysfunction   56
   Jeffrey J. Magnavita
4. Assessing the Dimensions of Personality Disorder   78
   Philip Erdberg
5. Borderline Personality Disorder and Borderline Personality
   Organization: Psychopathology and Psychotherapy   92
   Otto F. Kernberg
6. Personality Disorder or Relational Disconnection?   120
   Judith V. Jordan
7. Sociocultural Factors in the Treatment of Personality Disorders   135
   Joel Paris

SECTION TWO   CONTEMPORARY PSYCHOTHERAPEUTIC TREATMENT MODELS

8. Interpersonal Reconstructive Therapy (IRT) for Individuals
   with Personality Disorder   151
   Lorna Smith Benjamin
9. Cognitive Therapy of Personality Disorders   169
   James Pretzer
10. The Treatment of Personality Adaptations Using
    Redecision Therapy   194
    Vann S. Joines
11. Dialectical Behavior Therapy of Severe Personality Disorders   221
    Clive J. Robins and Cedar R. Koons

12. Time-Limited Dynamic Psychotherapy 254
    Hanna Levenson

13. Close Process Attention in Psychoanalytic Psychotherapy 280
    Frank Knoblauch

14. Application of Eye Movement Desensitization and
    Reprocessing (EMDR) to Personality Disorders 304
    Philip Manfield and Francine Shapiro

SECTION THREE   BROADENING THE SCOPE OF TREATMENT: SPECIAL
POPULATIONS AND SETTINGS

15. Pharmacotherapy of Personality Disorders 331
    Robert Grossman

16. Day Treatment of Personality Disorders 356
    John S. Ogrodniczuk and William E. Piper

17. Residential Treatment of Personality Disorders:
    The Containing Function 379
    Barri Belnap, Cuneyt Iscan, and Eric M. Plakun

18. Treatment of Personality Disorders with Co-occurring
    Substance Dependence: Dual Focus Schema Therapy 398
    Samuel A. Ball

19. Personality-Guided Therapy for Treating Medical Patients 426
    Ellen A. Dornelas

20. The Role of Trauma, Memory, Neurobiology, and the Self in
    the Formation of Personality Disorders 443
    Mark R. Elin

SECTION FOUR   EXPANDING THE RANGE OF TREATMENT: CHILD,
ADOLESCENT, AND ELDERLY MODELS

21. Treatment of Dramatic Personality Disorders in
    Children and Adolescents 467
    Efrain Bleiberg

22. Treatment of Personality Disorders in Older Adults:
    A Community Mental Health Model 498
    Rosemary Snapp Kean, Kathleen M. Hoey, and Stephen L. Pinals

SECTION FIVE   RESEARCH FINDINGS AND FUTURE CHALLENGES

23. Empirical Research on the Treatment of Personality Disorders 513
    Paul Crits-Christoph and Jacques P. Barber

24. Toward a Unified Model of Treatment for Personality Dysfunction 528
    Jeffrey J. Magnavita

Author Index 555

Subject Index 567

About the Editor

JEFFREY J. MAGNAVITA, PHD, ABPP, FAPA, is a licensed psychologist and marriage and family therapist in active clinical practice. A Diplomate of the American Board of Professional Psychology and Fellow of the American Psychological Association, he is the nominee or recipient of many awards for his work in the practice and theory of psychotherapy and personality disorders, on which he speaks at the national level. He is the founder of Glastonbury Psychological Associates, PC, and the Connecticut Center for Short-Term Dynamic Psychotherapy and is an adjunct professor of clinical psychology at the University of Hartford and lecturer at Smith College of Social Work. He authored *Restructuring Personality Disorders: A Short-Term Dynamic Approach; Relational Therapy for Personality Disorders*, and a text; *Theories of Personality: Contemporary Approaches to the Science of Personality* and was the volume editor of the *Comprehensive Handbook of Psychotherapy: Psychodynamic/Object Relations: Volume 1* and has extensive publications in the field. He is affiliate medical staff at a number of Hartford, Connecticut, area hospitals, where he consults and conducts training. He is an active member of the International Society for the Study of Personality Disorders, Society for Psychotherapy Research, New York Academy of Science, and Society for the Exploration and Integration of Psychotherapy and a founding member of the International Institute of Experiential Short-Term Dynamic Psychotherapy.

Contributors

Samuel A. Ball, PhD
Department of Psychiatry
Yale University School of Medicine
West Haven, Connecticut

Jacques P. Barber, PhD
Center for Psychotherapy Research
Department of Psychiatry
University of Pennsylvania
Philadelphia, Pennsylvania

Barri Belnap, MD
Erickson Institute of the Austen
   Riggs Center
Stockbridge, Massachusetts

Lorna Smith Benjamin, PhD, FDHC
Professor of Psychology
University of Utah
Salt Lake City, Utah

Efrain Bleiberg, MD
Medical Director
Professionals in Crises Program
Menninger Clinic
Professor and Director
Division of Child and Adolescent
   Psychiatry
Psychiatry Department of Psychiatry and
   Behavioral Sciences
Baylor College of Medicine
Houston, Texas

Paul Crits-Christoph, PhD
Center for Psychotherapy Research
Department of Psychiatry
University of Pennsylvania
Philadelphia, Pennsylvania

Ellen A. Dornelas, PhD
Director of Behavioral Health Programs
Preventive Cardiology, Hartford Hospital

Hartford, Connecticut
Assistant Professor of Clinical Medicine
University of Connecticut School of
   Medicine
Farmington, Connecticut

Mark R. Elin, PhD, ABPN
Assistant Professor of Psychiatry
Tutts University School of Medicine
Baystate Medical Center
Springfield, Massachusetts

Philip Erdberg, PhD
Assistant Clinical Professor
University of California
San Francisco, California

Robert Grossman, MD
Assistant Professor of Psychiatry
Medical Director, Traumatic Stress
   Treatment Program
Mt. Sinai School of Medicine
New York, New York

Seth D. Grossman, PsyD
Institute for Advanced Studies in
   Personology and Psychopathology
Coral Gables, Florida

Kathleen M. Hoey, LICSW
Senior Clinical Social Work Supervisor
   and Clinical Team Leader
Geriatric Service
Department of Psychiatry
Cambridge Health Alliance
Cambridge, Massachusetts

Cuneyt Iscan, MD
Erickson Institute of the Austen
   Riggs Center
Stockbridge, Massachusetts

Vann S. Joines, PhD
President and Director of the Southeast
    Institute for Group and Family Therapy
Chapel Hill, North Carolina

Judith V. Jordan, PhD
Assistant Professor
Harvard Medical School
Co-Director
Jean Baker Miller Training Institute
Wellesley College
Wellesley, Massachusetts

Rosemary Snapp Kean, MS, RNCS
Clinical Team Leader
Geriatric Service
Department of Psychiatry
Cambridge Heath Alliance
Cambridge, Massachusetts

Otto F. Kernberg, MD
New York Presbyterian Hospital,
    Westchester Division
White Plains, New York

Frank Knoblauch, MD
Western New England Institute for
    Psychoanalysis
Assistant Clinical Professor of Psychiatry
University of Connecticut School of
    Medicine
Farmington, Connecticut

Cedar R. Koons, MSW
Private Practice
Santa Fe, New Mexico

Hanna Levenson, PhD
Director, Brief Psychotherapy Program
Psychiatry Department
California Pacific Medical Center
Director, Levenson Institute for Training
    (LIFT)
San Francisco, California

Philip Manfield, PhD
Private Practice
Berkeley, California

Theodore Millon, PhD, DSc
Institute for Advanced Studies in
    Personology and Psychopathology
Coral Gables, Florida

John S. Ogrodniczuk, PhD
Department of Psychiatry
University of British Columbia
Vancouver, British Columbia, Canada

Joel Paris, MD
Professor of Psychiatry
McGill University
Quebec, Canada

Stephen L. Pinals, MD
Assistant Director of Geriatric Psychiatry
Director of the Geriatric Psychiatry
    Fellowship Program
Cambridge Health Alliance
Psychiatry Instructor
Harvard Medical School
Cambridge, Massachusetts

William E. Piper, PhD
Department of Psychiatry
University of British Columbia
Vancouver, British Columbia, Canada

Eric M. Plakun, MD
Erickson Institute of the Austen
    Riggs Center
Stockbridge, Massachusetts

James Pretzer, PhD
Cleveland Center for Cognitive Therapy
Beachwood, Ohio
Case Western Reserve University
Cleveland, Ohio

Clive J. Robins, PhD
Department of Psychiatry and Behavioral
    Sciences
Department of Psychology: Social and
    Health Sciences
Duke University
Durham, North Carolina

Francine Shapiro, PhD
Senior Research Fellow
Mental Research Institute
Palo Alto, California

ETIOLOGY, THEORY, PSYCHOPATHOLOGY, AND ASSESSMENT

Classification, Prevalence, and Etiology of Personality Disorders: Related Issues and Controversy

Jeffrey J. Magnavita

W E STAND POISED at the edge of a remarkable new era in contemporary clinical psychology. Multiple related scientific disciplines intersect at a point of important mutual interest—*the effective treatment of personality systems*—especially for those systems that are poorly functioning and/or inefficiently adapting to the requirements of contemporary society. Such systems comprise what clinical scientists call *personality disorders.* Personality and its disordered or dysfunctional states have been of interest to humankind since the early stages of civilization probably coinciding with the birth of consciousness or the point at which we could reflect upon our "self." As soon as we became conscious of the existence of the "self" and aware of the "other," we wanted to know what made us tick and what was happening with those around us; adaptation and survival would have depended, in part, on this kind of insight. Evolutionary processes have certainly shaped our wide array of personality adaptations, styles, and disorders, and will continue to do so.

Evidence of an interest in personality and psychopathology can be seen in earliest documented history. The early Egyptians were fascinated by a possible link between the uterus and emotional disorders, which the Greeks later called *hysteria* (Alexander & Selesnick, 1966; Stone, 1997). This clinical syndrome became a major impetus in the development of Freud's system of psychoanalysis, which is considered by many to be one of the main intellectual milestones of the twentieth century (Magnavita, 2002a; Wepman & Heine, 1963). Earlier efforts in the late nineteenth century were made to understand the etiology of and treatment for hysteria, which posed a scientific and clinical challenge to the major pioneers in medicine, psychology, and psychiatry. Jean Charcot (1889) devoted much of his scientific career to documenting this disorder. Using the newly discovered art of photography, he captured haunting images of this often grotesque disturbance.

Charcot also experimented with various forms of treatment, most notable of which was hypnosis. His interest in psychopathology, along with that of others such as Emil Kraepelin (1904), the great classifier of mental disorders, initiated modern nosology, much of which is still in use in current day diagnostic systems.

The study of personality is fueled by our relentless interest in knowing ourselves and has resulted in various theoretical systems. The most familiar of these is the four humors of the Greeks (Magnavita, 2002b), elements of which are still seen in some contemporary biological and psychological theories (Davis & Millon, 1999). Our interest in self-understanding and the theories associated with it converged with a fascination in the pathological states of adaptation that have plagued humankind from the time of documented history. Humans have always shown a desire to alleviate the suffering of those who experience mental disorders. The early Egyptians developed a system of treatment based on soul-searching on the part of ill patients (Alexander & Selesnick, 1966). The use of the word *psychotherapy* was first seen in the writings of Hippolyte Bernheim (1891) in his work entitled, *Hypnotisme, Suggestion, Psychotherapie* (Jackson, 1999). There has been great progress in developing personality theory, in understanding and classifying psychopathology, and in pioneering new methods of treatment for those suffering with disorders of personality, but developing cost-efficient and effective forms of treatment remains a challenge. This chapter presents some of the basic background information on classification, etiology, and prevalence of personality disorders and reviews some constructs and useful theoretical developments to guide you through the remainder of this volume. We begin with the classification of personality. How we categorize and label the clinical phenomenon has major implications for researchers and clinicians; there are multiple perspectives and approaches to consider.

CLASSIFICATION OF PERSONALITY

The classification of personality is a problematic area that has not been sufficiently resolved at this stage in development of the science of personality. Classification is a topic that can result in heated debates about what is, and what is not, a personality disorder and what the optimal treatment should be and how it should be delivered. Once a diagnosis is established, decisions must be made concerning "differential therapeutics" (Frances, Clarkin, & Perry, 1984): (1) *treatment format*—long-term, intermittent, intensive short-term, supportive; (2) *type/model*—cognitive, behavioral, interpersonal, psychodynamic, integrative, pharmacological; (3) *modalities*—group, individual, family, couples, mixed, sequential and; (4) *setting*—hospital, outpatient, partial, residential. The permutations seem overwhelming!

During one recent seminar, a participant raised his hand and announced that the cases being presented were not "truly personality disordered." A heated disagreement ensued regarding the diagnosis that the patient had been given. Even well-trained and experienced clinicians often disagree about what constitutes a "genuine" personality disorder. We all long for clear, meaningful diagnostic guidelines, potent treatment alternatives, and positive and preferably rapid outcomes. What we have to contend with in clinical reality is not nearly so clear, is often confusing, and lacks simple algorithms to help us neatly plot our course. Thus, what we do remains more a clinical art than a science. The models that clinicians adopt to depict patient systems and communicate via metaphorical language are often novel and flexible. Our models offer a way to organize the data, understand the phenomenology, and indicate the possibility of a "cure." Our primary concern is a way out for the patient who is suffering and the suffering of those others in his or her lives. Many of the dominant contemporary models are presented in this volume for you to study and possibly to incorporate into your clinical practice.

Personality disorder is first and foremost a *construct* that social and clinical scientists use in an attempt to deal with the complex phenomenon that results when the personality system is not functioning optimally. Some believe the construct should be jettisoned altogether and does more harm than good (Jordan, this volume, chapter 6). Is there any such thing as a personality disorder in reality? Those practitioners who have been in clinical practice can attest that there are certain individuals who demonstrate a capacity to engage in behavior that is clearly self-destructive, self-defeating, and self-sabotaging. Even when we *can* identify an inadequately functioning personality system, the challenges of measuring its severity and choosing a treatment approach must be tackled. We must account for the clinical reality that patients cut and mutilate themselves, use excessive amounts of substances to numb them, create chaos in their communities and families, and so forth. Personality remains a useful coherent construct to understand these and other disturbing phenomenon.

We find that, even with the best intentions on all sides, certain types of personality "dysfunction" are very difficult to modify or transform. So the term *personality disorder*, in spite of the stigma associated with conferring this label on another, does have clinical utility. This construct has remained a focus of attention for modern psychology for over a century, even though it had fallen in and out of vogue in some circles. It does seem to account for a clinical phenomenon that has not been replaced by a more useful construct. As this volume attests, most of the leading clinicians and theorists in the field choose to use the construct, with all its limitations. There are exceptions, such as Jean Baker Miller and Judith Jordan (Frager & Fadiman, 1998) from the Stone Center, who eschew pathological labeling as pejorative and demeaning. We return to this important issue later in this chapter.

What is a personality disorder? Before we try to answer this important question, we should first explore a related question, *What is personality?* As clinicians, theorists, and researchers, we are treating and studying people with unique personalities, although possibly poorly functioning, or functioning at any of the various levels of adaptive capacity. One definition of personality is "an individual's habitual way of thinking, feeling, perceiving, and reacting to the world" (Magnavita, 2002b, p. 16). There are problems with this classic textbook perspective drawn from academic psychology of the last century: with the focus on personology, which primarily investigates individual differences (Murray, 1938), it leaves the rest of the ecological matrix in the hands of sociologists, anthropologists, and social psychologists. This *individualistic* definition of personality is one whose primary focus is clearly on the individual personality system. As such, this definition is limiting and antiquated, especially if we, as we must, acknowledge that human personality is expressed within a context, an intrapsychic, dyadic, triadic, familial, sociopolitical, cultural, and ecological matrix. The components of this matrix are in an ongoing interaction, shaping and influencing the various subsystems, in multiple and complex feedback loops. To prepare ourselves for the challenges we are facing at the beginning of the new millennium, such as developing effective treatment for underserved minority groups, the elderly, substance abusers, severe personality dysfunction, and many others, we need to expand our perspective of personality from the individual system to the subsystems that operate within the total ecological system (Magnavita, in press). This requires an interdisciplinary collaboration among related scientific disciplines concerned with the study of human nature, relational science, neuroscience, affective science, the study of consciousness and personality (Magnavita, 2002b).

Does a personality disorder exist? The answer to this question depends on whom you ask. If you ask a clinical researcher who is trained to use empirical measures, a personality disorder represents a score on an objective measure that exceeds a statistically significant cut-off point or a designated score on a structured interview. With a score above the point, the clinician would say a personality disorder exists, and below it a disorder is not present. A psychopathologist might define the presence or absence of a personality disorder based on whether there exists a "harmful dysfunction" (Wakefield, 1999) or, in their terms, is the patient demonstrating signs of an *evolutionary maladaptive behavioral repertoire?* A clinician might look for whether there are long-standing, self-defeating aspects to the individual's interpersonal patterns, and whether there is an over-reliance on primitive defenses (Magnavita, 1997; McWilliams, 1994). A family clinician might be more interested in deciding how the individual or family's organization and function influences maladaptive or dysfunctional processes. A psychopharmacologist might investigate the response to various psychotropic medications. A forensic psychologist or psychiatrist would be interested in the results of a battery of objective and standardized tests, in-depth clinical interviews, and history that would support a diagnosis likely to be held to legal standards of evidence. The answer depends on the orientation of the professional answering the question, as well as the system or systems of classification that he or she employs, and has the most utility for the task on which they embark, such as producing academic papers, conducting epidemiological research or a forensic evaluation, planning clinical treatment, engaging in psychopathological research, and so forth.

There are various systems of classification that include (1) *categorical*, (2) *dimensional*, (3) *structural*, (4) *prototypal*, and (5) *relational*. They each have strengths and certain limitations. Each has a perspective and offers one view of reality.

1. CATEGORICAL CLASSIFICATION

The categorical classification is used predominantly by psychotherapists in research. For many clinicians, it is required to complete insurance forms for reimbursement of clinical services. The predominant categorical system for classification of personality disorders and other clinical syndromes is the *Diagnostic and Statistical Manual of Mental Disorders* (*DSM-IV*) published by the American Psychiatric Association (APA, 1994). The *DSM* defines personality disorder as: "an enduring pattern of inner experience and behavior that deviates markedly from the expectations of the individual's culture, is pervasive and inflexible, has an onset in adolescence or early adulthood, is stable over time, and lead to distress or impairment" (APA, 1994, p. 629). The multiaxial *DSM* has been a major development in the classification of personality disorders, particularly in its emphasis on placing personality disorders on their own axis—the second axis. The categorical system relies on establishing the presence of behaviorally observable and atheoretical criteria that indicate the presence of a diagnosable personality disorder. *DSM* categorizes personality disorders into three clusters, A, B, and C, as follows:

1. *Cluster A* is characterized by odd or eccentric behavior and includes paranoid, schizoid, and schizotypal personalities. This cluster tends to be the most treatment refractory and is probably the most likely to have underlying biogenetic factors.
2. *Cluster B* is characterized by erratic, emotional, and dramatic presentations and includes antisocial, borderline, histrionic, and narcissistic personalities. This cluster includes personality disorders often considered to be severe and that have mixed treatment results.
3. *Cluster C* is characterized by anxiety and fearfulness and includes avoidant, dependent, and obsessive-compulsive personalities. These are generally viewed as the most treatment responsive and have shown the best results with shorter duration treatment protocols (Beck, Freeman, et al., 1990; Winston et al., 1994).

There are several problems with *DSM*. One is the degree of overlap among the categories—many patients are diagnosed with more than one. In addition, many clinicians find *DSM* to be a very rough diagnostic schema that does not take into consideration the finer distinctions among those who are given the same diagnosis. For example, two patients diagnosed with an obsessive-compulsive personality disorder may be functioning at very different levels of adaptive functioning and thus treatment and prognosis might be very different. The usefulness for treatment planning is questionable and rightly so; how could the presence of six or seven criteria truly inform the complex treatment intervention that is most often required for the personality disordered patient?

2. DIMENSIONAL CLASSIFICATION

The dimensional classification of personality takes a different approach from the categorical. This system is based on the premise that personality does not exist in categories but rather along dimensions. Dimensional classification grew out of the study of normal personality using the trait approach developed by Gordon Allport (Allport & Odbert, 1936) that used factor analysis to reduce the over 17,000 words they identified in the dictionary to describe personality. Personality disorders are an example of normal traits amplified to an extreme, to the point of being maladaptive, and so they are well suited to the dimensional system. This system has been primarily used to investigate the construct of personality in both normal and disordered populations. The most dominant of the dimensional models is the five-factor model which has identified five empirically derived dimensions of personality that include: neuroticism, extraversion, openness, agreeableness, and conscientiousness (Costa & McCrae, 1992).

3. STRUCTURAL-DYNAMIC CLASSIFICATION

The structural-dynamic classification of personality is based on a psychodynamic understanding of personality structure and organization (McWilliams, 1994).

This system evolved from the character types developed by psychoanalytic pioneers of the last century and to a certain extent they are still present in many of the current *DSM* categories. In this system, personality organization is placed on a continuum from psychotic, borderline, neurotic to normal with each point representing a varying degree of structural integrity—how well the system can handle anxiety, conflict, and emotional experience before becoming overloaded and symptomatic—called *ego-adaptive capacity*. Thus, someone functioning at the right of the borderline position would be able to handle more anxiety and conflict than someone on the left side, toward the psychotic range whose tolerance is much lower. Each type or mixture of personality types can be organized at any position along the continuum. If you could overlay *DSM* on top of the structural continuum, you would see that the Cluster C disorders are equivalent to those at the neurotic level, Cluster B at the borderline level, and Cluster A at the psychotic level. A crucial part of personality in the structural-dynamic classification is the organization and use of defense mechanisms. Those at higher levels of organization and adaptation generally use more mature and neurotic defenses, those in the borderline range use more primitive defenses and those in the psychotic spectrum tend to use more primitive and psychotic mixes. O. Kernberg (1984) has advanced the structural-dynamic system in his work focusing primarily on the severe personality disorders.

4. Prototypal Classification

The prototypal classification of personality combines the categorical with the dimensional and lends itself to finer distinctions among various personality types and disorders. The most notable of the prototypal systems is Millon's (Millon & Davis, 1996) that retains categories of personality disorder but assesses them on three primary dimensions: self/other, active/passive, and pleasure/pain. Millon has developed highly valid and reliable instruments that can be used to assess the personality with standardized objective tests.

5. Relational Classification

The relational classification of personality has two main branches, the interpersonal model of Harry Stack Sullivan (1953) who dealt with *dyadic configurations* and the systemic model of Murray Bowen (1976) who dealt with *triadic configurations*. The interpersonal model has evolved in various forms from Leary's (1957) circumplex model to Benjamin's (1993) Structural Analysis of Social Behavior (SASB), and a systemically based relational model (Magnavita, 2000) of dysfunctional personologic systems. Most recently, there has been a movement to develop and codify a comprehensive relational model (Kaslow, 1996) and another to expand the use of relational diagnoses in *DSM* (Beach, 2002). Relational diagnosis looks at patterns of communication, themes, multigenerational processes, feedback loops, and interpersonal processes such as complimentarity.

Pathological Labels—Useful or Pejorative?

As mentioned earlier in this chapter, the label "personality disorder" can be pejorative and some clinicians eschew its use. In the worst case, labeling can be used to marginalize and control those who society finds unacceptable. We have seen evidence of this in the use of psychiatric labeling of dissidents in the communist Soviet Union. Most of us have had a representative from a managed care company deny a request for treatment of a patient who has been diagnosed with personality disorder. This is done on the grounds that these patients are not treatment responsive and that Axis II disorders are not covered under their policy. Most of us have been conditioned to report the secondary symptom complexes such as depression, anxiety, and substance abuse, which are generally more acceptable and covered by the policy. When we confer a label on a patient regardless of our intent it can be demoralizing or experienced as an act of devaluing that person, or even felt as a deeply wounding and moralistic attack. Language is indeed powerful and the way in which we use it can be constraining or freeing. Clinicians and diagnosticians must be aware of the effect of sloppy or inconsiderate use of diagnostic labeling. The term *personality disorder* is probably not the best one for the field to have adopted, but for now we have no choice as it has been codified in *DSM-IV*. It seems more acceptable to many to use the alternative label *personality dysfunction,* that occurs when a personality system is not adapting optimally or is overwhelmed or flooded with trauma or overwhelming stress. Personality dysfunction is a more fluid construct that allows for changes in the manner in which a person's personality functions. During times of trauma, war, or economic or political adversity, a person's personality may be reorganized to cope with the events. At these times, the person's personality may indeed be dysfunctional as it has become overwhelmed, but it seems a stretch to say that this is a personality disorder, which implies a long-standing dysfunction. If someone's personality is not functioning effectively, we can help them by enhancing defensive organization, restructuring cognitive schema and beliefs, metabolizing affect over traumatic experience, teaching interpersonal skills, offering alternative attachment experiences, increasing adaptive strategies, and so on.

Science likes labels and needs tools to organize and categorize that which it studies. The construct of personality disorder has indeed allowed researchers interested in personality to study the subject and get research funding. There has been a major increase in research interest and development of new models to treat personality disorders as can be seen by many of the contributions in this volume. Identifying a condition such as borderline personality disorder has drawn attention to those who suffer from affective dysregulation, identity confusion, and interpersonal instability that characterizes this disorder. It allows those who have these symptoms to educate themselves and seek the best treatment available. Identifying and labeling also allows clinicians to understand the commonalties among patients that might suggest a particular method or approach for treatment.

PREVALENCE OF PERSONALITY DISORDERS IN CONTEMPORARY SOCIETY

The prevalence of personality disorders in contemporary society depends on the validity of the classification system and diagnostic instruments used to establish the presence of a disorder. As we have discussed, there are problems with classification and nosology that make estimates of prevalence only approximate. Millon and Davis (1996) write: "No other area in the study of psychopathology is fraught with more controversy than the personality disorders" (p. 485). Nevertheless, epidemiological surveys do shed some light and provide some empirical evidence about the prevalence of personality disorders in the population. The most often cited study on the prevalence of personality disorders in the United States is by Weissman (1993) who found that approximately one out of 10 people fulfill the criteria for a personality disorder. Merikangas and Weissman (1986) found that approximately half of those receiving mental health treatment also suffered from a personality disorder. The Weissman study remains the most comprehensive report on the prevalence of personality disorders but was based on *DSM-III* and as Mattia and Zimmerman point out: "No epidemiological survey of the full range of personality disorders has been conducted in the post *DSM-III* era" (2001, p. 107). Further studies are warranted; the Merikangas and Weissman studies have illuminated the problem of quantifying the extent of personality disorders in the general and clinical population and will guide future research.

The finding that about half of those receiving mental health treatment are compromised in their personality functioning, enough to warrant a personality disorder diagnosis, underscores the importance of acknowledging the contribution of personality to relational disturbances such as marital dysfunction, spousal abuse, domestic violence, child abuse, as well as the most common clinical syndromes such as anxiety, depression, eating disorders, and addictions. The prevalence rates for personality disorders vary greatly. In a review of six studies, Mattia and Zimmerman (2001) found that the rates documented ranged from as low as 6.7% to as high as 33.3%. These findings are suggestive of a greater problem than is being acknowledged. There are few epidemiological studies that have investigated the prevalence of childhood and adolescent personality disorders. Bernstein et al. (1993) indicate that the rate of personality disorders between the ages of 9 and 19 is "high." They found that approximately 31% suffer from moderate personality disturbance and 17% can be classified as severe. In contrast, Lewinsohn, Rohde, Seeley, and Klein (1997), using a different methodology, only report 3.3% rate of prevalence in young adults; the discrepancy seems to be due to methodological and measurement issues but is useful in pointing the way for further studies.

Are we underestimating the prevalence of personality disorders? What does seem evident from clinical practice, although undocumented by empirical findings, is the increasing number of children, adolescents, and adults who are entering treatment with signs of personality dysfunction. This may be disguised because of a tendency for clinicians to use diagnostic nomenclature that is less pathology oriented and "more hopeful" in terms of prognosis. Many clinicians still believe that personality dysfunction is beyond the realm of treatment and will avoid it in favor of a less stigmatizing Axis I disorder. The presence of multiple co-occurring clinical syndromes is often a sign that personality dysfunction is at the root of the problem but may be obscured by the complex interrelationship of these clinical and relational disorders, and an unwillingness to address the personality component. With regards to childhood and adolescent personality disorders, P. F. Kernberg, Weiner, and Bardenstein (2000) write: "when PDs are looked for in children and adolescents, their prevalence can be considerable" (p. 4). Further, they state in their book *Personality Disorders in Children and Adolescents:* "Our purpose is to present the mounting and compelling evidence for the presence of PDs in children and adolescents so that they will be more readily recognized and treated" (p. ix).

Are we witnessing signs of an epidemic in process? If clinical, sociocultural, and political indices are accurate, we may be entering an unprecedented era for individual and social pathology caused by economic pressure, racism, and cultural fragmentation (West, 2001), which might be a harbinger for an epidemic in personality dysfunction. Cultural, political, and economic factors are putting undue strain on family and social institutions that were once able to mitigate some of the impact of increased anxiety from rapid cultural change and fragmentation that spawn social pathologies and promote personality dysfunction in individuals and families. In clinical settings, we see more and more severe cases of personality disorder at younger ages, along with fewer resources from the community with which to handle these, magnified by destabilization of the family. More and more, families are left without the necessary support to deal with disturbances in their family members. This is particularly evident to clinicians who have tried to find an appropriate hospital for a personality disturbed patient that will keep the patient more than a few days before returning the patient to the community and to a family ill-equipped to deal with the burden of acute episodes and chronic care. As more and more families are being forced into harsher economic conditions and poverty, the likelihood that there will be an epidemic in personality disorders is not far fetched. This may be especially true for groups that have already been marginalized by racism and economic disadvantage (West, 2001). West writes:

> The collapse of meaning in life—the eclipse of hope and absence of love of self and others, the breakdown of family and neighborhood bonds—leads to the social deracination and cultural denudement of urban dwellers, especially children. We have created rootless, dangling people with little link to the supportive networks—family, friends, school—that sustain some sense of purpose in life. We have witnessed the collapse of the spiritual communities that in the past helped Americans face despair, disease, and death that transmit through the generations dignity and decency, excellence and elegance. (p. 10)

West (2001) is concerned that unless there is significant attention paid to the problems of racism, sociocultural marginalization, and downward mobility of many groups in American society, the foundation of democracy will be threatened. There is no research that has investigated the presence of personality dysfunction in minority populations but it is clear that African American males as a group are experiencing severe stress to their personality systems.

IMPACT OF PERSONALITY DISORDERS

The total impact of personality disorders (PDs) on the individual, family, and society is substantial. Ruegg and Francis (1995) nicely summarized the impact:

> PDs are associated with crime, substance abuse, disability, increased need for medical care, suicide attempts, self-injurious behavior, assaults, delayed recovery from Axis I and medical illness, institutionalization, underachievement, underemployment, family disruption, child abuse and neglect, homelessness, illegitimacy, poverty, STDs, misdiagnosis and mistreatment of medical and psychiatric disorder, malpractice suits, medical and judicial recidivism, dissatisfaction with and disruption of psychiatric treatment settings, and dependency on public support. (pp. 16–17)

"As economic conditions worsen and the trend toward family breakdown continues, we can predict an increase in the incidence of personality disorder" (Magnavita, 1997). This development underscores the urgency of developing the science of personality, obtaining epidemiological findings concerning the prevalence, developing cogent theoretical models, and effective treatment interventions for this under served population. According to P. F. Kernberg et al. (2000): "Personality disorders (PDs) historically have received less attention from clinicians and researchers than other psychiatric disorders such as depression and schizophrenia" (p. 3).

Prevalence of Co-Occurring Conditions

Along with a discussion of the prevalence of personality disorders, we should also consider the associated topic of *comorbidity:* the co-occurrence of more than one clinical disorder. Dolan-Sewell, Krueger, and Shea (2001) believe there are inherent problems with the concept of comorbidity when applied to mental disorders. "Although the use of the term 'comorbidity' to refer to covariation among disorders is common, our understanding of mental disorders has not yet reached the level described as truly 'distinct' " (p. 85). Comorbidity reflects the use of the dominant medical model to conceptualize mental disorders and may not be as useful as it is with medical illness where two or more separate disease entities often co-exist. The relationship among personality disorders and clinical syndromes is not so clear and might not be separable. Personality disorders represent a dysfunction of the individual and family personality system and thus lead to the expression of clinical disturbances and relational dysfunction (Magnavita, 1997, 2000, in press). Dissecting psychopathological conditions into various syndromes may mean losing sight of the goal of treating the personality system of the individual, the family, and the broader ecosystem in which they function.

Regardless of the controversy, using the current dominant diagnostic system of classification (*DSM*), there is increasing empirical evidence of the likelihood that a personality disorder diagnosis suggests that another clinical disorder will also be present and that it will likely be the reason for treatment. Tyrer, Gunderson, Lyons, and Tohen (1997) in their review of the literature found some of the following associated comorbid conditions: Borderline PD and Depression; Depressive PD and Depression; Avoidant PD and Generalized Social Phobia: Cluster B PDs and Psychoactive Substance Abuse; Cluster B and C PDs and Eating Disorders, and Somatoform Disorders; Cluster C PDs and Anxiety Disorders and Hypochondriasis; and finally Cluster A PDs and Schizophrenia. Looking at this phenomenon of co-occurring disorders from another perspective suggests that 79% of those diagnosed with a personality disorder will also fulfill criteria for an Axis I disorder (Fabrega, Ulrich, Pilkonis, & Messich, 1992).

Relevance of Identifying Co-Occurring Disorders for Clinical Practice

Co-occurring disorders are not exhibited by chance but emerge out of the personality configuration of the patient's total ecological system from the microscopic level to the macroscopic level of analysis. The clinical syndrome, relational dysfunction, and personality characteristics and organization of each patient cannot be viewed separately. For example, we know that marital dissatisfaction is a cause of depression in women and that the personality characteristics and organization of a woman will influence how this complex constellation is handled. A woman with histrionic features may act out by having an affair and causing a marital showdown; a woman with obsessive features may become more perfectionistic and drive her spouse away; a woman with borderline features may become more self-destructive, increasing parasuicidal behavior such as cutting her arms; a dependent woman might triangulate a child by encouraging school phobia as she herself becomes increasingly agoraphobic. Millon (1999) has termed his model of treatment *personality-guided therapy*, which is an apt and useful description for how all therapy, regardless of the presenting complaint or treatment focus, should be conducted. The personality system, the central organizing system of a person, should be the cornerstone of treatment. Much of psychotherapy is concerned with pattern recognition, so that using personality as the central organizing system allows us to see patterns that are interconnected and, once discovered, are more readily restructured or modified. We next focus our attention on the causes of personality disorders.

ETIOLOGY OF PERSONALITY DISORDERS

The causes or etiology of personality disorders is a subject of great interest to clinical scientists and empirical researchers alike. There is no question that the etiology of personality disorders is multifactorial and complex, probably with multiple developmental pathways. Attempts to reduce the cause of a complex phenomenon to one level of abstraction such as trauma, biological, social, or interpersonal are likely to be fruitless. Most clinicians have faced the question posed by family members or patients with personality dysfunction: *What causes a personality disorder?* or, *How did I or my family member get it?* Aside from the clinical implications of knowing what the roots of a dysfunction are, being able to provide some reasonable psychoeducation to the family or individual is helpful. Useful models have been developed that can help us organize the etiological factors implicated in personality dysfunction. There are four models which, when blended, have extraordinary theoretical coherence and explanatory value when trying to understand the complex phenomenon of personality disorders. After reviewing these models, we will look at the most well-documented factors that have been empirically supported as etiological factors in the development or maintenance of personality dysfunction. These models are "atheoretical" in the sense that they cut across schools of theories of personality and psychotherapy and are building blocks for a unified personality-guided relational therapy (Magnavita, in press). We discuss some of the important advances in models that can guide the clinician regardless of his or her preferred treatment model.

Biopsychosocial Model

Engel (1980) reminded us of the importance of not ignoring any level of abstraction of the biopsychosocial model from the molecular to the ecological system. The biopsychosocial model views the individual holistically and does not ignore the potential contributing effects of various domains from the molecular to the ecological. This model reminds us of the fact that human functioning is complex and any reductionistic model is likely to explain only a portion of the variance that accounts for a certain personality organization, style, or clinical condition.

DIATHESIS-STRESS MODEL

The diathesis-stress model explains how we each have a certain threshold of biological and psychological vulnerability that when surpassed will result in symptom expression (Monroe & Simons, 1991). For example, when the level of stress in some individuals reaches a certain level they may develop lower back pain, while others may be subject to gastrointestinal disturbance. The most vulnerable biopsychological systems will be the channel for anxiety. These biopsychosocial systems are genetically determined to some degree. All people have a diathesis, or a genetically predisposed vulnerability, in one area or another. Some people have very hearty, euthymic temperaments, maintaining positive moods in bleak situations, while others tend more toward dysthymia. Some have a genetic predisposition to bipolar-affective or schizophrenic spectrum disorders. This model is very helpful in understanding and predicting how a schizophrenic illness may be precipitated in an individual, when stress and environmental conditions bring out the previously unexpressed phenotype. Paris (2001) applied this model to understanding personality functioning in a useful way. He suggested that temperamental vulnerabilities can be amplified by environmental challenges and trauma. The *diathesis* is the weak point where the organism "breaks down." Another way in which to apply the diathesis-stress model, which is of particular relevance for personality dysfunction, is to look at the overall personality system of an individual, dyad, or triadic configuration and to assess the impact of stress on the personality subsystems. For example, when viewing the individual personality at the intrapsychic system, we can observe that a patient with an obsessive compulsive personality configuration, when stressed by an external challenge, is likely to develop a symptom profile that is related to problems with anxiety suppression. Thus, it is common for these individuals to develop generalized anxiety disorder, sexual inhibition, and dysthymia.

GENERAL SYSTEM THEORY

A major development in social and biological sciences in the mid-twentieth century was the development of general system theory whose groundbreaking way of understanding complex systems was applied to communications theory, cybernetics, psychiatry, and was in part the impetus for the family therapy movement (von Bertalanffy, 1968). Von Bertalanffy's theoretical model has largely been incorporated into current psychological thought but remains of use. When we apply the tenets of general system theory to the elements of the biopsychosocial model, we have a powerful way of beginning to understand the interrelatedness of various elements and subsystems of the biopsychosocial model.

CHAOS AND COMPLEXITY THEORY

Another very useful development in science in the latter part of the twentieth century was *chaos theory*. Chaos theory deals with complex systems and demonstrates that the universe has many properties of what are called chaotic systems, which organize and re-organize in patterns (Gleick, 1987). If we can read the chaos, we see emergent patterns that reveal the self-organizing properties of the universe. The importance of chaos theory for our topic is in its ability to account for the interconnectedness of physical phenomenon. Early chaos theorists were very interested in studying and predicting weather patterns. This work revealed an important phenomenon known as the *Butterfly Effect*, which describes how a butterfly flapping her wings in China can create a violent weather pattern in North America. In other words, what they discovered was that small perturbations in parts of a system can have dramatic effects that can alter the system as a whole quite dramatically. Certain experiences are amplified in systems and create powerful effects.

Winter and Barenbaum (1999) write:

> In other fields of science, recognition of increased complexity has led to the development of "chaos theory" or "complexity theory," which is now being taken up by psychologists (e.g., Vallacher & Nowak, 1997). Because two basic postulates of personality psychology are (1) complexity of interaction among elements, and (2) that earlier experience affects later behavior in ways that are at least somewhat irreversible (or reversible with greater difficulty than acquisition), the field seems ideally situated to take advantage of these new theoretical and methodological tools. (p. 20)

COMPUTER MODELING

The computer has been used by many cognitive psychologists and neuroscientists as a model for human cognition and, more currently, for emotional functioning. Personality has also been likened to a computer by Winter and Barenbaum (1999) who describe their analogy:

> Personality may come to be seen as a series of Windows computer applications. Over time, different personality "applications" are installed, opened, moved between foreground and background, modified, closed, even deleted. Although the sum total of available "personality" elements may have limits that are specifiable (perhaps unique for each person), the current "on-line" personality may be complex and fluid. (p. 20)

COMPUTER NETWORK MODEL

An analogy that is more contemporaneous and in keeping with the movement toward unified personality (see Magnavita, chapter 24) is the analogy of a network composed of interconnected computers capable of interaction and communication. A computer network seems to reflect the way personality systems function on an *intrapsychic* level (individual computer hardware—genetic and neurobiological, and software capability—attachment and relational experience); *dyadic level* (communication process among two computers); *triadic + N* (communication among three computers); and also in the larger *mesosystem* (interconnected computer networks). A more powerful computer with greater processing and expanded memory is capable of utilizing more powerful and faster programs. A powerful computer will function at a high level with the proper software. If the software antiquated, poorly written, or has a virus (maladaptive personality patterns), the whole system will function poorly or may even crash. A system with limited hardware capacity will not do well even with the best available software; it will not be able to take advantage of its features and may become even slower or overwhelmed with demands. Interconnected computers may be arranged in networks that communicate to one another via hardware and software communication programs. An individual system with limited hardware and software can draw from the network. Any problem in the communication system could potentially cause a crash of the whole network.

ETIOLOGICAL FACTORS

We know with some degree of certainty the etiological factors that determine personality dysfunction. We are not, however, anywhere near having the ability to predict or pinpoint these with any degree of certainty. If we had the resources for a project comparable to the human genome project whereby we could focus many scientific resources on personality disorders, we could probably make advances in understanding similar to those we have made in understanding our genetic code. It is beyond the scope of this chapter to review in great detail the contributing factors to both functional and dysfunctional states of personality but it is critical for clinicians to have some familiarity with them. The broad categories include: (1) genetic predisposition, (2) attachment experience, (3) traumatic events, (4) family constellation, and (5) sociocultural and political forces. These factors are interactive, interrelated, and composed of complex biochemical/neuroanatomical-psychological-sociocultural feedback loops each evolutionarily shaping and being shaped by the others over the course of a lifetime and even across generations.

1. Genetic Predisposition   Will a gene ever be found for personality disorders? It is unlikely, but there are certainly multiple genes that predispose our neurobiological system and that influence who we are and how we behave. It is estimated that anywhere between 30% to 50% of personality variation is inherited (Buss, 1999). In comparison, intelligence, another component system of personality, has an estimated heritability of 60%, which has been extensively documented (Herrnstein & Murray, 1994). Biological variables such as genetic endowments influencing temperamental dispositions set the parameters for personality development. Using the diathesis-stress model, we can loosely predict the symptom constellations and personality adaptations that will ensue. Neurobiological systems have bias in the way they are organized and function and may have a relationship to later personality development (Cloninger, 1986a, 1986b). Cloninger views personality predispositions as an artifact of neurotransmitter action that is genetically predetermined. Depue and Lenzenweger (2001) "conceive of personality disorders as emergent phenotypes arising for the interaction of the foregoing neurobehavioral systems underlying major personality traits" (p. 165). These neurobiological dispositions are also called *temperament;* there is robust evidence to suggest that these temperamental differences are observed quite early in development. Greenspan and Benderly (1997) describe these as sensitivity, reactivity, and motor preference potentials. Thomas and Chess

(1977) assessed temperament on an array of observable responses in infants that include approach or withdrawal, adaptability, threshold of responsiveness, intensity of reaction, quality of mood, distractibility, attention span, and persistence. It is certain that both nature and nurture influence personality, though the extent of the contribution of each remains unclear.

2. *Attachment Experience*   One important developmental pathway to personality dysfunction is the quality and type of attachments that an individual forms as she progresses through her development. Bartholomew, Kwong, and Hart (2001) describe this process:

> From this perspective, personality disorder is viewed as a deviation from optimal development. Such deviation is presumed to have developed over an extended period and would be hypothesized to be associated with a number of interacting risk factors, which may defer across individuals and across disorders. Multiple pathways can lead to the same overt outcome—for instance, a particular form of personality disorder—and no specific risk factor would be expected to be necessary or sufficient for the development of a particular outcome. Attachment processes, in the past and present, may be one important factor affecting developmental pathways to personality disorder. (p. 211)

Thomas and Chess (1977) also realized that temperamental factors were not sufficient in explaining developmental shaping. They also believed that "goodness of fit" between the infant and child was crucial (Chess & Thomas, 1986). Winnicott believed that there is no such entity as an infant but only a mother-child dyad (Rayner, 1991).

3. *Traumatic Events*   There is little question that traumatic events are strongly implicated in the development of personality dysfunction. This is especially apparent in the research on severe personality disorders. This is not to say that everyone who experiences a traumatic event will inevitably develop personality pathology but this does appear to be one common pathway. There are mitigating resiliency factors that seem to inoculate some who have been traumatized. Paris (2001) states: "whereas most individuals are resilient to adversity, people who develop clinical symptoms have an underlying vulnerability to the same risk factor" (p. 231). There is a point, however, where even the most resilient individual will be markedly affected by trauma and it will have an enduring impact on personality development. Herman (1992) and van der Kolk, McFarlane, and Weisaeth (1996) have made advances in our understanding of the impact of trauma on personality functioning. It seems that early and severe trauma is overwhelming to the neurobiological system and may in a sense "scar" the brain leading to future disturbance and developmental psychopathology. The over-excitation of certain brain centers, particularly the limbic system, may lead to a kindling effect that creates an easily triggered intense and disorganizing emotional response.

4. *Family Constellation and Dysfunction*   Clinical observation and other evidence support the view that those who are raised in severely dysfunctional families are more likely to develop personality dysfunction (Magnavita & MacFarlane, in press; Magnavita, 2000). Although there is a paucity of empirical support for this

observation, in a review of the literature, Paris (2001) found that "parental psycho-pathology is associated with a variety of psychosocial adversities, such as trauma, family dysfunction, and family breakdown" (p. 234). Over the course of genera-tions, a multigenerational transmission effect can continue to produce dysfunc-tional personologic systems, which, in some cases, worsen over time (Magnavita, 2000). The interaction between genetics and family environment is an interesting area of investigation. Plomin and Caspi (1999) studied nondisordered personality and found: "The surprise is that genetic research consistently shows that family resemblance for personality is almost entirely due to shared heredity rather than shared family environment" (p. 256). They report that family constellation such as birth order and sibling spacing seem to have an imprint on personality.

5. Sociocultural and Political Forces   There is little in the way of documentation to assess the impact of sociocultural and political factors on personality dys-function. Erickson's (1950) seminal work focusing on contemporary society's influence on identity remains relevant today. Paris (2001) posits that the disin-tegration of society may be an important factor implicated in the development of personality pathology and further suggests that the effect may be "amplified by rapid social change" (p. 237). Other contemporary social commentators such as West (2001) observe that strong political and sociocultural forces negatively impact the identity of many people, especially minority groups. Winter and Barenbaum (1999) write:

> First, we believe that personality psychology will need to pay increased attention to matters of context. Whatever the evolutionary origins, genetic basis, or physio-logical substrate of any aspect of personality, both its *level* and *channels of expression* will be strongly affected, in complex ways, by the multiple dimensions of social context: not only by the immediate situational context but also the larger contexts of age cohort, family institution, social class, nation/culture, history, and (perhaps supremely) gender. We suggest that varying the social macrocontext will "constel-late," or completely change, all other variables of personality—much as in the clas-sic demonstrations of gestalt principles of perception. (p. 19)

THE MUTABILITY OF PERSONALITY

An often-debated topic within the discipline of personality is whether personal-ity is stable and how stable is it, and can it change, and whether it can be trans-formed slowly, rapidly, or at all (Heatherton & Weinberger, 1994; Magnavita, 1997). The mutability of personality is an academic research and clinical contro-versy that has yet to be adequately addressed. Standard measures of personality do support, to a degree, the consistency of personality over time and yet develop-mental processes entail continuous change. Whether or not personality is set and at what age it is consolidated has been the source of much speculation and contro-versy. The limited empirical work on this topic has been done in a naturalistic setting and suggests the possibility that "quantum change" or discontinuous transformational experiences do indeed occur at times (Miller & C'deBaca, 1994).

Why are some personality organizations so difficult to alter? It is unclear why certain manifestations of personality are so difficult to alter. The evidence seems to implicate the effect of interpersonal experience and trauma on the structuralization of the mind (Greenspan & Benderly, 1997; Grigsby & Stevens, 2000; Siegel, 1999). These researchers found that interpersonal experience, affective arousal, and trauma seem to alter neuronal pathways, making some connections stronger and pruning others. The complex interactions among the biopsychosocial elements such as trauma, attachment, and interpersonal experience are strongly implicated and are an area of great interest and speculation.

DEVELOPMENTAL PERSONOLOGY

The field of psychopathology traditionally attempts to isolate and study "specific" disorders by investigating the relevance and validity of various diagnostic categories. General psychopathology texts (Adams & Sutker, 2001; Millon, Blaney, & Davis, 1999; Turner & Hersen, 1997), as well as those specifically devoted to personality disorders, present the various *DSM-IV* disorders and psychopathological conditions in chapter after chapter. Although this trend in the study of psychopathology adds to our knowledge about these conditions and may be useful for understanding conditions with a known biogenetic basis such as schizophrenia and bipolar disorder, there are dangers in this approach. One problem with studying psychopathology through the fragmented lenses of various disorders and clinical syndromes is that the richness of the study of humankind is lost. This type of reductionism further separates professionals by specialty, each group using their own labels, having their own adherents and research teams. The mental health practitioner must not lose sight of the human being in this endeavor, just as the primary care physician will not relinquish his or her role to the medical specialists. Instead of employing the increasingly fragmented delineations of disorders as rallying points, we should begin the process of looking at psychopathology in a developmental framework.

Cummings, Davies, and Campbell (2000) suggest a new model for viewing psychopathological processes in their context:

> Thus, contextualism conceptualizes development as the ongoing interplay between an active, changing organism in a dynamic, changing context. Activity and change are thus basic, essential parts of development; that is, developmental processes are not reducible to a large number of disconnected, microscopic elements and explainable by the effect of some environmental force filtered through parts of a passive organism (i.e., a machine; p. 24).

PERSONALITY SYSTEMICS

Finally, let us consider one other, even more fluid model with which to study human functioning. It seems evident that most of the pioneers in the field of personality, as well as contemporary figures in personality theory and personality disorders, would agree that personality is a system of interrelated domains and subsystems. Personality can be placed at the center of human behavior. Thus, the term *personality systemics* emphasizes the study of personality systems in their various forms and associated processes. These include interrelated domains (neurobiological, affective, cognitive, defensive, interpersonal, familial, sociocultural, political) that can be viewed at the microscopic, macroscopic, or mesosystem level of organization in the context of the total ecological system (Magnavita, in press).

Cummings et al. (2000) write of the importance of this perspective for psychopathology, which they term "developmental psychopathology":

> contextualism regards development as embedded in series of nested, interconnected wholes or networks of activity at multiple levels of analysis, including the intraindividual subsystem (e.g., interplay between specific dimensions within a domain such as affect or cognition), the intraindividual system (e.g., family or peer relationship quality), and ecological or sociocultural system (e.g., community, subculture, culture). Thus, development regulates and is regulated by multiple factors, events, and processes at several levels that unfold over time. (p. 24)

Their language is surprisingly reminiscent of that of Ludwig von Bertalanffy's (1968) general system theory and Urie Bronfenbrenner's (1979) ecological model. Perhaps their models could now be applied to the field of personality theory and psychopathology. Their work as well as that of many other seminal pioneers from the last century needs to be revitalized through the lens of current research, practice, and theory, and perhaps their models can accommodate some of the recent discoveries that are continually changing the landscape during this exciting time for the study of personality disorders.

SUMMARY AND CONCLUSIONS

The field of personality, which embraces the study and treatment of personality disorders, is undergoing a renaissance. The classification of personality, an age-old interest of humankind, has more recently become a focus of serious scientific and clinical interest. This has led to a number of classification systems, each of which has utility for the clinician. The construct *personality disorder* is one that most clinicians have an inherent understanding of, but which is nonetheless problematic and complex. Some have suggested that personality is best conceptualized as a complex system, not as a static structure that is immutable over time and unaffected by developmental processes. The controversy continues and leaves the door open for clinical scientists to further delineate the structure and processes that make us all unique, while explaining the great similarities in how we have evolved. This chapter will prepare the reader for the exploration of many of the contemporary theories of personality and the treatment methods and techniques that clinicians use in addressing dysfunctional manifestations of personality.

REFERENCES

Adams, H. E., & Sutker, P. B. (Eds.). (2001). *Comprehensive handbook of psychopathology* (3rd ed.). New York: Plenum Press.

Alexander, F. G., & Selesnick, S. T. (1966). *The history of psychiatry: An evaluation of psychiatric thought and practice from prehistoric times to the present.* New York: Harper & Row.

Allport, G. W., & Odbert, H. S. (1936). Trait-names: A psych-lexical study. *Psychological Monographs, 47,* 1–171.

American Psychiatric Association. (1994). *Diagnostic and statistical manual of mental disorders* (4th ed.). Washington, DC: Author.

Bartholomew, K., Kwong, M. J., & Hart, S. D. (2001). Attachment. In W. J. Livesley (Ed.), *Handbook of personality disorders: Theory, research, and treatment* (pp. 196–230). New York: Guilford Press.

Beach, S. R. H. (2002). Family psychology and the new "relational diagnoses" of *DSM-V*. *Family Psychologist, 18*(2), 6–7.

Beck, A. T., Freeman, A., & Associates. (1990). *Cognitive therapy of personality disorders.* New York: Guilford Press.

Benjamin, L. S. (1993). *Interpersonal diagnosis and treatment of personality disorders.* New York: Guilford Press.

Bernheim, H. (1891). *Hypnotisme, suggestion, psychotherapie: Etudes nouvelles.* Paris: Octave Doin.

Bernstein, D., Cohen, P., Velex, N., Schwab-Stone, M., Siever, L., & Shinsato, L. (1993). Prevalence and stability of the *DSM-III* personality disorders in a community-based survey of adolescents. *American Journal of Psychiatry, 150,* 1237–1243.

Bowen, M. (1976). Theory and practice of family therapy. In P. J. Guerin Jr. (Ed.), *Family therapy: Theory and practice* (pp. 42–90). New York: Gardner Press.

Bronfenbrenner, U. (1979). *The ecology of developmental process: Experiments by nature and design.* Cambridge, MA: Harvard University Press.

Buss, D. M. (1999). Human nature and individual differences: The evolution of human personality. In L. A. Pervin & O. P. John (Eds.), *Handbook of personality: Theory and research* (2nd ed., pp. 31–56). New York: Guilford Press.

Charcot, J. M. (1889). *Clinical lectures on diseases of the nervous system* (T. Savil, Trans.). London: Sydenham Society.

Chess, S., & Thomas, A. (1986). *Temperament in clinical practice.* New York: Guilford Press.

Cloninger, C. R. (1986a). A systematic method for clinical description and classification of personality variants: A proposal. *Archives of General Psychiatry, 44,* 573–588.

Cloninger, C. R. (1986b). A unified biosocial of personality and its role in development of anxiety. *Psychiatric Developments, 3,* 167–226.

Costa, P. T., & McCrae, R. R. (1992). The five-factor model of personality and its relevance to personality disorders. *Journal of Personality Disorders, 6,* 343–359.

Cummings, E. M., Davies, P. T., & Campbell, S. B. (2000). *Developmental psychopathology and family process: Theory, research, and clinical implications.* New York: Guilford Press.

Davis, R. D., & Millon, T. (1999). Models of personality and its disorders. In T. Millon, P. H. Blaney, & R. D. Davis (Eds.), *Oxford textbook of psychopathology* (pp. 485–522). New York: Oxford University Press.

Depue, R. A., & Lenzenweger, M. F. (2001). A neurobiological dimensional model. In W. J. Livesly (Ed.), *Handbook of personality disorders: Theory, research, and treatment* (pp. 136–176). New York: Guilford Press.

Dolan-Sewell, R. T., Krueger, R. F., & Shea, M. T. (2001). Co-occurrence with syndrome disorders. In W. J. Livesley (Ed.), *Handbook of personality disorders: Theory, research, and treatment* (pp. 84–104). New York: Guilford Press.

Engel, G. L. (1980). The clinical application of the biopsychosocial model. *American Journal of Psychiatry, 137*(5), 535–544.

Erickson, E. H. (1950). *Childhood and society.* New York: Norton.

Fabrega, H., Ulrich, R., Pilkonis, P., & Messich, J. E. (1992). Pure personality disorders in an intake psychiatric setting. *Journal of Personality Disorders, 6,* 153–161.

Frager, R., & Fadiman, J. (1998). *Personality and personal growth.* New York: Longman.

Frances, A. J., Clarkin, J. F., & Perry, S. (1984). *Differential therapeutics in psychiatry.* New York: Brunner/Mazel.

Gleick, J. (1987). *Chaos: Making a new science.* New York: Viking/Penguin Books.

Greenspan, S. I., & Benderly, B. L. (1997). *The growth of the mind: And endangered origins of intelligence.* Reading, MA: Perseus Books.

Grigsby, J., & Stevens, D. (2000). *Neurodynamics of personality.* New York: Guilford Press.

Heatherton, T. F., & Weinberger, J. L. (Eds.). (1994). *Can personality change?* Washington, DC: American Psychological Association.

Herman, J. L. (1992). *Trauma and recovery.* New York: Basic Books.

Herrnstein, R. J., & Murray, C. (1994). *The bell curve: Intelligence and class structure in American life.* New York: Simon & Schuster.

Jackson, S. W. (1999). *Care of the psyche: A history of psychological healing.* New Haven, CT: Yale University Press.

Kaslow, F. W. (1996). *Handbook of relational diagnosis and dysfunctional family patterns.* New York: Guilford Press.

Kernberg, O. F. (1984). *Severe personality disorders: Psychotherapeutic strategies.* New Haven, CT: Yale University Press.

Kernberg, P. F., Weiner, A. S., & Bardenstein, K. K. (2000). *Personality disorders in children and adolescents.* New York: Basic Books.

Kraepelin, E. (1904). *Lectures on clinical psychiatry.* New York: Wood.

Leary, T. (1957). *Interpersonal diagnosis of personality.* New York: Ronald Press.

Lewinsohn, P., Rohde, P., Seeley, J., & Klein, D. (1997). Axis II psychopathology as a function of Axis I disorders in childhood and adolescence. *Journal of the American Academy of Child and Adolescent Psychiatry, 36,* 1752–1759.

Magnavita, J. J. (1997). *Restructuring personality disorders: A short-term dynamic approach.* New York: Guilford Press.

Magnavita, J. J. (2000). *Relational therapy for personality disorders.* New York: Wiley.

Magnavita, J. J. (2002a). Psychodynamic approaches to psychotherapy: A century of innovations. In F. W. Kaslow (Editor-in-Chief) & J. J. Magnavita (Eds.), *Comprehensive handbook of psychotherapy: Psychodynamic/object relations* (Vol. 1, pp. 1–12). New York: Wiley.

Magnavita, J. J. (2002b). *Theories of personality: Contemporary approaches to the science of personality.* New York: Wiley.

Magnavita, J. J. (in press). *Personality-guided relational therapy: A component systems model.* Washington, DC: American Psychological Association.

Magnavita, J. J., & MacFarlane, M. M. (in press). Family treatment of personality disorders: Historical overview and current perspectives. In M. MacFarlane (Ed.), *Family treatment of personality disorders: Interpersonal approaches to relationship change.* New York: Haworth Press.

Mattia, J. I., & Zimmerman, M. (2001). Epidemiology. In W. J. Livesley (Ed.), *Handbook of personality disorders: Theory, research, and treatment* (pp. 107–123). New York: Guilford Press.

McWilliams, N. (1994). *Psychoanalytic diagnosis: Understanding personality structure in clinical practice.* New York: Guilford Press.

Merikangas, K. R., & Weissman, M. M. (1986). Epidemiology of *DSM-III* Axis II personality disorders. In A. J. Francis & R. E. Hales (Eds.), *Psychiatric update: The American Psychiatric Association annual review* (Vol. 5). Washington, DC: American Psychiatric Press.

Miller, W. R., & C'deBaca, J. (1994). Quantum change: Toward a psychology of transformation. In T. F. Heatherton & J. L. Weinberger (Eds.), *Can personality change?* (pp. 253–280). Washington, DC: American Psychological Association.

Millon, T., Blaney, P. H., & Davis, R. D. (Eds.). (1999). *Oxford textbook of psychopathology.* New York: Oxford University Press.

Millon, T., & Davis, R. D. (1996). *Disorders of personality: DSM-IV and beyond.* New York: Wiley.

Millon, T. (with Grossman, S., Meagher, S., Millon, C., & Everly, G.). (1999). *Personality-guided therapy.* New York: Wiley.

Monroe, S. M., & Simons, A. D. (1991). Diathesis-stress theories in the context of life stress research. *Psychological Bulletin, 110,* 406–425.

Murray, H. A. (1938). *Explorations in personality.* New York: Oxford University Press.

Paris, J. (2001). Psychosocial adversity. In W. J. Lively (Ed.), *Handbook of personality disorders: Theory, research, and treatment* (pp. 231–241). New York: Guilford Press.

Plomin, R., & Caspi, A. (1999). Behavioral genetics and personality. In L. A. Pervin & O. P. John (Eds.), *Handbook of personality: Theory and research* (2nd ed., pp. 251–276). New York: Guilford Press.

Rayner, E. (1991). *The independent mind in British psychoanalysis.* Northvale, NJ: Aronson.

Ruegg, R., & Francis, A. (1995). New research in personality disorders. *Journal of Personality Disorders, 9*(1), 1–48.

Siegel, D. J. (1999). *The developing mind: Toward a neurobiology of interpersonal experience.* New York: Guilford Press.

Stone, M. M. (1997). *Healing the mind: A history of psychiatry from antiquity to the present.* New York: Norton.

Sullivan, H. S. (1953). *The interpersonal theory of psychiatry.* New York: Norton.

Thomas, A., & Chess, S. (1977). *Temperament and development.* New York: Brunner/Mazel.

Turner, S. M., & Hersen, M. (1997). *Adult psychopathology and diagnosis* (3rd ed.). New York: Wiley.

Tyrer, P., Gunderson, J., Lyons, M., & Tohen, M. (1997). Special feature: Extent of comorbidity between mental state and personality disorders. *Journal of Personality Disorders, 11*(3), 242–259.

Vallacher, R. R., & Nowak, A. (1997). The emergence of dynamical social psychology. *Psychological Inquiry, 8,* 73–99.

van der Kolk, B. A., McFarlane, A. C., & Weisaeth, L. (Eds.). (1996). *Traumatic stress: The effects of overwhelming experience on mind, body, and society.* New York: Guilford Press.

von Bertalanffy, L. (1968). *General system theory.* New York: Braziller.

Wakefield, J. C. (1999). Evolutionary versus prototype analyzes of the concept of disorder. *Journal of Abnormal Psychology, 108*(3), 374–399.

Weissman, M. M. (1993, Spring). The epidemiology of personality disorders: A 1990 update. *Journal of Personality Disorders* (Suppl. 7), 44–62.

Wepman, J. M., & Heine, R. W. (1963). *Concepts of personality.* Chicago: Aldine.

West, C. (2001). *Race matters.* New York: Vintage Books.

Winston, A., Laikin, M., Pollack, J., Samstag, L. W., McCullough, L., & Muran, C. (1994). Short-term psychotherapy of personality disorders. *American Journal of Psychiatry, 15*(2), 190–194.

Winter, D. G., & Barenbaum, N. B. (1999). History of modern personality theory and research. In L. A. Pervin & O. P. John (Eds.), *Handbook of personality: Theory and research* (2nd ed., pp. 3–27). New York: Guilford Press.

CHAPTER 2

Psychopathologic Assessment Can Usefully Inform Therapy: A View from the Study of Personality

Theodore Millon and Seth D. Grossman

A FREQUENTLY OVERHEARD DIALOGUE among psychologists and other human science professionals relates to the clinical utility of diagnostic classifications, be they via the accepted standard of the *DSM-IV* or alternate schemes. This debate pervades all venues and institutions, from committees currently drafting revisions of the *DSM* standard, to clinicians and researchers of diverse (often opposing) schools of thought, down to graduate training programs where it is commonly phrased as an essay question in basic psychopathology coursework. As diverse are the professionals and students discussing the matter, so, too, are the answers given to this question of "What purpose, good or bad, does classification serve?" Answers to such queries vary on a continuum from "the only true criteria for making sense of human presentation" to "we should do the world a favor and get rid of all classifications."

Meritorious arguments could be presented to favor nearly any thoughtful response to these queries, which should make the self-respecting professional stop to contemplate a number of important issues. If there is such uncertainty as to the utility of this diagnostic tradition, why do we continue to consider classification, in any form, viable? If it is of such paramount importance to some, how can it be derogated so thoroughly by others? Indeed, there is credibility to some arguments made by adherents of what we might call the "anarchistic" view of classification; that is, those who promote the view that any attempts at an organizational system that orders and names phenomena found in the domain of psychological disturbances should be abandoned. According to this paradigm's adherents, the diagnostic system merely slaps a label on a person for our "ease of handling" at the tremendous cost of saddling the individual with a bright "neon" insignia pervading any future attempts at health, individuality, or any potential pursuit of a life beyond the therapeutic environment. Furthermore, members of this persuasion may likely resonate with the belief that a diagnostically driven therapy may "flatten" any nuance of uniqueness vital to an effective intervention. Perhaps this is true to some extent. If, in fact, we treat every simple phobia with a protocol treatment, each OCD case with the intervention prescribed by the label, and so on, we effectively reduce ourselves to "cookie-cutter" style therapy. What, then, is the distinction between the services of the clinician thoroughly versed in individual personality dynamics and that of the "technician" who "applies" techniques after reading a treatment manual for an intervention "proven" effective in eradicating a given symptom?

On an even more immediate level, it is certainly obvious that psychiatric labels preceding treatment carry expectations for many clinicians, especially for those who are not aware that labels possess potential biases, and hence invite a scripted affective reaction or a blunted receptivity to patient presentations that fall outside of what may be anticipated for any given category. Might we then rightfully question whether or not we are doing a substantial disservice in, as some would have it, "force-fitting" such man-made constructs to individuals? May not the costs considerably outweigh the benefits?

Our immediate reaction to such issues is this: If the central purpose of our classification system was simply to label phenomena for "ease of handling" in the same sense as we organize cargo for economy of space and transit, the concerns just stated would be lent additional credence. As it stands now, the preceding arguments stand firmly on common knowledge of our human tendency to judge and reach conclusions based primarily on expectation and prior knowledge of a construct; in this sense, the anarchists are correct in their concerns. Unfortunately, for all of its attempts at inclusiveness and political correctness, the established diagnostic system does little to defend itself against such criticism, despite its imperative to do so. In any science, classification is not an arbitrary extension subject to being summarily and unequivocally dismissed; it is an inextricable component of the very structure of the science. In the absence of a system creating order among its elements, there would be no ability for investigators to advance knowledge, nor would there be any ability for them to communicate with each other (Barlow, 1991). Of course, this absence then undermines higher order "basics"; without a taxonomy, or any sort of benchmark, it is virtually impossible to operationalize, assess, or modify the disparate and chaotic elements and objects which would then be readily apparent (Millon, 1990; Millon & Davis, 1996).

The quandary presented in the previous paragraphs may seem to indict the notion of classification, in general, and indeed, this is how many well-intentioned members of our scientific community may view it. However, in examining the problem closer, it becomes more apparent that the finger-pointing may be more than slightly misguided. Certainly, as Westen (1998) indicates, many of the difficulties associated with psychiatric labeling are problems that lie with clinicians and training models. This may be addressed by a concerted effort to become aware of biases and other personal reactions to particular kinds of patients, both in training and in clinical practice. Suggestive of some modifications to our approach, this effort then begs some further unanswered questions. First, while we begin to realize that it may be the established diagnostic system, rather than the notion of classification itself, that is somehow incomplete, we concern ourselves with constructing a more useful means of assessing and identifying variables, compatible with the "industry standard," which will prove pragmatic in our intervention. As we will explain, a mature, scientific approach to therapeutic intervention *must* derive fluidly from the taxonomy. This begins to answer our second question: While awareness of personal biases may tell us what *not* to do, and what to watch for in ourselves as clinicians in reaction to certain patients, we must also begin to take a *balanced* and *informed* view of how therapeutic action may be predicated based on a particular presentation, manifest in a useful diagnosis.

The current diagnostic system is, by design, descriptive, empirical, and atheoretical. It purposely avoids assumptions of etiology or therapeutic direction, thereby aiming to accommodate clinicians and researchers of diverse persuasions. To be serviceable, and not an impediment, to as many factions as possible, it remains devoid of constructs that are "foreign" to a given persuasion (Blatt & Levy, 1998). Appealing and noble as this approach may sound, there are pronounced problems with this kind of taxonomy. First, if we remove all that is foreign to any school and permit only "empirical" constructs, we leave out the potentially fruitful addition of allowing our conceptualization of the patient and his or her difficulties to inform treatment, which was the intention of diagnosis in the first place. Second, by leaving out theory in this regard, we are encouraging the further splitting between modes of entry to effective therapeutic intervention by disallowing what might rightfully be learned from systems and interactions between data levels (e.g., behavior, cognition, intrapsychic, physiological). Finally, for all its political correctness and good intention, this atheoretical system does not succeed in bringing together these factions. An orthodox behaviorist will not accept personality as a construct and will therefore not acknowledge Axis II formulations. A staunch psychodynamicist will tend to eschew most diagnostic categories as they exist, and most humanists will ignore all of them, lest they disrupt the perception of the person's individuality via the danger of labeling. In essence, the *DSM*'s theory neutrality makes it irrelevant to those clinicians who do operate from theory, and the processes of conceptualization and diagnosis become separate and unrelated entities (Westen, 1998). We are then left with many clinicians who begrudge the system, utilizing it essentially for reimbursement purposes.

Perhaps not so ironically, then, the first of two major barriers standing in the way of integrative diagnostic considerations being pragmatic for guiding psychotherapy is the *DSM* itself. The current framework, inclusive of such innovations as diagnostic prototypes and broad and diverse viewpoints stemming from work groups intent on preventing any single perspective from foreclosing on the others, dates back to the preparation of 1980s *DSM-III* (American Psychiatric Association [APA], 1980). However, more than 20 years following its publication, the contemporary *DSM* still cannot interrelate and differentiate its complex constructs without officially endorsing an underlying set of deeper principles. To date, its concepts are manifest mainly by way of committee consensus, cloaked by the illusion of empirical research. Because the diagnostic criteria have *not* been explicitly constructed to facilitate treatment, the *DSM-IV* (APA, 1994) is relegated to its rather minimalistic function of classifying persons into categories, rather than encouraging an integrative understanding of the patient across all domains in which the person's mental impairments are expressed (Barron, 1998). The *DSM-IV* criteria is disproportionately weighted across these domains, nonexistent, in fact, in some, and therefore cannot perform this function.

The second barrier is the human habit system. Most therapists, whatever their orientation or mode of treatment, pay minimal attention to the possibility that diagnosis can inform the philosophy and technique they employ. The admonition that different therapeutic approaches should be pursued with different patients and different problems is practically self-evident to the point of being trite, but given no logical basis from which to design effective therapeutic sequences and composites, even the most self-consciously antidogmatic clinician must implicitly lean toward one orientation or another. Of little consequence is what the actual syndrome or disorder may be; a family therapist is likely to select and employ a variant of family therapy, a cognitively-oriented therapist will find that a cognitive approach will probably "work best," and so on, including integrative therapists who are beginning to become a "school" and join this unfortunate trend of asserting the "truth" that their approach is the most efficacious. In spite of the self-evident admonition against fitting our patients into the proverbial "Procrustean beds" of our therapeutic approaches, it appears that our approaches continue to resonate more with where training occurred than with the nature of the patients' difficulties.

A diagnostic system, be it categorical, dimensional, or a combination of the two (e.g., the prototypal *DSM* system as it was intended, or the augmented synergistic proposal to follow), may profitably categorize patients according to presenting personality styles, as well as overt symptomology. This does not negate the fact that patients, so categorized, will display differences in the presence and constellation of their characteristics. A half century ago, the philosopher, Grünbaum, illustrated this thesis (1952):

> Every individual is unique by virtue of being a distinctive assemblage of characteristics not precisely duplicated in any other individual. Nevertheless, it is quite conceivable that the following ... might hold: If a male child having specifiable characteristics is subjected to maternal hostility and has a strong paternal attachment at a certain stage of his development, he will develop paranoia during adult life. If this ... holds, then children who are subjected to the stipulated conditions in fact become paranoiacs, however much they may have differed in other respects in childhood and whatever their other differences may be once they are already insane. (p. 672)

The question that must be raised is whether placement in the category impedes or facilitates a variety of clinically relevant objectives. Thus, if this grouping of key characteristics simplifies the task of clinical analysis by alerting the diagnostician to features of the patient's past history and present functioning that he has not yet observed, or if it enables clinicians to communicate effectively about their patients, or guides their selection of beneficial therapeutic plans, or assists researchers in the design of experiments, then the existence of these syndromal categories has served many useful purposes. Furthermore, as has been argued here and elsewhere (Millon, 1988, 1999), we must, as a profession, understand that the methodology we utilize should not stem from our particular emphasis of training; rather, it should stem from an informed, organized conception of the nature of the person's problem and, deeper than that, the nature of the person's orientation to the world (e.g., personality).

What has been termed "Personality-Guided Therapy" (Millon et al., 1999), may serve as an example of an integrative, diagnostically informed treatment, as its integrative processes are dictated by the nature of personality itself. The actual content of this synergistic therapy, however, is and must be specified on some other basis. Psychopathology, and in particular, personality, is by definition the patterning of intraindividual variables, but the nature of these variables does not follow from the definition, but must be supplied by some principle or on some basis which is superordinate to the construct. In this model, for example, the content of personality and psychopathology are derived from evolutionary theory, a discipline that informs but exists apart from our clinical subject. In and of itself, pathologic personality is a structural-functional concept that refers to the intraorganismic patterning of variables; it does not in itself say what these variables are, nor can it.

Why should we formulate a synergistic therapeutic approach? The answer may perhaps be best grasped by examining the inherent nature of psychopathology. If clinical syndromes were anchored exclusively to one particular trait domain (as phobias are thought of by some as being primarily behavioral in nature), a single or modality-bound psychotherapy would always be appropriate and desirable. Psychopathology, however, does not exclusively hold to one or the other modality; rather, it is multioperational and systemic. Every part is tied to every other, such that a holographic synergism lends the whole an integrative tenacity that makes psychic pathology "real," a complex system of elements to be reckoned with in any therapeutic endeavor. Therapies, then, should mirror the configuration of the many trait and clinical domains of the syndromes and disorders they seek to remedy. If the scope of the therapy is insufficient relative to the scope of the pathology, the treatment system will have considerable difficulty fulfilling its goals of healthy adaptation.

In light of the intrinsically complex nature of pathology, it may be useful to think of the psychic elements of a person as analogous to the sections of an orchestra, and the trait domains of a patient as a clustering of discordant instruments that exhibit imbalances, deficiencies, or conflicts within these sections. To extend this analogy, therapists may be seen as conductors whose task is to bring forth a harmonious balance among all the sections, as well as their specifically discordant instruments, muting some here, accentuating others there, all to the end of fulfilling the conductor's knowledge of how "the composition" can best be made consonant. The task is not that of altering one instrument, but of all, *in concert*. What is sought in music, then, is a balanced score, one composed of harmonic counterpoints, rhythmic patterns, and melodic combinations. What is needed in therapy is a likewise balanced program, a coordinated strategy of counterpoised approaches designed to optimize sequential and combinatorial treatment effects.

FROM PHILOSOPHY TO THEORY

A good theory should allow techniques across many modalities to be dynamically adapted, or integrated as ongoing changes in the patient occur, or as new information comes to light. What has been termed *multimodal therapy* in the sense of "technical eclecticism" (e.g., see Lazarus, 1976) is a quantum leap in terms of opening formerly rigid eyes to the many possibilities of blending data levels from different psychotherapy "camps." However, eclecticism is an insufficient guide to effective synergistic therapy. It cannot prescribe the particular form of those modalities that will remedy the pathologies of persons and their syndromes; it is also too open with regard to content and too imprecise to achieve focused goals. The intrinsically configurational nature of psychopathology, its multioperationism, and the interwoven character of clinical domains, simply are not as integrated in eclecticism as they need be in treating psychopathology. An open-minded therapist is left, then, with several different modality combinations, each with some currency toward understanding the patient's pathology, but no real means of bringing these diverse conceptions together in a coherent model of what, exactly, to do. Modality techniques considered fundamental in one perspective may not be so regarded within another; further, their fundamental constructs are different. Rather than inherit the modality tactics of a particular perspective, then, a theory of psychotherapy as a total system should seek some set of principles that can be addressed to the patient's whole psyche, thereby capitalizing on the naturally organic system of the person.

Before proceeding to a reasonably detailed outline of assessment and treatment techniques that will foster an informed psychotherapy based on thoughtful, meaningful diagnosis, we would like to make some comments in favor of the utility of a theory of the person. Kurt Lewin's words of more than 60 years ago, that "there is nothing so practical as a good theory" (1936), still resonate soundly in this argument. In spite of those who would shun theory for its subjective qualities, it is simply impossible, despite the efforts of empiricists and others who would hold to only "pure" observable phenomena, to remove any theoretical bias. Furthermore, theory is unavoidable if you want a system that can be investigated both for its reliability and validity (Carson, 1991; Loevinger, 1957; Millon, 1991). Theory, when properly fashioned, ultimately provides more simplicity and clarity than unintegrated and scattered information. Unrelated knowledge and techniques, especially those based on surface similarities, are a sign of a primitive science, as has been effectively argued by modern philosophers of science (Hempel, 1961; Quine, 1961). The key lies in finding theoretical principles for psychotherapy that fall "beyond" the field of psychology proper. It is necessary, therefore, to go beyond current conceptual boundaries to more established, "adjacent" sciences. Not only may such steps bear new conceptual fruits, but they may provide a foundation that can guide our own discipline's explorations.

EVOLUTION AS A NATURAL FRAMEWORK

Such a search for fundamental principles, we maintain, should begin with human evolution. Just as each person is composed of a total patterning of variables across all domains of human expression, it is the total organism that survives and reproduces, carrying forth both its adaptive and maladaptive potentials into subsequent generations. As the evolutionary success of organisms is dependent on the entire configuration of the organism's characteristics and potentials, so, too, does psychological fitness derive from the relation of the entire configuration of personal characteristics to the environments in which the person functions.

The evolutionary theory comprises three imperatives, each of which is a necessary aspect of the progression of evolution:

1. Each organism must survive.
2. It must adapt to its environment.
3. It must reproduce.

Each of these imperatives relates to a polarity allowing for its expression in the individual's life. To survive, an organism seeks to maximize pleasure (enhance life circumstances), *and* minimize pain (avoid dangerous or threatening stimuli). To adapt, an organism must, at appropriate times, either passively conform to, or actively *re*form, the surrounding environment's constraints and opportunities. And finally, to regenerate, an organism must adopt either a self-oriented or other-oriented strategy, judiciously "choosing" to self-invest or nurture other significant organisms (Millon, 1990). Anywhere in the universe, these are the fundamental evolutionary concerns, and there are none more fundamental.

Polarities, that is, *contrasting* functional directions, representing these three phases (pleasure-pain, passive-active, other-self) are the basis of the theoretically anchored prototypal classification system of personality styles and clinical disorders (Millon & Davis, 1996) that we will demonstrate for its interventional utility. Such bipolar or dimensional schemes are almost universally present throughout the literatures of mankind, as well as in psychology-at-large (Millon, 1990). The earliest may be traced to ancient Eastern religions, most notably the Chinese *I Ching* texts and the Hebrew's *Kabala*. In the life of the individual organism, each individual organism moves through developmental stages that have functional goals related to their respective phases of evolution. Within each stage, every individual acquires character dispositions representing a balance or predilection toward one of the two polarity inclinations; which inclination emerges as dominant over time results from the inextricable and reciprocal interplay of intraorganismic and extraorganismic factors. For example, during early infancy, the primary organismic function is to "continue to exist." Here, evolution has supplied mechanisms that orient the infant toward life-enhancing environments (pleasure) and away from life-threatening ones (pain). So-called "normal" individuals exhibit a reasonable balance between each of the polarity pairs. Not all individuals fall at the center, of course. Individual differences in both personality features and overall style will reflect the relative positions and strengths of each polarity component. A particularly "healthy" person, for example, would be one who is high on both self and other, indicating a solid sense of self-worth, combined with a genuine sensitivity to the needs of others.

The expression of traits or dispositions acquired in early stages of development may have their expression transformed as later faculties or dispositions develop (Millon, 1969). Temperament is perhaps a classic example. An individual with an active temperament may develop, contingent on contextual factors, into several theoretically derived "prototypal" personality styles, for example, an avoidant or an antisocial style, the consequences being partly determined by whether the child has a fearful or a fearless temperament when dealing with a harsh environment. The transformation of earlier temperamental characteristics takes the form of what has been called "personological bifurcations" (Millon, 1990). Thus, if the individual is inclined toward a *passive* orientation and later learns to be self-focused, a prototypical narcissistic style ensues. But if the individual possesses an *active* orientation and later learns to be self-focused, a prototypical antisocial style may ensue. Thus, early developing dispositions may undergo "vicissitudes," whereby their meaning in the context of the whole organism is subsequently reformed into complex personality configurations.

At a slightly more finite level of specification are what we have termed the personality *subtypes*. This idea of subtypes recognizes two fundamental facts. The first derives from the chance side of the evolutionary equation, and draws on the long descriptive tradition in psychology and psychiatry, as perhaps best expressed in the works of the turn of the century nosologist Emil Kraepelin: In the ordinary course of clinical work, we find that every disorder seems to sort itself into ever finer subcategories, which rest on an a priori basis, but instead flow from cultural and social factors and their interaction with biological influences such as constitution, temperament, or perhaps even systematic neurological defects. Accordingly, if society were different, or if the neurotransmitters chosen by evolution to bathe the human brain were different, the subtypes would be different also. Such entities are the pristine product of clinical observation, and however sharp the classification boundaries may be drawn between them, they are, in fact, unusually soft.

While the concept of prototype and subtype allows the natural heterogeneity of persons to be accommodated within a classification system, there are as many ways to fulfill a given diagnosis as there are subsets of the number of diagnostic criteria required at the diagnostic threshold. For example, there are many ways to score five of a total of nine diagnostic criteria, whatever the actual syndrome. In the context of an idealized medical disease model, which Axis I approximates, the fact that two different individuals, both of whom are depressed, might possess substantially different sets of depressive symptoms is not really problematic. The symptoms may be expressed somewhat differently, but the underlying pathology process is the same and can be treated in the same way. For example, while one person gains weight and wakes early in the morning, and the other loses weight and sleeps long into the day, both may be treated with an antidepressant and cognitive therapy. Personality, however, as represented in Axis II of the *DSM*, should be seen to follow a fundamentally different conceptual model. Whereas variance from the prototypal ideal is usually considered irrelevant in the Axis I medical model of clinical syndromes, it is the very essence of Axis II. Personality styles or disorders are reified for clinical utility, but are most accurately thought of as variants of personality prototypes, a phrase that communicates their relatively unique clinical "complexion," without conveying the erroneous connotation of a distinct disease entity.

The evolutionary thesis may also be seen to provide a basis for deriving the so-called "clinical syndromes" of Axis-II, as well. To illustrate briefly, consider the anxiety disorders. Without explicating its several variants, a low pain threshold on the pleasure-pain polarity would dispose such individuals to be sensitive to punishments that, depending on covariant polarity positions, might result in the acquisition of complex syndromal characteristics, such as ease of discouragement, low self-esteem, cautiousness, and social phobias. Similarly, a low pleasure threshold on the same polarity might make such individuals prone to experience joy and satisfaction with great ease: again, depending on covariant polarity positions, such persons might be inclined toward impulsiveness and hedonic pursuits, be intolerant of frustration and delay, and, at the clinical level, give evidence of a susceptibility to manic episodes.

To use musical metaphors again, *DSM-IV*'s Axis I clinical syndromes are composed essentially of a single theme or subject (e.g., anxiety, depression), a salient melodic line that may vary in its rhythm and harmony, changing little except in its timing, cadence, and progression. In contrast, the diversely expressed domains that comprise Axis II seem constructed more in accord with the compositional structure known as the fugue where there is a dovetailing of two or more melodic lines. Framed in the sonata style, the opening exposition in the fugue begins when an introductory theme is announced (or analogously in psychopathology, a series of clinical symptoms become evident), following which a second and perhaps third, and essentially independent set of themes emerge in the form of "answers" to the first (akin to the unfolding expression of underlying personality traits). As the complexity of the fugue is revealed (we now have identified a full-blown personality disorder), variants of the introductory theme (that is, the initial symptom picture) develop *counter-subjects* (less observable, inferred traits) that are interwoven with the preceding in accord with well-known harmonic rules (comparably, mechanisms that regulate intrapsychic dynamics). This matrix of entwined melodic lines progresses over time in an episodic fashion, occasionally augmented, at other times diminished. It is sequenced to follow its evolving contrapuntal structure, unfolding an interlaced tapestry (the development and linkages of several psychological traits). To build this metaphorical elaboration further, not only may personality be viewed much like a fugue, but the melodic lines of its psychological counterpoints are comprised of the three evolutionary themes presented earlier (the polarities, that is). Thus, some fugues are rhythmically vigorous and rousing (high "active"), others kindle a sweet sentimentality (high "other"), still others evoke a somber and anguished mood (high "pain"), and so on. When the counterpoint of the first three polarities is harmonically balanced, we observe a well-functioning or so-called normal person; when deficiencies, imbalances, or conflicts exist among them, we observe one or another variant of the personality disorders.

CREATION OF A MEANINGFUL PERSONOLOGIC DIAGNOSIS

The validity of a pragmatic assessment and diagnosis depends on the validity of the system of categorized types and trait dimensions that might be brought to bear on the individual case. The prototype construct, which is one of the favorable attributes of the *DSM,* represents a synthesis of both categorical and dimensional models. Prototypal models assume that no necessary or sufficient criteria exist by which syndromes and disorders can be unequivocally diagnosed. The synthetic character of the prototypal model can be seen by comparing what is saved and discarded in the three approaches. The categorical model sacrifices quantitative variation in favor of the discrete, binary judgments. The dimensional model sacrifices qualitative distinctions in favor of quantitative scores. Of the three models, the prototypal is the only one that conserves both qualitative and quantitative clinical information.

However, the *DSM*'s personality prototypes represent an approach that is necessary, but not sufficient. It simply lists characteristics that have been found to accompany a particular disorder with some regularity and specificity. Although the *DSM* puts forth several domains in which personality is expressed (notably cognition, affectivity, interpersonal functioning, and impulse control), these psychological domains are neither comprehensive nor comparable, and this limits the utility of this approach. Because of this, the *DSM-IV* lacks a basis to organize these structures of personality meaningfully, in a manner amenable to intervention. Further, these problems exist both within and between disorders, so that different disorders evince different content distortions. Finally, theoretically derived "prototypes" are a good basis for understanding how "real world" blends of personality style appear, but the *DSM* does not provide the undergirding for understanding such blends. For example, it is relatively easy to identify a *schizoid* by checking off enough *DSM-IV* criteria for the construct, but it is impossible, by these criteria, to make finer and more useful distinctions as they are more likely to appear outside of textbook-style, theoretically derived prototypes (e.g., what subtype of schizoid a particular patient might be), since the criteria to discriminate between subgroups simply do not as yet exist. As will be seen, learning to conceptualize these blends of personality styles is a vital skill in formulating synergistic treatment plans.

Both the nature of the person and the laws of evolution require that the stylistic domains of personality be drawn together in a logical fashion. No domain is an autonomous entity. Instead, the evolution of the structure and content of personality is constrained by the evolutionary imperatives of survival, adaptation, and reproductive success, for it is always the whole organism that is selected and evolves. To synthesize the domains of the person as a coherent unity, we draw on the boundary between organism and environment. What we call *functional domains* relate the organism to the external world, while other domains serve as *structural* substrates for functioning, existing "inside" the organism. Table 2.1 lists and describes the domain matrix of the structures and functions of personality, as derived from the expression of evolutionary polarities.

The preceding issue points to the inadequacy of any approach that links classification to intervention without theoretical guidance. The argument is merely that diagnosis should constrain and guide therapy in a manner consonant with assumptions of the theoretically derived prototypal model; without a philosophical framework, there is no sound basis from which to derive principles that contextualize the person and his or her integrated structures and functions with a thorough intervention reflective of the complexity of this personality. The scope of the interventions that might be considered appropriate and the form of their application are left unattended. Any set of interventions or techniques might be applied singly or in combination, without regard to the diagnostic complexity of the treated disorder. In the actual practice of therapy, techniques within a particular pathological data level, that is, psychodynamic techniques, behavioral techniques, and so on, are, in fact, often applied conjointly. Thus, systematic desensitization might be followed by in vivo exposure, or a patient might keep a diary of his or her thoughts, while at the same time reframing those thoughts in accordance with the therapist's directions when they occur. In these formulations, however, there is no strong a priori reason why any two therapies or techniques should be combined at all. When techniques from different modalities are applied together successfully, it is because the combination mirrors the composition of the individual case, not because it derives its logic on the basis of a theory or the syndrome.

The whole clinical enterprise is thereby changed. The purpose is not to classify individuals into categories, but instead to augment the classification system in a more comprehensive attempt to capture the particular reality that is the person. The purpose is not to put persons in the classification system, but instead to reorient the system with respect to the person by determining how their unique, ontological constellation of attributes overflows and exceeds it. The classification thus becomes a point of departure for comparison and contrast, a way-station in achieving a total understanding of the complexity of the whole, not a destination in itself. When in the course of an assessment the clinician begins to feel that the subject is understood at a level where ordinary diagnostic labels no longer adequately apply, the classification system is well on its

Table 2.1

Expression of Personality Across the Domains of Clinical Science

Domain Disorder	Behavioral Acts	Interpersonal Conduct	Cognitive Style	Self-Image	Object Representations	Regulatory Mechanisms	Morphologic Organization	Mood/ Temperament
Schizoid	Impassive	Unengaged	Impoverished	Complacent	Meager	Intellectualization	Undifferentiated	Apathetic
Avoidant	Fretful	Aversive	Distracted	Alienated	Vexatious	Fantasy	Fragile	Anguished
Depressive	Disconsolate	Defenseless	Pessimistic	Worthless	Forsaken	Fantasy	Depleted	Melancholic
Dependent	Incompetent	Submissive	Naive	Inept	Immature	Introjection	Inchoate	Pacific
Histrionic	Dramatic	Attention-seeking	Flighty	Gregarious	Shallow	Dissociation	Disjointed	Fickle
Narcissistic	Haughty	Exploitive	Expansive	Admirable	Contrived	Rationalization	Spurious	Insouciant
Antisocial	Impulsive	Irresponsible	Deviant	Autonomous	Debased	Acting-out	Unruly	Callous
Sadistic	Precipitate	Abrasive	Dogmatic	Combative	Pernicious	Isolation	Eruptive	Hostile
Compulsive	Disciplined	Respectful	Constricted	Conscientious	Concealed	Reaction formation	Compartmentalized	Solemn
Negativistic	Resentful	Contrary	Skeptical	Discontented	Vacillating	Displacement	Divergent	Irritable
Masochistic	Abstinent	Deferential	Diffident	Undeserving	Discredited	Exaggeration	Inverted	Dysphoric
Schizotypal	Eccentric	Secretive	Autistic	Estranged	Chaotic	Undoing	Fragmented	Distraught or insentient
Borderline	Spasmodic	Paradoxical	Capricious	Uncertain	Incompatible	Regression	Split	Labile
Paranoid	Defensive	Provocative	Suspicious	Inviolable	Unalterable	Projection	Inelastic	Irascible

way to being falsified relative to the individual, and that a truly idiographic understanding of the person is close at hand, ready to be approached in a comprehensive and systematic way therapeutically.

Much of the confusion that has plagued diagnostic systems in the past can be attributed to the overlapping and changeability of symptom pictures; we argue that greater clarity can be achieved in classification if we focus on the person's basic personality *as a system* rather than limit ourselves to the particular dominant symptom the person manifests at any particular time. Moreover, by focusing our attention on enduring personality traits and pervasive clinical domains of expression, we may be able to deduce the cluster of different symptoms the patient is *likely* to display and the sequence of symptoms he or she may exhibit over time. For example, knowing the vulnerabilities and habitual coping strategies of a *paranoid* person, we would predict that he will evidence either together or in sequence both delusions and hostile mania, should he become psychotically disordered. Similarly, *compulsive* personalities may be expected to manifest cyclical swings between catatonic rigidity, agitated depression, and manic excitement, should they decompensate into a psychotic state. Focusing on ingrained personality patterns rather than transient symptoms enables us, then, to grasp both the patient's complex syndrome, and the symptoms he is likely to exhibit, as well as the possible sequence in which the symptoms will wax and wane.

Ideally, a diagnosis should function as a means of narrowing the universe of therapeutic techniques to some small set of choices. Within this small set, uniquely personal factors come into play between alternative techniques or the order in which these techniques might be applied. As we have stated, the concept of a system must be brought to the forefront, even when discussing simple behavioral reactions and symptoms. Systems function as a whole, but are composed of parts—in this case, the eight structural and functional domains in Millon's earlier writings (Millon, 1984, 1986a, 1990; Millon et al., 1999; Millon & Davis, 1996). They serve as a means of classifying the parts or constructs in accord with traditional historic therapeutic traditions. The nature and intensity of the constraints in each of these domains limit the potential number of states that the system can assume at any moment in time; this total configuration of operative domains results in each patient's distinctive pattern of individuality. Equally significant, this pattern of domain problems serves to construct a model for *synergistic treatment approaches* (Millon et al., 1999).

APPLICATION OF AN INFORMED CLASSIFICATION TO THERAPEUTIC STRATEGY

The evolutionary principles from which we derive our conceptualizations of personality, and the clinical domains that underlie personologic structure and function (and in cases of syndromal distress, psychopathology) do, in our judgment, provide a useful framework for identifying both goals and methods of treatment. Before operationally explicating these facets, however, we would like to briefly describe two general clinical constructs that pervade and help structure the blending of treatment techniques in Millon's synergistic model; the first relates to the goal of balancing uneven polarities, and the second, the use of techniques that counter thoughts, emotions, and behaviors that perpetuate the patient's difficulties (Millon & Davis, 1996).

As noted elsewhere (Millon, 1990), a theoretical basis is developed from the principles of evolution, to which three polarities are considered fundamental: the pain-pleasure, the active-passive, and the self-other. As a general philosophy, specific treatment techniques are selected as tactics to achieve polarity-oriented balances. Depending on the pathological polarity to be modified and the integrative treatment sequence one has in mind, the goals of therapy are, in general: to overcome *pleasure deficiencies* in schizoids, avoidants, and depressive styles and disorders; to reestablish *interpersonally imbalanced* polarity disturbances in dependents, histrionics, narcissists, and antisocials; to undo the *intrapsychic conflicts* in sadists, compulsives, masochists, and negativists; last, to reconstruct the *structural defects* in schizotypal, borderline, and paranoid persons (Millon et al., 1999). These goals are to be achieved by the use of modality tactics that are optimally suited to the clinical domains in which these pathologies are expressed (see the following section on domain assessment).

Our second superordinate therapeutic construct relates to continuity in personality and psychopathology that may be attributed in great measure to the stability of constitutional factors and the deeply ingrained character of early experiential learning. Every behavior, attitude, and feeling that is currently exhibited is a perpetuation, a remnant of the past that persists into the present. Not only do these residuals passively shape the present by temporal precedence, if nothing else, but they insidiously distort and transform ongoing life events to make them duplicates of the past. It is this self-perpetuating re-creative process that becomes so problematic in treating psychopathology. In other words, and as Millon (1969, 1981) has said previously, *psychopathology is itself pathogenic.* It sets into motion *new* life experiences that are further pathology-producing. A major goal of therapy, then, would be to stop these perpetuating inclinations, that is, to prevent the continued exacerbation and intensification of a patient's established problematic habits and attitudes. Much of what therapists must do is reverse self-pathogenesis, the intruding into the present of erroneous expectations, the perniciousness of maladaptive interpersonal conduct, the repetitive establishing of new, self-entrapping "vicious circles," as Horney has earlier described it (1945) and what Wachtel has referred to as "cyclical psychodynamics" (1973).

COMPLEX SYNDROME TREATMENT GOALS

Before commencing with an outline of domain-oriented assessment, we would like to make distinctions between three levels of pathogenic processes: simple reactions, complex syndromes, and personality patterns (styles/disorders; Millon et al., 1999). These three levels lie on a continuum such that the former is essentially a straightforward, often dramatic, but essentially singular symptom, unaffected by other psychosocial traits of which the-person-as-a-whole is composed (Millon, 1969). At the other extreme are personality patterns (styles and disorders) that comprise an interrelated mix of psychological traits, such as cognitive attitudes and interpersonal behaviors, as well as biological temperaments and intrapsychic processes. Complex syndromes lie in between, manifestly akin to simple reactions, but deeply interwoven and mediated by pervasive personality traits and embedded vulnerabilities. It is on this seemingly superficial level, which in fact encompasses many trait domains of personality, that we frequently find many of our most problematic and distressed patients; we focus our attention here in this section of the chapter.

Patients fall at varying levels of severity along the simple reaction, complex syndrome, personality pattern continuum, and adjustments may have to be made in following a synergistic plan to accommodate possible changes in our assessment of a case. Cognitive, behavioral, psychodynamic, and interpersonal approaches are *each* likely to demonstrate some level of therapeutic efficacy over waiting-list controls. Even though consistently channeled through a particular bias and directed at a *particular* symptom domain, many interventions will gather enough momentum to eventually change significant portions of the entire person. In cases where the whole complex of psychic processes is reconfigured, it is not likely to be the intervention per se that produces so vast a change, but a synergistic interaction between a syndrome intervention and the personologic context in which that intervention takes place. Therefore, it is the interdependent nature of the organismic system that compensates for the inadequacy of a single domain focus. The fact that systems spread the effect of any input throughout their entire infrastructure is likely to be a significant reason why no major school of therapy (that is, the behavioral, cognitive, interpersonal, intrapsychic, and biological) has yet to be judged a total failure, or has been able to demonstrate consistent superiority for all disorders.

Criteria used to select and develop the trait domains we have included are:

1. That they be varied in the features they embody: that is, not be limited just to behaviors or cognitions, but instead encompass a full range of clinically relevant characteristics.
2. That they *parallel,* if not correspond, to many of our profession's current therapeutic modalities (e.g., cognitively oriented techniques for altering dysfunctional beliefs; group treatment procedures for modifying interpersonal conduct).
3. That they not only be coordinated to the official *DSM* schema of personality and syndromal prototypes, but also that most syndromes and personality patterns be able to be characterized by a distinctive characteristic within each clinical domain.

In conducting a domain-oriented assessment, clinicians should be careful not to regard each domain as a concretized, independent entity, and thereby fall into a naïve operationism. Each domain is a legitimate, but highly contextualized, part of an integrated whole, one absolutely necessary if the integrity of the organism is to be maintained. Nevertheless, individuals differ with respect to which and how many domains of their pathology are expressed. Patients vary not only in degree to which their domain characteristics approximate a pathologic syndrome or personality disorder, but also in the extent to which the influences of each domain shape the patient's overall functioning. Conceptualizing each form of psychopathology as a system, we should recognize that different parts of the system may be salient for different individuals, even where those individuals share a diagnosis.

In the following paragraphs, we become more tangible in regard to our proposed diagnostically informed treatment approach. We outline the major clinical domains, which may be manifested singularly, or in complex syndromes, or in personality disorders. No less important, we outline their covariant and parallel treatment modalities. For the present, our focus is on characterizing each of *eight* clinical domains *and* illustrating the eight therapeutic modalities that parallel them. (See Millon et al., 1999, for a fuller discussion of what follows.)

Expressive Behaviors

These attributes relate to the observables seen at the *behavioral level* of data and are usually recorded by noting what and how the patient acts. Through inference, observations of overt behavior enable us to deduce either what the patient unknowingly reveals about him or herself or, often conversely, what he or she wishes others to think or to know about him or her. The range and character of these expressive behaviors are not only wide and diverse, but they convey both distinctive and worthwhile clinical information, from communicating a sense of personal incompetence to exhibiting general defensiveness, to demonstrating a disciplined self-control, and so on. This domain of clinical data is likely to be especially productive in differentiating patients on the passive-active polarity of Millon's (1990) theoretical model. Behavioral methods seem especially suitable to the elimination of problematic behaviors and the creation of more effective adaptations.

Parallel Behavior Therapies   As written previously, behaviorists contend that "other" therapeutic approaches are method-oriented rather than problem-oriented. Non-behaviorists are seen to proceed in a uniform and complicating fashion regardless of the particular character of the patient's difficulty, utilizing the same "psycho-analytic" or "cognitive" procedure with all forms and varieties of pathology. Not only do they claim that behavioral approaches are flexible and problem-oriented, but there is no "fixed" technique in pure behavior therapy. As we see it, behavioral techniques are extremely useful in counteracting simple clinical reactions that manifest themselves in overt behaviors. They distinguish the elements of each simple reaction and then fashion a procedure designed specifically to effect changes only in that problem. For example, if the patient complains of acute anxiety attacks, procedures are designed to eliminate just that symptom, and therapy is completed when the symptom has been removed.

Interpersonal/Relational Conduct

A patient's style of relating to others may be captured in a number of ways, such as how his or her actions impact on others, intended or otherwise, the attitudes that underlie, prompt, and give shape to these actions, the methods by which he or she engages others to meet his or her needs, or his or her way of coping with social tensions and conflicts. Extrapolating from these observations, the clinician may construct an image of how the patient functions in relation to others, be it antagonistically, respectfully, aversively, secretively, and so on.

Interpersonal Assessment Domains   Tenets of interpersonal theory, especially as encoded in the circumplex representation, make this taxonomy a promising one for the assessment of both personality traits and clusters and clinical syndromes. According to its most basic conception, each person constricts the response repertoire of others in order to evoke specifically those responses that confirm his or her perception of the self and world (Kiesler, 1982, 1997). Each party in the interpersonal system is co-opted by the other in an effort to elicit validation. Together, the parties must find a stable system state that mutually confirms, thereby maintaining and perpetuating their respective self-concepts. These system states can be based on either reciprocity (on the vertical axis) or correspondence (on the horizontal axis).

While usually presented two-dimensionally, the circumplex can also be visualized as a bivariate distribution with increasing densification toward the center, and increasing sparsity toward the edges. Healthy or flexible interpersonal styles appear as balanced patterns within the circle. Individuals usually possess a full range of styles by which to relate to others, regardless of the kinds of others with whom they find themselves involved. Psychic pathology can be expressed geometrically through distortions of the healthy circular and concentric pattern.

The interpersonal style of the schizoid, avoidant, dependent, histrionic, narcissistic, and antisocial personalities seem better assessed by the circumplex than do compulsive, borderline, negativistic (passive-aggressive), paranoid, and schizotypal individuals (Pincus & Wiggins, 1989). We would conclude then that any assessment of clinical syndromes and personality that is anchored *only* in the interpersonal domain, while informative, must be regarded as incomplete. Clinicians of an interpersonal bent must balance the increased specificity gained by using an exclusively interpersonally oriented instrument with the knowledge that the paradigm itself is acknowledged to be an incomplete representation of psychic pathology.

Parallel Interpersonal Therapies   There are three major variants of treatment that focus on the interpersonal domain. The first engages one patient exclusively at a time in a dyadic patient-therapist medium, but centers its attentions primarily on the patient's relationships with others; these techniques are known as *interpersonal psychotherapy.* The second set of techniques assembles an assortment of patients together in a group so that their habitual styles of relating to others can be observed and analyzed as the interactions among the participants unfold; these techniques are known as group psychotherapy. The third variant is *family therapy* where established and ostensibly problematic relationships are evaluated and treated.

To paraphrase Kiesler (1997), the essential problems of individuals reside in the person's recurrent transactions with significant others. These stem largely from disordered, inappropriate, or inadequate communications, and result from failing to attend and/or not correct the unsuccessful and self-defeating nature of these communications. The interpersonal approach centers its attention on the individual's closest relationships, notably current family interactions, the family of origin, past and present love affairs and friendships, as well as neighborhood and work relations. It is the patient's habitual interactive and hierarchical roles in these social systems that are the focus of interpersonal therapy. The dyadic treatment interaction, despite its uniqueness, is seen as paralleling other venues of human communication. The interpersonal therapist becomes sensitized to the intrusions of the patient's habitual styles of interaction by the manner in which he "draws out" or "pulls" the therapist's feelings and attitudes. It is these evocative responses that provide a good indication of how the patient continues to relate to others. This transactive process mirrors in many ways what psychoanalysts refer to in their concepts of transference and countertransference. More will be said on these matters when we discuss treatment modalities oriented to modifying the patient's "object relationships."

Once a past history assessment has been undertaken and its elements clarified, the task of the interpersonal therapist is to help patients identify the persons with whom they are currently having difficulties, what these difficulties are, and whether there are ways in which they can be resolved or made more satisfactory. Problems in the patient's current environment should be stated explicitly, for example, being intimidated on the job, arguing over trivia with their spouse, missing old friends, and shown to be derivations from past experiences and relationships.

Developed as a comprehensive modality of interpersonal treatment more than a half-century ago (e.g., see Slavson, 1943), the impact of *group psychotherapy* in molding and sustaining interpersonal behaviors has been thoroughly explored in recent decades. Clearly, there are several advantages to group, and also to family therapies. Perhaps most significant is the fact that the patient acquires his new behaviors in a setting that is the same or similar to his "natural" interpersonal world; relating to family or peer group members is a more realistic experience than that of the hierarchic therapist-patient dyad. It is easier to "generalize" to the extratherapeutic world what is learned in family and peer-group settings since it is closer to "reality" than is the individual treatment setting.

Cognitive Modes

How the patient focuses and allocates attention, encodes and processes information, organizes thoughts, makes attributions, and communicates reactions and ideas to others represents data at the "cognitive" level, and are among the most useful indices to the clinician of the patient's distinctive way of functioning. By synthesizing these signs and symptoms, it may be possible to identify indications of what may be termed an impoverished style, or distracted thinking, or cognitive flightiness, or constricted thought, and so on.

Cognitive Assessment Domains   Cognitivists place heavy emphasis on internal processes that mediate overt actions. Cognitivists also differ from both behavior and intrapsychic therapists with regard to which events and processes they consider central to pathogenesis and treatment. Cognitivists concern themselves with the reorientation of consciously discordant feelings and readily identifiable erroneous beliefs, and not to the modification of narrow behaviors or to disgorging the past and its associated unconscious derivatives.

Parallel Cognitive Therapies   Given their emphasis on conscious attitudes and perceptions, cognitive therapists are inclined to follow an insight-expressive rather than an action-suppressive treatment process. Both cognitive and intrapsychic therapists employ the insight-expressive approach, but the focus of their explorations differs, at least in theory. Cognitivists attend to dissonant assumptions and expectations that can be consciously acknowledged by an examination of the patient's everyday relationships and activities. The therapist may not only assume authority for deciding the objectives of treatment, but may confront the patient with the irrationalities of his thinking. For example, there is the practice of "exposing" the patient's erroneous or irrational attitudes, and the reworking of his or her belief structure into one with a more rational and stable composition.

In what he terms "rational-emotive" therapy, Ellis (1967) considers the primary objective of therapy to be countering the patient's tendency to perpetuate his difficulties through illogical and negative thinking. The patient, by reiterating these unrealistic and self-defeating beliefs in a self-dialogue, constantly reaffirms his irrationality and aggravates his distress. To overcome these implicit but pervasive attitudes, the therapist confronts the patient with them and induces him to think about them consciously and concertedly and to "attack them" forcefully and unequivocally until they no longer influence his behavior. By revealing and assailing these beliefs and by "commanding" the patient to engage in activities that run counter to them, their hold on his life is broken and new directions become possible.

The other highly regarded cognitive approach has been developed by Beck and his associates (Beck, Freeman, & Associates, 1990). Central to Beck's approach is the concept of *schema,* that is, specific rules that govern information processing and behavior. To Beck, the disentangling and clarification of these schemas lies at the heart of therapeutic work with psychopathology. They persist, despite their dysfunctional consequences, owing largely to the fact that they enable the patient to find ways to extract short-term benefits from them, thereby diverting the patient from pursuing more effective, long-term solutions. As with other sophisticated therapists, Beck emphasizes the therapist-patient relationship as a central element in the therapeutic process. As he notes further, considerable "artistry" is involved in unraveling the origins of the patient's beliefs and in exploring the meaning of significant past events.

Self-Image

One major configuration emerges during development to impose a measure of sameness on an otherwise fluid environment, the perception of self-as-object, a distinct, ever-present, and identifiable "I" or "me."

Self-Image Assessment Domains   Self-identity stems largely from conceptions formed at a cognitive level. The self is especially significant in that it provides a stable anchor to serve as a guidepost and to give continuity to changing experience. Most persons have an implicit sense of who they are, but differ greatly in clarity, accuracy, and complexity (Millon, 1986b) of their self-introspections.

The character and valuation of the self-image is often a problematic one, such as an unhappy and dismaying self-reality, seen in the *avoidant's* feeling of being alienated, or the *depressive's* image of worthlessness, or the *negativist's* sense of self-discontent. On the other hand, there are those whose self-image is one of complacence, as is seen in the *schizoid,* or that of being gregarious among *histrionics,* or admirable among *narcissists.* Thus, self-image, despite the many particulars of his or her character, appear to be predominantly either of a positive or a negative quality.

Parallel Self-Image Therapies   Self-actualization or humanistic therapists are those whose orientation is to "free" the patient to develop a more positive and confident image of her self-worth. Liberated in this manner, the patient ostensibly learned to act in ways that were "right" for her, and thereby enabled her to "actualize" her inherent potentials. To promote these objectives, the therapist views events from the patient's frame of reference and conveys both a "caring" attitude and a genuine respect for the patient's worth as a human being. According to Carl Rogers (1942, 1951, 1961, 1967), patient "growth" is a product neither of special treatment procedures nor professional know-how; rather, it emerges from the quality and character of the therapeutic relationship. More specifically, it occurs as a consequence of attitudes expressed on the part of the therapist, notably his *genuineness* and his unconditional positive regard.

Also suitable for those who have experienced the anguish of a chronically troubled life are the philosophies and techniques of modern-day "existential therapists," those who seek to enable the patient to deal with his unhappiness realistically, yet in a constructive and positive manner. The existential school possesses a less sanguine view of a person's inherent fate than do Rogerians, believing that he or she must struggle to find a valued meaning to life; therapy, then, attempts to strengthen the patient's capacity to choose an "authentic" existence. *Self-actualizing* therapists of this latter persuasion are committed to the view that a person must confront and accept the inevitable dilemmas of life if he is to achieve a measure of "authentic" self-realization. Mutual acceptance and self-revelation enables the patient to find an authentic meaning to his existence, despite the profound and inescapable contradictions that life presents. These existentially-oriented self-image therapies may be especially suitable for psychopathologies in which life has been a series of alienations and unhappiness, for example, *avoidants, depressives,* and so on. By contrast, the underlying assumption of the more humanistically oriented self-actualizing therapies, including client-centered, experiential, and Gestalt, is that man may have been too harsh with himself, tending to blame and judge his actions more severely than is necessary.

Intrapsychic Objects, Mechanisms, and Morphology

As noted previously, significant experiences from the past leave an inner imprint, a structural residue composed of memories, attitudes, and affects that serve as a substrate of dispositions for perceiving and reacting to life's ongoing events.

Intrapsychic Assessment Domains: Intrapsychic Objects Analogous to the various organ systems of which the body is composed, both the character and substance of these internalized representations of significant figures and relationships of the past can be differentiated and analyzed for clinical purposes. Variations in the nature and content of this inner world can be associated with one or another complex syndrome or personality pattern, and lead us to employ descriptive terms to represent them, such as shallow, vexatious, undifferentiated, concealed, and irreconcilable.

Intrapsychic Assessment Domains: Regulatory Mechanisms Although *mechanisms* of self-protection, need gratification, and conflict resolution are consciously recognized at times, they represent data derived primarily from intrapsychic sources. Because *regulatory mechanisms* also are internal processes, they are even more difficult to discern and describe than processes that are anchored a bit closer to the observable world. As such, they are not directly amenable to assessment by self-reflective appraisal in pure form, but only as derivatives many levels removed from their core conflicts and their dynamic regulation. By definition, dynamic regulatory mechanisms co-opt and transform both internal and external realities before they can enter conscious awareness in a robust and unaltered form. When chronically enacted, they often perpetuate a sequence of events that intensifies the very problems they were intended to circumvent.

Great care must be taken not to challenge or undo these intrapsychic mechanisms that regulate and balance the inner psychic system of a patient. Therapists must appraise the character of these regulatory functions so they can be quickly identified and handled in as beneficial a manner as possible. Moreover, these regulatory/defensive mechanisms may restrict the patient from dealing with her difficulties in a rational and honest fashion.

While the measurement of defense mechanisms, historically a troublesome and inconsistent procedure, has improved through content objectification and specification, current procedures still leave something to be desired. Because the size of the correlation coefficient that can be achieved between measures is limited by their reliabilities, it is likely that external validity of defensive measures will remain more difficult to establish than that of self-report inventories.

Intrapsychic Assessment Domains: Morphologic Organization   The overall architecture that serves as a framework for an individual's psychic interior may display weakness in its structural cohesion, exhibit deficient coordination among its components, and possess few mechanisms to maintain balance and harmony, regulate internal conflicts, or mediate external pressures; the concept of *morphologic organization* refers to the structural strength, interior congruity, and functional efficacy of the overall personality system. "Organization" of the mind is a concept almost exclusively derived from inferences at the *intrapsychic level* of analysis, one akin to and employed in conjunction with current psychoanalytic notions such as borderline and psychotic levels, but this usage tends to be limited, relating essentially to quantitative degrees of integrative pathology, not to qualitative variations in either integrative structure or configuration. *Stylistic* variants of this structural attribute may be employed to characterize each of the complex syndromes or personality disorder prototypes; their distinctive organizational attributes are represented with descriptors such an inchoate, disjoined, and compartmentalized.

Morphological structures represent deeply embedded and relatively enduring templates of imprinted memories, attitudes, needs, fears, conflicts, and so on, which guide experience and transform the nature of ongoing life events. Psychic structures are architectural in form. Moreover, they have an orienting and preemptive effect in that they alter the character of action and the impact of subsequent experiences in line with preformed inclinations and expectancies. By selectively lowering thresholds for transactions that are consonant with either constitutional proclivities or early learnings, future events are often experienced as variations of the past. Of course, the residuals of the past do more than passively contribute their share to the present. By temporal precedence, if nothing else, they guide, shape, or distort the character of current events and objective realities.

For purposes of definition, morphological organization represents structural domains that can be conceived as "substrates and action dispositions of a quasi-permanent nature." Possessing a network of interconnecting pathways, organisms contain the framework in which the internalized residues of the past are cast. These structures often serve to close the organism off to novel interpretations of the world, and tend to limit the possibilities of expression to those that have already become prepotent. Their preemptive and channeling character plays an important role in perpetuating the maladaptive behavior and vicious circles of pathology.

Parallel Intrapsychic Therapies   You are likely to have discussed both frequently and at length the history, rationale, and considerable heterogeneity of intrapsychic theory (Millon, 1990). Despite inevitable controversies and divergences in emphasis, often appearing more divisive upon first than later examination, intrapsychic therapists do share certain beliefs and goals in common that are worthy of note and distinguish them from other modality orientations; two are noted here.

First, all intrapsychic therapists focus on *internal mediating* processes (e.g., regulatory mechanisms) and structures (object representations) that ostensibly *underlie* and give rise to overt behavior. In contrast to cognitivists, however, their attention is directed to those mediating events that operate at the *unconscious* rather than the conscious level. To them, overt behaviors and cognitive reports are merely *surface* expressions of dynamically orchestrated, but deeply repressed emotions and associated defensive strategies (Magnavita, 1997), all framed in a distinctive structural morphology (Kernberg, 1984). Since these unconscious processes and structures are essentially impervious to surface maneuvers, techniques of behavior modification are seen as mere palliatives, and methods of cognitive reorientation are thought to resolve only those difficulties that are so trivial or painless as to be tolerated consciously. "True" therapy occurs only when these deeply ingrained elements of the unconscious are fully unearthed and analyzed. The task of intrapsychic therapy, then, is to circumvent or pierce resistances that shield these insidious structures and processes, bringing them into consciousness, and reworking them into more constructive forms.

Second, intrapsychic therapists see as their goal the *reconstruction* of the patient's complex syndrome or personality pattern, not the removal of a single domain syndrome, or the reframing of a superficial cognitive attitude. Disentangling the underlying structure of complex syndromes or personality pathology, forged of many interlocking elements that build into a network of pervasive strategies and mechanisms, is the object of their therapy. Reconstruction, then, rather than repair of a simple syndrome is the option chosen by intrapsychic therapists. They set for themselves the laborious task of rebuilding those functions (regulatory mechanisms) and structures (morphologic organization) that comprise the substance of the patient's psychic worlds, not merely its *facade*. Treatment approaches designed *merely* to modify behavioral conduct and cognitive complaints fail to deal with the root source of pathology and are bound therefore to be of short-lived efficacy. As they view it, therapy must reconstruct the *inner* structures and processes that underlie overt behaviors and beliefs. It does not sacrifice the goal of syndromal or personality reconstruction for short-term behavioral or cognitive relief. Reworking the source of the problem rather than controlling its effects is what distinguishes intrapsychic therapies as treatment procedures.

MOOD/TEMPERAMENT THERAPIES

Few observables are clinically more relevant from the *biophysical* level of data analysis than the predominant character of an individual's affect and the intensity and frequency with which he or she expresses it. The *meaning* of extreme emotions is easy to decode. This is not so with the more subtle moods and feelings that insidiously and repetitively pervade the patient's ongoing relationships and experiences. Not only are the expressive features of mood and drive conveyed by terms such as distraught, labile, fickle, or hostile communicated via self report, but they are revealed as well, albeit indirectly, in the patient's level of activity, speech quality, and physical appearance.

Parallel Mood/Temperament Therapies   Although the direct action of pharmacological medications is chemical and their effects formulable in terms of altered neurophysiological relationships, there are those who believe that the crucial variable is not chemical or neurophysiological, but psychological. To them, the factors that determine the patient's response are not molecular events or processes, but the patient's prior psychological state and the environment within which he currently functions. According to this view, biophysical changes induced by medications take on a "meaning" to the patient, and it is this meaning that determines his "final" clinical response.

Theorists of this persuasion pay less attention to specifying the mechanisms and pathways of biophysical change than to the impact of these changes on the patient's self-image, coping competencies, social relationships, and the like. To support their thesis, they note that barbiturates, which typically produce sedative reactions, often produce excitement and hyperactivity. Similarly, many persons exhibit a cheerful state of intoxication when given sodium amytal in a congenial social setting, but succumb to a hypnotic state when the drug is administered to them in a therapeutic environment.

Of even greater significance than social factors according to this view, is the patient's awareness of the energy and temperamental changes that have taken place as a consequence of drug action. Early in their development, Freyhan (1959), discussing the effect of "tranquilizers" in reducing mobility and drive, stated that patients with *compulsive* traits, who need intensified activity to control their anxiety, may react unfavorably to their loss of initiative, resulting thereby in an upsurge rather than a decrement in anxiety. Other patients, such as *avoidants* who are comforted by feelings of reduced activity and energy, may view the drug's tranquilizing effect as a welcome relief. Thus, even if a drug produced a uniform biophysical effect on all patients, its psychological impact would differ from patient to patient, depending on the meaning these changes have in the larger context of the patient's needs, attitudes, and coping strategies.

If a drug facilitates the control of disturbing impulses or if it activates a new sense of competence and adequacy, then it may be spoken of as beneficial. Conversely, if the effect is to weaken the patient's defenses and upset his self-image, it may prove detrimental. The key to a drug's effectiveness then, is not only its chemical impact, but the significance of the psychological changes it activates.

SYNERGISTIC INTEGRATION IN A
PERSONALITY-GUIDED CONTEXT

If no one subset of *DSM-IV* diagnostic criteria are necessary or sufficient for membership in a diagnostic class, and if the structure of the taxonomy and the planning and practice of therapy are to be linked in a meaningful way, it seems likely that *no* one therapy or technique can be regarded as a necessary or sufficient remediation as well. Diagnostic heterogeneity-therapeutic heterogeneity is a more intrinsically agreeable pairing than diagnostic heterogeneity-therapeutic homogeneity, which treats every person diagnosed the same way, ignoring individual differences. The argument is one of parallelism: The palette of methods and techniques available to the therapist must be commensurate with the idiographic heterogeneity of the patient for whom the methods and techniques are intended.

When translated into psychological terms, a theory of psychopathology should be able to generate answers to a number of key questions. For example, how do its essential constructs interrelate and combine to form specific syndromes and disorders? And, if it is to meet the criteria of an integrative or unifying schema, can it help derive all forms of personality and syndrome with the same set of constructs; that is, not employ one set of explanatory concepts for borderline personalities, another for somatoforms, a third for depressives, and so on. If we may recall, one of the great appeals of early analytic theory was its ability to explain several character types from a single developmental model of psychosexual stages. Can the same be said for other, more encompassing theories? Moreover, can these theories provide a structure and serve as a guide for planning psychotherapy with all varieties of psychopathologies?

A major treatment implication recorded earlier in the chapter noted that the polarity schema and the clinical domains can serve as useful points of focus for corresponding modalities of therapy. It would be ideal, of course, if patients were "pure" prototypes, and all expressive psychic domains were prototypal and invariably present. Were this so, each diagnosis would automatically match with its polarity configuration and corresponding therapeutic mode. Unfortunately, patients rarely are pure textbook prototypes; most, by far; are complex mixtures, exhibiting, for example, the deficient pain *and* pleasure polarities that typify the schizoid prototype, the interpersonal conduct and cognitive style features of the avoidant prototype, the self-image qualities that characterize the schizotypal, and so on. Further, the polarity configurations and their expressive domains are not likely to be of equal clinical relevance or prominence in a particular case: thus, interpersonal characteristics may be especially troublesome, whereas cognitive processes, though problematic, may be of lesser significance. Which domains and which polarities should be selected for therapeutic intervention requires a comprehensive assessment, one that appraises not only the overall configuration of polarities and domains, but differentiates their balance and degrees of salience.

The task of the therapist is to identify domain dysfunctions and to provide matching treatment modalities that derive logically from the "theory of that particular person," that is, to put together a related combination of treatment modalities that mirror the different domains in which that specific patient's pathology is expressed and configured. When techniques drawn from different modalities are applied together, it should be because that combination reflects the domains that comprise the individual person's characteristics, not because it is required by the logic of one or another theory or technological preference. The orchestration of diverse, yet synthesized techniques of intervention is what differentiates personality-guided synergism from other variants of psychotherapy. These two, parallel constructs emerging from different traditions and conceived in different venues, reflect shared philosophical perspectives, one oriented toward the understanding of complex psychopathologies, the other toward effecting their remediation. It is the very interwoven nature of the patient's problematic domains that define syndromes and personalities that make a multifaceted and integrated approach a necessity.

Potentiated Pairings and Catalytic Sequences

As the great neurological surgeon/psychologist Kurt Goldstein (1940) stated, patients whose brains have been altered to remedy a major neurological disorder do not simply lose the function that the disturbed or extirpated area subserved. Rather, the patient restructures and reorganizes his brain capacities so that he can maintain an integrated sense of self. In a similar way, when one or another major domain of ones habitual psychological makeup is removed or diminished (e.g., depression), the patient must reorganize himself, not only to compensate for the loss, but also to formulate a new reconstructed self.

There is a separateness among eclectically designed techniques; just a wise selectivity of what works best. In synergistic therapy, there are psychologically designed composites and progressions among diverse techniques. In an attempt to formulate them in current writings (Millon, 1988; Millon et al., 1999), terms such as "catalytic sequences" and "potentiating pairings" are employed to represent the nature and intent of these polarity- and domain-oriented treatment plans. In essence, they comprise therapeutic arrangements and timing series that will resolve polarity imbalances and effect clinical domain changes that would otherwise not occur by the use of several, essentially uncoordinated techniques.

The first of the *synergistic procedures* we recommend (Millon, 1988; Millon et al., 1999) has been termed "potentiated pairings"; they consist of treatment methods that are combined simultaneously to overcome problematic characteristics that might be refractory to each technique if they were administered separately. These composites pull and push for change on many different fronts, so that the therapy becomes as multioperational and as tenacious as the disorder itself. A popular illustration of these treatment pairings is found in what has been referred to as "cognitive-behavior" therapy, perhaps the first of the synergistic therapies (Craighead, Craighead, Kazdin, & Mahoney, 1994).

In the second synergistic procedure, termed *catalytic sequences,* we might seek first to alter a patient's humiliating and painful stuttering by *behavior modification* procedures that, if achieved, may facilitate the use of *cognitive or self-actualizing* methods to produce changes in self-confidence that may, in its turn, foster the utility of *interpersonal* techniques in effecting improvements in relationships with others. Catalytic sequences are timing series that should optimize the impact of changes that would be less effective if the sequential combination were otherwise arranged.

Of course, there are no discrete boundaries between potentiating pairings and catalytic sequences, just as there is no line between their respective pathological analogues, that is, adaptive inflexibility and vicious circles (Millon, 1969). Nor should therapists be concerned about when to use one rather than another. Instead, they are intrinsically interdependent phenomena whose application is intended to foster increased flexibility and, hopefully, a beneficent rather than a vicious circle. Potentiated pairings and catalytic sequences represent but the first-order of therapeutic synergism. The idea of a "potentiated sequence" or a "catalytic pairing" recognizes that these logical composites may build on each other in proportion to what the tenacity of the disorder requires.

One question we may want to ask concerns the limits to which the content of synergistic therapy can be specified in advance at a tactical level, that is, the extent to which specific potentiating pairings and catalytic sequences can be identified for each of the complex syndromes and personality disorders. To the extent that each patient's presentations are prototypal, the potentiating pairings and catalytic sequences that are actually used should derive from modality tactics oriented to alter several of the more problematic domains. That, however, probably represents the limits to which theory can guide practice in an abstract sense, that is, without knowing anything about the history and characteristics of the *specific* individual case to which the theory is to be applied. Just as individuality is ultimately so rich that it cannot be exhausted by any taxonomic schema, *synergistic therapy,* ideally performed, is full of specificities that cannot readily be resolved by generalities. Potentiating pairings, catalytic sequences, and whatever other higher order composites that therapists may evolve, are conducted at an idiographic rather than at a diagnostic level. Accordingly, their precise content is specified as much by the logic of the individual case as by the logic of the syndrome or disorder themselves. At an idiographic level, each of us must ultimately be "artful" and open-minded therapists, using simultaneous or alternately focused methods. The synergism and enhancement produced by such catalytic and potentiating processes is what comprise genuinely innovative treatment strategies.

Polarity Goals

As stated earlier, we should select our specific treatment techniques as tactics to achieve the evolution-theory based polarity-oriented goals. Depending on the pathological polarity, the domains to be modified, and the overall treatment sequence we have in mind, the goals of therapy should be oriented toward the improvement of imbalanced or deficient polarities by the use of techniques that are optimally suited to modify their expression in those clinical domains that are problematic.

Therapeutic efforts responsive to problems in the pain-pleasure polarity would, for example, have as their essential aim the enhancement of pleasure among schizoid, avoidant, and depressive personalities (+ pleasure). Given the probability of intrinsic deficits in this area, *schizoids* might require the use of pharmacologic agents designed to activate their "flat" mood/temperament. Increments in pleasure for *avoidants,* however, are likely to depend more on cognitive techniques designed to alter their "alienated" self-image, and behavioral methods oriented to counter their "aversive" interpersonal inclination. Equally important for avoidants is reducing their hypersensitivities especially to social rejection (− pain); this may be achieved by coordinating the use of anxiolytic medications for their characteristic "anguished" mood/temperament with cognitive-behavioral methods geared to desensitization. In the passive-active polarity, increments in the capacity and skills to take a less reactive and more proactive role in dealing with the affairs of their lives (− passive; + active) would be a major goal of treatment for schizoids, depressives, dependents, narcissists, masochists, and compulsives. Turning to the *other-self* polarity, imbalances found among narcissists and antisocials, for example, suggest that a major aim of their treatment would be a reduction in their predominant self-focus, and a corresponding augmentation of their sensitivity to the needs of others (+ other; − self).

To make unbalanced or deficient polarities the primary aim of therapy is a new focus and a goal only modestly tested. In contrast, the clinical domains in which problems are expressed lend themselves to a wide variety of therapeutic techniques, the efficacy of which must continue to be gauged by ongoing experience and future systematic research. Nevertheless, our repertoire here is a rich one. For example, there are numerous cognitive-behavior techniques (Bandura, 1969; Craighead et al., 1994; Goldfried & Davison, 1976), such as assertiveness training, that may fruitfully be employed to establish a greater sense of self-autonomy or an active rather than a passive stance with regard to life. Similarly, pharmaceuticals are notably efficacious in reducing the intensity of pain (anxiety, depression) when the pleasure-pain polarity is in marked imbalance.

DOMAIN TACTICS

Turning to the specific domains in which clinical problems exhibit themselves, we can address dysfunctions in the realm of interpersonal conduct by employing any number of family (Gurman & Kniskern, 1991) or group (Yalom, 1986) therapeutic methods, as well as a series of recently evolved and explicitly formulated interpersonal techniques (Benjamin, 1993; Kiesler, 1997). Methods of classical analysis or its more contemporary schools may be especially suited to the realm of *object representations* and *morphologic organization* as would the cognitively oriented methods of Beck (1976; Beck et al., 1990) and Ellis (1970; Ellis & MacLaren, 1998) be well chosen to modify difficulties of cognitive beliefs and self-esteem.

Tactics and strategies keep in balance the two conceptual ingredients of therapy, the first refers to what goes on with a particular focused intervention, while the second refers to the overall plan or design that characterizes the entire course of therapy. Both are required. Tactical specificity without strategic goals implies doing without knowing why in the big picture, while goals without specificity implies knowing where to go, but having no way to get there. Obviously, we use short-term modality tactics to accomplish higher-level strategies or goals over the long-term.

SYSTEM TRANSACTIONS

The distinction between interaction and transaction points to an important element in the practice of synergistic psychotherapy. Because the goal of therapy is personality and clinical change, patient and therapist cannot be satisfied merely to interact like billiard balls and emerge from therapy unchanged. Instead, we must invent modes of therapy that maximize the transactive potential of the therapeutic process. Because of its lack of structure and feedback, traditional psychotherapy may wander around essentially indefinitely, without ever reaching termination. In fact, since patient and therapist may not have previously determined what constitutes success, it is not inconceivable that appropriate points of termination might be reached without either the therapist or patient ever realizing it, only for new issues to be raised and the process to begin again.

Pessimistically speaking, it must be remembered that the primary function of any system is homeostasis. In an earlier conceptualization (Millon, 1981), personality was likened to an immune system for the psyche, such that stability, constancy, or internal equilibrium, become the "goals" of a personality. Obviously, these run directly in opposition to the explicit goal of therapy, which is change. Usually, the dialogue between patient and therapist is not so directly confrontational that it is experienced as particularly threatening. In these cases, the personality system functions for the patient as a form of passive resistance, albeit one that may be experienced as a positive force (or trait) by the therapist. In fact, the schematic nature of self-image and object representations are so preemptive and confirmation-seeking that the true meaning of the therapist's comments may never reach the level of conscious processing. Alternately, even if a patient's equilibrium is initially up-ended by a particular interpretation, his or her defensive mechanisms may kick in to ensure that a therapist's comments are somehow distorted, misunderstood, interpreted in a less threatening manner, or even ignored. The first is a passive form of resistance; the second an active form. No wonder that effective therapy is often considered anxiety provoking, for it is in situations where the patient really has no effective response, where the functioning of the immune system is temporarily suppressed, that the scope of his or her response repertoire is most likely to be broadened. Personality "goes with what it knows," and it is with the "unknown" where learning is most possible. Arguing essentially the same point, Kiesler (1997) has stated that the therapist is obliged to make the "asocial" response, one other than that which the patient is specifically trying to evoke. Here, the proposals of the early analyst, Sandor Ferenczi (1926) and the more recent "anxiety-provoking" ideas of Sifneos (1972) are worthy of note.

If the psychic make-up of a person is regarded as a system, then the question becomes: How can the characteristics that define systems be co-opted to facilitate rather than retard transactive change? A coordinated schema of strategic goals and tactical modalities for treatment that seek to accomplish these ends are what we mean by "synergistic psychotherapy." Through various coordinated approaches that mirror the system-based structure of pathology, an effort is made to select domain-focused tactics that will fulfill the strategic goals of treatment.

If interventions are unfocused, rambling, and diffuse, the patient will merely "lean forward a little," passively resisting change by using his or her own "weight," that is, habitual characteristics already intrinsic to the system. While creating rapport is always important, nothing happens unless the system is eventually "shook up" in some way. Therapists should not always be toiling to expose their patient's defenses, but sooner or later, something must happen that cannot be readily fielded by habitual processes, something that often will be experienced as uncomfortable or even threatening.

In fact, synergistic therapy appears in many ways to be like a "punctuated equilibrium" (Eldridge & Gould, 1972) rather than a slow and continuous process. The systems model argues for periods of rapid growth during which the psychic system reconfigures itself into a new gestalt, alternating with periods of relative constancy. The purpose of keeping to a domain or tactical focus, or knowing clearly what you are doing and why you are doing it, is to keep the whole of psychotherapy from becoming diffused. The person-focused systems model runs counter to the deterministic universe-as-machine model of the late nineteenth century, which featured slow but incremental gains. In a standard systems model, diffuse interventions are experienced simply as another input to be discharged homeostatically, producing zero change. In the machine model, in which conservation laws play a prominent role, diffuse interventions produce small increments of change, with the promise that therapeutic goals will be reached, given enough time and effort. In contrast, in the synergistic model, few therapeutic goals may be reached at all, unless something unusual is planned that has genuine transformational potential. This potential is optimized through what we have termed *potentiated pairings* and *catalytic sequences.*

Tactical specificity is required in part because the psychic level in which therapy is practiced is fairly explicit. Most often, the in-session dialogue between patient and therapist is dominated by a discussion of specific behaviors, specific feelings, and specific events, not by a broad discussion of personality traits or clinical syndromes. When the latter are discussed, they are often perceived by the patient as an ego-alien or intrusive characterization. A statement such as "You have a troublesome personality" conceives the patient as a vessel filled by some noxious substance. Under these conditions, the professional is expected to empty and refill the vessel with something more desirable; the patient has relinquished control and responsibility and simply waits passively for the therapist to perform some mystical ritual, one of the worst assumptive sets in which to carry out psychotherapy. Whatever the physical substrates and dynamic forces involved in creating and sustaining particular traits, traits terms are evoked as inferences from particular constituent behaviors. Behaviors can be changed; traits have a more permanent connotation.

MODALITY SELECTIONS

Despite the foregoing, viewing traits in an explicit way, that is, by anchoring them to *real* and *objective* events, is beneficial to both the patient and the therapist. Knowing what behaviors are descriptively linked to particular traits helps patients understand how others perceive them, and to realize that these behaviors should not be repeated. Additionally, if patients are led to understand that their personality traits are, or are derived from, their concrete behaviors, there is hope, since behavior is more easily controlled and changed than is a clinical diagnosis. In this latter sense, the diagnosis or trait ascription itself may become the enemy. There is, after all, a difference between what is practically impossible because it is at the limits of one's endurance or ability, and what is logically impossible. With support and courage, human beings can be coaxed into transcending their limitations, into doing what was before considered practically impossible. No one, however, can do what is logically impossible. When clinical syndromes and personality disorders are framed through the medical model, change is paradigmatically impossible. Individuals who see themselves as vessels for a diseased syndrome or personality should be disabused of this notion.

For the therapist, operationalizing traits as clusters of behavioral acts or cognitive expectancies can be especially beneficial in selecting tactical modalities. First, some behaviors are linked to multiple traits, and some of these traits are more desirable than others, so that some play exists in the interpretation or spin put on any particular behavior at the trait level. This play can be utilized by the therapist to reframe patient attributions about self and others in more positive ways. For example, the *avoidant's* social withdrawal can be seen as having enough pride in oneself to leave a humiliating situation, while the *dependent's* clinging to a significant other can be seen as having the strength to devote oneself to another's care. These reframes will not be sufficient in and of themselves to produce change. They do, however, bond with the patient by making positive attributions, and thereby raising self-esteem, while simultaneously working to disconfirm or make the patient re-examine other beliefs that lower esteem and function to keep the person closed off from trying on new roles and behaviors.

Second, understanding traits as clusters of behaviors and/or cognitions is just as beneficial for the therapist as for the patient when it comes to overturning the medical model of syndromal and personality pathology and replacing it with a synergistic systems model. One of the problems of complex syndromes and personality disorders is that their range of attributions and perceptions are too narrow to characterize the richness that in fact exists in their social environment. As a result, they end up perpetuating old problems by interpreting even innocuous behaviors and events as noxious. Modern therapists have a similar problem in that the range of paradigms they have to bring to their syndromal and disordered patients is too narrow to describe the rich set of possibilities that exist for every individual. The belief that personality pathologies are medical diseases, monolithically fixed and beyond remediation, should itself be viewed as a form of paradigmatic pathology.

As outlined previously, there are the *strategic goals* of therapy, that is, those that endure across numerous sessions and against which progress is measured; second, there are the specific *domain modality* tactics by which these goals are pursued. Ideally, strategies and tactics should be integrated, with the tactics chosen to accomplish strategic goals, and the strategies chosen on the basis of what tactics might actually achieve given other constraints, such as the number of therapy sessions and the nature of the problem. To illustrate, intrapsychic therapies are highly strategic, but tactically impoverished; pure behavioral therapies are highly tactical, but strategically narrow and inflexible. There are, in fact, many different ways that strategies might be operationalized. Just as diagnostic criteria are neither necessary nor sufficient for membership in a given class, it is likely that no technique is an inevitable consequence of a given clinical strategy. Subtle variations in technique and the ingenuity of individual therapists to invent techniques ad hoc assure that there exists an almost infinite number of ways to operationalize or put into action a given clinical strategy.

Ideally, in a truly integrated clinical science, the theoretical basis that lends complex syndromes and personality disorders their content, that is, the basis on which its taxonomy is generated and patients assessed and classified, would also provide the basis for the goals and modalities of therapy. Without such a basis, anarchy ensues, for we will have no rationale by which to select from an almost infinite number of specific domain tactics that can be used, except the dogmas of past traditions. The "truth" is what works in the end, a pragmatism based on what we would term a *synergistic integrationism*.

SUMMARY AND CONCLUSION

The system we have termed *synergistic therapy* may have raised concerns as to whether any one therapist can be sufficiently skilled, not only in employing a wide variety of therapeutic approaches, but also to synthesize them and to plan their sequence. As the senior author was asked at a conference some years ago: "Can a highly competent behavioral therapist employ cognitive techniques with any measure of efficacy; and can he prove able, when necessary, to function as an insightful intrapsychic therapist? Can we find people who are strongly self-actualizing in their orientation who can, at other times, be cognitively confronting?" Is there any wisdom in selecting different modalities in treating a patient if the therapist has not been trained diversely or is not particularly competent in more than one ore two therapeutic modalities?

It is our belief that the majority of therapists have the ability to break out of their single-minded or loosely eclectic frameworks, to overcome their prior limitations, and to acquire a solid working knowledge of diverse treatment modalities. Developing a measure of expertise with the widest possible range of modalities is highly likely to increase treatment efficacy with a therapist's primary goal of his or her professional career, that of helping patients and clients overcome their mental health difficulties.

REFERENCES

American Psychiatric Association. (1980). *Diagnostic and statistical manual of mental disorders* (3rd ed.). Washington, DC: Author.

American Psychiatric Association. (1994). *Diagnostic and statistical manual of mental disorders* (4th ed.). Washington, DC: Author.

Bandura, A. (1969). *Principles of behavior modification.* New York: Holt, Rinehart and Winston.

Barlow, D. H. (1991). Introduction to the special issues on diagnoses, dimensions, and *DSM-IV:* The science of classification. *Journal of Abnormal Psychology, 100,* 243–244.

Barron, J. W. (Ed.). (1998). *Making diagnosis meaningful: Enhancing evaluation and treatment of psychological disorders.* Washington, DC: American Psychological Association.

Beck, A. T. (1976). *Cognitive therapy and the emotional disorders.* New York: International Universities Press.

Beck, A. T., Freeman, A., & Associates. (1990). *Cognitive therapy of personality disorders.* New York: Guilford Press.

Benjamin, L. S. (1993). *Interpersonal diagnosis and treatment of personality disorders.* New York: Guilford Press.

Blatt, S. J., & Levy, K. N. (1998). A psychodynamic approach to the diagnosis of psychopathology. In J. W. Barron (Ed.), *Making diagnosis meaningful: Enhancing evaluation and treatment of psychological disorders* (pp. 73–110). Washington, DC: American Psychological Association.

Carson, R. C. (1991). Dilemmas in the pathway of the *DSM-IV. Journal of Abnormal Psychology, 100,* 302–307.

Craighead, L. W., Craighead, W. E., Kazdin, A. E., & Mahoney, M. J. (Eds.). (1994). *Cognitive and behavioral interventions: An empirical approach to mental health problems.* Boston: Allyn & Bacon.

Eldridge, N., & Gould, S. (1972). Punctuated equilibria: An alternative to phyletic gradualism. In T. Schopf (Ed.), *Models in paleobiology.* San Francisco: Freeman.

Ellis, A. (1967). *A guide to rational living.* Englewood, NJ: Prentice-Hall.

Ellis, A. (1970). *The essence of rational psychotherapy: A comprehensive approach to treatment.* New York: Institute for Rational Living.

Ellis, A., & MacLaren, C. (1998). *Rational emotive behavior therapy: A therapist's guide.* Atascadero, CA: Impact.

Ferenczi, S. (1926). *Further contributions to the theory and technique of psychoanalysis.* New York: Basic Books.

Freyhan, F. A. (1959). Clinical and integrative aspects. In N. S. Kline (Ed.), *Psychopharmacology frontiers* (pp. 214–230). Boston: Little, Brown.

Goldfried, M. R., & Davison, G. C. (1976). *Clinical behavior therapy*. New York: Holt, Rinehart and Winston.

Goldstein, K. (1940). *Human nature in the light of psychopathology*. Cambridge, MA: Harvard University Press.

Grünbaum, A. (1952). Causality and the science of human behavior. *American Scientist, 26,* 665–676.

Gurman, A. S., & Kniskern, K. (Eds.). (1991). *The handbook of family therapy* (2nd ed.). New York: Brunner/Mazel.

Hempel, C. G. (1961). Introduction to problems of taxonomy. In J. Zubin (Ed.), *Field studies in the mental disorders* (pp. 3–22). New York: Grune & Stratton.

Horney, K. (1945). *Our inner conflicts: A constructive theory of neurosis*. New York: Norton.

Kernberg, O. F. (1984). *Severe personality disorders*. New Haven, CT: Yale University Press.

Kiesler, D. J. (1982). The 1982 interpersonal circle: A taxonomy for complementarity in human transactions. *Psychological Review, 90,* 185–214.

Kiesler, D. J. (1997). *Contemporary interpersonal theory and research*. New York: Wiley.

Lazarus, A. A. (1976). *Multimodal behavior therapy*. New York: Springer.

Lewin, K. (1936). *Principles of topographical psychology*. New York: McGraw-Hill.

Loevinger, J. (1957). Objective tests on measurements of psychological theory. *Psychological Reports, 3,* 635–694.

Magnavita, J. J. (1997). *Restructuring personality disorders: A short-term dynamic approach*. New York: Guilford Press.

Millon, T. (1969). *Modern psychopathology: A biosocial approach to maladaptive learning and functioning*. Philadelphia: Saunders.

Millon, T. (1981). *Disorders of personality: DSM-III, Axis II*. New York: Wiley-Interscience.

Millon, T. (1984). On the renaissance of personality assessment and personality theory. *Journal of Personality Assessment, 48*(5), 450–466.

Millon, T. (1986a). Personality prototypes and their diagnostic criteria. In T. Millon & G. L. Klerman (Eds.), *Contemporary directions in psychopathology: Toward the DSM-IV* (pp. 671–712). New York: Guilford Press.

Millon, T. (1986b). A theoretical derivation of pathological personalities. In T. Millon & G. L. Klerman (Eds.), *Contemporary directions in psychopathology: Toward the DSM-IV* (pp. 639–669). New York: Guilford Press.

Millon, T. (1988). Personologic psychotherapy: Ten commandments for a posteclectic approach to integrative treatment. *Psychotherapy, 25,* 209–219.

Millon, T. (1990). *Toward a new personology: An evolutionary model*. New York: Wiley.

Millon, T. (1991). Classification in psychopathology: Rationale, alternative, and standards. *Journal of Abnormal Psychology, 100,* 245–261.

Millon, T. (with Grossman, S., Meagher, S., Millon, C., & Everly, G.). (1999). *Personality-guided therapy*. New York: Wiley.

Millon, T., & Davis, R. D. (1996). *Disorders of personality: DSM-IV and beyond*. New York: Wiley.

Pincus, A. L., & Wiggins, J. S. (1989). Conceptions of personality disorders and dimensions of personality. *Psychological Assessment, 1,* 305–316.

Quine, W. V. O. (1961). *From a logical point of view* (2nd ed.). New York: Harper & Row.

Rogers, C. R. (1942). *Counseling and psychotherapy*. Boston: Houghton Mifflin.

Rogers, C. R. (1951). *Client-centered therapy*. Boston: Houghton Mifflin.

Rogers, C. R. (1961). *On becoming a person*. Boston: Houghton Mifflin.

Rogers, C. R. (1967). *The therapeutic relationship and its impact*. Madison: University of Wisconsin Press.

Sifneos, P. E. (1972). *Short-term psychotherapy and emotional crisis.* Cambridge, MA: Harvard University Press.

Slavson, S. R. (1943). *An introduction to group therapy.* New York: Commonwealth Fund.

Wachtel, P. L. (1973). Psychodynamics, behavior therapy and the implacable experimenter: An inquiry into the consistency of personality. *Journal of Abnormal Psychology, 82,* 324–334.

Westen, D. (1998). Case formulation and personality diagnosis: Two processes or one. In J. W. Barron (Ed.), *Making diagnosis meaningful: Enhancing evaluation and treatment of psychological disorders* (pp. 111–138). Washington, DC: American Psychological Association.

Yalom, I. D. (1986). *The theory and practice of group psychotherapy* (3rd ed.). New York: Basic Books.

CHAPTER 3

The Relevance of Theory in
Treating Personality Dysfunction

Jeffrey J. Magnavita

T HE TREATMENT OF patients with personality dysfunction is an enormously
complex undertaking, even when aided by advanced education, training,
and experience. It is an often demanding, challenging, and confusing endeavor, but one that offers substantial rewards for both the clinician and patient. The multiplicity of variables and processes in operation are not readily
sorted out. Treating personality dysfunction requires making sense out of the
chaos of interrelated interactions among individual, couple, family, and social
systems. Theory is essential because it offers a system of organizing all the variables, the multiple channels of input and complex processes. Theory does so by
providing a guide for viewing the organization, structure, and process of complex systems and offering organizing principles from which to make sense of
the phenomena. Theories of personality and personality disorder are attempts
at charting neurobiological, intrapsychic, interpersonal, familial, and cultural
territory as expressed in human behavior, function, and adaptation. Some theoretical systems appear "simple" in that they concern themselves with only one
level of abstraction or process. Other theoretical constructions are daunting,
using esoteric language and multiple levels of the biopsychosocial model. Some
theory requires the student to learn what is essentially a new language. The explanatory value of a system may rely on the fit between the theory's terminology
and semantic expression and the therapists' sense of human functioning. Some
are intuitively drawn to cognitive, psychodynamic, interpersonal, behavioral, biological, or systemic models. Others seek more free-ranging integrative or unified
approaches. This volume emphasizes various contemporary approaches to treating
personality, as well as the variety of clinical syndromes that emerge or co-occur
with personality dysfunction. It is critical in a volume of this nature to understand the importance and the place of theory in contemporary clinical science.

Theory shapes our conceptualization of the patient's troubles but, more importantly, informs our intervention, determining how we select from the array of
clinical treatment methods and techniques. It is impossible to treat personality

dysfunction without a map; theory provides the map. A "good enough" theory is immensely valuable in this endeavor and "poor" theory potentially destructive and possibly lethal. The various theories offer different maps and even contradictory approaches; occasionally, we find methods and techniques that look familiar, but the language is new. On close inspection, even divergent approaches may reveal strong similarities in their underpinnings although technique and stance may be different. A clinician must select his or her maps—this volume assists in this regard. When embarking on such a complex endeavor as treating personality dysfunction, clinicians need all available help. This chapter concerns itself with issues of theory in the contemporary treatment of clinical syndromes and personality dysfunction. To gain a true appreciation of our topic, we must look at the major historical developments and the pioneering figures that brought them about. A good place to start is with a definition of *theory*.

The Random House College Dictionary (Stein, 1975) defines theory as "a coherent group of general propositions used as principles of explanation for a class of phenomenon" (p. 1362). The phenomenon that we are primarily concerned with is human behavior, with particular emphasis on dysfunctional adaptations, whether these are expressed as relationship disturbances, clinical disorders, or patterns of behavior that are maladaptive. Personality theory has attained and, for the most part of the past century, continued to hold a prominent position in the social and clinical sciences (Magnavita, 2002d). Only during the ascendancy of behaviorism, which eschewed the "fuzzy" construct of personality, was its utility challenged. Much of personality theory has emerged from the interest in understanding psychopathological conditions and developing effective treatment approaches. Personality disorder has roots in the various subdisciplines of psychology and psychiatry, nosology, diagnosis, psychopathology, psychotherapy, and social psychology. Personality disorders have primarily been considered the domain of psychopathology, and personality theory the domain of academic psychology. This artificial distinction unnecessarily fragments the field; they are indeed the same discipline and focus even though most personality theory has been derived from clinical and psychopathological investigation. Rychlak (1973), a leading intellectual force in personality theory, states, "it is not possible to grasp the full meaning of classical personality theory without also understanding the theories of psychopathology and psychotherapy within which they are framed" (p. 18).

Personality theory and theories of personality disorder share a close relationship with theories of psychotherapy. Rychlak wrote in the preface, "The area of personality theory is immense and confusing, and even the great thinkers in the field do not have a clear picture of one another." This volume is an indication that, in spite of exponential growth in the field of personality, the field is increasingly less fragmented and interdisciplinary collaboration is more common. The phase of parochialism is largely over—a new era has begun.

THE ISSUE OF COMPETING THEORETICAL MODELS

Why is it that there are competing theoretical models for treating personality dysfunction? Science is highly competitive; theorists, researchers, and clinical practitioners compete for financial support and public and professional recognition. Rivalry is a strong impetus in science because the best theoretical models are likely to survive and the others will fall by the wayside. (Remember, for example, the somatype personality theory and phrenology?) Theories with research application and clinical utility will be more likely to survive.

Interdisciplinary collaboration is necessary to advance beyond our rudimentary understanding of personality disorders and beyond the simplistic notion that personality can be fully understood in any one domain. Over a century ago, William James (1890) identified the many constituent domains of personality, and, after a productive century of work, many of these component domains have been delineated (Magnavita, 2002d). The major discoveries of the past century included additional developments in domains that are central to any metatheoretical model of personality. This volume is a testament to the array of often-divergent theoretical models for treating personality disorders and a trend toward eventual unification of theory and practice. Recently, many remarkable breakthroughs have occurred that influence how contemporary theorists and clinicians conceptualize theory and practice (Magnavita, 2002a), as is reflected by the chapters in this volume. In the next section of this chapter, a brief history of the field of personology and psychotherapy is presented.

HISTORY, TRENDS, AND EVOLUTION OF PERSONOLOGY AND PSYCHOTHERAPEUTIC APPROACHES

An entire volume, or even multiple volumes, could easily be devoted to the history of personality theory and its relationship to psychotherapy. For our purposes, a more modest review of the past century is sufficient. There are periods during the past 100 years that emerge as distinct and significant. A dialectic process has taken place, much as described by Kuhn (1962) in *The Structure of Scientific Revolutions,* as a common phenomenon in the development of any scientific endeavor. In this process, a theoretical model is developed and then a seemingly antithetical model is offered to challenge the first, dominant model. As scientific findings accumulate, there may be a merging of the two systems over time into a new, stronger amalgam, and so the dialectic process continues. The most valid contributions are absorbed, and the less useful fall by the wayside. Prominent examples of this process include the development of psychoanalysis, the rise of behaviorism, and the subsequent absorption of many of these principles into the dominant theoretical systems.

The history of *personology* is divided into four stages: (1) early modern begins in the 1890s, (2) later modern begins in 1950, (3) contemporary in 1980, and (4) unified at the beginning of the new millennium.

1. EARLY MODERN PERSONOLOGY AND PSYCHOTHERAPY (1890 TO 1949)

The Single School and Dueling School Phase   At the dawn of the development of modern personology in the late 1890s, psychiatry/psychology was emerging from its dominance by quasi-scientific models such as phrenology and its sister discipline, philosophy. Scientific methods of observation, classification, and statistical methods were just beginning to be applied to the study of humans and to the understanding of psychopathology. This exciting time was characterized by a number of theoreticians who sought to bring psychology and psychiatry into the modern period. The beginnings of modern psychology were primarily "single school" oriented, with the exception of William James (1890) in *The Principles of Psychology* that was an attempt to present a unified model drawing from the available knowledge. James was ahead of his time in striving for unification. However, not enough of the component systems of modern and contemporary personology had been discovered, such as systems and interpersonal and attachment theory; the cognitive revolution had not yet occurred, affective science had yet to be born, and temperamental and neurobiological models were simplistic. It would take nearly another century of effort to have these developments in place and to bring the field of personology within reach of unification.

It was not long before the major titans of this early phase started to clash, each claiming dominance of his system. One of these titans, John B. Watson (1924), assailed the tautological basis of psychoanalysis. Watson and Raynor (1920) demonstrated that neurotic conditions could be experimentally induced without the need for "esoteric" constructs such as the oedipal conflict, defense mechanisms, libido, unconscious, and so on. They succeeded in inducing a "neurosis" in a subject named Little Albert using classic conditioning and then were able to remove it with an extinction process. Paradoxically, Watson's attack may have done more for psychoanalysis than for his cause by increasing its exposure (Rilling, 2000).

Critical Developments   Several critical developments occurred during this phase of personology. The following is not meant to be inclusive but to highlight some of the major developments.

THE DEVELOPMENT OF PSYCHOANALYSIS   Psychoanalysis marks the beginning of modern personology and was a major point of departure from extant theoretical models. With Freud's (1900) publication of *Interpretation of Dreams,* a new system was proposed that later became an intellectual touchstone for the twentieth century. At its inception, psychoanalysis was a "grand" theory, one that was intrapsychic in orientation. It, therefore, was limited in its scope and offered only a partial explanation of personality and psychopathology. Although Freud paid some attention to culture and society, he saw the locus of his system as occurring "inside" the mind. Psychoanalysis, however, was a force to contend with, offering its adherents a novel theory of how the mind works that could help understand components of human suffering and adaptation. It quickly became the dominant model of personality, psychopathology, and psychotherapy. Original conceptualizations of character types were anchored to stages of psychosexual development. Today we see character types as useful although limiting. Rychlak (1973) describes the limitations: "A *typology* is, like our stereotype, a commentary on the *total* complex of behavioral tendencies we call 'the person.' These characteristics are really 'sophisticated stereotypes,' and we might call them *theorotypes* to capture the notion that they are really 'sophisticated stereotypes' of everyday thought" (p. 14).

Sandor Ferenczi (Ferenczi & Rank, 1925) developed active methods of psychotherapy that were attempts to accelerate treatment and applied them with the more difficult cases. He also continued to develop trauma theory that had been abandoned by Freud. Ferenczi believed that the root of most psychopathology was physical, sexual, or emotional abuse.

THE RISE OF BEHAVIORISM   Behaviorism's roots were in empiricism and became the domain of academic psychology, which pursued learning theory and conditioning paradigms. Behaviorism offered a model of human functioning that was contingent on the laws of behavior that were garnered through careful observation and animal research. In this way, its methods differed dramatically from the psychoanalytic methods of free association. Later, behavioral approaches were applied to clinical treatment of anxiety and other clinical syndromes but not to personality disorders. Behavioral approaches continue to offer empirically sound methods and techniques such as systematic desensitization and anxiety reduction techniques that are useful to incorporate into treatment.

THE EMERGENCE OF TRAIT PSYCHOLOGY AS A DOMINANT FORCE IN PSYCHOLOGY During this early phase in modern personology, Allport made significant advances in trait theory (1937; Allport & Odbert, 1936). Allport believed that normal personality and personality disorder were separate domains of scientific inquiry. At this point, academic psychology primarily became focused on normal personality, and disorders were the domain of the clinical theorists. This trait approach later led to various factor theories of personality that have more recently been gaining a presence in personality assessment (see chapter 4).

THE FORMAL STUDY OF PERSONALITY THEORY AS A SEPARATE DISCIPLINE During this period, the formal study of personality as a separate scientific discipline occurred. Henry Murray (1938) was interested in advancing the study of personality through systematic study of the individual and coined the term *personology*, which he defined as: "the branch of psychology which principally concerns itself with the study of human lives and the factors that influence their course, [and] which investigates individual differences and types of personality" (p. 4). He espoused his belief that the study of personality should be a scientific endeavor: "Absorbing this tradition, man may now explore his soul and observe the conduct of his fellows, dispassionate to the limit, yet ever animated by the faith that gaining mastery through knowledge he may eventually surmount himself" (p. 35).

THE DEVELOPMENT OF CHARACTER ANALYTIC APPROACHES Reich (1945) developed methods for directly treating the particular character of the patient and published his groundbreaking volume *Character Analysis*. Reich's methods were radical in that they directly addressed the nonverbal aspects of patient communication. He believed that with certain "character armored" individuals, treatment could not begin in the traditional manner. He felt it was necessary to penetrate the defense system first and bring the aggressive impulses to the surface. Reich continues to influence many contemporary workers who have developed short-term dynamic treatment methods with personality-disordered patients (Magnavita, 1993).

2. LATER MODERN PERSONOLOGY AND PSYCHOTHERAPY (1950 TO 1979)

Rapprochement among Dominant School Phase During the later modern stage of personology, the beginning of rapprochement among some theoretical systems was evident. Most notable was the bridge that was built between what many considered two diametrically opposed theoretical models: psychoanalysis and behaviorism. Dollard and Miller (1950) published the classic volume *Personality and Psychotherapy: An Analysis of Learning, Thinking, and Culture*. This remarkable interpretation of Freudian concepts into a learning paradigm showed how two systems were actually using similar language to describe personality. More importantly, this was evidence of rapprochement among intellectuals and theorists from different schools.

Critical Developments

THE DEVELOPMENT OF INTERPERSONAL PSYCHIATRY   Interpersonal theory was a significant departure from the intrapsychic model of the time. Sullivan (1953) published his volume *The Interpersonal Theory of Psychiatry*, changing the course of American psychiatry and psychology. He emphasized the dyad as the locus of psychopathology and psychotherapy and made remarkable gains with severely disturbed patients using his approach. He also emphasized the contribution of culture, society, and the family to mental dysfunction and collaborated with one of the eminent anthropologists of the time, Edward Sapir. Chrzanowski (1977) describes the essence of the difference between intrapsychic and interpersonal theory: "Instead of patient and therapist as separate units, we are more attuned to the evolving relational patterns between the parties, rather than to an exclusive focus on the patient's inner life" (p. 15). "Interpersonal theory distinguishes between two interrelated but inherently separate ecologic systems—man and his human environment" (p. 58).

THE EMERGENCE OF SYSTEM THEORY   A major paradigmatic shift occurred with the introduction of von Bertalanffy's (1968) general system theory because of its direct relevance to personality theory. General system theory offered a way of viewing complex systems as interrelated elements that affect one another holistically. Elements of these complex systems cannot be isolated without losing something important. It is not the separate elements of a system but the dynamic forces that exist and govern a system that are critical. Complex systems use feedback mechanisms that determine how the system functions. This development has major implications for understanding the personality system (Magnavita, in press).

THE BEGINNING OF PSYCHOTHERAPY RESEARCH   The field of psychotherapy research was spawned by Hans Eysenck's (1952) challenge to psychoanalysis and psychotherapy to demonstrate effectiveness. Eysenck did not stop with his criticism of psychoanalysis but presented research that actually demonstrated psychotherapy's ineffectiveness. This was clearly a wake-up call for the field and resulted in efforts to investigate scientifically the efficacy of psychotherapy (Magnavita, 2002d). Since that date, there has been strong interest in psychotherapy efficacy. Incidentally, several subsequent studies challenged Eysenck's findings (Smith, Glass, & Miller, 1980).

EMERGENCE OF PSYCHOPHARMACOLOGICAL TREATMENT OF MAJOR MENTAL DISORDERS   Major developments in psychopharmacological approaches to treating mental disorders occurred during this phase. Mental institutions were virtually emptied of patients when pharmacological agents, most notably lithium and thorazine, were found to be palliative in the treatment of bipolar and psychotic disturbances. This success demonstrated the biological basis of many psychological disorders previously viewed as purely psychological.

THE DEVELOPMENT OF ATTACHMENT THEORY   Attachment theory offered an exciting innovation during this phase, emerging from British object relations theory (Winnicott, Shepherd, & Davis, 1989). Bowlby's (1969, 1973, 1980) work in attachment demonstrated the importance of early relational experiences for the development of a healthy self. Enough naturalistic evidence and primate research conducted by Harry Harlow (Blum, 2002) had accumulated to demonstrate that severe attachment disruptions were life threatening to infants and constituted a massive assault to the personality system. Attachment theory has experienced a renewal of interest recently and is considered a unifying theoretical system.

3. Contemporary Personology and Psychotherapy (1980 to 1999)

The Integrative Movement Phase   The 1980s integrative phase was termed a *paradigmatic shift* in the field of personality (Sperry, 1995). The psychotherapy integration movement created a new stage of rapprochement among schools of psychotherapy, and a new awareness of the nature and impact of personality disorders was set into motion by *DSM's* classification system. Many new scientific disciplines began to bring a new perspective to the study of personality disorders such as affective science, neuroscience, and relational science. Advances in more sophisticated psychopharmacological treatments were being developed. Personality disorders became a popular topic of professional seminars, and many researchers, theorists, and clinicians were drawn to this exciting new field. The public also was exposed to the personality disturbances that were popularized in a number of movies such as *Fatal Attraction*, where Glenn Close did an excellent characterization of borderline phenomenon, and in *Girl Interrupted*, where various adolescent personality disorders were portrayed. This period of development also saw the organization of the *International Society for the Study of Personality Disorders* (ISSPD), the *Society for Exploration of Psychotherapy Integration* (SEPI), and *Society for Psychotherapy Researchers* (SPR), all of which have attracted some of the elite in the fields of theory, practice, and research. National and international conferences on the topics of personality disorders and new models of treatment became commonplace.

Critical Developments

The Development of *DSM* and the Emphasis on Personality Disorders *DSM*, even with all of its inherent flaws, spawned renewed interest in the personality disorders. According to Clarkin and Lenzenweger (1996), "The advent of *DSM-III* and its successors, which utilize a multiaxial diagnostic system that makes a distinction between clinical syndromes (Axis I) and personality disorders (Axis II), both brought into sharp focus and encapsulated the controversy concerning the nature and the role of personality pathology in the history of psychiatry and the history of modern personality research" (p. 5). *DSM* and its associated controversy engendered an interest in validating personality constructs, as well as differentiating between normal and disordered personality.

Advances in Psychopharmacology Treatment   Further advances in the development of psychopharmacological agents provided new and effective adjunctive treatments for personality disorders and co-occurring syndromes. Kramer (1993) wrote about his observations on the impact of new antidepressants in "altering" personality. He viewed Prozac as capable of being transformational in some cases.

The Rise of the Integrative Psychotherapy Movement   According to Norcross and Newman (1992), strong rivalry among various orientations has had a long "undistinguished history in psychotherapy" (p. 3). Allport (1968) challenged his peers to achieve what he called "systematic eclecticism." However, eclecticism was viewed by many as simply a hodgepodge of theoretically dissimilar constructs and methods. In the early 1980s, the psychotherapy integrative movement gained momentum, and there was a dramatic rise in interest in it (Norcross & Goldfried, 1992, p. 60). Allport's intentions were even more sophisticated than the term *eclectic* suggests. He was really setting the stage for the introduction of a unified model, which he describes as: "a system that seeks the solution of fundamental problems by selecting and uniting what it regards as true in the specialized approaches to psychological sciences" (pp. 5–6). Further, he wrote that the field was not ready to "synthesize all plausible theories," but he believed, "it is still an ideal and a challenge" (p. 6).

THE COGNITIVE REVOLUTION   The cognitive revolution is said to have had its origins in the 1950s in response to radical behaviorism, which eschewed mental constructs that were not observable (Magnavita, 2002d). Eventually, cognitive science replaced behaviorism as the main theoretical system in psychology. It was not until much later, primarily with the work of Aaron Beck, that the revolution invaded clinical psychiatry and psychology with the application of the information processing model to depression (Beck, Rush, Shaw, & Emery, 1979) and later to the treatment of personality disorders (Beck, Freeman, & Associates, 1990).

THE EMERGENCE OF AFFECTIVE SCIENCE   Emotion has generally been considered an area unworthy of psychological investigation. There are historical exceptions, however. Charles Darwin is considered the father of affective science (Magnavita, 2002d). The first systematic examination of the topic was published in his volume, *The Expression of Emotions in Man and Animal* (Darwin, 1998). Another champion of emotion was Harry Harlow, whose work in attachment was engendered by his interest in understanding love (Blum, 2002). Silvan Tomkins (1962, 1963, 1991) published his influential work that marked the "official" beginning of affective science, which now has reached a place of prominence in the social sciences. Affective science has supported the universality of human facial expression in communicating emotion (Ekman & Davidson, 1994), something that many clinicians have learned to use to guide their work.

THE REDISCOVERY OF TRAUMA THEORY   Freud's original discovery of trauma as the main etiological factor in the development of hysteria and its subsequent "suppression" remains controversial (Magnavita, 2002b). As noted earlier in this chapter, Ferenczi and Rank (1925) continued to view trauma as the major pathway to severe personality disturbance but, for the most part, this position was abandoned. Rachman (1997) suggests that Ferenczi's early work and his observations about trauma are consistent with contemporary views. The impact of trauma on personality is well documented with extensive clinical and naturalistic material (Herman, 1992).

THE EMERGENCE OF NEUROSCIENCE AND THE STUDY OF CONSCIOUSNESS   The study of consciousness has been taken up by neuroscience. Some feel human consciousness remains one of the last mysteries of science (Dennett, 1991). Neuroscience offers many exciting new tools with which to investigate the interface between the mind and body. New models of how the mind works (Pinker, 1997) are being developed. There is hope that neuroscience will offer a way to understand the pervasive impact of early trauma as well as how psychotherapy may alter or reorganize neuronal networks and brain structure.

4. UNIFIED PERSONOLOGY AND PSYCHOTHERAPY (2000 TO PRESENT)

The Unification Phase   The field of personality disorders is currently in the unification phase, which is characterized by an attempt to find the unifying processes that link the major domains of the personality systems. The trend toward unification of personology is apparent in the number of collaborative volumes on the topics of developmental psychopathology, personality, and personality disorder theory and treatment. What is evident in many of the contributions is the tremendous amount of cross-fertilization in the field. Certainly, this emphasis on unification could be challenged as being overly inclusive and lacking in sufficient support. This criticism is well taken, but in fact most clinicians actually use individualized unified systems when they conduct their work. Clinicians are resourceful at developing personalized systems and incorporating flexible models that mirror the real life phenomenon they struggle to understand.

Critical Developments

THE CALL FOR UNIFIED MODEL FOR SOCIAL AND BIOLOGICAL SCIENCE   E. O. Wilson (1998) created the concept of *consilience* in the study of human nature. His view of consilience entails the grand unification of science and all her disciplines. Wilson states, "The greatest challenge today, not just in cell biology and ecology but in all science, is the accurate and complete description of complex systems" (p. 85). He describes the following bridges:

1. Cognitive neuroscience attempting to solve the mystery of consciousness.
2. Human behavioral genetics attempting to tease apart hereditary bases of mental development.
3. Evolutionary biology attempting to explain the hereditary origins of social behavior.
4. Environmental science, the theater in which humans adapt (p. 193).

Wilber (2000) also approaches this topic but from a different perspective. He emphasizes the interconnected nature of knowledge. His view is one of synthesizing knowledge in a "holonic" view where whole-part relationships can be understood.

THE DEVELOPMENT OF MILLON'S MODEL FOR UNIFICATION   Millon, Grossman, Meagher, Millon, and Everly (1999) present a personality-guided model of therapy that places personality in the central position in their conceptual system. This represents a major shift in thinking from the single domain approaches of the early part of the past century and the integrative approaches of the latter half. Published at the turn of the century, their volume *Personality-Guided Therapy* (Millon et al., 1999) will likely stand as a clear landmark of the shift toward unification of personology. The authors emphasize the ways in which expressions of clinical syndromes, whether complex or simple, can be best understood by viewing the organization and structure of the personality. Furthermore, the book outlines ways in which to combine and sequence various treatment modalities and approaches in a synergistic manner. This approach seems to reflect the clinical reality of practicing clinicians who often combine modalities and methods. Perhaps as a unified model becomes more accepted, the processes involved in this complex treatment application will be more clearly understood.

STERNBERG'S CALL FOR UNIFICATION OF PSYCHOLOGY   *Unified psychology,* as proposed by Sternberg and Grigorenko (2001), describes a "multiparadigmatic, multidisciplinary, and integrated study of psychological phenomenon through converging operations" (p. 1069). They believe that the adherence to single paradigms unnecessarily compartmentalizes and artificially fragments the field. This seems particularly relevant to the fundamental concern of this volume and the future of the field of personology.

CONTEMPORARY THEORIES OF PERSONALITY DISORDERS AND TREATMENT

The dominant theoretical models for understanding and treating personality disorders are generally accepted and understood. There are various other models, too, one of the most exciting of which is Eye Movement Desensitization and Reprocessing (EMDR), that have been developed or are being developed that also have application and appear to offer innovative techniques (Manfield & Shapiro, this volume). Most models, however, fall within the spectrum of the following "schools": psychodynamic, cognitive, cognitive-behavioral, interpersonal, psychobiological, family, integrative, and "unified." The first four of these models are primary schools that emphasize the various domains with which they are associated, such as affect-anxiety-defense in psychodynamic, cognitive schema in the cognitive model, and neurotransmitters in the psychobiological. The psychodynamic and cognitive concentrate on the intrapsychic domain. The interpersonal, primarily dyadic, configurations and the cognitive-behavioral are concerned with external reinforcement contingencies. The family model concerns itself with triadic configurations as they exist in the nuclear and extended family and are carried forward by multigenerational transmission. Even in the dominant models, we can see evidence of a considerable amount of integration. Integrative models draw from several of these domains, combining several of the main elements from two or more schools. The permutations are much more prolific than is outlined here. Unified models are attempting to organize the domains into an overarching metatheory; they are still in the infancy of development. Irving Yalom, a major leader in existential therapy, writes, "The contemporary field is more pluralistic: many diverse approaches have proven therapeutically effective and the therapist of today is more apt to tailor the therapy to fit the particular clinical needs of each patient" (Rosenbluth, 1997, p. x). At this point in the evolution of these theoretical-treatment systems, there is a considerable amount of integration. Clarkin and Lenzenweger's (1996) *Major Theories of Personality Disorder* provides a more detailed presentation of the dominant schools.

PSYCHODYNAMIC MODELS

Psychodynamic psychotherapy has evolved into multiple forms and derivative models that are far beyond the scope of this chapter. The *Comprehensive Handbook of Psychotherapy: Psychodynamic/Object Relations* reviews some of the contemporary approaches (Magnavita, 2002b). Psychodynamic models have four primary evolutionary branches, all of which emphasize personality organization and developmental processes: (1) structural-drive theory, (2) object relations, (3) ego psychology, and (4) self psychology. Structural-drive theory deals with the triangle of affect-anxiety-defense. Object relations focuses on the internalized representations of the major attachment figures and the processes by which these are expressed defensively and interpersonally. Ego psychology is primarily concerned with the adaptation and functioning of the defense system. Self psychology deals with the development of the self in dyadic relationships. The integration and development of short-term treatment models (Magnavita, 2002b) have proven most promising in contemporary psychodynamic therapy.

Cognitive Models

Cognitive approaches to treating personality disorders gained ascendancy with the pioneering work of Aaron Beck and his associates. See the *Comprehensive Handbook of Psychotherapy: Cognitive-Behavioral Approaches* (Patterson, 2002) for a presentation of current models. The single most influential volume is *Cognitive Therapy of Personality Disorders* (Beck et al., 1990). The cognitive model emerged during the cognitive revolution when principles of information processing were applied to clinical practice for the treatment of depression and anxiety and later to the treatment of personality disorders. The cognitive model emphasizes the internalized schema, including individuals' guiding beliefs about themselves and the world, which are often dysfunctional. Personality-disordered individuals of various types have common schematic representations through which they filter experience and respond to self and others. Cognitive therapy offers a rich array of methods such as cognitive restructuring and techniques of challenging irrational or dysfunctional beliefs.

Cognitive-Behavioral Models

The cognitive-behavioral treatment of personality disorders is one of the newer treatments for personality disorders (Sperry, 1999). The dialectical behavior therapy (DBT) model of Marsha Linehan (1993) was developed specifically for Borderline Personality Disorder. Her approach, although based on behavioral principles, blends aspects of Eastern philosophy and many elements of the major schools.

Interpersonal Models

The interpersonal model for the treatment of personality disorders has multiple influences including Leary (1957), Sullivan (1953), and the contemporary work of Benjamin (1993, 2003) also presented in this volume (see chapter 8). The interpersonal model's focus is on dyadic configurations, the processes that occur between two individuals, and how these interpersonal processes influence the expression of personality. Interpersonal models of therapy tend to be highly integrative, drawing methods and techniques from various schools while holding to their belief that psychopathology emerges from, and is expressed in, the dyad.

Psychobiological Models

Psychobiological approaches to treating personality disorders have gained attention more recently as new biologic theories of personality have gained prominence that offer suggestions for addressing the underlying neurobiological substrates on which personality is based. Klein (1967, 1970) experimented using "chemical dissection": administering pharmacological agents in an attempt to distinguish between hysteroid-dysphoric and phobic-anxious types. Psychopharmacology, to some degree, continues to rely on his approach to clinical psychiatric diagnosis in many cases. This is especially evident in the treatment of personality dysfunction. Cloninger (1986a, 1986b) developed a three-factor (novelty seeking, harm avoidance, and reward dependence) biosocial model and Siever (Siever & Davis, 1991) a four-factor model (cognitive/perceptual organization, impulsivity/aggression, affective instability, and anxiety/inhibition) to explain how the neurobiological systems influence personality.

FAMILY MODELS

Family models were not generally applied to the understanding of personality as defined by academic and clinical scientists. However, the family model is one that is gaining more attention in contemporary theory and clinical practice (Magnavita & MacFarlane, in press). The most highly developed of the family models is Bowen's (1978) family systems theory. The key concepts include *triangles,* which are basic emotional units when there are unstable dyads, *level of differentiation* between self and other, and between intellectual and emotional. The drive in humans is not the instinctual aggression and sexual impulses of classic drive theory but the struggle between intimacy or connection and individuation and autonomy. "The degree of fusion of the intellectual and emotional systems within an individual parallels the degree to which that person fuses or loses self in relationship" (Kerr, 1981, p. 239). Various clinical types of families can be identified that, over generations, spawn personality dysfunction among their lineage (Magnavita, 2000). As stated previously, personality has traditionally been considered a construct used to explain the individual. There has been little cross-fertilization between the systemic and personality models, even though many have alluded to the importance of systemic thinking. More recently, the idea that personality disorder can be viewed and treated in the context of the family system has emerged. Perlmutter (1996) writes:

> Awareness of the family context of the disorders also introduces a degree of "relativism" to the criteria for personality disorder. It is common to find that the whole family has the same traits or idiosyncrasies found in the individual patient. The whole family may be avoidant, hysterical, or schizotypal. (p. 327)

In fact, there is little empirical evidence concerning the constellation of personality disorders within family systems. In another volume, I present the view that there are certain family themes around which families are organized, which will give rise to particular personality disorders that are more likely to occur (Magnavita, 2000).

INTEGRATIVE MODELS

Integrative treatment models for personality dysfunction and integrative models of personality (Magnavita, 2002d) have begun to emerge with the assimilation and blending of theories and methods. Integrative models became prominent during the 1980s and continue to be developed. Models such as these seem to come closer to reflecting what therapists do in their clinical practice. Very few clinicians practice "pure form" therapy (if such a thing exists outside research protocols). Even proponents of "single" school orientations have been known to practice more integratively than their descriptions suggest. This observation has been validated by my own observations and by a number of individuals in diverse training programs who have seen the tapes of prominent clinicians and trainers.

Single school treatment is primarily the domain of psychotherapy researchers who require adherence to a particular model.

Because there are numerous integrative models, only some of those applicable to personality disorders are mentioned. A major advance is Wachtel's (1977) "cyclical psychodynamic" model, an integrative approach applicable to the treatment of personality dysfunction. Johnson (1985) developed one of the earliest innovative integrative approaches to "transforming character." Magnavita (2000, 2002c) presented an integrative relational model that blends psychodynamic, cognitive, and systems theory and is the precursor to the unified model presented in this volume (chapter 24). Sperry (1995) offered an integrative approach to treating personality disorders, and Preston (1997) developed a brief integrative approach for treating borderline personality. Young (1994) advanced Beck's model and developed his schema-focused therapy for personality disorders, which he describes as integrating elements of various other systems (see Ball, chapter 18, this volume). These approaches and others all share a common belief that blending various theoretical elements, techniques, and modalities is preferable, especially for personality dysfunction.

UNIFIED MODELS

Unified models of personality and psychotherapy represent the next stage in evolution of the field. Rychlak (1973) believed in the necessity of an interdisciplinary approach: "Modern psychology must be able to provide generalizations which coalesce with the thinking of other sciences if it is to become an undisputed science." He suggested, "the best scheme and series of issues to unify personality theory would seem to be drawn from the history of philosophy and science" (preface). Millon, Meagher, and Grossman (2001) write:

> Quite evidently, the complexity and intricacy of personologic phenomena make it difficult not only to establish clear-cut relationships among phenomena but to find simple ways in which these phenomena can be classified or grouped. Should we artificially narrow our perspective to one data level to obtain at least a coherency of view? Or, should we trudge ahead with formulations which bridge domains but threaten to crumble by virtue of complexity and potentially low internal consistency? (p. 39)

Millon et al. (2001) offer their valuable perspective that overly precise theories may be narrow in their scope and oversimplified. On the other hand, the danger of broader scope theory is that precision may be lost and tautology rampant. Millon believes that "the natural direction of science is toward theories of greater and greater scope" (p. 55).

Millon (1990) bases his theory on an evolutionary model, but his work fits into a unified model: "Evolution is the logical choice as a scaffold from which to develop a science of personality" (Millon, 1990). "Just as personality is concerned with the total patterning of variables across the entire matrix of the person, it is the total organism that survives and reproduces, carrying forth both its adaptive and maladaptive potentials into future generations" (p. 55).

A unified model seeks connections among all the significant domain systems. Millon et al. (2001) state: "Rather than inherit the construct dimensions of a particular perspective, then, a theory of personality as a total phenomenon should seek some set of principles which can be addressed to the whole person, thereby capitalizing on the synthetic properties of personality as the total matrix of the person" (p. 55). Clarkin and Lenzenweger (1996) write: "To our minds, the tasks of future theorizing and empirical research in personality disorders will involve the effective integration of mind, brain, and behavior. Any comprehensive model of complex human behavior, particularly forms of psychopathology, will require a clear and genuine integration of ideas and research findings that cut across the levels of analysis linking mind, brain, and behavior" (p. 26).

Using a systemic framework that addresses the major domains of the personologic matrix, I am developing a model of a unified system (Magnavita, 2002d, in press; see Figure 3.1).

TREATMENT MODELS FOR SEVERE PERSONALITY DISORDERS

A major focus of the field recently has been to develop effective treatment methods for those patients who are "difficult" to treat or have a severe personality disorder. This trend began in the 1940s and 1950s when clinicians began to notice a group of patients who appeared neurotic at first but became highly regressed and explosive when in treatment (Waldinger & Gunderson, 1987). A new diagnostic term, *borderline,* was used to account for these individuals who seemed to be functioning at a point between neurotic and psychotic (Gunderson & Singer, 1975). There are two

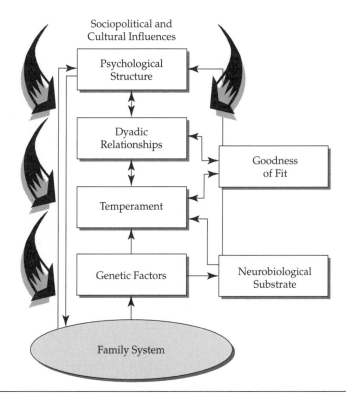

Figure 3.1 The Systemic Interrelationships among the Modular Components of Personality. [*Source:* From *Theories of Personality: Contemporary Approaches to the Science of Personality* (p. 398), by J. J. Magnavita, 2002, New York: Wiley.]

distinctive models that have been specifically developed for treating the severe personality disorders: Clarkin, Yeomans, and Kernberg's (1999) *transference focused therapy* (TFP), an object relational model using intensive individual psychodynamic psychotherapy (Clarkin, Levy, & Dammann, 2002), and Linehan's (1993) *dialectical behavior therapy* (DBT), an approach that uses cognitive-behavior therapy in a combination of group and individual formats.

The severe personality disorders take up a disproportionate amount of resources. They often require multidisciplinary treatment efforts and have a high rate of emergency room utilization. Severe personality disorder is often complicated by coexisting conditions such as substance abuse, which makes treatment extremely challenging. It seems likely that any effective programs will require a multidimensional approach that uses various treatment modalities and sequences of treatment (Millon et al., 1999).

PERSONALITY DISORDER AND SEVERE PSYCHIATRIC DISTURBANCE

The interrelationship among *biologically based* mental disorders and personality organization and type is a topic of tremendous importance to clinicians. Often, clinical syndromes that are considered to have a heavy biological loading such as schizophrenia and affective disorders, especially bipolar disorder, are treated in isolation without focus on the personality adaptation. Both clinical observation and experience underscore the importance of considering the personality as a central component of any clinical syndrome. For example, the personality system of an individual predisposed to psychiatric disorders will have a major impact on the treatment process. The manner in which an individual understands and accepts the constraints of chronic biologically based psychiatric disorder is highly contingent on the individual's personality and defensive structure. Whether medications will be taken as prescribed, the meaning of medication, and the acceptance of their limitations are central treatment issues. For example, patients with paranoid personality features suffering from a major affective disorder may view medication as an attempt to invade and control them, and/or medication compliance may be a problem because of paranoid delusions. On the other hand, individuals with obsessive-compulsive personality systems might be more likely to comply but may be hypervigilant about any physiological changes and continually phone the psychopharmacologist about various "side effects."

Another central issue is the impact of chronic mental illness on the personality system. Many individuals who are not treated or are not compliant with treatment and who have active clinical syndromes may begin to show gradual deterioration of the integrity of their personality system. Psychotic episodes or traumatic events certainly have major impact on personality functioning. It is imperative that the clinician working with individuals with severe trauma and psychotic disturbance do everything possible to maintain the integrity of the individual's personality system.

CHILD AND ADOLESCENT MODELS OF TREATMENT

A controversial issue in the treatment of personality disorders is whether children and adolescents ought to be diagnosed with personality disorders. Some believe that early identification and treatment of personality disorders in children and adolescents are critical to prevent more serious disturbances later in life. Masterson (1985) was one of the early clinical theorists whose work focused on adolescent personality disorders using an object relations-based developmental approach. Masterson hypothesized that borderline conditions in adolescents are the result of a failure of the separation-individuation phase of development. He summarizes:

> The heart of the theory is that separation for the Borderline patient does not evolve as a normal developmental experience but on the contrary entails such intense feelings of abandonment that it is experienced as truly a rendezvous with death. To defend against these feelings, the Borderline patient clings to the maternal figure, thus fails to progress through the normal developmental stages of separation-individuation to autonomy. (p. 19)

Masterson believes that the mother of the adolescent patient herself often suffers from a borderline condition. He writes, "Having been unable to separate from her own mother she fosters the symbiotic union with her child thus encouraging the continuance of his dependency to maintain her own emotional equilibrium" (p. 22). This individuation threatens her and makes it difficult for her to accept the separation. In adolescence, the child is unable to experience other people as a whole and so splits others into good and bad. He or she is unable to have satisfying interpersonal attachments because of the primitive defenses that develop to protect the ego. The emotional deprivation that ensues leads to abandonment sensitivity and a rage that interfere with all relationships.

Kernberg, Weiner, and Bardenstein (2000) present a developmentally based psychodynamic approach to assessment and treatment of child and adolescent personality disorders. Bleiberg (2001) has also developed an individually oriented relational approach, which blends psychodynamic and pharamacological elements presented in this volume (see Bleiberg, chapter 21). Fonagy and Target (2002) also use a psychodynamically based child therapy approach to treat child personality disorders.

TREATMENT MODELS FOR THE ELDERLY

An area of growing interest as the population ages is the treatment of personality disorders in the elderly. There is a dearth of epidemiological findings on the incidence and few treatment models for this population. Research on this subject is sorely needed. It is likely that as individuals age, there may be an exacerbation of personality dysfunction because of loss, increased stress, economic disadvantage, and the impact of aging and declining health. Many patients with personality disorders who have never been treated gravitate toward the medical system, where they unnecessarily burden medical providers. Assessing and treating these patients remain a challenge.

TREATMENT MODELS FOR MINORITIES

Treatment models for minorities have yet to be developed to address personality dysfunction. Possibly in an effort to avoid controversy over unnecessarily stigmatizing minority groups, most theorists and researchers have avoided this topic.

This has not served minorities well. A lack of attention to and research on minorities with personality dysfunction leaves few choices for social response. Unfortunately, many minorities with personality disorders, particularly African American males, fall under the domain of the penal system because of lack of access to the mental health system. The high incidence of substance abuse in disadvantaged populations may be generating increased interest in personality pathology, but little definitive has been shown at the present about these complicated interactions.

RYCHLAK'S GUIDELINES FOR EVALUATING THEORY

How are clinicians to decide what theoretical model or models to adopt? As clinical scientists concerned with human functioning, we have the responsibility to critically evaluate theory. Various approaches claim to treat personality disorders, but the empirical findings are scant. When a new theory of treatment is developed, it often takes years or decades before research support is available. In spite of these constraints, clinicians must select from available approaches to invest their resources in learning and practicing. It is important to be able to evaluate clinical theories of personality, psychopathology, and treatment. Rychlak (1973) offers us the following guidelines:

> A personality theory must answer four major questions: (1) What is the essential structure of personality? Or, if structure is to be disregarded, what are we to substitute? (2) On what basis does this structure behave? (3) Does this structure change over time, and if so, in what way? and (4) How does one account for the variety of human behavior among different individuals? If we can answer these four questions to our satisfaction, then we have fairly well exhausted the possible meanings which any theory or personality might be expected to generate. (pp. 20–21)

Further, he adds the following questions related to psychopathology and psychotherapy:

> Common sense would dictate that there are three questions which must be answered in this context: (1) How does a personality "get sick" or "become maladjusted" or "begin behaving in an unrewarding fashion"? (2) How does the therapist go about curing, resolving, or controlling (changing) the condition? and (3) Does he have any unique procedures in his approach distinguishing him from other psychotherapists? (p. 21)

The theory should also offer an explanation of change or an understanding of developmental progression.

CLINICAL UTILITY OF THEORY

One question that clinicians ask themselves is whether a particular theory has clinical utility: Does the theory serve a useful function in assisting the clinician in selecting treatment methods and techniques to guide treatment? Clinicians typically determine the clinical utility of a theory by trial and error rather than systematically. Clinicians look for theories that can organize the phenomenon they encounter in a fashion that will allow them to explain to their patients how treatment works. They try to formulate a problem in terms of a certain theory and then apply methods and techniques to see if change ensues. If the methods and techniques do not have any face validity, they are discarded and others tried. Over the course of clinical practice, their trials and errors shape clinicians' responses. Good theory tends to reduce the extent of the trial and error phase by offering a model of effectiveness.

ABILITY OF THEORY TO GENERATE RELEVANT RESEARCH

Theory must be able to generate research to be valuable to the science of personology. A theory that does not generate research to either support or invalidate its premises and constructs will eventually fade. Rychlak writes:

> The sophisticated scientist is not interested in "the truth," but rather in "the truth thus far" or "the truth as I view it from my theoretical stance." An attitude of this sort must help strengthen the kinds of empirical study the individual will engage in when he turns from theory to methodological test. He will be just as suspicious of his evidence as he is of his theory. This is the proper scientific attitude. It is tough-minded without being narrow-minded. (p. 17)

THE CLINICIAN AS CLINICAL THEORIST

All clinicians who treat patients with personality dysfunction are inherently clinical theorists. Every clinician has a model of the mind and of human relationships to help make clinical assessments and to organize treatment strategies. Very few follow any model of psychotherapy or personality theory that is endorsed by that model. Personality theory is filtered through the personality system of the clinician and so takes on a unique character of its own. Many clinicians have intuitive ways of understanding personality and human adaptation, whereas others use a formal system. One last caveat, although this chapter emphasizes the importance of theory: Never retreat into "pathological" theoretical certainty! Theory is a guide, but those we work with should not be forced into any artificial theoretical perspective.

SUMMARY AND CONCLUSIONS

This chapter presented an overview of the major developmental phases and critical events that have shaped the contemporary field of personology. The relevance of theory for clinical practice has been stressed, particularly for personality-disordered patients. Theory offers a way to understand the most complex phenomena of science: human behavior, consciousness, and human nature. Clinicians have to deal with an overwhelming amount of information that is communicated in multiple formats, which must be organized to be understood. Theory offers a way to systematize and distill material from the biopsychosocial realm of the patient. Some theory uses a narrow scope, emphasizing one domain or another; others are grand or unified, attempting to provide an overarching metatheory that allows for all aspects of the complex system, from the biological to the ecological. Theory also suggests methods and techniques for interventions and to reorganize or restructure dysfunctional personality systems. Over the past century, there have been substantial developments in the various domains of personality. We currently have identified the main domains and many of the processes by which they interrelate.

REFERENCES

Allport, G. W. (1937). *Personality: A psychological interpretation.* New York: Henry Holt.

Allport, G. W. (1968). *The person in psychology: Selected essays.* Boston: Beacon Press.

Allport, G. W., & Odbert, H. S. (1936). Trait-names: A psych-lexical study. *Psychological Monographs, 47,* 1–171.

Beck, A. T., Freeman, A., & Associates. (1990). *Cognitive therapy of personality disorders.* New York: Guilford Press.

Beck, A. T., Rush, A. J., Shaw, B. F., & Emery, G. (1979). *Cognitive therapy of depression.* New York: Guilford Press.

Benjamin, L. S. (1993). *Interpersonal diagnosis and treatment of personality disorders.* New York: Guilford Press.

Benjamin, L. S. (2003). *Interpersonal reconstructive therapy: Promoting change in nonresponders.* New York: Guilford Press.

Bleiberg, E. (2001). *Treating personality disorders in children and adolescents: A relational approach.* New York: Guilford Press.

Blum, D. (2002). *Love at Goon Park: Harry Harlow and the science of affection.* Cambridge, MA: Perseus.

Bowen, M. (1978). *Family therapy in clinical practice.* New York: Aronson.

Bowlby, J. (1969). *Attachment and loss. Volume I: Attachment.* New York: Basic Books.

Bowlby, J. (1973). *Attachment and loss. Volume II: Separation: Anxiety and anger.* New York: Basic Books.

Bowlby, J. (1980). *Attachment and loss. Volume III: Loss: Sadness and depression.* New York: Basic Books.

Chrzanowski, G. (1977). *Interpersonal approaches to psychoanalysis: Contemporary views of Harry Stack Sullivan.* New York: Gardner Press.

Clarkin, J. F., & Lenzenweger, M. F. (1996). *Major theories of personality disorder.* New York: Guilford Press.

Clarkin, J. F., Levy, K. N., & Dammann, G. W. (2002). An object-relations approach to the treatment of borderline patients. In F. W. Kaslow (Editor-in-Chief) & J. J. Magnavita (Vol. Ed.), *Comprehensive handbook of psychotherapy: Vol. I. Psychodynamic/object relations* (pp. 239–252). Hoboken, NJ: Wiley.

Clarkin, J. F., Yeomans, F. E., & Kernberg, O. F. (1999). *Psychotherapy for borderline personality.* New York: Wiley.

Cloninger, C. R. (1986a). A systematic method for clinical description and classification of personality variants: A proposal. *Archives of General Psychiatry, 44,* 573–588.

Cloninger, C. R. (1986b). A unified biosocial theory of personality and its role in the development of anxiety states. *Psychiatry Developments, 3,* 167–226.

Darwin, C. R. (1998). *The expression of the emotions in man and animal* (3rd ed.). New York: Oxford University Press. (Original work published 1872)

Dennett, D. C. (1991). *Consciousness explained.* Boston: Little, Brown.

Dollard, J., & Miller, N. E. (1950). *Personality and psychotherapy: An analysis in terms of learning, thinking, and culture.* New York: McGraw-Hill.

Ekman, P., & Davidson, R. J. (Eds.). (1994). *The nature of emotions: Fundamental questions.* New York: Oxford University Press.

Eysenck, H. J. (1952). The effects of psychotherapy: In evaluation. *Journal of Consulting Psychology, 16,* 319–324.

Ferenczi, S., & Rank, O. (1925). *The development of psychoanalysis.* New York: Nervous and Mental Disease Press.

Fonagy, P., & Target, M. (2002). Psychodynamic approaches to child therapy. In F. W. Kaslow (Editor-in-Chief) & J. J. Magnavita (Vol. Ed.), *Comprehensive handbook of psychotherapy: Vol. I. Psychodynamic/object relations* (pp. 105–129). Hoboken, NJ: Wiley.

Freud, S. (1900). The interpretation of dreams. In J. Strachey (Ed.), *The standard edition of the complete psychological works of Sigmund Freud* (Vols. 4–5, pp. 1–715). London: Hogarth Press.

Goldfried, M. R., & Newman, C. F. (1992). A history of psychotherapy integration. In J. C. Norcross & M. R. Goldfried (Eds.), *Handbook of integrative psychotherapy* (pp. 47–93). New York: Basic Books.

Gunderson, J. G., & Singer, M. T. (1975). Defining borderline patients: An overview. *American Journal of Psychiatry, 132,* 1–10.

Herman, J. L. (1992). *Trauma and recovery.* New York: Basic Books.

James, W. (1890). *The principles of psychology* (Vols. 1–2). New York: Henry Holt.

Johnson, S. M. (1985). *Characterological transformation: The hard work miracle.* New York: Norton.

Kerr, M. E. (1981). Family systems theory and therapy. In A. S. Gurman & D. P. Kniskern (Eds.), *Handbook of family therapy* (pp. 226–264). New York: Brunner/Mazel.

Kernberg, P. F., Weiner, A. S., & Bardenstein, K. K. (2000). *Treating personality disorders in children and adolescents.* New York: Guilford Press.

Klein, D. F. (1967). The importance of psychiatric diagnosis in prediction of critical drug effects. *Archives of General Psychiatry, 16,* 118–126.

Klein, D. F. (1970). Psychotropic drugs and regulation of behavior activation in psychiatric illness. In W. L. Smith (Ed.), *Drugs and cerebral function.* Springfield, IL: Charles C Thomas.

Kramer, P. D. (1993). *Listening to Prozac: A psychiatrist explores antidepressant drugs and the remaking of the self.* New York: Viking/Penguin Books.

Kuhn, T. S. (1962). *The structure of scientific revolutions.* Chicago: University of Chicago Press.

Leary, T. (1957). *Interpersonal diagnosis of personality: A functional theory and meta theory for personality evaluation.* New York: Ronald Press.

Linehan, M. M. (1993). *Cognitive-behavioral treatment of borderline personality disorder.* New York: Guilford Press.

Magnavita, J. J. (1993). The evolution of short-term dynamic psychotherapy: Treatment of the future? *Professional Psychology: Research and Practice, 24*(3), 360–365.

Magnavita, J. J. (2000). *Relational therapy for personality disorders.* New York: Wiley.

Magnavita, J. J. (2002a). Contemporary psychodynamics: Major issues, challenges, and future trends. In F. W. Kaslow (Editor-in-Chief) & J. J. Magnavita (Vol. Ed.), *Comprehensive handbook of psychotherapy: Vol. I. Psychodynamic/object relations* (pp. 587–604). Hoboken, NJ: Wiley.

Magnavita, J. J. (2002b). Psychodynamic approaches to psychotherapy: A century of innovations. In F. W. Kaslow (Editor-in-Chief) & J. J. Magnavita (Vol. Ed.), *Comprehensive handbook of psychotherapy: Vol. I. Psychodynamic/object relations* (pp. 1–12). Hoboken, NJ: Wiley.

Magnavita, J. J. (2002c). Relational psychodynamics for complex clinical syndromes. In F. W. Kaslow (Editor-in-Chief) & J. J. Magnavita (Vol. Ed.), *Comprehensive handbook of psychotherapy: Vol. I. Psychodynamic/object relations* (pp. 435–453). Hoboken, NJ: Wiley.

Magnavita, J. J. (2002d). *Theories of personality: Contemporary approaches to the science of personality.* Hoboken, NJ: Wiley.

Magnavita, J. J. (in press). *Personality-guided relational therapy.* Washington, DC: American Psychological Association.

Magnavita, J. J., & MacFarlane, M. M. (in press). Family treatment of personality disorders: Historical overview and current perspectives. In M. M. MacFarlane (Ed.), *Family treatment of personality disorders: Interpersonal approaches to relationship change.* New York: Haworth Press.

Masterson, J. F. (1985). *Treatment of the borderline adolescent: A developmental approach.* New York: Brunner/Mazel.

Millon, T. (1990). *Toward a new personology: An evolutionary model.* New York: Wiley.

Millon, T., Grossman, S. D., Meagher, S. E., Millon, C., & Everly, G. (1999). *Personality-guided therapy.* New York: Wiley.

Millon, T., Meagher, S. E., & Grossman, S. D. (2001). Theoretical perspectives. In W. J. Livesley (Ed.), *Handbook of personality disorders: Theory, research, and treatment* (pp. 39–59). New York: Guilford Press.

Murray, H. A. (1938). *Explorations in personality.* New York: Oxford University Press.

Norcross, J. C., & Goldfried, M. R. (Eds.). (1992). *Handbook of psychotherapy integration.* New York: Basic Books.

Norcross, J. C., & Newman, C. F. (1992). Psychotherapy integration: Setting the context. In J. C. Norcross & M. R. Goldfried (Eds.), *Handbook of psychotherapy integration* (pp. 3–45). New York: Basic Books.

Patterson, T. (Ed.). (2002). *Comprehensive handbook of psychotherapy: Cognitive-behavioral approaches.* Hoboken, NJ: Wiley.

Perlmutter, R. A. (1996). *A family approach to psychiatric disorders.* Washington, DC: American Psychiatric Press.

Pinker, S. (1997). *How the mind works.* New York: Basic Books.

Preston, J. D. (1997). *Shorter term treatments for borderline personality disorders.* Oakland, CA: New Harbinger.

Rachman, A. W. (1997). *Sandor Ferenczi: The psychotherapist of tenderness and passion.* Northvale, NJ: Aronson.

Reich, W. (1945). *Character analysis* (3rd ed.). New York: Noonday Press.

Rilling, M. (2000). John Watson's paradoxical struggle to explain Freud. *American Psychologist, 55*(3), 301–312.

Rosenbluth, M. (Ed.). (1997). *Treating difficult personality disorders.* San Francisco: Jossey-Bass.

Rychlak, J. F. (1973). *Introduction to personality and psychotherapy: A theory construction approach.* Boston: Houghton Mifflin.

Siever, L. J., & Davis, K. L. (1991). A psychobiological perspective on personality disorders. *American Journal of Psychiatry, 148,* 1647–1658.

Smith, M. L., Glass, G. V., & Miller, T. I. (1980). *The benefits of psychotherapy.* Baltimore: Johns Hopkins University Press.

Sperry, L. (1995). *Handbook of diagnosis and treatment of DSM-IV personality disorders.* New York: Brunner/Mazel.

Sperry, L. (1999). *Cognitive behavior therapy of DSM-IV personality disorders: Highly effective interventions for the most common personality problems.* Philadelphia: Brunner/Mazel.

Sternberg, R. J., & Grigorenko, E. L. (2001). Unified psychology. *American Psychologist, 56*(12), 1069–1079.

Sullivan, H. S. (1953). *The interpersonal theory of psychiatry.* New York: Norton.

Tomkins, S. S. (1962). *Affect imagery consciousness. Volume I: The positive affects.* New York: Springer.

Tomkins, S. S. (1963). *Affect imagery consciousness. Volume II: The negative affects.* New York: Springer.

Tomkins, S. S. (1991). *Affect imagery consciousness. Volume III: The negative affect: Anger and fear.* New York: Springer.

von Bertalanffy, L. (1968). *General system theory.* New York: Braziller.

Wachtel, P. L. (1977). *Psychoanalysis and behavior therapy: Toward an integration.* New York: Basic Books.

Waldinger, R. J., & Gunderson, J. G. (1987). *Effective psychotherapy with borderline patients: Case studies.* Washington, DC: American Psychiatric Press.

Watson, J. B. (1924). *Behaviorism.* New York: Norton.

Watson, J. B., & Raynor, R. (1920). Conditioned emotional reactions. *Journal of Experimental Psychology, 3,* 1–4.

Wilber, K. (2000). *A theory of everything: An integral vision for business, politics, and spirituality.* Boston: Shambhala.

Wilson, E. O. (1998). *Consilience: The unity of knowledge.* New York: Alfred A. Knopf.

Winnicott, C., Shepherd, R., & Davis, M. (Eds.). (1989). *Psychoanalytic explorations: D. W. Winnicott.* Cambridge, MA: Harvard University Press.

Young, J. E. (1994). *Cognitive therapy for personality disorders: A schema-focused approach* (Rev. ed.). Sarasota, FL: Professional Resource Exchange.

CHAPTER 4

Assessing the Dimensions of Personality Disorder

Philip Erdberg

FOR THE GREEK physician Hippocrates (460–400 B.C.), personality consisted of four dimensions and its disorders in their excesses or imbalances. Too much yellow bile resulted in an irritable temperament; too much black bile, in melancholia; too much blood, in an overly optimistic makeup; and too much phlegm, in an apathetic nature. Centuries later, Sigmund Freud dealt with the same question—the basic dimensions of personality—in the section of his 1915 metapsychology paper that he called "Instincts and Their Vicissitudes." "Our mental life as a whole is governed by three polarities," he wrote, identifying them as active versus passive, pleasure versus pain, and self versus other (1915/1925, pp. 76–77). Frustration or reinforcement of one or another of these elements resulted in potentially maladaptive personality styles skewed too much toward impacting the environment or accommodating to it, seeking new experiences or avoiding threat, or focusing on self versus concentrating on the welfare of others.

It is now nearly a century since Freud's 1915 paper, and the intervening decades have seen a multitude of new attempts to name the dimensions of personality. If we view personality disorders as "the maladaptive variants of personality traits that merge imperceptibly into normality and into one another" (American Psychiatric Association [APA], 2000, p. 689), the assessment of personality disorder becomes the assessment of these traits or dimensions, their interactions, and their dysfunctional extremes. This chapter presents four current—and conceptually diverse—approaches to identifying the dimensions of personality and surveys the associated instruments that have been developed to assess the normal and pathological manifestations of these dimensions.

MILLON'S EVOLUTIONARY MODEL

We begin with the work of Theodore Millon (1969), who drew on Freud's (1915/1925) explication to develop what he initially described as a biosocial-learning theory of personality and personality disorder. Later, Millon (1996) expanded his model to present the dimensions of personality as examples of universal evolutionary principles. The earlier biosocial-learning theory and the current evolutionary model share key elements that define Millon's thinking about the basic dimensions of personality.

Beginning with Freud's (1915/1925) active-passive, pleasure-pain, and self-other polarities, Millon (1969) identified a series of coping styles whose maladaptive extremes resulted in disorders similar to those identified on Axis II of the *DSM-III* (APA, 1980). In Millon's words (1996, p. 67): "These strategies reflect what kinds of reinforcements individuals learned to seek *or* to avoid (pleasure-pain), where individuals looked to obtain them (self-others), and how they learned to behave to elicit or to escape them (active-passive)." For example, Millon would characterize the *DSM* Histrionic Personality Disorder individual as someone inordinately high on both the "active" and the "other" dimensions. In his conceptualization, the histrionic individual endlessly and rather indiscriminately searches for the affection and stimulation that can be provided only from outside.

Millon (Millon & Davis, 1997) has suggested that all the *DSM* personality disorders can be included in this polarity model and viewed as representing one of three possible conditions. The *deficient* condition involves a style in which the individual is unable to emphasize either side of a polarity. The schizoid individual, for example, is deficient in his or her ability both to seek pleasurable experiences and to avoid painful ones. The *imbalanced* personality emphasizes one side of a polarity, often to the exclusion of the other. The dependent individual, for example, relies heavily on others for nurturance, with little ability to provide self-support. The *conflicted* personality oscillates between the two sides of one of the polarities. The passive-aggressive individual, for example, wavers between emphasizing the expectancies of others and focusing on his or her own wishes and needs.

Ultimately, Millon produced a series of psychological tests designed to quantify his constructs and make them available for researchers and clinicians. The *Millon Index of Personality Styles* (MIPS; Millon, Weiss, Millon, & Davis, 1994) represents Millon's attempt to operationalize the theoretically based latent personality elements articulated in his evolutionary model. It is a 180-item self-report measure whose scales identify various aspects of the polarities described previously. For example, a histrionic individual might emerge as high on the MIPS "active-modifying" and the MIPS "other-nurturing" latent construct scales. In Millon's words: "By focusing on these latent components, rather than their manifest derivations, the MIPS scales serve as a more direct gauge of the theory's evolutionary constructs than can be determined by the MCMI scales" (1996, p. 164).

As Millon suggests, the MCMI (Millon Clinical Multiaxial Inventory-III; Millon, Millon, & Davis, 1994) operates at a level above that of the latent elements of personality, focusing instead on the direct identification of personality disorders for diagnostic screening and clinical assessment purposes. It is now in the third version of what Millon calls "an evolving assessment instrument" (Millon & Davis, 1997, p. 69), a sequence that began in 1977 with the MCMI-I (Millon, 1977) and continued with the MCMI-II (Millon, 1987).

The current MCMI-III is a 175-item self-report inventory with 24 clinical scales and three additional scales—Disclosure, Desirability, and Debasement—which provide information about the person's impression management tendencies. The clinical scales encompass all the personality disorders listed in both *DSM-III-R*

(APA, 1987) and the *DSM-IV* (APA, 1994, 2000). They also include scales for possible Axis II syndromes listed in the "further study" appendixes of *DSM-III-R* and *DSM-IV*, namely Self-Defeating/Masochistic, Passive-Aggressive, Sadistic, and Depressive Personality disorders. The final sections of the MCMI-III consist of scales identifying a variety of Axis I presentations ranging from Schizophrenic Spectrum Disorders through drug and alcohol problems to Affect and Posttraumatic Stress Disorders.

Although the MCMI-III clinical scales carry the names of specific disorders, Millon notes that personality disorders are best conceptualized as prototypes, each encompassing several variations through which the basic personality style manifests itself. These subtypes can be represented by particular code-type configurations of the MCMI-III scales. For example, the subtypes of Narcissistic Personality Disorder might include what Millon calls the "Elitist subtype," whose code type would include an elevation only on the Narcissistic scale; the Amorous subtype, whose code type would include elevations on the Narcissistic and Histrionic scales; the Unprincipled subtype, whose code type would have elevations on the Narcissistic and Antisocial scales, and the Compensatory subtype, whose code type would include elevations on the Narcissistic and Avoidant and/or Passive-Aggressive scales (Millon & Davis, 1997).

Millon (Millon & Davis, 1997) views these subtypes as needing additional research to support their reliability and validity. He also notes that, unlike the basically invariant prototypes, the subtypes through which these prototypes manifest are shaped to some extent by the social forces of particular eras and cultures. Consequently, it would be expected that they would change over time and place, making code-type interpretation an ongoing combination of personality theory and context.

From a clinical standpoint, Millon's model allows the treating clinician to formulate specific intervention goals. For example, an important focus in the treatment of a narcissistic individual would be establishing a balance on the self-other polarity that moves toward more other-orientedness. Millon (1996) notes that the first therapeutic intervention must be to work toward a more realistic self-image. He writes: "As the patient comes to grasp the nonadaptive nature of the expansive narcissistic cognitive, preoccupation with immature fantasies may be decreased" (p. 423). At a tactical level, the therapist might work to help the client or patient move from unrealistic fantasy to a focus on more attainable goals that bring with them the potential for actual gratification.

In contrast, Millon's model would suggest that the crucial polarity changes for the avoidant individual involve the pleasure-pain and active-passive polarities. Millon (1996, p. 282) notes that a major therapeutic goal is to increase the client's active focus on pleasurable situations and decrease his or her withdrawal in the face of potential embarrassment. Armed with the understanding that avoidant individuals devote most of their energy to staying away from criticism, the therapist can begin with an unreservedly supportive approach. As trust develops, various successive approximation techniques can help the person develop more adaptive approaches to formerly threatening situations.

THE BIG FIVE MODEL AND THE FIVE-FACTOR MODEL

A very different approach to identifying the dimensions of personality takes leave of theory and instead draws on an assumption that Cattell articulated in

1943: "all aspects of human personality which are or have been of importance, interest, or utility have already become recorded in the substance of the language" (p. 483). This lexical hypothesis (Saucier & Goldberg, 1996) assumes that an examination of the natural language will yield a comprehensive taxonomy of personality attributes. It assumes that these attributes have become encoded in the natural language, describing the observable aspects of day-to-day personality function. The lexical approach makes no attempt to provide causal (nature versus nurture) explanations or delineate what Millon would call the latent constructs underlying these attributes.

The lexical approach assumes that, as a personality attribute becomes more important, it tends to have more synonyms in any single language and occurs more frequently across languages (Saucier & Goldberg, 1996). Within language, it is adjectives or their analogues that do the greater part of the work of describing personality attributes, with nouns ("she is a loner") sometimes serving this descriptive function as well. Drawing on this lexical hypothesis, exploratory factor analytic approaches have been applied to lexical data and have consistently and across many languages yielded a five-factor solution, the Big Five model (Goldberg, 1993). The factors have been named Extraversion, Agreeableness, Conscientiousness, Emotional Stability, and Intellect or Imagination. Although the five-factor solution is a robust one, the first three factors typically replicate more reliably than the last two (Saucier, 1995).

Costa and McCrae (1992) have combined some of the Big Five findings with their own analyses in what is now known as the five-factor model (FFM). Unlike the Big Five model, which is purely descriptive, the FFM suggests that its five factors encompass what McCrae and Costa (1996) describe as "endogenous basic tendencies" (p. 72). They suggest that these traits have a substantial genetic component, lending an explanatory, as opposed to a descriptive, component to the model.

The FFM, which has now become a very widely used model for delineating the basic dimensions of personality (Costa & McCrae, 1997; Costa & Widiger, 2002a), contains the following components: Neuroticism, Extraversion, Openness to Experience, Agreeableness, and Conscientiousness. Costa and McCrae sought to operationalize these constructs in a series of psychological tests, which began with the NEO Inventory (Costa & McCrae, 1980), continued with the NEO-PI (Costa & McCrae, 1985), and whose current version is the Revised NEO Personality Inventory (NEO-PI-R; Costa & McCrae, 1992). It has become the instrument most frequently associated with the FFM.

The NEO-PI-R includes domain scales for each of the five major factors described previously and six facet scales for each domain, allowing more fine-grained delineation in each of the dimensions. Reflecting the traits they measure, the domain and facet scales tend to be normally distributed, and Costa and McCrae (1992) suggest that scores can be characterized as being very low, low, average, high, and very high. Approximately 7% of individuals fall in the two extreme categories, 24% in the high and low ranges, and 38% in the average range (Costa & McCrae, 1992).

At the most far-reaching level, the NEO-PI-R domain scales provide an overall picture of an individual's personality style, whereas the facet scales allow more specific descriptions that detail the individual differences that can occur within domains. Given the increasingly widespread acceptance of the FFM in personality theory, it is useful to describe each of the domains and their associated facets in some detail. Several sources were helpful in generating the following descriptions (Costa & McCrae, 1992; Costa & Widiger, 2002b; Piedmont, 1998).

Neuroticism contrasts robust emotional adaptation with maladjustment. Individuals who are high on Neuroticism tend to manifest a variety of negative affects, including fear, distress, sadness, and anger. Although high scorers on Neuroticism may be vulnerable to psychological difficulties, a high score does not necessarily indicate the presence of psychopathology. Low scores on Neuroticism are associated with emotional stability and adequate stress tolerance.

The facet scales measuring different aspects of Neuroticism make it clear that two individuals with similar domain-level scores might manifest this trait differently. The facets include Anxiety, Angry Hostility, Depression, Self-Consciousness, Impulsiveness, and Vulnerability. High scorers on Anxiety tend to experience both specific fears and free-floating worries, leaving them tense and nervous. Angry Hostility is associated with greater likelihood of experiencing anger, which may be expressed in a variety of ways depending on other NEO-PI-R components such as Agreeableness. Individuals who are high on the Depression facet scale manifest as dejected, hopeless, and guilty. The Self-Consciousness facet taps the experience of interpersonal shame or embarrassment. Individuals who are high on Impulsiveness find it difficult to exercise control over cravings, and their frustration tolerance is low. The Vulnerability facet scale describes individuals who have real difficulty handling stressful situations and who become panicky in such circumstances. Low scorers on the Neuroticism facet scales are characterized by lower levels of these traits, emerging as relaxed, slow to anger, hopeful, comfortable, controlled, and with higher levels of stress tolerance.

The Extraversion domain contrasts a sort of gregarious sociability with a more reserved interpersonal style. Individuals who are high on Extraversion tend to be actively outgoing, assertive, and enthusiastic. The Extraversion domain scale is strongly correlated with vocational interest in enterprising occupations (Costa, McCrae, & Holland, 1984). Low scorers on Extraversion tend to be reserved, independent, and less exuberant. Individuals who are low on Extraversion are not necessarily introspective, reflective, or socially anxious; they are simply independent in their interpersonal style, comfortable being by themselves.

The facet scales measuring some of the characteristics of Extraversion cover the range through which this attribute can be expressed. They include Warmth, Gregariousness, Assertiveness, Activity, Excitement-Seeking, and Positive Emotions. The facet most associated with a potential for intimacy and close attachments is Warmth. Gregariousness taps a preference for being around others, whereas Assertiveness involves an interpersonally active, forthcoming style. Activity, Excitement-Seeking, and Positive Emotions all tap a sort of upbeat, outgoing style, with Activity specifically reflecting a high level of behavioral output, Excitement-Seeking a movement toward animated settings, and Positive Emotions an actively exuberant level of responsiveness.

The Openness to Experience domain, albeit the least extensively represented with linguistic descriptors, contrasts individuals who are curious and divergent in their approach with those who are more conventional with the familiar and traditional. Although this domain has some correlation with education, measured intelligence, and creativity (McCrae, 1987), Costa and McCrae (1992) emphasize that Openness to Experience and cognitive ability are not identical. Instead, this domain taps a willingness to take an "all bets are off" approach to a broad range of situations versus one that applies conventional templates as a way of understanding the world.

The facets of the Openness to Experience domain encompass some areas in which this "divergent approach" style can manifest. They include Fantasy, Aesthetics, Feelings, Actions, Ideas, and Values, each naming a particular area of experience that the individual is open to exploring. Fantasy involves openness to an individual's own mental life, whereas aesthetics involves an openness to the creative works of others. Individuals who are high on the Feelings facet scale are open to experiencing their own emotions and according them an important role in decision-making. Those who are high on Actions are willing to try new activities; those who are high on Ideas are willing to consider a variety of solutions before coming to decisions. For high Values individuals, there is a willingness to look at social and philosophical issues with no preconceived opinions.

The Agreeableness domain, like Extraversion, involves interpersonal style, but here the emphasis is on altruism as opposed to the sort of outgoing assertiveness that Extraversion describes. Individuals high on Agreeableness organize much of their function around a sort of empathic helpfulness, whereas those low on this domain tend to be much more self-focused and competitive.

The facet scales associated with Agreeableness—Trust, Straightforwardness, Altruism, Compliance, Modesty, and Tender-Mindedness—suggest that this attribute can play out in a variety of ways. Trust contrasts individuals who see the interpersonal world as cooperative and believable with those who see it as dangerous and disingenuous. Straightforwardness describes the distinction between frankness and a more guarded, although not necessarily dishonest, style. The Altruism facet taps perhaps the core aspect of the Agreeableness domain. Individuals who are high on Altruism are empathic in their interpersonal approach, willing to act on their concern for others. Compliance describes how the individual will respond to conflict, inhibiting competitiveness versus a willingness to confront and compete. Modesty is associated with a rather self-effacing, although not self-demeaning, style, and Tender-Mindedness describes a propensity for seeing the human as opposed to the more objective side of a variety of situations.

The Conscientiousness domain is associated with achievement motivation and a willingness to defer gratification for the sake of longer term goals. Adjectives such as *deliberate, purposeful,* and *planful* could well show up in the description of an individual who is high on Conscientiousness. Those lower on this domain might be described as less exacting and less determined.

The facet scales that provide more fine-grained descriptions of the manifestations of Conscientiousness include Competence, Order, Dutifulness, Achievement Striving, Self-Discipline, and Deliberation. Competence is associated with a concept of self as capable and prepared. Order refers to a methodical, well-organized style. Individuals with high scores on the Dutifulness facet scale have well-defined principles and act on a strong sense of ethical responsibility. Achievement Striving includes the high levels of aspiration that make up an important part of the Conscientiousness domain. Self-Discipline involves the capacity to initiate and complete tasks, even in the face of tediousness or distraction. Deliberation describes a thoughtful, "look before you leap" style characterized by careful consideration by individuals of the consequences of their actions.

The initial goal of the NEO-PI-R was to describe the basic dimensions of adult personality function, not to identify psychopathology or document its absence (Costa & McCrae, 1992). The question of whether the instrument is useful in the assessment of psychopathology in general and personality disorder in particular has been a controversial one. Ben-Porath and Waller (1992), for example, have suggested that instruments whose construction did not involve a focus on psychopathology should be required to demonstrate that they furnish data that adds "incrementally to the procurement of diagnostic information beyond that which is obtained from current clinical measures" (Ben-Porath & Waller, 1992).

A number of studies have suggested that the NEO-PI-R does provide such incremental value for Axis I disorders associated with substance abuse, anxiety, social phobia, and major depression (Trull & Sher, 1994) and for Axis II personality disorders (Trull, Useda, Costa, & McCrae, 1995). Clark and Harrison (2001) reported a meta-analysis done by Clark that included 17 studies in which correlations between an FFM instrument and a personality disorder-oriented instrument such as the MCMI were reported. They found the results "generally encouraging with regard to the utility of extending the FFM into the domain of personality pathology," and although they suggest that supplementary scales may be needed to provide more complete coverage, their conclusion was that "generic concerns about the appropriateness of the dimensions for characterizing personality pathology appear unfounded" (p. 297).

The NEO-PI-R appears to be of particular value in the assessment of personality disorder, a finding that is not surprising given a conceptualization of personality disorder as constellations of stable traits that move imperceptibly from "normal" to "pathological" to the extent that they become "inflexible and maladaptive and cause significant functional impairment or subjective distress" (APA, 2000, p. 686). Consequently, the past decade has seen an increasing interest in research and clinical applications of the NEO-PI-R.

Costa and McCrae began this trend in 1990 with an important article describing the utility of the FFM for the assessment of personality disorder. They correlated NEO-PI self-reports, peer ratings, and spouse ratings with MMPI personality scales and NEO-PI self-reports with MCMI-I and MCMI-II findings. In their words, the FFM "appears to account for the major dimensions underlying personality disorder scales developed by a number of different investigators" (p. 370). More recently, Costa and Widiger have brought together a diverse group of researchers and clinicians to address this topic in the edited book *Personality Disorders and the Five-Factor Model*, now in its second edition (1994, 2002b). A chapter by Widiger, Trull, Clarkin, Sanderson, and Costa (2002) presents a series of hypotheses about the relationship between the FFM and the *DSM-IV* personality disorders. A chapter by Widiger, Costa, and McCrae (2002) details a process for diagnosis of personality disorder with the FFM. These chapters form the basis for the following paragraphs.

The Cluster A (Paranoid, Schizoid, and Schizotypal) disorders can be conceptualized as low on the two domains associated with interpersonal comfort—Extraversion and Agreeableness. The more fine-grained facet level would help articulate similarities and differences among the three syndromes. Paranoid disorders could be viewed as high on Angry Hostility and low on Trust, Straightforwardness, and Compliance. For the schizoid individual, a translation of the *DSM-IV* descriptors into FFM terminology would produce a picture of low Warmth, Gregariousness, and Positive Emotions. The schizotypal individual would be characterized by high Anxiety and would differ from paranoid and schizoid individuals by having higher levels of openness to Fantasy, Action, and Ideas.

The Cluster B (Histrionic, Borderline, Narcissistic, and Antisocial) disorders are more diverse from a domain standpoint. For the histrionic individual, the primary loadings are on high Extraversion and Openness to Experience; for the borderline individual, there are extreme loadings throughout the Neuroticism domain; the narcissistic picture is one of low Agreeableness, more specifically low Altruism, Modesty, and Tender-Mindedness, whereas the antisocial individual can be characterized by a combination of very low Conscientiousness and very low Agreeableness. Harpur, Hart, and Hare (2002) report that as psychopathy, as assessed by the Psychopathy Checklist, increases, so does the likelihood of very low scores on Agreeableness.

The Cluster C (Dependent, Avoidant, and Obsessive-Compulsive) personality disorders appear to have two distinct threads from a domain standpoint. Avoidant and dependent individuals can be characterized by their high elevations throughout the Neuroticism domain, whereas obsessive-compulsive individuals would be more likely to load primarily on Conscientiousness. The high levels of Neuroticism help differentiate the Self-Conscious and Vulnerable avoidant from the behaviorally similar but less conflicted schizoid person, who, as noted previously, is characterized more by low Warmth and low Positive Emotions. Dependent individuals share the high Neuroticism of their avoidant counterparts, but their profile is likely to contain significant elements of high Agreeableness as well. For the obsessive-compulsive person, the high levels of Conscientiousness are most likely to manifest in Competence, Order, Dutifulness, and Achievement Striving, facets which at their extremes can become immobilizing. Additionally, the obsessive-compulsive person may be rather low on openness to new ideas or ways of solving problems.

The FFM has important implications for planning and monitoring intervention. Sanderson and Clarkin (2002) have suggested that the model can first be useful in making initial *macrotreatment* decisions such as those relating to the setting (inpatient, day treatment, outpatient), type, and duration and frequency of treatment. As intervention progresses, the model is helpful in guiding the clinician through what Sanderson and Clarkin call "microtreatment issues," the day-to-day decisions that form the basis of ongoing therapy (p. 359).

MacKenzie (2002) provides useful examples of the differential intervention approaches that can be developed from FFM findings. He suggests that an important first response for the patient with high Neuroticism findings would involve help in reestablishing control over maladaptive levels of anxiety and disorganization that occur as a function of heightened emotional reactivity. In contrast, he writes that individuals with low Neuroticism are likely to benefit from a more problem-oriented approach that focuses on day-to-day concerns and physical symptoms.

C. ROBERT CLONINGER'S SEVEN-FACTOR MODEL

Cloninger's work is noteworthy in terms of his conceptualization of the dimensions of personality along a very old dichotomy: nature versus nurture. Cloninger and his colleagues (Cloninger, Svrakic, Bayon, & Przybeck, 1999) have suggested that there are four components—*Temperament*, in their terminology—that are "... moderately heritable and stable throughout life regardless of culture or social learning" (p. 34). They include Novelty Seeking, Harm Avoidance, Reward Dependence, and Persistence. Novelty Seeking involves an active interest in new experiences, and Cloninger suggests that it is mediated by the dopamine neurotransmitter system. Harm Avoidance is a sort of thin-skinned sensitivity to aversive or threatening situations and is mediated, Cloninger suggests, by the serotonin system. Reward Dependence involves significant sensitivity to reinforcement contingencies, and Cloninger suggests it is mediated by the noradrenergic neurotransmitter system. Cloninger views Persistence, frustration tolerance in the face of difficult or tedious demands, as a temperament dimension but does not relate it to a specific neurotransmitter system.

Cloninger identifies three additional components—*Character* in his terminology—as more a function of child-rearing practices and individual experiences. These dimensions include Self-Directedness, Cooperativeness, and Self-Transcendence. Self-Directedness describes the person's level of responsibility and goal-focus; Cooperativeness describes the level of helpful empathy, and Self-Transcendence involves level of imaginative unconventionality.

Cloninger and his colleagues (1999) go on to suggest that various configurations of the different dimensions are associated with particular personality types. For example, Dependent Personality Disorder might be characterized by low findings on Self-Directedness and Self-Transcendence but a high finding in Cooperativeness.

Ultimately, Cloninger and his colleagues (Cloninger, Svrakic, & Przybeck, 1993) developed a psychological test, the Temperament and Character Inventory (TCI), to quantify the seven-factor model. In the decade following, there have been significant questions raised in terms of the model's replicability (Ball, Tennen, & Kranzler, 1999) and equivocal findings as to its reliability and validity. Braendstroem and his colleagues (1998; Braendstroem & Richter, 2001) have reported good test-retest findings and a factor structure that replicated the American seven-factor model in a large Swedish nonpatient sample. Allgulander, Cloninger, Przybeck, and Brandt (1998) administered the TCI to 29 individuals with Generalized Anxiety Disorder before they began treatment with paroxetine, a medication that works by increasing serotonin levels, and again after four to six months. They reported marked decreases in Harm Avoidance, consistent with Cloninger's hypothesis that this dimension is mediated by the serotonergic system. They also reported a marked increase in Self-Directedness and modest changes in Cooperativeness and Novelty Seeking.

On the other hand, a study by Katsuragi et al. (2001) failed to demonstrate a hypothesized relationship between the dopaminergic neurotransmitter system and Novelty Seeking in 205 normal volunteers. And although Svrakic, Whitehead, Przybeck, and Cloninger (1993) reported that Cluster A, B, and C personality disorders could be distinguished respectively by low Reward Dependence, high Novelty Seeking, and high Harm Avoidance, two subsequent studies (Ball, Tennen, Poling, Kranzler, & Rounsaville, 1997; Bayon, Hill, Svrakic, Przybeck, & Cloninger, 1996) did not replicate this distinction.

The significance of Cloninger's work lies in his division of the dimensions of personality into hard-wired, genetically determined traits and those that are more a function of individual, social, and cultural experiences. His hypotheses about the underlying neurochemical sources of some of the Temperament dimensions represents an important attempt to integrate neuroscience into our understanding of personality disorder.

At the clinical level, Cloninger's work foreshadows the importance of taking temperament issues into account when planning pharmacologic intervention. For example, Joyce, Mulder, and Cloninger (1999) studied 104 patients with a current major depressive episode who were treated with either clomipramine or desipramine in a six-week randomized double-blind trial. They found that patients with high Harm Avoidance and high Reward Dependence had favorable outcomes regardless of drug. More specifically, they found that for the women in their sample, high Reward Dependence predicted a good response to clomipramine whereas high Harm Avoidance predicted a good response to desipramine. Temperament measures accounted for 38% of the variance in treatment outcome for the entire sample and an even higher percentage (49%) for the severely depressed individuals in the sample. The authors conclude that "If the findings from this study can be replicated and temperament shown to be a major predictor of antidepressant response, then an important step in the validation of a system for understanding personality will have occurred" (p. 469).

THE RORSCHACH DESCRIPTIVE MODEL

The Rorschach goes about its task of providing personality descriptions using a technology very different from the various theory-based approaches that have been described so far. Instead, the Rorschach clinician presents patients or clients with a moderately ambiguous perceptual-cognitive task and codes the various ways they go about solving it. Then, using a series of concurrent validity studies that link Rorschach problem-solving approaches with real-world behavior, clinicians are able to make empirically based statements about a person's day-to-day function. For example, concurrent validity studies (Exner, 2003, pp. 356–358) suggest that individuals who solve the inkblots by breaking them into details that they integrate into meaningful relationships ("a lion walking over rocks in a pond with trees in the background") are likely to handle their day-to-day tasks in a similarly active, integrative way. Working at this molecular level, the Rorschach provides clinicians with a group of variables empirically related to specific behavioral tendencies.

Clinicians can use these molecular-level behavioral findings to describe important aspects of personality disorder. A good example is the Rorschach variable that describes an individual's preferred problem-solving style. Faced with everyday demands, some individuals (introversives) depend mostly on internal resources whereas others (extratensives) tend to interact with the outside world to deal with challenges. The Rorschach EB variable helps in discriminating these styles, and it would appear that the introversive-extratensive distinction is an important one in understanding personality disorder. For example, Exner (1986) compared borderline and schizotypal individuals and found that only a very small percentage (2.6%) of schizotypal individuals were extratensive, whereas nearly half (48.8%) of borderline individuals were characterized by this more interactive problem-solving style.

Another important Rorschach variable evaluates the level of stress the person is experiencing in relation to his or her organized coping resources. As this Rorschach variable, the D-score, moves into the minus range, it becomes more likely that the person's level of demand exceeds available resources for coping. Exner (1986) found that 57.1% of borderline individuals had D-scores in the minus range as compared with only 13.2% of schizotypal individuals. The finding suggests that fewer schizotypal individuals find their experience ego-alien, an important element in considering intervention approaches.

A study by Blais, Hilsenroth, and Fowler (1998) provides a good illustration of the specific applicability of the Rorschach to the assessment of personality disorder. They studied 79 patients from a university-based outpatient psychology clinic who met the *DSM-IV* criteria for an Axis II disorder and found significant correlations between Rorschach variables and seven of the eight *DSM-IV* criteria for Histrionic Personality Disorder. For example, the *DSM-IV* "excessively impressionistic" style of speech criterion correlated positively with Rorschach variables associated with affective volatility (chromatic color) and with interpersonal closeness (texture). The authors conclude that Rorschach elements are useful in identifying the specific behavioral markers of Histrionic Personality Disorder, allowing more precise personality disorder diagnoses.

The Rorschach thus provides a series of variables that can be used to describe likely real-world behavior of relevance in identifying intervention targets for individuals with personality disorder. If Rorschach variables such as the D-score suggest that the person is in an overload state, supportive approaches may be indicated. Other Rorschach variables can help in identifying problems with affective control, interpersonal accuracy, intensity of self-focus, or overinvolvement with details, and these findings pinpoint areas for which specific intervention is indicated.

SUMMARY AND CONCLUSION

This review suggests that, when researchers and theorists with widely different conceptual approaches attempt to identify and quantify the basic dimensions of personality and personality disorder, their findings are characterized by both overlap and divergence. Millon's Pleasure-Pain polarity seems very similar to Cloninger's Novelty Seeking and Harm Avoidance. Costa and McCrae's Agreeableness domain parallels Millon's Self-Other polarity and Cloninger's Character dimension of Cooperativeness. The Active side of Millon's Active-Passive polarity is similar to the FFM Extraversion domain. Cloninger's articulation of Persistence has its parallels in the FFM Conscientiousness domain. The Rorschach's description of overload comes close to high Neuroticism in the FFM.

On the other hand, each of these approaches accounts for some unique aspects of the variance in personality. Cloninger's approach attempts an integration of genetics and neuroscience with personality; Millon's, an integration with evolutionary theory; and Costa and McCrae's, an integration of the empirical and conceptual progress that has characterized the past two decades of personality research. Implicit in current Rorschach research is an atheoretical, descriptive approach that links test-taking approaches with relevant molecular-level real-world behavior.

The test instruments that have come from these approaches both overlap one another and contribute unique variance. Clark and Harrison (2001) have provided an extensive survey of assessment instruments for personality disorder and suggest that a multimethod approach that includes interview, psychological test, and collateral data sources allows the most comprehensive picture from both a clinical and a research standpoint.

What does seem clear is that personality disorders can be appropriately conceptualized as variants of basic personality dimensions that, in particular settings, can impair interpersonal or occupational function. Instruments such as the MCMI and the Schedule for Nonadaptive and Adaptive Personality (SNAP; Clark,

1993) that are linked with a nosology such as the *DSM* are certainly important for clinicians faced with the diagnostic demands of everyday practice. But it is at the level of their underlying dimensions that our understanding of the problematic adaptations we call personality disorder will likely best be enhanced.

REFERENCES

Allgulander, C., Cloninger, C. R., Przybeck, T. R., & Brandt, L. (1998). Changes on the Temperament and Character Inventory after paroxetine treatment in volunteers with generalized anxiety disorder. *Psychopharmacology Bulletin, 34,* 165–166.

American Psychiatric Association. (1980). *Diagnostic and statistical manual of mental disorders* (3rd ed.). Washington, DC: Author.

American Psychiatric Association. (1987). *Diagnostic and statistical manual of mental disorders* (3rd ed., rev.). Washington, DC: Author.

American Psychiatric Association. (1994). *Diagnostic and statistical manual of mental disorders* (4th ed.). Washington, DC: Author.

American Psychiatric Association. (2000). *Diagnostic and statistical manual of mental disorders* (4th ed., text rev.). Washington, DC: Author.

Ball, S. A., Tennen, H., & Kranzler, H. R. (1999). Factor replicability and validity of the Temperament and Character Inventory in substance-dependent patients. *Psychological Assessment, 11,* 514–524.

Ball, S. A., Tennen, H., Poling, J. C., Kranzler, H. R., & Rounsaville, B. J. (1997). Personality, temperament, and character dimensions and the *DSM-IV* personality disorders in substance abusers. *Journal of Abnormal Psychology, 106,* 545–553.

Bayon, C., Hill, K., Svrakic, D. M., Przybeck, T. R., & Cloninger, C. R. (1996). Dimensional assessment of personality in an outpatient sample: Relations of the systems of Millon and Cloninger. *Journal of Psychiatric Research, 30,* 341–352.

Ben-Porath, Y. S., & Waller, N. G. (1992). "Normal" personality inventories in clinical assessment: General requirements and the potential for using the NEO Personality Inventory. *Psychological Assessment, 4,* 14–19.

Blais, M. A., Hilsenroth, M. J., & Fowler, J. C. (1998). Rorschach correlates of the *DSM-IV* histrionic personality disorder. *Journal of Personality Assessment, 70*(2), 355–364.

Braendstroem, S., & Richter, J. (2001). Distributions by age and sex of the dimensions of Temperament and Character Inventory in a cross-cultural perspective among Sweden, Germany, and the United States. *Psychological Reports, 89,* 747–758.

Braendstroem, S., Schlette, P., Przybeck, T. R., Lundberg, M., Forsgren, T., Sigvardsson, S., et al. (1998). Swedish normative data on personality using the Temperament and Character Inventory. *Comprehensive Psychiatry, 39,* 122–128.

Cattell, R. B. (1943). The description of personality: Basic traits resolved into clusters. *Journal of Abnormal and Social Psychology, 38,* 476–506.

Clark, L. A. (1993). *Manual for the Schedule for Nonadaptive and Adaptive Personality.* Minneapolis: University of Minnesota Press.

Clark, L. A., & Harrison, J. A. (2001). Assessment instruments. In W. J. Livesley (Ed.), *Handbook of personality disorders* (pp. 277–306). New York: Guilford Press.

Cloninger, C. R., Svrakic, D. M., Bayon, C., & Przybeck, T. R. (1999). Measurement of psychopathology as variants of personality. In C. R. Cloninger (Ed.), *Personality and psychopathology* (pp. 33–65). Washington, DC: American Psychiatric Press.

Cloninger, C. R., Svrakic, D. M., & Przybeck, T. R. (1993). A psychobiological model of temperament and character. *Archives of General Psychiatry, 50,* 975–990.

Costa, P. T., & McCrae, R. R. (1980). Still stable after all these years: Personality as a key to some issues in adulthood and old age. In P. B. Baltes & O. G. Brim (Eds.), *Life span development and behavior* (pp. 65–102). New York: Academic Press.

Costa, P. T., & McCrae, R. R. (1985). *The NEO Personality Inventory manual.* Odessa, FL: Psychological Assessment Resources.

Costa, P. T., & McCrae, R. R. (1990). Personality disorders and the five-factor model of personality. *Journal of Personality Disorders, 4,* 362–371.

Costa, P. T., & McCrae, R. R. (1992). *Revised NEO Personality Inventory (NEO-PI-R) and NEO Five-Factor Inventory (NEO-FFI) professional manual.* Odessa, FL: Psychological Assessment Resources.

Costa, P. T., & McCrae, R. R. (1997). Stability and change in personality assessment: The Revised NEO Personality Inventory in the year 2000. *Journal of Personality Assessment, 68,* 86–94.

Costa, P. T., McCrae, R. R., & Holland, J. L. (1984). Personality and vocational interests in an adult sample. *Journal of Applied Psychology, 69,* 390–400.

Costa, P. T., & Widiger, T. A. (Eds.). (1994). *Personality disorders and the five-factor model of personality.* Washington, DC: American Psychological Association.

Costa, P. T., & Widiger, T. A. (2002a). Introduction: Personality disorders and the five-factor model of personality. In P. T. Costa & T. A. Widiger (Eds.), *Personality disorders and the five-factor model of personality* (2nd ed., pp. 3–14). Washington, DC: American Psychological Association.

Costa, P. T., & Widiger, T. A. (Eds.). (2002b). *Personality disorders and the five-factor model of personality* (2nd ed.). Washington, DC: American Psychological Association.

Exner, J. E. (1986). Some Rorschach data comparing schizophrenics with borderline and schizotypal personality disorders. *Journal of Personality Assessment, 50*(3), 455–471.

Exner, J. E. (2003). *The Rorschach: A comprehensive system: Volume 1 Basic foundations* (4th ed.). Hoboken, NJ: Wiley.

Freud, S. (1925). The instincts and their vicissitudes. In J. Strachey (Ed.), *The standard edition of the complete psychological works of Sigmund Freud* (Vol. 14, pp. 109–140). London: Hogarth Press. (Original work published 1915)

Goldberg, L. R. (1993). The structure of phenotypic personality traits. *American Psychologist, 48,* 26–34.

Harpur, T. J., Hart, S. D., & Hare, R. D. (2002). Personality of the psychopath. In P. T. Costa & T. A. Widiger (Eds.), *Personality disorders and the five-factor model of personality* (2nd ed., pp. 299–324). Washington, DC: American Psychological Association.

Joyce, P. R., Mulder, R. T., & Cloninger, C. R. (1999). Temperament and the pharmacotherapy of depression. In C. R. Cloninger (Ed.), *Personality and psychopathology* (pp. 457–473). Washington, DC: American Psychiatric Press.

Katsuragi, S., Kiyota, A., Tsutsumi, T., Isogawa, K., Nagayama, H., & Arinami, T. (2001). Lack of association between a polymorphism in the promoter region of the dopamine D2 receptor and personality traits. *Psychiatry Research, 105,* 123–127.

MacKenzie, K. R. (2002). Using personality measurements in clinical practice. In P. T. Costa & T. A. Widiger (Eds.), *Personality disorders and the five-factor model of personality* (2nd ed., pp. 377–390). Washington, DC: American Psychological Association.

McCrae, R. R. (1987). Creativity, divergent thinking, and openness to experience. *Journal of Personality and Social Psychology, 52,* 1258–1265.

McCrae, R. R., & Costa, P. T. (1996). Toward a new generation of personality theories: Theoretical contexts for the five-factor model. In J. S. Wiggins (Ed.), *The five-factor model of personality: Theoretical perspectives* (pp. 51–87). New York: Guilford Press.

Millon, T. (1969). *Modern psychopathology: A biosocial approach to maladaptive learning and functioning.* Philadelphia: Saunders.

Millon, T. (1977). *Millon Clinical Multiaxial Inventory manual.* Minneapolis, MN: National Computer Systems.

Millon, T. (1987). *Millon Clinical Multiaxial Inventory manual II.* Minneapolis, MN: National Computer Systems.

Millon, T. (1996). *Disorders of personality: DSM-IV and beyond.* New York: Wiley.

Millon, T., & Davis, R. (1997). The MCMI-III: Present and future directions. *Journal of Personality Assessment, 68*(1), 69–85.

Millon, T., Millon, C., & Davis, R. D. (1994). *Millon Clinical Multiaxial Inventory-III.* Minneapolis, MN: National Computer Systems.

Millon, T., Weiss, L., Millon, C., & Davis, R. (1994). *Millon Index of Personality Styles (MIPS) manual.* San Antonio, TX: Psychological Corporation.

Piedmont, R. L. (1998). *The Revised NEO Personality Inventory: Clinical and research applications.* New York: Plenum Press.

Sanderson, C., & Clarkin, J. F. (2002). Further use of the NEO-PI-R personality dimensions in differential treatment planning. In P. T. Costa & T. A. Widiger (Eds.), *Personality disorders and the five-factor model of personality* (2nd ed., pp. 351–375). Washington, DC: American Psychological Association.

Saucier, G. (1995). *Sampling the latent structure of person descriptors.* Paper presented at the 103rd annual meeting of the American Psychological Association, New York.

Saucier, G., & Goldberg, L. R. (1996). The language of personality: Lexical perspectives on the five-factor model. In J. S. Wiggins (Ed.), *The five-factor model of personality: Theoretical perspectives* (pp. 21–50). New York: Guilford Press.

Svrakic, D. M., Whitehead, C., Przybeck, T. R., & Cloninger, C. R. (1993). Differential diagnosis of personality disorders by the seven-factor model of temperament and character. *Archives of General Psychiatry, 50,* 991–999.

Trull, T. J., & Sher, K. J. (1994). Relationship between the five-factor model of personality and Axis I disorders in a nonclinical sample. *Journal of Abnormal Psychology, 103,* 350–360.

Trull, T. J., Useda, D. C., Costa, P. T., & McCrae, R. R. (1995). Comparison of the MMPI-2 Personality Psychopathology Five (PSY-5), the NEO-PI, and the NEO-PI-R. *Psychological Assessment, 7,* 508–516.

Widiger, T. A., Costa, P. T., & McCrae, R. R. (2002). A proposal for Axis II: Diagnosing personality disorders using the five-factor model. In P. T. Costa & T. A. Widiger (Eds.), *Personality disorders and the five-factor model of personality* (2nd ed., pp. 431–456). Washington, DC: American Psychological Association.

Widiger, T. A., Trull, T. J., Clarkin, J. F., Sanderson, C., & Costa, P. T. (2002). A description of the *DSM-IV* personality disorders with the five-factor model of personality. In P. T. Costa & T. A. Widiger (Eds.), *Personality disorders and the five-factor model of personality* (2nd ed., pp. 89–99). Washington, DC: American Psychological Association.

CHAPTER 5

Borderline Personality Disorder and Borderline Personality Organization: Psychopathology and Psychotherapy

Otto F. Kernberg

TEMPERAMENT, CHARACTER, AND THE STRUCTURE OF THE NORMAL PERSONALITY

TEMPERAMENT AND CHARACTER are crucial aspects of personality. *Temperament* refers to the constitutionally given and largely genetically determined inborn disposition to particular reactions to environmental stimuli, particularly to the intensity, rhythm, and thresholds of affective responses. I consider affective responses, particularly under conditions of peak affect states, crucial determinants of the organization of the personality. Inborn thresholds concerning the activation of positive, pleasurable, and rewarding, as well as negative, painful, and aggressive affects represent the most important bridge between biological and psychological determinants of the personality (Kernberg, 1994). Temperament also includes inborn dispositions to cognitive organization and to motor behavior, such as, for example, the hormonal, particularly testosterone-derived differences in cognitive functions and aspects of gender role identity that differentiate male and female behavior patterns. As to the etiology of personality disorders, however, the affective aspects of temperament appear of fundamental importance.

Cloninger (Cloninger, Svrakic, & Przybeck, 1993) related particular neurochemical systems to temperamental dispositions he called "novelty seeking," "harm avoidance," "reward dependence," and "persistence," offering one such avenue. However, I question Cloninger's direct translations of such dispositions into the specific types of personality disorders of the *DSM-IV* classification system. Torgersen, on the basis of his twin studies of genetic and environmental influences on the development of personality disorders (1985, 1994), found genetic influences significant only for the Schizotypal Personality Disorder; for practical purposes, they are significantly related to normal personality characteristics but have very little relationship with specific personality disorders.

In addition to temperament, character is another major component of personality. *Character* refers to the particular dynamic organization of behavior patterns of each individual that reflects the overall degree and level of organization of such patterns. Whereas academic psychology differentiates character from personality, the clinically relevant terminology of character pathology, character neurosis, and neurotic character refers to the same conditions, also called *personality trait* and *personality pattern* disturbances in earlier *DSM* classifications and to *personality disorders* in *DSM-III* and *DSM-IV*. From a psychoanalytic perspective, I propose that character refers to the behavioral manifestations of ego identity, whereas the subjective aspects of ego identity, that is, the integration of the self concept and of the concept of significant others, are the intrapsychic structures that determine the dynamics. Organization of character also includes all the behavioral aspects of what in psychoanalytic terminology is called *ego functions* and *ego structures*, that is, habitual behavior patterns that serve both adaptive and defensive functions/and derive from the interaction of temperamental disposition with relationships with significant others ("object relations").

From a psychoanalytic viewpoint, the personality is codetermined by temperament and character, but also by an additional intrapsychic structure, the superego. The integration of value systems, the moral and ethical dimension of the personality—from a psychoanalytic viewpoint, the integration of the various layers of the superego—is an important component of the total personality. Personality itself, then, may be considered the dynamic integration of all behavior patterns derived from temperament, character, and internalized value systems (Kernberg, 1976, 1980). In addition, the dynamic unconscious or the id constitutes the dominant, and potentially conflictive, motivational system of the personality. The extent to which sublimatory integration of id impulses into ego and superego functions has taken place reflects the normally adaptive potential of the personality.

My proposed psychoanalytic model for the classification of personality disorders incorporates significant contributions to this particular approach from other psychoanalytic researchers and theoreticians such as Salman Akhtar (1989, 1992), Rainer Krause (Krause, 1988; Krause & Lutolf, 1988), Michael Stone (1980, 1990, 1993a), and Vamik Volkan (1976, 1987). First, the normal personality is characterized by an integrated concept of the self and an integrated concept of significant others. These structural characteristics, jointly called *ego identity* (Erikson, 1956; Jacobson, 1964), are reflected in an internal sense and an external appearance of self-coherence and are a fundamental precondition for normal self-esteem, self-enjoyment, and zest for life. An integrated view of an individual's self ensures the capacity for a realization of his or her desires, capacities, and long-range capacity for an appropriate evaluation of others, empathy, and an emotional investment in others that implies a capacity for mature dependency while maintaining a consistent sense of autonomy as well.

A second structural characteristic of the normal personality, largely derived from and an expression of ego identity, is the presence of ego strength, particularly reflected in a broad spectrum of affect dispositions, capacity for affect and impulse control, and the capacity for sublimation in work and values (also contributed to importantly by superego integration). Consistency, persistence, and creativity in work as well as in interpersonal relations are also largely derived from normal ego identity, as are the capacity for trust, reciprocity, and commitment to others, also importantly codetermined by superego functions (Kernberg, 1975).

A third aspect of the normal personality is an integrated and mature superego, representing an internalization of value systems that is stable, depersonificated, abstract, individualized, and not excessively dependent on unconscious infantile prohibitions. Such a superego structure is reflected in a sense of personal responsibility; a capacity for realistic self-criticism; integrity as well as flexibility in dealing with the ethical aspects of decision making; a commitment to standards, values, and ideals; and the contribution to ego functions such as reciprocity, trust, and investment in depth.

A fourth aspect of the normal personality is an appropriate and satisfactory management of libidinal and aggressive impulses. It involves the capacity for a full expression of sensual and sexual needs integrated with tenderness and emotional commitment to a loved other and a normal degree of idealization of the other and the relationship. Here, a freedom of sexual expression is integrated with ego identity and the ego ideal. As to aggression, a normal personality structure includes capacity for sublimation in the form of self-assertion, for withstanding attacks without excessive reaction, to react protectively, and to avoid turning aggression against the self. Again, ego and superego functions contribute to such an equilibrium.

Underlying these aspects of the normal personality—summarized in a set of scales of psychological capacities by Wallerstein (1991)—are significant structural and dynamic preconditions. The structural preconditions refer to the developmental processes by which the earliest internalization of interactions with significant others—that is, of object relations—leads to the completion of a series of successive steps that transform these internalized object relations into the normal ego identity previously described. The sequence of internalization of object relations into the early ego starts with the symbiotic phase described by Mahler (Mahler & Furer, 1968; Mahler, Pine, & Bergman, 1975)—the internalization of fused self- and object representations under the dominance of a positive or negative peak affect state that leads to "all good" and "all bad" fused self- and object representations. Such states of symbiotic fusion alternate with other states of internalization of differentiated self- and object representations under conditions of low affect activation, which provides ordinary internalized models of interaction between self and others, whereas the initially fused internalized object relations under conditions of peak affect states lead to the basic structures of the dynamic unconscious, the id. My definition of the *id* characterizes it as the sum total of repressed, dissociated and projected, consciously unacceptable, internalized object relations under conditions of peak affect states. Libido and aggression are the hierarchically supraordinate motivational systems representing the integration of, respectively, positive or rewarding and negative or aversive peak affect states (Kernberg, 1992, 1994).

At a second stage of ego development, again under conditions of peak affect states, a gradual differentiation occurs between self- and object representations under conditions of all good and all bad interactions, which lead to internal units constituted by self-representation/object representation/dominant affect. These

units constitute the basic structures of the original ego-id matrix that characterizes the stage of separation-individuation described by Mahler.

Eventually, under normal conditions, in a third stage of development, all good
and all bad representations of self are integrated into a concept of the self that tol-
erates a realistic view of self as potentially imbued with both loving and hating
impulses. A parallel integration occurs of representations of significant others
into combined all good-all bad representations of each of the important persons in
the child's life, mostly parental figures but also siblings. These developments determine the capacity for experiencing integrated, ambivalent relationships with
others, in contrast to splitting object relationships into idealized and persecutory
ones. This marks the stage of object constancy or of total internalized object relations contrasted to the earlier stage of separation-individuation in which mutually
split-off, part object relations dominated psychic experience. Normal ego identity
as defined constitutes the core of the integrated ego, now differentiated by repres-
sive barriers from both superego and id.

This psychoanalytic model thus includes a developmental series of consecutive
psychic structures. It starts with the parallel development of realistic object relations under low affect activation and symbiotic object relations under conditions of
peak affect activation. These are followed by the phase of separation-individuation,
which is characterized by continuous growth of realistic relations under low affective conditions but significant splitting operations and related defensive mechanisms under activation of intense affect states. This finally leads to the phase of
object constancy in which a more realistic integrated concept of self and significant
others evolves in the context of ego identity, and, at the same time, repression eliminates from consciousness the more extreme manifestations of sexual and aggressive impulses that can no longer be tolerated under the effect of the integration of
the normal superego.

This structural and developmental model also conceives of the superego as
constituted by successive layers of internalized self- and object representations
(Jacobson, 1964; Kernberg, 1984). A first layer of all bad, "persecutory" internalized object relations reflects a demanding and prohibitive, primitive morality as
experienced by the child when environmental demands and prohibitions run
against the expression of aggressive, dependent, and sexual impulses. A second
layer of superego precursors is constituted by the ideal representations of self
and others reflecting early childhood ideals that promise the assurance of love
and dependency if the child lives up to them. The mutual toning down of the
earliest, persecutory level and the later idealizing level of superego functions
and the corresponding decrease in the tendency to reproject these superego precursors then brings about the capacity for internalizing more realistic, toned
down, ego's stage of object constancy. The integrative processes of the ego facilitate, in fact, this parallel development of the superego. An integrated superego,
as mentioned, in turn strengthens the capacity for object relatedness as well as
autonomy: An internalized value system makes the individual less dependent on
external confirmation or behavior control, while it facilitates a deeper commitment of relationships with others. In short, autonomy demands and prohibitions
from the parental figures lead to the third layer of the superego corresponding
to independence and a capacity for mature dependence in the sense of an internalized, autonomous values system, and the capacity to appreciate, trust, and relate to such systems in significant others.

With this summary of my model of the development of the psychic apparatus that derives the structures of id, ego, and superego from successive levels of internalization, differentiation, and integration of object relations, I next discuss the dynamic aspect of this development—the motivational factors underlying these structuralized developments, that is, an ego psychology object relations theory of drives.

THE MOTIVATIONAL ASPECTS OF PERSONALITY ORGANIZATION: AFFECTS AND DRIVES

I consider the drives of libido and aggression the hierarchically supraordinate integration of corresponding pleasurable and rewarding, and painful and aversive affect states (Kernberg, 1992, 1994). Affects are instinctive components of human behavior, that is, inborn dispositions common to all individuals of the human species. They emerge in the early stages of development and are gradually organized into drives as they are activated as part of early object relations. Gratifying, rewarding, pleasurable affects are integrated as libido as an overarching drive; and painful, aversive, negative affects are integrated as inborn, constitutionally and genetically determined models of reaction that are triggered first by physiological and bodily experiences and then gradually in the context of the development of object relations.

Rage represents the core affect of aggression as drive, and the vicissitudes of rage explain the origins of hatred and envy—the dominant affects of severe personality disorders—as well as of normal anger and irritability. Similarly, the affect of sexual excitement constitutes the core affect of libido. Sexual excitement slowly and gradually crystallizes from the primitive affect of elation. The early sensual responses to intimate bodily contact dominate the development of libido in parallel to that of aggression.

Krause (1988) has proposed that affects constitute a phylogenetically recent biological system evolved in mammals as a way for the infant animal to signal emergency needs to its mother, corresponding to a parallel inborn capacity of the mother to read and respond to the infant's affective signals, thus protecting the early development of the dependent infant mammal. This instinctive system reaches increasing complexity and dominance in controlling the social behavior of higher mammals, particularly primates.

Affectively driven development of object relations—that is, real and fantasized interpersonal interactions that are internalized as a complex world of self- and object representations in the context of affective interactions—I propose, constitute the determinants of unconscious mental life and of the structure of the psychic apparatus. Affects, in short, are both the building blocks of the drives and the signals of the activation of drives in the context of the activation of a particular internalized object relation, as typically expressed in the transference developments during psychoanalysis and psychoanalytic psychotherapy.

In contrast to other contemporary psychoanalytic object relations theories, I have argued that we still need a theory of drives because a theory of motivation based on affects alone would unnecessarily complicate the analysis of the transference relationship to the dominant objects of infancy and childhood. Multiple positive and negative affects are expressed toward the same significant others, and an affect theory placing motives on affects only would fail to consider the developmental lines of libidinal and aggressive strivings organizing the history of past internalized object relations that we have clarified in the context of psychoanalytic exploration.

This theory of motivation permits us to account for the concept of inborn dispositions to excessive or inadequate affect activation, thereby doing justice to the genetic and constitutional variations of intensity of drives reflected, for example, in the intensity, rhythm, and thresholds of affect activation commonly designated as temperament. This theory equally permits us to incorporate the effects of physical pain, psychic trauma, and severe disturbances in early object relations as contributing to intensifying aggression as a drive by triggering intense negative affects. In short, I believe the theory does justice to Freud's (1915/1925) statement that drives occupy an intermediate realm between the physical and the psychic realms.

Studies of alteration in neurotransmitter systems in severe personality disorders, particularly in the Borderline Personality Disorder, although still tentative and open to varying interpretations, point to the possibility that neurotransmitters are related to specific distortions in affect activation (Stone, 1993a, 1993b). Abnormalities in the adrenergic and cholinergic systems, for example, may be related to general affective instability; deficits in the dopaminergic system may be related to a general disposition toward transient psychotic symptoms in borderline patients; and impulsive, aggressive, self-destructive behavior may be facilitated by a lowered function of the serotonergic system (deVegvar, Siever, & Trestman, 1994; Yehuda, Southwick, Perry, & Giller, 1994). In general, genetic dispositions to temperamental variations in affect activation would seem to be mediated by alterations in neurotransmitter systems, providing a potential link between the biological determinants of affective response and the psychological triggers of specific affects.

These aspects of inborn dispositions to the activation of aggression mediated by the activation of aggressive affect states are complementary to the now well-established findings that structured aggressive behavior in infants may derive from early, severe, chronic physical pain and that habitual aggressive teasing interactions with the mother are followed by similar behaviors of infants, as we know from the work of Galenson (1986) and Fraiberg (1983). Grossman's convincing arguments (1986, 1991) in favor of the direct transformation of chronic intense pain into aggression provide a theoretical context for the earlier observations of the battered-child syndrome. The impressive findings of the prevalence of physical sexual abuse in the history of borderline patients confirmed by investigators both in the United States and abroad (Marziali, 1992; Perry & Herman, 1993; van der Kolk, Hostetler, Herron, & Fisler, 1994) provide additional evidence of the influence of trauma on the development of severe manifestations of aggression.

I stress the importance of this model for our understanding of the pathology of aggression because the exploration of severe personality disorders consistently finds the presence of pathological aggression predominating. One key dynamic of the normal personality is the dominance of libidinal striving over aggressive ones. Drive neutralization, according to my formulation, implies the integration of libidinal and aggressively invested originally split, idealized, and persecutory internalized object relations. This process leads from the state of separation-individuation to that of object constancy and culminates in integrated concepts of the self and of significant others and the integration of derivative affect states from the aggressive and libidinal series into the toned-down, discrete, elaborated, and complex affect disposition of the phase of object constancy.

Whereas a central motivational aspect of severe personality disorders is development of inordinate aggression and the related psychopathology of aggressive affect expression, the dominant pathology of the less severe personality disorders, in contrast to borderline personality organization (Kernberg, 1975, 1976, 1980, 1984), is the pathology of libido or of sexuality. This field includes particularly the hysterical, the obsessive-compulsive, and the depressive-masochistic personalities, although it is most evident in the Hysterical Personality Disorder (Kernberg, 1984). Although these three are all frequent personality disorders in outpatient practice, only the obsessive-compulsive personality is included in *DSM-IV* (American Psychiatric Association [APA], 1968) while the depressive personality disorder is relegated to the Appendix. The neglected hysterical personality disorder, it is hoped, will be rediscovered in *DSM-V* (institutional politics permitting). In these disorders, in the context of the achievement of object constancy, an integrated superego, a well-developed ego identity, and an advanced level of defensive operations centering on repression, the typical pathology of sexual inhibition, Oedipalization of object relations, and acting out of unconscious guilt over infantile sexual impulses dominate the pathological personality traits. In contrast, sexuality is usually "co-opted" by aggression in borderline personality organization; that is, sexual behavior and interaction are intimately condensed with aggressive aims, which severely limit or distort sexual intimacy and love relations and foster the abnormal development of paraphilias with their heightened condensation of sensual and aggressive aims.

An early classification of personality disorders stemming from Freud (1908, 1931) and Abraham (1920, 1921–1925) described oral, anal, and genital characters; a classification of that in practice has gradually been abandoned because psychoanalytic exploration found that severe personality disorders present pathological condensations of conflicts from all of these stages. The classification proposed by Freud and Abraham seems to have value when limited to the less severe constellations of these disorders (Kernberg, 1976). At the same time, however, their description of the relationship among oral conflicts, pathological dependency, a tendency toward depression, and self-directed aggression is eminently relevant for personality disorders along the entire developmental spectrum and can be observed most specifically in the depressive-masochistic personality (Kernberg, 1992). This personality disorder, while reflecting an advanced level of neurotic personality organization, transports, so to speak, an oral constellation of conflicts in a relatively unmodified fashion into the oedipal realm. Similarly, anal conflicts are most clearly observable in the Obsessive-Compulsive Personality Disorder, which, in parallel to the Depressive-Masochistic one, transports anal conflicts into the context of the Oedipal conflicts of object constancy. Yet, anal conflicts are also relevant along the entire spectrum of personality disorders.

Fenichel (1945) attempted a psychoanalytic classification of character constellations into sublimatory and reactive types. Reactive types include avoidance (phobias) and opposition (reaction formations). He then classified personality disorders or character pathology into pathological behavior toward the id (oral, anal, and phallic conflicts), toward the superego (moral masochism, psychopathy, acting out), and toward external objects (pathological inhibitions, pathological jealousy, pseudohypersexuality). This classification also was abandoned in practice, mainly because it became evident that all character pathology presents simultaneously pathological behavior toward these psychic structures.

A PSYCHOANALYTIC MODEL OF NOSOLOGY

My classification of personality disorders centers on the dimension of severity (Kernberg, 1976). Severity ranges from (1) psychotic personality organization, to (2) borderline personality organization, to (3) neurotic personality organization.

PSYCHOTIC PERSONALITY ORGANIZATION

Psychotic personality organization is characterized by lack of integration of the concept of self and significant others, that is, identity diffusion, a predominance of primitive defensive operations centering on splitting and loss of reality testing. The defensive operations of splitting and its derivatives (projective identification, denial, primitive idealization, omnipotence, omnipotent control, devaluation) have as a basic function to maintain separate the idealized and persecutory internalized object relations derived from the early developmental phases predating object constancy—that is, when aggressively determined internalizations strongly dominate the internal world of object relations, to prevent the overwhelming control or destruction of ideal object relations by aggressively infiltrated ones. This primitive constellation of defensive operations centering around splitting thus attempts to protect the capacity to depend on good objects and escape from terrifying aggression. This basic function of the primitive constellation of defensive operations actually dominates most clearly in the borderline personality organization, whereas an additional, most primitive function of these mechanisms in the case of psychotic personality organization is to compensate for the loss of reality testing in these patients.

Reality testing refers to the capacity to differentiate self from nonself and intrapsychic from external stimuli and to maintain empathy with ordinary social criteria of reality, all of which are typically lost in the psychoses and manifested particularly in hallucinations and delusions (Kernberg, 1976, 1984). The loss of reality testing reflects the lack of differentiation between self- and object representations under conditions of peak affect states, that is, a structural persistence of the symbiotic stage of development, its pathological hypertrophy, so to speak. The primitive defenses centering on splitting attempt to protect these patients from the chaos in all object relations derived from their loss of ego boundaries in intense relationships with others. All patients with psychotic personality organization really represent atypical forms of psychosis. Therefore, strictly speaking, psychotic personality organization represents an exclusion criterion for the personality disorders in a clinical sense.

BORDERLINE PERSONALITY ORGANIZATION

Borderline personality organization is also characterized by identity diffusion and the same predominance of primitive defensive operations centering on splitting, but it is distinguished by the presence of good reality testing, reflecting the differentiation between self- and object representation in the idealized and persecutory sector, characteristic of the separation-individuation phase (Kernberg, 1975). Actually, this category includes all the severe personality disorders in clinical practice. Typical personality disorders included here are the Borderline Personality Disorder, the Schizoid and Schizotypal Personality Disorders, the Paranoid Personality Disorder, the Hypomanic Personality Disorder, Hypochondriasis (a syndrome with many characteristics of a personality disorder proper), the Narcissistic Personality Disorder (including the Malignant Narcissism Syndrome [Kernberg, 1992]), and the Antisocial Personality Disorder.

All patients with these disorders present identity diffusion, the manifestations of primitive defensive operations, and varying degrees of superego deterioration (antisocial behavior). A particular group of patients typically suffers from significant disorganization of the superego, namely, the Narcissistic Personality Disorder, the Malignant Narcissism Syndrome, and the Antisocial Personality Disorder.

All the personality disorders within the borderline spectrum present, because of identity diffusion, severe distortions in their interpersonal relations—particularly problems in intimate relations with others, lack of consistent goals in terms of commitment to work or profession, uncertainty and lack of direction in their lives in many areas, and varying degrees of pathology in their sexual lives. They often present an incapacity to integrate tenderness and sexual feelings, and they may show a chaotic sexual life with multiple polymorphous perverse infantile tendencies. The most severe cases, however, may present with a generalized inhibition of all sexual responses because of a lack of sufficient activation of sensuous responses in the early relation with the caregiver, an overwhelming predominance of aggression that interferes with sensuality (rather than even recruiting it for aggressive aims). All these patients also evince nonspecific manifestations of ego weakness, that is, lack of anxiety tolerance, impulse control, and sublimatory functioning in terms of an incapacity for consistency, persistence, and creativity in work.

A particular group of personality disorders presents the characteristics of borderline personality organization, but these patients are able to maintain more satisfactory social adaptation and are usually more effective in obtaining some degree of intimacy in object relations and in integrating sexual and tender impulses. Thus, in spite of presenting identity diffusion, they also evince sufficient nonconflictual development of some ego functions, superego integration, and a benign cycle of intimate involvements, capacity for dependency gratification, and a better adaptation to work that make for significant quantitative differences. They constitute what might be called a "higher level" of borderline personality organization or an intermediate level of personality disorder. This group includes the cyclothymic personality, the sadomasochistic personality, the infantile or histrionic personality, and the dependent personalities, as well as some better functioning Narcissistic Personality Disorders.

NEUROTIC PERSONALITY ORGANIZATION

The next level of personality disorder, the *neurotic personality organization,* is characterized by normal ego identity and the related capacity for object relations in depth, ego strength reflecting in anxiety tolerance, impulse control, sublimatory functioning, effectiveness and creativity in work, and a capacity for sexual love and emotional intimacy disrupted only by unconscious guilt feelings reflected in specific pathological patterns of interaction in relation to sexual intimacy. This group includes the hysterical personality, the depressive-masochistic personality, the obsessive personality, and many so-called "avoidant personality disorders," that is, the phobic character of psychoanalytic literature (which remains a problematic entity). As mentioned, significant social inhibition or phobias may be found in several different types of personality disorder, and the underlying hysterical character structure typical for the phobic personality as described in early psychoanalytic literature applies only to some cases.

ETIOLOGY AND PSYCHOPATHOLOGY

Research findings have pointed to the prevalence among patients with borderline pathology of early traumatic experiences, such as prolonged, painful physical illness, experience or witnessing of physical or sexual abuse, severe early loss and abandonment, or a chaotic family structure (Kernberg, 1994). A biological predisposition to the activation of excessive aggressive and depressive affects because of dysfunctional biochemical neurotransmitter systems, particularly the serotonergic system (but also the adrenergic, noradrenergic, and dopaminergic systems) may be reflected in abnormal activation of negative affects and hyperreactivity to stimuli that would ordinarily generate anxiety or depression, thus fostering the distortion of early affective experiences in the direction of aggressively invested relations with significant others that are internalized as such. Thus, biological determinants in the predisposition to negative affect activation reflected in temperament and the internalization of object relations may eventually influence the concept of self and others (Depue, 1996).

Under the impact of the etiological forces previously outlined, the psychopathology of these patients emerges as dominated by aggressively invested internalized object relations. These threaten their libidinally invested internalized object relations and determine a protective fixation and exaggeration of the early defensive operations of splitting and related mechanisms described previously. Splitting mechanisms protect idealized representations of self and object against their contamination with the aggressive ones and sustain, therefore, a certain hope for internal well-being, safety, and gratifying relations with others when the dominance of aggressively invested internalized object relations threatens these patients with massive and pervasive distrust of others, with fear of the eruption of violent aggressive behavior from within or from others, and with the confusing distortions of a world view derived from the lack of integration of the concept of self and others.

The development of stable characterological patterns that reflect such early learning experiences under conditions that foster excessive splitting leads to consolidation of the syndrome of identity diffusion and dominance of the primitive defenses mentioned. Additional etiological factors, particularly, predominant tendencies toward introversion or extroversion, and the extent to which a constitutional disposition to excessive activation of depressive or euphoric affects is present may codetermine the various characterological constellations under which the basic syndrome of identity diffusion emerges in clinical practice. The classification of personality disorders proposed here combines a structural and developmental concept of the psychic apparatus based on the theory of internalized object relations, which permits classifying personality disorders according to the severity of the pathology, the extent to which the pathology is dominated by aggression, the extent to which pathological affective dispositions influence personality development, the effect of the development of a pathological grandiose self-structure, and the potential influence of a temperamental disposition to extroversion-introversion. The temperamentally determined tendency toward extroversion or introversion permits organization of the overall domain of personality disorders into two major groups, whereas the syndrome of identity diffusion, in turn, leads to a classification based on the severity of the personality disorders. In a combined analysis of the vicissitudes of instinctual conflicts between love and aggression and of the development of ego and superego structures, these overall features permit us to differentiate the various pathological personalities as well as relate them to one another. (Figure 5.1 summarizes the relationships among the various personality disorders.)

This classification also illuminates the advantages of combining categorical and dimensional criteria. There are developmental factors relating several personality disorders to one another, particularly along an axis of severity. Thus, a developmental line links the Borderline, the Hypomanic, the Cyclothymic, and the Depressive-Masochistic Personality Disorders. Another developmental line links the Borderline, the Histrionic or Infantile, the Dependent, and the Hysterical Personality Disorders. Still another developmental line links, in complex

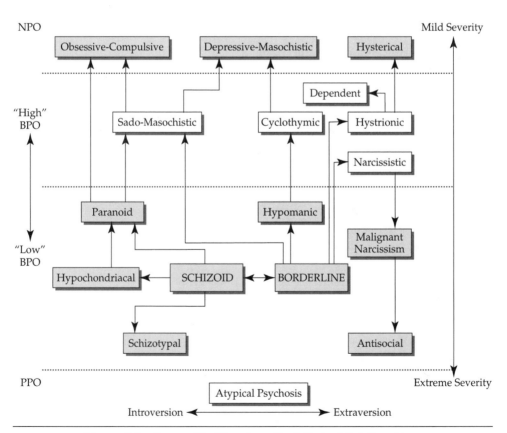

Figure 5.1　Personality Disorders: Their Mutual Relationships.

ways, the Schizoid, Schizotypal, Paranoid, and Hypochondriacal Personality Disorders and, at a higher developmental level, the Obsessive-Compulsive Personality Disorder. Finally, a developmental line links the Antisocial Personality, the Malignant Narcissism Syndrome, and the Narcissistic Personality Disorders (the latter, in turn, containing a broad spectrum of severity). Further relationships of all prevalent personality disorders are indicated in Figure 5.1. The vicissitudes of internalized object relations and of the development of affective responses emerge as basic components of a contemporary psychoanalytic approach to the personality disorders. I have proposed elsewhere (Kernberg, 1992) the concept of drives as supraordinate integration of the corresponding series of aggressive and libidinal affects and applied it to an overall developmental and psychostructural model. At the same time, the developmental vicissitudes of internalized object relations permit us to deepen understanding of these patients' affective responses.

Affects always include a cognitive component, a subjective component, a subjective experience of a highly pleasurable or unpleasurable nature, neurovegetative discharge phenomena, psychomotor activation, and, very crucially, a distinctive pattern of facial expression that originally served a communicative function directed to the caregiver. The cognitive aspect of affective responses always reflects the relationships between a self-representation and an object representation, which facilitates the diagnosis of the activated object relationship in each affect state that emerges in the therapeutic relationships.

This classification also helps to clarify the vicissitudes of the development of the sexual and aggressive drives. From the initial response of rage as a basic affect develops the structured affect of hatred as the central affect state in severe personality disorders. Hatred, in turn, may take the form of conscious or unconscious envy or an inordinate need for revenge that will color the corresponding transference developments. Similarly, as to the sexual response, the psychoanalytic understanding of the internalized object relations activated in sexual fantasy and experience facilitates the diagnosis and treatment of abnormal condensations of sexual excitement and hatred such as in the perversions or paraphilias and the diagnosis and treatment of inhibitions of sexuality and restrictions in the sexual responsiveness derived from its absorption in the patient's conflicts around extremely aggressive and traumatic internalized object relations.

The unconscious identification of the patient with the roles of both victim and victimizer in cases of severe trauma and abuse can also be better diagnosed, understood, and worked through in transference and countertransference in the light of the theory of internalized object relations that underlies this classification. In addition, the understanding of the structural determinants of pathological narcissism permits resolution of the apparent incapacity of narcissistic patients to develop differentiated transference reactions in parallel to their severe distortions of object relations in general.

One crucial advantage of the proposed classification of personality disorders is that the underlying structural concepts permit the therapist to translate the patient's affect states into the object relationship being activated in the transference and to "read" this transference in terms of the activation of a relationship that typically alternates in the projection of self- and object representations. The more severe the patient's pathology, the more readily does the patient project either his or her self-representation or this object representation onto the therapist, while enacting the reciprocal object or self-representation. This makes it possible to clarify, in the midst of intense affect activation, the nature of the relationship and to integrate the patient's previously split-off representations of self and significant others by gradual interpretation of these developments in the transference. This conceptualization, therefore, has direct implications for the therapeutic approach to personality disorders (Kernberg, 1992).

THERAPEUTIC STRATEGY

From a therapeutic perspective, the main objective of the psychodynamic psychotherapy is to focus on the syndrome of identity diffusion, its expression in the form of the activation of primitive object relations in the transference, and the exploration of these primitive transferences as they reflect early internalized object relations of an idealized and persecutory kind. The goal of this strategy is to identify such primitive transference paradigms and then to facilitate their gradual integration, so that splitting and other primitive defensive operations are replaced by more mature defensive operations, and identity diffusion is eventually resolved (Kernberg, 1984).

The essential strategy takes place in three consecutive steps:

1. The dominant primitive object relation is identified in the transference and described in an appropriate metaphorical statement that includes a hypothesized relation between two people linked by a dominant peak affective state.
2. In this dominant relationship, the patient's representation of self-relating to the representation of a significant other (object representation) is described, and the patient is shown how that self-representation, linked to its corresponding object representation by a specific affect, is activated with frequent role reversals in the transference. These role reversals show themselves in the corresponding object, identification unconsciously activated in the patient at this point, while projecting the other member of the internalized object relationship onto the therapist. In this second phase, patients learn not only to understand the different ways in which the same transference disposition may show in completely contradictory behaviors, but also to gradually tolerate their identification with both self- and object representations in this interaction.
3. The idealized internalized object relations are interpretively integrated with their corresponding, opposite, split-off persecutory ones, so that patients, who already have learned to accept their identification with contradictory internalized representations of self and object at different points of the treatment experience, now learn to integrate them, to accept that they harbor both loving and hateful feelings toward the same object, that their self-concept is both good and bad, and that their objects are neither as exclusively good or bad as they originally perceived them.

This gradual integration of the internal world of object relations leads toward the tolerance of ambivalence, a toning down and maturing of all affective experiences and emotional relations with significant others, a decrease in impulsive behaviors, and a growing capacity for self-reflection and empathy with significant others as patients' self-concept consolidates in an integrated view of themselves, and they experience the relationships with significant others in a new, integrated way.

The objective of this psychodynamic psychotherapy, in summary, is the resolution of identity diffusion and primitive defensive mechanisms. In practice, this development shows up in several successive steps: At first, in successfully treated cases, a significant decrease in impulsive behavior may be observed; later, a toning down of the patient's contradictory and explosive affects, and, eventually, the integration of normal ego identity may be seen.

THERAPEUTIC TECHNIQUES

The psychodynamic psychotherapy for borderline personality organization just outlined derives from psychoanalytic technique, using essential concepts and techniques derived from psychoanalysis, but modifying them in specific ways that make this treatment clearly different from psychoanalysis proper. In fact, one of the origins of this treatment was the failure of standard psychoanalysis to help many patients with severe personality disorders and the need to modify the psychoanalytic treatment in the light of that experience (captured particularly in the psychotherapy research project of the Menninger Foundation; Kernberg et al., 1972). The essential techniques taken from psychoanalysis that, in their respective modification, characterize the technique of this psychodynamic psychotherapy, are: (1) interpretation, (2) transference analysis, and (3) technical neutrality.

The *technique of interpretation* includes clarification of patients' subjective experience, tactful confrontation of those aspects of patients' nonverbal behavior that are dissociated or split off from their subjective experience, interpretation in the "here and now" of hypothesized unconscious meanings of patients' total behavior and their implicit conflictual nature, and interpretation of a hypothesized origin in the patient's past of that unconscious meaning in the here and now.

In psychodynamic psychotherapy, clarification, confrontation, and interpretation of unconscious meanings in the here and now predominate in the early stages, whereas emphasis on the linkage to the patient's unconscious past takes place only in advanced stages of the treatment. The initial avoidance of genetic interpretations protects the patient from confusion between present and past and from defensive intellectualization.

Transference analysis refers to the clarification, confrontation, and interpretation of unconscious, pathogenic internalized object relations from the past that are typically activated very early in the relationship with the therapist. In simplest terms, the transference reflects the distortion of the initial therapist-patient relationship by the emergence of an unconscious, fantasized relationship from the past that the patient unwittingly or unwillingly enacts in the present treatment situation. In psychoanalysis, a systemic analysis of transference developments is an essential technical tool; in psychoanalytic psychotherapy, transference analysis is modified by an ongoing linking of the relationship of such transference activations in the therapy hours with the patient's pathological enactments outside the treatment situation, while pathological interactions outside the treatment situation are also immediately explored in terms of their corresponding transference implications. This modification of the technique of transference analysis protects the treatment from the splitting of treatment hours from the patient's external life.

Technical neutrality refers to the therapist's not taking sides as to the patient's unconscious conflicts, but helping the patient to understand these conflicts by maintaining a neutral position. The therapist, in total emotional reaction to the patient, that is, his or her countertransference reaction, may experience powerful feelings and the temptation to react in specific ways in response to the patient's transference challenges. Using this countertransference response to better understand the transference without reacting to it, the therapist interprets the meanings of the transference from a position of concerned objectivity, which is the most important application of the therapist's position of technical neutrality.

In the psychodynamic psychotherapy of borderline patients, tendencies toward expression in action rather than through verbal communication—that is, "acting out"—may threaten the patient's life, other peoples' lives, the continuity of the treatment, or the frame of the psychotherapeutic sessions. The therapist may have to establish limits to the patient's behavior, both within and outside the sessions, which implies a movement away from technical neutrality. That is, the therapist takes the side of preserving life and safety when the patient's behavior places these in jeopardy. Interpretation of the transference conflict that has motivated such abandonment of technical neutrality, interpretation of the patient's interpretation of the therapist's intervention, and the gradual reinstatement of technical neutrality because of such interpretations is an essential sequence, often performed repeatedly in psychodynamic psychotherapy, differentiating it from psychoanalysis where technical neutrality can be maintained in a much more stable and consistent way. In summary, clarification, confrontation, and interpretation in the here and now are the essential techniques in the psychodynamic psychotherapy of borderline patients that make possible the resolution of primitive internalized object relations in the transference.

The establishment of an overall therapeutic relationship that determines a realistic relationship between patient and therapist—and also permits the diagnosis of its distortion by means of transference activation—is reflected by the treatment setting and the therapeutic frame. *Treatment setting* refers to the time, space, and regularity of therapeutic sessions. *Therapeutic frame* refers to specific tasks assigned to patient and therapist, namely free and full communication of the patient's subjective experiences (free association) and consistently attentive, respectful, concerned, and objective exploration of the patient's communication and the total treatment situation on the part of the therapist. These arrangements differ from standard psychoanalysis in the frequency of sessions (a minimum of two or three in psychotherapy in contrast to three to five in standard psychoanalysis) and in the physical positioning of face-to-face interviews in psychodynamic psychotherapy in contrast to the use of the couch in standard psychoanalysis. The establishment of the minimal (and, in most cases, sufficient) frequency of two sessions per week permits the simultaneous analysis of the patient's external life as well as in the transference. Fewer than two sessions per week tends to weaken the possibility of full grasp of either external reality or the transference.

The more severe the personality disorder, the more the patient's pathological behavior patterns and transference enactments show up in nonverbal behavior; the face-to-face position permits a full observation of this behavior. In fact, the database for the therapist's therapeutic interventions may be classified as originating from three *channels:*

- Channel 1, the patient's verbal communication of his or her subjective experience.
- Channel 2, the patient's nonverbal behavior, including his or her communicative style.
- Channel 3, the countertransference.

Whereas in standard psychoanalytic treatment most information derives from Channel 1 (although Channels 2 and 3 are important sources of information as well), in psychoanalytic psychotherapy more information stems from Channels 2 and 3, that is, the patient's nonverbal behavior and the emotional responses of the therapist to it. The therapist's emotional response to the patient at times reflects empathy with the patient's central subjective experience (concordant identification in the countertransference) and reflects at other times the therapist's identification with what the patient cannot tolerate in himself or herself and is projecting onto the therapist (complementary identification in the countertransference). Both reactions, when the therapist is able to identify and observe them, serve as valuable sources of information.

Countertransference analysis is, in fact, an essential aspect of this psychotherapy. The countertransference, defined as the total emotional reaction of the therapist to the patient at any particular time, needs to be explored fully by the therapist's self-reflective function, controlled by the therapist's firmly staying in role, and used as material to be integrated into the therapist's interpretative interventions. Thus, the therapist's "metabolism" of the countertransference as part of the total material of each hour, rather than its communication to the patient, characterizes this psychotherapeutic approach.

The tendency to severe acting out of the transference characteristic of borderline patients has been mentioned already; in addition to its management by the modification of technical neutrality and limit-setting in the hours mentioned before, treatment begins with the setting up of a treatment contract, which includes not only the treatment setting and frame, but also specific, highly individualized conditions for the treatment that derive from life-threatening and potentially treatment-threatening aspects of the patient's psychopathology. Particularly, the establishment of realistic controls and limit-setting that protects the patient from suicidal behavior and other destructive or self-destructive patterns of behavior are typical objectives of contract-setting. The initial contract-setting is a major aspect of the psychodynamic psychotherapy of borderline patients and can constitute a formidable preventive against the tendency to premature dropout of treatment typical for all psychotherapies of patients with borderline personality organization.

Tactical Approaches in Each Hour

The general strategy of treatment and the techniques mentioned previously are complemented by tactical approaches in each session that facilitate the strategic and general technical approach to transference analysis. The tactical aspects include the effort to establish, first, a joint view of reality with the patient, thus reinforcing reality testing before interpreting unconscious meanings in the patient's present behavior. The patient's relationship to the interpretation and his or her interpretation of the therapist's interpretations need to be clarified, as well as the extent to which his or her experiences reflect fantasies or acquire, at times, delusional characteristics. In each session, as implied earlier, both positive and negative transference dispositions are analyzed, primitive defensive mechanisms activated as part of transference enactments are interpreted, acting out is controlled, and the patient's capacity for self-observation and reflection is tested as part of each interpretative effort.

In general, the interpretative focus in each session is determined by what is effectively dominant at any point. Affect dominance takes precedence over transference dominance in the sense that transference analysis is not a unique, exclusive focus; when extratransferential issues are effectively dominant, they take priority.

Because of the severity of complicating symptoms that these patients frequently present—particularly destructive and self-destructive behaviors, suicidal and parasuicidal tendencies, eating disturbances, abuse of drugs and/or alcohol and antisocial behavior—a set of priorities of intervention has been established as another essential aspect of the psychodynamic psychotherapy of borderline patients (Kernberg, 1992). This set of priorities protects the patient and the treatment from the effects of such complications, while highlighting the need for their interpretative resolution as part of transference analysis. In practice, the following priories should override other affectively present material as the first focus of the therapist's attention.

Whenever a sense of danger to the patient's life, other people's lives, or the patient's physical integrity emerges in the session, that particular subject represents the highest priority for immediate therapeutic intervention; threatened interruptions of the treatment constitute the second highest priority; the presence of severe distortions in verbal communications, particularly chronic deceptiveness (which is typical for patients with both antisocial behavior and severe paranoid tendencies) constitutes a third priority; severe acting out, both in and outside the sessions, is a fourth priority; and the development of severe narcissistic resistance is a fifth priority. The analysis of narcissistic resistances follows the general principles of psychoanalytically derived techniques of dealing with such narcissistic defenses in the transference. In essence, narcissistic defenses become specific transference resistances against an authentic dependency on the therapist because such a dependency would threaten the narcissistic patient's pathological, grandiose self, and expose him or her to the activation of underlying conflicts with unconscious aggression, particularly severe conflicts around envy that need to be elaborated in the transference.

The treatment also includes particular techniques to deal with severe paranoid regressions and the development of delusional and hallucinatory manifestations in the sessions, techniques that are specific contributions of this psychotherapeutic approach to the treatment of severe regressions in the transference in the case of all patients subjected to psychodynamic or psychoanalytic treatment. The analysis of "incompatible realities" (Kernberg, 1992) as part of the exploration of transference psychosis usually makes it possible to resolve severe paranoid regressions in the transference and the shift into depressive transference developments.

A general classification of transferences into predominantly psychopathic, paranoid, and depressive transferences signals three degrees of severity of transference regression. In patients with significant antisocial behavior and corresponding superego pathology, psychopathic transferences are particularly likely to emerge. Their systemic interpretation tends to transform them into paranoid transferences, which, when successfully interpreted, give way to depressive transferences. The latter constitutes the more normal levels of development that characterize the advanced stages of the treatment, in which the patient is able to experience ambivalence, guilt, and concern; acknowledge his or her own aggressive tendencies toward self and others; mourn lost opportunities; and express wishes for reparation and sublimatory trends in general. At this stage, the patient is on the way to improvement. Excessively severe depressive transferences, however, indicate pathological submission to unconscious guilt, and this may constitute a problem in advanced stages of the treatment. The general principle applies that psychopathic transferences need to be resolved before paranoid ones and paranoid ones before depressive ones: This principle reflects another aspect of the general strategy of transference interpretation.

As may be rightly concluded from the previous discussion, transference analysis is a central aspect of this psychodynamic psychotherapy for borderline conditions. It implies the transformation of the patient's pathological expression of intolerable unconscious conflict between love and hate derived from pathogenic experiences in the past into conscious elaboration of these conflicts in the context of transference analysis. The gradual transformation of pathological character patterns into an emotional experience and self-reflection in the transference imply the therapist's active effort throughout the entire treatment to retranslate repetitive, pathological behaviors and acting out, on the one hand, and defensive somatizations, hypochondriacal reactions, and attacks on the patient's own body, on the other, into emotional developments in the transference.

In the course of this process, it will be necessary to face very primitive traumatic experiences from the past reactivated as traumatic transference episodes in which, unconsciously, the patient may express traumautophilic tendencies in an effort to repeat past traumas to overcome them. Primitive fears and fantasies about murderous and sexual attacks, primitive hatred, and efforts to deny all psychological reality to escape from psychic pain are the order of the day in the psychodynamic psychotherapy of these patients. Severely traumatized patients, whose past experience of physical abuse, sexual abuse, and/or witnessing such abuse has had significant etiological influence on their present psychopathology—particularly in a severe personality disorder with borderline, narcissistic, and/or antisocial features—typically present a specific constellation of internalized object relations (Kernberg, 1994). They evince the unconscious dominance of hateful, paralyzed, panic-ridden victim self-representation relating to a hateful, overpowering, sadistic object representation, a perpetrator-persecutor object representation linked to the self-representation by hatred and sadistic pleasure with the objective of inducing pain, sadistic control, humiliation, and destruction.

This internalized object relation, which has transformed the primitive affect of rage into characterologically anchored, chronic disposition of hatred, is activated in the transference with alternating role distribution: The patient's identification, for periods of time, with his or her victim self, while projecting the sadistic persecutor onto the therapist, will be followed, rapidly, in equally extended periods by the projection of his or her victimized self onto the therapist while the patient identifies, unconsciously, with the sadistic perpetrator. Only a systematic interpretation of the patient's unconscious identification with both victim and perpetrator may resolve this pathological constellation and lead to a gradual integration of dissociated or split-off self-representation into the patient's normal self. The effects of the traumatic past reside in the patient's internalized object relations; the key to its therapeutic resolution is coming to terms with this double identification.

To explore and resolve such conflicts, the therapist has to maintain a stable and steady treatment frame and, at times, may require ongoing supervision or consultation if intense and chronic countertransference reactions develop. The very sheltered nature of the therapeutic situation fosters the patient's expression of his or her unconscious conflictual needs and conflicts in this relationship. When everything goes well, severe regression in the psychotherapeutic sessions goes hand in hand with dramatic improvement in the patient's life, often observed very early on in the treatment. If either no such intense enactments occur in the hours or intense transference regression coincides with unremitting manifestations of these behavior patterns outside the hours as well, these are indications that the treatment is not going well and, by the same token, provide alarm signals to explore and correct the therapeutic approach. Ongoing supervision and consultation may resolve therapeutic statements, if and when such alarm signals are duly registered and taken into consideration.

A major question frequently raised is: What does it take to become a psychotherapist expert in this treatment? Psychiatric residents who have a good background and general training in psychodynamic techniques are able to advance stages of their training to carry out such treatment under supervision; I have similar experiences with postdoctoral fellows in clinical psychology who also have a good background and training in psychodynamic psychotherapy and are under appropriate supervision. Undoubtedly, there are some residents and young graduates with more talents than others to carry out this treatment, and a parallel psychoanalytic training provides an in-depth knowledge and experience with psychodynamic concepts that enormously help the talented psychotherapist to improve his or her technical approach. This treatment modality follows very naturally the lines of general psychodynamic psychotherapy and, as such, is easier to be taught than the complexity of the treatment approach would seem to indicate.

Insofar as the treatment requires at least two sessions per week over many months of treatment, it would appear to be an expensive form of long-term psychotherapy. The fact is, however, that these patients typically require repeated hospitalizations, they present chronic failure at work, and they need medical attention for the specific symptomatic complications. Their need for expensive, long-term social support may lead, if unchecked, to secondary gain and social parasitism. Psychotherapy geared to resolving severe personality disorders rather than simply providing an ongoing social support system may be less expensive than it would seem on the surface. Also, because this treatment aims at fundamental changes in patients' personalities as well as in their dominant symptoms, it has therapeutic aims unmatched by other treatments geared to the specific symptoms of severe personality disorders but not at modification of the personality structure per se. Ongoing present research on the effectiveness, the process, and outcome of this treatment is underway, and the manual currently being expanded should assist both researchers and clinicians in the field to become acquainted with a specific methodology geared to deal with one of our most challenging pathologies in clinical practice.

SUICIDAL RISK MANAGEMENT

In addition to these strategies and techniques, some particular tactics apply when this treatment is performed with patients presenting characterologically anchored suicidal tendencies. First is the preliminary development of a treatment contract that includes common features for all patients, such as agreeing on meeting times, financial arrangements, protocol for vacations and cancellations, potential involvement of third parties, and so on. Patients receive instructions to communicate their thoughts, feelings, and perceptions freely in the therapy hours, and therapists clarify their own responsibility for sharing with patients information that may help them increase their knowledge of self. To these, general features must be added for suicidal patients: specific arrangements that delimit clearly the responsibilities of patient and therapist in the management of the suicidal behavior (Yeomans, Selzer, & Clarkin, 1992). The treatment contract must include the setting up of conditions that ensure the patient's survival. To this end, patient and therapist must reach an understanding about the management of whatever suicidal behavior may emerge.

The treatment contract establishes conditions that protect both life and the treatment frame, practically limiting the therapeutic contacts to the treatment hours, thus permitting the therapist to maintain an interpretive, technically neutral stance. Concretely, patients are encouraged to communicate all suicidal fantasies, desires, and intentions in the therapy hours and to commit themselves to refraining from any action on these desires between the hours. The understanding is that, should patients consider themselves incapable of controlling the suicidal behavior, they would go to an emergency service of a psychiatric hospital to be examined and, if necessary, be hospitalized until considered safe by the hospital staff for continuing treatment as an outpatient.

Patients' responsibilities consist of either controlling their suicidal behavior and reserving its discussion to the treatment hours or, if unable to do that, to assume the responsibility themselves to be evaluated at an emergency service. Patients are discouraged from attempting to contact the therapist outside the treatment hours to avoid secondary gain of the symptom and to maintain the therapeutic communications in the context of the sessions themselves.

Often patients' suicidal threats, expressed to family members or other persons, may promote powerful secondary gain that feeds into the suicidal symptomatology. The therapist may have to meet with the entire family to explain the treatment arrangements and to explicitly liberate them from responsibility for the patient's survival. It needs to be stressed that should the therapist be concerned about the patient's reliability as protector of his or her own survival between the sessions, it is preferable to hospitalize the patient until a definite diagnosis is achieved and the patient's capacity for responsible participation in the treatment is reliably assessed.

In practice, the fact that the suicidal behavior of these patients cannot be predicted and is either impulsive or responds to the kind of cold planning discussed previously should provide the therapist with certainty that this unpredictable suicidal behavior cannot be controlled by any external measures, not even hospitalization. Only patients' cooperation and the elimination of secondary gain can prevent the suicide of patients whose suicidal tendencies are anchored in their character structure.

To perform the treatment effectively, therapists must assure themselves of their own security (physical, legal, and psychological) by explaining to the families the rationale for making patients responsible for their own safety. It must be very clear to patients and to the relatives why long-term hospitalization does not seem indicated under the circumstances and why outpatient treatment is recommended, despite the ongoing, uncontrollable risk for suicidal behavior. Therapists also need to spell out these arrangements in writing for their own legal protection. It is essential that therapists achieve a therapeutic frame and conditions for the treatment that permit them to remain calm under conditions of explicit or implicit suicidal threats from patients or pressures from patients' family members.

A further specific tactical measure and an absolutely essential aspect of this treatment approach is that therapists must interpret the transference implications of the treatment conditions for suicide control from the very start of the treatment. Thus, the therapist interprets, as far as possible based on total knowledge of the patient's present personality structure and history, the potential meaning that the patient may be giving to the therapist's intervention—as an act of invasive control, hostile dominance, or an arbitrary restriction. The therapist then attempts to link this interpretation with the more general transference interpretations that may be warranted. An essential tactic of this treatment approach is the combination of structuring the treatment, setting limits on the patient's suicidal behavior, and immediate interpretation of the transference implications of this limit-setting until such transference implications can be fully explored and resolved.

The underlying theoretical assumption is that, regardless of the particular psychodynamic issues activated in each case, a common feature of chronic suicidal or parasuicidal behavior is an implicit activation in the patient's mind of an object representation of a sadistic, murderous quality and the complementary activation of a victim representation of that object representation—a defeated, mistreated, threatened self-representation. The relationship between these two representations (self and object) is marked by intense hatred and is revealed in a relationship of the patient with his or her own body. Chronic suicidal and parasuicidal behavior reflect a somatization of an intrapsychic conflict: The limit-setting as part of the structure of the treatment arrangements and the interpretative approach to the corresponding implications for the therapeutic relationship transform such a somatized, internalized object relation into a transference-activated, internalized object relation that permits the suicidal conflict to be approached directly.

The patient temptation for suicidal behavior is thus transformed into a potentially hateful relation between one aspect of the patient's self and one aspect of his or her projected object representation that is attributed to the therapist. This transformation may dramatically eliminate long-standing suicidal behavior from the beginning of treatment; and while the transference rapidly shifts into a dominantly negative one, the containment, interpretive working through, and gradual resolution of that primitive transference may resolve suicidal behavior in the early stages of the patient's psychotherapeutic treatment.

TRANSFERENCE-FOCUSED MANAGEMENT OF AFFECT STORMS

In initial interviews, borderline patients usually show far better control of affect than they are able to maintain during effective treatment. The likelihood of periods of inordinate violence of the patient's affect and its expression in action and/or countertransference requires, however, that patient and therapist agree in advance on the conditions of the treatment that will make management of such episodes possible. These conditions must include the maintenance of a clear and stable boundary of the therapeutic setting. This boundary involves not only the fixed time and space of the psychotherapeutic relationship, but also the extent to which the patient may yell or not, the requirement to avoid any destructive action against the therapist, his or her belongings, the office, and the space in which the treatment takes place, as well as protecting the patient from any dangerously destructive action against the self. The patient must understand that physical contact between patient and therapist is prohibited as a condition of treatment.

With these boundaries in place, it begins to be possible to carry out the diagnosis and interpretation of the dominant object relation and of the corresponding primitive defensive operation (particularly projective identification) as these become activated in the sessions. When affect storms occur, however, the patient may not be able to accept any interpretation, particularly of projective identification, perceiving the interpretation as a traumatizing assault. Here the recommendation of John Steiner (1993)—to interpret the nature of what is projected as "object centered," spelling out the patient's perception of the therapist in great detail, without either accepting that perception nor rejecting it—gradually facilitates the patient's better tolerance of what he or she is projecting, as well as clarifying the nature of what is projected and the reasons for it, before interpretation of the projection proper "back into the patient."

Affect storms place a special strain on the therapist's tolerance of the countertransference; it is necessary both to keep an open mind to exploring (mentally) the implications of the strong feelings aroused by the patient's behavior and to protect against acting them out. The therapist has to attempt to stay in role, even when responding with corresponding intensity to the intensity of the patient's affect.

In my borderline psychotherapy research project, some therapists, whose interpretive interventions seem relevant, clear, in sufficient depth, and expressed at an appropriate tempo in moment-to-moment contact with the patient, nevertheless have difficulty in their treatments because of a pronounced discrepancy between the intense affective activation in the patient and the outward serenity of the therapist. Nothing is more effective in further inflaming an affect storm than a wooden, or unresponsive or soft-spoken, therapist, whose behavior suggests either that he or she doesn't "get it" or that he or she is contemptuous of the patient's loss of control or else terrified and paralyzed by the intensity of the patient's feelings. The therapist must be willing and able to engage the patient at an affective level that recognizes, has an appropriate intensity, and yet "contains" the affect of the patient.

This situation, in which patient and therapist are expressing themselves at the same affective level, is not infrequent in the treatment of severely disturbed patients. It may reflect Matte-Blanco's (1975, 1988) concept of a primitive level of symmetric logical functioning, where the self's very intensity of affect determines the combination of generalization and symmetric thinking, with the result that only a related, somewhat corresponding intensity of affect on the part of the object enables communication to be maintained.

It may seem obvious to state that the therapist's affective response must be sensitive to that of the patient, particularly when the dominant affects are so extremely aggressive or invasive. The fact remains that, at certain points, technical neutrality, in the sense of not taking sides on the issues in conflict in the patient, may be perfectly commensurate with an intensity of affect expression that signals the therapist's availability, responsiveness, and survival, without contamination by the patient's hatred. The enactment in the transference-countertransference bind that intense types of projective identification provoke may be functional in the sense of permitting the diagnosis of the primitive object relationship being enacted.

The effective management of affect storms eventually makes it possible to interpret the dominant set of object relations from surface to depth, that is, from the defensive to the impulsive side, starting from the patient's conscious, ego-syntonic experience, and proceeding to the unconscious, dissociated, repressed, or projected aspects of the patient's experience and the motivations for the defenses against it. This process permits the transformation of the affect storm, with its components of action and bodily responses, into a representational experience, a linkage of affect and cognition in terms of the clarification of the relationship between self- and object representation within the frame of a dominant affect (Clarkin, Yeomans, & Kernberg, 1999).

The psychoanalyst whose patients can tolerate a standard psychoanalytic technique may never have to address the occasional affect storm in the manner just described. But it may be an essential application of psychoanalytic technique to those cases for whom most psychoanalysts would see standard psychoanalysis as contraindicated and where a transference-focused psychoanalytic psychotherapy may be the treatment of choice (Kernberg, 1999).

The deadening calmness with which some patients defend against affect is a chronic behavioral enactment that is split off from the content of verbal communication. Seemingly just the opposite of an affect storm, it nevertheless evokes an intense countertransference reaction that may be understood in the relation to the patient's nonverbal behavior but is much more difficult to relate to what he communicates verbally, because the therapist tends to get lulled over time into accepting the patient's monotonous behavior. The therapist's problem is not so much the containment of an intolerably intense countertransference reaction but rather the sense of internal paralysis or guilt over increasing loss of interest in a patient who, at the surface, seems to be "so uncommunicative."

For example, a patient spoke in an aggressive and derogatory tone of voice, almost never looking at the therapist, while talking about various subjects apparently unrelated to this chronic aggressive demeanor. Another patient used to slouch on a couch, sipping from a water bottle, almost conveying the impression of a sleepy baby expecting to be soothed and comforted into total sleep, while filling the hours with trivial contents. The first patient reported chronic experiences of hostile reactions by other people toward her, which she interpreted as directed against everybody having her racial characteristics. The second patient would exasperate health personnel because of her effective way of extracting supplies and support for her totally passive, indolent, and parasitic lifestyle. The task in both cases, obviously, was how to bring into consciousness an aspect of the therapeutic interaction that was totally dissociated from the verbal communication and yet central both in the transference and in the patient's life experience outside the sessions.

The indication is for a clear, noncritical focus on what is going on in the session, raising patients' interest in their nonverbal behavior, and gradually facilitating the explanation of its transferential function. Such an approach tends to evoke strong denial, or else the patient may simply ignore the therapist's comments, smile indulgently, and maintain the behavior that has been highlighted. The patient may be accustomed to receiving similar confrontations from others in less friendly ways and be prepared to neutralize them. It may be helpful to analyze the patient's view of the motivation of those others: This information provides a preview of how the patient will experience the therapist's confrontations. The therapist's persistence in analyzing what is going on in the session eventually transforms the monotony of behavior into a storm of affect: This represents a moment of truth, in which the violent reaction reflects the object relation against which the monotonous behavior had been defending. At such points, the therapist may interpret that underlying object relation in what John Steiner (1993) has proposed as an "object centered" way. Object-centered interventions facilitate an immediate analysis of the total object relationship, such as: "Because you perceive me as having such hostile and derogatory ways of treating you, it is natural that your own reaction to me at this point should be like that of an enraged child scolded by a cold and cruel father."

In these situations, Winnicott's (1958) concept of "holding" or Bion's (1970) concept of "containing" are useful ways to conceptualize therapists' capacity to integrate, in their interpretive interventions, a combined understanding of patients' behavior and their own countertransference, without enacting the countertransference. However, partial enactment of countertransference responses are almost unavoidable under the trying circumstances created by repeated affect storms or the deadening defensive patterns against them. Such partial enactments or even acting out of the countertransference do not represent a serious danger to the treatment or a significant distortion of technical neutrality.

To the contrary, if therapists feel comfortable with their overall approach to patients and can honestly acknowledge, without excessive guilt or defensiveness, having lost control over their affect expression at a certain point, this may convey to patients that affect storms are not that dangerous, that some mild loss of control is only human, and that it doesn't preclude a return to an objective and concerned treatment relationship. At times, therapists' expressions of outrage at something outrageous communicated with a provocative calmness by patients may be an appropriate way of maintaining contact. These patients may require, as part of the analysis of the underlying dynamics, an affectively intense investment on the part of the therapist in pointing, moment by moment, to the hidden violence behind the deadening monotony. Observed from the outside, it is as if a totally phlegmatic and controlled patient were in treatment with a hysterical or even violent therapist. Therapists themselves may feel uneasy in a role that they may experience as supportive (because of the intense activity required) or even controlling or manipulative. However, therapists may have good reasons to reassure themselves that their intensity is not in the service of controlling patients' actions or of "moving" patients into any particular direction, but is rather designed to clarify what is going on through accentuating the emotional exploration of a development in the session at that moment. Therapists work, to use Bion's terms, "without memory nor desire" in exploring in-depth the hidden violence in the present interaction (manifest in their reading of patients' behavior and the countertransference). Therapists' manifest affective investment may be an important way in which they assert their standing on the side of life and of investment in object relations, as opposed to deadly "de-objectalization." Insofar as therapists are not "pushing" or "encouraging" or "demanding" in their responses to patients, but verbalizing their perception of the present interaction, this is still an *exploratory* and not a *supportive* approach.

At points of intense affect storms, whether spontaneous or following the confrontation of deadening dissociative behavior patterns in the hours, the patient may not be able to listen at all to the therapist. It is as if the patient's intolerance for developing representational expression of his or her own affects now includes efforts to destroy the therapist's representational expression of the patient's affective experience. In other words, the patient's destructive impulses may take the path of efforts to destroy the therapist's capacity for cognitive functioning.

Therapists have to differentiate their incapacity to listen, at the height of affect storms, from the chronic dismissing of everything the therapist says as an expression of the "syndrome of arrogance" described by Bion (1970). As part of this syndrome, a combination of pseudo-stupidity, curiosity (about the therapist), and arrogance reflects the dominance of primitive hatred in the transference, together with patients' incapacity to tolerate the awareness of their own hatred. Here, acting out totally replaces the ordinary subjective awareness of affective experience. There are still other patients whose chronic dismissal of what comes from the therapist is part of narcissistic resistances in the transference that need to be resolved with the usual interpretive approaches to the intolerance of a dependent relationship to the therapist (Kernberg, 1984).

Returning to the problem of affect storms, at times, therapists have to wait until the intensity of the affect storm subsides before making an interpretive comment; at other times, it may be helpful simply to ask patients if they believe that they would be able to tolerate a comment from the therapist at that point. I find it helpful, at times, to tell patients that I have thoughts on my mind that I am hesitant to spell out, because I do not know whether they might react to those thoughts with such vehement anger that they would have difficulty even to understand what I am trying to say. If a patient then tells me, ragefully, that he or she does not want to hear anything from me, I may remain silent for the moment and only interpret later what the reasons might be for the patient's intolerance of any communication from me.

Under such circumstances, it is helpful if the therapist first ascertains whether the intervention already includes the elaboration of the countertransference disposition that is part of the material included in the planned intervention. If therapists experience themselves as controlled by the countertransference, this is an indication for waiting and internal elaboration before intervening. It is also extremely important that therapists feel safe in their intervention, because to be afraid of patients is a powerful message that cannot but increase fear in patients; at such times, patients' rage is a defense against their fear of their own aggression. The therapist's physical, psychological, professional, and legal safety are indispensable preconditions for work with very regressed patients, and the therapist must take whatever measures are necessary to ensure that safety: This is a precondition for effective concern over the safety of the patient.

One important complication in the psychodynamic psychotherapy of borderline patients is the danger of "spilling over" of severe affect storms from the sessions into the patient's life outside the sessions. For example, one patient developed an intensely erotic attachment to the therapist, feeling that if the therapist were not to leave his wife and all other emotional commitments and dedicate himself solely to the patient, her life would no longer be worth living. This intense erotic transference contained, as may seem obvious, significantly pre-Oedipal elements, the desperate claim of a baby to have the exclusive attention of her mother. On the surface, however, it took the form of a "falling in love" that became so disturbing to the patient that she expressed to her husband her despair over the therapist's failure to respond to her love. This threatened her marriage as well as the treatment.

Under such circumstances, it may become important to set limits to the patient's behavior outside the hours or even to intervene directly in the patient's life, with a clear understanding that this means a significant move away from technical neutrality, requiring its interpretive reinstatement later (Clarkin et al.,

1999). These, fortunately, are rare complications when general concern is taken to maintain clear treatment boundaries. If, however, the therapist ignores or does not systematically interpret acting out of the transference, major "spilling over" into the patient's external life becomes much more likely. For example, one patient lingered on in the therapist's waiting room over a period of hours. Because this transference acting out was not addressed in the sessions, the patient ended up practically sleeping in the waiting room all day long, creating serious complications both for the patient and for the therapist's professional practice.

At the end, in successful treatments, affects are translated into a relationship between self- and object representations. The result of integrative interpretation of primitive transferences is resolution of identity diffusion and the integration of the internal world of objects. In the process, we expect those who are able to benefit from this treatment to be able to resume a satisfactory love life, intimacy and friendship, creativity and effectiveness in work, and the finding of their own ways of satisfaction and creativity in other areas of their lives.

REFERENCES

Abraham, K. (1920). Manifestation of the female castration complex. In *Selected papers on psychoanalysis* (pp. 338–369). London: Hogarth Press.

Abraham, K. (1921–1925). Psycho-analytical studies on character formation. In *Selected papers on psychoanalysis* (pp. 370–417). London: Hogarth Press.

Akhtar, S. (1989). Narcissistic personality disorder: Descriptive features and differential diagnosis. *Psychiatric Clinics of North America, 12,* 505–530.

Akhtar, S. (1992). *Broken structures.* Northvale, NJ: Aronson.

Bion, W. R. (1970). *Attention and interpretation.* London: Heinemann.

Clarkin, J. F., Yeomans, F. E., & Kernberg, O. F. (1999). *Psychotherapy for borderline personality.* New York: Wiley.

Cloninger, C. R., Svrakic, D. M., & Przybeck, T. R. (1993). A psychobiological model of temperament and character. *Archives of General Psychiatry, 50,* 975–990.

Depue, R. A. (1996). A neurobiological framework for the structure of personality and emotion: Implications for personality disorders. In J. F. Clarkin & M. F. Lenzenweger (Eds.), *Major theories of personality disorders* (pp. 347–383). New York: Guildford Press.

deVegvar, M. L., Siever, L. J., & Trestman, R. L. (1994). Impulsivity and serotonin in borderline personality disorder. In K. R. Silk (Ed.), *Biological and neurobehavioral studies of borderline personality disorder* (pp. 23–40). Washington, DC: American Psychiatric Press.

Erikson, E. H. (1956). The problem of ego identity. *American Psychoanalytic Association, 4,* 56–121.

Fenichel, O. (1945). *The psychoanalytic theory of neurosis.* New York: Norton.

Fraiberg, A. (1983). Pathological defenses in infancy. *Psychoanalytic Quarterly, 60,* 612–635.

Freud, S. (1925). The instincts and their vicissitudes. In J. Strachey (Ed.), *The standard edition of the complete psychological works of Sigmund Freud* (Vol. 14, pp. 109–140). London: Hogarth Press. (Original work published 1915)

Freud, S. (1931). Libidinal types. In J. Strachey (Ed.), *The standard edition of the complete psychological works of Sigmund Freud* (Vol. 21, pp. 215–220). London: Hogarth Press.

Freud, S. (1959). Character and anal eroticism. In J. Strachey (Ed.), *The standard edition of the complete psychological works of Sigmund Freud* (Vol. 9, pp. 169–175). London: Hogarth Press. (Original work published 1908)

Galenson, E. (1986). Some thoughts about infant psychopathology and aggressive development. *International Review of Psychoanalysis, 13,* 349–354.

Grossman, W. (1986). Notes on masochism: A discussion of the history and development of a psychoanalytic concept 1. *Psychoanalytic Quarterly, 55,* 379–413.

Grossman, W. (1991). Pain, aggression, fantasy, and concepts of sadomasochism. *Psychoanalytic Quarterly, 60,* 22–52.

Jacobson, E. (1964). *The self and object world.* New York: International Universities Press.

Kernberg, O. F. (1975). *Borderline conditions and pathological narcissism.* New York: Aronson.

Kernberg, O. F. (1976). *Object relations theory and clinical psychoanalysis.* New York: Aronson.

Kernberg, O. F. (1980). *Internal world and external reality: Object relations theory applied.* New York: Aronson.

Kernberg, O. F. (1984). *Severe personality disorders: Psychotherapeutic strategies.* New Haven, CT: Yale University Press.

Kernberg, O. F. (1989). The narcissistic personality disorder and the differential diagnosis of antisocial behavior. *Psychiatric Clinics of North America, 12,* 553–570.

Kernberg, O. F. (1992). *Aggression in personality disorder and perversions.* New Haven, CT: Yale University Press.

Kernberg, O. F. (1994). Aggression, trauma, and hatred in the treatment of borderline patients. *Psychiatric Clinics of North America, 17,* 701–714.

Kernberg, O. F. (1999). Psychoanalysis, psychoanalytic psychotherapy and supportive psychotherapy: Contemporary controversies. *International Journal of Psychoanalysis, 80*(6), 1075–1091.

Kernberg, O. F., Burnstein, E. D., Coyne, L., Appelbaum, A., Horowitz, L., & Voth, H. (1972). Psychotherapy and psychoanalysis: Final report of the Menninger Foundation's Psychotherapy Research Project. *Bulletin of the Menninger Clinic, 36,* 1–275.

Krause, R. (1988). A taxonomy of affects and its utilization for the understanding of early disorders [Eine Taxonomie der Affekte und ihre Anwendung auf das Verständnis der frühen Störungen]. *Psychotherapie und Medizinische Psychologie, 38,* 77–86.

Krause, R., & Lutolf, P. (1988). Facial indicators of transference processes in psychoanalytical treatment. In H. Dahl & H. Kachele (Eds.), *Psychoanalytic process research strategies* (pp. 257–272). Heidelberg, Germany: Springer.

Mahler, M., & Furer, M. (1968). *On human symbiosis and the vicissitudes of individuation.* New York: International Universities Press.

Mahler, M., Pine, F., & Bergman, A. (1975). *The psychological birth of the human infant.* New York: Basic Books.

Marziali, E. (1992). The etiology of borderline personality disorder: Developmental factors. In J. F. Clarkin, E. Marziali, & H. Munroe-Blum (Eds.), *Borderline personality disorder: Clinical implications* (pp. 27–44). New York: Guilford Press.

Matte-Blanco, I. (1975). *The unconscious as infinite sets.* London: Duckworth.

Matte-Blanco, I. (1988). *Thinking, feeling, and being.* London: Routledge.

Perry, J. C., & Herman, J. L. (1993). Trauma and defense in the etiology of borderline personality disorder. In J. Paris (Ed.), *Borderline personality disorder: Etiology and treatment* (pp. 123–140). Washington, DC: American Psychiatric Press.

Steiner, J. (1993). *Psychic retreats: Pathological organizations in psychotic, neurotic and borderline patients.* London: Routledge.

Stone, M. (1980). *The borderline syndromes.* New York: McGraw-Hill.

Stone, M. (1990). *The fate of borderline patients.* New York: Guilford Press.

Stone, M. (1993a). *Abnormalities of personality.* New York: Norton.

Stone, M. (1993b). Etiology of borderline personality disorder: Psychobiological factors contributing to an underlying irritability. In J. Paris (Ed.), *Borderline personality disorder: Etiology and treatment* (pp. 87–102). Washington, DC: American Psychiatric Press.

Torgersen, A. M. (1985). Temperamental differences in infants and 6-year-old children: A follow-up study of twins. In J. Strelau, F. H. Farley, & A. Gale (Eds.), *The biological basis of personality and behavior: Theories, measurement, techniques, and development* (pp. 227–239). Washington, DC: Hemisphere.

Torgersen, A. M. (1994, June). *Genetics of personality disorder.* Paper presented at the First European Congress on Disorders of Personality, Nijmegen, The Netherlands.

van der Kolk, B. A., Hostetler, A., Herron, N., & Fisler, R. E. (1994). Trauma and the development of borderline personality disorder. *Psychiatric Clinics of North America, 17,* 715–730.

Volkan, V. (1976). *Primitive internalized object relations.* New York: International Universities Press.

Volkan, V. (1987). *Six steps in the treatment of borderline personality organization.* Northvale, NJ: Aronson.

Wallerstein, R. (1991). *Scales of psychological capacity.* Unpublished manuscript.

Winnicott, D. (1958). *Collected papers: Through pediatrics to psycho-analysis.* New York: Basic Books.

Yehuda, R., Southwick, S. M., Perry, B. D., & Giller, E. L. (1994). Peripheral catecholamine alterations in borderline personality disorder. In R. Silk (Ed.), *Biological and neurobehavioral studies of borderline personality disorder* (pp. 63–90). Washington, DC: American Psychiatric Press.

Yeomans, F. E., Selzer, M. A., & Clarkin, J. F. (1992). *Treating the borderline patient: A contract-based approach.* New York: Basic Books.

CHAPTER 6

Personality Disorder or Relational Disconnection?

Judith V. Jordan

T HE *DSM-III-R* (AMERICAN PSYCHIATRIC ASSOCIATION [APA], 1987) defines personality traits as "enduring patterns of perceiving, relating to and thinking about the environment and oneself," which "are exhibited in a wide range of important social and personal contexts" (p. 335). It further states that personality disorders develop when "personality traits are inflexible and maladaptive and cause either significant functional impairment or subjective distress" (p. 335). *DSM-IV* (APA, 1994) adds attention to cultural factors in its revision: "An enduring pattern of inner experience and behavior that deviates markedly from the expectations of the individual's culture" and "the enduring pattern is inflexible and pervasive across a broad range of personal and social situations" (p. 275). It continues, "The pattern is stable and of long duration and its onset can be traced back at least to adolescence or early adulthood" (p. 276). From the point of view of the *relational-cultural model of development and therapy*, the diagnoses known as *personality disorders* invite serious rethinking and revision. This chapter explores these issues and offers an alternative view that eschews the use of the construct *personality disorders* and alternatively considers relational disconnection as the crucial phenomenon.

RELATIONAL-CULTURAL THEORY

Relational-cultural theory (RCT) challenges many of the traditional psychological theories of personality in terms of their emphasis on the growth of a separate self, their exclusive focus on intrapsychic phenomenon, and their espousal of enduring internal traits (Jordan, 1997; Jordan, Kaplan, Miller, Stiver, & Surrey, 1991; Miller & Stiver, 1997). A failure to appreciate the power of context to shape people's lives characterizes many of these traditional psychodynamic models where tribute is paid to autonomy, separation, and a separate self-status (Freud, 1920/1955; Klein, 1953; Kohut, 1984; Winnicott, 1960). Alternatively, RCT suggests that people grow through and toward connection throughout the life span; the ideal of *separation* is seen as illusory and defeating because the human condition is inevitably one of ongoing interdependence. Rather than tracing the trajectory of psychological development from dependence to independence and the development of self from merged to separate, RCT looks at development as involving increasing elaboration and differentiation of relational patterns and capacities. RCT suggests that human beings seek engagement in relationship in which both people are receiving and giving. There is movement toward relational authenticity, mutual empathy, and mutual empowerment. The capacity for mutuality and empathy is explicitly valued. In growth-fostering relationships, there are clear outcomes, known as the "five good things" (Miller & Stiver, 1997):

1. Increased sense of energy or zest.
2. Increased knowledge of self, other, and relationship, known as clarity.
3. Ability to act and create.
4. Sense of worth, feeling good about self and others.
5. Desire for more connection with others, creating widening circles of connection or community.

These relational outcomes are not the result of enduring internal traits or personality organization but arise in relationship. In the RCT model, isolation is viewed as the greatest source of psychological suffering for individuals; chronic isolation limits growth and contributes to a sense of immobilization and self-blame. Whereas the emphasis of understanding is on relational development and patterns of disconnections, other sources of psychological pain are acknowledged; some of these are caused by chemical imbalances and are typically represented in the Axis I diagnoses. The quality of relationship and injuries in relationships, however, also clearly affect psychobiology (Banks, 2001; van der Kolk, 1988). The goal of treatment is to bring people out of chronic disconnection (isolation) and back into the growth and movement of mutual relationship (Jordan, 1992).

ROLE OF MUTUAL EMPATHY IN THE THERAPEUTIC PROCESS

The path of healing and growth both in and out of therapy is via empathy. Mutual empathy involves mutual impact, mutual care, and mutual responsiveness. It depends on repair of empathic failures and altering relational expectations created in earlier formative and nonresponsive relationships. Simply put, therapy involves a dance of responsiveness: "I (therapist) empathize with you (patient), with your pain (for instance), and I let you see that your pain has affected me. In short, you have affected me and you matter to me." The patient sees, knows, and feels (empathizes with) the therapist's empathy and thereby begins to experience a sense of relational competence and efficacy. The patient finds and experiences the ability to create a caring response in the other person at the same time that there is a diminished sense of isolation. Both patient and therapist begin to move into growth-fostering connection (Jordan, 2000, 2002a, 2002b). Because RCT posits that chronic disconnections result from repeatedly not being empathically responded to or, at the more extreme, being violated, abused, or neglected, the healing intervention is one of responsiveness and empathy. Acute disconnections happen all the time in relationships; we are hurt, misunderstood, not listened to, overlooked. If in the moment we can represent our response to these failures, authentically share their impact on us, and find a caring response in the other person, we feel as though we "matter." We are taken seriously, respected, and listened to, and we feel relationally competent. We participate in changing the relationship in a more growthful direction for others and ourselves. We also experience the five good things mentioned previously (zest, clarity, creativity, a sense of worth, and a desire for more connection). In such resilient and reparative interactions, specific relationships are strengthened, and our faith or trust in relationships in general is also deepened. In fact, as acute disconnections are negotiated, we come more fully and confidently into connection.

If, however, we are empathically failed, misunderstood, humiliated, violated, or abused and we attempt to protest or to register our injury and we are not responded to but are ignored, further hurt, punished, and so forth, we learn that we cannot authentically represent ourselves in this relationship. If this occurs in a relationship with a powerful and important other (e.g., parent, teacher, boss) on whom we are dependent, we begin to distort our experience to try to fit in. We begin to deny our own pain to be accepted by this other person. As a result, we disconnect from ourselves. As Gilligan (1982) notes, we begin to keep ourselves out of relationship to stay in relationship. We move out of authenticity to stay in the semblance of connection. Authentic connection, however, suffers; both our connection with the other and the connection with our own experience are weakened. We can trace the effect of chronic disconnection most clearly in cases of childhood abuse, the most obvious and egregious example of relational injury. For instance, in the case of childhood sexual or physical abuse, children are hurt or abused; they initially try to protest, to state their reality. Their reality is denied, or they are threatened with dangerous consequences, further injury, isolation, the loss of loved ones, even death. To stay alive, psychologically and sometimes physically, they develop what RCT labels "strategies of disconnection" (Miller & Stiver, 1997); that is, they disconnect from their own real affective-cognitive experience and begin to twist themselves to be acceptable to literally stay alive in this abusive but needed relationship. Their inner experience gets frozen, immobilized; they feel isolated and endangered. They begin to lose track of their own real affect. As affect is split off, they are vulnerable to not knowing their own feelings. The necessary learning about the complexity of feelings cannot happen when they are left alone with strong affect. Furthermore, their biochemistry is altered in ways that leave them more vulnerable to affective instability and traumatic disconnections. Thus, a small hurt may lead to a big chemical and behavioral reaction as the overreactive amygdala short-circuits the cortical mediation of pain. The relational images of "If I register my hurt or anger, I am shunned, abandoned, or endangered" begin to generalize to all other relationships, and slowly children learn to bring only partial aspects of themselves into relationship. Their vulnerability in particular is not safe. They also experience the opposite of the five good things: a drop of energy (depression), confusion (lack of clarity), decreased productivity, a drop of self-worth, and a withdrawal from relationships in general. In the case of abuse, they also experience the more alarming symptoms of Posttraumatic Stress Disorder (PTSD) characterized by hyperarousal, panic, nightmares, self-destructive behavior, flashbacks, and intrusive thoughts, which further isolate and confuse them. It could be argued that some of the more painful consequences of these symptoms (the startle response, affective lability, inauthenticity, lack of trust, self-harm, substance abuse, and eating disorders) are the deepening sense of isolation, shame, and helplessness. These symptoms make the possibility of reparative connection even more elusive.

SHAME, DISCONNECTION, AND ISOLATION

The shame accompanying these issues is enormous, and shame is a major source of disconnection and isolation for many patients. Shame (Jordan, 1989) involves a sense of feeling unworthy of empathic responsiveness, an individual's conviction that he or she is unlovable, that his or her being is unacceptable. Shame also contributes to the cycle of isolation because the individual cannot easily bring the split-off or shamed parts into relationship without fearing that he or she will lose the empathy and caring that is so needed. Secrecy and distortion interfere with the establishment of authentic connection in which individuals might actually get the feedback that they are acceptable and even lovable. Shame thus becomes an obstacle to expanding the ways in which they are known and, therefore, the ways in which they can grow.

RELATIONAL DEVELOPMENT VERSUS PERSONALITY DEVELOPMENT

Rather than looking at *personality development* in understanding an individual's suffering, RCT looks at *relational development,* the capacity to be resilient in relationship (Jordan & Hartling, 2002), the increasing ability to move toward mutuality. This is the process of growth in connection (Jordan et al., 1991). The people engaged in the relationship, as well as the relationship itself, change, move, develop. RCT questions the notion of *separate self.* Self is a metaphor, which exists at a conceptual level only. The metaphor of self that is popular in Western psychology is spatial and essentially separate. The *mature* self is portrayed as bounded, separate, contained, autonomous, and actively initiating. Boundaries are seen as protecting the self from a possibly distorting context. Freud once observed, "Protection against stimuli is almost more important than reception of stimuli" (Freud, 1920/1955, p. 27). The model of science that psychology embraced in its infancy was that of Newtonian physics. The unit of separation (the atom, the molecule) was the focus of study and was felt to represent the basic unit of reality. At the psychological level in this traditional model, independence, separation, and autonomy are valued, elevated, and sought. The "new physics" has since posited relatedness, not separation, as the primary condition of matter. Similarly so-called one-person psychologies are giving way to two-person psychologies. Has the notion of *personality* and *personality disorders* kept up with the general movement of psychology toward relationship, or does it represent the atomistic, molecular view arising from Newtonian physics and the illusion of separation?

The more fluid metaphor of voice better captures an interactive notion of *who we are* than the static and spatially determined metaphor of *the self.* Voice is created in context; there is always a speaker and listener. We are listened into voice; how we are listened to significantly affects how and what we present. With empathic presence, we feel empowered, can be more authentic, take risks, and connect in new ways. We become who we are in different contexts, and our voices differ enormously in different contexts. People sometimes comment on being "smarter than they are smart" or "dumber than they are dumb" depending on whom they are speaking with. The notion of personality and personality disorders seems too static, too solid, too bounded. Most seem to partake of the premises of separate self-models. They do not sufficiently acknowledge the power of sociopolitical, cultural, and economic factors in people's lives. They do not acknowledge the power of privilege and the power of the dominant group to define norms and deviance (Walker, 1999). But if we suggest discarding or revising self and personality, how can we address the clear experience of uniqueness and continuity that most human beings experience?

THE NEED TO CONSIDER THE SOCIOCULTURAL, ECONOMIC, AND POLITICAL FACTORS

Relational-cultural theory clearly acknowledges that people experience a *sense of self* (particularly in a culture that so celebrates separate self). We have a sense of history, continuity, and personal predictability—subjective knowledge about our thoughts, feelings, and actions. We set goals, have intentions, and move with some purpose toward these goals. We have certain expectations, moods, likes, and dislikes that seem somewhat patterned and familiar. What gets lost in traditional models is that we always exist in contexts (either supportive and creative or destructive), and we grow in connection. We are profoundly influenced by our social contexts, and our sense of coherence and meaning is extremely dependent on many chance factors of our being. These factors also change, often with little control on our part. For instance, there are enormous sources of "unearned privilege" that impact our functioning (e.g., being White in a racist culture, male in a sexist culture, heterosexual in a heterosexist system). Belonging to the dominant and valued group in any stratified culture bestows enormous advantage to those in the privileged group (McIntosh, 1989). These advantages profoundly impact our paths of development. Often these influences are not acknowledged. In fact, the dominant experience is often assumed to be normative and "best," and this goes unexamined and unquestioned. In the mental health field, this can lead to pathologizing of difference (e.g., dependent personality in a culture that celebrates independence; hysterical personality in a culture that esteems rational, logical functioning more than emotional responsiveness). The marginalized groups of "difference" are often seen as less "mature," less evolved (Brown, 2002; Brown & Ballou, 2002; Lerman, 1996; Miller, 1976).

EMPHASIZING CHRONIC DISCONNECTION INSTEAD OF PSYCHOPATHOLOGY

In addition to looking at the personal sources of chronic disconnections (often termed *psychopathology* by other theories), RCT examines the sociocultural sources of disconnection and isolation. In particular, there is an analysis of power differences and the impact of privilege and stratification on an individual's development. Unequal distribution of power and stratification based on *difference* named by the dominant group (race, sex, sexual orientation, class, physical intactness) create significant disconnection and contribute to isolation and disempowerment. Those at the "margin" (hooks, 1984) are shamed for their difference; those at the "center" essentially make the judgment: "Your reality is inferior to mine." Silenced by shame and pushed into isolation, marginalized groups experience enormous pressures and suffering at economic, political, and personal levels. In systems reinforcing the dominance and privilege of White people, people of color are made to feel "less than." In systems supporting male dominance, women are seen as "less than," weak, and too needy. Any system based on dominance and subordination creates pain for both the dominant group and subordinate group. The subordinate group, however, enjoy none of the rewards of the dominant group and are further invited into inauthenticity and disconnection from their inner experience. Dominance is predicated on the inauthenticity of the nondominant group because the reality of the nondominant group (e.g., anger at being oppressed) creates conflict or threatens the reality of the dominant group. The strengths of the subordinate group sometimes develop from the need to create community to resist the destructive forces of subordination. In models of human behavior based on the celebration of "power over," strength is often framed as highly individualistic; standing on your own two feet is the place of safety. These models invite movement into isolation. RCT suggests instead that safety and growth reside in connection—not in isolation and power over others.

Most of the personality disorder diagnoses fail to examine the importance of context beyond the traditional nuclear family and often beyond the influence of the early mother-infant relationship. This can lead to real failures in understanding. The problem is then located in the individual; social conditions and the relational failures emanating from these social conditions are rarely examined as the source of the problem. Furthermore, many personality diagnoses fail to encompass the effects of abuse of power and social factors leading to disconnection. For instance, physical and sexual abuses are predicated on a massive abuse of power and violation of trust. The healing of chronic disconnections depends heavily on establishing good, safe connection, not on analyzing or reworking personality traits or simply eliminating bothersome symptoms. Furthermore, trauma is a normal response to abnormal stress (van der Kolk, 1996). Understanding PTSD as a "normal response" to chronic disconnection, stress, and terror provides a very different understanding than if we locate the problem in the individual's personality.

BORDERLINE PERSONALITY DISORDER: A CRITIQUE

We now examine Borderline Personality Disorder as an example of a personality disorder diagnosis that, it could be argued, fails in the intended goals of any diagnosis to clarify etiology, indicate treatment interventions, and determine prognosis. This diagnosis in particular may also have iatrogenic effects on many patients. For instance, one patient commented that other treaters had called her "a borderline," and she added that she knew that wasn't "good." In fact, she felt they were maligning her and taking an adversarial position with her of distance and guardedness; she felt that under such conditions, she actually was triggered more easily into traumatic disconnections and "acting crazy." In short, she felt unsafe. Applying a pathology-based label such as *borderline* does not contribute to the creation of a healing connection in therapy with people who have been severely harmed in violating interpersonal relationships. The emphasis conveyed by this label on the disturbance, as located in the personality of the patient, avoids a confrontation with the larger societal factors that make physical and sexual abuse of children almost normative. Some have noted that as many as 25% of all females suffer some form of sexual abuse before they reach the age of 18 (Russell, 1986). Locating the problem within the individual or even within the pathology of the nuclear family often leaves the larger societal conditions that directly produce the problems unexamined and untouched (Root, 1992).

A diagnosis is meant to be a descriptive device to capture symptom clusters, to provide a core understanding of etiology, and to suggest some useful prescriptions for treatment as well as offer some prognostic guidelines. Serious questions can be raised about how well personality disorders meet these criteria. But with personality diagnoses, the diagnosis also often sets a tone for treatment. For instance, when meeting with a patient with the borderline diagnosis, therapists often assume a distanced, judging, and adversarial stance. Their empathic attitude may actually decrease. Clinicians treating "borderline" patients tend to take a "doctor knows best" stance, expecting the client to be manipulative, angry, and characterized by rapid mood shifts and unstable interpersonal relationships. Most therapists also expect this will be a "challenging" treatment with someone who will "take up a lot of space and energy." An attitude of respect, curiosity, and working toward connection is easily lost with such a set of expectations on the part of the therapist. The frustration and anger of the therapist is most evident in case descriptions of "flaming borderlines" or "black holes." Some have even suggested that the borderline diagnosis is more a statement of the clinician's feelings of anger and frustration toward the patient than of etiology, treatment recommendations, or prognoses. Others have indicated that the borderline diagnosis may be synonymous with "the difficult patient" (Kernberg, Selzer, Koenigsberg, Carr, & Appelbaum, 1989).

Kernberg's (1975) understanding of etiology of the borderline personality disorder described an excess of instinctual aggression or faulty regulation on the part of the mother, particularly maternal failures in the rapprochement stage. There was no acknowledgment of the role of childhood abuse. Kernberg's hypotheses represented the prevailing wisdom about borderline diagnoses until the late 1980s (Kernberg et al., 1989; Stone, 1980). Despite new information, particularly about the role of abuse and relational violation in the lives of those diagnosed with borderline personality, the theory and clinical protocols built on this erroneous understanding of etiology have not been sufficiently altered to reflect this new evidence.

The prevalence of sexual abuse in the etiology of patients diagnosed as borderline has become well established in the past decade (Herman & van der Kolk, 1987). In those diagnosed as borderline, as many as 55% to 80% have been found to have a history of childhood sexual and/or physical abuse. An appreciation of the role of trauma in the development of people diagnosed with borderline personality organization renders a very different picture of their dynamics. Rather than focusing on maladaptive internal traits, resulting from failures of the mother in rapprochement and leading to failed separation and individuation, we begin to appreciate the impact and centrality of relationship and disconnection on the individual's ability to function in many life arenas. Thus, we see that the chronic stress and violation that is created by physical and sexual abuse of a small child leads to the most dramatic and cruel disconnections from others. There is obvious isolation, shame, immobilization, and affective instability (Herman, 1992). Furthermore, we begin to understand that some of these symptoms are normal reactions to an abnormal level of threat; they are physiologically determined, sometimes part of strategic adaptation to aversive conditions that threaten the lives of the victims. These adaptations involve an extreme survival effort (van der Kolk, McFarlane, & Weisaeth, 1996). Many of these strategies of disconnection and responses are etched in the biochemistry of the abuse survivor and lead to symptoms and behaviors that interfere with healing through connection, which survivors so desperately want and need. For instance, these strategies can involve a complete closing down emotionally at the first hint of interpersonal disappointment; the withdrawal can leave the person with an immediate sense of safety, but the larger movement toward the deeper safety of connection is compromised by these strategies. The paradox of longing for authentic, healing connection at the same time that the individual is terrified of the vulnerability necessary to move into real connection is dramatically played out in the lives of trauma survivors. There are traumatic disconnections in therapy and elsewhere, which are sudden, bewildering, and isolating for the PTSD survivor and the therapist. Ironically for the trauma survivor, connection does not equal safety. Each step toward trust and toward relinquishing protective strategies of disconnection reawakens the early fear of being injured and violated. Just as empathic failures stimulate anxiety and abrupt movement out of connection, so does the gradual movement toward more connection stimulate terror and closing down. In working through the patterns of disconnection, both survivor and therapist experience a series of whiplash shifts in direction. Relational stability is lacking. But safety ultimately for these most injured individuals arises in beginning to establish closer, mutual relationships, not in retreating into "power over" relationships, where they either seek protection from a powerful other or exercise some coercive control over the other person. The control battles emanating from either person's efforts to get the upper hand or exercise power do not lead to safety. Being in a relationship with a powerful and needed other usually initially triggers panic for the PTSD survivor. Connection in which the clinician or therapist is responsive, real, engaged, and working toward mutual empathy and respect offers the path out of fear and chronic disconnection. The "cure" arises in relational resilience, reestablishing the capacity for mutuality, finding "empathic possibility" (Jordan, 1989, 1999).

Relational images and expectations guide the movement of relationship for all of us (e.g., "If I am vulnerable, I will be injured or abandoned" versus "If I am vulnerable, I will be welcomed and respected"). These images are not static traits or internal characteristics but are constantly being affected by context and current relationships. We create each other and ourselves in relationship in an ongoing way. Where there have been early, chronic violations of trust and safety, the negative and fear-filled expectations for relationships often become rigid and overgeneralized. Developing some capacity to move back into connection following disconnection and getting clear about which relationships are safe and which are not are central to growth. For the PTSD patient and others violated in early relationships, we must first establish the possibility of empathic responsiveness and safe connection. This involves reworking relational patterns and establishing mutual respect and empathy (Jordan, 2000).

Therapy is about movement toward mutual connection, not about control and power. This is not to deny that, at times of danger, therapists move in to protect and support the healthy functioning of patients. But the larger work of therapy is not directed toward getting someone "under control" or exercising control over others to get them to "shape up" to some ideal we hold, however subtle or blatant that may be. When therapists move into a position of trying to establish control, we often move out of connection and into a place of power over others. Although chronic disconnection is almost always problematic, it creates special problems when working with patients who have PTSD. The language of limit setting and control is often evoked in treating the so-called borderline patient: "They need authority, firmness, to know they cannot run things"; "If you give an inch, they'll take a mile"; "They will always test you, so set limits clearly." What is seen as a control battle, infringing on the therapist's need to be in charge, does often involve a kind of testing, but it might better be described as "trying to find the real person" in the therapist and trying to find out what real responses are evoked in the other person (Jordan, 1995).

THE RELATIONAL STANCE

The more the therapist practices from some theory of "blank screen," neutrality, silence, or distance, the more the PTSD patient will feel anxious pressure to find "the real person" in the therapist to feel safe and the more the therapist will be setting limits and demarcating boundaries. Although it may seem like a question of semantics, the distinction between *stating limits* and *setting limits* gets to the heart of the way authenticity, real engagement, and mutuality operate in relational-cultural therapy. Rather than setting limits, which involves use of power over the other and often carries connotations of the pathological and overwhelming nature of the patient's needs, it is important for the therapist (and patient) to state their limits. This involves making use of the therapist's authentic responsiveness and inviting the patient into a relationship where there is respect for difference, tolerance, and learning about how each person affects the other. Both therapist and patient hold some accountability and responsibility for their impact on the other and on the relationship. For instance, as to the question of phone calls, therapists speak of setting limits on the number of phone calls that a patient can make to the therapist between sessions. Often, there is the implication that there is a big black hole, an endless void, a bottomless pit of need, and an insatiable desire for contact that is "sick," impossible, and frustrating. Therapists often feel angry about the patient's "excessive" need for contact between sessions. This is not to suggest that the anger is wrong but that the frustration of this situation, rather than being treated as occurring because of the patient's insatiability, is seen as a dilemma for the relationship. The need for contact can be honored at the same time that the realistic limit on such frequent contact can be managed by patient and therapist. For instance, the therapist really cannot attend to five phone calls a day from a patient; but the patient genuinely feels the need for the contact and reassurance at certain times in the therapy. It is important that the therapist state his or her limits: "I realize you really need to talk with me frequently during the day to feel connected and safe, but I simply cannot physically do it. I wish I had a clone or I had that kind of time, but since I don't, we have to figure out together how to make sure you get what you need and I don't feel so pressured or bad about not being able to be there for you. Together we have to be responsible for making this relationship work for both of us." This is not offered as a technique but as an example of how authentic responsiveness may make more sense than attempting to control or set limits. It is important that people get to know the impact of their actions on others. Patients inevitably must learn to grapple with the frustrations of not always being able to get exactly what they want; but it is essential that people have their needs and desires respected. People must also learn to negotiate conflict in a way that is respectful. In these encounters, patients learn that they can say no, while still caring about the impact of that no on the other person. They also discover in the process that the connection can endure.

The neutral, objective, authoritative stance of a traditional therapist feels dangerous and hurtful to the abuse survivor. This withholding stance can trigger panic and traumatic disconnection. Although all relationships initially feel terrifying for the PTSD patient, where there is authenticity and responsiveness, trust will slowly but, *not* necessarily, steadily grow. In RCT, both members of the therapeutic dyad will learn ways to trust each other; this is a mutual journey. It is natural that anger will be a part of this relationship; carefully modulated and thoughtful sharing of the therapist's anger or frustration will be of use to patients as they struggle to find a voice for their own anger and protest. The "borderline rage" that many talk about is best understood as the pent-up protest about awful relational injury that the child was unable to protect himself or herself from. In tolerating the intensity of this communication and experiencing it as a mere echo of the earlier pain, a deeper appreciation for the patient's suffering develops and leads to enhanced empathic connection. If the therapist can better grasp the terror and helplessness of the child victim, perhaps the therapist will find ways to be with that terrified anger, respect it, and help the patient find useful ways to express it. Therapists must honor both the desire for connection and the strategies of disconnection.

Similarly, the therapist must grasp the depth of shame and isolation that many people with PTSD struggle with. Shame seeks isolation and dwells in silence. It interferes with movement back into relationship. Our shamed parts are the last we want anyone to see or know. In shame, there is no hope for empathic possibility; we feel no one could possibly resonate with us. We are alone in shame. We lack self-empathy and compassion as we blame ourselves for what was done to us. We are disconnected from others and from ourselves.

In working with all of these challenges, therapists need to learn about relationships, relational failures, chronic disconnections, relational images, reestablishing empathic possibility, and relational resilience. We need to find ways to help people move from disconnection to connection. Therein lies hope. To help build connection and create the possibility for reconnection, we must work from a place of deep respect for our patients, with humility about our own efforts and openness to being moved and affected, which creates a nonjudgmental, nondefensive, and empathic presence.

Some of the personality diagnoses seem subtly disrespectful, some explicitly so. There is always the danger of the we-they dichotomy in treatment of patients. Objectification or assuming a position of "better than" is profoundly nonrelational and does not contribute to healing. In fact, it may push the patient into deeper isolation and despair. Often, therapists participate unwittingly in the illusion of having transcended difficulty in their own lives ("Oh yes, I was once a person who suffered and stumbled, but having been through my own therapy, better yet, analysis and training, I am beyond ordinary human suffering. I have achieved 'mental health'"). Mystification enhances the power and idealization about the therapist. Myths about the attainment of what psychoanalysts called "the pure gold of mental health" characterized by impossible standards of independence, strength, and conflict-free functioning shame both the inevitably imperfect therapist and the patient.

AVOIDING THE RETREAT INTO DIAGNOSIS, LABELS, AND THEORY

When we as therapists retreat to absolutes, dictums, categories, theories, or diagnoses in treatment, we probably most need to examine the relationship between therapist and patient. Beginning therapists feel enormous pressure to master a field characterized by uncertainty. As a beginning student said recently: "There was so little I knew about what I was doing. I only had the sense that this was a powerful role, and I was so scared of doing or saying the wrong thing. So I clung to the 'frame' issues of where I placed my chair, where the tissue was, what I would say when they asked where I was going on vacation." I support this student's honesty and truth saying. This is a difficult field to work in, filled as it necessarily is with uncertainty and urgency; it is particularly challenging in a larger cultural context that privileges knowledge, certainty, and agency. The combination of uncertainty and urgency often ignites inflexibility, disconnection, and sometimes arrogance in the therapist. Supervisors need to be sensitive to the tensions involved for beginning therapists who are trying to learn how to help people alleviate their suffering. We all need touchstones, anchors, and comforting guidelines such as, "Well at least I know my chair should be here or I stop exactly at 50 minutes." But when these anchors become elevated to the status of absolutes or knowns, we run the risk of losing our real, clinical responsiveness in the service of the frame. Note again, the therapist's responsiveness is carefully navigated and thoughtfully used in the therapy; so few of the parameters of therapy are knowns in this empirical, complexity-filled field. Attention to clinical judgment and ongoing supervision is essential.

Retreat into theory on the part of the therapist can lead to disconnection and impasse. Similarly, personality disorder diagnoses run the danger of reifying, pathologizing, and objectifying the individual: "She's a hysteric, a borderline, a dependent personality"; "He's a narcissist, a sociopath." Despite the descriptions in *DSM-III* and *DSM-IV*, which should make it clear that relationships play a large part in the pain and dysfunction of the people who carry these diagnoses, the notion is still that these are the most enduring, internal states and that once you have the label, you know what you're dealing with. This can lead to so many misunderstandings, distancing, and, ultimately, impasses. Perhaps we might begin to look at relational dysfunctions rather than personality disorders to aid us in our efforts to alleviate suffering.

The use of all diagnoses stems from a medical model. There are clearly psychological problems that have strong medical, biochemical, and physical components. There is no real separation between chemistry and psychology and no way to answer the ever-present questions about nature versus nurture. The patient in medicine is the physical person, the body host to the organ systems and to invasive organisms. Whereas the environment is seen as affecting the body, it is not seen as "the patient," probably to the detriment of understanding environmental factors in illness and to the detriment of preventive measures. In psychology, "the patient" is so much more complicated: Systems, relationships, and social categories are all involved. Who, what are we treating? What really contributes to change?

EMPIRICAL SUPPORT OF RELATIONAL-CULTURAL THEORY

Data from empirical research increasingly supports the power of connection to protect and to heal. The literature on resilience shows that a connection with one adult (parent or teacher) is the single best protection against high-risk behaviors of drinking, violence, depression, and suicide in adolescents (Resnick et al., 1997). Students who felt connected were less likely to use cigarettes, alcohol, or drugs; less likely to engage in early sexual activity, violence, or become pregnant; and less likely to experience emotional distress. These studies do not point to personality traits or diagnostic categories as the best predictors of outcome; they clearly and strongly point to the centrality of connection.

In addition to empirical findings, the relational-cultural model is based on values; we cannot, nor do we necessarily want to, claim, so-called *objectivity* and freedom from these values. We urge instead awareness of values and biases and their possible impact on observations. RCT values growth-fostering connection, social justice, and appreciation of the power of sociopolitical forces to shape peoples lives; we also acknowledge the importance of community and a model of psychology built on relationship rather than separation. A relational psychology calls for a change of paradigm from one of primary separation to one of primary relatedness, and it seeks to resist the destructive forces of separation and objectification for all people. It seems to me that, in clinical work, humility and an attitude of openness to learning serves us best. The same is true in our model building. It is essential to acknowledge as best we can our biases.

In our theory building as well as in our clinical practices, we need to be responsive to the messages we receive from patients, colleagues, supporters, and critics. Only when we remain interested and open to feedback following mistakes can we provide the possibility of empathic repair with our patients. We do not pretend to possess perfect knowledge; rather than pursuing some ideal of absolute attunement, we need to commit to working on our errors, blind spots, and lack of clarity with others. If the personality diagnoses help a therapist be really present, nondefensive, and curious in the difficult moments, they may serve as benign signposts. If, however, they become sources of objectification or distancing and distortion, they make real connection and healing less likely. Furthermore, if they obfuscate the larger social imbalances and injustices that are creating suffering for large groups of people, their usefulness is seriously compromised. Perhaps we need to keep asking the hard questions: How do the personality disorder diagnoses help? How do they hurt? Is there a better way to assess the human conditions that we seek to illuminate with these diagnoses? And most importantly, how can we further our understanding of how to alleviate human suffering to create personal and social change so that all human beings may live more resilient, satisfying, and connected lives?

SUMMARY AND CONCLUSIONS

Written from the bias of both feminist and relational-cultural psychology, this chapter critiques aspects of the construct of personality disorder. It suggests that personality disorders may be too anchored in a Eurocentric, limiting model of *separate self*. Traditional personality disorder models are built on the notion that separation is the desired and ultimate goal of personality development. They rely heavily on an understanding of personality as constructed of stable internalized traits, and they do not adequately explore the impact of the sociopolitical, cultural context on the individual's functioning. The relational-cultural model offers another way to think about psychopathology.

The relational model emphasizes that we grow in and through connection and seeks to understand relational development rather than personality development. RCT views chronic disconnection and isolation as the source of profound human suffering and what has been called psychopathology. The work of therapy is to bring people back into connection through mutual empathy and empowerment. As chronically disconnected individuals begin to find ways to represent themselves more fully and authentically in relationship with the therapist, they begin to experience *empathic possibility*, the hope that another human being will understand, resonate with, and respond positively to them. The work of therapy is to honor the patient's strategies of disconnection while safety in connection is created. Slowly, the patient relinquishes strategies of disconnection and begins to move out of shame and isolation into the fullness of authentic connection.

Although the relational-cultural model was originally developed to better understand women's experience, it has increasingly been used to understand boys and men, as well as most marginalized groups. It challenges many of the core premises of traditional Western psychology (e.g., the primacy of separation, the illusion of objectivity in the field of human behavior). It is a model that seeks not only to inform individual change in psychotherapy but also social change and a shift in the prevailing highly individualistic paradigm in psychology and ultimately in the dominant North American culture. According to RCT, the need for connection and community and the desire to be part of meaningful, responsive relationships is at the heart of human experience.

REFERENCES

American Psychiatric Association. (1987). *Diagnostic and statistical manual of mental disorders* (3rd ed., rev.). Washington, DC: Author.

American Psychiatric Association. (1994). *Desk Reference to the Diagnostic Criteria from DSM-IV* (4th ed.). Washington, DC: Author.

Banks, A. (2001). *Posttraumatic stress disorder: Relationships and brain chemistry.* (Project Report No. 8). Wellesley, MA: Stone Center Working Paper Series.

Brown, L. S. (2002). Discomforts of the powerless: Feminist constructions of distress. In R. A. Neimeyer & J. D. Rasking (Eds.), *Construction of disorder: Meaning making frameworks for psychotherapy* (pp. 287–308). Washington, DC: American Psychological Association.

Brown, L. S., & Ballou, M. (Eds.). (2002). *Rethinking mental health and disorder: Feminist perspectives.* New York: Guilford Press.

Freud, S. (1955). Beyond the pleasure principle. In J. Strachey (Ed.), *The standard edition of the complete psychological works of Sigmund Freud* (Vol. 18, pp. 3–64). London: Hogarth Press. (Original work published 1920)

Gilligan, C. (1982). *In a different voice.* Cambridge, MA: Harvard University Press.

Herman, J. (1992). *Trauma and recovery.* New York: Basic Books.

Herman, J., & van der Kolk, B. A. (1987). Traumatic antecedents of borderline personality disorder. In B. A. van der Kolk (Ed.), *Psychological trauma* (pp. 111–126). Washington, DC: American Psychiatric Press.

hooks, b. (1984). *Feminist theory from margin to center.* Boston: South End Press.

Jordan, J. V. (1989). *Relational development: Therapeutic implications of empathy and shame* (Work in progress, No. 57). Wellesley, MA: Stone Center Working Paper Series.

Jordan, J. V. (1992). *Relational resilience* (Work in progress, No. 57). Wellesley, MA: Stone Center Working Paper Series.

Jordan, J. V. (1995). Boundaries: A relational perspective. *Psychotherapy Forum, 1*(2), 1–4.

Jordan, J. V. (Ed.). (1997). *Women's growth in diversity.* New York: Guilford Press.

Jordan, J. V. (1999). *Toward connection and competence* (Work in progress, No. 83). Wellesley, MA: Stone Center Working Paper Series.

Jordan, J. V. (2000). The role of mutual empathy in relational: Cultural therapy. *Journal of Clinical Psychology/In Session: Psychotherapy Practice, 56*(80), 1005–1016.

Jordan, J. V. (2002a). *Learning at the margin: New models of strength* (Work in progress, No. 98). Wellesley, MA: Stone Center Working Paper Series.

Jordan, J. V. (2002b). A relational-cultural perspective in therapy. In F. Kazlow (Ed.), *Comprehensive handbook of psychotherapy* (Vol. 3, pp. 233–254). Hoboken, NJ: Wiley.

Jordan, J., & Hartling, L. (2002). New developments in relational-cultural theory. In M. Ballou & L. S. Brown (Eds.), *Rethinking mental health and disorder: Feminist perspectives* (pp. 48–70). New York: Guilford Press.

Jordan, J. V., Kaplan, A. G., Miller, J. B., Stiver, I. P., & Surrey, J. (1991). *Women's growth in connection.* New York: Guilford Press.

Kernberg, O. F. (1975). *Borderline conditions and pathological narcissism.* New York: Aronson.

Kernberg, O. F., Selzer, M. A., Koenigsberg, H., Carr, A., & Appelbaum, A. (1989). *Psychodynamic psychotherapy of borderline patients.* New York: Basic Books.

Klein, M. (with Riviere, J.). (1953). *Love, hate and reparation.* London: Hogarth Press.

Kohut, H. (1984). *How does analysis cure?* Chicago: University of Chicago Press.

Lerman, H. (1996). *Pigeonholing women's misery: A history and critical analysis of the psychodiagnosis of women in the twentieth century.* New York: Basic Books.

McIntosh, P. (1989, July/August). White privilege: Unpacking the invisible knapsack. *Peace and Freedom,* 10–12.

Miller, J. B. (1976). *Toward a new psychology of women.* Boston: Beacon Press.

Miller, J. B., & Stiver, I. P. (1997). *The healing connection: How women form relationships in therapy and in life.* Boston: Beacon Press.

Resnick, M., Bearman, P., Blum, R., Bauman, K., Harris, K., Jones, J., et al. (1997). Protecting adolescents from harm: Findings from the National Longitudinal study of Adolescent Health. *Journal of the American Medical Association, 278*(10), 823–832.

Root, M. (1992). Reconstructing the impact of trauma on personality. In L. S. Brown & M. Ballou (Eds.), *Personality and psychopathology: Feminist reappraisal* (pp. 229–265). New York: Guilford Press.

Russell, D. (1986). *The secret trauma.* New York: Basic Books.

Stone, M. (1980). *The borderline syndromes.* New York: McGraw-Hill.

van der Kolk, B. A. (1988). The trauma spectrum: The interaction of biological and social events in the genesis of the trauma response. *Journal of Traumatic Stress, 1*(3), 273–290.

van der Kolk, B. A. (1996). The complexity of adaptation to trauma: Self regulation, stimulus, discrimination and characterological development. In B. A. van der Kolk, A. C. McFarlane, & L. Weisaeth (Eds.), *Traumatic stress: The effects of overwhelming experience on mind, body and society* (pp. 182–213). New York: Guilford Press.

van der Kolk, B. A., McFarlane, A. C., & Weisaeth, L. (Eds.). (1996). *Traumatic stress: The effects of overwhelming experience on mind, body and society.* New York: Guilford Press.

Walker, M. (1999). *Race, self and society: Relational challenges in a culture of disconnection* (Work in progress, No 85). Wellesley, MA: Stone Center Working Paper Series.

Winnicott, D. (1960). The theory of the parent-infant relationship. *International Journal of Psychoanalysis, 41,* 585–595.

CHAPTER 7

Sociocultural Factors in the Treatment of Personality Disorders

Joel Paris

MENTAL ILLNESS DEVELOPS in a sociocultural context. Disorders can present with different symptoms in different cultures; some categories of illness are seen only in specific societies (Tsai, Butcher, Munoz, & Vitousek, 2001). These principles apply to common psychiatric symptoms such as depression (Kleinman, 1986), and personality disorders should be no exception. Because disorders are pathological amplifications of normal traits (Livesley, Schroeder, Jackson, & Jang, 1994) and because traits demonstrate sociocultural variation, personality disorders can present with different symptoms in different social contexts, and some categories may even be *culture-bound*.

Cross-cultural research sheds light on these issues. The broader dimensions of personality are similar in many different societies, even in cultures as different as North America and contemporary China (McCrae et al., 2001). Although there are differences between cultures in trait intensity, their magnitude is generally no greater than half a standard deviation (Eysenck, 1982). The personality disorders described by *DSM-IV* (American Psychiatric Association [APA], 1994) and ICD-10 (World Health Organization [WHO], 1992) can be identified in clinical settings all over the world (Loranger, Hirschfeld, Sartorius, & Regier, 1991).

Personality disorders are common, and they cause serious morbidity (Skodol et al., 2002). Several studies suggest these disorders have an overall prevalence of about 10% (Samuels et al., in press; Weissman, 1993). Although there is little research on the community prevalence of specific categories, a recent survey (Samuels et al., in press) indicates that antisocial personality is the most common category in community populations. Unfortunately, we lack good epidemiological data on cross-cultural differences in the community prevalence of personality disorders.

PERSONALITY DISORDERS AND
SOCIAL SENSITIVITY

Mental disorders whose prevalence changes with time and circumstance can be described as being *socially sensitive*. Disorders that have a stable prevalence across cultures and time can be described as being *socially insensitive*. Many of the socially sensitive disorders (e.g., substance abuse, eating disorders, antisocial personality, borderline personality) have externalizing symptoms. Impulsive traits, which tend to be contained by structure and limits and amplified by their absence, are particularly responsive to social context. At the same time, disorders characterized by internalizing symptoms (e.g., unipolar depression, anxiety disorders) are also socially sensitive. Anxious and depressive traits can be either contained or amplified by social supports.

The strongest evidence for sociocultural factors in mental disorders comes from epidemiological research documenting changes in prevalence over short periods of time. In particular, impulsive symptoms in adolescents and young adults (substance abuse, antisocial behavior, and depression) have increased, both in North America and Europe, since World War II (Millon, 1993; Paris, 1996; Rutter & Smith, 1995). These cohort effects are paralleled by increases in the prevalence of parasuicide and completed suicide (Bland, Dyck, Newman, & Orn, 1998).

A second line of evidence supporting the role of sociocultural factors in mental disorders comes from cross-cultural studies. Social scientists (e.g., see Lerner, 1958) have distinguished traditional societies, which have high social cohesion, fixed social roles, and intergenerational continuity, from modern societies, with lower social cohesion, fluid social roles, and less continuity between generations. Through history, social structures have usually been traditional. Although there are few societies left in the world that can still be described in this way, some are clearly more traditional than others.

CULTURAL DIFFERENCES AND
YOUNG ADULTHOOD

Socially sensitive disorders characterized by impulsivity tend to be less prevalent in traditional societies. For example, in Taiwan (Hwu, Yeh, & Change, 1989) and Japan (Sato & Takeichi, 1993), there is a low prevalence of substance abuse and antisocial personality among young people. The increasing prevalence of these same disorders among young adults in modern societies suggests that contemporary social conditions may be stressful. Even if many, or most, young people thrive under modernity, a vulnerable minority is at risk for mental disorders.

Socially sensitive disorders tend to begin in adolescence and youth. Although puberty is universal, adolescence as a separate developmental stage is largely a social construction (Furstenberg, 2000). Throughout most of history, young people assumed adult roles earlier in life. Traditionally, people lived in extended families, villages, and tribes and rarely traveled far. Those who did not fit into social structures left early and searched for a niche elsewhere. The majority stayed put, doing the same work as their parents and their grandparents. Most people did not have to search very far to find intimate relationships. Marriage was arranged early in life, with partners chosen from the same or from neighboring communities.

Adolescence emerged only in modern societies, which expect the younger generation to postpone maturity to learn complex skills and to develop their own unique identity. Not everyone is cut out for this challenge. Adolescence is a stressful time for those who are vulnerable to stress. In traditional societies, young people are provided social roles and networks. In modern societies, adolescents give up the protection of assigned roles and networks. They must spend many years learning how to function as adults. Instead of identifying with family and community values, they are expected to find their own, developing a unique identity. Young people rarely do the same work as their parents and must learn necessary skills from strangers. Families may not even understand the nature of their children's careers. Finally, young people are expected to find their own mates. Because there is no guarantee that this search will be successful, the young need to deal with the vicissitudes of mistaken choices, hurtful rejections, and intermittent loneliness.

Contemporary Western culture values individualism, and most of us would be thoroughly miserable in a traditional society. But the situation is different for individuals who are temperamentally vulnerable. How can impulsive adolescents choose a career without structure and guidance? How can moody adolescents deal with the cruelty and rejection of peers without social supports? How can shy adolescents find intimate relationships when they can barely introduce themselves to a stranger? These questions are relevant for understanding some of the causes of personality disorders.

SOCIAL FACTORS IN PERSONALITY DISORDERS

Personality disorders are dysfunctional exaggerations of normal traits. The amplification of traits to disorders depends on a combination of factors: unusually strong temperamental characteristics, psychosocial adversities, as well as discordance between traits and social demands. The following sections examine the role of social factors in four common categories of personality disorder: (1) antisocial, (2) borderline, (3) narcissistic, and (4) avoidant.

1. Antisocial Personality Disorder (ASPD)

The impulsive behavioral patterns seen in ASPD are rooted in temperamental abnormalities that can be observed early in childhood (Caspi, Moffitt, Newman, & Silva, 1996). At the same time, antisocial patients come from dysfunctional families that are unable to establish clear and consistent discipline (Robins, 1966). The role of social factors in ASPD has been supported by surveys (Kessler et al., 1994; Robins & Regier, 1991) showing that the disorder has increased in prevalence in recent decades. As noted previously, ASPD has a low prevalence in traditional societies, such as Taiwan and Japan.

Which factors are responsible for increasing rates of disorder? One likely cultural explanation is that postwar Western society is characterized by the breakdown of social networks, as well as by increases in family dissolution, unbuffered by social supports, such as extended family and community. In contrast, East Asian cultures that have a low prevalence of ASPD have cultural and family structures that are protective against antisocial behavior by maintaining high levels of cohesion. These families are a veritable mirror image of the risk factors for psychopathy: Fathers are strong and authoritative, expectations of children are high, and family loyalty is prized.

2. Borderline Personality Disorder (BPD)

This disorder is rooted in traits of impulsivity and affective instability (Siever & Davis, 1991). These characteristics can become exaggerated in the presence of psychosocial stressors (Paris, 1996). Both impulsivity and affective instability are "socially sensitive." BPD should, therefore, show cohort effects and cross-cultural differences similar to those observed for ASPD. Indirect evidence points to an increasing prevalence of BPD (Millon, 1993; Paris, 1996). A large percentage of youth suicides, which have increased dramatically, can be diagnosed with BPD (Lesage et al., 1994). Parasuicide, a key clinical feature of BPD, is also on the increase (Bland et al., 1998).

The social factors affecting prevalence resemble those previously described for ASPD. BPD becomes more common when there is a higher rate of family breakdown, a loss of social cohesion, and when social roles are less readily available. These stressors have greater effects on those who are temperamentally vulnerable (Paris, 1996). Impulsivity is amplified under circumstances where social structures fail to contain and buffer acting-out behaviors. Decreases in social support, interfering with a normal process of buffering, may also amplify affective instability (Linehan, 1993).

3. Narcissistic Personality Disorder (NPD)

This disorder is rooted in narcissistic traits, amplified by psychosocial stressors (Paris, 1997). Although we have no good community studies of its prevalence, some clinicians (e.g., see Kohut, 1977) have suggested that more cases of NPD are being seen over time.

Social networks are much less cohesive in modern society, and the absence of structure interferes with normal channeling of narcissistic traits into fruitful ambition. The trait of narcissism has probably not changed, but its consequences have. In traditional society, family and community buffered the effects of personal selfishness. On the one hand, modern society rewards individualism. To some degree, it also encourages narcissism. However, when interpersonal relationships are less stable, those who fail to invest in them can become socially isolated.

4. Avoidant Personality Disorder (APD)

This disorder is rooted in anxious traits, amplified to dysfunctional proportions. For example, Kagan (1994) has described a temperamental syndrome of "behavioral inhibition," which can be amplified by overprotective parenting. But most of these cases do not go on to develop APD, which can be understood only in a social context (Paris, 1997).

In a traditional society, anxious traits are buffered when family and community members are available to "cover" for unusually shy individuals. But it is more difficult for shy children to cope in modern society, given its low cohesion and less accessible social roles. As a result, anxious traits are more likely to be disabling, pervasive, and to lead to diagnosable disorders.

CLINICAL IMPLICATIONS OF THE MODEL

Personality disorders are, by definition, chronic. Ultimately, the chronicity of these disorders reflects the underlying stability of traits. As people grow older, their personality gradually becomes more fixed (Costa & McCrae, 1988). The course of time, as well as psychotherapy, may soften or modify traits, but does not produce basic change. Most people come to accept that, as adults, they must work their way around whatever traits they have. But patients with personality disorders have coping strategies that are narrow and fixed and tend to repeat the same mistakes in different forms.

There are two factors behind trait stability. One is the fact that 50% of the variance in personality traits is heritable (Plomin, DeFries, McClearn, & Rutter, 2000). Similar levels of heritability apply to personality disorders (Torgersen et al., 2000). The other factor derives from the effects of social learning (Bandura, 1977) in which self-reinforcing feedback loops emerge between traits and behavior. These risks interact so that family and interpersonal experiences—as well as social context—shape, reinforce, and amplify a genetic-temperamental matrix.

In this context, how should therapists think about treating patients with personality disorders? We do not, at this point, have drugs to change traits. In general, pharmacological interventions have a limited value in this population, in that they reduce symptoms but rarely change dysfunctional behavior (Soloff, 2000). At the same time, psychotherapy has also had a somewhat shaky record in treating personality disorders. Although there have been a multitude of reports from clinicians suggesting that radical change can be achieved, these claims have rarely been supported by evidence. A handful of controlled trials have been carried out, some of which have been subjected to meta-analysis (Perry, Banon, & Ianni, 1999). This area of research is reviewed elsewhere in this book (chapter 23, by Crits-Christoph & Barber), and there have been a number of encouraging findings. However, most data-based reports derive from selected cases; we lack evidence for consistent results in most patients who meet criteria for a personality disorder diagnosis. There are several reasons for this problem, all related to the chronicity of psychopathology. Understanding the past, as in psychodynamic therapy, does not necessarily break well-established feedback loops between traits and behavior. It, therefore, makes sense to apply a cognitive model, as several authors have suggested (e.g., see Beck, Freeman, & Associates, 1990). Some of the best results have emerged from cognitive therapy for borderline personality (e.g., see Linehan, 1993), although we do not know how broadly these findings can be generalized.

Although we can note the impact of social circumstances on personality pathology, this does not necessarily point to a way out for individuals. Nonetheless, a sociocultural perspective on personality disorders suggests a useful context for conducting therapy. The same traits can be adaptive or nonadaptive in different contexts (Beck et al., 1990). Therefore, without changing these characteristics, patients can learn to use them in more effective ways. In other words, although therapy does not change personality, traits can be modified in ways that affect their behavioral expression.

Specifically, patients can learn to make more judicious and selective use of existing traits and put these characteristics to better use. They can capitalize on strong points by selecting environments in which traits are most likely to be useful. For example, individuals with traits of impulsivity may benefit from choosing occupations where rapid reactions to environmental challenges are beneficial. Similarly, individuals with traits of affective instability may choose work in which emotional responsiveness is advantageous. Finally, individuals with traits of social anxiety may benefit from occupations that involve working alone. People can also minimize their weak points by avoiding environments in which traits are not useful.

For example, individuals with traits of impulsivity may choose to avoid situations that require enormous patience and persistence. Similarly, those with traits of affective instability may choose work in which high levels of emotional responsiveness interfere with task performance. Finally, individuals with traits of social anxiety may avoid occupations that require high levels of interaction with strangers.

In considering how to manage patients with personality disorders, we first examine how they improve naturalistically, even without treatment. Recovery is most striking in BPD. About 10% of these patients commit suicide, but the rest improve gradually over time, with less than 10% meeting criteria by age 50 (Paris & Zweig-Frank, 2001; Zweig-Frank & Paris, 2002). These patients eventually learn to modulate behaviors and find more adaptive solutions to problems. The goal of therapy is to speed up this process. But the process by which such a goal is accomplished is very complex.

Psychotherapy is ultimately a form of education. In personality disorders, the curriculum consists of showing patients how to make better and more adaptive use of traits. This process has cognitive, affective, interpersonal, and behavioral components. Formal teaching takes place in the therapist's office. Life outside the sessions is the laboratory. Learning and applying new behaviors to old situations is the homework. But like all teachers, therapists must recognize that learning is different for every student. Modifications in the behavioral expression of personality can be achieved only by taking trait profiles into account. Understanding these characteristics helps the therapist to predict which types of behavioral change will be easiest to master and which types will be most difficult.

These principles for the treatment for personality disorders fit best into a cognitive-behavioral model (Beck et al., 1990; Linehan, 1993; Young, 1999). They also support the importance of structured treatment, as demonstrated by positive results for day treatment programs in personality disorders (Bateman & Fonagy, 1999; Piper, Rosie, & Joyce, 1996). The concept of psychotherapy as trait modification (Paris, 1997, in press) involves four steps:

1. Identifying when traits are maladaptive.
2. Observing emotional states that lead to problematic behaviors.
3. Experimenting with more effective alternatives to see how they work.
4. Practicing new strategies once they are learned.

The following discussion illustrates these principles by describing the treatment of two common personality disorders: the borderline and narcissistic categories.

THERAPY IN BORDERLINE PERSONALITY DISORDER

Treatment requires the modification of two underlying traits: impulsivity and affective instability. To modulate these characteristics, patients need to understand the communicative functions of actions, identify emotional states, and learn alternative ways of handling conflict. These skills are basic elements in Linehan's (1993) dialectical behavior therapy.

The traits associated with borderline personality lead to problems at work or at school. Often, conflicts emerge with supervisors, colleagues, or teachers, who are seen as uncaring or abusive. These perceptions are filtered through all-or-nothing cognitive schema (splitting). These perceptions, typical of borderline patients, involve seeing the world as made up of people who are either unconditionally loving or totally untrustworthy. The therapist must help the borderline to correct such distortions, to see others with normal ambivalence, and to negotiate interpersonal conflict effectively.

Whatever difficulties they have in their intimate lives, borderline patients need a stable and independent source of self-esteem outside the conflictual arena of interpersonal conflict. Follow-up studies show that the ability to work is strongly related to recovery (McGlashan, 1993). Moreover, once work is stabilized, it becomes easier to deal with the problems of intimacy.

Much of the therapy with borderline patients focuses on problems in intimacy: relationships with lovers, with close friends, and with family members. Patients with BPD are quick to move close to other people and quick to be disappointed with them. This pattern, once identified, needs to be modified by learning to slow down emotionally when they meet new people and to take the necessary time to assess their good and bad qualities. Eventually, some borderline patients can learn how to absorb the inevitable disappointments associated with any close relationship.

As shown by long-term follow-up studies (Paris & Zweig-Frank, 2001), about half of patients with BPD improve in spite of failing to establish stable intimacy. This is not necessarily a bad thing. Given their difficulty with these types of relationships, borderline patients need to find alternatives. Sometimes, these attachments are attained through less demanding friendships. Often, given their need for structure, borderline patients benefit from establishing ties to a larger community, making use of social institutions such as religious organizations. These trajectories, observed in naturalistic research on recovery from BPD, can be actively encouraged by therapists.

Impulsivity in BPD is related to suicidality, the most troubling problem in this population. Paradoxically, suicidality has to be tolerated because it is the borderline patient's way of communicating distress. The therapist should respond to suicidal thoughts and behaviors as *communications* to be understood rather than threats to be acted on. Thus, when patients slash their wrists, the therapist should spend more time talking about distress and less time on cutting. Similarly, after an overdose of pills, once medical treatment has been carried out, the therapist should quickly resume the tasks of therapy and explore the circumstances leading up to the attempt. This approach does not ignore suicidality. Rather, it concentrates on what the patient is trying to say through such behaviors. Instead of letting the threat of suicide dominate the agenda of therapy, treatment moves into a problem-solving mode.

Borderline patients show a broad range of impulsive behaviors. They may abuse substances, be sexually promiscuous, or have tantrums in which they destroy property. In each of these situations, the task of the therapist is much the same—to identify underlying emotions and to examine in what alternative way the patient might have handled dysphoria.

Impulsivity in BPD is also associated with behaviors that interfere with the process of therapy itself. Some, such as severe substance abuse, have to be controlled before any substantive therapy can take place. Other common "therapy-interfering behaviors" (Linehan, 1993) can include coming late or missing sessions entirely. At some levels of impulsivity, therapy becomes impossible. The patient needs to know there are limits beyond which treatment may have to be discontinued.

The other aspect of treating BPD involves modulating affective instability. Therapists who work well with borderline patients know how to empathize with their highly dysphoric feelings, even when they are far from ordinary experience. Borderline patients are famous for their anger but are just as likely to be chronically depressed and anxious. Accepting and working with these emotions offers an implicit holding environment for the patient and often provides containment.

Helping borderline patients to manage dysphoric emotions is a central element of any treatment. *Short-range* strategies include distraction and positively reinforcing activities. Each patient has to learn on an individual basis what works best when he or she is upset. *Long-range* strategies involve identifying and solving the problems that produce these emotions. The crucial point is to learn that there are ways, other than impulsive actions, to relieve dysphoria.

THERAPY IN NARCISSISTIC PERSONALITY DISORDER

Grandiosity is the central characteristic of NPD. Life normally modifies these traits. We must all deal with disappointment and failure and come to terms with limitations; this is the essence of maturity. But narcissistic patients have trouble remaining on this trajectory. When they are young, they seem attractive and promising. But as they age, they are unable to deal with losses, so that their later years become marked by disappointment and bitterness (Kernberg, 1987). In spite of overtly high self-esteem, narcissistic individuals tend to "crash" when they fail.

Torgersen (1995) has observed that patients with NPD have a surprisingly high level of dysphoria, largely due to unsatisfactory intimate relationships. Most frequently, they seek treatment after a series of setbacks in intimacy. Torgersen also reported that patients with NPD have unstable long-term relationships, with a low rate of marriage, and a high rate of divorce when they do marry.

Narcissists can have special talents or qualities. Some are successful at work and have serious difficulties only in intimate relationships. Others also fail to meet expectations at the workplace. These difficulties result from a lack of persistence and an inability to collaborate with others. Narcissistic patients also tend to respond to negative feedback with anger, a reaction that makes bad situations worse. They may not understand that other people's evaluations are often valid.

Narcissists are strikingly lacking in empathy. One of the primary goals of therapy is to teach this skill. This is not easy because individuals with low empathy fail to observe how their behavior affects other people. They also present distorted or self-serving versions of events to the therapist. Unless patients learn to take responsibility for their mistakes, they will continue to make the same ones. This is one reason that therapy for this group is so often ineffective and/or interminable.

The concept of a healing empathic environment (Kohut, 1977) is in accord with research on the role of nonspecific factors in successful therapy. But by itself, empathy from a therapist is rarely sufficient to control consistently maladaptive behavior. Often, the most crucial interventions involve demonstrating the consequences of narcissistic behavior. These patients require confrontations to identify problem behaviors and to develop adaptive alternatives.

Narcissistic patients typically believe that their personality does not need to change very much and that other people should treat them better. Thinking well of yourself without brooding unduly on your defects can be associated with success, but patients come for treatment when these traits stop working for them, usually in intimate relationships.

Therapists must be cautious about validating the worldview of the narcissist. Usually, we lack sufficient information to determine how these patients are actually behaving. Like borderline patients, they can present the therapist with a distorted picture of their interpersonal world. It takes a good deal of skill to read between the lines and reconstruct what actually happened. Sometimes the picture remains cloudy and can only be clarified by interviewing key informants.

The most difficult problem in treating NPD involves getting patients to identify maladaptive patterns. Tactful confrontations are needed to help these patients perceive and acknowledge problems. They also have to be taught how to see interpersonal conflicts from other people's points of view and not to attribute other people's reactions to neglect or malevolence. Narcissistic patients are often poor at knowing what other people want and negotiating compromises so that each person gets to meet some portion of their needs. At the same time, they need to see that self-serving behaviors work to their own disservice. Finally, in parallel with the problems seen in impulsive patients with borderline personality, narcissism can be tamed by commitments to social institutions and to causes that lie outside their immediate interest. These attachments, which are less demanding and conflictual than intimate relationships, have a stabilizing effect and should be encouraged by therapists.

THE ROLE OF SOCIAL STRUCTURES IN THE TREATMENT OF PATIENTS WITH PERSONALITY DISORDERS

The social factors affecting personality disorders are structurally rooted in modern society and cannot be changed by clinicians. Thus, patients with personality disorders have difficulty in finding social roles and are more likely to recover if they establish such roles. But there is no way to provide a full range of opportunities for patients. Nor can we offer them the structures provided by traditional families and communities. Nonetheless, personality-disordered patients usually benefit from establishing better social networks and supports. Therefore, clinicians can encourage their patients to establish more connections with community organizations. Support groups, often based on the model of Alcoholics Anonymous, target individuals suffering from social isolation.

Patients in the A cluster (schizoid, schizotypal, paranoid) are particularly difficult to manage. They do not often seek psychotherapy, and we lack data demonstrating that it is useful for them. Most of these patients are not capable of sustained relationships but would benefit most from steady employment, preferably in settings that are interpersonally undemanding.

In traditional societies, some of these individuals might have worked as farmhands, and others might have obtained employment in factories. Thus, the current job market works against their mental health because postindustrial society, with its service economy, has fewer positions that require repetitive attention to a task. These jobs demand the very cognitive and interpersonal skills that these patients lack. As a result, Cluster A patients are likely to be marginal and unemployed.

For patients in Cluster B, psychotherapy is difficult, but remains the mainstay of treatment planning. (The main exception is ASPD, patients who rarely benefit from talking therapy, and those who are usually managed in the criminal justice system.)

Treatment of Cluster B patients must be pragmatic. In one long-term outcome study of BPD (Bardenstein & McGlashan, 1989), the ability to work was most strongly associated with stable recovery, whereas a greater investment in intimate relationships led to even more instability. Many patients have experienced insufficient structures in family life and in their social milieu. They need greater structure in their lives and in their therapy. Social structures that encourage persistence, competence, and achievement in work, as well as secure attachments in intimate relationships, can help Cluster B patients become less dependent on ephemeral reinforcers, such as sexual attractiveness or power. Therapists also need to help narcissistic patients by increasing commitments to work, relationships, and community—external structures that often act as buffers for narcissism.

Patients in Cluster C present a different set of problems. Their anxiety leads to long-term social difficulties that are self-reinforcing. One of the most important clinical issues involves preventing these patients from using avoidance, dependence, and procrastination in the therapy situation. Nonetheless, social networks can be important in planning treatment. Not all lonely people, with or without diagnosable personality disorders, are capable of establishing stable intimacy. For this reason, it is particularly important for them to find other satisfactions in life. They require stable and reasonably satisfying employment, as well as a social network consisting of less intimate extrafamilial attachments.

There is great individual variability in personality traits, as well as variation in what people need to feel fulfilled in their lives. Some patients attain the ultimate mental health goals (love and work), whereas others do not. When faced with patients with a diagnosis of personality disorder, treatment goals can be realistic and modest. It might even be useful to think about personality-disordered patients in the same way as we view those with other chronic disorders. If there are biological factors that prevent adaptation, treatment methods might be framed in terms of rehabilitation, that is, helping those who lack adaptive skills to meet social expectations. Clinicians need to take account of the depth of pathology in the personality disorders and consider partial recoveries as successes.

SUMMARY AND CONCLUSION

It is imperative to consider the sociocultural contributions in conceptualizing and treating personality disorders. Various personality traits can be modified, but in cases where this is difficult, patients can learn to put these characteristics to better use. Although many commonalities among these disorders exist cross-culturally, modern society shapes their expression with the concomitant loss of social cohesion and traditional social structures. Clinicians who are familiar with a sociocultural context are more adapt at conducting effective therapy.

REFERENCES

American Psychiatric Association. (1994). *Diagnostic and statistical manual of mental disorders* (4th ed.). Washington, DC: Author.

Bandura, A. (1977). *Social learning theory.* Englewood Cliffs, NJ: Prentice-Hall.

Bardenstein, K. K., & McGlashan, T. H. (1989). The natural history of a residentially treated borderline sample: Gender differences. *Journal of Personality Disorders, 3,* 69–83.

Bateman, A., & Fonagy, P. (1999). Effectiveness of partial hospitalization in the treatment of borderline personality disorder: A randomized controlled trial. *American Journal of Psychiatry, 156,* 1563–1569.

Beck, A. T., Freeman, A., & Associates. (1990). *Cognitive therapy of personality disorders.* New York: Guilford Press.

Bland, R. C., Dyck, R. J., Newman, S. C., & Orn, H. (1998). Attempted suicide in Edmonton. In A. A. Leenaars, S. Wenckstern, I. Sakinofsky, R. J. Dyck, M. J. Kral, & R. C. Bland (Eds.), *Suicide in Canada* (pp. 136–150). Toronto, Ontario, Canada: University of Toronto Press.

Caspi, A., Moffitt, T. E., Newman, D. L., & Silva, P. A. (1996). Behavioral observations at age three predict adult psychiatric disorders: Longitudinal evidence from a birth cohort. *Archives of General Psychiatry, 53,* 1033–1039.

Costa, P. T., & McCrae, R. R. (1988). From catalog to Murray's needs and the five factor model. *Journal of Personality and Social Psychology, 55,* 258–265.

Eysenck, H. J. (1982). Culture and personality abnormalities. In I. Al-Issa (Ed.), *Culture and psychopathology* (pp. 277–308). Baltimore: University Park Press.

Furstenberg, F. F. (2000). The sociology of adolescence and youth in the 1990s: A critical commentary. *Journal of Marriage and the Family, 62,* 896–910.

Hwu, H. G., Yeh, E. K., & Change, L. Y. (1989). Prevalence of psychiatric disorders in Taiwan defined by the Chinese Diagnostic Interview Schedule. *Acta Psychiatrica Scandinavica, 79,* 136–147.

Kagan, J. (1994). *Galen's prophecy.* New York: Basic Books.

Kernberg, O. F. (1987). *Severe personality disorders.* New York: Basic Books.

Kessler, R. C., McGonagle, K. A., Nelson, C. B., Hughes, M., Eshelman, S., Wittchen, H. U., et al. (1994). Lifetime and 12-month prevalence of *DSM-III-R* psychiatric disorders in the United States. *Archives of General Psychiatry, 51,* 8–19.

Kleinman, A. (1986). *Social origins of distress and disease.* New Haven, CT: Yale University Press.

Kohut, H. (1977). *The restoration of the self.* New York: International Universities Press.

Lerner, D. (1958). *The passing of traditional society.* New York: Free Press.

Lesage, A. D., Boyer, R., Grunberg, F., Morrisette, R., Vanier, C., Morrisette, R., et al. (1994). Suicide and mental disorders: A case control study of young men. *American Journal of Psychiatry, 151,* 1063–1068.

Linehan, M. M. (1993). *Dialectical behavioral therapy of borderline personality disorder.* New York: Guilford Press.

Livesley, W. J., Schroeder, M. L., Jackson, D. N., & Jang, K. (1994). Categorical distinctions in the study of personality disorder: Implications for classification. *Journal of Abnormal Psychology, 103,* 6–17.

Loranger, A. W., Hirschfeld, R. M. A., Sartorius, N., & Regier, D. A. (1991). The WHO/ADAMHA International Pilot Study of Personality Disorders: Background and purpose. *Journal of Personality Disorders, 5,* 296–306.

McCrae, R. R., Yang, J., Costa, P. T., Dai, X., Yao, S., Cai, T., et al. (2001). Personality profiles and the prediction of categorical personality disorders. *Journal of Personality, 69,* 155–174.

McGlashan, T. H. (1993). Implications of outcome research for the treatment of borderline personality disorder. In J. Paris (Ed.), *Borderline personality disorder: Etiology and treatment* (pp. 235–260). Washington, DC: American Psychiatric Press.

Millon, T. (1993). Borderline personality disorder: A psychosocial epidemic. In J. Paris (Ed.), *Borderline personality disorder: Etiology and treatment* (pp. 197–210). Washington, DC: American Psychiatric Press.

Paris, J. (1996). *Social factors in the personality disorders.* Cambridge, UK: Cambridge University Press.

Paris, J. (1997). *Working with traits.* Northvale, NJ: Aronson.

Paris, J. (in press). *Personality disorders over time.* Washington, DC: American Psychiatric Press.

Paris, J., & Zweig-Frank, H. (2001). A twenty-seven year follow-up of borderline patients. *Comprehensive Psychiatry, 42,* 482–487.

Perry, J. C., Banon, E., & Ianni, F. (1999). Effectiveness of psychotherapy for personality disorders. *American Journal of Psychiatry, 156,* 1312–1321.

Piper, W. E., Rosie, J. S., & Joyce, A. S. (1996). *Time-limited day treatment for personality disorders: Integration of research and practice in a group program.* Washington, DC: American Psychological Association.

Plomin, R., DeFries, J. C., McClearn, G. E., & Rutter, M. M. (2000). *Behavioral genetics: A primer* (3rd ed.). New York: Freeman.

Robins, L. N. (1966). *Deviant children grown up.* Baltimore: Williams & Wilkins.

Robins, L. N., & Regier, D. A. (Eds.). (1991). *Psychiatric disorders in America.* New York: Free Press.

Rutter, M., & Smith, D. J. (1995). *Psychosocial problems in young people.* Cambridge, MA: Cambridge University Press.

Samuels, J., Eaton, W. W., Bienvenu, O. J., Brown, C. H., Costa, P. T., & Nestadt, G. (in press). Prevalence and correlates of personality disorders in a community sample. *British Journal of Psychiatry.*

Sato, T., & Takeichi, M. (1993). Lifetime prevalence of specific psychiatric disorders in a general medicine clinic. *General Hospital Psychiatry, 15,* 224–233.

Siever, L. J., & Davis, K. L. (1991). A psychobiological perspective on the personality disorders. *American Journal of Psychiatry, 148,* 1647–1658.

Skodol, A. E., Gunderson, J. G., McGlashan, T. H., Dyck, I. R., Stout, R. L., Bender, D. S., et al. (2002). Functional impairment in patients with schizotypal, borderline, avoidant, or obsessive-compulsive personality disorder. *American Journal of Psychiatry, 159,* 276–283.

Soloff, P. H. (2000). Psychopharmacological treatment of borderline personality disorder. *Psychiatric Clinics North America, 23,* 169–192.

Torgersen, S. (1995, June). *Correlates of personality disorder diagnoses.* Presentation to International Society for the Study of Personality Disorders, Dublin, Ireland.

Torgersen, S., Lygren, S., Oien, P. A., Skre, I., Onstad, S., Edvardsen, J., et al. (2000). A twin study of personality disorders. *Comprehensive Psychiatry, 41,* 416–425.

Tsai, J. L., Butcher, J. N., Munoz, R. F., & Vitousek, K. (2001). Culture, ethnicity, and psychopathology. In H. C. Adams & P. B. Sutker (Eds.), *Comprehensive handbook of psychopathology* (pp. 105–127). New York: Kluwer Academic/Plenum.

Weissman, M. M. (1993, Spring). The epidemiology of personality disorders: A 1990 update. *Journal of Personality Disorders* (Suppl. 7), 44–62.

World Health Organization. (1992). *International classification of diseases* (10th ed.). Geneva, Switzerland: Author.

Young, J. E. (1999). *Cognitive therapy for personality disorders: A schema-focused approach* (3rd ed.). Sarasota, FL: Professional Resource Press.

Zweig-Frank, H., & Paris, J. (2002). Predictors of outcomes in a 27 year follow-up of patients with borderline personality disorder. *Comprehensive Psychiatry, 43,* 103–107.

CONTEMPORARY PSYCHOTHERAPEUTIC TREATMENT MODELS

Interpersonal Reconstructive Therapy (IRT) for Individuals with Personality Disorder

Lorna Smith Benjamin

INTERPERSONAL RECONSTRUCTIVE THERAPY (IRT; Benjamin, 2003) is designed to promote change in the nonresponder population, which includes, but is not limited to, individuals with personality disorder. In this chapter, principles of IRT are summarized and then illustrated by the case of Jillian, a psychiatric inpatient with a long history of "borderline" behaviors.

THEORETICAL COMPONENTS OF THE MODEL

The theoretical components of the IRT model are summarized in terms of the underlying theory of psychopathology and the theory of change.

THEORY OF PSYCHOPATHOLOGY

Interpersonal reconstructive therapy draws heavily on Bowlby's (1969, 1977) observations on the role of attachment in human development. His perspective is clinically compelling and has received broad support in many research contexts (Cassidy & Shaver, 1999). Applications of attachment theory in IRT concentrate on two of Bowlby's propositions. First, basic security is most affected by reliable proximity to the caregiver and by what Harlow and Harlow (1967) called "contact comfort." Second, experiences with caregivers shape children's internal working models of self and others. The case formulation method in IRT requires that presenting problems be linked to internal working models and that internal working

---

This chapter derives from and summarizes portions of L. S. Benjamin (2003). *Interpersonal Reconstructive Therapy: Promoting Change in Nonresponders.* New York: Guilford Press.

models be connected to relationships with specific loved ones. The IRT treatment method seeks to transform those internal working models in a way that allows the patient to become free to behave in new, more desirable ways.

Interpersonal reconstructive therapy theory operationalizes the definition of internal working models and provides specific methods to link them to presenting problems. In its most formal form, the case formulation method uses Structural Analysis of Social Behavior (SASB; Benjamin, 1979) to define and link key figures to presenting problems (Benjamin, 2003, chapters 2, 4, and appendix 4). Links involve one or more of three copy processes:

1. Be like him or her.
2. Act as if he or she is still there and in control.
3. Treat yourself as he or she treated you.

The three copy processes have these respective names: identification, recapitulation, and introjection. Using the SASB model and an early version of IRT procedures, Benjamin (1996) proposed that each of the symptoms of the *DSM-IV* personality disorders can be accounted for by specific copy processes usually found in their respective prototypic interpersonal histories. For example, if a child lives with a parent who unrealistically adores and serves him or her, the child is likely to develop a "pervasive pattern of grandiosity, a need for admiration, and lack of empathy," as is characteristic of Narcissistic Personality Disorder defined in the *DSM-IV* (American Psychiatric Association [APA], 1994).

Copying exists in normal as well as disordered individuals. The SASB model defines *normal* in terms of behaviors that are friendly and that show moderate degrees of enmeshment (one person is in control and the other submits) and differentiation (one person emancipates and the other separates). Pathological behavior includes characteristic positions that are hostile and/or that are extremely enmeshed or differentiated. A normal person can be hostile or extreme, too, but only in appropriate time-limited contexts. By contrast, a disordered person is characteristically hostile or occupies positions of extreme enmeshment or differentiation regardless of context. For example, consider the characteristic positions of personality-disordered individuals. Paranoid and antisocial patients are characteristically hostile. Schizoid and avoidant persons show extreme differentiation. Borderline, histrionic, dependent, and obsessive-compulsive individuals too often can be described as extremely enmeshed. Passive-aggressive and narcissistic persons are likely to alternate between the extremes of enmeshment and differentiation.

A core assumption in IRT is that copy processes are maintained by the wish that the internal working models, called *important persons and their internalized representations* (IPIRs), will forgive, forget, apologize, wake up, make restitution, relent—or otherwise make it possible for there to be rapprochement and blissful reunion. The usually unconscious plan in relation to the internalizations is that by providing living testimony to the IPIR's rules and values, the IPIR will become more loving, affirming, and nurturing. For example, the child who identifies with the parent is saying, "See, I am just like you. I agree with your views and apply them to myself. I love you so much. Please love me." The child who recapitulates the patterns he or she showed with the parent "says" to the internalization, "I love you so much, I agree to maintain the rules and values we always had. I hope I am doing it well enough to receive more and better love from you."

Children who treat themselves as the parent or other caregiver treated them engage in similar emotional logic.

These often unconscious wishes to be affirmed by, to achieve psychic proximity to the IPIRs, is called the *gift of love* (GOL). This may seem to be a strange interpretation for cases that engage in endless destruction of self and others. How can hostile and self-destructive patterns be based on love? Unfortunately, the conceptual problem is not whether, but why this is so. Copy process connections to relationships with attachment figures usually become apparent when IRT procedures for case formulation are followed. Even when the relationship to an IPIR seems dominated by pain, patients acknowledge copy process and the gift of love with remarks such as: "I thought I hated him, but I see that I am just like him. That really upsets me. But, you know, he *is* my father. I do love him."

In IRT, pathological patterns that are driven by wishes to have proximity to and the love of IPIRs are named the *regressive loyalist* or the *Red*. Therapy goal behaviors, which are the normative patterns of friendliness and moderate enmeshment or differentiation, are called the *growth collaborator* or the *Green*. A conflict between the Red and the Green is always present. For the nonresponder population, the Red part is disproportionately large. The goal of IRT therapy is to reduce the magnitude of the Red and enhance the Green to the point where the patient is comfortable relating to self and others in normal ways.

An IRT case formulation must be developed in collaboration with and confirmed by the patient, else it is incomplete. Because the case formulation is so central to the choice of interventions, it is vital to revise and update it if warranted by the continuing therapy narrative. Often, changes in the case formulation involve the addition of IPIRs, such as a big brother or a grandmother, to the original formulation.

THEORY OF CHANGE

Because the patient's relationship with the internalization sustains the problem patterns, treatment focuses consistently on activities that facilitate grieving and letting go of the residuals of Red attachments so that the Green parts can grow stronger. The overall IRT therapy process is described simply by *The Learning Speech*: "Therapy involves learning about your patterns, where they are from and what they are for. Understanding your patterns might lead you to decide to change, and then you can begin work on learning new patterns that may work better for you" (Benjamin, 2003, chapter 3).

The most difficult phase of IRT is enabling the wish to change. The patient has to decide to let go of the wishes and grieve the loss of what never was and never can be (or cannot again be) so that he or she can be more appropriately present in the here and now. Once the fantasies in relation to the internalization are abandoned, opportunities for learning more constructive alternatives can be used to provide new emotional learning for how to relate to others in ways that have a chance to result in reciprocal and genuine (i.e., uncoerced) love and affection.

RANGE OF PSYCHOPATHOLOGY AND PERSONALITY DISORDERS WITHIN SCOPE OF TREATMENT

Interpersonal reconstructive therapy was designed for use with the so-called nonresponder population, defined as individuals who have not responded to treatment with medications or psychotherapy. It has long been recognized that personality-disordered individuals are likely to be nonresponders (Shea, 1993). More recently, there has been additional concern about treatment-resistant depression (Thase, Friedman, & Howland, 2001). There is considerable discussion in the literature about what makes a nonresponder unresponsive. It is commonly thought that the right mix of medications (cocktail) or the development of better drugs will resolve this problem. There is no doubt that medications are becoming increasingly effective, but IRT theory holds that loyalty to IPIRs trumps all available chemistry. When the relationship with the internalization is appropriately modified, nonresponders can become more responsive to medication in general.

IRT is most appropriate for treatment-resistant cases of personality disorder and for Axis I disorders that are comorbid with personality disorder, such as depression, anxiety, or certain forms of thought disorder such as delusions, dissociations, and transient hallucinations. Detail on how to link Axis I and Axis II problems appears in Benjamin, 2003, chapter 2. Because IRT fundamentally is a learning process, it is not appropriate for individuals whose capacity to learn is compromised. It is, therefore, not appropriate for individuals with severely limited cognitive skills—whether the limitations are due to trauma or inherited factors that compromise learning ability. Uncontrolled use of drugs or alcohol also interferes with IRT, so users are required to participate successfully in concurrent programs designed specifically for management of substance abuse.

TREATMENT METHODS AND TECHNICAL ASPECTS OR INTERVENTIONS

Interpersonal reconstructive therapy provides flowcharts for developing a case formulation (Benjamin, 2003; figures 2–1, 2–2, & 2–3), for transforming relationships with the IPIRs (figure 3–2), for coming "unstuck" (figure 3–3), and for crisis management (figures 7–1 & 3–4). These procedures are executed by following a core algorithm, which has six rules:

1. Work from a baseline of accurate empathy.
2. Support the growth collaborator (Green) more than the regressive loyalist (Red).
3. Relate every intervention to the case formulation.
4. Seek concrete illustrative detail about input, response, impact on self.
5. Include the ABCs: Affect (A), Behavior (B), and Cognition (C).
6. Relate each intervention to one or more of five therapy steps (Benjamin, 2003; figure 3–1).

Each of the five therapy steps requires activities that facilitate self-discovery (psychodynamic techniques) and self-management (cognitive-behavioral techniques). These five steps are:

1. Collaboration (the therapy relationship).
2. Learning about patterns, where they are from, and what they are for (insight).
3. Blocking problem patterns (crisis and stalemate management).

4. Enabling the will to change in steps that compare to Prochaska's transtheoretical stages of change (Prochaska, DiClemente, & Norcross, 1992).
5. Learning new patterns (via standard behavioral technology).

The core algorithm, including the five steps, is illustrated by the case of Jillian.

PROCESS OF THERAPEUTIC CHANGE

The process of therapeutic change will be illustrated by a clinical case example discussed in terms of: her current living situation and circumstances, background and history, clinical presentation, diagnostic formulation, treatment process, and a dialogue that illustrates the basic components of the model.

CLINICAL CASE EXAMPLE

Jillian was a 26-year-old married, Caucasian female, who was bonded as a housekeeper but not currently employed. Jillian had not finished high school and, at age 16, married an unfaithful and violent man, whom she soon divorced. At the time of her present hospitalization, she was living with a female roommate while her second husband worked overseas for an oil company. The marital relationship had been stormy, largely because of the husband's reported infidelity. For example, when Jillian discovered him with another woman, she assaulted the intruder and broke her jaw.

BACKGROUND AND HISTORY

Jillian grew up with her mother, older brother, younger sister, and stepfather. Her mother had divorced her biological father when Jillian was a baby, and the patient hardly ever saw him. Jillian was fond of her mother, saying "She is the only one I can trust," but her mother was rarely home because she had to work to support the family. This left Jillian in the care of an older brother, who was somewhat abusive. Her stepfather insisted the house be in perfect order, else there would be yelling and violent beatings. Often unemployed, he was fond of alcohol and frequently woke the children in the night as he carried on about missing items of his that they were to find in this "mess of a house." When they could not produce the requested items, the beatings followed. Because Jillian did not finish high school, the stepfather refused to speak to her for years and had forbidden her to visit the family home. She was hurt by the fact that her mother had not overruled him in this.

CLINICAL PRESENTATION

Jillian had multiple hospitalizations, a record of assaulting others followed by jail time, a pattern of cutting herself, chronic suicidal ideation, and debilitating depression. She was admitted to the hospital this time for detoxification from pain medications and for escalating suicidal ideation. There were many signs of depression, including increased irritability, weight loss, and fatigue. She was highly stressed by severe financial difficulties. Shortly before her admission, she had an argument with an officer at the bank that stemmed from her opinion that he had arbitrarily and unfairly frozen her account and then angrily cut three neat slashes on her arm. She said she felt better afterward.

DIAGNOSTIC FORMULATION

Jillian had been diagnosed with Bipolar Disorder (aggressiveness without mania) on two previous hospitalizations and presently met criteria for Major Depressive Disorder, severe. Despite the affective volatility and instability that was suggestive of Borderline Personality Disorder (BPD), Jillian was better described by the label Oppositional Disorder—a *DSM-IV* category closely related to the description of Passive Aggressive Personality Disorder (PAG) from the *DSM-III-R* (APA, 1987). Her patterns that were independent of mood disorder and that supported this label included the following specific *DSM-IV* items: (1) She often lost her temper, (3) she typically refused to comply with rules and requests, (5) she frequently blamed others for her mistakes or misbehavior, (6) she was touchy and easily annoyed by others, (7) she was often angry and resentful. The proper way to define the PAG category has been so controversial that in the *DSM-IV*, it was moved from Axis II in the *DSM-III-R* to a provisional category marked for further research. Nonetheless, Benjamin's (1996) interpersonal translation of the *DSM-IV* description of PAG often applies to nonresponders, including Jillian. According to IRT, the treatment implications for BPD and for PAG are different, so the distinction is important and is discussed later. The following discussion is a simplified version of the IRT-based case formulation for Jillian.

Jillian's financial situation was so dire that she felt helpless, angry, and depressed enough to be driven to cut herself and contemplate suicide. She attributed her situation to her husband's dereliction of duty and to the fact that her grandmother would not help her even as she generously supported others in the family. Jillian's early learning had fostered the perception that demands on her would be unreasonable (e.g., stepfather's relentless perfectionistic and unreasonable demands), and they would be backed up by extreme violence (attacks from stepfather and brother). Moreover, people who could and should be helping (mother, grandmother) would not. After she burned out from trying to meet impossible expectations, Jillian had adopted the strategy of resisting coercion at all costs. Following demands of a boss at work, for example, was out of the question. Like her brother and stepfather, she was willing to use violence to make her point when necessary.

Given that her husband had abandoned her physically, financially, and emotionally and that creditors were making strong demands she could not meet, Jillian felt enraged, helpless, and depressed. Cutting herself after the bank refused to help was, in her mind, a way of showing them, like her stepfather, how much harm they had done. Cutting and the ultimate escape through suicide might make him sorry and perhaps would be followed by amends-making. In this way, she could "win by losing," which is the mantra for individuals with PAG. It felt good to deliver that message, however fanciful the medium of communication. If the PAG kills the individual, however, there can be no reunion and rapprochement. However, PAG after-death fantasies often include features that do support the plan.

This brief case formulation attempts, then, to relate as many of the presenting problems as possible to Jillian's IPIRs. It touches on her chronic unemployment, aggressiveness, depression, cutting, and suicidality. The idea that she will be guided by a strategy of winning by losing (in relation to authorities and care-givers who are seen as abusive and negligent) has significant impact on the choice of interventions in IRT (Benjamin, 1996, chapter 11). An individual with BPD has an altogether different agenda (Benjamin, 1996, chapter 5).

TREATMENT PROCESS

While an inpatient, Jillian was treated with an antipsychotic medication, antide-pressants, and a variety of anxiolyics in an effort to find a combination to which she might show more favorable responses. Although she had been in outpatient therapy for some time, Jillian had been highly dismissive of and unreliable in her participation in psychotherapy, as well as in her compliance with medications prescribed. During hospitalization, she was seen for a consultation with me and then treated for the balance of her stay in the hospital by an IRT therapist in train-ing. At discharge, Jillian gave that therapist maximally high ratings on a service satisfaction measure. The IRT treatment narrative that follows focuses only on her cutting and suicidal behaviors and is based on material gathered during Jillian's case formulation consultation. Because she had only a brief inpatient treatment, some of the therapy exchanges in the vignette here represent a concatenation of events from PAG cases that have successfully completed IRT over a much longer period of time.

PATIENT-THERAPIST DIALOGUE THAT ILLUSTRATES
RULES IN THE CORE ALGORITHM

The vignette demonstrates IRT procedures that usually bring rapid management of cutting behavior in individuals with PAG:

1. **JILLIAN:** After the bank officer said I could not have access to my account, I was so frustrated, I went home and took a knife and cut on myself as hard as I could.
2. **THERAPIST:** You felt completely blocked and helpless.
3. **JILLIAN:** Yes, I was furious. I was beside myself.
4. **THERAPIST:** So when the bank officer unfairly withheld what was due you, you became so outraged, you had to cut on yourself.
5. **JILLIAN:** Yes.
6. **THERAPIST:** Can you say more about your feelings and thoughts just before you cut on yourself?
7. **JILLIAN:** It was so unfair. I just could not stand it.
8. **THERAPIST:** So the unfairness of it hurt the most. Do you have any idea why cutting on yourself helped you feel better?
9. **JILLIAN:** No.
10. **THERAPIST:** I believe this must somehow make sense. May we try to figure this out?
11. **JILLIAN:** I suppose so.
12. **THERAPIST:** Good. So let's imagine the bank officer could somehow know what you did after talking to him. What do you imagine he would think and feel?

13. **JILLIAN:**   I don't know if he would, but he ought to know that he really hurt me when he was so unfair.

14. **THERAPIST:**   So the most painful part of this is the unfairness. It would be good if he knew how much he harmed you.

15. **JILLIAN:**   Yes. That is exactly it.

16. **THERAPIST:**   In other words, you cut on yourself to let an unfair person know the harmful consequences of his action.

17. **JILLIAN:**   Yes.

18. **THERAPIST:**   How do you feel about that?

19. **JILLIAN:**   Really angry.

20. **THERAPIST:**   I believe that anger has a purpose, and usually it is either to help a person gain control, or it is to create some distance. If that is true, what might your anger be for?

21. **JILLIAN:**   Control. I want to control him.

22. **THERAPIST:**   How should that control work?

23. **JILLIAN:**   Well, he should see what he has done, feel bad about it, and then let me have my money.

24. **THERAPIST:**   Okay, so in your mind, hurting yourself punishes him by showing him how harmful he was, and should make him become more helpful.

25. **JILLIAN:**   Well yeah, but it does not work that way.

26. **THERAPIST:**   Right. In fact, it got you here in the hospital.

27. **JILLIAN:**   Maybe so. But I hope to get some help here.

28. **THERAPIST:**   Okay, it can be helpful to learn about your patterns, where they are from, and what they are for. Once you see that clearly, you might decide to try other ways of responding—ones that might work better for you.

29. **JILLIAN:**   Yeah . . .

30. **THERAPIST:**   So let's see if we can understand better what this pattern is and where it is from. I expect that it does make sense.

31. **JILLIAN:**   Okay.

32. **THERAPIST:**   Remember how you felt when he said no, and you became so angry at the unfairness of it. Is that a familiar feeling for you?

33. **JILLIAN:**   Yeah. I have it often.

34. **THERAPIST:**   Can you remember an earlier experience that felt like this?

35. **JILLIAN:**   Sure. With my stepdad. He would get all mad at us if we could not find his checkbook for him. He'd smack us around and say we could not have allowance for three weeks. We hadn't touched his checkbook, but it did not matter. If he couldn't find what he wanted, we had to pay. And Mom was intimidated by him so she couldn't help.

36. **THERAPIST:**   So withholding your money unfairly and hurting you physically when you had done nothing wrong was something he often did to you.

37. **JILLIAN:**   For sure.

38. **THERAPIST:**   Do you see any connection here? For no good reason, somebody withholds your money and you get punished physically.

39. **JILLIAN:**   Maybe. I see the bank guy didn't give me the money, and I hurt myself.

40. **THERAPIST:**   Loss of money that is yours and painful punishment go together in your experience.

41. **JILLIAN:**   Yes. It happened a lot.

42. **THERAPIST:**   So with the bank officer, you re-created the pattern you had so often with your stepfather. In your mind, hurting yourself punished and hurt him, just as your stepfather used to punish and hurt you.

43. **JILLIAN:**   I never thought of it that way.

44. **THERAPIST:**   You know what you know. You have taken in your stepfather's rules here. His rule was that he could unfairly accuse and punish you by taking away your money as he hurt you physically, too. So that is what you did when the bank officer refused to let you have what you are certain was yours. In your mind, you hurt yourself as your stepfather would, and at the same time, you were trying to punish him, too. Does that make sense?

45. **JILLIAN:**   Yes.

46. **THERAPIST:**   How do you feel about that?

47. **JILLIAN:**   Awful. I hate the idea that I am being like him in any way.

48. **THERAPIST:**   Good. Let's agree to work on developing your own rules and your own ways of dealing with a situation like this. For starters, how about remembering that hurting yourself to punish him really represents letting him decide on the rules that govern your behavior.

49. **JILLIAN:**   I can't let him do that to me.

50. **THERAPIST:**   So let's see if you can take control of your own mind. Let's step aside from the feelings you need to be punished, combined with the need to punish the one who is unfair to you, and work on figuring out less self-destructive ways you might deal with your money troubles.

51. **JILLIAN:**   Sounds okay, but how do I do that?

In this segment of IRT, the therapy task was to understand what set off the self-cutting and escalated suicidality, as well as to uncover the motivation that supported it. The next challenge was to interfere with the motivation to self-destruct and use feelings about the relevant IPIR to motivate better self-care. The dialogue introduced the idea that rather than win by losing as she cut and became suicidal, Jillian was actually being controlled by her stepfather's rules and values. Given her oppositional nature, this strategy of giving ownership of her cutting and suicidality to her stepfather's internalization made it very unattractive. Instead of using his own rules to strike back at him, now it is clear his rules have once again been used against her. Motivational interventions such as this give patients conceptual tools that help them resist their ingrained dangerous habits. As in any learning process, one trial is not enough. Sustained control of such self-destructive behaviors is dependent on many reiterations of these ideas developed within a trustworthy therapy relationship. With practice and with time, new patterns and better rules can become stable and intrinsic. In this example, the therapist used each of the six rules of the core algorithm in the effort to contain the cutting behavior.

Rule 1 Work from a Baseline of Accurate Empathy   Accurate empathy provides the foundation for all interventions in IRT. If an intervention does not include empathy at least implicitly, it probably is not IRT-adherent. Empathy, as expressed in line 2, frequently heightens affect. This kind of support increases understanding and can enhance the effect of later requests to activate state-dependent memories, as was done in line 32 ("Remember how you felt when he said no, and you became so angry at the unfairness of it. Is that a familiar feeling for you?"). In addition, empathic responses that include interpersonal contexts can help build understanding of patterns and the motivations for them. For example, line 4 ("So when the bank officer unfairly withheld what was due you, you became so outraged, you had to cut on yourself") provides a succinct and accurate summary of centrally important interpersonal and intrapsychic patterns.

Rule 2 Support the Growth Collaborator (Green) More than the Regressive Loyalist (Red)
As noted previously, disordered individuals, including nonresponders, are more concerned in their relationships with their internalizations than they are with what is actually happening. This is the reason IRT places such high value on consideration of the conflict between the Red and the Green and on diminishing Red while enhancing Green.

Consider line 7, when Jillian says: "It was so unfair. I just could not stand it." There are many possible responses to this statement. A therapist working with a cathartic model might have said: "You needed to get out your anger." A therapist using a behavioral model (e.g., see Ellis, 1973) might have worked toward helping her realize that her response of anger and cutting was not actually determined by the bank officer's action. Rather, it was a consequence of whatever she told herself about his actions. Hence, by changing her self-talk, she could change her feelings and behavior.

The IRT therapist said in line 8: "So the unfairness of it hurt the most. Do you have any idea why cutting on yourself helped you feel better?" The first part of this statement underscores a crucial component of the Red pattern. The second part, "Do you have any idea why cutting on yourself helped you feel better?" calls on Jillian's Green. Like the entire vignette, Line 8 implements the sequence: acknowledge Red and then activate Green. This is one, but not the only, way to minimize Red and maximize Green. Other possibilities are mentioned in Benjamin, 2003, chapter 3.

Rule 3 Relate Every Intervention to the Case Formulation   In lines 16 ("In other words, you cut on yourself to let an unfair person know the harmful consequences of his action") and 18 ("How do you feel about that?"), the therapist heightens her anger at the bank officer. Then, rather than facilitate further expression, the therapist moves toward a functional analysis of it. In IRT, the case formulation provides the quintessential functional analysis: Problem patterns are connected to wishes in relation to an IPIR. The quest to discover the function of the anger begins in line 20, when the therapist explains: "I believe that anger has a purpose, and usually it is either to help a person gain control or to create some distance. If that is true, what might your anger be for here?" Jillian responds: "Control. I want to control him." The therapist asks: "How should that control work?" Jillian explains: "Well, he should see what he has done, feel bad about it, and then let me have my money."

Having used Jillian's own words to establish the motivation for the cutting, the therapist then magnifies the pattern in line 24 so that Jillian's Green may see it clearly: "Okay, so in your mind, hurting yourself punishes him by showing him how harmful he was, and that should make him become more helpful." As her purpose is reflected so clearly back to her, she can look at it in a realistic rather than fanciful way. She says in line 25: "Well yeah, but it does not work that way."

At this point, Jillian's anger has been clearly related to the case formulation (Rule 3). Moreover, by encouraging her to note the failure of the anger to create the desired result, the series of interventions has reduced the strength of the Red and enhanced her Green (Rule 2).

Rule 4 Seek Concrete Illustrative Detail about Input, Response, and Impact on Self A number of the therapist's comments in the vignette include Rule 4, which requires that as many exchanges as possible be framed in terms of an interpersonal perception (input), a response to that perception (response), and the effect of the interpersonal scenario on the self-concept (impact on self). Consider line 14: "So the most painful part of this is the unfairness. It would be good if he knew how much he harmed you." This summary of what she has just said tags the input (unfairness), the response (strike back), and the impact on the self (great harm). Consistent attention to the interpersonal paradigm ensures that the therapy dialogue will be concrete and specific enough to be accurately understood by both therapist and patient and that the exchanges will be about patterns most relevant to the case formulation and the therapy learning.

Rule 5 Include Affect (A), Behavior (B), and Cognition (C) Learning about patterns in IRT takes place in all domains: affect, behavior, and cognition. The three parallel domains are called the ABCs. IRT assumes that affect, behavior, and cognition evolved together, each supporting the common goal of survival (Benjamin, 2003, chapters 2 & 4, and appendix 4–1). Affects and cognitions that enhance survival support behaviors that enhance survival and vice versa.

Full appreciation of the case formulation requires that the patient add the dimensions of affective experience (A) and behavior (B) to his or her ability to describe input, response, and impact on the self (C). For example, Jillian needs to learn to understand at the levels of A and B as well as C that she punishes herself and others just as her stepfather did. In so doing, she seeks his affirmation and love. This gift of love aspect of the case formulation usually emerges at later stages of IRT. The wish for restitution and affirmation from the oppressive IPIR is very difficult to admit and then to give up. Changes in this wish are dependent on learning and relearning in many different contexts at all possible levels of A, B, and C.

Rule 6 Relate the Intervention to the Five Steps The sixth rule is the most complex component of the core algorithm because it includes five therapy steps. These comprise the stages of therapy process that begin with establishing a therapy contract at Step 1 and continue through learning new patterns at Step 5. The five steps are discussed in the next section on therapy process.

COMMENT ON PROCESS AND TECHNIQUE—TECHNICAL INTERVENTIONS

The five therapy steps describe various components to the general task of identifying and relinquishing Red and growing the Green. Each step is shaped by the case formulation, which it must be remembered, centers on the presenting problems. Every session addresses whatever theme the patient brings in. If the case formulation is accurate, it will be useful in working with the theme of any arbitrarily selected day. The presenting problem addressed in the vignette is cutting and other self-destructive behaviors. The case formulation suggests that if she damages herself, the message sent to the internalized representation of her stepfather would affect him in ways that she would enjoy. Cutting and escalation to suicidality would expose his unfairness and his cruelty for all to see. It also would provide testimony to the stepfather's belief that she "deserved" punishment. It will ensure that he gets his just deserts by exposure and shame for having a destroyed daughter. And on top of that, her success in nailing him will show that she is a "chip off the old block." According to the fantasy, restitution and affirmation ultimately will follow the realization that he has been unfair and that she really is trying to please him. Meanwhile, the current representative for the stepfather, namely, the bank officer, surely will deliver the money. If not, he will be punished, perhaps by lawsuits subsequent to her death.

When working with fantasies in relation to presenting problems and themes of the day, the IRT therapist needs to be comfortable with multiple layers of meanings, some contradictory. Fantasies do not, as Freud (1900/1938, pp. 535–536) noted, always conform to secondary process. Neither do messages from loved ones to patients. However, in all instances, the hypotheses about the fantasies and their relation to the presenting problems must make sense to the patient and be confirmed by concrete patient statements in the therapy narrative. Patients are never said to "resist" interpretations in IRT. Rather, a rejected formulation is sent "back to the drawing board" for further work by both patient and therapist.

Step 1 Collaboration   Eliciting Jillian's collaboration to build Green and constrain the Red is a vital early step in IRT. In the vignette, the task was to elicit her collaboration in exploring the meaning of her cutting to her and to engage her interest in realigning her motives.

Collaboration was elicited in line 10, as the therapist said: "I believe this must somehow make sense. May we try to figure this out?" Following the explanation of the reason for these questions, the therapist then asked for permission to proceed. Such disclosure of rationale and requests for permission to continue reduce the likelihood the interview will degenerate to therapist questions and patient answers. If Jillian actively participates in the quest to develop her case formulation, that in itself begins to strengthen her Green.

Step 2 Learn about Your Patterns, Where They Are From, and What They Are For   This step involves the development of insight from the perspective of IRT. The description of input, response, and impact on self in line 4 ("So when the bank officer unfairly withheld what was due you, you became so outraged, you had to cut on yourself") clearly established a key pattern. Understanding of her motivation developed in line 14: "So the most painful part of this is the unfairness. It would be good if he knew how much he harmed you." That information had been elicited by the question in line 12: "So let's imagine the bank officer could somehow know what you did after talking to him. What do you think he would think and feel?" The motivation was further developed in line 23, when Jillian said: "Well, he should see what he has done, feel bad about it, say he is sorry, and then let me have my money."

The link to an IPIR was made first by explaining the purpose of further inquiry in lines 28 ("Okay, it can be helpful to learn about your patterns, where they are from, and what they are for. Once you see that clearly, you might decide to try other ways of responding—ones that might work better for you") and 30 ("So let's see if we can understand better what this pattern is and where it is from. I expect that it does make sense"). With these statements, the therapist explains Step 2 and establishes the IRT model of therapy as a learning process.

Then, the therapist heightens the related affect explicitly in line 32: "Remember how you felt when he said no, and you became so angry at the unfairness of it?" A link to an IPIR is elicited by the question: "Is that a familiar feeling for you?" After only two more exchanges, Jillian relates the feeling to her stepfather in line 35 ("Sure. With my stepdad. He would get all mad at us if we could not find his checkbook for him. He'd smack us around and say we could not have allowance for three weeks. We hadn't touched his checkbook, but it did not matter. If he couldn't find what he wanted, we had to pay. And Mom was intimidated by him so she couldn't help"). Because of the sequencing here that led directly from problem pattern to memories of the stepfather, he is defined as an IPIR connected to the problem pattern under discussion. That link is requested in line 38 ("Do you see any connection here? For no good reason, somebody withholds your money and you get punished physically") and consolidated in line 42 ("So with the bank officer, you re-created the pattern you had so often with your stepfather. In your mind, hurting yourself punished and hurt him, just as your stepfather used to punish and hurt you").

Such rapid closing of the loop from problem to IPIR back to problem is characteristic of an inpatient consultative interview, but not of a slower, longer term outpatient treatment. Reasons for this, including patient safety, are discussed at length in Benjamin, 2003, chapter 2. In an outpatient treatment, several sessions are needed to develop a case formulation and to fully outline Step 2. Relatively complete affective, cognitive, and behavioral learning about the details of the case formulation typically takes the better part of a year. Giving up the associated wishes and building new patterns frequently takes another year or two in the nonresponder population that typically has been in treatment for decades or more.

Step 3 Block Problem Patterns   Once the case formulation is well understood by the patient, he or she is better able to manage dangerous symptoms. The process of containing cutting and suicidality begins in line 48. The therapist says: "Let's agree to work on developing your own rules and your own ways of dealing with a situation like this. For starters, how about remembering that hurting yourself to punish him as well as you really represents letting him decide on the rules that govern your behavior." Jillian responds: "I can't let him do that to me." She shows interest in developing alternative responses, and the therapy process can turn to focus on strategies for containing harmful behaviors and developing better alternatives. For more detail, see Benjamin, 2003, chapters 7, 8, and 9.

As mentioned previously, these motivationally focused interventions that block problem patterns can be sustained only if there is an ongoing, effective therapy relationship. Without that, the old wishes to please rather than defy the internalization are highly likely to reclaim the patient's psyche.

Step 4 Enable the Will to Change   Helping a patient like Jillian give up the plan of winning by losing is at the heart of reconstructive therapy. Two of the traditionally recognized therapy change factors are prerequisites to Step 4. These are a strong therapy relationship (enhanced by Step 1, described in Benjamin, 2003, chapter 5) and insight (Step 2, described in Benjamin, 2003, chapter 6). The emotional support that evolves in a good collaboration helps provide the basic security necessary to give up old ways of coping and to try new ones. The perspective provided by insight frequently engages the patient's interest in changing the problem patterns. For example, the thought that her stepfather's attacks on her were the model for her self-harm made Jillian angry. This, in turn, helped engage her will to change.

The five steps in IRT are approximately sequential, but there is substantial overlap. Already it is clear that collaboration (Step 1) and insight (Step 2) contribute to the will to change (Step 4). Step 4 itself implicitly includes earlier steps because it consists of substages such as those described in Prochaska et al.'s (1992) transtheoretical model. First, there is precontemplation, when the patient does not know there is a problem. People who are working on collaboration (Step 1) and learning about patterns (Step 2) are in that stage. After gaining insight (Step 2), the patient is aware of the connections between problem patterns and internalized representations of loved ones and begins to think seriously about change. The action stage comes when the patient reliably blocks problem patterns without needing cheerleading from the therapist and collaboratively works to come to terms with and relinquish the wishes that sustain the patterns.

As patients take action and successfully give up old wishes, it is common for them to become frightened and say: "If I am not what I have been, then I don't exist. Who am I? How and what shall I be?" The answers to those questions must come from the patient himself or herself. The uncertainty about identity raises a special challenge for the last part of Step 4, the maintenance stage. That fear creates strong urges to reclaim the old ways, to go back and indulge the old wishes. Such a regression is just as threatening in reconstructive therapy as it is in treatment of misuse of alcohol and drugs. The old wishes are addictions, and it does not take much to tempt newly recovered nonresponders to go back to their old ways. Once again, Red must be blocked and Green supported. Step 4 poses a difficult challenge for both patient and therapist in each of its subphases.

Step 5 Learning New Patterns   After the grip of the old wishes is loosened, nonresponders become more amenable to medications and standard cognitive behavioral techniques, assertiveness training, communication skills lessons, and so on. After Jillian gives up her wishes for restitution and affirmation from her stepfather, she will be much more willing and able to restrain her wishes to aggress against herself and others. She will be more willing to submit to normative social demands to develop functional skills that let her keep a job and work her own way out of financial difficulty. She will show more give and take in relationships and diminish her certainty that her only options are to prevail, be defeated, or leave.

HOW THERAPEUTIC CHALLENGES ARE CONCEPTUALIZED AND MANAGED

The preceding review of the core algorithm, including the therapy steps, emphasized that Jillian's major challenge was to give up the idea of winning by losing—of receiving affirmation and restitution in relation to the problem IPIR. This is "easier said than done." Learning in IRT requires repetition in many modes (A, B, C), using all aspects of the core algorithm. From patients, this requires hard work, willingness to challenge themselves to try new and, therefore, frightening ways, tolerance of the boredom that comes with repeated practice of desired but unfamiliar patterns, ability to bear the pain of full realization of all that has been lost, and the energy to fully engage with the challenge of developing a new identity.

For the therapist, the most difficult challenge is in making sure the case formulation is correct and using it to minimize Red and maximize Green by implementing as many of the facets of the core algorithm as possible. Prototypic differences between the self-mutilation and suicidal behaviors of individuals with PAG and BPD help illustrate the point that in IRT, interventions are directed by the case formulation. Without a case formulation, IRT cannot begin. There is no universally prescribed treatment for a specific symptom such as self-mutilation.

BPD and PAG have many symptoms in common. They usually present with chronic depression, nonfunctionality, comorbid drug abuse, repeated suicidal episodes, self-harm as in cutting themselves or being reckless in obviously dangerous ways, and outbursts of rage. Benjamin (1996) suggests that patients with BPD are preoccupied with coercing nurturance and proximity from powerful, nurturant, yet exploitative caregivers to allay their ultimate fear—abandonment. The BPD's desperate self-destructive and impulsive actions are triggered by perceived abandonment and are to force the caregiver to rescue, soothe, stay with, and protect the BPD. By contrast, patients with PAG are more likely to be preoccupied with oppressive, cruel, and negligent caregivers who exert inordinate control and/or withhold what the PAG needs and deserves. They are devoted to defying the control and extorting what is withheld. Their suffering and failure indict the caregiver's authority.

These formulations predict that the BPD and PAG diagnostic groups will have different needs and give different reactions to any given intervention, such as structure offered by caregivers and authorities. The BPD is hungry for powerful nurturance but will try to manage it in reckless ways. The PAG asks for help but also hates and defies any form of power, even if nurturant. He or she also is primed to feel shortchanged, regardless of what is delivered.

From the perspective of IRT, then, therapy rules for self-mutilation (e.g., see Linehan, 1993) will be followed by BPD if required to maintain proximity to and approval of the therapist and therapy group. After following the rules, the therapist and the group provide the desperately needed antidotes to abandonment for the BPD. The BPD is helped to internalize the needed therapy standards for self-regulation and soothing.

On the other hand, those same rules may be seen by the PAG individual as cruel and unfair. The PAG is vulnerable to engage in self-destructive actions just to demonstrate he or she cannot be helped by or controlled by any "simpleminded, stupid" procedures. The therapist should realize that his or her help is worse than useless and that he or she cannot "win." For this reason, the therapist working with an individual with PAG needs to avoid taking positions that can be seen as controlling and instead offer a basic orientation described by the term *cat therapy*. Under this model, structure is available, but interventions are placed on the therapy doorstep with explicit acknowledgment this may not be what is needed. Maybe the PAG "cat" will choose not to try it. That point had been clearly made to Jillian long before the session described occurred. If the PAG "cat" decides to sample the therapy offerings, perhaps the therapy "tuna fish" will bring comfort—perhaps not. And if he or she does participate, it is vital that any progress in therapy clearly belong to the PAG. In no way can progress in therapy be seen as any kind of success on the therapist's part.

These analyses of very different meanings of self-mutilation demonstrate that the IRT therapist must have clear understanding of the rules and values of IPIRs associated with the problem patterns before deciding which interventions will be effective in managing self-destructive and other undesirable behaviors. In Benjamin, 1996, the IRT case formulation methods were applied to categories of personality disorder. In Benjamin, 2003, the methods are described in ways that permit the clinician to develop original case formulations uniquely tailored to each individual, regardless of diagnostic category.

MECHANISMS OF CHANGE AND THERAPEUTIC ACTION

As already noted, change hinges on transforming the wishes in relation to the IPIRs that are most directly associated with the problem patterns. Change is facilitated by efforts to maximize Green and minimize Red. Therapy procedures are specified by the core algorithm and always relate back to the case formulation.

RESEARCH AND EMPIRICAL SUPPORT

For the past few years, a pilot program at the University of Utah has had graduate student IRT therapists provide brief inpatient therapy for clearly defined nonresponders after the IRT supervisor developed the case formulation. There were more than 50 such brief inpatient treatments, and most were seen by the patients and their referring therapists as very helpful. More recently, cases that did not have other placements were transferred outpatient follow-up by IRT student therapists for between 4 months and 2½ years. There were five outpatient treatments by students following discharge. None has committed suicide. Only one attempted suicide. No other patients in the practicum were rehospitalized, despite long records of many previous hospitalizations and multiple suicide attempts. Three of these erstwhile nonresponders completed before-and-after measures of symptoms. Data show that all three returned to full function that matched or exceeded levels before their assessment at discharge.

In addition, about 20 student outpatient IRT treatments of "ordinary" cases from the hospital outpatient clinic wait list did not begin with IRT inpatient work. These were assessed and treated by the IRT students, and many showed clear progress during their semester-long treatments. None made a suicide attempt or needed hospitalization. There were six more supervisions of students with severely disordered cases from another university that had been handed down over the years from therapist to therapist. Although some were suicidal and two were homicidal, none made any attempts, and none was hospitalized. Most made obvious constructive changes.

This list of results, some of which were properly based on objective, symptom-oriented self-rating data gathered before and after treatment under an IRT-approved training protocol, does not comprise a formal clinical trial. However, the data are a step above the "testimonial" or isolated "case report" methods of validation.

A more formal study of the effectiveness of IRT is presently in place at the University of Utah Neuropsychiatric Institute, which has created an IRT clinic. That clinic has three purposes:

1. IRT service to patients.
2. IRT training for therapists.
3. Research on the nature and effects of IRT.

The research has three goals: (1) Did the treatment adhere closely to the rules of IRT? (2) Was the treatment effective in improving function and relieving suffering? and (3) What therapy interventions were least and most helpful? This project is, in effect, a study of the nature and impact of a service and educational clinic. Results will be used to apply for support for a randomized, full clinical trial of the effectiveness of IRT.

SUMMARY AND CONCLUSIONS

The interpersonal reconstructive therapy (IRT; Benjamin, 2003) case formulation method requires that problem patterns be linked to learning with important early loved ones via one or more of three copy processes: (1) Be like him or her, (2) act as if he or she is still there and in control, and (3) treat yourself as he or she treated you. The processes are respectively named: identification, recapitulation, and introjection. The copying is maintained by fantasies that important persons' internalized representation (IPIR) ultimately will provide the desired love if the patient's living testimony to the IPIR's rules and values is good enough. Such consistent implementation of perceived parental values suggests a continuing wish to please that parent or other important caregiver. Because the relationship with the internalization sustains the problem patterns, treatment must focus sharply on grieving and letting go of these fantasy residuals of early attachments. In IRT, there are flowcharts that guide the clinician in using the theory to develop the individual case formulation and to choose optimal treatment interventions. A core algorithm with six rules directs the moment-to-moment focus. Overall therapy progress is described by five steps, each of which requires activities that facilitate self-discovery (psychodynamic techniques) and self-management (cognitive-behavioral techniques). All therapy steps address a basic conflict between the regressive loyalist (Red, the part that seeks the approval of the IPIRs) and the growth collaborator (Green, the part that comes to therapy for constructive change). The five steps are: (1) collaboration (the therapy relationship); (2) learning about patterns, where they are from, and what they are for (insight); (3) blocking problem patterns (crisis and stalemate management); (4) enabling the will to change (in steps that compare to Prochaska's transtheoretical stages of change); and (5) learning new patterns (via standard behavioral and communications training technology).

REFERENCES

American Psychiatric Association. (1987). *Diagnostic and statistical manual of mental disorders* (3rd ed., rev.). Washington, DC: Author.

American Psychiatric Association. (1994). *Diagnostic and statistical manual of mental disorders* (4th ed.). Washington, DC: Author.

Benjamin, L. S. (1979). Structural analysis of differentiation failure. *Psychiatry, Journal for the Study of Interpersonal Process, 42,* 1–23.

Benjamin, L. S. (1996). *Interpersonal diagnosis and treatment of personality disorders* (2nd ed.). New York: Guilford Press.

Benjamin, L. S. (2003). *Interpersonal reconstructive therapy: Promoting change in nonresponders.* New York: Guilford Press.

Bowlby, J. (1969). *Attachment and loss: Vol. I. Attachment.* New York: Basic Books.

Bowlby, J. (1977). The making and breaking of affectional bonds. *British Journal of Psychiatry, 130,* 201–210.

Cassidy, J. R., & Shaver, P. E. (Eds.). (1999). *Handbook of attachment: Theory, research and clinical applications.* New York: Guilford Press.

Ellis, A. (1973). *Humanistic psychotherapy: The rational emotive approach.* New York: Julian Press.

Freud, S. (1938). The interpretation of dreams (pp. 179–549). In A. A. Brill (Ed. & Trans.) *The basic writings of Sigmund Freud.* New York: The Modern Library. (Original work published 1900)

Harlow, H., & Harlow, M. (1967). The young monkeys. *Psychology Today, 1,* 40–47.

Linehan, M. (1993). *Cognitive-behavioral treatment of borderline personality disorder.* New York: Guilford Press.

Prochaska, J. O., DiClemente, C. C., & Norcross, J. C. (1992). In search of how people change: Applications to addictive behaviors. *American Psychologist, 47,* 1102–1114.

Shea, M. T. (1993). Psychosocial treatment of personality disorders. *Journal of Personality Disorders, 7*(Suppl.), 167–180.

Thase, M. E., Friedman, E. S., & Howland, R. H. (2001). Management of treatment-resistant depression: Psychotherapeutic perspectives. *Journal of Clinical Psychiatry, 62*(Suppl. 18), 18–24.

CHAPTER 9

Cognitive Therapy of Personality Disorders

James Pretzer

C LIENTS WITH PERSONALITY disorders present a challenge to therapists of any orientation. These individuals can be hard to understand, therapy often is complex and difficult, and treatment outcome is often poorer than would be desired. Cognitive therapy* is widely known as an effective, relatively short-term approach to treating depression and other Axis I disorders. If it can provide an effective approach to treating individuals with personality disorders, this would be quite valuable. However, many see cognitive therapy and other cognitive-behavioral therapies as achieving symptomatic improvement but not the "deep" change needed to alleviate personality disorders. Is cognitive therapy a promising approach to understanding and treating personality disorders?

THEORETICAL COMPONENTS OF THE MODEL

Cognitive therapy is based on a contemporary understanding of the relationships among thought, emotion, and behavior. It presumes that individuals are constantly and automatically appraising the situations they encounter and that these "automatic thoughts" (immediate, spontaneous appraisals) play a central role in eliciting and shaping an individual's emotional and behavioral response to a situation. For example, if I arrive on time for an appointment with my physician and am kept waiting for a long time, I might interpret this event in a variety of ways. I could conclude "This shows how little I matter," or "This

---

*A number of different cognitive and cognitive-behavioral approaches to therapy have been developed in recent years. While these various approaches have much in common, there are important conceptual and technical differences among them. To minimize confusion, the specific approach developed by Aaron T. Beck and his colleagues (Beck, Rush, Shaw, & Emery, 1979) is referred to as *cognitive therapy* whereas the term *cognitive-behavioral* will be used to refer to the full range of cognitive and cognitive-behavioral approaches.

Table 9.1
Common Cognitive Distortions

Dichotomous thinking: Viewing experiences in terms of two mutually exclusive categories with no shades of gray in between. For example, believing that you are *either* a success *or* a failure and that anything short of a perfect performance is a total failure.

Over-generalization: Perceiving a particular event as being characteristic of life in general rather than as being one event among many. For example, concluding that an inconsiderate response from your spouse shows that she doesn't care despite her having showed consideration on other occasions.

Selective abstraction: Focusing on one aspect of a complex situation to the exclusion of other relevant aspects of the situation. For example, focusing on the one negative comment in a performance evaluation received at work and overlooking the positive comments contained in the evaluation.

Disqualifying the positive: Discounting positive experiences that would conflict with the individual's negative views. For example, rejecting positive feedback from friends and colleagues on the grounds that: "They're only saying that to be nice" rather than considering whether the feedback could be valid.

Mind-reading: Assuming that you know what others are thinking or how others are reacting despite having little or no evidence. For example, thinking: "I just know he thought I was an idiot!" despite the other person's having given no apparent indications of his or her reactions.

Fortune-telling: Reacting as though expectations about future events are established facts rather than recognizing them as fears, hopes, or predictions. For example, thinking: "He's leaving me, I just know it!" and acting as though this is definitely true.

Catastrophizing: Treating actual or anticipated negative events as intolerable catastrophes rather than seeing them in perspective. For example, thinking: "What if I faint?" without considering that while fainting may be unpleasant or embarrassing, it is not terribly dangerous.

Maximization/Minimization: Treating some aspects of the situation, personal characteristics, or experiences as trivial and others as very important independent of their actual significance. For example, thinking: "Sure, I'm good at my job, but so what, my parents don't respect me."

Emotional reasoning: Assuming that your emotional reactions necessarily reflect the true situation. For example, concluding that since you feel hopeless, the situation must really be hopeless.

"Should" statements: The use of "should" and "have to" statements that are not actually true to provide motivation or control over your behavior. For example, thinking: "I shouldn't feel aggravated. She's my mother, I have to listen to her."

Labeling: Attaching a global label to yourself rather than referring to specific events or actions. For example, thinking: "I'm a failure!" rather than "Wow, I blew that one!"

Personalization: Assuming that you are the cause of a particular external event when, in fact, other factors are responsible. For example, thinking: "She wasn't very friendly today, she must be mad at me," without considering that factors other than your own behavior may affect the other individual's mood.

shows how poor he is at managing his time," or perhaps "This shows how busy he is." My interpretation of the long wait shapes my emotional and behavioral responses. When an individual's interpretation of the situation is accurate, emotional and behavioral responses are likely to prove to be appropriate and adaptive. When the situation is misinterpreted, the individual's responses are more likely to prove dysfunctional.

According to cognitive therapy, each of us interprets experiences on the basis of beliefs and assumptions we acquired through previous experience. These include unconditional core beliefs, or schemas, such as "I don't count," conditional beliefs such as "If I speak up for what I want, no one will take me seriously," and interpersonal strategies such as "To get what I want, I have to *make* people take me seriously." These beliefs and assumptions lie dormant until a relevant situation arises and then automatically become active and shape the individual's responses when a relevant situation is encountered. This often occurs without the individual's being aware of his or her beliefs and assumptions.

Another aspect of cognition that can contribute to misperceptions of situations is the errors in reasoning that cognitive therapy refers to as *cognitive distortions*. These errors in logic (see Table 9.1) can seriously distort interpretations of events and amplify the impact of beliefs and assumptions. To continue our previous example: If I am prone to "dichotomous thinking," I will be more likely to react as though being kept waiting reveals *total* disregard for my feelings. This, in turn, elicits a much stronger reaction than would be elicited by a more moderate evaluation of the situation.

While the cognitive model assumes that the individual's automatic thoughts shape his or her emotional response to the situation, we also hypothesize that the individual's emotional state has important effects on cognition (see Figure 9.1). A large body of research has demonstrated that affect tends to influence both cognition and behavior in mood-congruent ways (Isen, 1984). For example, a number of studies have demonstrated that even a mild, experimentally induced depressed mood biases perception and recall in a depression-congruent way (Watkins, Mathews, Williamson, & Fuller, 1992). If negative automatic thoughts tend to elicit a depressed mood and a depressed mood biases cognition in a depression-congruent way, this sets the stage for a self-perpetuating cycle in which a depressed mood increases the likelihood of negative automatic thoughts, these negative thoughts

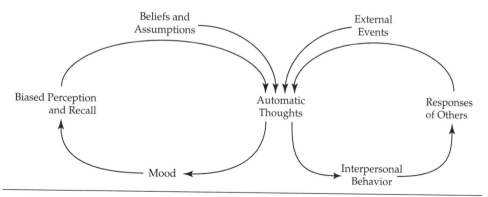

Figure 9.1 Cognitive-Interpersonal Cycle.

elicit more of a depressed mood, the increasingly depressed mood further biases cognition, and so on. This type of self-perpetuating cycle can perpetuate a mood and the mood's biasing effect on perception and recall until something happens to disrupt the cycle.

The cognitive model does *not* simply assert that dysfunctional cognitions cause psychopathology. We view cognition as an important part of the cycle through which humans perceive and respond to events and thus as having an important role in pathological responses to events. However, we view cognition as part of a cycle and as a promising point for intervention, not as the cause of psychopathology.

As shown in Figure 9.1, cognitive therapy's model is not exclusively cognitive. Rather, the cognitive model focuses on the interplay among cognition, affect, and behavior in psychopathology. The individual's beliefs and assumptions and his or her cognitive distortions shape perception of events, and the interpretation of those events shapes the individual's emotional response and interpersonal behavior, but the cycle does not end here. A person's interpersonal behavior influences the responses of others, and their responses can, in turn, result in experiences that influence the individual's beliefs and assumptions. For example, if I passively tolerate being kept waiting and my physician makes no comment about my wait, the fact that he did not apologize for keeping me waiting is likely to reinforce my conclusion that he has no regard for my feelings. However, if I comment about the long wait and my physician explains why I was kept waiting so long in a way that shows consideration for my feelings, this response may lead me to different conclusions. When an individual interacts with others in ways that elicit responses that reinforce his or her beliefs and assumptions, those beliefs and assumptions are likely to be persistent.

How does cognitive therapy's view of psychopathology apply to understanding personality disorders? If we examine the individual's momentary interpretations of events and the assumptions under which they operate, the cognitive perspective helps us understand his or her reactions in specific situations, but this does not explain the persistence of dysfunctional behavior. If we consider the way in which moods bias cognition in mood-congruent ways, we can understand how a disturbed mood and dysfunctional cognitions can persist during a particular episode, but it does little to explain the broad, persistent patterns of dysfunctional cognition and behavior that are observed in individuals diagnosed with personality disorders. However, if we also consider the impact of self-perpetuating cognitive-interpersonal cycle such as described previously, this provides one way of understanding how dysfunctional behavior can be so persistent and resistant to change.

For example (continuing the scenario discussed previously), if I conclude that my physician has no regard for my feelings and believe that I *have* to make people take me seriously, I am likely to react strongly to his lack of punctuality. If he responds to my tirade in a way that leaves me feeling that he understands my dissatisfaction and is taking me seriously, I am likely to be satisfied for the time being but this also reinforces my conviction that I have to *make* people take me seriously. If he responds in a way that leaves me feeling that he is not taking me seriously, this reinforces my conviction that "I don't count" and I am likely to redouble my efforts to *make* him care. If my efforts to *make* him care end with his refusing to continue as my physician or with my stomping out angrily, this reinforces my conviction that "I don't count" and "If I speak up for what I want, no one will take me seriously." Once one of these cognitive-interpersonal cycles is established, the individual's beliefs and assumptions tend to bias his or her perception of events. Experiences that should contradict his or her assumptions are overlooked, discounted, or misinterpreted. At the same time, his or her interpersonal behavior results in experiences that seem to confirm the dysfunctional beliefs.

The cognitive and interpersonal processes that occur in individuals who qualify for Axis II diagnoses are the same as occur in any other nonpsychotic, neurologically intact individual except that, in individuals with Axis II diagnoses, strongly self-perpetuating, dysfunctional cognitive-interpersonal cycles have evolved. The cognitive view of *personality disorder*, is that this term is the label currently used to refer to individuals with pervasive, self-perpetuating cognitive-interpersonal cycles that are dysfunctional enough to come to the attention of mental health professionals (Pretzer & Beck, 1996).

RANGE OF PSYCHOPATHOLOGY AND PERSONALITY DISORDERS WITHIN SCOPE OF TREATMENT

Cognitive therapy was initially developed as a treatment for depression (A. T. Beck, Rush, Shaw, & Emery, 1979) and has subsequently been applied with a wide range of disorders such as anxiety disorders (A. T. Beck & Emery, 1985), substance abuse (A. T. Beck, Wright, Newman, & Liese, 1993), marital and family problems (Epstein & Baucom, 2002), and even schizophrenia (Perris & McGorry, 1998). However, although the principles of cognitive therapy apply across the full range of psychiatric problems, the treatment approach needs to be modified to take into account the characteristics of the individuals being treated. Some have argued that cognitive therapy of depression (A. T. Beck et al., 1979) is not an appropriate treatment for individuals with personality disorders (McGinn & Young, 1996; Rothstein & Vallis, 1991; Young, 1990) and this is indeed the case. Cognitive therapy of depression is a protocol for treating depression and somewhat different protocols are used in treating other disorders. Cognitive therapy of personality disorders (A. T. Beck et al., 1990; Freeman, Pretzer, Fleming, & Simon, 1990; Pretzer, 1998; Pretzer & Beck, 1996) would be used in treating personality disorders and we would combine the two approaches in treating an individual who manifests both depression and a personality disorder.

There is a consensus among investigators developing cognitive therapy approaches to the treatment of personality disorders that it is important to develop conceptualizations and treatment approaches tailored to specific personality disorders rather than relying on a generic approach that does not distinguish between the various personality disorders. Unfortunately, a discussion of cognitive therapy with each of the personality disorders is beyond the scope of this chapter. This chapter discusses the general principles of cognitive therapy with personality disorders. For approaches to understanding and treating each of the personality disorders, see A. T. Beck et al. (1990) and Freeman et al. (1990).

TREATMENT METHODS AND TECHNICAL ASPECTS OR INTERVENTIONS

The cognitive model of psychopathology emphasizes dysfunctional automatic thoughts, dysfunctional beliefs and assumptions, and dysfunctional interpersonal

Table 9.2
A Client's Record of Thoughts and Feelings in a Problem Situation

Situation	Emotion(s)	Automatic Thoughts
Briefly describe the situation	Rate 0% to 100%	Try to quote thoughts then rate belief in each thought 0% to 100%
Rick left my apartment angry at me.	Depressed 90%	1. He'll never be back. (75%)
	Desperate 75%	
		2. I can't go on without him. (85%)
		3. No one will ever really love me. (95%)

behavior. Not surprisingly, all of these are important targets for intervention in cognitive therapy. The initial goal of cognitive therapy is to break the cycle or cycles that perpetuate and amplify the client's problems (see Table 9.2). This could potentially be done by modifying the client's automatic thoughts, by improving the client's mood, by working to counteract the biasing impact of mood on recall and perception, and/or by changing the client's behavior. These interventions may break the cycle or cycles that perpetuate the client's problems and alleviate the client's immediate distress. However, if therapy stops at this point, the client would be at risk for a relapse whenever he or she experienced events similar to the ones that precipitated the current problems. To achieve lasting results, it would also be important to modify the factors that predispose the client to his or her problems and to help the client plan effective ways to handle situations that might precipitate a relapse.

The basic principles of cognitive therapy are summarized in Table 9.3. Cognitive therapy is an "eclectic" approach in the sense that cognitive therapy provides a coherent conceptual framework within which a wide range of intervention techniques

Table 9.3
General Principles of Cognitive Therapy

- Therapist and client work collaboratively towards clear goals.
- The therapist takes an active, directive role.
- Interventions are based on an individualized conceptualization.
- The focus is on specific problem situations and on specific thoughts, feelings, and actions.
- Therapist and client focus on modifying thoughts, coping with emotions, and/or changing behavior as needed.
- The client continues the work of therapy between sessions.
- Interventions later in therapy focus on identifying and modifying predisposing factors including schemas and core beliefs.
- At the close of treatment, therapist and client work explicitly on relapse prevention.

can be used. As therapist and client endeavor to work together toward shared goals, the therapist is free to select from a wide range of intervention techniques.

GUIDED DISCOVERY

One part of cognitive therapy's collaborative approach is an emphasis on a process of *guided discovery*. The therapist guides the client by asking questions, making observations, and asking the client to monitor relevant aspects of the situation. This helps therapist and client to develop an understanding of the problems, to explore possible solutions, to develop plans for dealing with the problems, and to implement the plans effectively. Guided discovery has an advantage over approaches in which the therapist unilaterally develops an understanding of the problems and proposes solutions in that it maximizes client involvement in therapy sessions and minimizes the possibility of the client's feeling that the therapist's ideas are being imposed on him or her. In addition, because the client is actively involved in the process of developing an understanding of the problems and coming up with a solution, he or she has an opportunity to learn to deal with problems effectively and should be better able to handle future problems as they arise.

SELF-MONITORING

One of the primary interventions used in cognitive therapy is helping the client to identify the specific automatic thoughts that occur in problem situations and to recognize the effects these thoughts have on the client's emotions and behavior (A. T. Beck et al., 1979, chapter 8; A. T. Beck et al., 1990, pp. 80–90; Freeman et al., 1990, pp. 49–68). Negative, self-deprecating, or other problematic thoughts typically are a habitual part of the client's life and come "fast and furious" without the client's necessarily being aware of their presence or their relationship to his or her distress. It is possible to identify these cognitions through guided discovery during the therapy session. However, this involves relying on the client's retrospective recall of his or her thoughts, feelings, and actions. Frequently, cognitive therapists have clients observe their thoughts, feelings, and actions as they occur in problem situations and write them down in the hope of providing more complete, detailed information. Many different formats can be used for self-monitoring. One of the formats used most frequently is illustrated in Table 9.2, which shows the thoughts and feelings a client with Dependent Personality Disorder recorded in response to a fight with her boyfriend.

RATIONAL RESPONSES

One technique for helping clients learn to deal effectively with thoughts that prove problematic is to help them develop the ability to look critically at the thoughts and to formulate more realistic alternative views, which are termed *rational responses*. Table 9.4 shows rational responses to the thoughts from Table 9.2, which the client developed with her therapist's help. A detailed discussion of the process through which therapists help clients master the process of "talking back" to their dysfunctional thoughts is beyond the scope of this chapter. Detailed discussions of this process can be found in a number of sources (e.g., see J. Beck, 1995; Freeman et al., 1990; Greenberger & Padesky, 1995).

Table 9.4
"Rational Responses" Developed with the Therapist's Assistance

Situation	Emotion(s) Rate	Automatic Thoughts	Rational Response	Outcome
Briefly describe the situation	0% to 100%	Try to quote thoughts then rate belief in each thought 0% to 100%	Rate degree of belief 0% to 100%	Rerate emotions
Rick left my apartment angry at me.	Depressed 90% Desperate 75%	1. He'll never be back. (75%)	1. We've had lots of fights before, and he always comes back when he cools down. (90%)	Depressed 50% Desperation 10%
		2. I can't go on without him. (85%)	2. I managed OK before I met him. (75%) He actually doesn't help take care of me; I end up having to take care of him. (95%)	
		3. No one will ever really love me. (95%)	3. People have cared for me in the past (including Rick). (90%)	

Behavioral Experiments

Although verbal discussions in the office can be helpful, insight alone is usually not sufficient to produce lasting change. Cognitive therapy incorporates many experiential interventions intended to increase the impact of therapy. One experiential intervention that cognitive therapy uses extensively is the *behavioral experiment*. The therapist selects one of the client's important thoughts or beliefs and frames it as a testable hypothesis. He or she then helps the client find a practical way to collect observations to test the thought or belief. For example, when a client expresses the view, "There's no point to asking for what I want, no one will take me seriously," his or her therapist may coach the client through the process of testing this belief by selecting situations in which to make requests, observing the responses of others, and discovering whether it is true that no one takes the requests seriously.

Changing Interpersonal Behavior

The dramatic interpersonal problems encountered by many individuals with personality disorders make it clear that behavior change is needed in addition to changes in thoughts and feelings. It might seem that changes in thoughts and feelings would inevitably lead to changes in behavior, but this is not necessarily the case. Cognitive therapy often includes explicitly working to change the client's interpersonal behavior in real-life situations. Often, this coaching on behavior change needs to be done in combination with cognitive interventions that address the individual's fears and behavioral experiments that test how significant others respond to the behavior change.

IDENTIFYING AND MODIFYING CORE BELIEFS

In the early stages of therapy, cognitive therapists usually focus on the client's thoughts, feelings, and actions in problem situations in the hope of providing some immediate relief. However, it usually is important to also address dysfunctional beliefs and assumptions that contribute to the individual's ongoing problems. A variety of techniques for doing this have been developed (J. Beck, 1995, chapter 11; A. T. Beck et al., 1979, chapter 12).

RELAPSE PREVENTION

Cognitive therapy ends by explicitly working to prepare the client to maintain the gains they have made and to deal with future setbacks (A. T. Beck et al., 1979, chapter 15). This work, based on Marlatt and Gordon's (1985) research on relapse

Table 9.5
A Typical Relapse Prevention Plan

Warning signs:

Getting to work late (even one time).

Missing a day of work without a clear physical illness.

Having to drag myself out of bed in the morning.

Skipping meals because I'm just not hungry.

Having difficulty sleeping through the night.

Even starting to think about suicide.

Feeling like I'm not having any fun.

Agreeing with Rick when I don't really mean it.

What to do if I notice a warning sign:

Start writing out thought sheets again (and sticking with it until my responses seem convincing).

Reread the summary thought sheets in my therapy folder.

Make an effort to be assertive with Rick, even with small things.

Force myself to do several fun things (from my list of ideas) every day, even if I don't really feel like it.

Spend extra time just relaxing and playing with my son.

Call and talk to a friend.

Reread relevant chapters from *Feeling Good*.

If I try the above steps for one week and it's not helping, or if I go one week without trying these steps, call Dr. Jones at _____.

---

prevention, consists of helping the client to understand the importance of actively maintaining gains, to recognize high-risk situations, and to identify early warning signs of impending relapse. Therapist and client develop explicit plans for maintaining gains, handling high-risk situations, and heading off potential relapse. An example of a typical relapse prevention plan is shown in Table 9.5.

Cognitive therapy is not a one-size-fits-all approach in which standard techniques are applied to all clients. Interventions are selected on the basis of the therapist's understanding of the individual and his or her problems, the specific treatment approaches that have been developed for specific disorders, and collaborative decisions made between therapist and client.

PROCESS OF THERAPEUTIC APPROACH

The approach used in cognitive therapy has been described as "collaborative empiricism" (A. T. Beck et al., 1979, chapter 3). The therapist endeavors to work *with* the client to help him or her recognize the factors that contribute to problems, to test the validity of the thoughts, beliefs, and assumptions that prove important, and to make the necessary changes in cognition and behavior. Although it is clear that very different therapeutic approaches, ranging from philosophical debate to operant conditioning, can be effective with at least some clients, collaborative empiricism has substantial advantages. By actively collaborating with the client, the therapist minimizes the resistance and oppositionality that is often elicited by taking an authoritarian role, yet the therapist is still in a position to structure each session as well as the overall course of therapy to be as efficient and effective as possible (A. T. Beck et al., 1979, chapter 4).

ASSESSMENT PHASE

In cognitive therapy, a strategic approach to intervention is emphasized (Persons, 1991). Our view is that therapy is most effective and most efficient when the therapist uses a clear conceptualization of the client's problems as a basis for selecting the most productive targets for intervention and the most appropriate intervention techniques. To take a strategic approach to therapy, the therapist must develop an initial understanding of the client and his or her problems. Therefore, the first step in cognitive therapy is an initial assessment, which provides a foundation for intervention (A. T. Beck et al., 1979, chapter 5). By beginning with a systematic evaluation, the therapist can develop an initial conceptualization quickly and thus be in a position to intervene effectively early in therapy. This initial conceptualization is then refined as therapy proceeds.

The assessment process also continues throughout the course of therapy as therapist and client work together to identify the automatic thoughts and core beliefs that play a role in the client's problems. A variety of questionnaires and assessment procedures are used from time to time. However, cognitive therapists rely most heavily on the clinical interview, on guided discovery, and on self-monitoring on the part of the client.

ALLIANCE BUILDING

In cognitive therapy, the initial therapy sessions are also important because they provide an opportunity for the therapist to establish a solid foundation for subsequent interventions (A. T. Beck et al., 1979, chapter 3; A. T. Beck et al., 1990, pp. 64–79; Wright & Davis, 1994). The effectiveness of any psychotherapy depends on a relationship of confidence, openness, caring, and trust established between client and therapist. The cognitive therapist takes an active, directive role in treatment and thus can work actively to develop the therapeutic relationship rather than waiting for it to develop gradually over time. With many clients, this is more easily said than done. The complexities and difficulties encountered in the therapeutic relationship are particularly important in the treatment of clients with personality disorders.

To collaborate effectively, therapist and client must agree on what they are trying to accomplish. Therefore, following the initial evaluation, the therapist works with the client to specify and prioritize goals for therapy. These goals include the problems that the client wishes to overcome and the positive changes he or she wants to work toward and should be operationalized clearly and specifically enough so that both therapist and client can tell if progress is being made.

There is considerable advantage in working initially toward a goal that appears manageable even if it is not the goal that is most important to the client. If it proves possible to make demonstrable progress toward a valued goal, the client will be encouraged, which will increase his or her motivation for therapy. The process of jointly agreeing on goals and priorities maximizes the likelihood that therapy will accomplish what the client is seeking. At the same time, it establishes the precedent of the therapist's soliciting and respecting the client's input while being open about his or her own views. Thus, it lays the foundation for therapist and client to work together collaboratively, and it makes it clear to the client that his or her concerns are understood and respected. The time and effort spent on establishing mutually agreed on goals and priorities are more than compensated for by the resulting increase in client involvement, decrease in resistance, and decrease in time and effort wasted on peripheral topics.

With clients who do not have personality disorders, the development of a collaborative relationship usually is straightforward. With personality-disordered clients, the process may be much more complex. Clients may have difficulty trusting the therapist and may be reluctant to disclose the thoughts and feelings they experience in problem situations. The client's perception of the therapist may be biased at times, and the dysfunctional interpersonal behaviors that clients manifest in relationships outside therapy may be manifested in the therapist-client relationship as well. The therapist is likely to need to allow extra time for developing a good working relationship. In particular, the therapist may need to persistently be alert for misperceptions and misunderstandings and to clear them up before they disrupt therapy. Although the interpersonal difficulties that are manifested in the therapist-client relationship can disrupt therapy if they are not addressed effectively, they also provide the therapist with the opportunity to do in-vivo observation and intervention (Freeman et al., 1990; Linehan, 1987; Mays, 1985; Padesky, 1986).

One important issue in a collaborative approach to therapy is for the therapist to share his or her understanding of the client's problems with the client. It is much easier to get clients to follow through on interventions if what they are asked to do "makes sense" to them, especially if they are being asked to do something that is difficult or scary. In the guided discovery approach to develop an understanding of the client's problems presents many natural opportunities for the therapist to share an explanation of the role the client's thoughts, feelings, and actions play in his or her problems and of the steps the client can take to overcome the problems (Freeman et al., 1990, pp. 94–95).

"Homework assignments" are used extensively throughout cognitive therapy (A. T. Beck et al., 1979, chapter 13). Clients who actively engage in some of the work of therapy between sessions have been found to accomplish more than those who passively wait for their weekly hour with the therapist (Persons, Burns, & Perloff, 1988). In addition, clients are in a position to collect data and test the effects of cognitive and behavioral changes in daily life in ways that would be difficult to duplicate in the therapy session. Noncompliance often occurs when homework assignments are used. However, rather than being a problem, noncompliance is often useful in identifying problems in the therapist-client relationship and in identifying the factors that block the client from making the desired changes (A. T. Beck et al., 1990, pp. 66–77).

MIDDLE PHASE

Clients with personality disorders often enter therapy at times of crisis, and initial interventions often are directed toward achieving enough stability so that therapist and client can work systematically toward achieving the client's goals. Following this stabilization, cognitive therapy typically focuses on the specific thoughts, feelings, and behaviors that occur in problem situations and works to achieve symptomatic relief. Once the client is having fewer crises and is feeling better, cognitive therapy moves on to the middle phase where the focus shifts to identifying and addressing the factors that perpetuate the client's problems. These typically include dysfunctional interaction patterns, family and/or support system problems, and dysfunctional beliefs and assumptions. The focus of therapy typically shifts from finding solutions for specific problem situations to identifying issues that are persistently manifested across problem situations and addressing them. This does not mean that specific cognitive and behavioral interventions are abandoned. Rather, specific intervention techniques are used to challenge dysfunctional beliefs, to develop more adaptive alternatives, and to test the adaptive alternatives in real-life situations.

TERMINATION

When the client has attained his or her goals for therapy, work on relapse prevention has been completed, and the client's progress has been maintained long enough to have a reasonable amount of confidence that the client is able to cope with problems as they arise, the decision to terminate is made jointly between therapist and client. With clients who do not have personality disorders, the termination process usually is fairly straightforward. Clients with personality disorders are more prone to have strong emotional reactions to the idea of terminating therapy, and it is important to recognize these reactions and address them. The client's reaction to termination can also be eased if therapy is tapered off by shifting from weekly sessions to biweekly and, possibly, monthly sessions as the time for termination approaches. This not only makes the ending of therapy less abrupt but also provides therapist and client with an opportunity to discover how well the client handles problems without the therapist's help and to discover whether any additional issues need to be addressed. Also, termination can be framed as shifting from regularly scheduled appointments to meeting as needed rather than making it sound as though termination means that the client can never consult the therapist again.

FOLLOW-UP

In cognitive therapy, the client is typically offered the opportunity to return for "booster sessions" if problems arise, in the hopes that early intervention with future problems may forestall major difficulties. Planned follow-up sessions are not routinely scheduled but can be planned if the client wishes or if the therapist sees a need for systematic follow-up.

CLINICAL CASE EXAMPLE

Georgia, a recently divorced woman in her mid-40s, initially called and left a message asking a psychologist (the author) to call, telling his secretary, "I may want to hire him." She started her initial session by saying, "I have a bunch of problems" and described having recently been diagnosed with a recurrence of skin cancer. She continued, "I think I'm borderline" and described a history of verbal and physical abuse both during childhood and in her marriage. She reported having recurrent problems in romantic relationships, saying, "I keep marrying my father" and also reported having had negative experiences with previous therapists. Georgia stated her primary goal for therapy as, "I want to live without psychic pain." She was correct in thinking that she met criteria for a diagnosis of Borderline Personality Disorder, and her understandable difficulty coping with the recurrence of her cancer also qualified for a diagnosis of Adjustment Disorder.

Initially, therapy focused on clarifying Georgia's goals for therapy and developing an understanding of Georgia's reactions in specific situations where she encountered difficulty. For example, when she was kept waiting for a scheduled appointment with her physician, her interpretation was, "He thinks I don't count." She became very angry and demanded to be seen, threatening to leave if she was not seen promptly. On that occasion, the nurse responded respectfully to Georgia's outburst and persuaded her to wait a bit longer, but on many other occasions Georgia's intense reactions to perceived slights had disrupted relationships with physicians, therapists, friends, and business associates. In the heat of the moment, it seemed self-evident to Georgia that the delay in being seen by her physician occurred because, "I don't count" and that the appropriate response was to become irate. It was only after she was treated with respect by the nurse and then by the physician that she considered other possibilities such as, "He must be busy," or "Their scheduling is inefficient."

As Georgia and her therapist worked to develop an understanding of her reactions in problem situations, Georgia explained that she often dealt with painful emotions by "not letting myself feel anything." Her therapist's response was to explore the consequences of relying on this strategy and to highlight the drawbacks it had for her. He then helped her recognize the advantages of developing the ability to tolerate intense emotions and introduced the idea that individuals can face intense emotions "in manageable chunks" so that they feel less overwhelming. In addition to this discussion, her therapist proposed a program of gradually tolerating painful emotions both in therapy and in daily life to increase her affect tolerance.

Georgia's intense outbursts when she felt slighted often created interpersonal problems for her. The outbursts intimidated some people and alienated others. On the occasions when her intense reactions intimidated others, it seemed to her that her outburst "worked," which reinforced her assumption that this was the way to make people take her seriously. On the occasions when her reactions alienated others, it seemed to prove that she didn't count to them, and she would either redouble her efforts to make them take her seriously or would break off the relationship. Although it might seem that therapy should focus on getting Georgia to react more mildly when slighted, part of the problem was that she would try to avoid conflict by tolerating slights as long as possible and *then* would react intensely. Rather than trying to get Georgia to respond mildly to slights, her therapist encouraged her to stand up for herself sooner but more moderately rather than tolerating slights as long as possible. When Georgia tried setting limits and speaking up for herself in more moderate ways, she was pleased to discover that others often took her seriously and considered her feelings.

One unexpected side effect of Georgia's speaking up for herself in moderate ways rather than tolerating mistreatment until she exploded was that people reacted more positively to her. She began to feel more a part of the group, was included in more activities, and started getting more invitations from friends. While she was pleased with this, she also found it uncomfortable in some ways:

GEORGIA: I'm not sure how I feel about all these friends and invitations.

THERAPIST: Is there something uncomfortable about it?

GEORGIA: I guess so.

THERAPIST: Can you think of a recent time when this came up?

GEORGIA: Just the other day Maryann asked me to lunch, but the restaurant she picked is one I really don't like because it's way too noisy and the service is bad.

THERAPIST: So think back to when she invited you to lunch . . . how did you feel?

GEORGIA: Annoyed, I guess. I have better things to do than put up with bad service and noise.

THERAPIST: Do you remember what ran through your head when she invited you to lunch at that restaurant?

GEORGIA: It was, "Why there? I hate going there."

THERAPIST: What got to you the most about her invitation?

GEORGIA: I ended up feeling like I'm not in control of my life any more. Somebody can just call me up and there go all my plans.

THERAPIST: It sounds as though having somebody like you and invite you to something means you're stuck doing what they want.

GEORGIA: How can I say no when they're being nice to me?

THERAPIST: Good question. If someone's being nice to me, am I stuck doing what they suggest whether I want to or not?

GEORGIA: Won't they get mad if I say no?

THERAPIST: What's your experience been? If you were to politely turn down an invitation or to suggest an alternative, how do you think your friends would react?

GEORGIA: Maybe it wouldn't be that big a deal.

Therapist: One idea would be to test this out. Instead of trying to guess how people will react, a person could pick an invitation or two that aren't a big deal and try saying something like, "I'd love to but I can't go on Saturday" or "I'm not really into bowling; could we go to a movie instead?" to see how people react.

Georgia: I guess so.

Therapist: How do you think it would go if you were to try this with one or two minor invitations?

Georgia: That would be okay.

Therapist: It seems like it would be really useful to find out if its okay to politely turn down an invitation or not. If it's okay, then I don't have to worry about being invited to something I don't want to go to. If it's not okay, then either I'm stuck doing whatever they suggest or I have to find a way not to get invited in the first place. How about testing this out?

Georgia: Okay.

In subsequent sessions, her therapist followed up by checking to see if Georgia had indeed tried politely turning down invitations and how her friends had responded. Over the course of a few weeks, she discovered that she could exercise control over her schedule and her life without alienating her friends. This left her more comfortable with developing friendships.

Therapy also addressed many issues not directly related to her personality disorder as Georgia underwent chemotherapy, experienced ups and downs in relationships, and dealt with stressful situations at work. In addressing each of these situations, her therapist was alert for manifestations of her underlying conviction that her feelings didn't count and that drastic action was needed to get others to take her seriously. When possible, her therapist helped Georgia plan *behavioral experiments* in which she used real-life situations to test the validity of her assumptions and/or to experiment with new approaches to problem situations. For example, after her life had been going well for several weeks, Georgia found herself thinking, "I'm going to pay for this." It turned out that she had a strong conviction that if her life went well and she was happy, something bad would happen because she didn't deserve to be happy. In addition to addressing this belief verbally during the session, her therapist proposed keeping tabs on the number of "bad" things that happened when she was happy and comparing this with the number of "bad" things that happened when she was unhappy. It turned out that negative events were no more likely when she was happy than when she was unhappy.

At this point, Georgia has been seen for a total of 56 sessions over the course of four years and has experienced major improvements in many important areas of life. She has been able to cope with two recurrences of cancer, with the end of an important romantic relationship, and the ups and downs of starting her own business. She has experienced major improvements in her mood and in many areas of life. Most notably, the quality of her interpersonal relationships has undergone a substantial change. At the beginning of therapy, she often felt mistreated by others and reacted intensely to perceived slights. She began a recent session by saying, "There's a new theme in my life . . . I have friends!" She described having friends reach out to her during a recent hospitalization and described both situations where she went out of her way to reach out to others and situations where she set appropriate limits without having to be upset.

The intervention approach used with Georgia is specific to her, and there would be major differences in both the conceptualization and the intervention approach used to treat an individual with a different personality disorder. A discussion of cognitive therapy with each of the personality disorders is beyond the scope of this chapter. Interested readers can find detailed discussions of cognitive therapy with each of the personality disorders in *Cognitive Therapy of Personality Disorders* (A. T. Beck et al., 1990) and *Clinical Applications of Cognitive Therapy* (Freeman et al., 1990).

HOW THERAPEUTIC CHALLENGES ARE CONCEPTUALIZED AND MANAGED

Although cognitive therapy may seem simple and straightforward when it is presented in a textbook or a workshop, there is no shortage of therapeutic challenges when applying cognitive therapy to the treatment of personality disorders. The complex, deeply ingrained, persistent, and inflexible problems presented by clients with personality disorders are, by all clinical accounts, difficult to treat. Authors often note that a number of problems arise in the course of treatment, including difficulty obtaining clear reports of thoughts and emotions, low tolerance for strong emotion, poor compliance with homework assignments, and questionable motivation for change (McGinn & Young, 1996; Padesky, 1986; Rothstein & Vallis, 1991).

Behavioral and cognitive-behavioral therapists are generally accustomed to being able to establish a fairly straightforward therapeutic relationship at the outset of therapy and then proceeding without much attention to the interpersonal aspects of therapy. However, this is generally not the case when working with clients who have personality disorders because the dysfunctional interpersonal behaviors that the clients manifest in relationships outside therapy are likely to emerge within the therapist-client relationship as well. For example, if an individual believes, "I don't count" and anticipates that others will not take him or her seriously, this is likely to have much the same impact in therapy as it has in daily life. The individual may well react strongly to perceived slights by the therapist and may have difficulty being appropriately assertive in therapy.

Linehan (1993) has emphasized the importance of what she calls "therapy-interfering behaviors" in the treatment of Borderline Personality Disorder, and the same point applies in the treatment of other personality disorders as well. A variety of interpersonal behaviors such as inconsistent attendance, angry outbursts during therapy sessions, and recurrent crises can greatly interfere with the effectiveness of therapy. Although we do not presume that the client's intent is to undercut the effectiveness of therapy, that is the effect these behaviors have if they are not addressed effectively. Cognitive therapists endeavor to recognize therapy-interfering behaviors as soon as they are manifested and to work with the client to address them promptly. Sometimes all the therapist needs to do is to call the client's attention to the consequences of his or her behavior (i.e., "I know it seems reasonable to come in to see me when you are feeling bad and to cancel sessions when you are feeling okay, but how does that work out in real life?"). At other times, the therapist needs to set clear, consistent limits (i.e., "We now know from experience that when you've had a few drinks before your appointment, we accomplish very little. Our policy needs to be no drinking before therapy. That would mean that if you show up for an appointment and have drunk any alcohol that day, we'll reschedule the appointment, but you'll be charged since you didn't cancel 24 hours in advance. How does that sound to you? Do we need to schedule our appointments earlier in the day?"). On yet other occasions, focusing on the consequences of therapy-interfering behavior and setting limits may not be sufficient, and therapist and client may need to devote significant time and effort to developing a solution.

One type of problem that is more common when working with clients who have personality disorders is the extreme and/or persistent misperception of the therapist by the client, which psychoanalytically oriented therapists have long termed *transference.* This phenomenon can easily be understood in cognitive-behavioral terms. In interpersonal interactions, an individual's behavior is shaped by his or her perception of the current interpersonal interaction, by expectations based on previous experiences in similar interpersonal situations, and by generalized expectations and beliefs about interpersonal relationships. In an ambiguous or novel interpersonal situation, such as psychoanalytic psychotherapy, many of the individual's responses are based on generalized beliefs and expectancies because the other person's behavior is difficult to interpret. The active, directive style used by most behavioral and cognitive-behavioral therapists minimizes misperceptions of the therapist because the therapist takes on a relatively straightforward, unambiguous role. However, clients with personality disorders are often vigilant for any indications that their hopes or fears may be realized and can react very dramatically when the therapist's behavior appears to confirm their anticipations. When these strongly emotional responses occur, it is important for the therapist to recognize what is happening, to quickly develop a clear understanding of what the client is thinking, and to clear up the misconceptions and misunderstandings directly but sensitively. Otherwise, these reactions can greatly complicate therapy.

The interpersonal complexities encountered in the course of therapy with individuals who have personality disorders are likely to disrupt therapy if they are not addressed successfully. However, the emergence of these issues also provides an opportunity for more effective intervention. When working with an individual, it can often be difficult to accurately assess the client's interpersonal behavior because the client's reports during therapy sessions may be of limited validity. This makes it difficult to design effective interventions and gauge their impact. However, when the client's interpersonal difficulties are manifested in the therapist-client relationship, the therapist has the opportunity to directly observe the client's behavior and to intervene (Freeman et al., 1990; Linehan, 1987; Mays, 1985; Padesky, 1986). With clients who have interpersonal problems of the magnitude common among clients with personality disorders, the effectiveness and efficiency of intervention can be substantially increased if problems in the therapist-client relationship are used as opportunities for intervention rather than being viewed only as problems to be eliminated as quickly as possible.

Many factors contribute to a high rate of noncompliance among clients with personality disorders. In addition to the complexities in the therapist-client relationship discussed previously, the dysfunctional behaviors of clients with personality disorders are strongly ingrained and often are reinforced by aspects of the client's environment. Also, each personality disorder produces its own problems with compliance. For example, the individual with Avoidant Personality

Disorder is likely to resist any assignments that involve social interaction, and the client with Borderline Personality Disorder is likely to feel compelled to prove his or her autonomy through noncompliance. Rather than simply being an impediment to progress, episodes of noncompliance can provide an opportunity for effective intervention. When noncompliance is predictable, addressing the issues beforehand may not only improve compliance with that particular assignment but also prove helpful with other situations where similar issues arise. When noncompliance arises unexpectedly, it provides an opportunity to identify issues that are impeding progress in therapy by identifying the thoughts and feelings that occur at the point where the client considers doing the assignment and chooses not to. In some ways, noncompliance can be more useful than compliance when working with personality disorder clients. When the client performs an assignment and it goes as expected, the result is progress toward the client's goals, but it only confirms what is already known. When the client fails to perform an assignment or encounters problems with it, an important problem that may not have been recognized or considered previously is often identified.

MECHANISMS OF CHANGE AND THERAPEUTIC ACTION

Cognitive therapy's view of the mechanisms of change focuses on understanding the persistence of dysfunctional cognitions and behaviors. Many dysfunctional cognitions persist because:

- Many individuals are unaware of the role their thoughts play in their problems.
- The dysfunctional cognitions often seem so plausible that individuals fail to examine them critically.
- Selective perception and cognitive biases often result in the individual's ignoring or discounting experiences that would otherwise conflict with the dysfunctional cognitions.
- Cognitive distortions often lead to erroneous conclusions.
- The individual's dysfunctional interpersonal behavior often can produce experiences that seem to confirm dysfunctional cognitions.
- Individuals who are reluctant to tolerate aversive affect may consciously or nonconsciously avoid memories, perceptions, and/or conclusions that would elicit strong emotional responses.

Thus, cognitive interventions focus on identifying the specific dysfunctional cognitions that play a role in the individual's problems and examining them critically. The therapist works to correct for the effects of selective perception, biased cognition, and cognitive distortions and to help the individual to face and tolerate aversive affect.

Many dysfunctional behaviors persist because:

- They are a product of persistent dysfunctional beliefs.
- Expectations about the consequences of possible actions encourage behaviors that actually prove to be dysfunctional and/or discourage behaviors that would prove adaptive.

- The individual lacks the skills needed to engage in potentially adaptive behavior.
- The environment reinforces dysfunctional behavior and/or punishes adaptive behavior.

To change dysfunctional behavior, it may be necessary to modify long-standing cognitions, to examine the individual's expectations about the consequences of his or her actions, to modify the individual's environment, or to help the individual master the cognitive or behavioral skills needed to successfully engage in more adaptive behavior. When dysfunctional behavior is strongly maintained by dysfunctional cognitions, it may be necessary to modify the cognitions first.

When dysfunctional cognitions are strongly supported by interpersonal experience, it may be necessary to accomplish changes in interpersonal behavior and/or in the individual's environment to challenge the cognitions effectively. Because personality disorders are characterized by self-perpetuating cognitive-interpersonal cycles where dysfunctional cognitions strongly maintain dysfunctional behavior and dysfunctional behavior strongly maintains dysfunctional cognition, it sometimes can be difficult to find ways to intervene effectively. A strategic approach based on a clear conceptualization is often necessary to allow effective intervention.

RESEARCH AND EMPIRICAL SUPPORT

One of the strengths of cognitive therapy is that the approach is based on extensive research. In addition, both the adequacy of cognitive conceptualizations and the effectiveness of cognitive therapy have been tested empirically.

THE VALIDITY OF COGNITIVE CONCEPTUALIZATIONS OF PERSONALITY DISORDER

Cognitive conceptualizations of personality disorders are of recent vintage and, consequently, only limited research into the validity of these conceptualizations has been reported. Recent studies have examined the relationships between the sets of beliefs hypothesized to play a role in each of the personality disorders and diagnostic status. These hypotheses have been supported for Borderline Personality Disorder (Arntz, Dietzel, & Dreesen, 1999) and for Avoidant, Dependent, Obsessive-Compulsive, Narcissistic, and Paranoid Personality Disorders (A. T. Beck et al., 2001). The other personality disorders were not studied because of an inadequate number of subjects. These studies show that dysfunctional beliefs are related to personality disorders in ways that are consistent with cognitive theory but do not provide grounds for conclusions about causality and do not provide a comprehensive test of cognitive conceptualizations of personality disorders.

THE EFFECTIVENESS OF COGNITIVE THERAPY WITH PERSONALITY DISORDERS

Cognitive therapy has been found to provide effective treatment for a wide range of Axis I disorders. However, research into the effectiveness of cognitive-behavioral approaches to treating individuals with personality disorders is more limited. Table 9.6 provides an overview of the available evidence about the effectiveness of cognitive-behavioral interventions with individuals diagnosed as having personality disorders. It is immediately apparent from this table that there have been many uncontrolled clinical reports that assert that cognitive-behavioral therapy can provide effective treatment for personality disorders but fewer controlled outcome studies.

A number of single-case design studies (Nelson-Gray, Johnson, Foyle, Daniel, & Harmon, 1996; Turkat & Maisto, 1985) have provided evidence that some clients with personality disorders can be treated effectively, but also have shown that other clients do not respond to treatment or show mixed results. Springer, Lohr, Buchtel, and Silk (1995) report that a short-term cognitive-behavioral therapy group produced significant improvement in a sample of hospitalized subjects

Table 9.6
The Effectiveness of Cognitive-Behavioral Treatment with Personality Disorders

	Uncontrolled Clinical Reports	Single-Case Design Studies	Studies of the Effects of Personality Disorders on Treatment Outcome	Controlled Outcome Studies
Antisocial	+	−	+	*
Avoidant	+	+	±	+
Borderline	±	−	+	±
Dependent	+	+	+	
Histrionic	+		−	
Narcissistic	+	+		
Obsessive-Compulsive	+	−		
Paranoid	+	+		
Passive-Aggressive	+		+	
Schizoid	+			
Schizotypal				

+ Cognitive-behavioral interventions found to be effective.
− Cognitive-behavioral interventions found not to be effective.
± Mixed findings.
* Cognitive-behavioral interventions were effective with Antisocial Personality Disorder subjects only when the individual was depressed at pretest.

with various personality disorders and that a secondary analysis of a subset of subjects with Borderline Personality Disorder revealed similar findings. They also report that clients evaluated the group as being useful in their life outside the hospital.

At least three personality disorders have been the subject of controlled outcome studies. In a study of the treatment of opiate addicts in a methadone maintenance program, Woody, McLellan, Luborsky, and O'Brien (1985) found that subjects who met *DSM-III* diagnostic criteria for both Major Depression and Antisocial Personality Disorder responded well both to cognitive therapy and to a supportive-expressive psychotherapy systematized by Luborsky (Luborsky, McLellan, Woody, O'Brien, & Auerbach, 1985). The subjects showed statistically significant improvement on 11 of 22 outcome variables, including psychiatric symptoms, drug use, employment, and illegal activity. Subjects who met criteria for Antisocial Personality Disorder but not Major Depression showed little response to treatment, improving on only 3 of 22 variables. This pattern of results was maintained at a seven-month follow-up. Although subjects not diagnosed as Antisocial Personality Disorder responded to treatment better than the sociopaths did, sociopaths who were initially depressed did only slightly worse than the nonsociopaths while the nondepressed sociopaths did much worse.

Studies of the treatment of Avoidant Personality Disorder have shown that short-term social skills training and social skills training combined with cognitive interventions have been effective in increasing the frequency of social interaction and decreasing social anxiety (Stravynski, Marks, & Yule, 1982). Stravynski and his colleagues interpreted this finding as demonstrating the "lack of value" of cognitive interventions. However, the two treatments were equally effective, all treatments were provided by a single therapist (who was also principal investigator), and only one of many possible cognitive interventions (disputation of irrational beliefs) was used. In a subsequent study, Greenberg and Stravynski (1985) report that the avoidant client's fear of ridicule appears to contribute to premature termination in many cases, and they suggest that interventions that modify relevant aspects of clients' cognitions might add substantially to the effectiveness of intervention.

Studies by Linehan and her colleagues (Linehan, Armstrong, Suarez, Allmon, & Heard, 1991; Linehan, Heard, & Armstrong, 1993; Linehan, Tutek, & Heard, 1992) on the treatment of Borderline Personality Disorder have been widely recognized as providing evidence that cognitive-behavioral interventions can be effective with clients who have severe personality disorders. The finding that one year of cognitive-behavioral treatment can produce significant improvement in subjects who not only met diagnostic criteria for Borderline Personality Disorder but also were chronically parasuicidal, had histories of multiple psychiatric hospitalizations, and were unable to maintain employment due to their psychiatric symptoms is encouraging. However, Linehan's approach to the treatment of Borderline Personality Disorder is a very specific protocol for the treatment of one specific personality disorder, and evidence of the effectiveness of her approach does not necessarily provide general support for cognitive therapy with personality disorders.

Controlled outcome studies are sometimes criticized because, in clinical practice, most therapists do not apply a standardized treatment protocol with a homogeneous sample of individuals who share a common diagnosis. Instead, clinicians face a variety of clients and take an individualized approach to treatment. A study of the effectiveness of cognitive therapy under such real-world conditions provides important support for the clinical use of cognitive therapy with clients who are diagnosed as having personality disorders. Persons and her colleagues (1988) conducted an interesting empirical study of clients receiving cognitive therapy for depression in private practice settings. The subjects were 70 consecutive individuals seeking treatment from Burns or Persons in their own practices. Both therapists are established cognitive therapists who have taught and published extensively. In this study, both therapists conducted cognitive therapy as they normally do in their practices. This meant that treatment was open-ended, it was individualized rather than standardized, and medication and inpatient treatment were used as needed.

The primary focus of the study was on identifying predictors of dropout and treatment outcome in cognitive therapy for depression. However, it is interesting for our purposes that 54.3% of the subjects met *DSM-III* criteria for a personality disorder diagnosis and that the investigators considered the presence of a personality disorder diagnosis as a potential predictor of both premature termination of therapy and therapy outcome. The investigators found that, although patients with personality disorders were significantly more likely to drop out of therapy prematurely than patients without personality disorders, those patients with personality disorder diagnoses who persisted in therapy through the completion of treatment showed substantial improvement and did not differ significantly in degree of improvement from patients without personality disorders. Similar findings were reported by Sanderson, Beck, and McGinn (1994) in a study of cognitive therapy for generalized anxiety disorder. Subjects diagnosed with a comorbid personality disorder were more likely to drop out of treatment, but treatment was effective in reducing both anxiety and depression for those who completed a minimum course of treatment.

Little research is available that compares cognitive therapy with other approaches to the treatment of individuals with personality disorders. In the study of the treatment of heroin addicts with and without Antisocial Personality Disorder cited previously, Woody et al. (1985) found that both cognitive therapy and supportive-expressive psychotherapy were effective for antisocial subjects who were depressed at the beginning of treatment and that neither approach was effective with antisocial subjects who were not depressed. In a large, multisite outcome study, the National Institute of Mental Health Treatment of Depression Collaborative Program found a nonsignificant trend for patients with personality disorders to do slightly better than other patients in cognitive therapy whereas they did worse than other patients in interpersonal psychotherapy and pharmacotherapy (Shea et al., 1990). Finally, Hardy et al. (1995) found that individuals with Cluster B personality disorders had significantly poorer outcomes in interpersonal psychotherapy than in cognitive therapy (they did not assess Cluster A or Cluster C personality disorders). These three studies are encouraging but do not provide adequate grounds for drawing conclusions about how cognitive therapy compares with other treatments for individuals with personality disorders.

SUMMARY AND CONCLUSIONS

The available empirical support for cognitive therapy with personality disorders is encouraging. However, cognitive therapy for personality disorders is still under development and is in need of continued theoretical refinement, clinical innovation, and empirical research. With some personality disorders, such as Paranoid Personality Disorder, cognitive conceptualizations have been developed in considerable detail and specific treatment approaches have been proposed. These disorders are ripe for empirical tests of the validity of the conceptualization, of the overall effectiveness of the proposed treatment approach, and of the effects of particular interventions. With other personality disorders, such as Schizotypal Personality Disorder, both the conceptualization and the treatment approach are much less developed and would need further refinement to be suitable for empirical testing.

One area that needs theoretical attention and empirical investigation is the question of how to best conceptualize and treat individuals who are diagnosed as having Mixed Personality Disorder or who satisfy diagnostic criteria for more than one personality disorder. Can we best conceptualize and treat an individual who meets *DSM-IV* criteria for both Paranoid Personality Disorder and Histrionic Personality Disorder, for example, simply by combining the conceptualizations and treatment approaches that have been developed for each disorder separately, or is some other approach needed? If it is possible to develop a comprehensive cognitive typology of the personality disorders, this could simplify the task of exploring the similarities and differences among the personality disorders and make it easier to develop clear conceptualizations of individuals who merit more than one personality disorder diagnosis.

Given the prevalence of personality disorders and the consensus that treatment of clients with personality disorders is difficult and complex no matter which treatment approach is used, it is important that these disorders be a continued focus of empirical research, theoretical innovation, and clinical experimentation. In the meantime, treatment recommendations based on clinical observation and a limited empirical base are the best that cognitive therapy can offer to clinicians who must try to work with personality disorder clients today rather than waiting for empirically validated treatment protocols to be developed. Fortunately, when cognitive-behavioral interventions are based on an individualized conceptualization of the client's problems and the interpersonal aspects of therapy receive sufficient attention, many clients with personality disorders can be treated effectively.

REFERENCES

Arntz, A., Dietzel, R., & Dreesen, L. (1999). Assumptions in borderline personality disorder: Specificity, stability and relationship with etiological factors. *Behavior Research and Therapy, 37,* 545–557.

Beck, A. T., Butler, A. C., Brown, G. K., Dahlsgaard, K. K., Newman, C. F., & Beck, J. S. (2001). Dysfunctional beliefs discriminate personality disorders. *Behavior Research and Therapy, 39,* 1213–1225.

Beck, A. T., & Emery, G. (1985). *Anxiety disorders and phobias: A cognitive perspective.* New York: Basic Books.

Beck, A. T., Freeman, A., Pretzer, J. L., Davis, D. D., Fleming, B., Ottaviani, R., et al. (1990). *Cognitive therapy of the personality disorders.* New York: Guilford Press.

Beck, A. T., Rush, A. J., Shaw, B. F., & Emery, G. (1979). *Cognitive therapy of depression.* New York: Guilford Press.

Beck, A. T., Wright, F. D., Newman, C. F., & Liese, B. S. (1993). *Cognitive therapy of substance abuse.* New York: Guilford Press.

Beck, J. S. (1995). *Cognitive therapy: Basics and beyond.* New York: Guilford Press.

Epstein, N. B., & Baucom, D. H. (2002). *Enhanced cognitive-behavioral therapy for couples: A contextual approach.* Washington, DC: American Psychological Association.

Freeman, A., Pretzer, J. L., Fleming, B., & Simon, K. M. (1990). *Clinical applications of cognitive therapy.* New York: Plenum Press.

Greenberg, D., & Stravynski, A. (1985). Patients who complain of social dysfunction: I. Clinical and demographic features. *Canadian Journal of Psychiatry, 30,* 206–211.

Greenberger, D., & Padesky, C. A. (1995). *Mind over mood: A cognitive therapy treatment manual for clients.* New York: Guilford Press.

Hardy, G. E., Barkham, M., Shapiro, D. A., Stiles, W. B., Rees, A., & Reynolds, S. (1995). Impact of Cluster C personality disorders on outcomes of contrasting brief therapies for depression. *Journal of Consulting and Clinical Psychology, 63,* 997–1004.

Isen, A. M. (1984). Toward understanding the role of affect in cognition. In R. S. Wyer & T. K. Skrull (Eds.), *Handbook of social cognition* (pp. 179–236). Hillsdale, NJ: Erlbaum.

Linehan, M. M. (1987). Commentaries on "The inner experience of the borderline self-mutilator": A cognitive behavioral approach. *Journal of Personality Disorders, 1,* 328–333.

Linehan, M. M. (1993). *Cognitive-behavioral treatment of borderline personality disorder.* New York: Guilford Press.

Linehan, M. M., Armstrong, H. E., Suarez, A., Allmon, D. J., & Heard, H. L. (1991). Cognitive-behavioral treatment of chronically suicidal borderline patients. *Archives of General Psychiatry, 48,* 1060–1064.

Linehan, M. M., Heard, H. L., & Armstrong, H. E. (1993). Naturalistic follow-up of a behavioral treatment for chronically parasuicidal borderline patients. *Archives of General Psychiatry, 50,* 971–974.

Linehan, M. M., Tutek, D. A., & Heard, H. L. (1992, November). *Interpersonal and social treatment outcomes in borderline personality disorder.* Paper presented at the 26th annual conference of the Association for the Advancement of Behavior Therapy, Boston.

Luborsky, L., McLellan, A. T., Woody, G. E., O'Brien, C. P., & Auerbach, A. (1985). Therapist success and its determinants. *Archives of General Psychiatry, 42,* 602–611.

Marlatt, G. A., & Gordon, J. M. (Eds.). (1985). *Relapse prevention: Maintenance strategies in the treatment of addictive behaviors.* New York: Guilford Press.

Mays, D. T. (1985). Behavior therapy with borderline personality disorders: One clinician's perspective. In D. T. Mays & C. M. Franks (Eds.), *Negative outcome in psychotherapy and what to do about it* (pp. 301–311). New York: Springer.

McGinn, L. K., & Young, J. E. (1996). Schema-focused therapy. In P. M. Salkovskis (Ed.), *Frontiers of cognitive therapy* (pp. 183–207). New York: Guilford Press.

Nelson-Gray, R. O., Johnson, D., Foyle, L. W., Daniel, S. S., & Harmon, R. (1996). The effectiveness of cognitive therapy tailored to depressives with personality disorders. *Journal of Personality Disorders, 10,* 132–152.

Padesky, C. A. (1986, September, 18–20). *Personality disorders: Cognitive therapy into the 90's.* Paper presented at the second International Conference on Cognitive Psychotherapy, Umeå, Sweden.

Perris, C., & McGorry, P. D. (1998). *Cognitive psychotherapy of psychotic and personality disorders: Handbook of theory and practice.* New York: Wiley.

Persons, J. B. (1991). *Cognitive therapy in practice: A case formulation approach.* New York: Norton.

Persons, J. B., Burns, B. D., & Perloff, J. M. (1988). Predictors of drop-out and outcome in cognitive therapy for depression in a private practice setting. *Cognitive Therapy and Research, 12,* 557–575.

Pretzer, J. L. (1998). Cognitive-behavioral approaches to the treatment of personality disorders. In C. Perris & P. D. McGorry (Eds.), *Cognitive psychotherapy of psychotic and personality disorders: Handbook of theory and practice* (pp. 269–292). New York: Wiley.

Pretzer, J. L., & Beck, A. T. (1996). A cognitive theory of personality disorders. In J. F. Clarkin & M. F. Lenzenweger (Eds.), *Major theories of personality disorder* (pp. 36–105). New York: Guilford Press.

Rothstein, M. M., & Vallis, T. M. (1991). The application of cognitive therapy to patients with personality disorders. In T. M. Vallis, J. L. Howes, & P. C. Miller (Eds.), *The challenge of cognitive therapy: Applications to nontraditional populations* (pp. 59–84). New York: Plenum Press.

Sanderson, W. C., Beck, A. T., & McGinn, L. K. (1994). Cognitive therapy for generalized anxiety disorder: Significance of co-morbid personality disorders. *Journal of Cognitive Psychotherapy: An International Quarterly, 8,* 13–18.

Shea, M. T., Pilkonis, P. A., Beckham, E., Collins, J. F., Elkin, I., Sotsky, S. M., et al. (1990). Personality disorders and treatment outcome in the NIMH treatment of depression collaborative research program. *American Journal of Psychiatry, 147,* 711–718.

Springer, T., Lohr, N. E., Buchtel, H. A., & Silk, K. R. (1995). A preliminary report of short-term cognitive-behavioral group therapy for inpatients with personality disorders. *Journal of Psychotherapy Practice and Research, 5,* 57–71.

Stravynski, A., Marks, I., & Yule, W. (1982). Social skills problems in neurotic outpatients: Social skills training with and without cognitive modification. *Archives of General Psychiatry, 39,* 1378–1385.

Turkat, I. D., & Maisto, S. A. (1985). Personality disorders: Application of the experimental method to the formulation and modification of personality disorders. In D. H. Barlow (Ed.), *Clinical handbook of psychological disorders: A step by step treatment manual* (pp. 502–570). New York: Guilford Press.

Watkins, P. C., Mathews, A., Williamson, D. A., & Fuller, R. D. (1992). Mood-congruent memory in depression: Emotional priming or elaboration? *Journal of Abnormal Psychology, 101,* 581–586.

Woody, G. E., McLellan, A. T., Luborsky, L., & O'Brien, C. P. (1985). Sociopathy and psychotherapy outcome. *Archives of General Psychiatry, 42,* 1081–1086.

Wright, J. H., & Davis, D. (1994). The therapeutic relationship in cognitive-behavioral therapy: Patient perceptions and therapist responses. *Cognitive and Behavioral Practice, 1,* 25–46.

Young, J. (1990). *Cognitive therapy for personality disorders: A schema-focused approach.* Sarasota, FL: Professional Resource Exchange.

CHAPTER 10

The Treatment of Personality Adaptations Using Redecision Therapy

Vann S. Joines

THIS CHAPTER EXPLORES the theory of personality adaptations and how these adaptations can be treated using redecision therapy. This is a nonpathological approach to working with personality. The assumption of this approach is that the psychological symptoms or problems that people have in the present represent the best options that these individuals had in childhood, both to survive and to meet the expectations of their parents and other significant authority figures. Furthermore, the part of the self that exercises these options in the present operates unconsciously and autonomously and is oriented to feelings rather than time and place. The conscious part of the personality has little or no appreciation for the survival value of these options and is usually critical of and attempting to eliminate these symptoms or behaviors. Thus, an inevitable impasse is set up between these two parts. By assisting individuals in *experiencing* their unconscious "emotional truth" concerning these options, they can consciously appreciate their previously unconscious survival strategies (adaptations) and make new decisions (redecisions) about the best way to operate in the present. These *redecisions* may involve the realization that what worked best in childhood is no longer necessary given the resources the individual has now that he or she did not have as a child or the realization that the original option is still the best one in the present and is no longer to be regarded as a problem.

The concept of personality adaptations was first developed by two colleagues who were observing similar phenomena in different settings. Paul Ware (1983) was directing an inpatient treatment program for adolescents. Growing out of his work with transactional analysis (Berne, 1961), Ware began to realize that there are just so many possible ways individuals can adapt in their family of origin to survive psychologically and to meet the expectations of their parents. Ware identified six basic adaptations that seemed to be universal among human beings:

Schizoid, Antisocial, Paranoid, Passive-Aggressive, Obsessive-Compulsive, and Hysteric.

Taibi Kahler (1972) had been conducting a questionnaire-based research project into various aspects of personality, using some of the ideas of transactional analysis. He was interested both in the process of personality—how people do things—as well as the content—what people do. On the basis of his research, Kahler also identified the same six personality patterns.

As colleagues in the International Transactional Analysis Association and personal friends, Ware and Kahler began to share what they were observing with each other and together developed a new theory they called "personality adaptations." After hearing them present this information, I began to work with this model in the early 1980s and contributed many additional insights, as well as a questionnaire for assessing the adaptations and a recent book on the topic (Joines, 1986, 1988; Joines & Stewart, 2002b).

Redecision therapy (Goulding & Goulding, 1978, 1979; Kadis, 1985), a powerful and highly effective in-depth, brief therapy approach combining cognitive, affective, and behavioral work, was developed by Robert Goulding and Mary Goulding as a result of their training with Fritz Perls and Eric Berne in the early 1960s. The Gouldings recognized what a powerful combination Berne's transactional analysis (1961), with its clear conceptual framework, and Perl's Gestalt therapy (Perls, 1969; Perls, Hefferline, & Goodman, 1951), with its powerful experiential tools, would make when integrated. They added many of their own discoveries, and redecision therapy was born.

Combining the model of personality adaptations with redecision therapy offers a unique and powerful nonpathological approach to working with the issues of personality.

THEORETICAL COMPONENTS OF THE COMBINED MODEL

The six personality adaptations identified by Ware were given more descriptive names by Kahler:

1. Schizoid (Kahler—dreamers).
2. Antisocial (Kahler—promoters).
3. Paranoid (Kahler—persisters).
4. Passive-aggressive (Kahler—rebels).
5. Obsessive-compulsive (Kahler—workaholics).
6. Hysteric (more currently histrionic, Kahler—reactors).

The adaptations are seen as resulting from a combination of what is innate and what is shaped by the environment. The first three Ware termed "surviving" adaptations because they are believed to begin developing in the first 18 months of life as a way individuals take care of themselves when trust breaks down and infants believe that they cannot rely on the environment to take care of them and must figure out how to do that on their own. The latter three Ware called "performing" adaptations because they are seen as the way toddlers and young children adapt to meet the expectations of their parents from 18 months to 6 years of age (Joines & Stewart, 2002b).

These adaptations are viewed as universal and as forming the basic building blocks of personality. They do not imply pathology but rather adaptive *style* and, therefore, are seen across the spectrum from completely healthy to totally dysfunctional. Each adaptation has positive as well as negative characteristics. Both Kahler (1977a) and Joines (1986) have given colloquial names to Ware's original types. Kahler's are listed with Ware's. Joines's titles suggesting both the positive and negative aspects of the adaptations are:

1. Creative-daydreamer (Schizoid).
2. Charming-manipulator (Antisocial).
3. Brilliant-skeptic (Paranoid).
4. Playful-resister (Passive-Aggressive).
5. Responsible-workaholic (Obsessive-Compulsive).
6. Enthusiastic-overreactor (Histrionic).

The *DSM-IV-TR* (American Psychiatric Association [APA], 2000) *personality disorders* depict the negative characteristics of the adaptations used in a chronic, maladaptive way. These personality disorders are composed of: (1) pure adaptations, (2) different degrees of the adaptations, and (3) various combinations of the adaptations. For example, Avoidant Personality Disorder is composed of both the Schizoid and Paranoid adaptations and represents the mildest version of the Schizoid Personality Disorder. Schizoid Personality Disorder represents the mid-range of the Schizoid adaptation, whereas Schizotypal is the most severe. Dependent Personality Disorder is viewed as resulting from a combination of the Schizoid and Passive-Aggressive adaptations. Borderline Personality Disorder is seen as a combination of the Antisocial and Passive-Aggressive adaptations. Narcissistic Personality Disorder results from a combination of the Paranoid and Antisocial adaptations.

Every individual has at least one of the "surviving" and at least one of the "performing" adaptations that are preferred over the others. These preferred styles represent what worked best in an individual's family of origin to survive psychologically and to meet the expectations of his or her parents. Because each adaptation represents the best option for a given situation, individuals usually know how to do the behaviors of all the adaptations, but certain ones are preferred because they worked best in their household.

CONTACT DOORS

Each person can be contacted in one of three areas: feeling, thinking, or behavior. Ware (1983) pointed out that each adaptation has a preferred area for initial contact, a target area for growth and change, and a trap area in which the person has the greatest defenses. He called these the "doors" (p. 11) to therapy, and they vary for each adaptation. By knowing the doors for each adaptation, the therapist can quickly establish rapport, target interventions to the area that will have the greatest effect, and avoid becoming trapped in the client's defenses.

REDECISION THERAPY

As mentioned earlier, redecision therapy is an integration of the theory of transactional analysis with the experiential techniques of Gestalt therapy. Several basic assumptions guide this process:

1. *Okayness:* Okayness is a statement of essence rather than behavior. It refers to the fact that each of us has basic worth, value, and dignity as a human being. The redecision therapist works from the stance of both therapist and client being okay.
2. *Autonomy:* The belief is that all individuals can think and decide what they want for their own lives. Therefore, the therapy is *contractual* rather than the therapist deciding what is best for the client.
3. *Responsibility:* A major assumption is that "the power is in the patient" (Goulding & Goulding, 1978, p. 10); that is, it is the patient, not the therapist, who really has the power to change. The therapist's role is to make explicit the choices and how and why the person may be stopping himself or herself from changing in the present and to create the conditions necessary for change.
4. *Protection:* Another assumption is that the behaviors the client has been using have been in the interest of protecting himself or herself on an emotional level in the best way the client has known up to now. By bringing that realization into conscious awareness, clients can have empathy for themselves and informed choice about how they want to live now.
5. *Authenticity:* A final assumption is that "people change at the point at which they become fully who they are (experience and own their emotional truth) rather than trying to be what they are not" (trying to fool themselves and others; Fagan & Sheppard, 1967 Workshop). The experiential techniques of Gestalt therapy are used to help clients experience their own emotional truth.

GESTALT TECHNIQUES

Gestalt techniques used in redecision therapy include:

1. *The use of fantasy:* Fantasy is used to allow the client to "try on" new behaviors by experiencing them in fantasy before implementing them in reality. The person can experience what a positive change would be like or what it would be like to continue with a current bad feeling state over time. Both can increase commitment to change.
2. *Putting words with body language:* Perls believed that "the truth is in the body" (Fagan & Sheppard, 1967 Workshop). Awareness can often be facilitated by having the client be aware of and put words with various aspects of body language. Frequently, clients will show with their bodies what the main issue is long before they are aware on a conscious level. Thus, the body can provide significant shortcuts in therapy.
3. *Using active present tense:* Having clients speak in first person, active present tense allows them to experience what they are saying rather than merely talking about it. As a result, the content is much more immediate and alive in that the person is emotionally connected to what he or she is saying.
4. *Making the rounds:* In a group setting, when a member is projecting a certain judgment of himself or herself onto other members of the group, it can be very therapeutic to have that person go around the group and tell all the others what they are feeling or thinking about the individual as though it were true. The person will discover that the disowned feelings and thoughts are coming from inside. The person will also realize that the other members of the group are actually very supportive.

5. *Gestalt dialogues:* Perls pointed out how we identify with one part of our- selves and split off another part that feels unacceptable. Gestalt dialogues are used to integrate the parts of self that have been split off. These dia- logues can be set up in a number of ways: (1) between two symbolic parts of the body (left hand versus right hand), (2) between conflicting parts that have been expressed verbally ("I want to" versus "I don't want to"), (3) be- tween self and a part projected onto a current person (using two chairs), and (4) between self and a part projected onto a parent or other historical figure (again using two chairs).

TRANSACTIONAL ANALYSIS CONCEPTS

Redecision therapy also uses the transactional analysis concepts of ego states, rackets, games, counterinjunctions, injunctions, life positions, early decisions, life scripts, and escape hatches to identify critical elements in the process.

EGO STATES

Transactional Analysis views the personality structure in terms of ego states: Parent, Adult, and Child. An ego state is a consistent, coherent system of feeling and thinking with a correlated set of behavior patterns. The Parent is what we have internalized from our parents and significant other authority figures. It includes both nurturing and limit-setting functions along with ethical guide- lines and value judgments. The Adult is our capacity for here and now reality testing. It mediates between the desires of the Child and the concerns of the Parent. The Child is the original part of self—our feelings, intuitive perceptions, and decisions based on early experience. It is the most enjoyable part and the part that is spontaneous and capable of forming warm intimate relationships with others.

RACKETS

Rackets are the feelings that people learn to feel in a situation of stress in their family of origin and that are used now to elicit support from the environment. They are the feelings that the parents modeled and/or responded to and, there- fore, reinforced. Rackets are frequently substituted for other feelings. For exam- ple, if an individual's parents responded to stress by getting angry and paying the most attention to the individual when he or she was angry but ignored him or her when the individual was feeling sad, the racket feeling the person is likely to develop is anger. The person may now get angry when he or she is actually feeling sad. He or she is likely to seek out justification for feeling angry in current situa- tions because anger is the feeling that elicited attention and support from his or her parents.

GAMES

Games are the process that Freud referred to as the "compulsion to repeat" (1920/1955, p. 35). Games are used to re-create a similar situation repeatedly to (1) try to "undo" the original situation, albeit unsuccessfully and (2) justify what individuals are already feeling and believing about themselves, others, and their destiny. Games are created by setting up an interaction based on implicit assumptions that the other party does not hold and then feeling tricked when the assumptions that the other party does hold becomes explicit. The first individual then tries to blame the other party for not holding the same assumptions that he or she had.

COUNTERINJUNCTIONS

Counterinjunctions are the directives from an individual's parents about what he or she should do to meet their expectations and be someone the family would be proud of. "Drivers" are a particular set of counterinjunctions that carry with them a conditional sense of okayness. For example, "You can be okay if you are perfect." There are five of these drivers: "Be perfect," "Try hard," "Be strong," "Hurry up," and "Please others" (Kahler & Capers, 1974). Individuals strive to follow these counterinjunctions to be okay with their parents.

INJUNCTIONS

Injunctions are secret, implied messages from an individual's parents that are conveyed when the parents feel threatened by and react negatively to the existence, feelings, or behavior of the child. This process is usually not within the parents' awareness. The Gouldings (1979) identified three categories of injunctions: behavior, feeling, and thinking. The behavioral injunctions are:

1. Don't be or don't exist.
2. Don't be well or don't be sane.
3. Don't make it or don't succeed.
4. Don't be you.
5. Don't be close or don't trust.
6. Don't be a child.
7. Don't grow up.
8. Don't be important.
9. Don't belong.
10. Don't enjoy.
11. Don't.

The feeling injunctions include:

1. Don't feel.
2. Don't feel "x."
3. Don't feel what you feel; feel what I feel.

The thinking injunctions are:

1. Don't think.
2. Don't think "x."
3. Don't think what you think; think what I think.

LIFE POSITIONS

Life positions are the conclusions about self, others, and destiny that children come to as a result of how they are interacted with by their parents. The life position includes a feeling, a statement about self, a statement about the other, and a statement about the individual's destiny. For example, in response to being treated harshly, a child might feel sad, think "You're mean, I'm unlovable," and conclude, "I'll never get what I want."

EARLY DECISIONS

The early decision is a plan of action the child decides on to try to correct a bad situation the child is experiencing; for example, if the child feels ignored and wants to get his or her parents to love him or her, the child may decide, "I'll feel sad until you change, and if things get bad enough, I'll kill myself, then you'll miss me and want me back." Early decisions are acted out unconsciously as a way to try to make people or situations change, keep safe, or, if all else fails, get even.

LIFE SCRIPTS

A life script is the overall unconscious plan for how individuals attempt to get unconditional love from their parents or, if that doesn't seem possible, to get revenge. This plan is based on the early decision and governs much of what people do in life and, by definition, is outside of awareness. All the previous elements discussed are seen as part of that life script. The goal is to bring these elements into awareness so that the person can exercise conscious choice over what he or she does in the present.

Each of the personality adaptations has a certain pattern of striving or life script that individuals use to try to protect themselves and be okay with their parents and other significant persons in their life. Although most people believe that they direct their lives consciously, the reality is that their most significant behavior is autonomously directed by an unconscious part of themselves that decided how best to take care of themselves, given their experiences in childhood. As that part is integrated in to conscious awareness, individuals can then in fact exercise conscious choice over their behavior.

ESCAPE HATCHES

Escape hatches are specific decisions individuals make in childhood about how they will get out of situations that seem unbearable. Examples are:

- Out of sadness, a person may decide, "If things get bad enough, I'll just kill myself."
- Out of anger, an individual may decide, "If things get bad enough, I'll kill you."
- Out of fear, a person may decide, "If things get bad enough, I'll go crazy."

Whenever any of these escape hatches are open, clients do not make progress in therapy because a part of them is unconsciously working to justify the early decision. If they allowed their lives to get better, they would not have a way to justify the option. Therefore, it is important to make sure that clients have closed all the escape hatches to free their energy for change.

RANGE OF PSYCHOPATHOLOGY AND PERSONALITY DISORDERS WITHIN THE SCOPE OF TREATMENT

Because working with the personality adaptations involves a nonpathological approach to treatment and focuses on teaching clients to use their adaptive styles in the way that will serve them best in the present, this approach is applicable to a wide range of treatment issues. Essentially, the personality adaptations are seen across the spectrum from health to dysfunction. At the healthier end of the spectrum, more of the positive aspects of the adaptations are seen. As an individual moves toward the dysfunctional end of the spectrum, more of the negative aspects of the adaptations become apparent.

Adjustment disorders can occur with any of the personality adaptations. In terms of subtypes, adjustment disorders with anxious or depressed mood are likely to be seen across the spectrum in individuals with Histrionic, Obsessive-Compulsive, Passive-Aggressive, Schizoid, or Paranoid adaptations. Adjustment disorders with disturbance of conduct are most likely to be seen in individuals with an Antisocial adaptation.

The personality adaptations that are most likely to experience anxiety and mood disorders are the performing adaptations (Histrionic, Obsessive-Compulsive, and Passive-Aggressive). When the symptoms of anxiety and depression are more severe, the surviving adaptations of Schizoid and Paranoid are likely to be involved as well. The Antisocial adaptation will tend to act out rather than experience anxiety and depression.

At the level of the personality disorders, the negative sides of the adaptations are used as a chronic maladaptive style. Pure types of adaptations are seen along with various degrees and combinations of the adaptations. For example, Schizoid, Antisocial, Paranoid, Passive-Aggressive, Obsessive-Compulsive, and Histrionic Personality Disorders are seen as the pure types of the adaptations. As to the Schizoid adaptation, three levels of personality disorders are apparent: (1) Avoidant, which is the mildest version, (2) Schizoid, which is in the middle, and (3) Schizotypal, which is the most severe. The other personality disorders represent different combinations of the adaptations. For example, Dependent Personality Disorder involves a combination of the Schizoid and Passive-Aggressive adaptations. Avoidant Personality Disorder represents a combination of the Paranoid and Schizoid adaptations. Borderline Personality Disorder has aspects of both the Antisocial and Passive-Aggressive adaptations. Narcissistic Personality Disorder involves both the Antisocial and Paranoid adaptations.

The dysfunctional extremes of the different adaptations are seen at the psychotic level. For example, the different types of schizophrenia seem to be different adaptations combined with the Schizoid adaptation. In the paranoid type, the extreme of the Paranoid adaptation is seen along with the Schizoid. In the disorganized type (previously known as hebephrenia), the Antisocial adaptation is seen along with the Schizoid. In the catatonic type, the Passive-Aggressive adaptation is seen along with the Schizoid.

TREATMENT METHODS AND
TECHNICAL ASPECTS OR INTERVENTIONS

The primary goal in using redecision therapy to treat the different personality adaptations is to help the individual achieve autonomy, that is, to consciously choose how he or she wants to live in the present rather than operate on the basis of archaic, unconscious survival strategies. The personality adaptations represent what was once the best option for individuals taking care of themselves in their family of origin. In the present, the positive sides of the adaptations can still serve the individual well. What is important is to let go of the negative sides. The process for doing so is to help the client experientially bring into awareness the old strategies and their survival value in childhood and spontaneously create new options in the present.

CONTACT

Contact is a concept from Gestalt therapy that means as full a meeting between self and another person that is possible in the present moment (Perls et al., 1951). As noted previously, each of the personality adaptations has a certain preferred way of making contact. By joining clients in their preferred area, the therapist can quickly establish rapport and eliminate a barrier to effective therapy. The "open door" for making contact with each of the adaptations is as follows:

1. *Schizoid:* Invade their withdrawn passivity.
2. *Paranoid:* Join them in their thinking.
3. *Antisocial:* Playfully make explicit the way in which they are not being straight.
4. *Passive-Aggressive:* Playfully stroke their rebellious child behavior.
5. *Obsessive-Compulsive:* Join them in their thinking.
6. *Histrionic:* Be nurturing and playful.

FRAMING THE PRESENTING PROBLEM SO THAT IT IS SOLVABLE

Sometimes clients frame problems in ways that are unsolvable, for example: (1) trying to change someone else, (2) trying to force yourself to change against your will, and (3) trying to stop yourself from doing something rather than choosing to do something different. If a client has framed a problem in a way that is unsolvable, it is important to help him or her frame it in a way that is solvable. For example, if individuals are pushing themselves to stop procrastinating, they may be helped to see that they procrastinate more when they push themselves and they actually get more done when they get off their back.

CONTRACTING

Berne defined a contract as "an explicit bilateral commitment to a well-defined course of action" (1966, p. 362). Contracting is the process of specifying the goal(s) of the therapy and entering into a cooperative rather than a competitive process. It further seeds the idea of positive change by focusing on the desired outcome of therapy rather than on the problem. Contracting is also an opportunity to make explicit how a person might sabotage the desired change and to take corrective action instead. It is important to make sure that the contract is congruent on both the social (explicit) and psychological (implicit) levels.

CONFRONTING CONS

Cons are the ways clients attempt to keep themselves in a victim position and justify not solving the problem. Originally, maintaining such a position was important in childhood when taking direct action meant the possibility of getting hurt in some way. The first con is the most important to confront because it usually establishes the psychological level contract. For example, if clients say that they want "to be able to" do something, the psychological level, the implicit message is that the therapist is suppose to "make the client able to," which is an exercise in frustration because the real issue is not their ability but their willingness. In this case, it is useful to say, for example: "I'm aware that you are already 'able to,' are you willing to?"

DECONTAMINATION WORK

Often the beliefs that clients hold "contaminate" or interfere with clear, adult ego state data processing. By challenging those beliefs, the therapist can assist the client in seeing the situation more objectively. For example, ask a client who says she is "bad" where she learned to think that way; then, as she realizes that one of her parents taught her that, ask what she believes now.

RACKET ANALYSIS

For clients who are maintaining a familiar, unpleasant feeling, it is important to find out what the spontaneous feeling is underneath that is being avoided by the racket. That can be done by finding out the existential position (belief about self, other, and an individual's destiny) the client moves into when he or she is feeling the familiar feeling. The existential position can then be traced back to an early experience in which the person first learned to feel the familiar feeling. As the client describes the early experience, the natural spontaneous feeling that wasn't permitted can easily be discovered.

GAME ANALYSIS

To maintain the familiar unpleasant feeling, a client unconsciously re-creates the same situation repeatedly. The therapist can ask for a recent specific example of when the client felt the familiar unpleasant feeling, listen to the dynamics, and then diagram the game in terms of both the social and psychological levels of communication. Doing so helps clients bring into awareness how they invite responses that they do not really want. The familiar unpleasant feeling(s) at the end of the game will be the racket.

EARLY SCENE WORK

The racket can be traced back to an early scene in which the client first felt the feeling(s), and the therapist can have the client reexperience the scene in first person, active, present tense as though it is happening now. By working with the scene in present tense, the therapist can identify the counterinjunctions, injunctions, and early decision clients made so to take care of themselves.

TARGETING INTERVENTIONS

Because each of the personality adaptations has a target area (feeling, thinking, or behavior), which will enable maximum change, the therapist can work in the mode that matches the target area for the client's adaptation(s) to achieve maximum results. The target areas for the adaptations are:

1. *Schizoids:* Thinking. Ask them to share their thinking aloud and bring it to closure by taking action to get their needs met.
2. *Paranoids:* Feeling. Inquire about what they are feeling.
3. *Antisocials:* Feeling. Find out what they really want that they presume they can't get so they try to con others instead.
4. *Passive-Aggressives:* Feeling. Find out what they are feeling and wanting.
5. *Obsessive-Compulsives:* Feeling. Help them identify and deal with their feelings.
6. *Histrionics:* Thinking. Help them to think about what they are feeling.

REDECISION WORK

Helping clients make explicit the early decision by verbalizing it and telling the parent or other significant figure(s) what they are deciding to do in the early scene allows them to experience the clever way in which they took care of themselves as children. This realization helps shift the client's energy to a free, spontaneous place. At the same time, clients experience how the decision is no longer necessary in light of the resources they have now. As a result, clients are assisted in spontaneously redeciding to do things differently in the present.

ANCHORING AND REINFORCING THE REDECISION

Humor is often used to anchor the redecision because the person is likely to remember something humorous, and humor helps access the individual's spontaneity and positive feelings. An example of an anchor for a woman who decides to take back her power might be to sing "I Am Woman, Hear Me Roar!"

Positive stroking is used to reinforce the new behavior whenever the client reports a positive change or the therapist notices the client using the new behavior.

PROCESS OF THE THERAPEUTIC APPROACH

The process of using redecision therapy with the different personality adaptations consists of first establishing effective contact with the client. Assessment of the individual's personality adaptations is important to know which area (thinking, feeling, or behavior) is the "open door" for the client. This assessment can be done intuitively, by observing "driver" behavior, or by using a questionnaire. When the therapist puts his or her energy in the same area as clients put theirs, effective contact and rapport can be established very easily.

The next step is to find out the presenting problem and whether the client has framed it in a way that is solvable or unsolvable. Almost inevitably, the client is attempting to solve the problem in his or her own "trap area," which is why the client has not been able to solve it himself or herself. That is, the client has been critical of himself or herself in the area that feels most vulnerable to the client. The therapist wants to position himself or herself on the side of clients' natural child ego state (the original, spontaneous part of the individual) and help clients experience the original value of what they have been doing to try to protect themselves so they have empathy for themselves rather than criticism.

Once the problem has been clarified and possibly reframed in a way that is solvable, the therapist finds out how clients want to change the problem and negotiates a very clear, behaviorally specific contract. Ways in which clients may be giving away their power and responsibility and clients' unconscious defenses are carefully tracked and made explicit. Clients are invited to give a current example of the problem they are experiencing and to use first person, active, present tense to experience in the here and now what they are describing. Clients are also asked to describe what they are feeling and what they are telling themselves about themselves, the other people involved, and their destiny. The assumption is that in conflictual situations in the present, we reexperience a familiar existential position resulting from early decisions we made in childhood about ourselves, others, and our destiny. These decisions represent the very best option we perceived at the time for taking care of ourselves. The difficulty in the present is that we keep limiting ourselves to this one option when other options would work better for solving the current problem. The redecision process allows us to free ourselves from those past decisions and pursue new options in the present.

Clients are next asked if this existential position is a familiar way of feeling and who they were in this position with as a child. Then clients are asked to be in the early scene, again using first person, active, present tense and describe what is happening. The therapist works with the "target area" (feeling, thinking, or behavior) of clients' adaptation so that the interventions will be most effective. Clients are also asked what they are feeling, telling themselves, and deciding to do as a child to take care of themselves, given what is taking place. The therapist then works with the client using Gestalt dialogues to talk out with the early figures the emotional issues that did not get resolved to resolve them now and come to a new decision (redecision) about how they will take care of themselves in the present. The therapist looks for evidence of clients' change in the session by observing their body, emotional states, and energy shifts. The goal is for clients to experience the change in the present moment so they are feeling, thinking, and behaving differently. The therapist works to anchor the new decision in clients' memory. Clients are then asked to make a specific adult plan for how to implement that new decision outside the session as well. In subsequent sessions, clients report on their successes and receive reinforcement, as well as do additional work on areas that do not yet feel resolved. Once clients have achieved the changes they desire, the sessions are spread out until they feel ready to say goodbye.

The goodbye process consists of processing anything in the relationship with the therapist that feels unfinished, reviewing and celebrating clients' changes, sharing appreciations, and saying goodbye.

Throughout the redecision process, knowledge about the adaptations is used to guide the therapy in terms of key issues to be addressed, the target areas for intervention, and the trap areas to be avoided. Some of the key elements for each of the adaptations follow.

Creative-Daydreamer (Schizoid)   For creative-daydreamers, the open door is behavior. The type of behavior they use is withdrawn passivity. As kids, they saw their parents as overwhelmed and were afraid of being too much for their parents to handle, so they learned to not cause trouble for their parents. They learned to be supportive of their parents in hopes that their parents would be okay and in turn take care of them. When that did not work, they simply withdrew and substituted fantasy for getting their needs met by interacting with others in reality.

For the therapist to make effective contact with creative-daydreamers, he or she needs to invade their withdrawn passivity by going in after them and bringing them out. The way to do that is to convey firm expectations that they be active, participate, and ask for what they want. Creative-daydreamers are the only adaptation that will respond positively to such firm expectations. When they experience firm expectations from the therapist, they feel safe because they know that they are not going to overwhelm him or her.

Once contact and rapport have been established, the target area for the therapist to focus on is thinking. It is important to get creative-daydreamers to share their thinking aloud and to bring it to closure by taking action to get their needs met in reality. Feelings are the area to avoid because they are the trap area for creative-daydreamers. The *driver* for creative-daydreamers is "Be strong" (not have feelings and needs). When individuals with this adaptation feel bad, they withdraw to try to get away from those bad feelings, which only makes them feel worse, and that is how they get stuck. As they take action to get their needs met, they feel good and become animated and excited.

Impasse clarification is a key part of the redecision process with creative-daydreamers and often necessary before they can contract clearly for change. Because they try to avoid problems rather than solve them, the therapist needs to continually bring them back to the problem with a strong affirmation that they are competent and can solve it. Creative-daydreamers need to learn to be as supportive of their own feelings and needs as they are of everyone else's. The redecision work itself is done primarily in the thinking mode, helping them decontaminate their early beliefs and claim their rightful place in the world today.

Typical *cons* used by creative-daydreamers are substituting the pronoun "it" for "I" and using passive rather than active verbs. It is important to have them change those to experience their own personal power and responsibility in the situation. The *rackets* they use are numbness, confusion, and frustration to cover more intense feelings such as hurt, rage, and excitement. Their major *injunctions* are: "Don't think," "Don't be important," "Don't feel angry or excited," "Don't enjoy," "Don't belong," and "Don't be sane." The *escape hatch* to close is going crazy. The primary therapeutic goal is to help them reclaim their birthright to take up space, have feelings and needs, and take action to get those needs met.

Charming-Manipulators (Antisocial)   Behavior is also the open door for charming-manipulators, but it is the opposite behavior from the creative-daydreamers. Charming-manipulators are actively aggressive. They attempt to charm or intimidate others into giving them what they want. They often grew up in competitive situations where it was "survival of the fittest." To make genuine contact with them, the therapist has to make explicit what they are doing without being critical. It helps to be matter-of-fact or playful. Because they are playing a *game* called "Catch Me If You Can," their behavior is very predictable and the therapist can anticipate where they are going and get there before they do. They are intrigued by how the therapist was able to do that and initially become engaged in therapy to find out. When they cannot outwit the therapist, they respect him or her. Such respect is earned through continual testing over time. It usually takes some time before charming-manipulators make a real commitment to therapy.

Once genuine contact has been established, the target area to work with is feeling. It is useful to ask charming-manipulators when they first decided to stop trusting people and what they really want that they presume they can't get so they try devious tactics instead. As they allow themselves to feel and be real rather than to pretend, the greatest change is seen in their thinking. They begin to look at long-range consequences rather than outsmarting others in the moment, and they begin to make commitments in relationships.

Because charming-manipulators experienced abandonment from parents in childhood and will fight against being in a vulnerable position again, initially they will not genuinely engage in the redecision process per se. They may attempt to fool the therapist by pretending. Therefore, the early stages of redecision therapy with them consist mainly of confronting their *cons* until they begin to transact in a straight way. Impasse clarification comprises the bulk of the work with redecision work in the latter stages to help them grieve the early abandonment they experienced. It is important to leave the burden of proof on them to demonstrate the sincerity of what they are saying they want to change. Charming-manipulators need to learn to clean up their act and to stop abandoning themselves.

The *rackets* charming-manipulators use are anger and confusion covering sadness and scare. The major *injunctions* they received are: "Don't trust," "Don't make it," "Don't feel sad or scared," and "Don't think" (to problem-solve, think to outsmart and make fools of others). The *escape hatch* to close is homicide. The primary therapeutic goal is to help them to be real and get their needs met in a cooperative way with others.

Brilliant-Skeptic (Paranoid)   Thinking is the open door for brilliant-skeptics. They tend to think in a very careful, detailed manner and are often initially skeptical of other's motives. They grew up in unpredictable situations and had to be vigilant to take care of themselves. As a result, they don't like surprises. They want things to be reliable and consistent and to know everything that is going to happen ahead of time.

To make effective contact, the therapist needs to engage brilliant-skeptics by thinking with them and by being very predictable. As rapport is established, the target area of feeling can be explored in a nurturing manner. It is important to not initiate being playful with them too early because they will view that as silly and childish and be skeptical of the therapist's motives. It is better to wait until the therapist sees some sign of playfulness from them to support. As the therapist does so, they will begin to relax and let go of being so controlling. The result is that they gain some spontaneity.

The trap area to avoid is behavior. Brilliant-skeptics were supposed to "be perfect" and to "be strong," and they are attempting to behave in a way that no one could find fault with. If you comment on their behavior, they become very self-conscious and all their defenses go up. They retreat into what feels like a concrete silo that is impossible to get through. Under normal circumstances, it takes a while before brilliant-skeptics decide that they can trust the therapist enough to be vulnerable with him or her. Helping them deal with their fear by checking out their fantasies so they feel safe and supported is a major issue.

The redecision process proceeds slowly with brilliant-skeptics. They will not engage in double-chair work initially because it seems too unpredictable to them. It is helpful to explain everything ahead of time that the therapist wants them to do so there are no surprises. As they learn to trust that the therapist will not surprise them and that they are not going to feel humiliated, they begin to allow the therapist enough control to lead them in the therapeutic process. Much of the early work involves helping them create a safe and trusting relationship. That is done both by the therapist's being reliable and consistent and by helping them decontaminate their Adult ego state from their rigid Controlling-Parent beliefs to make it safe for their Child ego state to emerge. The critical redecision work often involves working through the ways they were inappropriately intruded on as kids and experiencing how they can protect themselves now.

Typical *cons* to be aware of are the "shoulds," "oughts," "musts," "need tos," and "wanting to know why" of the Parent ego state and the *"be able tos"* of the Child. The *racket* is usually anger covering scare. Major *injunctions* include: "Don't feel," "Don't trust," and "Don't be a child." The *escape hatch* to close is homicide. The primary therapeutic goal is learning to feel safe in the world.

Playful-Resister (Passive-Aggressive)   Behavior is the open door for playful-resisters, but it is very different behavior from that of the creative-daydreamers or charming-manipulators. Playful-resistors approach the world in an aggressively passive manner. For example, they might say, "Gosh, it sure is hot in here!" and expect someone else to do something about it. They are often one of the adaptations that therapists have the most difficulty working with because playful-resisters want someone else to make things better but resist any attempt by others at directing them to do something to make a change. Their resistance comes from having been overcontrolled in childhood. Others often wind up very frustrated in dealing with them. To make effective contact, the therapist has to engage their Rebellious-Child behavior in a playful manner. As the therapist is playful, playful-resisters experience that the therapist is not trying to control them.

Once the therapist has achieved rapport, he or she can move to being nurturing and find out what the playful-resister is feeling and wanting, which is the target area. In that way, the therapist can help the client be more direct and ask for what he or she wants from others. Playful-resisters need to experience that others will be cooperative with them now rather than get into power struggles with them the way their parents did.

The trap area to avoid is thinking because the message they got as kids was to "try hard," and they are already doing so in their thinking. They tend to frame things as either/or, all or nothing, and struggle in their thinking. Neither choice feels good because both involve giving up something. The original dilemma was feeling as though they had to give up what they wanted to get—their parents' love. They often push themselves from their Parent ego state and resist from their Child. Decisions for them feel like "damned if I do and damned if I don't." It is important for them to learn that there are always more than two choices in any situation and that when they limit their choices to two, they create an inevitable dilemma. What works best is for the therapist to work from the stance that the client is okay with him or her without having to change anything. In fact, the therapist can actually discourage them from changing to take over the resistant position. Doing so frees the playful-resister to go in a positive direction.

The redecision process with playful-resisters requires staying on the side of their Natural Child ego state by continually being playful with them. It is often fruitless to attempt to do contracting or anything else that involves engaging their thinking in a direct way. Playful-resisters are painfully aware of their impasse, and the play helps free their energy. As they get in touch with the pain of the power struggles they experienced with their parents, redecision work can help them release that pain and further free their energy.

Typical *cons* for the playful-resister are: "I don't know" and the use of "yes, but." The *rackets* are frustration and confusion covering hurt and anger. The major *injunctions* are: "Don't make it," "Don't grow up," "Don't feel," and "Don't be close." The *escape hatch* to close is going crazy. It is important to help them learn to say "no" directly rather than to passively resist. The primary therapeutic goal is letting go of struggling.

Responsible-Workaholics (Obsessive-Compulsive)   Thinking is the open door for responsible-workaholics. They were supposed to be "good boys" and "good girls" and do everything right. Worth and value were equated with "doing." They learned to work hard to be "model citizens." They want to know that others approve of what they do and will see them as good. Therefore, they think about everything they do.

To make effective contact, the therapist must engage responsible-workaholics in thinking. Much of the early work involves helping them decontaminate their Adult ego state from their oppressive internal Parent by pointing out how hard they are on themselves. Once rapport has been established, the therapist can move to nurturing or playful behavior to find out what they are feeling, which is the target area. By integrating their feelings with their thinking, they begin to loosen up and become more playful.

The trap area to avoid with responsible-workaholics is behavior. Because they believe that they have to "be perfect" to be okay, any behavioral confrontation feels to them as though they are not doing something right and they become defensive very quickly. By helping them to experience the oppressiveness of their internal Parent ego state demands, they begin to let go of their perfection and relax. It is also useful to encourage them to make at least one mistake a day and have fun doing so. They never got to be openly rebellious and need permission to do that. They also need to experience that they can be valued apart from what they do.

Redecision therapy with responsible-workaholics is fairly straightforward because their open door is thinking and their target door is feeling. The work moves from contracting to impasse clarification, to redecision work per se, which frees their emotions. In many ways, they are model clients who come on time, are cooperative, pay their bills, and want to do what the therapist is directing them to do. One pitfall to watch out for is their tendency to overadapt to what they think the therapist wants rather than think about what they really want. The *cons* they use are the qualifiers "more," "better," and "be able to" as in "I want to be able to be more relaxed." Because they are supposed to be perfect and they know that they can't really do that, they are always wanting to be better, rather than realizing that they can be "good enough" and don't have to keep working at it. Their *rackets* are anxiety, guilt, and depression, which cover sadness and anger. Their major *injunctions* are: "Don't be a child," "Don't be important," and "Don't feel." The *escape hatch* to close is working themselves to death. The major therapeutic goal for them is learning to "be."

Enthusiastic-Overreactors (Histrionic)   Enthusiastic-overreactors make contact with the world through feeling, which is their open door. They learned to be attentive to other people's feelings and needs and to try to make them happy and feel good by being cute, playful, and entertaining. That was the primary way they received validation in childhood.

To make effective contact with enthusiastic-overreactors, the therapist has to engage their feelings by being nurturing or playful. They want to know that others care about their feelings and are pleased by them. They love attention and tend to equate attention with love. Once rapport has been established, the therapist can then engage them in thinking, which is their target door. Their Adult ego state needs to be decontaminated from their Child feelings. They tend to equate reality with what they feel, and they need to know that just because something feels true, it doesn't necessarily make it true in reality.

The trap door to avoid with enthusiastic-overreactors is behavior. Because they are doing everything they know how to please others, any behavioral confrontation feels to them as though they are not being pleasing, and they become very defensive. As they integrate their thinking in with their feelings, they stop overreacting.

The redecision process usually flows easily with enthusiastic-overreactors because they feel naturally, and contracting and impasse clarification elicits their thinking. Redecision work per se is used to help them take back the personal power they had to give up in childhood, express their anger, own their own thinking, and allow themselves to grow up. The primary *cons* they use are: "I guess," "I think I want to," and "I can't." Their *rackets* are scare, sadness, confusion, and guilt, which cover their anger. Their major *injunctions* are: "Don't think," "Don't grow up," and "Don't be important." The *escape hatch* to close is running away and suicide. They need to learn to use their anger appropriately to set limits with others. The major therapeutic goal is reclaiming their personal power.

Combined Adaptations   Because everyone has at least one surviving and one performing adaptation, it is important to be able to track when the person moves from one adaptation to another or when the individual is actually using a combination of adaptations. By knowing the behaviors, developmental issues, and drivers for each adaptation, it is fairly easy to track the adaptations. The drivers for each of the adaptations are:

1. *Creative-daydreamer:* Be strong.
2. *Charming-manipulator:* Be strong and please others.
3. *Brilliant-skeptics:* Be strong and be perfect.
4. *Playful-resister:* Try hard.
5. *Responsible-workaholic:* Be perfect.
6. *Enthusiastic-overreactor:* Please others.

The way the adaptations appear differ slightly depending on what adaptation they are combined with. For example, charming-manipulator combined with enthusiastic-overreactor is very flamboyant whereas charming-manipulator combined with responsible-workaholic is more subdued. Some therapeutic issues involve primarily one adaptation. Others involve a combination of adaptations. The case presented in the next section is an example of an issue involving a combination of adaptations.

CLINICAL CASE EXAMPLE

The client in this case is a married, Caucasian female in her 30s, who has been in an ongoing group for about six months. She is very bright, articulate, and uses intellectualization as a defense. She initially tended to withdraw whenever anything emotional was going on in the group and often appeared anxious. She originally came because she was "burned out" in her job and wanted to switch careers. She has both the brilliant-skeptic and charming-manipulator adaptations on the surviving level and the responsible-workaholic adaptation on the performing level.

This is an interesting combination of adaptations to work with because the brilliant-skeptic and responsible-workaholic adaptations have thinking as the open door and behavior as the trap, whereas the charming-manipulator adaptation has behavior as the open door and thinking as the trap. The problem becomes how to establish rapport. If the therapist starts with thinking, the danger is getting into the trap area of the charming-manipulator. If the therapist starts with behavior, the problem is getting into the trap area of the brilliant-skeptic and responsible-workaholic. Fortunately, the target area for all three adaptations is feeling.

Given this difficulty, it was important for the therapist to put a lot of energy into being reliable and consistent for the client to feel safe and build trust. In addition, the therapist had to carefully track the adaptations, joining the client in thinking when she was in brilliant-skeptic or responsible-workaholic and playfully confronting her when she moved into charming-manipulator. The following is an example of this work:

THERAPIST: Who has something they want to change?

This question is used in redecision therapy to emphasize that change is possible and can be done in the present session.

CLIENT: I'm withdrawing. I don't like that I'm withdrawing. It would be real easy for me to let the rest of the afternoon go by and just sit here.

She doesn't respond directly to the question, which is a ploy of the charming-manipulator to invite the therapist to chase her (initiating a game of "Catch Me If You Can"). She is displaying a "be strong" driver by the use of "it" instead of "I." She also criticizes herself from her brilliant-skeptic adaptation. I choose to playfully and subtly point out that she has already moved out of withdrawing.

THERAPIST: (Playfully) It would have been . . . (Laughter)
CLIENT: (Laughter) It would have been. It would have been much easier than this is. I'm much more comfortable withdrawing.

She is saying something that is true for her brilliant-skeptic adaptation, but she is saying it in a somewhat seductive way from her charming-manipulator adaptation. It is obvious that she wants me to coax her out. Again, I choose to subtly and playfully confront her behavior, which is the open door for the charming-manipulator. By doing this subtly, I avoid the trap area of the brilliant-skeptic.

THERAPIST: Part of you is.
CLIENT: The part I'm familiar with is more comfortable. The part I'm not familiar with is not comfortable.
THERAPIST: At one point, it would have been the other way around.

I want to point out that her behavior is adapted rather than spontaneous.

CLIENT: At one point, I was willing to tough it out.

She describes the "Be strong" driver of both her charming-manipulator and brilliant-skeptic adaptations. I point out that I was talking about the spontaneous part of herself.

THERAPIST: No, at one point you were spontaneous and free.
CLIENT: It's been so long, I don't remember that.
THERAPIST: Right . . . consciously . . . so what do you want to change for you?

I go back to the original question she never answered. This time she answers straight.

CLIENT: I'd like to trust me.
THERAPIST: Tell me what you mean.
CLIENT: To be spontaneous . . . this is getting old. Why don't I feel free to be me?

She again is critical of herself from her brilliant-skeptic adaptation by wanting to know "why" she is in the place she is in as though knowing "why" might make a difference.

THERAPIST: Well, most people don't feel free to be spontaneous when someone is criticizing them.
CLIENT: (Smiling) That is true.
THERAPIST: So you want to give that (critical) part of you a new job assignment?
CLIENT: Well, I was thinking about that, too . . . how do I decrease the critical part and increase something else? . . . and I couldn't think of a way of doing it.

She is trying from her brilliant-skeptic adaptation to figure all of this out intellectually so that she doesn't have to feel and be vulnerable.

THERAPIST: (Playfully) Well, thinking is not going to do it. "Doing it" will do it.
CLIENT: Alright. How am I going to do it? I'm willing, if I know what to do, but my conscious mind doesn't know what to do.

She is being evasive from her charming-manipulator, which I confront.

THERAPIST: That's really not true.
CLIENT: My conscious mind does know what to do?
THERAPIST: You know how to nurture yourself. You know how to give yourself positive strokes rather than negative strokes.

CLIENT: Then why don't I do it?

> This is another "con" from her charming-manipulator adaptation, trying to get me to take responsibility for her work. I playfully let her know that I know what she is doing by stroking her cleverness.

THERAPIST: (Laughing) You are good!

CLIENT: (Laughing) I am good! You said that the first time I met you. "You're good!" I'm not even conscious of doing it. It's so automatic.

THERAPIST: So let yourself imagine being spontaneous and free and let yourself experience what feels scary or potentially dangerous about that.

> The idea behind this intervention is that if the client allows herself to experience in fantasy the behavior she desires, the unconscious protective reasons for not doing it will automatically surface. I then feed back her words in first person, active, present tense so that she will stay in the experience.

CLIENT: Immediately when you say let yourself experience being spontaneous and free, I get a knot in my throat, I start feeling tight in my chest and stomach, and I start scaring myself that I don't know how to do this.

THERAPIST: So, "If I'm spontaneous and free, I won't know what to do."

CLIENT: (Nodding) I won't know what to do. I won't know how to act. I won't know what is safe . . . and whatever I do or say might be wrong.

THERAPIST: That's always a possibility.

CLIENT: Uh huh, and I've tried so hard to be perfect . . . that I don't want to be wrong.

> This is the "Be perfect" driver of the brilliant-skeptic and responsible-workaholic adaptations.

THERAPIST: And what else? . . . if you are wrong?

CLIENT: Somebody will criticize me.

THERAPIST: And . . . I'll feel?

> Now that the therapist has rapport and the client is being sincere, he moves to the target area for all of her adaptations—feeling.

CLIENT: I'll feel real sad.

THERAPIST: (Checking out an intuitive hunch) Is there also a part of you who will feel shame?

CLIENT: Uh huh . . . maybe I've eliminated shame consciously . . . yeah, if somebody criticizes me, I'll feel shame.

THERAPIST: And when kids feel shame, they want the floor to open up and they disappear so they don't have to face those people.

CLIENT: And maybe if I withdraw, I won't have to experience all that.

> Here she makes explicit the defense.

THERAPIST: Yeah . . . so who are you in that position with as a child?

> I invite her to go back to the early scene where all this started to work through the early difficulty and free her from the bind she feels.

CLIENT: Uh . . . I don't do things wrong so I don't get in trouble.

THERAPIST: Yeah.

CLIENT: I do the right thing. I say the right thing. I protect myself so I never have to feel that.

Here we see the reason she had to develop the brilliant-skeptic and responsible-workaholic adaptations.

THERAPIST: Who are you in that position with as a child? Who is the "somebody" that criticized you?
CLIENT: I don't remember being criticized that much. As far back as I can remember, I was doing what was expected of me.

She redefines my question from "who" to "how much?" She is working hard to stay away from her painful feelings. I use humor to encourage her on and once again move to the target area of feeling.

THERAPIST: You know, you didn't come out of the womb doing that.
CLIENT: I know . . . but before I can't remember, I learned to do it.
THERAPIST: If you let yourself experience being criticized and feeling shamed, what's your sense of who's doing it?
CLIENT: I suspect I'm trying to please my father more than I'm trying to please my mother. I don't know why.

She would prefer to stay with her thinking. I encourage her to let her feelings guide her.

THERAPIST: Does that feel right?
CLIENT: Yeah, it does . . . I can remember as a teenager doing things to please him. (Bites her bottom lip)

She is on the verge of tears now and trying to hold them back by biting her bottom lip. I again feed back her experience in first person, active, present tense to keep her in the experience so that she can experience her own emotional truth.

THERAPIST: So the risk is, "I'll feel shame and I'll lose father."
CLIENT: (Nodding) Yeah (Looking and sounding very sad now) . . . he'll be disappointed and I'll lose him. He won't love me.
THERAPIST: What are you feeling?
CLIENT: Very uncomfortable. I want to get up and run away. I want to go somewhere and protect myself from these feelings. I don't want to feel them.

Here she is describing the importance of the charming-manipulator adaptation to protect herself from her pain and fear of abandonment.

THERAPIST: Because . . . ?
CLIENT: I feel alone and if I'm going to protect myself, I might as well cut them off.

She is talking out what she is feeling now rather than acting it out so I know she will continue. I invite her to talk directly to her father in fantasy to bring out her suppressed feelings.

THERAPIST: So just see your father . . . and see what you want to say to him.
CLIENT: I'm just a little girl. I'm not a grownup.
THERAPIST: Tell him more.
CLIENT: I'm just a little girl. I'm not a grownup. I can't do everything right.

THERAPIST:　How does he respond?

CLIENT:　(As father) "You're supposed to act better than that. (Tearing) You're not supposed to do that. You embarrass me."

THERAPIST:　Hmmm, so father is feeling shame.

CLIENT:　(Obviously moved) Oh shit . . . Oh shit!

THERAPIST:　What are you experiencing?

CLIENT:　Well, I just . . . I knew something . . . I just put two and two together.

THERAPIST:　Which is . . . ?

CLIENT:　Well . . . my dad was blind in one eye, and when I was a child, old enough to know he was blind but . . . big family secret that we didn't talk about . . . one summer day, I was sitting on the swing at my grandmother's and I asked, "Why is Daddy blind?" and my mother told me how my dad got blind, and my grandmother and dad were not there. When he was a child, about 5 or 6, he was being spontaneous and free and playing in some mud puddles on a dirt road and his mother had told him not to do that and so his punishment was that he got whipped with a piece of wood from the wood box, and a splinter got in his eye and blinded him. No wonder . . . he was not spontaneous and free . . . he passed it on to me! I've known he was blind and I've known why he was blind . . .

She has just made an important breakthrough and her body is trembling. My next intervention is to help her express the feeling that has been locked in her body.

THERAPIST:　(Pulling up a chair) Just put him out here and tell him.

CLIENT:　There's more to the story. There's a really, really sad part to the story. (Begins to cry) Oh, Daddy . . . Oh, Daddy (Shaking her head from side to side)

THERAPIST:　Breathe and make as much noise as you want to . . .

CLIENT:　(Begins to sob as her body is shaking)

THERAPIST:　Just let that out . . .

CLIENT:　(Cries more freely holding her head in her hands)

THERAPIST:　What else do you want to tell him?

CLIENT:　I feel so sorry for you . . . that you could never see it as an accident. Oh, Daddy! Oh, Daddy, Daddy, Daddy, Daddy (Shaking her head and crying). It's really not true that you were punished. (Repeating) It's really not true that you were punished.

THERAPIST:　Who told him that?

CLIENT:　I don't know but it was his belief that God punished him for disobeying his mother. You can't be spontaneous or God will punish you. (Cries deeply as her body continues shaking)

THERAPIST:　No wonder he was so scared.

CLIENT:　All his life he was scared.

THERAPIST:　And he invited you to carry that also.

CLIENT:　I never saw my shame as his shame.

By staying in the experience, she realizes that it is really her father's shame that she has been carrying. Working through fear and shame is a primary issue for the brilliant-skeptic.

THERAPIST:　And all along, you didn't have anything to be ashamed of.

CLIENT:　No, as a little kid, I didn't have anything to be ashamed of.

THERAPIST:　And "God's not going to punish me if I am spontaneous and free."

Client: No, he's not . . . (Becoming spontaneous) or she's not (Laughing). She'll probably be really happy!

This is the redecision—that she can be spontaneous and free now and God is not going to punish her as her dad believed. Her humor and laughter and spontaneity signal her moving into her Natural Child ego state.

Therapist: Yep!

Client: Wow!

Therapist: What are you experiencing now?

Client: My arms are still shaking.

Therapist: That's energy! You're freeing up all that energy you've been holding back . . . all that held-back spontaneity!

Client: (Laughs and throws a pillow up into the air) Oh damn! I never made the connection with my spontaneity being tied down. I can think of one instance when I was about 8 years old in church. You know how girls used to kick off their shoes and kind of dangle the back of them on their foot? I was down really close to the front of the church, and my dad and mom were in the choir and could see me and I was dangling my shoe on my foot, and thank God the minister didn't have any daughters and really liked me. He was my dad's closest friend at that time period, and my dad was so embarrassed by what I was doing. He was furious and he was going to take me home and spank me, and the minister heard my dad getting angry at me and he said, "Don't do that. She's just being a kid."

Therapist: Right! Exactly! Good for him!

Client: But my dad was ashamed, and I think that was about the age he was feeling.

She is now integrating her redecision in her Adult ego state. Her experience as a child is a good example of how parents often move into their Parent ego state without thinking and do to their kids what was done to them when they encounter some behavior on their child's part that they got punished for.

Therapist: So will you remember that phrase? "Don't do that. She's just being a kid."

This is an example of an anchor—a phrase that the person is likely to hold on to as a reminder of his or her redecision.

Client: (Laughs) Nice phrase to remember!

Therapist: Yeah, and any time you begin to hear any critical message, just say that phrase, "Don't do that. She's just being a kid."

Client: I'll do that. Whew!

Therapist: Looks like there's some relief with that.

Client: There is.

Therapist: Good. Really nice work!

Client: Thanks.

Therapist: You're welcome!

By making contact with the client in the open doors of her adaptations, the therapist quickly established rapport. Next, the therapist moved to the target area to help the client make a change. By going back and experiencing the early situation where the problem began, the client could appreciate both why she adapted in the way she did and the new choices she has in the present and reclaim the parts of herself that she had to give up as a child. At that point, she could easily redecide to behave differently in the present. Thus, combining the information on personality adaptations with the redecision therapy process creates a powerful and effective combination for change.

RESEARCH AND EMPIRICAL SUPPORT

Lieberman, Yalom, and Miles (1973), as reported in *Encounter Groups: First Facts*, conducted the first research involving redecision therapy. This was a study of the effectiveness of different approaches to group therapy and included 17 different types of groups. The most productive by far was the redecision therapy group led by R. Goulding. Ten of the 12 members showed positive change with no causalities (being worse off at the end). The members were enthusiastic about the group, and the group ranked first on the criterion that the members reported having personally learned a great deal. The group also tied for first in the members' ratings as a constructive experience. Their ratings of the leader were equally high, with Goulding ranked highest in overall leader dimensions. The leader behaviors correlated with the highest outcomes were:

1. High caring.
2. High meaning-attribution (offering explanations of what they observed and information on how to change).
3. Moderate emotional stimulation (did not seduce the clients with charisma).
4. Moderate executive function (use of structured exercises and group management).

McNeel (1977a, 1977b, 1982) examined the effects of an intensive weekend group workshop conducted by R. Goulding and M. Goulding to determine if people changed as a result of that event. The 15 participants changed substantially as evidenced by scores on the Personal Orientation Inventory (POI) and the Personal Growth Checklist (PGC) administered just before the workshop and again three months after the workshop. On the POI, the change was significant at the .01 level on seven of the scales and at the .05 level on the other three. On the PGC, the change was at the .01 level on two of the scales and at the .05 level on the other three. Interviews before and after the workshop provided qualitative verification for the changes indicated on the assessment instruments. Participants also indicated distinct changes they made as a result of specific segments of work they had done. Overall, the experience proved very positive for participants.

Bader (1976, 1982) studied the outcomes of five families who participated in a seven-day residential family therapy workshop using redecision therapy as compared with five similar families who served as controls. She found significant changes at the .05 level on the Cohesiveness, Expressiveness, and Independence scales of the Family Environment Scale (FES). She also found significant positive changes at the .05 level on a self-report questionnaire designed to identify changes that family members perceived in themselves or other family members. "The results obtained demonstrated that family therapy using TA with Redecision techniques is successful in effecting family systems change" (1982, p. 37).

Kadis and McClendon (1981) reported the results from using their intensive multiple family therapy group model in which they used redecision family therapy with 59 families over a seven-year period. A follow-up survey indicated that 57.7% of the parents and 74.4% of the children did not seek further therapy, that 80% of the parents and 76% of the children thought that their family had changed, and that 89% of the parents believed that they had changed in personal growth whereas 23.3% of the children believed that they themselves had not changed.

The primary research on personality adaptations theory has been the development of two personality adaptations assessment instruments, one by Joines (Joines Personality Adaptation Questionnaire [3rd Edition], © 2002) and the other by Kahler (Kahler Personality Assessment Profile, © 1982).

Joines developed a 72-item questionnaire (12 items for each of the six adaptations), which was administered to 1,500 individuals (both clinical and normal populations). The reliabilities for the different subscales using Cronbach's alphas for the standardized variables were as follows: creative-daydreamer (Schizoid) 0.79, charming-manipulator (Antisocial) 0.68, brilliant-skeptic (Paranoid) 0.59, playful-resister (Passive-Aggressive) 0.73, responsible-workaholic (Obsessive-Compulsive) 0.62, and enthusiastic-overreactor (Histrionic) 0.61. An exploratory factor analysis conducted on the three surviving adaptations and again on the three performing adaptations revealed that they all loaded on their respective factors. Based on this research, there is good evidence that the six adaptations exist in reality and can be measured using the questionnaire developed.

Kahler found significant correlations between reactors (enthusiastic-overreactors) and emotions, workaholics (responsible-workaholics) and thoughts, persisters (brilliant-skeptics) and opinions, promoters (charming-manipulators) and actions, rebels (playful-resisters) and reactions, and dreamers (creative-daydreamers) and inactions, thus validating Ware's concept of "doors."

Kahler also had three "experts" in assessing the personality adaptations independently interview 100 people. All six personality types were represented in the sample. The three judges agreed on 97 assessments, yielding an interjudge reliability significant at > .001. An additional number of people were assessed and selected by the judges independently so that a minimum number of 30 individuals were available for each personality type, yielding a total sample of 180 identified "assessed" people. Two hundred and thirteen items were administered to 112 randomly selected subjects. Analysis of this data indicated once again a natural loading on six criteria—the six personality adaptations.

Two hundred and four of these items were administered to the 180 identified personality types. Only items that had a correlation of greater than .60 (significant at > .01) were accepted for inclusion in the final Personality Pattern Inventory (PPI).

Gilbert (1999) found that educators are predominantly reactor (enthusiastic-overreactor), workaholic (responsible-workaholic), and persister (brilliant-skeptic) personality types, who demonstrate little potential to interact with the three other personality types—dreamer (creative-daydreamer), rebel (playful-resister), and promoter (charming-manipulator), which comprise 35% of the general (student) population.

Bailey's (1998) study demonstrated statistically significant differences between student personality designations and the inattentive and hyperactive-impulse subscales. The combined findings suggested that there were personality characteristics within a student's personality that predisposed him or her toward exhibiting what were perceived by teachers as inattentive and/or hyperactive-impulsive behaviors. The most compelling finding was that miscommunication between teachers and students due to a difference in personality type may be the reason many students are referred for and consequently labeled with Attention-Deficit Hyperactivity Disorder.

Joines's and Kahler's studies indicate that there is good evidence that the six personality adaptations both exist in reality and can be measured using appropriate assessment tools.

Gilbert's and Bailey's studies suggest that differences in personality types play a significant role in perception about what is considered normal versus pathological behavior. Additional research in this area is needed to determine to what extent conventional "treatment" is an attempt to make others conform to the therapist's preferences versus an effort to help individuals achieve their own potential, given their unique personality styles.

SUMMARY AND CONCLUSIONS

Personality is an extremely important factor to consider in treatment not only with the personality disorders but across the diagnostic spectrum. An understanding of the particular personality adaptations of the individuals being treated is crucial in appreciating the value of how they have learned to survive psychologically and in knowing how best to work with them in therapy. By knowing their adaptations, the therapist can quickly establish rapport, target interventions to the area (thinking, feeling, or behavior) that will be most effective in enabling them to change, and avoid becoming trapped in the person's defenses. When this information is combined with redecision therapy, the therapist has a very powerful tool for enabling change. The combined approach offers a non-pathological method of allowing clients to experience their own emotional truth, which both helps them to appreciate the original value of their behavior and frees them to make new choices in the present.

REFERENCES

American Psychiatric Association. (2000). *Diagnostic and statistical manual of mental disorders* (4th ed., text rev.). Washington, DC: Author.

Bader, E. (1976). Redecision in family therapy: A study of change in an intensive family therapy workshop (Doctoral dissertation, California School of Professional Psychology, 1976). *Dissertation Abstracts International, 37,* 05B, 2491.

Bader, E. (1982). Redecisions in family therapy: A study of change in an intensive family therapy workshop. *Transactional Analysis Journal, 12*(1), 27–38.

Bailey, R. (1998). *An Investigation of personality types of adolescents who have been rated by classroom teachers to exhibit inattentive and/or hyperactive-impulse behaviors.* Unpublished doctoral dissertation, University of Arkansas at Little Rock.

Berne, E. (1961). *Transactional analysis in psychotherapy: A systematic individual and social psychiatry.* New York: Grove Press.

Berne, E. (1966). *Principles of group treatment.* New York: Grove Press.

Fagan, J., & Sheppard, I. (1967, July). *Two-hour workshop on Gestalt therapy.* Atlanta: Georgia Mental Health Institute.

Freud, S. (1955). Beyond the pleasure principle. In J. Strachey (Ed.), *The standard edition of the complete psychological works of Sigmund Freud* (Vol. 18, pp. 3–64). London: Hogarth Press. (Original work published 1920)

Gilbert, M. (1999). Why educators have problems with some students: Understanding frames of reference. *Journal of Educational Administration, 37*(3), 243–256.

Goulding, R., & Goulding, M. (1978). *The power is in the patient.* San Francisco: TA Press.

Goulding, R., & Goulding, M. (1979). *Changing lives through redecision therapy.* New York: Brunner/Mazel.

Joines, V. (1986). Using redecision therapy with different personality adaptations. *Transactional Analysis Journal, 16*(3), 152–160.

Joines, V. (1988). Diagnosis and treatment planning using a transactional analysis framework. *Transactional Analysis Journal, 18*(3), 185–190.

Joines, V. (2002a). *Joines personality adaptations questionnaire* (3rd ed.). Chapel Hill, NC: Southeast Institute for Group and Family Therapy.

Joines, V., & Stewart, I. (2002b). *Personality adaptations: A new guide to human understanding in psychotherapy and counseling.* Chapel Hill, NC: Lifespace.

Kadis, L. B. (Ed.). (1985). *Redecision therapy: Expanded perspectives.* Watsonville, CA: Western Institute for Group and Family Therapy.

Kadis, L. B., & McClendon, R. (1981). Redecision family therapy: Its use with intensive multiple family groups. *American Journal of Family Therapy, 9*(2), 75–83.

Kahler, T. (1972). *Predicting academic underachievement in ninth and twelfth grade males with the Kahler Transactional Analysis Script Checklist.* Unpublished doctoral dissertation, West Lafayette, IN, Purdue University.

Kahler, T. (1977a). *The transactional analysis script profile (TSAP).* Little Rock, AR: Taibi Kahler Associates.

Kahler, T. (1977b). *The transactional analysis script profile (TSAP): A guide for the therapist.* Little Rock, AR: Taibi Kahler Associates.

Kahler, T. (1982). *Personality pattern inventory validation studies.* Little Rock, AR: Kahler Communications.

Kahler, T., & Capers, H. (1974). The miniscript. *Transactional Analysis Journal, 4*(1), 26–42.

Liberman, M. A., Yalom, I. D., & Miles, M. B. (1973). *Encounter groups: First facts.* New York: Basic Books.

McNeel, J. (1977a). Redecisions in psychotherapy: A study of the effects of an intensive weekend group workshop (Doctoral dissertation, California School of Professional Psychology, 1976). *Dissertation Abstracts International, 36,* 9-B, 4700.

McNeel, J. (1977b). The seven components of redecision therapy. In G. Barnes (Ed.), *Transactional analysis after Eric Berne: Teachings and practices of three TA schools* (pp. 425–441). New York: Harper & Row.

McNeel, J. (1982). Redecisions in psychotherapy: A study of the effects of an intensive weekend group workshop. *Transactional Analysis Journal, 12*(1), 10–26.

Perls, F. S. (1969). *Gestalt therapy verbatim.* Moab, UT: Real People Press.

Perls, F. S., Hefferline, R. F., & Goodman, P. (1951). *Gestalt therapy.* New York: Dell.

Stewart, I., & Joines, V. (1987). *TA today: A new introduction to transactional analysis.* Chapel Hill, NC: Lifespace.

Ware, P. (1983). Personality adaptations: Doors to therapy. *Transactional Analysis Journal, 13*(1), 11–19.

CHAPTER 11

Dialectical Behavior Therapy of Severe Personality Disorders

Clive J. Robins and Cedar R. Koons

PATIENTS WHO MEET criteria for borderline personality disorder (BPD) are prevalent in clinical practice, comprising about 10% of psychiatric outpatients. They often present with multiple severe and chronic behavioral problems, including suicidal and other self-injurious behaviors. Most persons with BPD gradually improve, but changes are usually slow, and about 50% still meet criteria at follow-ups four to seven years later (Links, Heslegrave, & van Reekum, 1998; Zanarini, Frankenburg, Hennen, & Silk, 2003). They usually are difficult to treat and some forms of treatment even may lead to their problems becoming more severe; therefore, treating clinicians may feel frustrated, incompetent, or hopeless about the patient. Furthermore, behaviors such as suicide attempts or anger directed at the therapist may elicit fear, anger, and other emotions that the therapist needs to manage appropriately to maintain an effective therapeutic relationship.

THEORETICAL COMPONENTS OF MODEL

Dialectical behavior therapy (DBT) has evolved over more than 20 years from Marsha Linehan's attempts to understand and develop effective treatment for chronically suicidal women (Linehan, 1987) and borderline personality disorder (Linehan, 1993a). It integrates behavioral and cognitive treatment principles and strategies with others derived from client-centered and process-experiential therapies, Zen Buddhism, and dialectical philosophy (Robins, Ivanoff, & Linehan, 2001). Currently, it is the only form of outpatient psychotherapy shown in randomized trials to have some efficacy for patients diagnosed with BPD.

The term *dialectical* in the name of the treatment reflects its emphasis on synthesis of apparent polarities or oppositions. The primary polarity addressed is that of acceptance and change. If the therapist focuses only on change strategies, BPD patients often feel that their level of distress is not understood or even that they are being blamed for their problems. They may respond with anger at the therapist or withdrawal from treatment. Linehan, therefore, modified standard cognitive-behavioral treatment to include a greater emphasis on validating aspects of the patient's experience. A second way in which the dialectic of acceptance and change is important in DBT is that borderline patients have great difficulty accepting themselves, other people, and life generally. Although cognitive-behavioral treatment strategies can help patients to change many behaviors, they usually have not focused on promoting acceptance (Sanderson & Linehan, 1999). DBT attempts to do so, in part by teaching and encouraging patients to practice mindfulness, that is, to cultivate nonjudgmental, focused, in-this-moment awareness and to behave in ways consistent with their important goals and values (Robins, 2002).

The theoretical foundations of DBT include: (1) A biosocial theory of BPD and (2) treatment principles drawn from behavior therapy, Zen, and dialectics.

A BIOSOCIAL THEORY OF BORDERLINE PERSONALITY DISORDER

In DBT, the development and maintenance of BPD behaviors is viewed as resulting from a transaction of a biological component, namely dysfunction of the emotion regulation system, and a social-environmental component, namely an invalidating environment.

Emotion Dysregulation   Borderline personality disorder may involve a dysfunction of parts of the central nervous system involved in regulation of emotions. Twin studies suggest a genetic influence on emotion dysregulation specifically (Livesley, Jang, & Vernon, 1998) and on BPD (Torgersen et al., 2000). Other causal factors might include events during fetal development and early life trauma, which can have enduring structural effects on the developing limbic system (Sapolsky, 1996). DBT proposes that individuals with BPD are biologically vulnerable to experiencing emotions more intensely than the average person and also have more difficulty modulating their intensity.

Invalidating Environment   The primary environmental influence on the disorder is considered by Linehan (1993a) to be an invalidating environment, in which the person's communications about private experiences frequently are met with responses that suggest they are invalid, faulty, or inappropriate or that oversimplify the ease of solving the problem. Communications of negative emotions may be ignored or punished, but extreme communications are taken more seriously. Consequently, the individual may come to self-invalidate; not learn to set appropriate goals; not learn how to accurately label, communicate about, or regulate emotions; and learn instead to inhibit emotional expression or respond to distress with extreme behaviors.

Dialectical Transaction of Emotion Dysregulation and Invalidation   Over time, as the individual's behavior becomes more extreme, in attempts to regulate emotion or to communicate, he or she is increasingly likely to experience invalidation from the environment, including from the mental health system. His or her responses are likely to be puzzling to others, who may conclude that the person is faking his or her response to manipulate a situation, or is being entirely unreasonable and "crazy," or is not trying to control his or her behavior. If this belief is communicated, explicitly or implicitly, the sensitive individual is likely to feel even more emotionally vulnerable. Thus, in this transactional model, the individual and those in his or her interpersonal environment continuously influence one another.

A Dialectical Behavior Therapy Perspective on the Borderline Personality Disorder Diagnostic Criteria   Dialectical behavior therapy organizes the nine *DSM-IV* criteria for BPD, of which at least five must be met (American Psychiatric Association [APA], 1994), into five broad areas of dysregulation because this clarifies what skills the patient needs to learn and practice.

1. EMOTION DYSREGULATION   In addition to the reactivity and instability of mood described in the *DSM*, the baseline mood usually is chronic dysphoria, and about 50% meet criteria for major depression (Gunderson & Elliot, 1985). *DSM-IV* specifies intense, inappropriate expressions of anger as a separate criterion. However, our own clinical experience is that borderline patients are at least as likely to be underexpressive of anger. DBT views borderline patients as having as much difficulty regulating sadness, anxiety, guilt, and shame as they do regulating anger. So why is anger singled out in the *DSM-IV*? One possibility is that clinicians find patients' expressions of anger more aversive than expressions of other emotions, so they are particularly salient.

2. RELATIONSHIP DYSREGULATION   Unstable, intense relationships may result from patients' intense emotions and accompanying behaviors such as anger outbursts or self-injury, which lead others to withdraw, or from their own difficulty in being assertive about relationship problems, which leads them to withdraw. Frantic efforts to avoid abandonment may reflect this relationship history and/or rejection, neglect, or abandonment in childhood. Individuals who are helpful or nurturing may be idealized and those who fail to meet these needs devalued. Strong emotions tend to produce extreme and biased cognitions, so borderline patients, who experience strong emotions frequently, tend to view themselves and others in extreme and mood-dependent ways.

3. SELF-DYSREGULATION   The experience of intense and frequently changing emotions and associated behaviors makes it difficult for individuals to predict their own behavior, probably an important component of developing a coherent sense of self. In addition, borderline patients' repeated experience of invalidation is hypothesized to lead to self-invalidation of their own preferences, goals, perceptions, and so on, which, therefore, do not become well developed or stable.

4. BEHAVIOR DYSREGULATION   *DSM-IV* criteria include suicidal and other self-injurious behaviors specifically and other impulsive and potentially harmful behaviors generally, such as substance abuse, reckless driving, or binge eating. These behaviors may serve a variety of functions. For example, although parasuicide can serve an interpersonal communication function, as implied by phrases such as "suicide gesture" and "manipulative suicide attempt," its most common function seems to be to escape or decrease aversive emotions (Brown, Comtois, & Linehan, 2002). Substance abuse, binge eating, and other "impulsive" behaviors can serve the same function. Treatment, therefore, needs to help patients develop more adaptive ways to regulate and/or to tolerate strong emotions.

5. COGNITIVE DYSREGULATION   A subset of these patients may experience transient paranoia, dissociation, or hallucinations when under stress. These biased or distorted perceptions and beliefs may reflect the influence of strong emotions on cognitive processes.

CORE TREATMENT PRINCIPLES

The principles on which the treatment strategies are based derive from three primary sources: learning theory, Zen Buddhism, and dialectical philosophy.

Learning Theory   DBT assumes that many maladaptive behaviors, both overt and private (thoughts, feelings), are learned and, therefore, can, in principle, be replaced by new learning. Three primary ways in which organisms learn are through respondent or classical conditioning, operant or instrumental conditioning, and modeling.

1. RESPONDENT (CLASSICAL) CONDITIONING   When two or more stimuli repeatedly co-occur, they become associated, so that the natural response to one becomes a learned response to the other, famously illustrated by the salivation of Pavlov's dogs in response to a tone previously paired with food. After a person is raped in a dark alley, being near a dark alley may elicit a fear response. Maladaptive positive emotional responses may also be learned in this way, such as an association between the sight of a knife used previously to self-injure and emotional relief. It is primarily involuntary responses such as emotional reactions that are learned through classical conditioning.

2. OPERANT (INSTRUMENTAL) CONDITIONING   Consequences following a behavior may lead reliably to a subsequent increase or decrease in that behavior, processes referred to as *reinforcement* and *punishment,* respectively. When previously reinforced behavior no longer is reinforced, the behavior will decrease, a process called *extinction.* When desired or adaptive behavior does not occur and, therefore, cannot be reinforced, reinforcement of successively closer approximations of the behavior can lead to the desired behavior, a process referred to as *shaping.* These and other operant learning principles, though widely known, often are not considered by therapists in relation to patient behaviors and therapist-patient interactions. DBT, like many other behavioral therapies, pays considerable attention to behavior-consequence contingencies.

3. MODELING   Humans and other organisms learn both emotional responses and overt behaviors by observing the responses of others and the consequences of those responses. Maladaptive behaviors may have been learned through modeling by parents, siblings, other patients, and others. Characteristics of the model that increase the probability that the observer will enact the behavior include perceived expertise or credibility and perceived similarity between model and observer. In the context of a strong therapeutic alliance, therapists can serve as effective models of skillful behavior.

Zen   Whereas learning theory emphasizes how behavior can change, an important principle of Zen Buddhism is that everything is as it should be at this moment. Approaching life with this attitude is the epitome of accepting yourself, other people, and the universe. The realities or perceived realities of BPD patients often are painful and difficult or impossible to change, as they are at times for all of us. We cannot change the past, some aspects of our current situation may not be immediately changeable, or the costs of changing may be too high. Acceptance is helpful because it reduces suffering that results from continually telling yourself that the situation should not be the way it nonetheless is. Lack of acceptance can even stand in the way of change. For example, strong self-blame and guilt over self-injury, substance abuse, or binge eating do not usually lead to positive change and may even lead to further problem behaviors such as self-punishment. It is more productive to describe undesired behaviors nonjudgmentally to yourself (i.e., accept that they happened), note their discrepancy from behaviors that are more effective for reaching your goals, and develop a plan for changing them.

Zen principles and practices that guide DBT therapists' attitudes and behaviors and are taught to patients include: the importance of being mindful of the current moment, seeing reality without delusion, accepting reality without judgment, letting go of attachments that cause suffering, and finding a middle way. Zen is also characterized by the humanistic assumption that everyone has an inherent capacity for wisdom, referred to in DBT skills teaching as "Wise Mind."

Dialectics   An overarching goal in DBT is for the patient to develop more dialectical patterns of thinking and behavior. Linehan (1993a) discusses three characteristics of a dialectical worldview.

1. PRINCIPLE OF INTERRELATEDNESS AND WHOLENESS   Everything is connected to everything else, and objects or individuals cannot be understood in terms of their parts but only by considering the relationships among the parts. Our sense of identity is defined largely in relation to others, despite the individualistic emphasis of our culture.

2. PRINCIPLE OF POLARITY   Nature consists of opposing forces or elements (thesis and antithesis), and the essence of growth is in the coming together (synthesis) of these divisions. For any idea with merit, an idea that opposes it in some way may also have merit, and integration of the two may be useful. Even patients' maladaptive behaviors serve a purpose.

3. PRINCIPLE OF CONTINUOUS CHANGE   Because polarities give rise to syntheses and everything is connected, it follows that everything is continually in a state of change. As one person or object influences another, so, too, is he, she, or it influenced by the other, and both are changed.

This dialectical worldview is reflected in DBT in a transactional and systemic biosocial theory, in a view of the patient and therapist as being in a bidirectional, transactional relationship, in the use of both acceptance-oriented and change-oriented treatment strategies, and in teaching acceptance-oriented and change-oriented skills.

RANGE OF PSYCHOPATHOLOGY WITHIN SCOPE OF TREATMENT

DBT was developed as an outpatient treatment for chronically suicidal and/or otherwise self-injurious women with BPD. As we discuss in a later section, it has been shown to be effective in improving the lives of not only this population, but also borderline women who are not necessarily parasuicidal, women with BPD and substance abuse problems, women with binge eating disorder or bulimia, and depressed elders. Clinical experience suggests that it may also be a useful treatment approach for men with BPD and for multiproblem patients generally, particularly those with emotion regulation difficulties and/or impulsive behaviors.

Investigators currently are evaluating DBT for couples in which one member is diagnosed with BPD or there is domestic violence (Fruzzetti & Levensky, 2000) and for men and women in correctional facilities (McCann, Ball, & Ivanoff, 2000). DBT also has been adapted for use in psychiatric inpatient settings (Barley et al., 1993; Bohus et al., 2000; Swenson, Sanderson, Dulit, & Linehan, 2001) and day treatment programs (Simpson et al., 1998). It is not clear for whom this treatment might be contraindicated.

TREATMENT METHODS AND TECHNICAL ASPECTS AND INTERVENTIONS

In this section, we describe the several modalities that comprise the treatment and their functions. We also describe the sets of treatment strategies, including the core strategies of validation and problem solving, communication style strategies, case management strategies, and dialectical strategies.

TREATMENT MODES AND THEIR FUNCTIONS IN DIALECTICAL BEHAVIOR THERAPY

A comprehensive treatment for patients with BPD needs to do at least four things: (1) help patients develop new skills, (2) address motivational obstacles to skills use, (3) help patients generalize what they learn to their daily lives, and (4) keep therapists motivated and skilled in treating a difficult-to-treat population. In standard outpatient DBT, these four functions are addressed through four treatment components or modes.

Developing Skills: Skills-Training Group   Linehan's (1993b) skills-training manual covers four sets of skills: mindfulness, distress tolerance, emotion regulation, and interpersonal effectiveness (assertiveness). These skills usually are taught in a group format. Sessions begin with review and troubleshooting of homework from the previous week, followed by presentation and discussion of new material, behavior rehearsal, and homework assignments. The curriculum can be covered in about six months of weekly two-hour sessions, and most patients go through the sequence twice. Because of patients' emotional sensitivity, skills trainers (usually two) discourage detailed descriptions of problem behaviors and group "process" discussions and maintain a focus on the skills to be learned.

Problem-Solving Motivational Obstacles: Individual Therapy   A primary function of individual therapy in DBT is to address the situations, emotions, beliefs, and consequences that lead to or maintain a patient's problem behaviors or interfere with his or her use of skills. The individual therapist helps the patient use whatever skills he or she has to more effectively navigate crises and reduce problem behaviors. Frequently, this occurs in the context of a behavioral analysis of a recent incident of problem behavior, which we discuss in detail later. Whereas the goal of skills training is to get the skills into the patient, the goal of individual therapy is to get the skills out of him or her.

Generalizing Learning: Telephone Coaching   Skills learned in the treatment setting may not generalize to the patient's natural environment. The purpose of telephone coaching between sessions is to promote such generalization. Patients are instructed to call their individual therapist when they are in crisis or having difficulty controlling urges to self-injure, drink alcohol, stay in bed, or engage in some other problem behavior. The therapist coaches the patient, in a brief period (e.g., 10 minutes), in how to respond. Patients are expected to call before, rather than after, engaging in high-priority target behaviors, when they have already "solved the problem," and they are not to call their therapist within 24 hours of self-injury because therapist attention contingent on that behavior may reinforce it. If the patient does call in that circumstance, the therapist only assesses and responds to possible medical risk. Other than the 24-hour rule and the principle that there must be some availability for coaching, therapists determine and observe their own limits as to patients' use of telephone, e-mail, or other out-of-session contacts.

Motivating Therapists and Enhancing Their Skill: Consultation Team Meeting Patients with BPD are difficult to treat, and therapists (including skills trainers) working with them may have emotional reactions that may lead them to feel burned out or to extreme or unbalanced use of treatment strategies. DBT, therefore, includes a consultation team, the purpose of which is to keep therapists motivated and to provide guidance in conducting the treatment. Team members agree to accept a dialectical philosophy in which useful truths are seen as emerging from the transactions between opposing ideas. The team tries to apply the Zen principles of nonjudgmental observation and description of both the therapist's and the patient's behavior and to help each therapist find an optimal balance of acceptance and change strategies.

BALANCING TREATMENT STRATEGIES

The borderline patient's typically stressful or barren life circumstances, destructive behavior patterns, and high level of distress seem to call out for a relentless focus on potent change strategies, yet these may lead him or her to feel misunderstood, hurt or angry, or to become self-castigating. If, alternatively, the therapist focuses primarily on validating the patient's pain and helping him or her to accept problem behaviors and difficult circumstances, the patient may be upset that his or her sense of desperation about the need for change is not being taken seriously. In DBT, therefore, the therapist strives to achieve the most effective balance or dialectical synthesis of change and acceptance strategies in each moment. Balance does not always mean finding a middle way. It also can involve movement between strong polarities. For example, the therapist may point out that it is understandable that the patient is afraid of going to a job interview, and she needs to go anyway. Another example is that the therapist is completely committed to the treatment goal of keeping the patient out of the hospital and will hospitalize the patient if he or she is at imminent high risk of suicide.

There are four primary sets of DBT strategies, each of which includes both acceptance-oriented and change-oriented strategies. *Core strategies* are problem solving (change) and validation (acceptance). *Dialectical strategies* present or highlight extreme positions that then tend to elicit their antithesis. *Communication style strategies* include a reciprocal style (acceptance) and an irreverent one (change). *Case management strategies* include being a consultant to the patient (change), intervening in the environment for the patient (acceptance), and obtaining consultation from the team (balancing acceptance and change).

PROBLEM-SOLVING STRATEGIES

The first step in helping the patient to change a problem behavior pattern is to conduct a *behavioral analysis* of a particular instance of it (usually recent), that is, attempt to understand the variables that maintain the behavior by examining its antecedents and its consequences. A helpful behavioral analysis will point to one or more solutions, that is, changes that would lead to more desired outcomes. To facilitate those changes, the therapist uses standard cognitive-behavior therapy procedures, which can be usefully classified into four groups:

1. *Skills training,* if the patient does not know how to behave more skillfully.
2. *Contingency management,* if the patient's maladaptive behavior is being reinforced or adaptive behavior is being punished or not reinforced.
3. *Exposure,* if conditioned emotional reactions to particular stimuli interfere with adaptive behavior.
4. *Cognitive modification,* if the patient's beliefs, attitudes, and thoughts interfere with adaptive behavior.

We describe each of these sets of procedures.

Behavioral Analysis   The goal of a behavioral analysis is to recreate the sequence of vulnerability factors, prompting events, thoughts, feelings, action urges, and observable behaviors that led up to an instance of a problem behavior and the personal, interpersonal, and other consequences that followed it. The first step is to describe the problem behavior objectively, specifically, and nonjudgmentally. For example, "Friday evening, between 11 and 11:30, scratched ankles repeatedly with fingernails, enough to draw blood but not requiring stitches."

It is most helpful next to identify a prompting environmental event. The patient may initially be unable to identify one and, for example, respond with "I always feel suicidal." One useful strategy is to identify the time at which the urge increased. Solutions directed at the prompting event include avoiding such events (stimulus control) or changing them. It is often helpful to identify vulnerability factors that made the prompting event more difficult for the patient to cope with, such as other recent stressors, moods, lack of sleep, or inadequate nutrition impairing cognitive functioning. Solutions may then include attempts to reduce vulnerability factors.

The therapist and patient identify the chain from the prompting event to the problem behavior. Links in the chain may include thoughts about the event, emotional reactions, subsequent behaviors, and reactions to those behaviors by the patient and others. The greater the number of links identified, the greater the number of potential solutions. Patients may need repeated controlled exposure to the situation to allow their emotional response to habituate, to change what they tell themselves about the situation, use interpersonal skills, or use distress tolerance skills to cope with urges to engage in the problem behavior. The therapist also inquires about consequences of the problem behavior, including changes in the patient's emotions, responses of other people, and environmental changes. This may identify reinforcers that the therapist may be able to remove and negative consequences that the therapist can highlight.

Skills Training Solutions to a problem behavior pattern may involve the patient's being more interpersonally assertive, regulating emotions in more adaptive ways, or finding ways to tolerate distress. Mindfulness—nonjudgmental awareness of present experience—facilitates all of these capabilities. Dialectical behavior therapy teaches these skills in four modules: Mindfulness and distress tolerance are primarily acceptance-oriented; emotion regulation and interpersonal effectiveness are primarily change-oriented.

Mindfulness skills are taught in DBT because they can have clinically significant benefits. Among others, these benefits can include becoming less scattered and distractible, particularly at times of strong emotion, more able to let go of rumination, more aware of action urges before acting on them, and experiencing life more fully.

Like other skills, mindfulness can be developed with practice, setting aside time deliberately to be mindful, thereby strengthening the ability to do so. In the Zen tradition, the most common basic practice is to sit comfortably with eyes closed, focusing the mind on the inhalations and exhalations of the breath, and noticing the thoughts, images, sensations, and action urges that enter your awareness, allowing them to come and go freely without judging, holding onto, or trying to suppress them. Other objects of focus may also be used, such as external objects, a particular idea or class of thoughts, or activities such as walking. Such practice sometimes results in physical and mental relaxation, which can allow the individual's "wise mind" to be more accessible. However, relaxation is not a primary goal of mindfulness practice. In fact, awareness during mindfulness practice may at times be painful. These experiences are not to be avoided nor are pleasant experiences to be sought. The individual learns that thoughts, emotions, action urges, and so on come and go like the waves of an ocean, but the observing self remains present.

In DBT, mindfulness is taught as a set of *what* skills (what to do) and a set of *how* skills (how to do it). The *what* skills are *observing* your sense experiences, *describing* what you observe (e.g., "I am aware of an urge to move"), and *participating*, that is, interacting with the world. Practice in observing and describing are helpful steps toward participating mindfully. The *how* skills are *one-mindfully*, focusing on one thing at a time with full awareness; *nonjudgmentally*, without labeling experiences or behaviors as good or bad; and *effectively*, behaving in ways that are consistent with your important goals and values, rather than getting caught up in goals such as proving a point. Some of the practical issues involved in teaching mindfulness skills in DBT groups are discussed in Robins (2002).

Distress tolerance skills include crisis strategies to be used in place of self-injury, substance use, binging and purging, or other maladaptive behaviors the patient uses to decrease distress. These include various distracting activities, self-soothing activities, use of imagery, self-encouragement, and considering the pros and cons of acting on urges and of not acting on them. Other distress tolerance strategies have the goal of greater acceptance of reality. These include practicing mindfulness of daily life, such as following the breath while having a conversation, half-smiling, being mindful of your bodily movements, and turning acceptance into willingness to do what is needed in a situation, rather than being willful.

Emotion regulation skills taught include: *understanding* the nature and functions of emotions; *describing* emotions accurately and nonjudgmentally; *reducing vulnerability* factors for emotions, such as poor sleep, exercise, and diet; and *increasing resilience* by engaging in pleasant or mastery-enhancing activities. Skills for coping with emotions when they occur include mindfulness of the emotion (acceptance strategy) and opposite action (change strategy). *Being mindful of the emotion,* observing it come and go, without fighting, holding onto, or amplifying it, can decrease its duration or intensity because unless "fueled" by thoughts or other behaviors, emotional responses are naturally short-lived. *Acting opposite* to the action urge that is part of the emotional response to a situation can reduce the emotion. For fear, opposite action is to not avoid or escape the situation, but instead approach it and allow fear to habituate. Similarly, shame may be reduced by revealing instead of hiding; sadness, by getting active rather than withdrawing; unjustified guilt, by repeating the behavior that elicits it rather than apologizing (justified guilt by apologizing or repairing the situation); and anger, by gently withdrawing and by thinking and acting empathically rather than attacking.

Interpersonal effectiveness skills focus on making requests, refusing requests, and negotiating solutions to interpersonal conflicts while appropriately balancing the relative importance of achieving the immediate objective, maintaining or developing a good relationship, and maintaining self-respect. Acronyms are used to help patients remember components that are often helpful to include in an assertive statement. For example, the acronym for skills for obtaining their objective is DEAR MAN—Describe the situation, Express how you feel about it, Assert what you want the other person to do, and Reinforce them ahead of time, doing all this Mindfully, Appearing confident, and with willingness to Negotiate. Groups provide excellent opportunities to role-play and to rehearse these skills.

Contingency Management   If problem behavior seems to be maintained by reinforcing consequences, the therapist tries to arrange for them to cease, for punishing consequences to occur or be highlighted, or for incompatible adaptive behaviors to be reinforced. The therapist has little direct control over many of these consequences, so eliciting commitment from the patient and/or significant others to change reinforcement contingencies often is important. The therapist does have control over his or her own behavior toward the patient and can deliberately and contingently use this to influence the patient if he or she has developed a strong therapeutic relationship that the patient values. Although the consequences that will reinforce or punish a given behavior of a particular patient cannot be known definitively ahead of time (e.g., for some patients, praise initially may not serve as a reinforcer), for most patients, therapist expressions of approval, interest, concern, caring, liking, admiration, reassurance, validation, and attention from the therapist are reinforcers and their opposites are punishers. Therapists need to take care that they do not engage in such reinforcing behaviors immediately following maladaptive behavior, despite urges to help the patient to feel better in the moment.

When reinforcing consequences of a behavior are withdrawn, it may show an "extinction burst," an increase before it decreases. It is essential for the therapist not to back down and provide the reinforcer because he or she will have reinforced an increased intensity of the behavior. Instead, the therapist can soothe and validate the patient about how difficult it is to be on the extinction schedule and help the patient find another response that will be reinforced.

Punishment is usually not a preferred strategy, because it (1) can lead to strong emotional reactions that interfere with learning, (2) can strengthen a self-invalidating style, (3) can make the therapist a more negatively valenced stimulus, and (4) does not teach specific adaptive behavior. In some situations, however, particularly when the therapist cannot withdraw the reinforcers, such as the emotion-regulating effects of self-injury, he or she may need to use aversive consequences. The most common punishers in DBT are the therapist's disapproval, confrontation, or reduction in therapist availability. Other aversive consequences include overcorrection (doing the reverse behavior or undoing the effects of the behavior and going beyond that), taking a "vacation from therapy," return from which is contingent on some commitment or behavior change, and, as a last resort, termination from therapy. Termination usually can be avoided by earlier use of other contingencies.

Exposure   The core of behavioral treatments for anxiety disorders, which have been shown to be highly effective, is repeated exposure to the anxiety-provoking stimuli and prevention of the normal escape or avoidance response. This approach is extended in DBT to other emotions such as guilt, shame, and anger when they are problematic in intensity, lead to dysfunctional avoidance behavior, or inhibit the use of skills. The important elements are (1) to orient the patient to the strategy and its rationale, (2) to arrange for repeated exposure that does not lead to an outcome that could reinforce the problematic emotional response, (3) to block the action and expressive tendencies associated with the problem emotion, such as avoidance, and (4) to enhance the patient's sense of control over exposure by graduating the intensity or difficulty of the stimulus. It is important that the patient not terminate exposures prematurely by escape.

There are innumerable opportunities to help patients decrease maladaptive emotional reactions through exposure in the course of other DBT change strategies and acceptance strategies. For example, behavioral analysis of a recent incident of problem behavior may generate some of the emotions that were present during the incident or feelings of shame about the behavior. In skills training, rehearsing new interpersonal behaviors often generates anxiety. Therapist disapproval or approval may set off feelings of shame or fear, anger or pride. In mindfulness practice, the contents of awareness may generate anxiety or other emotions.

Cognitive Modification   Treatment targets may include both cognitive content and cognitive style. *Content* refers to negative automatic thoughts and maladaptive beliefs, attitudes, or schemas, which in BPD frequently concern self as worthless, defective, unlovable, and vulnerable, and others as excessively admired, despised, or feared. Common problems of cognitive style in BPD include dichotomous thinking (splitting) and dysfunctional allocation of attention (e.g., ruminating, dissociating), among others. The therapist tries to help patients to change these contents and styles by (1) teaching self-observation through mindfulness practice and written assignments; (2) identifying maladaptive cognitions and pointing to nondialectical thinking; (3) having patients generate alternative, more adaptive cognitions in session and for homework assignments; and (4) developing guidelines for when they should trust versus suspect their own interpretations, because self-validation is often also a goal.

VALIDATION STRATEGIES

Validation, which is used in DBT to balance problem solving, simply means communicating to the patient that his or her response makes sense, is understood, or is reasonable. It is important to validate only that which is, in fact, valid. Validation does not mean saying positive things about the patient, certainly if they are not true. Some things always are valid and, therefore, always can be validated, such as emotional responses, which are always understandable reactions to a perception or thought, even if the perception or thought itself is not valid. Other things are invalid, such as a belief that all other drivers on the road intend to harm the patient. Many things, however, can be valid in some way but not valid in another. For example, self-injury may regulate a patient's emotions. The behavior, therefore, is valid in terms of a short-term consequence. It makes sense. On the other hand, the behavior probably has various negative consequences and is not effective in helping patients reach their longer term goals in life. Early in treatment, it may be helpful to validate self-injury in the sense of communicating that it is understandable. This may be unnecessary or undesirable later in treatment.

Validation strategies involve looking for the nugget of gold (what is valid) in the bucket of sand (what is not valid). In validation, the therapist actively accepts patients as they are, does not discount, pathologize, trivialize, or interpret their responses, but instead searches for what is valid, true, and relevant; amplifies it if necessary; and reflects it back to the patient.

Validation can occur at a number of levels. Level one is unbiased listening and observing. This communicates to patients that they are important and worth listening to carefully. Level two validation is accurate reflection of the patient's communications. Summarizing and paraphrasing communicates to patients that they have been understood. Level three validation involves accurately articulating emotions, thoughts, and behavior patterns that patients have not yet put into words, with statements such as "I see I made you angry" or "If I were in that situation, I'd be really mad." Patients may feel particularly understood if they did not even have to communicate their reaction. If the therapist's inference is incorrect, it is likely to be experienced as invalidating, so it is important not to stray far from the observable data. Level four validation refers to the patient's past learning history or biological dysfunction. For example, the therapist might state, "I think it is understandable that you often find it difficult to focus because of your diagnosed attention-deficit/hyperactivity disorder" or "It makes sense that you would have difficulty trusting me. I'm a man, and men have treated you very badly in the past." However, this last example also illustrates that implicit in the therapist's statement is the notion that the patient's reaction involves a distortion (i.e., is a transference reaction). At times, it may be more helpful to validate in terms of the present context or normative functioning (level five), as in: "It makes sense that you would be having difficulty trusting me. We have met only a few times. It takes some time for most people to trust their therapist." The sixth level of validation described in DBT is radical genuineness. The therapist responds as his or her natural self, rather than with role-prescribed behavior, and does not treat the patient as overly fragile, but instead as able to tolerate the therapist's natural reactions. This validates the patient's capability.

DIALECTICAL STRATEGIES

As we noted earlier, a dialectical philosophy influences all aspects of the treatment, including its theory of the etiology of borderline personality disorder, view of the therapeutic relationship, balance of treatment strategies, and balance of skills taught to patients. In addition, Linehan (1993) has described several specific dialectical strategies.

Balancing Treatment Strategies   Balancing validation and problem solving, as well as other strategies, as the needs of patient and situation constantly shift, is the most fundamental dialectical strategy.

Entering the Paradox   The therapist highlights paradoxes in the patient's life and in treatment, without attempting to resolve them. The therapist models and teaches that "both this and that" are true, rather than "this or that." For example, if the patient states that the therapist does not really care about her because the therapist is just doing a paid job, the therapist might respond that both are true (if they are)—that he or she cares very much about the patient *and* would not continue to treat her if there were no payment.

Metaphor   These often can have greater impact or be more memorable than direct, literal communications, particularly when collaboration has broken down, when the patient is feeling hopeless, and in many other difficult situations. Treatment progress is like climbing a mountain. Practicing mindfulness is like strengthening a muscle. A patient who wants a better life, but will not learn the DBT skills because they are boring, may be told that he or she is like an aspiring house builder who does not do foundations because they are boring.

Devil's Advocate   This strategy may be used to strengthen a patient's belief or commitment. The therapist notes arguments for the opposing point of view, without arguing strongly for them. For example, when a patient makes an initial commitment to stop self-harm, the therapist might point out that this may be very difficult, because self-harm has "worked" so well to reduce the patient's distress. The intention is that the patient then will emphasize how self-harm has created problems for him or her or how important it is to stop the behavior.

Extending   This strategy borrows a concept from the martial art Aikido, in which the partner's blow is not opposed, but rather flowed with and pulled beyond its intended target. For example, the patient's statement "If I don't get X . . . I may as well kill myself" might be met with "This is very serious. How can we talk about X, when your life is at stake. Perhaps we should think about hospitalization." This strategy can be helpful when the patient is very hopeless or when the therapist believes the patient is exaggerating or being overly dramatic.

Wise Mind   The therapist communicates to the patient his or her belief that each person has inherent wisdom about what is best for him or her in each situation, and that the patient can learn to attend to wise mind once emotional dysregulation is controlled.

Making Lemonade out of Lemons   This refers to looking for the positive or helpful side of a difficult situation, the silver lining in the cloud. To avoid invalidating the patient, it is helpful to remember that to make lemonade, you also need sugar (validation of the difficulty).

Allowing Natural Change   A dialectical worldview assumes that everything is constantly changing. Patients must learn to cope successfully with change. The therapist, therefore, makes no special effort to shield the patient from change in the treatment parameters or the environment.

Dialectical Assessment   The therapist continuously seeks to understand the patient's problems in a situational context, including contributions from the treatment environment, rather than focusing only on the patient's contribution.

COMMUNICATION STYLE STRATEGIES

Dialectical behavior therapists strategically vary their communication style between being reciprocal (acceptance) and being irreverent (change).

Reciprocal Communication   This is the modal style in DBT. It involves being warm, genuine, and empathic. It may include therapist self-disclosure, which is used in behavior therapies in several ways. One is to respond to the patient's queries about professional or personal information. In DBT, we do not take the position that disclosing such information is a "boundary violation." Instead, a decision about self-disclosure is based on whether the information might be helpful to the patient, whether it might be harmful to him or her, and whether the therapist personally is comfortable with revealing it. Self-disclosure can also take the form of modeling. Therapists may describe how they coped with a situation in their own life. Finally, DBT therapists frequently disclose their reactions to the patient (self-involving self-disclosure) to clarify their own limits, to reinforce or punish a behavior, or to provide patients with useful feedback they rarely receive from others about the impact of their behavior.

Irreverent Communication   This refers to deliberately being out of synch with the patient, saying or doing something unexpected, humorous, or confrontational. Used judiciously, it can help a patient look at a situation from a new perspective or back away from a course of action. For example, if a patient tells her therapist that she is going to quit the skills-training group, which she must continue to stay in this individual therapy, the therapist might simply state, "I'm really going to miss working with you."

CASE MANAGEMENT STRATEGIES

In helping patients more successfully manage their social and professional relationships and interactions with social service agencies and other institutions, DBT therapists attempt to appropriately balance use of two strategies: consultation to the patient and environmental intervention. Use of the consultation team, discussed elsewhere, is also a case management strategy.

Consultation to the Patient This is the primary case management strategy in DBT. The strategy has three main objectives: (1) to teach patients the essential skills needed to manage their own lives, (2) to demonstrate respect for the patients' abilities and foster their self-respect, and (3) to decrease splitting among persons in the patient's network. For example, if the patient is experiencing side effects of sexual dysfunction from medication, the therapist would not contact the prescribing physician, but might instead address any fears the patient has about discussing it with his or her physician and coach and rehearse with the patient how to do so. In the long run, it is more helpful to teach people to fish than to give them a fish.

The DBT therapist generally does not consult with anyone outside the DBT team about the patient unless the patient is present, which may be a different stance on consultation than that of some other professionals, so the therapist needs to orient others in the patient's network to the rationale for this policy. If the therapist is contacted by police, rescue squads, emergency room personnel, inpatient treating clinicians, or housing supervisors for recommendations about what to do with the patient, the DBT therapist asks for information about the current situation, provides or corrects any necessary information the patient cannot give, and suggests that the other person follow his or her usual procedures. The therapist then asks to speak with the patient and coaches the patient on how best to interact or to cope with the situation.

Environmental Intervention Sometimes the consultation to the patient strategy is not ethical, feasible, or effective. When patients are unable or unwilling to act on their own, no matter how well coached, and the outcome is very important, intervening in the environment on the patient's behalf may be worth the lost learning opportunity. Examples include situations in which patients might die, lose public assistance or access to health care, or be committed involuntarily to a state hospital when it is not in their best interests. Statutes also require the therapist to intervene in certain situations involving patients who are minors. There are also times when intervening is the humane thing to do and will cause no harm, such as going to get the patient when his or her car breaks down on the way to therapy.

PROCESS OF THERAPEUTIC APPROACH

Because individuals who meet criteria for borderline personality disorder typically present with multiple problems, therapists need to prioritize and decide which problems are better addressed early in treatment and which are better left until later. Similarly, within a treatment session, decisions must be made about which problems to prioritize. In this section, we discuss the concept of stages of treatment and a hierarchy of targets within each stage.

Pretreatment Stage: Assessment

Whether an individual meets BPD criteria can be evaluated using a structured diagnostic interview, but diagnostic information alone is of limited utility for developing a treatment plan. The therapist needs to know the specific patterns of behavior (including thoughts and feelings) that are creating difficulty for this particular individual and which variables influence them. This information can be assessed in a variety of ways, including through verbal report during sessions, questionnaires, and direct observation. Daily written self-monitoring, often employed in behavioral and cognitive therapies, is considered essential in DBT. Patients are given diary cards or sheets on which to record the occurrence, frequency, or intensity of a number of target behaviors, emotions, and so on that are determined by the therapist and patient together, based on that patient's hierarchy of target priorities. The accuracy of these daily written reports probably is much greater than that of weekly verbal reports in which patients are more likely to omit important occurrences. Information provided by the diary card at the beginning of each session is critical to determining the agenda of that session.

PRETREATMENT STAGE: COMMITMENT

Before commencing treatment, the therapist and the patient need to agree about the most important goals and methods of treatment. The agreements that the DBT therapist requires depend, in part, on the patient's behavior patterns. For example, if the patient has a recent history of suicidal or other self-injurious behaviors, the therapist will require that the patient commit to stopping the behavior. A commitment is not a contract that, if broken, results in termination from treatment. Rather, it concerns the patient's goals and intentions, and explicit commitments are likely to influence behavior. Verbal agreements usually are preferred because they are natural and appropriate to the relationship, whereas patients may view written agreements as more coercive or primarily as the therapist's attempt to limit their legal liability. If self-injury is not an issue for this patient, the therapist may require an explicit commitment to work on changing a different high priority behavior, such as substance use, binging and purging, or aggressive behavior. Patients also must agree to be willing to address behaviors that interfere with treatment and to attend both individual therapy and skills training groups regularly.

Linehan (1993a) suggests strategies for increasing patients' commitments. Some are drawn from social psychology research on persuasion, such as "foot-in-the-door" and "door-in-the-face." Some are similar to strategies used in motivational interviewing, such as evaluating both the pros and cons of changing and of not changing, playing devil's advocate, and highlighting the patient's freedom to choose while acknowledging the consequences of his or her choices.

STAGES OF TREATMENT

It is common for BPD patients to have multiple problems, such as self-injurious behavior, disordered eating and sleeping, substance abuse, intrusive aversive memories, conflictual relationships or an absence of meaningful relationships, and difficulty sustaining employment or schooling. The therapist may try to focus on one problem at a time, but frequent crises easily can shift the focus from session to session and lead to the therapist's feeling overwhelmed. DBT addresses this challenge with the concept of treatment stages that are determined by the current level of dysfunction and with a clear hierarchy of treatment targets within each stage. Not all patients need or want all treatment stages, but treatment should not focus on problems associated with a later stage if problems associated with an earlier stage are prominent.

Stage 1 treatment focuses on severe behavioral dyscontrol, such as self-injury, severe eating disorder or substance abuse, or repeated hospitalizations. The primary goal is to help the patient stop these escape behaviors and develop greater behavioral control. This stage may be brief, protracted, or not needed at all, depending on the patient's initial level of dysfunction, existing skills, and ability and willingness to work hard in treatment.

Stage 2 treatment focuses on patients' problematic avoidance of emotional experiences, including, but not limited to, their avoidance of cues associated with earlier traumata, when relevant. The goal is to increase appropriate experiencing of emotions by exposing the patient to the relevant cues. In the case of trauma history, this might involve, among other things, having the patient repeatedly describe the trauma in detail. Cognitive restructuring of beliefs related to the trauma that are associated with guilt, shame, anger, lack of trust, and so on is also useful. Trauma history would not be a focus with a patient who has severe behavioral dyscontrol because it would likely generate very strong emotions and thereby increase attempts to regulate those emotions through problem behaviors including suicidal behaviors. Exposure for Post-Traumatic Stress Disorder (PTSD) would be conducted only when the patient demonstrates reasonable control over extreme behaviors.

The goals of Stage 3 treatment include helping patients to improve their relationships and self-esteem or make other changes that will increase the experience of ordinary happiness and unhappiness rather than misery. Stage 4 treatment moves away from amelioration of problems to promotion of an increased capacity for joy and sense of connection to the universe.

Stage 2 treatment primarily is standard cognitive-behavioral therapy for PTSD. It is likely that many forms of treatment are helpful to patients in Stage 3 and that many approaches to spiritual development are helpful in Stage 4. It is in treating Stage 1 behaviors that DBT probably is most unique. We, therefore, describe the targets of Stage 1 in greater detail.

STAGE 1 TREATMENT TARGETS

Patients in Stage 1 treatment typically have multiple serious difficulties. The DBT therapist maintains a clear focus in each session by following a standard hierarchy of treatment target priorities:

1. Decrease life-threatening behaviors.
2. Decrease treatment-interfering behaviors.
3. Decrease quality-of-life-interfering behaviors.
4. Increase knowledge and performance of skilled behaviors.

Information about these behaviors is obtained from the diary card, from the patient's or others' verbal reports, or from the therapist's direct observation of behaviors in session. Once a behavior is chosen to focus on, the patient and therapist conduct a detailed behavioral analysis of it and develop potential solutions that the patient could implement in the future.

Decrease Life-Threatening and Other Self-Injurious Behaviors   These behaviors include suicide attempts, suicide threats, nonsuicidal self-injury, urges to engage in these behaviors, and marked increases or decreases in suicidal ideation (as well as behaviors that threaten or harm others). Even minor self-injuries are taken seriously because they can otherwise escalate over time, similar to addictive behaviors. Whenever any of these behaviors has occurred since the last session, it is the primary focus of the current session.

Decrease Therapy-Interfering Behaviors   Approximately 50% of BPD patients drop out of most treatments within one year, often because of their frustration or dissatisfaction with the provider or their provider's frustration with them. These frustrations usually result from therapy-interfering behaviors of one or both parties, that is, behaviors that interfere with the progress of treatment. Because a therapist cannot help a BPD patient who does not attend treatment for very long, DBT assigns a high priority to explicitly addressing such problems when they arise. In Linehan, Armstrong, Suarez, Allmon, and Heard's (1991) initial outcome study, only 17% of patients in DBT dropped out of treatment with their initially assigned therapist, compared with 58% of those in treatment as usual. In our own outcome study (Koons et al., 2001), the dropout rate for DBT was 23%.

Therapy-interfering behaviors of patients can include:

- Behaviors that interfere with receiving the treatment, such as not attending regularly, repeatedly being very late, being overmedicated or intoxicated during session, and dissociating during session.
- Behaviors that interfere with other patients' treatment, such as hostile behaviors toward other patients, selling them drugs, and discussing details of self-injuries with them.
- Behaviors that reduce the therapist's motivation or cross his or her personal limits, such as repeated hostility toward the therapist, not completing diary cards or doing other agreed-on assignments, calling the therapist too frequently, or not calling when it would have been appropriate.

Therapists differ in their own particular limits and tolerances, so what is therapy-interfering for one therapist may not be for another. The consultation team can help the therapist become more aware of whether his or her limits are being stretched. Unlike individual therapy, treating therapy-interfering behaviors is a low priority in skills-training groups, because attending to them in depth leaves too little time for teaching and rehearsing skills.

Therapists also engage in therapy-interfering behaviors, such as being late for appointments, being distracted or sleepy during sessions, not returning phone calls, or forgetting important information about the patient. Therapists also may be too oriented toward change or too oriented toward acceptance and may need guidance from the consultation team and the ability to constructively use feedback from the patient to find a more optimal balance.

Decrease Quality-of-Life-Interfering Behaviors   The third priority is to decrease behaviors that seriously interfere with the patient's having a reasonable quality of life. These might include substance abuse, binging and/or purging, panic attacks, or other psychopathology, unsafe sexual behaviors, or shoplifting. They may also include ongoing external situations in the patient's life such as homelessness or not having any activities or social contacts beyond therapy.

Increase Skilled Behaviors   The fourth priority of Stage 1 DBT as a whole and of the individual therapy component is skills acquisition and strengthening. However, it is the main priority of the skills-training group (trumped only by the rare incident of behaviors that could destroy, rather than just interfere with, therapy for that patient or others). If a particular skill that the patient has not yet learned in the group would be helpful in a current situation, the individual therapist may do some skills training, but this is usually in the context of treating a higher priority target.

Overarching Goal: Dialectical Synthesis   The thoughts and beliefs of BPD patients, which influence their behaviors and feelings, are often extreme and polarized. A patient who makes a mistake may label himself or herself completely worthless and become suicidal. A patient whose presence is not acknowledged by someone may conclude that the other person hates him or her or is a mean person. Patients also may view positive events and behaviors of others in equally extreme ways. An overarching goal in DBT, therefore, is to help the patient to think more dialectically, in terms of both/and rather than either/or. The therapist points out the extreme nature of these patterns and helps the person to think of and practice alternatives. The therapist also models dialectical thinking and behavior.

Linehan (1993a) has described a number of dialectical dilemmas that are common among patients with BPD, which can be considered secondary targets in DBT because they often contribute to the occurrence of primary target behaviors. These include the dialectics of (1) emotional vulnerability (e.g., "I'm in so much pain, you've got to help me") versus self-invalidation (e.g., "I should be able to handle this myself—I hate myself for being a wimp"), (2) crisis generation (poor judgment and impulsive behavior that create or exacerbate distressing situations) versus inhibited grieving (inability or unwillingness to experience distressing emotions or thoughts), and (3) active passivity (acting helpless and pushing others to solve the problem) versus apparent competence (voluntarily or involuntarily appearing more competent or less distressed than is actually the case). To decrease these patterns, the therapist attempts to help the patient to (1) improve emotion regulation skills, (2) increase his or her ability to self-validate, (3) improve realistic decision-making and decrease impulsivity, (4) increase emotional experiencing rather than avoidance, (5) become a better problem solver, and (6) improve accurate identification and communication of feelings to get appropriate help.

CLINICAL CASE EXAMPLE

Rachel is a 33-year-old White female college graduate. The following history is based on her self-report. (The case description refers to the therapist, C. Koons, in the first person singular.) Rachel has never been married, has no children, and lives alone in her own condo with her three cats. Her closest relationship is with her former college roommate, whom she sees about every two months. She is estranged from her mother, who lives about 40 miles distant, and from her one brother, who lives in a neighboring state. Her father is deceased.

Rachel's mother was a homemaker who was often depressed and was addicted to Valium. Rachel's brother, Ralph, who was often left in charge of Rachel while their mother "rested," physically and emotionally abused her from age 8 until she was 13, when Ralph left home. Rachel's father, a dentist, worked long hours and was not very engaged with the family. He favored Ralph over Rachel and said so directly and indirectly numerous times during Rachel's childhood.

In elementary and secondary school, Rachel was an average student, but social anxiety prevented her from making friends. Rachel described herself in high school as "a pudgy nerd." At age 17, she began purging, experiencing suicidal ideation, and intermittently self-harming, mainly by superficial scratches and cuts with a knife, which she kept secret.

In her senior year of college, Rachel left home to live with a roommate. That year, her mother was diagnosed and treated for breast cancer. Rachel felt overwhelmed with pressure to graduate, cut her wrists, and was admitted to the university hospital. Her father was outraged that Rachel could be so focused on her own difficulties during her mother's illness. He threatened to cut off her support unless she "pulled herself together." Rachel dropped out of school and moved back home after discharge from the hospital. She finally finished her degree in sociology at age 26. During that time, she developed panic disorder with agoraphobia and obsessive-compulsive disorder (OCD). After completing her BA, Rachel continued to live at home, though her relationship with her parents deteriorated.

Eventually, Rachel got a job in the field of computers and moved out of her parents' home. Shortly after, her father died of a heart attack. Rachel reported no grief at this sudden death, only a kind of numbness. She put all her attention on her job and performed well, other than problems with attendance. Rachel was laid off from her first job after three years and was unemployed for about 18 months. She was still unemployed when she entered DBT treatment. She was hired at her current job two months into treatment and has been in this job for eight months. Since her first hospitalization, Rachel had received medication management and supportive psychotherapy one to two times per month from the same psychiatrist who previously treated her mother.

CLINICAL PRESENTATION

Rachel's psychiatrist, who referred her for DBT, had been treating her for depression and had also diagnosed her with OCD, panic disorder, and bulimia nervosa and began to suspect she might also meet criteria for BPD. At the time of referral, Rachel was taking 100 mg of Zoloft and 6 mg of Klonopin per day.

Rachel arrived for her first appointment early, dressed in blue jeans, a sweatshirt, and flip-flops. She appeared younger than her stated age. She is of medium height with short brown hair, brown eyes, and acne scars. She is moderately obese and speaks in a very soft voice.

I had her fill out the Beck Depression Inventory, Beck Hopelessness Scale, and the BPD section of the SCID II screening questionnaire. Rachel was moderately depressed and very hopeless. She endorsed seven of nine BPD criteria, including mood swings, problems with anger, chaotic relationships, fear of abandonment, impulsivity, suicide ideation and self-harm behavior, and feelings of emptiness. In our interview, Rachel denied dissociation, paranoia or psychosis, and denied current suicidal intent or plan. It was clear that she was meeting with me solely on the advice of her psychiatrist. She very much wanted to feel better and felt that the medications "are not helping, so I might as well give this a try." She also indicated that she was desperate to find employment.

It was difficult for Rachel to identify goals other than feeling better and getting a job. She said she would like, one day, to get married and have children, but felt that was unlikely due to her age, her appearance, her moods, and her OCD. I introduced DBT treatment as a way for Rachel to become more skillful at pursuing and attaining her goals. She was skeptical at first, feeling that she would fail at treatment and that her goals were unattainable. But she decided she wanted to at least explore DBT further and see if she wanted to commit to it. We made four more appointments that day, and I told her that we could use that time to see if this treatment was a good fit for her.

In the next four sessions, I oriented Rachel to what DBT involves, specifically that we would work on eliminating self-harm behaviors, reducing behaviors that might interfere with therapy, and reducing behaviors that seriously interfere with an adequate quality of life—in her case, including panic attacks, purging, and not having a job. She would be expected to meet with me individually at least once each week, to attend a weekly DBT skills group, to complete all homework from individual and group therapy, and commit to one year of treatment. Rachel immediately agreed to all of these things, but in further discussion it became clear that she abhorred groups, especially psychotherapy groups, which she had attended in the hospital. She admitted that it would be nearly impossible for her to make herself go to group if it proved at all confrontational. I pointed out that DBT skills group is more like a class than a traditional psychotherapy group. Then, using the DBT commitment strategies of alternately highlighting both the potential benefits of the treatment and the difficulties she was likely to experience, I nudged her toward a more realistic consideration of and firmer commitment to the treatment.

At the end of the four initial sessions, Rachel said she wanted to commit to DBT. She approved of the fact that DBT was very structured and believed it might help her. She was also beginning to feel attached to me. By the fifth session, we were ready to prepare her diary card and start her in skills group.

At the outset of treatment, Rachel's most important problem behaviors included self-harm, suicide ideation, panic attacks, and purging. She reported suicide ideation and self-harm urges daily and cut herself superficially two to three times per week. She had no firm suicide plan or intent. Rachel's panic attacks, which she reported were severe and occurred two to three times per week, seemed to be linked to her job search and fears of rejection. Her purging consisted of vomiting one to two times per week, usually on weekends after large meals. Excessive hand washing and frequent long showers had greatly decreased since she had been taking Zoloft, but we still put them on her diary card. Because alcohol, street drugs, and over-the-counter medications had never been a problem for Rachel, we eliminated these from the standard DBT card. We did monitor prescription drug use, even though she was compliant with her medications. On entering treatment, Rachel was miserable most days, maintained a regular schedule only one to two days a week, and engaged in few activities outside her apartment, so her diary card included misery ratings, schedule maintenance, and activities.

Diagnostic Formulation

In addition to her *DSM-IV* diagnoses and primary behavioral targets, Rachel's behavior patterns can be described in terms of the dialectical dilemmas commonly seen in BPD patients, which are often secondary targets of treatment, as in her case.

Rachel's panic attacks and frequent misery are forms of *emotion dysregulation*, and her suicidal ideation, self-injury, and purging are maladaptive efforts to escape or regulate intense emotions. Developmentally, her shy, anxious temperament and her difficulties observing, labeling, and regulating her emotions were exacerbated by being raised by a depressed mother and an absent father and by abuse from her brother. Rachel also has a strong tendency to self-invalidate. She holds herself to perfectionist standards she learned growing up and blames herself and gives up when she cannot meet these standards. She often describes herself as a "loser" and a "crybaby," invalidating terms that may have been applied to her by others during her childhood. This self-invalidation also contributes to her cutting, purging, isolating, and thinking about killing herself. I, therefore, try to be alert to any self-invalidation that occurs in session and link it directly to worsening emotion regulation and encourage Rachel to reward herself for any new behaviors rather than hold out for perfect performance. I also teach and encourage her to identify self-invalidating thoughts such as "I am a crybaby" and replace them with more accurate and encouraging statements such as "I'm feeling kind of emotional right now; this will pass."

Rachel engages in some problem behaviors to *inhibit emotional experiencing*, especially fear and sadness, which she describes as intolerable. These behaviors, including going numb when she is upset and not going out of the house all weekend, have contributed (are on the chain) to her most serious problem behaviors, including cutting and purging, and also contribute to her profound loneliness. Rachel's inhibited emotional experiencing is directly linked to *crisis-generating behaviors*. For example, when she is consumed with loneliness and isolates herself, Rachel often proceeds from numbness to strong suicidal thoughts, which distract her from her loneliness. Another example is that when she perceives criticism from a peer at work and feels shame, Rachel tries to avoid the peer and the feelings by arriving to work late and leaving early. However, soon the attendance problem provokes her supervisor to speak with her. The fear of unemployment (not as unpleasant an emotion for her as shame) distracts her from her shame. I focus on these two secondary targets of inhibited emotional experience and crisis generation by exposing Rachel in session to cues that elicit loneliness or shame, and I encourage the use of emotion regulation skills to label, identify, and manage her emotions.

Although she often appears competent, Rachel actually lacks some of the problem-solving and interpersonal skills she needs to accomplish her job. This *apparent competence* causes her peers to believe she is lazy and/or malingering, judgments that Rachel finds extremely painful, yet believes are accurate. Apparent competence appears often in therapy sessions, as evidenced by the many social interaction assignments I gave early in treatment that Rachel was unable to complete. I now always assess her actual skill level during problem solving, rather than assume that she has the capacity to do what she has agreed to.

Rachel also demonstrates *active passivity*. Because she lacks, or believes she lacks, some skills to complete jobs at work, she relies on help from others. She has a few "friends" in her work environment that will "help her out," but Rachel quickly becomes dependent on these individuals, who sometimes tire of repeatedly rescuing her. This also crops up in the therapeutic relationship, and Rachel and I frequently struggle with it. I have oriented her to the principle that I do not want to rescue her when she has the skills to rescue herself, and I want to teach and coach her in skills needed to solve her problems herself.

Progress in Treatment

During the first weeks of treatment, my focus was primarily on reducing self-harm behavior and supporting Rachel's search for and maintenance of employment. In the second month, she was hired as a data technician at a large corporation. The move to employed status was very difficult, especially because Rachel had been asleep in the day and awake at night while she was unemployed. She also had an increase in panic symptoms and in purging. After about two months of employment, she was able to get her sleep schedule normalized.

Since entering treatment 10 months ago, Rachel has attended group and individual therapy regularly, always fills out her diary cards, and usually does her homework. She continues to be compliant with her medications and has succeeded (with much coaching on my part) in convincing her psychiatrist to discontinue the Klonopin and to add Buspar because we both believed the Klonopin was contributing to her oversleeping. Rachel is still in Stage 1 DBT, as would be expected at this point in treatment.

Level One Targets: Life-Threatening Behaviors   Rachel's episodes of self-harm have reduced from one per week to about one per month and still consist of superficial cuts. She has gotten rid of her straight razor, but urges to self-harm remain high. She continues to have passive suicide ideation such as "I wish I were dead" many days each week, triggered by hopeless thoughts and loneliness. The urges to self-harm appear to result most often from intense shame generated by perceived criticism or rejection by others and by self-invalidation. Most of the time, Rachel is able to use skills to overcome her self-harm urges. Her misery, however, remains very high.

Level Two Targets: Therapy-Interfering Behaviors   Rachel is a model client in many ways. However, because she is very avoidant, conducting behavioral analyses with her can be like pulling teeth. "I don't remember," "I don't know," "I'm not sure" are her most frequent first answers to questions about what her thoughts, feelings, and sensations were around a particular episode. She also finds it very difficult to generate solutions to problems, making solution analysis agonizingly slow.

Level Three Targets: Quality-of-Life-Interfering Behaviors   Rachel's OCD behaviors remain in remission. She is purging much less frequently, about one to two times per month, often in response to overeating and the sensation of fullness. In the past, it also brought relief from negative emotions, but Rachel says that it no longer does so. Panic episodes remain a problem. There appear to be many cues for a panic response, such as being asked to talk at a staff meeting and lying awake at night before a busy workday. We have recently begun meeting an extra session per week, devoted to panic control treatment. Rachel continues to have problems with maintaining a schedule on weekends and a low activity level. Perhaps the biggest problem contributing to her low quality of life has been her low level of social interaction. She has been unable to complete many assignments that generate social anxiety, such as asking a colleague to spend time together outside work, attending a lecture or workshop, or even spending an hour or two sitting in a coffee shop. Some of the problem has been that I may have made assignments too difficult, and some is therapy-interfering behaviors on her part.

Level Four Targets: Acquiring Dialectical Behavior Therapy Skills   Rachel has attended group regularly and is a favorite of both leaders. She says she hates group, mainly because one of the participants reminds her of a girl who used to tease her in high school, but the leaders report that she is cheerful and pleasant to everyone. Rachel has a good grasp of many of the more concrete DBT skills, especially the crisis survival skills and some of the mindfulness skills, though she still has difficulty producing them when she is seriously distressed. She is weakest at the interpersonal and emotion regulation skills.

Treatment Process

I illustrate aspects of Rachel's treatment with a transcript from one session, the diary card for which follows on page 245.

Rachel arrived on time and had her diary card as usual. We greeted each other warmly, and she installed her audiotape while I looked over her diary card. I first looked at the columns for self-harm and saw that none had occurred. We needed to discuss an instance of therapy-interfering behavior, namely, that she had not been practicing progressive muscle relaxation as she had agreed to do. She reported a panic attack every day at work and left work early on two days when they were most severe. During this vignette, I continually focus on primary target two (therapy-interfering behavior) and the secondary targets of self-invalidation and inhibited emotional experiencing, which for her lead to emotion-dysregulation and crisis-generating behaviors.

Therapist: No self-harm this week and no urges. That is great!

Comment on process and technique: Therapist goes directly to the highest target, notes improvement, and attempts to reinforce it with praise.

Technical interventions: Targeting. Reinforcement.

Therapist: No purging, great. Hmm, one day of an extra shower. Looks like that was the day you had a very bad panic attack at work?
Client: Yes, that is why I starred it. I took a 30-minute shower when I got home, I felt so yucky.
Therapist: You have had a panic attack every single day at work. And your suicide ideation is up slightly. Why do you think that is?
Client: I don't know.
Therapist: (Says nothing, tucks chin, and lifts eyebrows)

Comment on process and technique: Therapist recognizes the importance of her approval to this client and shows mild disapproval of the avoidance response.

Date	Prescription Medications #	Specify	Panic Episodes #	Specify	Handwashing Extra Showers #	Specify	Vomit #	Specify	Relaxation Practice (Y/N)	Suicide Ideation (0–5)	Self-Harm Urges (0–5)	Self-Harm Actions (Y/N)	Avoidance Impulses Urges (0–5)	Action
Mon		100 Zoloft Buspar	2	At work	0		0		A little	5	0	No	4	Go home (did)
Tues		100 Zoloft Buspar	1	At home	0		0		No	5	0	No	3	Skip work (went)
Wed		100 Zoloft Buspar	1	At work	0		0		No	5	0	No		
Thu		100 Zoloft Buspar	2	At work At grocery	0		0		No	5	0	No	5	Skip work (went late)
Fri		Forgot	1	At work	2	Extra shower	0		No	5	0	No	5	Go home (did)
Sat		100 Zoloft Buspar	0		0		0		No	3	0	No		
Sun		100 Zoloft Buspar	0		0		0		Fell asleep	4	0	No	3	Sleep all day (got up at noon)

Technical interventions: Targeting suicidal ideation. Targeting in-session therapy-interfering behavior. Contingency management. Irreverent communication style.

CLIENT: Probably because I am so miserable at work. But don't worry. I'm not planning on anything. I just noticed the thoughts more. I think they are worse when I have more panic.

THERAPIST: Good, I'm glad you aren't planning on doing anything. Still, the increase is troublesome. We've seen this happen before when you were very anxious. Do the thoughts decrease the anxiety?

CLIENT: No. They make it worse.

Comment on process and technique: Because suicidal ideation has been linked in past analyses with panic, the therapist does not do a full behavioral analysis but goes directly to solution analysis (following).

Technical interventions: Highlighting problem behavior. Pattern recognition (part of behavioral analysis). Hypothesis testing.

THERAPIST: So, what skills have you been using with the suicidal thoughts?

CLIENT: Not any, really. When I feel that bad, I just completely forget the skills.

THERAPIST: (Looks to the back of the card where skills use is recorded) You say you have been using the distraction skills most days. Do they work to decrease the suicidal thoughts?

CLIENT: Yeah, but they keep coming back.

THERAPIST: Yeah, you have to keep using them, over and over and over. What about the mindfulness skills, like "Teflon mind" or "observe, describe?"

CLIENT: Yeah, I could use those.

THERAPIST: What gets in the way of using them?

Comment on process and technique: Because of the client's desire to please the therapist, she will often agree right away to any solutions generated.

Technical interventions: Troubleshooting the solution.

CLIENT: I am so jittery and nervous.

THERAPIST: Okay, so the anxiety is getting in the way of using skills?

CLIENT: Yeah, it's been terrible. I've had to go home early every day last week. I don't want to go in the mornings either.

THERAPIST: Sounds really miserable. Clearly, we have to get this panic under control. It is getting in the way of you using skills, and it makes your suicide ideation worse. And it could jeopardize your job.

CLIENT: I can't afford to lose this job. My supervisor wants to speak with me tomorrow morning, and I know it's about leaving early. I'm probably going to lose my job. (Smiles)

THERAPIST: Why are you smiling?

CLIENT: Was I smiling?

THERAPIST: Yes. What were you feeling?

Comment on process and technique: Therapist agrees that panic attacks make her life miserable and highlights their negative consequences to increase commitment to a solution. Therapist then comments on the incongruity between the client's verbal and facial expression.

Technical interventions: Validation. Highlighting negative consequences. Targeting in-session behavior. Exposure to emotions.

CLIENT: Oh, I don't know. I guess it would be a relief not to have to go in there. But I know it would really be a disaster. I really, really need to keep the job. I guess I was afraid.

THERAPIST: So you are leaving early because of anxiety and panic and now your supervisor wants to speak with you. Have you had any criticism about your work?

CLIENT: No, I'm sure it's about leaving early. It's the damn panic attacks. One morning I even had one before going to work. I was at home! I don't know what to do. Maybe I should ask Dr. Jones to increase my Zoloft. That probably won't work either. (Sighs)

THERAPIST: Rachel, I see here that you haven't been practicing the progressive relaxation. Why is that?

CLIENT: I just couldn't lie still long enough to do it. I am such a screw-up.

THERAPIST: (Squeezes squeeze toy, which makes a squeak)

CLIENT: I knew you'd do that. Okay, so I self-invalidated.

THERAPIST: Can you reframe that?

CLIENT: It is really hard to make myself lie down and do progressive relaxation when I am so nervous, so I avoid.

Comment on process and technique: Therapist is using a squeeze toy to highlight for the client her self-critical comments and asks her to modify them.

Technical interventions: Irreverent communication style. Targeting a secondary target. Cognitive modification. Activating new behavior in session.

THERAPIST: How many days did you try?

CLIENT: (Sighs heavily) I left the tape in my cubicle at work, and I kept forgetting it. I never actually took it home. I'm such an idiot.

THERAPIST: (Squeak)

CLIENT: I know. But it's true! I *am* an idiot. I cannot do this job and that is why I am panicking and now I'm going to lose this job. . . . (Begins to cry)

THERAPIST: Wait. Hold on. Can you see the relationship between invalidating yourself and feeling hopeless?

CLIENT: Yes, I do see it. (Takes a deep breath and begins to try to regulate emotion)

THERAPIST: Okay. Good. Now, about the progressive relaxation, did you not practice at all this week?

CLIENT: Well, I never listened to the tape. I tried to remember the way you taught me but I couldn't remember all the muscle groups. Anyway, we used to do that in the hospital and it never worked for me.

THERAPIST: Rachel, do you remember when we reviewed the panic protocol and you agreed to do it?

Comment on process and technique: Therapist is targeting commitment.

Technical intervention: Highlighting prior commitment.

CLIENT: Yes. But you don't understand how hard it is for me. I am not sure I can even do this or if I do it whether or not it will help. I feel like I'll never get past this anxiety.

THERAPIST: I know it feels that way. You've been anxious most of your life and it has really been a struggle. And it probably seems impossible to start with daily relaxation practice when the problem seems so insurmountable.

Comment on process and technique: Therapist validates client's feeling about task difficulty.

Technical intervention: Validation in terms of past learning history and current disorder.

CLIENT: I wish I could just take a pill and make it go away. But I don't want to end up like my mother. My mother is a worse fuck-up than I am.

THERAPIST: (Squeezes toy and laughs) There you go again.

Comment on process and technique: Therapist is humorous in contrast to client's escalating negative emotion.

Technical intervention: Irreverent communication style.

CLIENT: (Laughs) You need an electric shock you can give me.

THERAPIST: Whew. Can you reframe that?

CLIENT: (Laughs) Okay. "Thanks for reminding me!"

THERAPIST: Fabulous. Now, back to the panic protocol. It starts with the relaxation piece. What do you say? Can you practice two times next week?

CLIENT: Only twice?

THERAPIST: At least twice, for sure?

Comment on process and technique: It is important to give an assignment that the client is not likely to fail. Success can then be reinforced and built on (shaping).

Technical intervention: Foot in the door (a commitment strategy).

CLIENT: Okay. I can for sure do that.

THERAPIST: How will you remember to get the tape from work?

CLIENT: I've got it in my purse now. I picked it up from my desk before coming here.

THERAPIST: Good. Now, what is going to get in the way of you doing it?

Comment on process and technique: Because of the patient's pattern of agreeing to things she may not follow though with, the therapist refuses to take client's immediate agreement.

Technical interventions: Devil's advocate. Troubleshooting the solution.

CLIENT: I'm not sure.

THERAPIST: Think it over.

CLIENT: Now that I've got the tape, nothing, I don't think. I promise I'll do it. (Smiles) I give you my word.

THERAPIST: Okay, I'll take that. How many days are you agreeing to?

CLIENT: I don't know.

THERAPIST: Look, Rachel, the data say that very regular practice is essential to overcoming the panic. You want to overcome the panic, don't you?

Comment on process and technique: Therapist is linking the targeted behavior (practicing relaxation) to the client's goals (overcoming panic).

Technical interventions: Didactic strategy. Commitment strengthening.

CLIENT: Yes, I do. I will do it every day. It is just so boring!

THERAPIST: How do you know, if you haven't even done it yet?

CLIENT: Good point. I guess I just have the idea that it is boring. Boring is kind of like anxiety-provoking.

THERAPIST: Yeah. I think that is true. So, are you sure you want to do it every day?

CLIENT: Yes, I'll do it.

THERAPIST: Great. Now let's do behavior analysis of yesterday's panic episode. (Session continues down the target hierarchy)

HOW THERAPEUTIC CHALLENGES ARE CONCEPTUALIZED AND MANAGED

Difficulties in the therapy relationship are conceptualized in DBT as arising from multiple sources, including the patient, the therapist, the treatment setting, and the patient's environment (Robins & Koons, 2000). As we described earlier, treatment-interfering behaviors are given high priority in DBT, second only to life-threatening behaviors. They are treated exactly the same as other problems targeted in therapy. The therapist attempts to understand the situation within the framework of the biosocial theory of BPD and from a dialectical perspective. The therapist validates what is valid about the patient's behavior or feelings, conducts a behavioral analysis to understand the influences on the problem, and then uses strategies that include some combination of skills training, contingency management, exposure, and cognitive restructuring. For example, if the frequency or nature of the patient's calls crosses the therapist's personal limits, the therapist might tell the patient that his or her desire to receive support or help in coping is understandable, yet the therapist does not have enough time to be so available. Furthermore, a treatment goal is for the patient to develop better coping skills, so it is important for the patient to try various coping strategies before calling. Specific strategies that the patient will try before calling might be rehearsed. If the frequency of calls does not diminish despite the patient having needed coping skills, contingency management strategies might be used. For example, the patient might be allowed only a fixed maximum number of calls per week, with the length of the next therapy session being contingent on whether the rule is followed.

MECHANISMS OF CHANGE AND THERAPEUTIC ACTION

Adaptive change may occur through a variety of mechanisms in DBT. One mechanism may be skills acquisition and strengthening. Patients develop greater capabilities to interact assertively, to regulate their emotions, to tolerate emotional distress and inhibit maladaptive escape behaviors, to be aware of their current internal states and external environment, and to be nonjudgmental, among other skills. Skillful behavior will be reinforced more than unskillful behavior, on average and, therefore, should become self-sustaining. The relationship of changes in skills knowledge, competence, and use to changes in symptoms and functioning has not yet been studied systematically.

Dialectical behavior therapy involves several treatment modes, and there are few empirical data as to the relative importance of each to outcomes. Linehan (1993a, p. 25) reported that, compared with 8 patients who received non-DBT individual therapy only, 11 patients who also received group DBT skills training did not have better outcomes, so DBT individual therapy may be essential for patients to benefit from group skills training. However, these are data from just one small study. Larger treatment component analysis studies are needed. It is likely that patients benefit from the individual therapy focus on repeated behavioral analyses. In our experience, patients who benefit the most learn to do behavioral analyses of their own behaviors and develop solutions; that is, over time, they become their own therapists.

RESEARCH AND EMPIRICAL SUPPORT

The efficacy of DBT has been supported in several published randomized controlled trials (RCTs) for BPD, substance abuse and BPD, eating disorders, and depression in the elderly.

Parasuicidal women with BPD who received DBT for one year had significantly greater reductions in self-harming behaviors (including suicide attempts), in the medical risk of those behaviors, and in the frequency and duration of psychiatric hospitalizations, and lower treatment dropout rates than women receiving treatment-as-usual (TAU) in the community (Linehan et al., 1991). They also had greater reductions in trait anger and higher Global Assessment Scale (GAS) scores and social adjustment (Linehan, Tutek, Heard, & Armstrong, 1994). Improved symptoms and functioning were maintained at 6- and 12-month follow-ups (Linehan, Heard, & Armstrong, 1993).

Women veterans with BPD (40% with recent parasuicide) who were randomly assigned to DBT for six months had significantly greater decreases in suicidal ideation, hopelessness, depression, and anger expression than those assigned to TAU, and only the DBT group showed significant decreases in number of parasuicidal acts, anger experienced but not expressed, and dissociation (Koons et al., 2001).

For women with BPD and drug abuse, Linehan et al. (1999) found that DBT resulted in fewer treatment dropouts and greater reductions in drug use as assessed both by interview and by urinalyses than TAU. DBT patients also had better social role adjustment and GAS scores at a four-month follow-up. In a later study treating women with BPD and heroin dependence, Linehan et al. (2002) evaluated DBT against a more rigorous control condition, Comprehensive Validation Therapy with 12-Step (CVT+12S), in which therapists used only the acceptance-oriented strategies of DBT. Patients in both conditions received opiate replacement medication. Both treatments resulted in significant and equivalent reductions in opiate and other drug use, although CVT+12S showed increased opiate use during the last four months of the 12-month treatment. Only 36% of DBT participants dropped out, but none dropped out of CVT+12, suggesting that a heavily acceptance-oriented treatment may help retain in treatment a population that typically has a very high dropout rate.

Adaptations of DBT have been shown in RCTs to be effective for non-BPD patients with other disorders. Telch, Agras, and Linehan (2001) compared group DBT (skills training and behavioral analyses) with a waiting list control condition for women with binge eating disorder. DBT was associated with greater decreases in binge frequency, concerns about weight, shape, and eating and anger, and 89% of DBT participants were abstinent from binges at posttreatment compared with 12.5% of controls. Safer, Telch, and Agras (2001) evaluated the same treatment delivered in an individual format for women with bulimia. Compared with the waiting list, DBT resulted in greater decreases in frequencies of both binging and purging. At the end of treatment, only 36% of DBT participants still met criteria for bulimia, compared with 80% of those on the waiting list. Lynch, Morse, Mendelson, and Robins (2003) examined the efficacy of adding group DBT skills training and individual telephone coaching to treatment with antidepressant medication in a sample of depressed elders. Although the groups did not significantly differ in changes in depression during treatment (both had significant reductions), the DBT adaptation was associated with a higher rate of remission at a six-month follow-up.

In addition to these RCTs, nonrandomized but controlled trials suggest that DBT may have efficacy for the treatment of suicidal adolescents (Rathus & Miller, 2002) and inpatients with BPD (Barley et al., 1993).

SUMMARY AND CONCLUSIONS

Dialectical behavior therapy combines standard cognitive and behavioral treatment strategies with acceptance strategies drawn from client-centered and other humanistic therapies and from Zen principles and practice. It has been found to be effective for treatment of BPD and other difficult-to-treat disorders. It should be emphasized, however, that in the treatment research studies, most patients with BPD, though significantly improved, still reported clinically significant levels of dysphoria. Our clinical experience suggests that further therapeutic gains may occur with longer term DBT treatment than has been evaluated in studies to date. Our experiences with the developer(s), trainers, and practitioners of DBT suggest that the treatment will itself continue to evolve dialectically, better to meet the challenge of helping multiproblem, difficult-to-treat patients.

REFERENCES

American Psychiatric Association. (1994). *Diagnostic and statistical manual of mental disorders* (4th ed.). Washington, DC: Author.

Barley, W. D., Buie, S. E., Peterson, E. W., Hollingsworth, A. S., Griva, M., Hickerson, S. C., et al. (1993). The development of an inpatient cognitive-behavioral treatment program for borderline personality disorder. *Journal of Personality Disorders, 7,* 232–240.

Bohus, M., Haaf, B., Stiglmayr, C., Pohl, U., Bohme, R., & Linehan, M. (2000). Evaluation of inpatient dialectical behavior therapy for borderline personality disorder: A prospective study. *Behavior Research and Therapy, 38,* 875–887.

Brown, M. Z., Comtois, K. A., & Linehan, M. M. (2002). Reasons for suicide attempts and nonsuicidal self-injury in women with borderline personality disorder. *Journal of Abnormal Psychology, 111,* 198–202.

Fruzzetti, A. E., & Levensky, E. R. (2000). Dialectical behavior therapy for domestic violence: Rationale and procedures. *Cognitive and Behavioral Practice, 7,* 435–447.

Gunderson, J. G., & Elliott, G. R. (1985). The interface between borderline personality disorder and affective disorder. *American Journal of Psychiatry, 142,* 277–288.

Koons, C., Robins, C. J., Tweed, J. L., Lynch, T. R., Gonzalez, A. M., Morse, J. Q., et al. (2001). Efficacy of dialectical behavior therapy in women veterans with borderline personality disorder. *Behavior Therapy, 32,* 371–390.

Linehan, M. M. (1987). Dialectical behavior therapy: A cognitive-behavioral approach to parasuicide. *Journal of Personality Disorders, 1,* 328–333.

Linehan, M. M. (1993a). *Cognitive-behavioral treatment of borderline personality disorder.* New York: Guilford Press.

Linehan, M. M. (1993b). *Skills training manual for treating borderline personality disorder.* New York: Guilford Press.

Linehan, M. M., Armstrong, H. E., Suarez, A., Allmon, D., & Heard, H. L. (1991). Cognitive-behavioral treatment of chronically suicidal borderline patients. *Archives of General Psychiatry, 48,* 1060–1064.

Linehan, M. M., Dimeff, L. A., Reynolds, S. K., Comtois, K. A., Welch, S. S., Heagerty, P., et al. (2002). Dialectical behavior therapy versus comprehensive validation therapy plus 12-step for the treatment of opioid dependent women meeting criteria for borderline personality disorder. *Drug and Alcohol Dependence, 67,* 13–26.

Linehan, M. M., Heard, H. L., & Armstrong, H. E. (1993). Naturalistic follow-up of a behavioral treatment for chronically parasuicidal borderline patients. *Archives of General Psychiatry, 50,* 157–158.

Linehan, M. M., Schmidt, H. I., Dimeff, L. A., Craft, J. C., Kanter, J., & Comtois, K. A. (1999). Dialectical behavior therapy for patients with borderline personality disorder and drug-dependence. *American Journal on Addictions, 8,* 279–292.

Linehan, M. M., Tutek, D. A., Heard, H. L., & Armstrong, H. E. (1994). Interpersonal outcome of cognitive-behavioral treatment for chronically suicidal borderline patients. *American Journal of Psychiatry, 151,* 1771–1776.

Links, P. S., Heslegrave, R., & van Reekum, R. (1998). Prospective follow-up study of borderline personality disorder: Prognosis, prediction of outcome, and Axis II comorbidity. *Canadian Journal of Psychiatry, 43,* 251–259.

Livesley, W. J., Jang, K. L., & Vernon, P. A. (1998). Phenotypic and genetic structure of traits delineating personality disorder. *Archives of General Psychiatry, 55,* 941–948.

Lynch, T. R., Morse, J. Q., Mendelson, T., & Robins, C. J. (2003). Dialectical behavior therapy for depressed older adults: A randomized pilot study. *American Journal of Geriatric Psychiatry, 11,* 33–45.

McCann, R. A., Ball, E. M., & Ivanoff, A. (2000). DBT with an inpatient forensic population: The CMHIP forensic model. *Cognitive and Behavioral Practice, 7,* 447–456.

Rathus, J. H., & Miller, A. L. (2002). Dialectical behavior therapy adapted for suicidal adolescents. *Suicide and Life Threatening Behavior, 32,* 146–157.

Robins, C. J. (2002). Zen principles and mindfulness practice in dialectical behavior therapy. *Cognitive and Behavioral Practice, 9,* 50–57.

Robins, C. J., Ivanoff, A. M., & Linehan, M. M. (2001). Dialectical behavior therapy. In W. J. Livesley (Ed.), *Handbook of personality disorders: Theory, research, and treatment* (pp. 117–139). New York: Guilford Press.

Robins, C. J., & Koons, C. R. (2000). The therapeutic relationship in dialectical behavior therapy. In A. N. Sabo & L. Havens (Eds.), *The real world guide to psychotherapy practice* (pp. 237–266). Cambridge, MA: Harvard University Press.

Safer, D. L., Telch, C. F., & Agras, W. S. (2001). Dialectical behavior therapy for bulimia nervosa. *American Journal of Psychiatry, 158,* 632–634.

Sanderson, C., & Linehan, M. M. (1999). Acceptance and forgiveness. In W. R. Miller (Ed.), *Integrating spirituality into treatment: Resources for practitioners* (pp. 199–216). Washington, DC: American Psychological Association.

Sapolsky, R. M. (1996). Why stress is bad for your brain. *Science, 273,* 749–750.

Simpson, E. B., Pistorello, J., Begin, A., Costello, E., Levinson, H., Mulberry, S., et al. (1998). Use of dialectical behavior therapy in a partial hospital program for women with borderline personality disorder. *Psychiatric Services, 49,* 669–673.

Swenson, C. R., Sanderson, C., Dulit, R. A., & Linehan, M. M. (2001). The application of dialectical behavior therapy for patients with borderline personality disorder on inpatient units. *Psychiatric Quarterly, 72,* 307–324.

Telch, C. F., Agras, W. S., & Linehan, M. M. (2001). Dialectical behavior therapy for binge eating disorder. *Journal of Consulting and Clinical Psychology, 69,* 1061–1065.

Torgersen, S., Lygren, S., Oien, P. A., Skre, I., Onstad, S., Edvardsen, J., et al. (2000). A twin study of personality disorders. *Comprehensive Psychiatry, 41,* 416–425.

Zanarini, M. C., Frankenburg, M. D., Hennen, J., & Silk, K. R. (2003). The longitudinal course of borderline psychopathology: 6-year prospective follow-up of the phenomenology of borderline personality disorder. *American Journal of Psychiatry, 160,* 274–283.

CHAPTER 12

Time-Limited
Dynamic Psychotherapy

Hanna Levenson

TIME-LIMITED DYNAMIC psychotherapy (TLDP) is a form of brief, focused therapy that was developed by Hans Strupp and Jeffrey Binder (1984). It is an interpersonal, time-sensitive approach for patients with chronic, pervasive, dysfunctional ways of relating to others. Its premises and techniques are broadly applicable regardless of time limits. However, its method of formulating and intervening makes it particularly well suited for so-called difficult patients (e.g., those with diagnoses of personality disorder) seen in a brief or time-limited therapy. The brevity of the treatment promotes therapist pragmatism, flexibility, and accountability (Levenson, Butler, Powers, & Beitman, 2002). Furthermore, time pressures help keep the therapist attuned to circumscribed goals using an active, directive stance (Levenson, Butler, & Bein, 2002). The focus is not on the reduction of symptoms per se (although such improvements are expected to occur), but rather on changing ingrained patterns of interpersonal relatedness or personality style. Time-limited dynamic psychotherapy makes use of the relationship that develops between therapist and patient to kindle fundamental changes in the way a person interacts with others and himself or herself.

TLDP was first formalized in a treatment manual written for an empirical investigation on briefer ways of intervening with challenging patients. This manual eventually was reproduced in book form—*Psychotherapy in a New Key: A Guide to Time-Limited Dynamic Psychotherapy* (Strupp & Binder, 1984). In a more recently published clinical casebook, *Time-Limited Dynamic Psychotherapy: A Guide to Clinical Practice*, Levenson (1995) translates TLDP principles and strategies into pragmatically

Some material in this chapter is from *Time-Limited Dynamic Psychotherapy: A Guide to Clinical Practice,* by Hanna Levenson, 1995, New York: Basic Books, copyright © 1995, reprinted by permission of Basic Books, a member of Perseus Books. Other material is from "Time-Limited Dynamic Psychotherapy: An Integrationist Approach," by Hanna Levenson, in press, *Journal of Psychotherapy Integration,* reprinted by permission of Kluwer Academic/Plenum.

useful ways of thinking and intervening for the practitioner. The Levenson text places more emphasis on behavioral changes through experiential learning than insight through interpretation. It maintains continuity with psychoanalytic modalities by highlighting the role of the therapeutic relationship in evoking and resolving past problem patterns.

Historically, TLDP is rooted in an object-relations framework. According to object-relations theory, images of the self and others evolve from human interactions rather than from biologically derived tensions. The search for and maintenance of human relatedness is considered to be a major motivating force in all human beings. Specifically, the self is seen as an internalization of interactions with significant others. This relational view sharply contrasts with that of classical psychoanalysis, which emphasizes the role of innate mental structures in mediating conflicts between the gratification of instinctual impulses and societal constraints. Indeed, the TLDP interpersonal perspective reflects a larger paradigm shift occurring within psychoanalytic theory and practice from a one-person to a two-person psychology (Messer & Warren, 1995).

TLDP is consistent with the views of modern interpersonal theorists (Anchin & Kiesler, 1982; Benjamin, 1993; Greenberg & Mitchell, 1983), originating with the early work of Sullivan (1953). Strupp and Binder (1984) make clear that their "purpose is neither to construct a new theory of personality development nor to attempt a systematic integration of existing theories. Rather, we have chosen interpersonal conceptions as a framework for the proposed form of psychotherapy because of their hypothesized relevance and utility" (p. 28). The relational view of TLDP focuses on transactional patterns in which the therapist is embedded in the therapeutic relationship as a participant observer. Transference (the repetition of past interpersonal scenarios within the therapeutic relationship) is not considered a distortion, but rather a patient's plausible perceptions of the therapist's behavior and intent. Similarly, countertransference (the emergence of a therapist's emotional patterns within the therapy) does not indicate a failure on the part of the therapist. Rather, it represents his or her natural reactions to the pushes and pulls from interacting with a specific patient.

Other theories of psychotherapy are also incorporating interpersonal perspectives in their conceptualizations and practice. This can be seen in cognitive therapy (Safran & Segal, 1990), behavior therapy (Kohlenberg & Tsai, 1991), and gestalt therapy (Glickhauf-Hughes, Reviere, Clance, & Jones, 1996). Data from child development research (e.g., see Stern, 1985) point to how an individual's world is essentially interpersonal. Recent information from the field of neurobiology suggests that "relationships early in life may shape the *very structures* that create representations of experience and allow a coherent view of the world. Interpersonal experiences directly influence how we mentally construct reality" (emphasis added, Siegel, 1999, p. 4). This growing recognition of the import of interpersonal relatedness promotes compatibility across a variety of theoretical and strategic viewpoints, allowing for meaningful psychotherapy integration (Anchin, 1982).

RANGE OF PSYCHOPATHOLOGY AND PERSONALITY DISORDERS WITHIN SCOPE OF TREATMENT

The background of TLDP stems from a series of empirical studies begun in the early 1950s (Strupp, 1955a, 1955b, 1955c). Strupp asked practicing therapists to pretend they were responding to patients' statements, which were presented in written form or on film. He was initially interested in the relationship between technique and therapist variables, but became intrigued with results that indicated that the therapists' immediate negative attitudes toward the patient were associated with a loss of empathy and unfavorable clinical judgments. "On the basis of these data, I hypothesized that the therapist's initial attitude toward the patient might give rise to a self-fulfilling prophecy and that the therapist's communications embodied both technical and personal elements" (Strupp, 1993, p. 431). Results from later studies revealed that patients who were negativistic, inflexible, mistrusting, or otherwise highly resistant uniformly had poor outcomes (Strupp, 1980a, 1980b, 1980c, 1980d) because even trained therapists were rendered relatively inept in adapting their approach to the needs of these difficult patients.

Strupp reasoned that such patients had characterological styles that made it very hard for them to negotiate a good working relationship with their therapists. In such cases, the therapists' skill in managing the interpersonal therapeutic climate was severely taxed. Because the therapies were brief, this inability to readily form a therapeutic alliance had deleterious effects on the entire therapy. As an outgrowth of these findings, Strupp and colleagues (Strupp & Binder, 1984) at Vanderbilt University designed a program of specialized training in TLDP to help therapists deal with patients who have trouble forming working alliances because of their lifelong dysfunctional interpersonal difficulties (those usually diagnosed as having personality disorders). However, TLDP is also applicable for anyone who is having symptoms (e.g., depression, anxiety) that affect their relatedness to self and other.

According to Strupp and Binder (1984), there are five major selection criteria for determining a patient's appropriateness for TLDP:

1. Patients must be in *emotional discomfort* so they are motivated to endure the often challenging and painful change process and to make sacrifices of time, effort, and money as required by therapy.

2. Patients must *come for appointments and engage with the therapist*—or at least talk. Initially, such an attitude may be fostered by hope or faith in a positive outcome. Later, it might stem from actual experiences of the therapist as a helpful partner.

3. Patients must be *willing to consider how their relationships have contributed* to distressing symptoms, negative attitudes, and/or behavioral difficulties. The operative word here is *willing*. Suitable patients do not actually have to walk in the door indicating that they have made this connection. Rather, in the give-and-take of the therapeutic encounters, they evidence signs of being willing to entertain the possibility. It should be noted that they do not have to understand the nature of interpersonal difficulties or admit responsibility for them to meet this selection criterion.

4. Patients need to be *willing to examine feelings* that may hinder more successful relationships and may foster more dysfunctional ones.

5. Patients should be capable of having a *meaningful relationship* with the therapist. Again, it is not expected that the patient initially relates in a collaborative manner. But the potential for establishing such a relationship should exist. Patients cannot be out of touch with reality or so impaired that they have difficulty appreciating that their therapists are separate people.

Although previously I endorsed these selection criteria (Levenson, 1995), clinical experience suggests that TLDP may be helpful to patients even when they do not quite meet these criteria as long as adequate descriptions of their interpersonal transactions can be elicited. Specific diagnoses are not mentioned per se as part of the selection decision.

TREATMENT METHODS AND
TECHNICAL ASPECTS AND INTERVENTIONS

ASSUMPTIONS ESSENTIAL TO TIME-LIMITED
DYNAMIC PSYCHOTHERAPY TREATMENT

The TLDP model makes five basic assumptions that greatly affect treatment:

1. *Maladaptive relationship patterns are learned in the past.* Disturbances in adult interpersonal relatedness typically stem from faulty relationships with early caregivers—usually in the parental home. Bowlby (1973) elaborated that early experiences with parental figures result in mental representations of these relationships or working models of an individual's interpersonal world. These models, or schemata, inform the individual about the nature of human relatedness and what is generally necessary to sustain and maintain emotional connectedness to others. Children filter the world through the lenses of these schemata, which allow them to interpret the present, understand the past, and anticipate the future.

2. *Such maladaptive patterns are maintained in the present.* This emphasis on early childhood experiences is consistent with much of psychoanalytic thinking. From a TLDP framework, however, the individual's personality is not seen as fixed at a certain point, but rather as continually changing as it interacts with others. Data from neurobiology appear to confirm that, although relationships play a crucial role in the early years, this "shaping process occurs throughout life" (Siegel, 1999, p. 4). Although an individual's dysfunctional interactive style is learned early in life, this style must be supported in the person's present adult life for the interpersonal difficulties to continue. For example, if a child has learned to be placating and deferential because he grew up in a home with authoritarian parents, he will unwittingly and inadvertently attempt to maintain this role as an adult by pulling for others to act harshly toward him.

This focus is consistent with a systems-oriented approach, which stresses the context of a situation and the circular processes surrounding it. "Pathology" does not reside within an individual, but rather is created by all the components within the (pathological) system (von Bertalanffy, 1969). Maladaptive patterns are maintained through their enactment in the current social system, as others unwittingly replicate familiar responses from a person's troubled past.

3. *Dysfunctional relationship patterns are reenacted in vivo in the therapy.* A third assumption is that the patient interacts with the therapist in the same dysfunctional way that characterizes his or her interactions with significant others (i.e., transference) and tries to enlist the therapist into playing a complementary role. This reenactment is an ideal therapeutic opportunity because it permits the therapist to observe the playing out of the maladaptive interactional pattern and to experience what it is like to try to relate to that individual. Because dysfunctional interactions are presumably sustained in the present, including the current patient-therapist relationship, the therapist can concentrate on the present to

alter the patient's dysfunctional interactive style. Working in the present allows change to happen more quickly because there is no assumption that the individual needs to work through childhood conflicts and discover historical truths. This emphasis on the present has tremendous implications for treating interpersonal difficulties in a brief time frame.

4. *The therapist responds countertransferentially.* A corollary assumption to the TLDP concept of transference is that the therapist also enters into the relationship and becomes a part of the reenactment of the dysfunctional interpersonal interaction. In Sullivan's terms (1953), the therapist becomes a *participant observer.* The relational-interactionist position of TLDP holds that the therapist cannot help but react to the patient—that is, the therapist inevitably will be pushed and pulled by the patient's dysfunctional style and will respond accordingly. This transactional type of reciprocity and complementarity (what I call *interactional countertransference*) does not indicate a failure on the part of the therapist, but rather represents his or her "role responsiveness" (Sandler, 1976) or "interpersonal empathy" (Strupp & Binder, 1984). The therapist inevitably becomes "hooked" into acting out the corresponding response to the patient's inflexible, maladaptive pattern (Kiesler, 1988), or, in Wachtel's terms (1987), patients induce therapists to act as "accomplices."

That the therapist is invited repeatedly by the patient (unconsciously) to become a partner in a well-rehearsed, maladaptive two-step has its parallels in the recursive aspect of mental development. For example, children who have experienced serious family dysfunction are thought to have disorganized internal mental structures and processes as a result. These disorganized processes impair the child's behavior with others, which causes others not to respond in empathic ways, thereby disorganizing the development of the mind still further (Lyons-Ruth & Jacobwitz, 1999).

To get an individual unhooked, it is essential that the therapist realize how he or she is fostering a replication of the dysfunctional pattern. The TLDP therapist uses this information to attempt to change the nature of the interaction in a positive way, thereby engaging the patient in a healthier mode of relating. In addition, the therapist can collaboratively invite the patient to look at what is happening between them (i.e., metacommunicate), either highlighting the dysfunctional reenactment while it is occurring or solidifying new experiential learning following a more functionally adaptive interactive process.

5. *The TLDP focus is on the chief problematic relationship pattern.* Although patients may have a repertoire of different interpersonal patterns, the emphasis in TLDP is on discerning a patient's most pervasive and problematic style of relating (which may need to incorporate several divergent views of self and other). This is not to say that other relationship patterns may not be important. However, focusing on the most frequently troublesome type of interaction should have ramifications for other less central interpersonal schemas and is pragmatically essential when time is of the essence. The presence of a clear interpersonal focus is an important element distinguishing time-limited psychoanalytic therapy from longer term efforts at personality reconstruction.

GOALS

The TLDP therapist seeks two overriding goals with patients: *new experiences* and *new understandings.*

1. New Experience   The first and major goal in conducting TLDP is offering the patient a new relational experience. *New* is meant in the sense of being different and more functional (i.e., healthier) than the maladaptive pattern to which the person has become accustomed. *Experience* emphasizes the affective-action component of change—behaving and feeling differently and emotionally appreciating the difference. From a TLDP perspective, behaviors are encouraged that signify a new manner of interacting (e.g., more flexibly, more independently) rather than specific, content-based behaviors (e.g., going to a movie alone). The new experience is actually composed of a set of focused experiences throughout the therapy in which the patient gains a different appreciation of self, of therapist, and of their interaction. These new experiences provide the patient with experiential learning so that old patterns may be relinquished and new patterns may evolve.

The focus of these new experiences centers on those that are particularly helpful to a patient based on the therapist's formulation of the case (see later discussion). The therapist identifies what he or she could say or do (within the therapeutic role) that would most likely subvert or interrupt the patient's maladaptive interactive style. The therapist's behavior gives the patient the opportunity to disconfirm his or her interpersonal schemata. The patient can actively try out (consciously or unconsciously) new behaviors in the therapy, see how they feel, and notice how the therapist responds. This information then informs the patient's internal representations of what can be expected from self and others. This in vivo learning is a critical component in the practice of TLDP.

These experiential forays into what for the patient has been frightening territory make for heightened affective learning. A tension is created when the familiar (though detrimental) responses to the patient's presentation are not provided. From this tension new learning takes place. Such an emotionally intense, here-and-now process is thought to "heat up" the therapeutic process and permit progress to be made more quickly than in therapies that depend solely on more abstract learning (usually through interpretation and clarification). This experiential learning is important for doing brief therapy and becomes critical when working with patients who have difficulties establishing a therapeutic alliance, exploring relational issues in the here-and-now, or evidencing the capacity for introspection and insight. As Frieda Fromm-Reichmann is credited with saying, what the patient needs is an experience, not an explanation.

There are definite parallels between the goal of a new experience and procedures used in some behavioral techniques (e.g., exposure therapy) where clients are exposed to feared stimuli without the expected negative consequences. Modern cognitive theorists voice analogous perspectives (Safran & Segal, 1990) when they talk about interpersonal processes that lead to *experiential disconfirmation.* Similarities can also be found in the plan formulation method (Sampson & Weiss, 1986; Weiss, 1993), in which opportunities for change occur when patients test their pathogenic beliefs in the context of the therapeutic relationship.

The concept of a *corrective emotional experience* described more than 50 years ago is also applicable (Alexander & French, 1946). In their classic book, *Psychoanalytic Therapy: Principles and Applications,* Alexander and French challenged the then-prevalent assumption concerning the therapeutic importance of exposing repressed memories and providing a genetic reconstruction. By focusing on the importance of experiential learning, they suggested that change could take place even without the patient's insight into the etiology of their problems.

Decades of clinical and empirical data within psychology clearly support this conclusion (Bergin & Garfield, 1994; Fisher & Greenberg, 1997). Now there appear to be neurobiological data indicating that *most* learning is done without conscious awareness (Siegel, 1999). This view has major implications for the techniques used. It questions the pursuit of insight as a necessary goal and thereby challenges the use of interpretation as the cornerstone of psychodynamic technique. From an empirical standpoint, data suggest that transference interpretations in particular may not be as effective as previously thought (Henry, Strupp, Schacht, & Gaston, 1994; Piper, Joyce, McCallum, & Azim, 1993).

Alexander and French's (1946) concept of the corrective emotional experience has been criticized for promoting manipulation of the transference by suggesting that the therapist should respond in a way diametrically opposite to that expected by the patient. For example, if the child had been raised by an intrusive mother, the therapist should maintain a more restrained stance. The TLDP concept of the new relational experience does not involve a direct manipulation of the transference; nor is it solely accomplished by the offering of a "good enough" therapeutic relationship. Specifically, a therapist can help provide a new experience by selectively choosing from all of the helpful, mature, and respectful ways of being present in a session those particular aspects that would most effectively undermine a specific patient's dysfunctional style. A warm stance that supports a patient's independence, for example, may counter expectations of intrusiveness as readily as a stance of restraint.

2. New Understanding   The second goal of providing a new understanding focuses more specifically on cognitive changes than the first goal just discussed, which emphasizes the affective-behavioral arena. The patient's new understanding usually involves an identification and comprehension of his or her dysfunctional patterns. To facilitate such a new understanding, the TLDP therapist can point out repetitive patterns that have originated in experiences with past significant others, with present significant others, and in the here-and-now with the therapist. This is similar to Menniger's (1958) concept of the triangle of insight. Therapists' judicious disclosing of their own reactions to patients' behaviors can also be beneficial. If undertaken in a constructive and sensitive manner, such disclosure allows patients to recognize similar relationship patterns with different people in their lives. This new perspective enables them to examine their active role in perpetuating dysfunctional interactions.

Differentiating between the idea of a new experience and a new understanding helps the clinician attend to aspects of the change process that would be most helpful in formulating and intervening as efficiently and effectively as possible. In addition, because psychodynamically trained therapists are so ready to intervene with an interpretation, placing the new experience in the foreground helps them regroup and focus on the "big picture"—how not to reenact a dysfunctional scenario with the patient. This emphasis on the new experience is a departure from the central role of understanding through interpretation in the original TLDP model (Strupp & Binder, 1984). Focusing on experiential learning broadens the range of patients who can benefit from brief therapies, leads to more generalization to the outside world, and permits therapists to incorporate a variety of techniques or strategies that might be helpful.

THE CYCLICAL MALADAPTIVE PATTERN

In the past, psychodynamic brief therapists used their intuition, insight, and clinical savvy to devise formulations of cases. Although these methods may work wonderfully for the gifted or experienced therapist, they are impossible to teach explicitly. One remedy for this situation was the development of a procedure for deriving a dynamic, interpersonal focus—the cyclical maladaptive pattern (CMP; Binder & Strupp, 1991). Briefly, the CMP outlines the idiosyncratic vicious cycle (Wachtel, 1997) of maladaptive interactions that a particular patient manifests with others. These cycles or patterns involve inflexible, self-defeating expectations and behaviors and negative self-appraisals that lead to dysfunctional and maladaptive interactions with others (Butler & Binder, 1987; Butler, Strupp, & Binder, 1993). Such maladaptive patterns are of central importance for understanding and treating people with personality disorders.

Development and use of the CMP in treatment is essential to TLDP. It is not necessarily shared with the patient but may well be, depending on the patient's abilities to deal with the material. For some patients with minimal capacity for introspection and abstraction, the problematic interpersonal scenario may never be stated per se. Rather, the content may stay very close to the presenting problems and concerns of the patient. Other patients enter therapy with a fairly good understanding of their self-perpetuating interpersonal patterns. In these cases, the therapist and patient can jointly articulate the parameters that foster such behavior, generalize to other situations where applicable, and readily recognize its occurrence in the therapy.

In either case, the CMP plays a key role in guiding the clinician in formulating a treatment plan. It provides an organizational framework that makes a large mass of data comprehensible and leads to fruitful hypotheses. A CMP should not be seen as an encapsulated version of Truth, but rather as a plausible narrative, incorporating major components of a person's current and historical interactive world. It is a map of the territory—not the territory itself (Strupp & Binder, 1984). A successful TLDP formulation should provide a *blueprint* for the therapy. It describes the nature of the problem, leads to the delineation of goals, serves as a guide for interventions, and enables the therapist to anticipate reenactments within the context of the therapeutic interaction. The CMP also provides a way to assess whether the therapy is on the right track, both in terms of outcome at termination as well as in-session mini-outcomes. The focus provided by the CMP permits the therapist to intervene in ways that have the greatest likelihood of being therapeutic. Thus, there are possibilities for the therapy to be briefer *and* more effective.

PROCESS OF THERAPEUTIC APPROACH

FORMULATION

In the first phase of TLDP, the therapist formulates the case by constructing the CMP. There are roughly nine interlocking steps in this process. These steps should not be thought of as separate techniques applied in a linear, rigid fashion, but rather as guidelines for the therapist to be used in a fluid and interactive manner (see Table 12.1; Levenson & Strupp, 1997).

Table 12.1
TLDP Steps in TLDP Case Formulation

1. Let patients tell their stories in their own words.
2. Explore the interpersonal context related to symptoms or problems.
3. Obtain data for the CMP.
4. Listen for themes in the patient's content and manner of interacting (in past and present relationships as well as with the therapist).
5. Be aware of reciprocal reactions (countertransferential pushes and pulls).
6. Develop a CMP narrative describing the patient's predominant dysfunctional interactive pattern.
7. Use the CMP to formulate what new experience might lead to more adaptive relating within the therapeutic relationship (Goal 1).
8. Use the CMP to formulate what new understanding might lead to the patient's increased awareness of dysfunctional patterns as they occur with the therapist and others (Goal 2).
9. Revise and refine the CMP throughout therapy.

To derive a TLDP formulation, the therapist lets the patient tell his or her own story (Step 1) in the initial sessions rather than relying on the traditional psychiatric interview that structures the patient's responses into categories of information (e.g., developmental history, education). By listening to *how* the patient tells his or her story (e.g., deferentially, cautiously, dramatically) as well as to the content, the therapist can learn much about the patient's interpersonal style. The therapist then explores the interpersonal context of the patient's symptoms or problems (Step 2). When did the problems begin? What else was going on in the patient's life at that time, especially of an interpersonal nature?

The clinician obtains data that will be used to construct a CMP (Step 3). This process is facilitated by using four categories to gather, organize, and probe for clinical information:

1. *Acts of the Self:* These acts include the thoughts, feelings, motives, perceptions, and behaviors of the patient of an interpersonal nature. For example, "When I meet strangers, I think they wouldn't want to have anything to do with me" (thought). "I am afraid to take the promotion" (feeling). "I wish I were the life of the party" (motive). Sometimes these acts are conscious as the previous ones, and sometimes they are outside awareness, as in the case of the woman who does not realize how jealous she is of her sister's accomplishments.
2. *Expectations of Others' Reactions:* This category pertains to all the statements having to do with how the patient imagines others will react to him or her in response to some interpersonal behavior (act of the self). "My boss will fire me if I make a mistake." "If I go to the dance, no one will ask me to dance."
3. *Acts of Others toward the Self:* This third grouping consists of the actual behaviors of other people, as observed (or assumed) and interpreted by the patient. "When I made a mistake at work, my boss shunned me for the rest

of the day." "When I went to the dance, guys asked me to dance, but only because they felt sorry for me."

4. *Acts of the Self toward the Self (Introject):* In this section belong all of the patient's behaviors or attitudes toward himself or herself—when the self is the object of the interpersonal pattern. How does the patient treat himself or herself? "When I made the mistake, I berated myself so much I had difficulty sleeping that night." "When no one asked me to dance, I told myself it's because I'm fat, ugly, and unlovable."

For the fourth step, the therapist then listens for themes in the emerging material by being sensitive to commonalities and redundancies in the patient's transactional patterns over person, time, and place. As part of interacting with the patient, the therapist will be pulled into responding in a complementary fashion, recreating a dysfunctional dance with the patient. By examining the patterns of the here-and-now interaction and by using the *Expectations of Others' Reactions* and the *Acts of Others* components of the CMP, the therapist becomes more aware of his or her countertransferential reenactments (Step 5).

A therapist's reactions to the patient should make sense given the patient's interpersonal pattern. Each therapist has a unique personality that might contribute to the particular shading of the reaction that is elicited by the patient. The TLDP perspective, however, is that the therapist's behavior is *predominantly* shaped by the patient's evoking patterns (i.e., the influence of the therapist's personal conflicts is not so paramount as to undermine the therapy).

By using the four categories of the CMP and the therapist's own reactions to the developing transactional relationship with the client, a CMP narrative is developed describing the patient's predominant dysfunctional interactive pattern (Step 6). The CMP can be used to foresee likely transference-countertransference reenactments that might inhibit treatment progress. By anticipating patient resistances, ruptures in the therapeutic alliance, and so on, the therapist is able to plan appropriately. Thus, when therapeutic impasses occur, the therapist is not caught off guard, but rather is prepared to capitalize on the situation and maximize its clinical impact—a necessity when time is of the essence.

From the CMP formulation, the therapist then discerns the goals for treatment. The first goal involves determining the nature of the new experience (Step 7). This new experience should contain *specific* patient-therapist interactions (Gill, 1993) that disconfirm existing negative expectations. After determining the nature of the new experience, the therapist can use the CMP formulation to determine the second goal for treatment, the new understanding (Step 8) of the client's dysfunctional pattern as it occurs in relationships.

The last step (9) in the formulation process involves the continuous refinement of the CMP throughout the therapy. In a brief therapy, the therapist cannot wait to have all the "facts" before formulating the case and intervening. As the therapy proceeds, new content and interactional data become available that might strengthen, modify, or negate the working formulation.

Time-Limited Dynamic Psychotherapy Strategies

Implementation of TLDP does not rely on a set of techniques. Rather, it depends on therapeutic *strategies* that are useful only to the extent that they are *embedded in a larger interpersonal relationship.* The Vanderbilt Therapeutic Strategies Scale (VTSS) was designed by members of the Center for Psychotherapy Research Team at Vanderbilt University (Butler et al., 1986) as a measure of the degree to which therapists adhere to TLDP principles. Research indicates that the VTSS is able to reflect changes in therapists' behaviors following training in TLDP (Butler, Lane, & Strupp, 1988; Butler & Strupp, 1989; Butler, Strupp, & Lane, 1987; Henry, Strupp, Butler, Schacht, & Binder, 1993). The VTSS is divided into two sections: The first is concerned with a general approach to psychodynamic interviewing; the second, with therapist actions specific to TLDP. Table 12.2 contains the 10 TLDP specific strategies from the VTSS.

In TLDP, the therapist specifically addresses transactions in the patient-therapist relationship (Strategy 1). This focus on the here-and-now provides the building blocks for understanding how the interaction may be a microcosm of interpersonal difficulties. The therapist actively encourages the patient to explore thoughts and feelings about the therapist (Strategy 2) and conversely to discuss how the patient imagines the therapist might think or feel about the patient (Strategy 3). It can often be helpful for the therapist actually to self-disclose his or her countertransferential pull to the patient's specific behaviors (Strategy 4). In this way, the therapist can guide exploration of possible distortions in the patient's perceptions of others or help the patient appreciate his or her impact on others ("When you did X just now, I felt like doing Y. Can we take a look at this situation?").

Throughout the therapy, the therapist attempts to discover and discuss with the patient any themes emerging in the content and process of the patient's

Table 12.2
Vanderbilt Therapeutic Strategies Scale

TLDP Specific Strategies

1. Therapist specifically addresses transactions in the patient-therapist relationship.
2. Therapist encourages the patient to explore feelings and thoughts about the therapist or the therapeutic relationship.
3. Therapist encourages the patient to discuss how the therapist might feel or think about the patient.
4. Therapist discusses own reactions to some aspect of the patient's behavior in relation to the therapist.
5. Therapist attempts to explore patterns that might constitute a cyclical maladaptive pattern in the patient's interpersonal relationships.
6. Therapist asks about the patient's introject (how the patient feels about and treats himself or herself).
7. Therapist links a recurrent pattern of behavior or interpersonal conflict to transactions between the patient and therapist.
8. Therapist addresses obstacles (e.g., silences, coming late, avoidance of meaningful topics) that might influence the therapeutic process.
9. Therapist provides the opportunity for the patient to have a new experience of oneself and/or the therapist relevant to the patient's particular cyclical maladaptive pattern.
10. Therapist discusses an aspect of the time-limited nature of TLDP or termination.

*Reprinted with permission of S. F. Butler, & the Center for Psychotherapy Research Team (1995). Vanderbilt Therapeutic Strategies Scale. In H. Levenson (Ed.), *Time-limited dynamic psychotherapy: A guide to clinical practice* (pp. 240–242). New York: Basic Books.

relationships (Strategy 5). These explorations enable the patient to become more aware of problematic patterns of behavior (CMP). Asking about how the patient treats himself or herself (Strategy 6) can further be used to understand how interpersonal processes affect self-structures and vice versa.

The therapist can help depathologize the patient's CMP by guiding him or her in understanding its historical development. From the TLDP point of view, symptoms and dysfunctional behaviors are the individual's attempt to adapt to situations threatening interpersonal relatedness. For example, in therapy a passive, anxious client began to understand that as a child he had to be subservient and hypervigilant to avoid beatings. This realization enabled him to view his present interpersonal style from a different perspective and allowed him to have some empathy for his childhood plight.

In TLDP, the most potent intervention capable of providing a new understanding is thought to be the therapist's linking the patient's recurrent patterns of behavior to transactions between the therapist and patient (Strategy 7). Although most of the therapy will be devoted to examining the patient's problems in relationships *outside the therapy* (as discussed previously), it is chiefly through the therapist's observations and interpretations about the reenactment of the cyclical maladaptive pattern *in the sessions* that patients begin to have an in vivo understanding of their behaviors and stimulus value. By ascertaining how an interpersonal pattern has emerged in the therapeutic relationship, the patient has perhaps for the first time the opportunity to examine the nature of such behaviors in a safe environment.

An often-asked question is how early in the therapy the therapist can make observations having to do with transactions in the patient-therapist relationship as manifestations of the CMP (e.g., transference-countertransference reenactments). The rule of thumb is that the therapist needs to allow ample time for the therapeutic relationship to evolve. That is, the therapist *and* patient need to have sufficient experiences in which particular dynamic interactions have played out repeatedly. In this way, the interactive pattern is recognized not only by the therapist, but also by the patient.

A common error in technique is for the therapist, who is alert to discerning relationship themes, to point out such patterns to the patient long before the patient has had the opportunity to experience such redundancies in interacting with the therapist. These types of premature interpretations are usually met with surprise, hostility, and/or confusion on the part of the patient and can lead to gross ruptures in the working alliance. If the therapist has decided it is the apt time to link a recurrent pattern of behavior with others to transactions between the patient and himself or herself, the therapist should make them as detailed and concrete as possible. Such specificity helps the patient experientially recognize himself or herself in the situation.

In Strategy 8, the therapist addresses obstacles (e.g., coming late) that might influence the therapeutic process. In TLDP, these obstacles often are the meat surrounding the CMP skeletal structure. That is, such defensive maneuvers help the therapist discover the manner in which the patient tries to maintain a familiar, albeit dysfunctional, pattern. Resistance from the perspective of TLDP is viewed within the interpersonal sphere—as one of a number of transactions between therapist and patient. The assumption is that the patient is attempting to retain personal integrity and ingrained perceptions of himself or herself and others.

The patient's perceptions support his or her understanding of what is required to maintain interpersonal connectedness. Resistance in this light is the patient's attempt to do the best he or she can with how he or she construes the world.

Therefore, the manner in which the patient "resists" will be informative as to the patient's interactive style. The therapist often has the experience of hitting a wall when confronted with the patient's resistance. This wall often demarcates the boundaries of the patient's CMP. Rather than continue to hit the wall in an attempt to break through it, the TLDP therapist can stand back, appreciate the wall, and invite the patient to look at the wall also (i.e., metacommunication). Such an approach often avoids power plays with hostile patients and helps to promote empathy and collaboration. Because the focus in TLDP is on the interpersonal interaction, the therapist always has the process (between therapist and patient) to talk about when a therapeutic impasse has occurred. It is this focus on the interactive process that is the sine qua non of TLDP.

One of the most important treatment strategies is providing the opportunity for patients to have a new experience of themselves and/or the therapist that helps undermine patients' CMP (Strategy 9). The following examples of how to intervene with two patients with seemingly similar behaviors but differing experiential goals illustrate the strategy.

Marjorie's maladaptive interpersonal pattern suggested she had deeply ingrained beliefs that she could not be appreciated unless she were the charming, effervescent ingenue. When she attempted to joke throughout most of the fifth session, her therapist directed her attention to the contrast between her joking and her anxiously twisting her handkerchief. (New experience: The therapist invites the possibility that he can be interested in her even if she were anxious and not entertaining.)

Susan's lifelong dysfunctional pattern, on the other hand, revealed a meek stance fostered by repeated ridicule from her alcoholic father. She also attempted to joke in the fifth session, nervously twisting her handkerchief. Susan's therapist listened with engaged interest to the jokes and did not interrupt. (New experience: The therapist can appreciate her taking center stage and not humiliate her when she is so vulnerable.) In both cases, the therapist's interventions (observing nonverbal behavior, listening) were well within the psychodynamic therapist's acceptable repertoire. There was no need to do anything feigned (e.g., laugh uproariously at Susan's joke), nor was there a demand to respond with a similar therapeutic stance to both presentations.

In these cases, the therapists' behavior gave the patients a new interpersonal experience—an opportunity to disconfirm their own interpersonal schemata. With sufficient quality and/or quantity of these experiences, patients can develop different internalized working models of relationships. In this way, TLDP promotes change by altering the basic infrastructure of the patient's transactional world, which then reverberates to influence the concept of self.

TERMINATION

The last strategy is designed to support exploration of the patient's reactions to the time-limited nature of TLDP and termination (Strategy 10). Because TLDP is based on an interpersonal model, with roots in attachment theory and object relations, issues of loss are interwoven through the therapy and do not solely appear in the termination phase. Toward the end of therapy, the best advice for the

TLDP therapist is to maintain the dynamic focus and the goals for treatment, while examining how these patterns appear when loss and separation issues are most salient.

How does the TLDP therapist know when the patient has had "enough" therapy? In doing TLDP, I use five sets of questions to help the therapist judge when termination is appropriate:

1. Has the patient evidenced interactional changes with significant others in his or her life? Does the patient report more rewarding transactions?
2. Has the patient had a new experience (or a series of new experiences) of himself or herself and the therapist within the therapy?
3. Has there been a change in the level on which the therapist and patient are relating (from parent-child to adult-adult)?
4. Has the therapist's countertransferential reaction to the patient shifted (usually from negative to positive)?
5. Does the patient manifest some understanding about his or her dynamics and the role he or she was playing to maintain them?

If the answer is no to more than one of these questions, the therapist should seriously consider whether the patient has had an adequate course of therapy. The therapist should reflect why this has been the case and weigh the possible benefits of alternative therapies, another course of TLDP, a different therapist, nonprofessional alternatives, and so on.

As with most brief therapies, TLDP is not considered the final or definitive intervention. At some point in the future, the patient may feel the need to obtain more therapy for similar or different issues. Such additional therapy would not be viewed as evidence of a TLDP treatment failure. In fact, it is hoped that patients will view their TLDP therapies as helpful and as a resource to which they could return over time. This view of the availability of multiple, short-term therapies over the individual's life span is consistent with the position of the therapist as family practitioner (Cummings, 1995).

CLINICAL CASE EXAMPLE

Mr. Pedotti was a short, thin, 62-year-old, diabetic man of Italian descent. At the time of his referral to the outpatient psychiatry service of a large medical center, he had had diabetic retinopathy and kidney failure and was receiving hemodialysis three times a week. Mr. Pedotti was referred by his primary care physician for help with depression, insomnia, and anxiety. Mr. Pedotti felt that he was dying and that his life was over. His physician had been treating him with antianxiety agents (lorazepam) for his chronic anxiety.

At the age of 15, Mr. Pedotti emigrated from Italy with his parents and three older brothers. As a small child, he was overprotected by his mother and largely ignored by his father, who favored the older boys. As a youth, Mr. Pedotti was a lightweight boxer, turning professional for a short time until his diabetes began to incapacitate him in his early 20s. While he was boxing, his father (who also had diabetes) praised him for being strong, but withdrew his attention when his son's health began failing. At the time of his therapy, Mr. Pedotti had been married for 40 years and had four, healthy, grown children. His wife supported the family as a cook in a restaurant.

Mr. Pedotti was referred to the Brief Therapy Program—a training component of the outpatient services. He was assigned to work with Claire Vann, a psychology predoctoral intern under my supervision. Following a two-session assessment, he was offered 16 additional sessions of once-a-week therapy. He missed three of these appointments (once when his father died).

SESSION 1

Mr. Pedotti was accompanied by his wife in the waiting room. He appeared haggard. When the therapist entered, Mrs. Pedotti immediately began telling her about Mr. Pedotti's difficulties. While his wife talked, Mr. Pedotti remained silent, looking sullen and dejected. Finally, the therapist was able to extricate the patient from his wife, and he followed her slowly to the therapy room. During his first visit, Mr. Pedotti described his history of medical problems and his sadness over how they limited his activities. His affect was restricted, and he was tearful at times. He said that his three brothers were all in good health, and he wondered if he inherited his "condition" from his father. Mr. Pedotti said that at times he would withdraw from others ("shun people"), not take care of his appearance, and question the reasons for his "misfortune." During these periods, Mr. Pedotti said his children typically responded by leaving him alone, and his wife assumed more of his responsibilities such as making his medical appointments.

Mr. Pedotti talked about having thoughts of death but denied suicidal ideation or plans. He seemed to Ms. Vann to be more interested in help with his physical needs than with his emotional difficulties. During the first session, Mr. Pedotti was so physically distressed that he stood for part of it. He usually waited for the therapist to ask questions; at times when she did not, he became anxious. He spoke softly and slowly staring at the floor.

By allowing Mr. Pedotti to tell his own story, Ms. Vann observed and reacted to the patient's passivity. Mr. Pedotti seemed comfortable letting his wife and the therapist take control.

THERAPIST: What made you decide to seek therapy now?
PATIENT: The dialysis nurse said that my behavior was peculiar. My wife said it was a good idea, and she called and made the appointment and brought me here. (Patient stops and waits for therapist to ask the next question.)

Ms. Vann's countertransferential reactions to the patient included feelings of uselessness ("Perhaps he just needs consultation around his medical condition"), emotional distance ("I felt somewhat bored during the session"), and pity. Ms. Vann began to suspect that Mr. Pedotti's passivity and powerlessness had much to do with his depression and anxiety but was still unsure of the appropriateness and efficacy of TLDP, given Mr. Pedotti's preoccupation with his physical condition.

SESSION 2

Mr. Pedotti arrived promptly for his appointment, again accompanied by his wife. An important theme in this visit was his discussion of the way others responded to him.

THERAPIST: I'm hearing that when your physical problems interfere with your activities, you get depressed?

PATIENT: Yes, quite a bit.

THERAPIST: And what happens then?

PATIENT: I go to my room and don't feel like talking.

THERAPIST: And when you leave to go to your room and don't talk, how do other people react?

PATIENT: The kids understand I'm sick and don't pay attention to me.

THERAPIST: So when you close down and don't talk, they stop paying attention to you.

Comments on process and technique: In this vignette, the therapist is asking for specific behavioral details to understand the patient's interpersonal scenarios, which will eventually lead to a formulation (CMP). By following the patient's input closely and reflecting back what she has heard, the therapist begins to understand the patient's patterns while building rapport. Making causative links between what the patient does and others' actions helps the patient become aware of how his behavior has interpersonal consequences.

Technical interventions:

- Ask for details (actions) describing social interchanges.
- Explore the interpersonal context related to symptoms.
- Inquire about factors related to selection criteria.
- Obtain data for the CMP.
- Link patient's action to the complementary action of others in a coherent narrative.

Following this session, Ms. Vann assessed that Mr. Pedotti would be appropriate for TLDP. He seemed willing to talk about his problems in interpersonal terms and not solely stay focused on his medical condition. Furthermore, and most importantly, the therapist was beginning to see how the patient's repetitive, maladaptive pattern was evidenced not only in his current relationships, but also in the here-and-now interaction with her. Mr. Pedotti turned to the therapist for constant direction and yet withdrew from interacting with her in a way that discouraged her active collaboration. In fact, Ms. Vann felt useless and pulled to withdraw from him—a pattern that Mr. Pedotti said happened with his wife and children. Mr. Pedotti, however, was not aware of how his own interpersonal behaviors (e.g., avoiding contact and isolating himself when depressed) promoted the very responses (e.g., inattention, infantilization), which made him feel worthless and abandoned.

After these two evaluation sessions, Ms. Vann delineated a working conceptualization of Mr. Pedotti's CMP and derived the goals for treatment.

Acts of the Self Mr. Pedotti is a man who assumes a passive and sometimes depressive or withdrawn stance in the face of stressful circumstances to avoid being seen by others as crazy and as a failure. Part of this stance involves closing himself off emotionally (especially his anger), and part involves underfunctioning and giving his voice and power to others.

Expectations of Others' Reactions   Mr. Pedotti expects that others will show a lack of understanding, concern, and involvement with him. He believes others are no longer influenced by him and see him as useless or blameworthy—"a loser." He believes his family worries about his being a sick man; he expects they will take over his responsibilities when he does not feel well. He also expects if he shows his feelings, he will be judged crazy or as not trying.

Acts of Others toward the Self   Mr. Pedotti's suppression of emotions and accompanying withdrawal leads to others' feeling a lack of connection. They respond by staying physically distant, communicating with him through his spokesperson (wife). This confirms Mr. Pedotti's fears that he cannot express his true feelings. His passivity is seen by others as a failure to try, and sometimes they blame him or become angry. Others pick up the responsibilities he drops and are not influenced by him.

Introject   Mr. Pedotti sees himself as a helpless, powerless victim. Because he views his strong emotions as a sign he is crazy, he suppresses them. He feels weak and considers himself as useless and emasculated—just existing. He is disappointed in himself and treats himself like a loser, rather than the fighter he once was.

Goals

1. The new experience Mr. Pedotti needs in the context of the therapeutic relationship is to have more autonomy, control, and influence—to experience himself as a fighter again. Mr. Pedotti should have the experience of expressing his strong emotions to the therapist without being judged crazy. For the therapist, this means not taking control for him in sessions, being directive *only* in examining process and encouraging affective expression, responding positively to patient expressions of control and influence during sessions, staying with his feelings, and not being frightened of Mr. Pedotti's strong emotions—especially anger.
2. The new understanding focuses on helping Mr. Pedotti see how his passive, distancing stance serves only to drive others away, and no matter how devastating his physical condition, he is still a worthwhile person with much to offer his loved ones.

From this formulation, Ms. Vann was able to anticipate transference-countertransference problems (e.g., the pull for the therapist to be overly solicitous or emotionally distant, the patient's heightened dependency needs as termination nears).

SESSIONS 3 TO 6

Mr. Pedotti continued to come in with "no agenda," preferring that the therapist direct the session. Mr. Pedotti talked about how, as a boy, he and his brothers worked picking grapes. The highlight of his life was clearly when he was a boxer. With the therapist's help, Mr. Pedotti was able to relate how his self-esteem had been tied to his physical abilities and how, now that he was so physically limited, he considered himself worthless.

Mr. Pedotti admitted that he did not communicate how depressed he was to his family. He preferred to withdraw to avoid revealing his "weakness." He was afraid others would see him as "crazy," or as "not trying." Although Mr. Pedotti said he could talk about his depression and anxiety in the sessions, the therapist observed that he showed little affective expression of his distress. As the therapist was able to get Mr. Pedotti to focus on his emotions in the sessions, Mr. Pedotti reported that he was feeling "better," but did not know why. He attributed it to his dialysis.

In the waiting room before the beginning of the fifth session, Mr. Pedotti's wife told Ms. Vann that her husband had to end the session early because of another commitment. The therapist (in keeping with her treatment goals) replied, "It is up to your husband." However, in the session, she took responsibility for clarifying when the session would end.

THERAPIST: I understand that you'll be needing to end the session early today.
PATIENT: I think I have a doctor's appointment.
THERAPIST: (Realizing what she had done) How do you feel about the fact that I brought up your leaving early, rather than waiting for you to bring it up?
PATIENT: (Matter-of-factly) Oh, fine.
THERAPIST: Hmm. (Pause) I wonder why I took the responsibility for mentioning it.
PATIENT: Why? It's fine.
THERAPIST: Yes, I hear that it is fine with you, but sometimes, like right now, I think I end up treating you like you are not capable of determining your own direction in here. Sort of like how your wife takes over for you sometimes.
PATIENT: Hmm.
THERAPIST: (Pause) And I don't think it always feels good to you to have others treating you like you are incapable. Does it?

Comments on process and technique: The aim of the therapist's sharing of her own countertransferential reactions is to help the patient recognize the potential downside of his behavior, in terms of inviting the very reaction he finds so humiliating and depressing.

Technical interventions:

- Self-disclose countertransferential reactions.
- Link patient-therapist transaction to recurrent pattern of behavior with others.
- Metacommunicate about interaction in the here-and-now.

In the sixth session, Mr. Pedotti was able to talk about how he suppressed his feelings even in the session because he was afraid that Ms. Vann would "lock me up" in a psychiatric unit, "never to be released." Again, another opportunity presented itself in the here-and-now of the therapeutic relationship, this time for the therapist to support Mr. Pedotti's willingness to reveal himself. Ms. Vann pointed out to the patient how he had taken a risk in revealing his concerns to her in the session.

SESSIONS 7 TO 10

In the middle portion of his brief therapy, Mr. Pedotti talked about his father's situation, which the therapist could see dramatically paralleled his own. Mr. Pedotti viewed his father as docile and powerless in a relationship in which his father's new wife insulated, controlled, and spoke for him. Mr. Pedotti found this to be more true when his father (who also had diabetes) was more physically compromised. Mr. Pedotti talked about anger toward this woman, but denied any similarities to his own situation. A discussion about anger ensued, in which it became clear that Mr. Pedotti feared expressing his anger because he expected it would be met with disapproval. However, the times he could recall having been angry, he thought that others listened to him and took him seriously. Mr. Pedotti was intrigued with this disparity between what he expected and what he experienced.

Ms. Vann suggested that, in the past, Mr. Pedotti may have behaved as though the worst would happen and that perhaps he was just waiting to die. She contrasted this attitude with the patient's identity as a boxer and a fighter. The patient readily expanded the metaphor and expressed that his opponent, which he saw as his physical problem, was "very big," and he was at a loss to know how to fight it. In subsequent sessions, the therapist worked on reframing the "fight" as not against his disease but rather as against his emotionally and mentally "giving up." At the end of the eighth session, Mr. Pedotti talked about the possibility of getting a kidney transplant, and he wondered whether one of his three brothers would donate a kidney.

Mr. Pedotti missed his next appointment because of the death of his sickly father. In the 10th session, he talked about his anger toward both his father and his father's wife. "My father died years before his death." During this session, when the therapist drew parallels between his father's situation and his own, Mr. Pedotti was able to acknowledge how his own passivity and withdrawal were also rendering him almost dead. He spoke about wanting increased interaction with his family and, for the first time, expressed hope about receiving a transplant.

SESSIONS 11 TO 15

During the last third of his therapy, Mr. Pedotti spent much of his time talking about his growing awareness of similarities between his father's emotional-social reaction to severe illness and his own. He described his desire to live as fully as long as possible rather than to withdraw into a premature emotional death. During these last sessions, the focus repeatedly returned to the termination of the therapy and the relationship that had evolved between Mr. Pedotti and Ms. Vann. Mr. Pedotti discussed his desire to remain in psychotherapy and requested that it be continued. Although his therapist acknowledged Mr. Pedotti's assertiveness, she told him that his present therapy could not continue but that the decision about subsequent treatment was his to make. However, Ms. Vann also said she welcomed hearing his thoughts and feelings about their therapy's coming to a close.

Mr. Pedotti initially replied that he did not have the time to think about the ending of the therapy because of difficulties he was having at the medical center getting a second opinion about a proposed cataract procedure. He described his treatment by various medical staff disparagingly: "Intern students who just leave me up in the air." His therapist (a trainee) used this opportunity to ask Mr. Pedotti about parallels between this recent experience and feelings of being left without her help and support.

THERAPIST: We have two more sessions. I'm wondering how you are feeling about our ending.
PATIENT: I was thinking about it today, but not too much.
THERAPIST: And your feelings about our ending?
PATIENT: Good to have a break to reflect on things—to relax. I'm telling my wife how I feel—things I want and don't want, also I'm talking more with my children. They say they miss me when they leave, and that makes me feel good. Also, I'm trying to think positively about my health. I'm on the wait list for a kidney transplant.
THERAPIST: (10 minutes further into the session) In a previous session, you said you didn't want to think about when our therapy is going to end.
PATIENT: I'm sorry it's gonna end. Not sure how much further I can go to get better on my own. Not sure I can do it by myself. I'm not confident.
THERAPIST: So this is scary for you to think about. I can understand that it is hard to stop since you have found it helpful, and I appreciate your telling me how you feel about it.
PATIENT: Yeah. (Pause) I'll miss you.

Comment on process and technique: The patient is reluctant to talk about stopping therapy, but the therapist is persistent in her efforts to help the patient express his sad, scared, and (eventually) angry feelings about ending.

Technical interventions:

- Challenge the defense (avoidance).
- Address aspects of the termination as they reflect on the therapeutic process and patient's CMP.
- Maintain the focus.

With some difficulty, Mr. Pedotti was able to discuss his anxiety, sadness, and even some anger about termination. Ms. Vann validated his feelings by stating that they were understandable given the circumstances (i.e., the closeness that had evolved between them and the help the patient had received from their work together), but she steadfastly maintained the termination date.

Although Ms. Vann was not totally sure that Mr. Pedotti would continue to make the gains he had during his therapy, she assessed that to extend the length of the therapy would probably be more antitherapeutic than helpful. By sticking to the planned termination, the therapist hoped to convey the message to Mr. Pedotti that she thought of him as a "fighter" who was able to be victorious. In addition, termination provided an opportunity for Mr. Pedotti to understand his readiness to suppress negative affect and to allow the expression of feelings about losing his relationship with his therapist.

By the end of the 15-session therapy, Mr. Pedotti seemed to find a purpose "in making a difference" to loved ones, especially his grandchildren. He reestablished intimate contacts with his immediate and extended family. He became more assertive with his wife about his own medical treatment. He became involved in more social activities. In sum, he was able to regain a sense of himself as a fighter who, rather than fighting a disease, was fighting the pull to give up and stop living.

Two months after his last brief therapy session, Mr. Pedotti had a successful kidney transplant. His mental status as recorded by his physician one month following his transplant was: "Soft spoken, friendly, good eye contact, mildly restricted affect, denies depression, goal directed, future oriented."

HOW THERAPEUTIC CHALLENGES ARE CONCEPTUALIZED AND MANAGED

As stated previously, TLDP was devised to help therapists deal with challenging patients and situations. Rather than viewing therapeutic ruptures and misalliances as instances where the therapy has gone awry, the TLDP therapist sees them as examples of problematic communication patterns that unavoidably emerge with personality-disordered patients (i.e., reenactments). For the TLDP therapist, they are golden opportunities to provide the patient with a healthier interpersonal experience and/or a new understanding. Virtually any of the TLDP intervention strategies outlined in Table 12.2 could be used to help transform the therapeutic relationship into a specialized context for reflecting on and changing interpersonal patterns (Levenson, Schacht, & Strupp, 2002).

RESEARCH AND EMPIRICAL SUPPORT

A series of studies done at Vanderbilt University in the 1970s (Vanderbilt I) demonstrates that therapists become entrapped into reacting with negativity, hostility, and disrespect, and, in general, antitherapeutically when patients are negative and hostile. Moreover, the nature of therapists' and patients' behavior in relation to each other has been shown to be associated with the quality of therapeutic outcome. Henry, Schacht, and Strupp (1986) reexamined several cases from the Vanderbilt I project using the Statistical Analysis of Social Behavior (SASB) method (Benjamin, 1982). The SASB employs a circumplex model to discern and code patterns of transactions as distributed along the two axes of affiliation-disaffiliation and independence-interdependence. Findings indicate that in the cases with better outcomes, the therapists were significantly more "affirming and understanding," more "helpful and protecting," and less "belittling and blaming." Patients who had poorer outcomes were significantly less "disclosing and expressing," more "trusting and relying" (passively and deferentially so), and more "walling off and avoiding." Further, multiple communications (e.g., simultaneously accepting and rejecting) by both the patients and therapists were related to poorer outcomes.

In another series of findings on the therapeutic process and its impact, Quintana and Meara (1990) found that patients' intrapsychic activity became similar to the way they perceived their therapists treated them in short-term therapy. Going one step further, Harrist, Quintana, Strupp, and Henry (1994) found that patients internalized both their own and their therapists' contributions to the therapeutic interaction and that these internalizations were associated with better outcomes. A recent study examining relational change (Travis, Binder, Bliwise, & Horne-Moyer, 2001) found that following TLDP, patients significantly shifted in their attachment styles (from insecure to secure) and significantly increased the number of their secure attachment themes.

The VA Short-Term Psychotherapy Research Project—the VAST Project—examined TLDP process and outcome with a personality-disordered population (Levenson & Bein, 1993). As part of that project, Overstreet (1993) found that approximately 60% of the 89 male patients achieved positive interpersonal or symptomatic outcomes following TLDP (average of 14 sessions). At termination, 71% of patients felt their problems had lessened. One-fifth of the patients moved into the normal range of scores on a measure of interpersonal problems.

In the VAST Project long-term follow-up study (Bein, Levenson, & Overstreet, 1994), patients were reassessed a mean of three years after their TLDP therapies. Findings reveal that patient gains from treatment (measured by symptom and interpersonal inventories) were maintained and slightly bolstered. In addition, at the time of follow-up, 80% of the patients thought their therapies had helped them deal more effectively with their problems. Other analyses indicate that patients were more likely to value their therapies the more they perceived that sessions focused on TLDP-congruent strategies (i.e., trying to understand their typical patterns of relating to people, exploring childhood relationships, and trying to relate in a new and better way with their therapists).

Using the VAST Project data, Hartmann and Levenson (1995) examined the meaningfulness of TLDP case formulation in a real clinical situation. CMPs (written by the treating therapists after the first one or two sessions with their patients) were read by five clinicians who did not know anything about the patients or their therapies. These raters were able to agree on the patients' interpersonal problems solely based on the information contained in the CMP narratives. A study by Johnson, Popp, Schacht, Mellon, and Strupp (1989) warrants attention in this context as well insofar as it addressed, from a different vantage point, the clinical meaningfulness and reliability of CMP formulation. They found that the relationship themes identified with a modification of the CMP coded by the SASB were similar to themes derived using the core conflictual relationship theme (CCRT) method, providing an important demonstration that concurrence exists in relationship themes identified by different methods for assessing maladaptive interpersonal patterns.

The study by Hartmann and Levenson (1995) using the VAST Project data also revealed important relationships between patients' CMPs and facets of clinical process and outcome. Specifically, their data indicate that there is a statistically significant relationship between what interpersonal problems the raters felt *should* have been discussed in the therapy (based only on the patients' CMPs) and those topics the therapists said actually *were* discussed. Perhaps most meaningful is the finding that better outcomes were achieved the more these therapies stayed focused on topics relevant to the patients' CMPs. Thus, these preliminary findings indicate that the TLDP case formulations convey reliable interpersonal information to clinicians otherwise unfamiliar with the case, guide the issues that are discussed in the therapy, and lead to better outcomes the more therapists can adhere to them.

Research has also demonstrated specific effects of TLDP training on therapists who are learning this approach. In a three-year investigation of the effects of TLDP training on therapist performance (Vanderbilt II), Henry, Strupp, et al. (1993) found that the training program was successful in changing therapists' interventions congruent with TLDP strategies and that these changes held even with the more difficult patients (Henry, Schacht, Strupp, Butler, & Binder, 1993). However, a later study discovered that many of the project therapists did not reach an acceptable level of TLDP mastery (Bein et al., 2000). The Vanderbilt II findings also revealed some unintended and potentially untoward training effects. For example, after training, the activity level of the therapists increased, giving them more of an opportunity to make "mistakes." As a consequence, these therapists appeared less approving and less supportive and delivered more disaffiliative and complex communications to patients.

In another training study, Levenson and Bolter (1988) examined the values and attitudes of psychiatry residents and psychology interns before and after a six-month seminar and group supervision in TLDP. They found that after training, there were significant changes in the students' attitudes (e.g., willingness to be more active) as measured by a questionnaire designed to highlight value differences between short-term and long-term therapists (Bolter, Levenson, & Alvarez, 1990). Other research has supported these findings (Levenson & Strupp, 1999; Neff, Lambert, Lunnen, Budman, & Levenson, 1997).

SUMMARY AND CONCLUSIONS

Time-limited dynamic psychotherapy is designed to help therapists treat difficult patients (primarily those suffering from personality disorders) within a time-limited format. The therapist discerns the patient's cyclical, maladaptive pattern (CMP) to understand the patient's inflexible, self-perpetuating, and self-defeating expectations and negative self-appraisals that lead to maladaptive interactions with others. This CMP becomes the focus of the work. The goal of TLDP is to disrupt these patterns and thereby alter the very schemata (introject) that maintain them. Treatment strategies include observing the inevitable reenactment of those characteristic dysfunctional patterns in the therapeutic relationship, metacommunicating about them, and providing opportunities for experiential learning.

REFERENCES

Alexander, F., & French, T. M. (1946). *Psychoanalytic therapy: Principles and applications.* New York: Ronald Press.

Anchin, J. C. (1982). Sequence, pattern, and style: Integration and treatment implications of some interpersonal concepts. In J. C. Anchin & D. J. Kiesler (Eds.), *Handbook of interpersonal psychotherapy* (pp. 95–131). New York: Pergamon Press.

Anchin, J. C., & Kiesler, D. J. (Eds.). (1982). *Handbook of interpersonal psychotherapy.* New York: Pergamon Press.

Bein, E., Anderson, T., Strupp, H. H., Henry, W. P., Schacht, T. E., Binder, J. L., et al. (2000). The effects of training in time-limited dynamic psychotherapy: Changes in therapeutic outcome. *Psychotherapy Research, 10,* 119–132.

Bein, E., Levenson, H., & Overstreet, D. (1994, June). *Outcome and follow-up data from the VAST project.* Paper presented at the annual international meeting of the Society for Psychotherapy Research, York, England.

Benjamin, L. S. (1982). Use of Structural Analysis of Social Behavior (SASB) to guide intervention in psychotherapy. In J. C. Anchin & D. J. Kiesler (Eds.), *Handbook of interpersonal psychotherapy* (pp. 190–212). New York: Pergamon Press.

Benjamin, L. S. (1993). *Interpersonal diagnosis and treatment of personality disorders*. New York: Guilford Press.

Bergin, A. E., & Garfield, S. L. (Eds.). (1994). *Handbook of psychotherapy and behavior change*. New York: Wiley.

Binder, J. L., & Strupp, H. H. (1991). The Vanderbilt approach to time-limited dynamic psychotherapy. In P. Crits-Christoph & J. P. Barber (Eds.), *Handbook of short-term dynamic psychotherapy* (pp. 137–165). New York: Basic Books.

Bolter, K., Levenson, H., & Alvarez, W. (1990). Differences in values between short term and long term therapists. *Professional Psychology: Research and Practice, 4,* 285–290.

Bowlby, J. (1973). *Attachment and loss: Volume II. Separation: Anxiety and anger*. New York: Basic Books.

Butler, S. F., & Binder, J. L. (1987). Cyclical psychodynamics and the triangle of insight: An integration. *Psychiatry, 50,* 218–231.

Butler, S. F., & the Center for Psychotherapy Research Team. (1986). *Working manual for the Vanderbilt Therapeutic Strategies Scale*. Unpublished manuscript, Vanderbilt University, Nashville, TN.

Butler, S. F., Lane, T. W., & Strupp, H. H. (1988, June). *Patterns of therapeutic skill acquisition as a result of training in time-limited dynamic psychotherapy*. Paper presented at the annual meeting of the Society for Psychotherapy Research, Santa Fe, NM.

Butler, S. F., & Strupp, H. H. (1989, June). *Issues in training therapists to competency: The Vanderbilt experience*. Paper presented at the annual meeting of the Society for Psychotherapy Research, Toronto, Ontario, Canada.

Butler, S. F., Strupp, H. H., & Binder, J. L. (1993). Time-limited dynamic psychotherapy. In S. Budman, M. Hoyt, & S. Friedman (Eds.), *The first session in brief therapy* (pp. 87–110). New York: Guilford Press.

Butler, S. F., Strupp, H. H., & Lane, T. W. (1987, June). *The Time-Limited Dynamic Psychotherapy Therapeutic Strategies Scale: Development of an adherence measure*. Paper presented to the international meeting of the Society for Psychotherapy Research, Ulm, West Germany.

Cummings, N. A. (1995). Impact of managed care on employment and training: A primer for survival. *Professional Psychology: Research and Practice, 26,* 10–15.

Fisher, S., & Greenberg, R. P. (1997). *Freud scientifically reappraised: Testing theories and therapy*. New York: Wiley.

Gill, M. M. (1993). Interaction and interpretation. *Psychoanalytic Dialogues, 3,* 111–122.

Glickhauf-Hughes, C., Reviere, S. L., Clance, P. R., & Jones, R. A. (1996). An integration of object relations theory with gestalt techniques to promote structuralization of the self. *Journal of Psychotherapy Integration, 6,* 39–59.

Greenberg, J. R., & Mitchell, S. A. (1983). *Object relations in psychoanalytic theory*. Cambridge, MA: Harvard University Press.

Harrist, R. S., Quintana, S. M., Strupp, H. H., & Henry, W. P. (1994). Internalization of interpersonal process in time-limited dynamic psychotherapy. *Psychotherapy, 31,* 49–57.

Hartmann, K., & Levenson, H. (1995, June). *Case formulation in TLDP*. Paper presented at the annual international meeting of the Society for Psychotherapy Research meeting, Vancouver, British Columbia, Canada.

Henry, W. P., Schacht, T. E., & Strupp, H. H. (1986). Structural analysis of social behavior: Application to a study of interpersonal process in differential psychoanalytic outcome. *Journal of Consulting and Clinical Psychology, 54,* 27–31.

Henry, W. P., Schacht, T. E., Strupp, H. H., Butler, S. F., & Binder, J. L. (1993). Effects of training in time-limited dynamic psychotherapy: Mediators of therapists' responses to training. *Journal of Consulting and Clinical Psychology, 61,* 441–447.

Henry, W. P., Strupp, H. H., Butler, S. F., Schacht, T. E., & Binder, J. L. (1993). Effects of training in time-limited dynamic psychotherapy: Changes in therapist behavior. *Journal of Counseling and Clinical Psychology, 61,* 434–440.

Henry, W. P., Strupp, H. H., Schacht, T. E., & Gaston, L. (1994). Psychodynamic approaches. In A. E. Bergin & S. L. Garfield (Eds.), *Handbook of psychotherapy and behavior change* (pp. 467–508). New York: Wiley.

Johnson, M. E., Popp, C., Schacht, T. E., Mellon, J., & Strupp, H. H. (1989). Converging evidence for identification of recurrent relationship themes: Comparison of two methods. *Psychiatry, 52,* 275–288.

Kiesler, D. J. (1988). *Therapeutic metacommunication: Therapist impact disclosure as feedback in psychotherapy.* Palo Alto, CA: Consulting Psychologists Press.

Kohlenberg, R. J., & Tsai, M. (1991). *FAP: Functional analytic psychotherapy.* New York: Plenum Press.

Levenson, H. (1995). *Time-limited dynamic psychotherapy: A guide to clinical practice.* New York: Basic Books.

Levenson, H., & Bein, E. (1993, June). *VA short-term psychotherapy research project: Outcome.* Paper presented at the annual international meeting of the Society for Psychotherapy Research, Pittsburgh, PA.

Levenson, H., & Bolter, K. (1988, August). *Short-term psychotherapy values and attitudes: Changes with training.* Paper presented at the annual convention of the American Psychological Association, Atlanta, GA.

Levenson, H., Butler, S. F., & Bein, E. (2002). Brief dynamic individual psychotherapy. In R. E. Hales, S. C. Yudofsky, & J. A. Talbott (Eds.), *The American Psychiatric Press textbook of psychiatry* (4th ed., pp. 1151–1176). Washington, DC: American Psychiatric Press.

Levenson, H., Butler, S. F., Powers, T., & Beitman, B. (2002). *Concise guide to brief dynamic and interpersonal psychotherapy.* Washington, DC: American Psychiatric Press.

Levenson, H., Schacht, T. E., & Strupp, H. H. (2002). Time-limited dynamic psychotherapy. In M. Hersen & W. H. Sledge (Eds.), *Encyclopedia of psychotherapy* (pp. 807–814). New York: Elsevier Science.

Levenson, H., & Strupp, H. H. (1997). Cyclical maladaptive patterns in time-limited dynamic psychotherapy. In T. D. Eells (Ed.), *Handbook of psychotherapy case formulation* (pp. 84–115). New York: Guilford Press.

Levenson, H., & Strupp, H. H. (1999). Recommendations for the future of training in brief dynamic psychotherapy. *Journal of Clinical Psychology, 55,* 385–391.

Lyons-Ruth, K., & Jacobwitz, D. (1999). Attachment disorganization: Unresolved loss, relational violence, and lapses in behavioral and attentional strategies. In J. Cassidy & P. R. Shaver (Eds.), *Handbook of attachment: Theory, research, and clinical applications* (pp. 520–554). New York: Guilford Press.

Menninger, K. (1958). *Theory of psychoanalytic technique.* London: Imago.

Messer, S. B., & Warren, C. S. (1995). *Models of brief psychodynamic therapy: A comparative approach.* New York: Guilford Press.

Neff, W. L., Lambert, M. J., Lunnen, K. M., Budman, S. H., & Levenson, H. (1997). Therapists' attitudes toward short-term therapy: Changes with training. *Employee Assistance Quarterly, 11,* 67–77.

Overstreet, D. L. (1993). *Patient contribution to differential outcome in time-limited dynamic psychotherapy: An empirical analysis.* Unpublished doctoral dissertation, Wright Institute, Berkeley, CA.

Piper, W. E., Joyce, A. S., McCallum, M., & Azim, H. F. A. (1993). Concentration and correspondence of transference interpretations in short-term psychotherapy. *Journal of Consulting and Clinical Psychology, 61,* 586–595.

Quintana, S. M., & Meara, N. M. (1990). Internalization of the therapeutic relationship in short term psychotherapy. *Journal of Counseling Psychology, 37,* 123–130.

Safran, J. D., & Segal, Z. V. (1990). *Interpersonal process in cognitive therapy.* New York: Basic Books.

Sampson, H., & Weiss, J. (1986). Testing hypotheses: The approach of the Mount Zion Psychotherapy Research Group. In L. S. Greenberg & N. M. Pinsof (Eds.), *The psychotherapeutic process: A research handbook* (pp. 591–614). New York: Guilford Press.

Sandler, J. (1976). Countertransference and role-responsiveness. *International Review of Psycho-Analysis, 3,* 43–47.

Siegel, D. J. (1999). *The developing mind: Toward a neurobiology of interpersonal experience.* New York: Guilford Press.

Stern, D. (1985). *The interpersonal world of the infant.* New York: Basic Books.

Strupp, H. H. (1955a). An objective comparison of Rogerian and psychoanalytic techniques. *Journal of Consulting Psychology, 19,* 1–7.

Strupp, H. H. (1955b). The effect of the psychotherapist's personal analysis upon his techniques. *Journal of Consulting Psychology, 19,* 197–204.

Strupp, H. H. (1955c). Psychotherapeutic technique, professional affiliations, and experience level. *Journal of Consulting Psychology, 19,* 97–102.

Strupp, H. H. (1980a). Success and failure in time-limited psychotherapy: A systematic comparison of two cases (Comparison 1). *Archives of General Psychiatry, 37,* 595–603.

Strupp, H. H. (1980b). Success and failure in time-limited psychotherapy: A systematic comparison of two cases (Comparison 2). *Archives of General Psychiatry, 37,* 708–716.

Strupp, H. H. (1980c). Success and failure in time-limited psychotherapy: With special reference to the performance of a lay counselor (Comparison 3). *Archives of General Psychiatry, 37,* 831–841.

Strupp, H. H. (1980d). Success and failure in time-limited psychotherapy: Further evidence (Comparison 4). *Archives of General Psychiatry, 37,* 947–954.

Strupp, H. H. (1993). The Vanderbilt psychotherapy studies: Synopsis. *Journal of Consulting and Clinical Psychology, 61,* 431–433.

Strupp, H. H., & Binder, J. L. (1984). *Psychotherapy in a new key.* New York: Basic Books.

Sullivan, H. S. (1953). *The interpersonal theory of psychiatry.* New York: Norton.

Travis, L. A., Binder, J. L., Bliwise, N. G., & Horne-Moyer, H. L. (2001). Changes in clients' attachment styles over the course of time-limited dynamic psychotherapy. *Psychotherapy, 38,* 149–159.

von Bertalanffy, L. (1969). *General systems theory: Essays on its foundation and development* (Rev. ed.). New York: Braziller.

Wachtel, P. L. (1987). *Action and insight.* New York: Guilford Press.

Wachtel, P. L. (1997). *Psychoanalysis, behavior theory, and the relational world.* Washington, DC: American Psychological Association.

Weiss, J. (1993). *How psychotherapy works.* New York: Guilford Press.

CHAPTER 13

Close Process Attention in Psychoanalytic Psychotherapy

Frank Knoblauch

WITH HIS WRITINGS and teaching over the past 20 years, Paul Gray defined a method of modern psychoanalytic technique, which has served both as a clarification and extension of existing ego-psychological techniques and as a challenge to those practicing from other clinical-theoretical points of view. In this chapter, I introduce in a condensed way some of Gray's important contributions to psychoanalysis and attempt to show how many of these ideas, though derived from psychoanalysis, can apply as well to the practice of psychoanalytic psychotherapy. Gray often spoke of the "widening scope" of patients being treated by psychoanalytic or psychoanalytically inspired methods. He referred to attempts to employ psychoanalytic methods to clinical situations not originally thought suitable for psychoanalysis. He often emphasized that he was primarily addressing his own writings to those "narrower scope" patients who could benefit from a rigorously applied ego-psychological analysis. Of particular interest for this present volume, however, are questions as to how the kinds of insights and advances in technique emerging from the work of Gray and others in psychoanalysis relate to methods of psychotherapy for patients with personality disorder. As a way of contrasting Gray's method, which came to be called *close process attention*, with some other approaches being used in the treatment of personality disorders, I look at Horowitz's work on Histrionic Personality Disorder and Meissner's work on the paranoid process. (Horowitz's patients could be seen as nearer to Gray's "narrow scope," and Meissner's patients would be in Kernberg's borderline personality organization group and, in some instances, were psychotic.) I conclude with a return to some further comments on close process attention and its relevance for most forms of psychodynamic psychotherapy.

I begin with a summary of Gray's central clinical-theoretical innovations and clarifications and then illustrate these by looking at extended excerpts of process material (concerning five consecutive psychoanalytic sessions) published by a group of Gray's colleagues (Davison et al., 1996). Gray's *The Ego and Analysis of Defense* (1994) in many sections traces in close detail the evolution of his thought and his views of how other analysts have come to think about psychoanalytic treatment and remains the best starting point for those wanting to learn about close process attention. I do not retrace the development of Gray's ideas in detail here but begin instead with where Gray ended, with a consideration of three of his central clinical concepts: *close process attention* (and the related *inside focus*), the *analysis of defense*, and the analyst's *analysis of, rather than use of, the superego function*.

CLOSE PROCESS ATTENTION

With his "Psychoanalytic Technique and the Ego's Capacity for Viewing Intrapsychic Activity" in 1973, Gray introduced the cast of characters we would see repeatedly over the next 29 years as he developed and progressively refined his ideas until the time of his death in 2002. The phrase "the ego's capacity for viewing intrapsychic activity" heralded much of what was to come. The mind, he reminds us, is activity, and his recommended method takes advantage of the fact that the unceasingly active mind can also turn its attention on itself, on its own activity.

Gray is talking in this way about both the analysand's mind and the analyst's mind. He begins with remarks to the analyst:

> It is a curious fact that the central, most necessary part of psychoanalytic technique is one of the least discussed, certainly one of the least well conceptualized aspects of psychoanalysis. I am referring to analytic listening or, more accurately, analytic perception. . . . The observations that follow concern that portion of the complex of functions here designated as the analyst's perspective of attention, or perceptual focus, in particular, the uses of such perspectives of attention that are receptive to the derivatives of thoughts or affects or processes of which the patient is unaware. (Gray, 1994, p. 5)

Gray picks his battles as he enters his century's psychoanalytic debates over who the analyst is, what he or she does, and how he or she should listen. He begins with *attention*. Like his book title *The Ego and Analysis of Defense*, meant to echo Anna Freud's (1936) *The Ego and the Mechanism of Defense*, his attention to "attention" in his first paragraph echoes the terms "free floating" and "evenly hovering" attention. In the next 29 years, he respectfully but unceasingly battles against psychoanalytic technical recommendations that would have the analyst loosely floating along as he listens or listening with a "third ear" (Reik, 1948). Gray thinks we should sharpen our focus and spell out more clearly what we are looking for:

> In listening, we give priority to maintaining a close and even focus on the audible flow of words and affects for manifestations of instinctual derivatives emerging into consciousness. Once a derivative appears, the analyst continues to listen to the *subsequent sequence* of material for changes (alterations in context, content, etc.) that indicate, by their content, that the ego has initiated a defense in order to stem a rising or anticipated discomfort (anxiety, sense of risk) because of conflict over exposing a specific part of the material containing some drive derivatives. (Gray, 1994, p. 176)

Central to Gray's emerging emphasis of attention to the ego in the process of defending itself is his belief that analysts in their clinical work have been slow to incorporate the implications of advances made in psychoanalytic theory. In particular, he focuses on the psychoanalytic theories of defense and anxiety and, analyzing the analyst, he notes resistance to assimilating and employing what he considers important theoretical advances such as the structural theory (seen as superceding the topographic theory) and Sigmund Freud's 1926 theory of anxiety. Analysts, he tells us, have their own "fixations" and have been caught up in a "developmental lag" (Gray, 1982).

THE INSIDE FOCUS

Gray (1982) began to call this approach "close process technique" to emphasize that the analyst attends closely to the instant-to-instant workings of the patient's mind. The subject of the analysis is the patient as seen *in* the moment in the session—not the patient's life, history, or problems because these occurred outside the session. This distinction is a powerful discriminator of therapeutic methods in that most psychotherapies occupy themselves with various "objects" of interest located in a wide variety of psychic or actual locales. Gray argues for consistent, persistent focusing on what is occurring *in* the session. He would have us remain attentive to the mind in the here and now and observed with the ego metaphor in mind—namely, observed with the assumption that the mind is continuously encountering threats and dangers and finding defenses and solutions. The *surface* attracting our attention is chosen to include drive derivative triggers and defensive responses so that the paths between them can be retraced. Even as patients turn their attention away from observing themselves and the listening, observing analyst to focus on the past or a dream or elsewhere, the close process analyst keeps an eye on the sequence, the timing of the shift, and looks for a useful moment to intervene. His intervention ordinarily points to such shifts and raises questions about the felt threats that preceded.

ANALYSIS OF DEFENSE

In 1982, Gray wrote *"Developmental Lag" in the Evolution of Technique for Psychoanalysis of Neurotic Conflict*, in which he argued that analysts in their techniques of psychoanalysis were lagging behind the advances that had already occurred in their theories (e.g., of anxiety or of defense or resistance). As to our clinical approach to defense analysis, he argued that we would do better to follow Anna Freud and her important insights since *The Ego and the Mechanisms of Defense* (1936) than to follow Sigmund Freud himself and many others in their tendencies to revert to topographic models and even id analysis. Sigmund Freud's (1926) "Inhibitions, Symptoms, and Anxiety" moved his theories of anxieties beyond and away from their origins and to the concept of signal anxiety. Freud revised his earlier ideas in a way that included his "structural" understanding of the mind, which understood the ego as serving a mediating role in devising compromises between impulses and dangers of various sorts. Pray focuses on this issue in detail in his "Two Different Methods of Analyzing Defense" (1996).

Pray (1996) "compares Anna Freud's 1936 ideas on analyzing defense with mainstream traditional psychoanalytic thinking, represented . . . by Brenner's views in his *The Mind in Conflict* (1982) and other writings, as well as the views of other analysts consistent with his point of view." Working with detailed psychoanalytic process material published by Silverman (1987) in *Psychoanalytic Inquiry*, Pray contrasts the analysis of defense done by Silverman in these hours with an approach to the analysis of defense, which he argues is consistent with Anna Freud's insights about the nature of the ego, of anxiety, and of defense. Silverman's method and discussions of it by Brenner are seen as representative of "mainstream traditional psychoanalytic thinking." Pray's rendition of Anna Freud's approach is also similar to the understanding of defense in Gray's "close process attention."

Pray illustrates the Anna Freud-Paul Gray approach to analytic attention with the opening segment of Silverman's material. Bold type indicates material immediately following the two moments of defense discussed by Pray:

Friday

Patient: The rain woke me up early this morning. It was beating down on my air Conditioner so loudly it woke me up. I looked at the clock. It was 5:30. I Thought in an hour I have to come here. I didn't want to come today. I've Been mad at you all week. **It's not that I'm mad at you.** I wanted to stay Away from all this stuff I think I feel here. I also got angry at R. [her room-Mate] yesterday. In the bathroom, she takes two towel bars and a hook. And I have just one towel bar. I didn't say anything for a long time. I Finally, got up the courage and told her we have to change the arrangements In the bathroom. **It sounds so silly.** I get so worked up over such things. I Get so angry. (Pray, 1996, p. 58; from Silverman, 1987, p. 151)

In two moments of what Anna Freud (1936) might call "fresh conflict," the patient switches from expressions of anger and self-assertion to self-effacement and self-control. Central to Anna Freud's and Gray's ideas is that such moments involve not just defense but "transference of defense" including transference of defenses related to unconscious superego issues. With such a patient, close process treatment might lead, for example, to her realizing more and more that she tends to have a defensive response to mounting aggressive and angry feelings. One common sequence that she would learn to see herself repeating would involve her turning, at such moments, to ideas that others and, in particular, her analyst wouldn't approve of and that, therefore, such expressions need to be quickly inhibited or transformed.

Pray uses parts of the following material from the same analytic hour to illustrate Silverman's approach, which is consistent with Brenner's writings about analyzing defense:

In this sequence, the patient first talks about how she had been intimidated by a hairdresser who cut her hair and then about tipping a girl who had shampooed her hair.

PATIENT: Why? (Slight pause) I can't figure it out. There's no rhyme or reason. I don't understand it.

ANALYST: So long as you take that attitude, so long as you don't think it out and find out the rhyme and reason . . .

PATIENT: Well, *he* cut my hair. He *cut* me. But she just put her fingers into my hair. I don't understand.

ANALYST: He stuck scissors into your hair, and she stuck fingers into your hair. You were talking before about avoiding sexual excitement. Scissors and fingers into your hair sounds sexual. You turn away and avoid the excitement, pain, and hurt with men, and when you turn away from men altogether and turn toward a woman, you get scared all over again.

The patient talks about how and why some of Silverman's interpretation "doesn't fit" and soon has recalled a masturbation fantasy she had mentioned earlier in the analysis and then later had avoided. In the fantasy, a mad scientist doctor and a nurse tie her down and "do things" to her.

PATIENT: I don't know what this has to do with being intimidated by the hairdresser and feeling inhibited tipping the girl who washes my hair but not the manicurist. It makes no sense. (Pause)

ANALYST: You blocked yourself from hearing the answer you gave: the hairdresser sticking scissors into your hair and cutting you; the young woman preparing you for the haircut; they're the mad scientist doctor and his nurse.

Charles Brenner in his discussion of the material writes:

> Dr. Silverman and I think alike on this point. His patient is a sexually inhibited, masochistic woman who, at the time of the report, wished to stay in the same sort of relationship to Silverman that she'd had for years with her father: one which was unconsciously gratifying in a masochistic, submissive way ("You teach me; you tell me what to do.") and at the same time was not consciously sexually exciting. (Brenner, 1987, p. 168)

Brenner and Silverman want to help the patient look beyond the surface memories of the haircut and mad scientist fantasies to understand compromise formations employed in dealing with her conflictual sexual and aggressive feelings, her anxieties, and her inhibitions and prohibitions. Silverman tells the patient both that she is defending against understanding her own experiences and the hidden meaning of them, in this instance, that she blocked her own sexual desire. His approach, which is not based on close process attention to the immediate conscious surface, warrants reading his entire clinical text (covering four sessions) because for classical structural psychoanalysts, the surface toward which interpretations will be directed could be thought of as spreading out much more broadly and extensively than the close process surface. The *third ear* is important in that an analyst's skill and helpfulness depend to a substantial degree on ability to *hear* what isn't said, what lies below or beyond an extended surface of this sort.

THE ANALYTIC SURFACE

As Pray makes clear in his contrasting representations of traditional psychoanalytic technique and the Anna Freud-Paul Gray technique, what individuals bracket as "defense" and what they say about it exert powerful effects on what the analysis will be about. In these discussions of defense, in another way, we are still concerned with attention and what Gray called "analytic perception": "The analyst's primary goal is always the analysis of the patient's psyche, not the patient's life" (Gray, 1994, p. 9).

In another passage, Gray describes his selection among various possible foci of intervention:

The perceptual focus is in terms of an immediate danger (of the emerging drive derivative) *in that hour*. The patient could perceive that the analyst's perceptual focus was on the psychological phenomena (i.e., the psychic realities) occurring at the moment, "inside" the analysis, and not on aspects of potential behavior (acting out) at another time and place, that is, "outside" the fundamental analytic setting. (Gray, 1994, p. 12)

In a subtle yet powerful shift of attention, Gray moves the therapist off the outermost surface of the patient's verbal stream and one small, yet significant, level down to the level of difficulties and conflict encountered by the patient at that very moment as the patient attempts to talk openly, honestly, and spontaneously to the therapist. In most psychotherapies, that outermost surface—the manifest verbal content of the moment—will typically offer to focus patient and therapist somewhere "out there": onto a remembered experience, onto a dream or a fantasy, perhaps onto some collection of ideas thought to represent crucial aspects of the patient's dynamics. The close process focus is toward the patient and analyst in the therapeutic interaction. It often asks what danger or problem the patient encountered "just then" as he or she attempted the task of free association. That danger and the person's response to it become central aspects of the immediate surface of attention. Silverman's patient in the first passage cited previously, for example, rapidly switches from "I've been mad at you all week" to "It's not that I'm mad at you." Gray would hope to open up that brief moment further with questions such as: "How were you imagining just then that I would react to your comment or to what might have been about to emerge next?" Or, "Was there some danger or threat in continuing to talk about your angry feelings?"

Following closely on this issue of where to focus comes another central emphasis of the close process technique as it has evolved from the writings of Gray, namely, that when the analyst interrupts the patient's "attempted spontaneity," he or she does so to "intervene," not to "interpret." These interventions are related in one way to a visible surface within the verbal stream (for example, a shift or change of voice noted by the therapist) but in another crucial way to the generally unspoken, unknown surface of the patient's moment-to-moment representations of the therapist. Of special interest are the patient's ideas and pictures of that therapist, who is looking on just then as the patient attempts spontaneity. These representations constitute the crucial aspect of the patient's *immediate reality* we hope better to understand. Invariably, an initially unconscious, because not-reflected-on, aspect of that reality is the idea that the patient is performing his or her task for and in the presence of an authority figure.

ANALYSIS OF, RATHER THAN USE OF, THE ANALYST'S SUPEREGO FUNCTION

Clearly focused *within* the therapeutic situation with his eye consistently on the analysand's attempts at spontaneity, Gray watches for the emergence of a drive derivative (which especially means to him a derivative of aggression) and, in close succession, the emergence of defense. And defense, in the therapeutic situation, often means apparent submission to the therapist's authority. One important form of resistance is the patient's resistance to awareness of his or her experience of the therapist. In "The Patient's Resistance to Awareness of the Analyst's Presence," Levenson (2003) focuses on just such resistances:

[W]hen patients experience their aggressive urges as particularly threatening, the transference fantasy of the analyst's criticism and disapproval may not provide enough safety. The intrusion of aggressive wishes, feelings, or fantasies into conscious awareness, even for the briefest moments and even if promptly self-directed, may be so distressing and produce self-critical feelings so dystonic that further defense measures are required. The additional defensive step that I am describing involves the patient creating the self-protective illusion that he is largely alone rather than in the presence of, and speaking to, the analyst. By not allowing himself full conscious awareness of relating to the analyst, the patient gains additional protection against his aggressive wishes. (pp. 3–4)

With respect to patients' resistances to becoming aware of their tendencies to transfer onto the therapist parental-supervisory attitudes, Gray remarks:

It should not come as a surprise that patients show considerable reluctance to recognize and analyze that aspect of transference the ego finds so effective for restraining *disclosure*. Once children have made *self-civilizing* use of a perception of a parent as an auxiliary guardian of their morals, of their struggle against their dangerous instinctual drives ("my mother/father would *never* let me do, or say, that"), they do not want to believe that the authoritative figures are, in fact, usually less inhibiting than illusion would have them believe. Further, they do not want to face their God-equivalents, to see them too clearly, they only want them to always "be there" serving their controlling role. (1994, p. 183)

A major emphasis in close process monitoring is attending to the ongoing apparent representations of and psychological uses of the analyst as the analysand attempts to talk spontaneously. It is taken for granted that the therapeutic situation is not really an "atmosphere of safety" but, on the contrary, "an unfamiliar situation" and one to which, Gray tells us, the ego has a "predictable response":

In an analytic situation, there is a constant threat that the *inner* measures will not provide a sufficient sense of "safety." This is because analysands are deliberately placed into circumstances that promote—through intrapsychic stimulations and external conditions enhancing a form of permissiveness—a continual atmosphere of potential risk; the risk that they may experience and reveal to another individual conflicted ("uncivilized") wishes and impulses. This unusual, unremitting condition exists owing to the accepted *task* (not "rule") that they *verbalize* for the analyst's attention everything coming into consciousness. (1994, p. 204, Gray's italics)

We are guided by the theory that much is *transferred* into this new situation. Of particular interest in the close process approach is the way in which old dangers and defenses are given a new form. In Sigmund Freud's earliest methods, the scientist-detective sought out traumatic old situations, hoping to release strangulated affects and reconstruct for the patient what happened or must have happened way back then. Modern psychotherapeutic techniques tend to stay closer to the present in one sense as therapists look *there* for emerging signs of old problems. Modern neuroscience has lent support to an idea, which has also evolved in clinical work: There are different kinds of memories. The episodic or declarative versus procedural memory distinction suggests that as our patients talk, at times they are operating with memories of episodes or moments in their earlier life that now attract consciousness; but at the same time, their minds consist, too, of procedures that they have learned and now employ (such as riding a bike) as if automatically. The kind of defenses picked out via close process attention similarly could be thought of as old, well-learned skills or procedures that the patient now employs instantly as he or she responds to something associated with an old trigger. One type of therapeutic action of the method occurs via myriad opportunities to look at these habitual procedures and to reflect on and try out currently available alternatives.

CLOSE PROCESS MONITORING IN PSYCHOANALYSIS

Goldberger (1996) has edited a volume titled *Danger and Defense: The Technique of Close Process Attention,* a Festschrift published in honor of Gray, which continues his work in many useful ways. The first chapter, *Defense Analysis and Mutative Interpretation,* by Walter Todd Davison, Monroe Pray, Curtis Bristol, and Robert Wexler, is especially recommended for those interested in clinical material in which the close process technique is employed. The authors publish their process notes for an entire week of psychoanalysis, an unusually extensive clinical text.

Davison et al. (1996) help to extend Gray's concepts and theoretical ideas by attempting to specify succinctly some basic principles and guidelines for the close process analyst in action:

Four Steps to a Mutative Interpretation

Step One: State what the patient is saying now.

Step Two: State what that seems to be shifted away from. If the analysand can hear these suggestions and followed them, then . . .

Step Three: Inquire about the perceived risk or danger in holding the first thought or feeling. Listen for the transferred superego imago that was the stimulus for defense.

Step Four: Review the picture of the transferred superego imago. (p. 19)

In abstract or summary form, as analysands attempt to talk spontaneously, they soon stimulate feelings and urges, which they rapidly censor, conceal, and oppose. These are often accompanied by the barely noticed idea that the analyst would not approve of, would criticize, or would even attack them for such talk or for expression of such feelings. The task of the analyst is to notice such potential openings into the analysand's rapid defensive activities and intervene at the most promising of such openings to invite analysands to look retrospectively at such a sequence to try to reconstruct what danger they encountered at that very moment when that feeling emerged. In particular, analysands are invited to consider the possibility that their handling of that moment may relate to how they were perceiving the analyst. The goal here is the familiar *reintrojection* of a projection. Or, as Ritvo (in press) describes the process in *Conflicts of Aggression in Coming of Age:*

The ego reacts defensively to the affect signal it receives when a conflicted aggressive drive derivative presses toward discharge. The analysand responds with an interruption in the free expression of his thoughts in the presence of the analyst to whom the defensive functions of the superego are transferred. This offers an opportunity for the analyst to draw attention to the defensive response in close proximity to the drive derivative. The therapeutic aim is to strengthen the autonomy of the ego by increasing its tolerance of drive derivatives in awareness without resorting to habitual defenses, enabling the analysand to choose more adaptive ways of coping with conflict. (p. 7)

CLINICAL CASE EXAMPLE: CLOSE PROCESS TECHNIQUE

In the next section of this chapter, a condensed version of the Davison et al. material is summarized. Portions of the clinical material in the form of extended excerpts serve to move from the level of general principles to an actual clinical period of treatment. I comment in sidebars on many of the analyst's interventions in an attempt to relate these clinical choices to the technical ideas reviewed previously.

MONDAY

In the week before the sessions published, the analyst had informed the patient that he would be away on the Monday 11 days from then. The analysand, Mrs. M, begins the *Monday* session saying that it had not been a good weekend, and she soon begins to talk about a dream in which she was supposed to give her daughter a shot and was helped in that by a doctor. Associations lead to a childhood experience in which she compared her own attempted stoicism about getting a shot of anesthetic at the dentist's office with her brother's wild fighting against it. Mrs. M then becomes sarcastic and verbally attacks the analyst. Then she becomes more reflective:

MRS. M: It sounds like I want to pick a fight with you. No, that's not right. I know you won't fight back and I can needle you all I want. I guess I just feel like needling you.

ANALYST: If you experienced yourself on the receiving end of that, at an earlier time, then doing it to me may seem natural to you.

The analyst refers to a shift, turning passive into active, which he relates to the drive derivative needling.

MRS. M: I remember how still I was. What a fool. I want to please you, but I won't hold still for that—not the needle—not ever again, not even for you.

ANALYST: You experience me as needling you following a moment when you were freer to think of doing that to me.

Another defense, now active to passive. Same drive derivative.

MRS. M: Yes, your calmness seems insulting, even condescending, like you are saying to me, "I have calmness and you don't." Damn it. It makes me mad . . . I felt like I needed you this weekend. You were probably home with your wife. (Pause) If that fat-mouthed law student gives me a hard time today, he's going to get a fat lip. (She delivered a short punch to the air.)

ANALYST: Now you are punching someone outside the room, just before you were thinking of doing something to me; can you sense the danger there?

The defense is now the displacement from analyst to another object and from "here" to "there."

MRS. M: Are you a glutton for punishment? Would you feel better if I thought of giving you a chubby jowl? I feel really wound up today, and I guess I don't want to take it all out on you. I don't know when David (her husband) will be home. I need him. C (her daughter) needs him, too. I guess I am afraid that if I am too hard on you, you won't be there for me.

TUESDAY

Mrs. M begins talking of feeling jittery, of looking forward to her husband's return home from a trip but feeling nervous. Soon she has recalled a dream in which she slammed a laundry hamper closed on her husband's bathrobe belt. The analyst reports that "her voice trailed off; a minute or so passed."

ANALYST: Does your hesitation include a feeling regarding the dream imagery?

The analyst points to a moment in time, her hesitation, and asks the analysand to "think back." Can she reconstruct what she had felt just then?

MRS. M: Yes, it's sexual. It makes me nervous. David stopped using condoms. I have to use a diaphragm. I hate it. I feel exposed, like I'm the one making the first move toward sex. (A few moments silence) That belt may have to do with a (Mumble, mumble) hanging out.
ANALYST: Some tension about that word.

Again, the analyst picks a focal point but his intervention is to ask, not to tell.

MRS. M: Uh huh. (She clenched her fists and put her hands behind her head. She sighed.) It sounds like I want to cut someone's penis off.
ANALYST: And maybe you feel concern about speaking of that wish in my presence.

The patient, as Gray sometimes put it, was able to reengage the initially avoided material. The analyst hopes to clarify why the avoidance had been necessary.

MRS. M: You might think I was after you. Maybe I am. I have been cutting to you lately.
ANALYST: And the risk involved in speaking of cutting me?

An issue of clinical style and judgment in such sequences involves both the analyst's decisions as to when dangers have been clarified and understood enough but also when patients are likely to be able to carry forward these sorts of clarifications on their own.

MRS. M: Just that if I am cutting to you, you may be sharp with me. (Pause) Sometimes when David gets on top of me, his penis slips out and bends back. He shrivels up. Men seem so brittle to me. So delicate. (Mockery replaced concern) It probably wouldn't take much to break one off. (Pause) That reminds me I had a fantasy last weekend that David was home, and he tied my hands and had intercourse with me. I was surprised that it didn't hurt, which is weird because I don't remember a time when intercourse hurt though suddenly it seems possible. Like I might not be able to stretch enough. (She shuddered.)

ANALYST: One way to view this train of thoughts is that uncertainty about your elasticity and being tied up follows a moment when you spoke of advantage over a man.

As in the author's four steps, the shift is identified and described. The emerging danger, which seemed to require such a shift, is here left for the analysand to ponder if she feels the need. Or, she may have other thoughts she wants to get to.

Mrs. M went on to remember an experience that occurred when she was 11 and a man exposed his erect penis to her and later recalled her father and his puffy jowls as he seemed not to believe her report of the incident.

WEDNESDAY

Mrs. M began by recounting that she "had the best time ever in bed with David last night," she felt that her analyst has really helped her a lot, and she feels grateful to him. But her husband had to leave suddenly, and Mrs. M felt sick to her stomach and got drunk. In this hour, she expressed wanting "a woman to nurse me . . . to cuddle me in bed like a baby," "slamming that clothes hamper on the belt," then fears she'll ruin it with her husband (by "screaming like I do at you sometimes or like I used to at C").

ANALYST: As if you might have to concern yourself with sparing me?

The analysand here might have been moving back and forth in her focus between describing feelings and experiences with her husband and with the analyst. His comment again points toward the moment of defense—in this case, inhibition of her verbally aggressive behaviors—and asks about the analysand's "concern" at that moment.

MRS. M: I know, but it's hard to believe that anything's different. Only boys were allowed to raise hell. I'm afraid that I might spew all this resentment out all over David for leaving me last night . . . I just pictured myself as a big penis spewing all over him. He has trouble with my raising my voice. Someday you may just leave me, too. How much of this can you put up with?

THURSDAY

MRS. M: When I said goodbye yesterday, you looked so tired and sallow. I thought you must really be sick. Could you have cancer? Maybe that was why you were wearing all that awful smelling cologne, to cover up the smell of your shrinking and dying.

Mrs. M expressed that she had felt angry with her analyst for his comments about her diminishing herself yesterday when she wanted to talk about suckling a woman's breast. She felt the analyst wasn't in touch with what she had wanted to talk about. And Mrs. M has a fantasy that her analyst is dying of cancer.

Mrs. M: You said that you would be away Monday, didn't you? Maybe you need the rest. Maybe you are getting treatment for cancer. If you had cancer, then I wouldn't have to be angry at you. Yesterday I had a thought that I couldn't tell you. After I got drunk, I threw up and smelled up the whole bedroom. I guess I feel stinking and rotten . . . unless I might have done that to myself rather than complain to you how unfair it is of you to just announce you are leaving with absolutely no hint of why or where. It has always bothered me that I tell you everything and you share almost nothing of yourself with me.

Analyst: Something that seemed dangerous to complain about before that now seems safer.

The analyst focuses on a sequence mentioned right here but experienced yesterday. He invites the analysand to think back about why she "couldn't tell" him. "Seemed dangerous" invites the analysand to try to spell out what sort of danger she had imagined.

Mrs. M: I have complained about it before, but yesterday the way you looked startled me. I think I was worried that you might really be sick. Then it would be unfair to burden you with my complaints. I really did a job on myself. It affected my work. I had to give a lecture that I have given many times before, but it seemed that I had forgotten something and couldn't get emotionally in touch with what I was doing.

Analyst: Something difficult to get in touch with. Something forgotten.

Like the analyst's last comment, this intervention takes up a sequence just mentioned but which occurred yesterday. The "switch" in it was from feeling a confident grasp of what she was thinking and experiencing to forgetting something or feeling out of touch. Again, the intervention serves to point toward something and respects the reality that only the analysand has a chance of "finding out" what might have happened.

Mrs. M: Well, I never saw anyone look the way you did yesterday when I left. Certainly my father never looked that way. He was big, brown, robust, *not* shriveled . . .

Analyst: If he was *not* shriveled, then you would not have to worry about speaking of feelings associated with something shriveled.

The analyst helps keep a perspective of attention in which the focus is not just on what the patient is saying but on what might have upset her. The analyst is not working toward making a summary, interpretive statement about the analysand's presumed dynamics.

Mrs. M: Absolutely! He was *not* shriveled! He was healthy looking even when he was sick. He kept pushing himself, going to work every day until the last week . . . Then he just withered before my very eyes. Everything but his jowls; they remained fleshy and baggy. When I was left in the room with him, there were times when his genitals were exposed. I was nervous about looking. What a time for my mother to leave us alone. For years, she couldn't stand for us to be together without her; then she leaves me with him as he is just about gone. He looked to me for comfort. I felt awkward being near him. I didn't know how to help him. I felt so alone. It's a similar feeling that I have with you sometimes when you miss the point . . . I try to go along with your direction but I resent it so much and feel so alone. I saw his genitals . . . his penis and testicles were all shriveled . . . not big like I expected. It was awful.

FRIDAY

MRS. M: I had a dream last night. I had a skinned, bloody beagle under my arm. It came to life. It looked like a penis becoming erect. I hate to see dead bodies, any kind of dead animal. Yesterday you looked dead. (Silence)

The analyst focuses attention on Mrs. M's trouble with speaking about some of this. She soon has an association to seeing her brother's flabby penis become erect in the bathtub and imagines herself yanking it off. In a rapid shift, she is feeling "all boxed in." Later, she talks of her husband's falling from a ladder and then of her binding him to "a beag . . . I mean bed." The analyst's focus on the moment the slip occurred leads to further memories, finally of a cat on a three-day (sexual) binge.

ANALYST: A cat on a three-day binge?

Gray argued that we should not "leap over the repression barrier" to tell analysands what was behind or beyond what they are saying. Here the analyst may hear in "cat on a three-day binge" an unrecognized reference to himself and his upcoming extra day off, but his intervention primarily brackets a portion of the surface and invites the analysand to reflect or pay attention there, too.

MRS. M: (Chuckle) You're going away for three days. Guess what I have in store for you when you return . . . if you dare? (She made a slashing motion in the air.)

ANALYST: There you express something in action that may seem dangerous to put into words.

The emergent thought here, the *drive derivative,* is about cutting (maybe castrating) the analyst. The analysand's ego rapidly, as if reflexively, transforms that sort of emerging comment into making the analyst guess, then into a gesture.

MRS. M: I'll cut your nuts . . . your penis, too. (She said with considerably less anxiety than on Monday.)

ANALYST: Now that you have told me that fantasy, could we look at your anxiety over it?

The analysand has been able, retracing her steps, to reconstruct what she might have been about to say when, instead, she made the slashing gesture. The analyst didn't choose to tell her why he thought she drew back from making such a comment in the first place, but instead invites her to reflect on that moment, to try to reengage the material.

MRS. M: I really care for you . . . and it's hard to believe that you won't withdraw from my cutting thoughts.

CLOSE PROCESS ATTENTION AND THE
TREATMENT OF PERSONALITY DISORDERS

Gray's *The Ego and Analysis of Defense* as well as many of the writings in a second book about close process attention, *Danger and Defense: The Technique of Close Process Attention, A Festschrift in Honor of Paul Gray* (Goldberger, 1996), describe a technique of psychoanalysis. This technique as it emerged first in the thoughts of Gray was believed to be particularly suitable to "analysands of the narrower scope." Whether such techniques might also be optimal ones for patients of many other sorts and if they are not optimal in these other cases, why not? are questions that remain to be answered.

In the next sections of this chapter, I raise some questions of this sort by undertaking a close process reading of descriptions of treatments published by Horowitz and Meissner. I clarify some of the similarities and differences between close process technique and these two examples of techniques of psychoanalytic psychotherapy and, at the same time, consider how and whether close process ideas need to be modified as we move into different forms of psychotherapeutic work. Can we, for example, use the perspectives of attention described by Gray even if, in the end, we do not choose exclusively close process interventions? Are Gray's recommendations as to the analysis of, rather than the therapist's influential use of, his authority less helpful as we move outward on the scope of therapies and patients treated? How should we think in these psychotherapy cases about the place of suggestion in the treatment? I begin with a look at three summaries provided by Horowitz concerning patients with Histrionic Personality Disorder. These summaries of traits and symptoms and of clinical observations and therapeutic changes provide a window to help us ask: What is it after all that we want to be looking at?

HOROWITZ ON THE TREATMENT OF
HISTRIONIC PERSONALITY DISORDER

Horowitz (1991) in *Hysterical Personality Style and the Histrionic Personality Disorder* introduces his subject with a chapter titled "Core Traits of Hysterical or Histrionic Personality Disorders." We could think of his discourse in this chapter as attempting to describe and delineate common hysterical or histrionic traits, signs, symptoms, and behaviors. For example:

> Patients who seek treatment for a hysterical personality disorder may complain of recurrent and uncontrolled episodes of emotional flooding of conscious experience. Feelings emerge involuntarily and then are hard to dispel. Thought is sometimes jumbled but seldom grossly irrational or delusional. Such patients complain that their interpersonal relationships are unsatisfactory.
>
> Aims at satisfying long-term relationships are periodically frustrated. There may be a sense of desperation and inability to "wait" for new relationships to develop gradually. The insistent need for attention can alienate others. Values may fluctuate according to the interests of current companions rather than the self. Naivete may be maintained, leading to poor interpersonal decisions and, eventually, to plummeting self-esteem. (p. 4)

I was impressed in reading Horowitz at the sense of familiarity I felt reading his descriptions and at the clarity and succinctness of description. But how do we best show these patients about traits? And how do we get into thinking with them about why these behaviors and feelings occur, how they came about, what functions they serve, and the like. Foucault (1972), in his extensive writings about medical and psychiatric discourses, notes, among many other criticisms, the tendency in such speech to summarize and unify. He would have reminded us that our signs and symptoms here and our related taxonomies, these apparent unities, are really models or attempted summarizations of aspects of countless specific experiences occurring in many people. They are "totalizing statements," attempts to substitute—for meanings dispersed over vast domains—simple supposed units of organization. Those of us who are not so zealously deconstructing nor operating primarily as philosophers or intellectual pioneers need our unities and our provisional certainties, but one advantage of Gray's method of focusing in on immediate, short time sequences is that he moves the observers (both patient and therapist) away from broad domains of speculation about and unification of now distant objects of interest toward events and sequences that, at least in temporal terms, are less dispersed though still dense and complex.

Horowitz does not use such descriptive, even taxonomic units to analyze his patients. As to his approach to clinical observation, consider his Table 5–2 concerning "Patterns and Change in Attention":

1. On wholes rather than details.
2. On persons' surface attitudes toward her rather than their intentions.
3. Selective inattention to some of her own actions.
4. Dominated by stimuli relevant to active, wishful, or fearful person schemas. (1991, p. 225)

Horowitz's "perspective of attention" is now not on traits but on his patient in a session. He is noticing how *the patient* pays attention. In this respect, his clinical vision resembles Gray's in that both analysts are tracking the patient's observing, "information processing" mind as it operates in the session. Horowitz's description of the patient's change in treatment shows a similar attention to observing ego: "Learned to attend to details, her own acts, contexts of interpersonal situations, and to clues to motives of self and other" (1991, p. 225).

Horowitz here and Gray are both in what Gray termed "the narrower scope" of traditional psychoanalyses. They both are impressed with the importance of encouraging development of nascent observing capacities. Horowitz's following summary, however, of his style of work in the first year of analysis of a patient with hysterical personality shows some significant differences in technical approach from close process attention:

> During the analytic hours she demanded and pleaded for help. She found it hard to verbalize her ideas and feelings and wanted the analyst to disclose his personal weaknesses so that she would feel comfortable enough to reveal hers. She reported many other kinds of treatment in which therapists were more revealing, kinder, more giving, faster, and better. She admitted that she consciously withheld information about current happenings. The analyst's response to these various maneuvers was to clarify what she was saying, largely by repetition. For example, with

transference issues he might say, "You want me to do something more active to help you," or "You don't think you can stand it if I just keep listening and tell you what I think is going on." With outside issues, the analyst attempted to clarify patterns of interaction and cause and effect. Again, the style involved short repetitions of what she had said and occasional requests for more detail. (1991, p. 206)

If before we were picturing Gray and Horowitz as interested in promoting observing ego, here Horowitz seems to function as if an auxiliary observing ego clarifying what the patient, too, might be beginning to see about herself. Most close process attention therapists would make fewer comments in the form: "You want . . ." or "You don't think . . ." to try to speak less *for* their patients and to try to raise more of a question about a moment of feeling and defense that the patient is invited to reflect on and perhaps speak about. *Sequences* within the patient's immediate working memory of the session are given priority over potential clarification of general patterns of behavior, thought, or feeling. And poorly recognized moments of danger-defense are selected for attention rather than presumed feeling or attitude states, which, in other methods, would be named.

I have not here attempted to bring out some of the advantages of Horowitz's methods but have selected passages intended to help point to contrasts that likely occur between his approaches and those I have been describing. Many different clinical techniques can be effective—at least in some cases—and it remains to be determined which methods have the most success with which patients. Horowitz's outcome reports are of great interest in this respect in that they might be showing how convergent various different but effective therapies can be in their results. And they hint at research waiting to be done, which could profitably look at the effectiveness of differing treatment approaches. As to the kind of somewhat specifiable treatment goals described by Horowitz (1991), consider his Table 5–5, "Patterns and Change in Associational Connections and Appraisal of Input Style":

1. Erroneously and excessively perceived present situations by associations organized by desired and dreaded role relationship models.
2. Inhibited her associations when she experienced negative affect (which was easily aroused).
3. Avoided designation of self as instigator of thoughts, feelings, or actions.
4. Inhibited threatening memories, but with concomitant tendency to intrusive representation of them, resulting in feeling a loss of conscious control.
5. Changed meaning of events by shifting schemas of self and object between active and passive roles or by losing reflective self-awareness in altered state of consciousness.
6. Poor chaining of concepts, memories, and plans into cause-and-effect sequences. (p. 236)

Change During Treatment

Learned to suppress and recall selectively, learned to tolerate uncertainty and continue problem-solving over time, learned to allow increased network of associations, less avoidance with less intrusion of warded-off contents, more realistic appraisals of own and others' roles with ability to model and check cause-and-effect sequences and events. (p. 236)

Though Horowitz and Gray, for example, would proceed in somewhat different ways with the kind of patient discussed, both roads seem to converge on the kind of changes that would tend to occur. All psychoanalytic methods and most psychotherapies, if sustained enough, may have in common that they promote self-observation and reflection.

MEISSNER'S TREATMENT OF THE PARANOID PROCESS

A different sort of contrast emerges if we compare therapeutic techniques used with one type of "wider scope" patients as described by Meissner (1986) in *Psychotherapy and the Paranoid Process*. Consider, for example, the surface chosen by the analyst in Meissner's "psychotherapeutic schema" recommended for work with "the paranoid process":

> The term "paranoid process" refers to a set of mechanisms that have both developmental and defensive components but which operate most critically in gradually delineating the individual's inner psychic world and his experience of an emerging sense of self. Correlatively, the paranoid process contributes to shaping the individual's experience of the significant objects in his experiential world. Consequently, the paranoid process contributes in important ways to the progressive individuation of a sense of inner cohesiveness and self-awareness, while at the same time it shapes and directs the progressive and continuing interaction with significant objects. (p. 17)

The schema is organized around the principle that the externalized elements of the paranoid process—specifically, the paranoid construction with its component projections—must be traced back to the underlying organization of introjects from which they derive and on which they depend. The organization and supporting forces contributing to the shaping and maintenance of the introjects can then be effectively worked through (Meissner, 1986, p. 39).

Meissner's theories are related to systematic ego psychology, object relations, and self-psychological points of view. In discussing the proposed "mechanisms of the paranoid process" (1986, p. 17), he emphasizes the roles of introjection, projection, and paranoid construction. In his therapy, then, he observes as if with a goal of separating and distinguishing reflections of introjects from the apparent products of projection or of paranoid constructive processes. His resulting focus gives priority to helping an understanding emerge of how paranoid patients experience themselves and their bodies and their "objects" and external world.

Meissner's technique aims to "identify the elements of the paranoid construction, and elicit and define within them the projective aspects, enabling us to shift back to an inner frame of reference and deal with the organization of the introjects as a central issue of the therapeutic endeavor." His language here (e.g., paranoid construction, projective aspects, introjects) is somewhat more abstract, theoretical, and inferential than that favored by Gray, but the key issue may be related to the question of what an individual does with his or her own theoretical and other ideas, which might not be very close to what our patients are actually thinking and "seeing." Gray wants us to maintain the patient's point of view in the sense of attempting to track along as the patient encounters objects and impulses and obstacles within his own thinking and feeling, which interfere with maximal self-expressiveness. And these inner objects and so on will be represented, including verbally in the patient's own terms.

Meissner, in his chapter on the psychotherapy of the paranoid patient, provides a kind of summary of how the therapist might work. In brackets, I have commented on some points of major contrast with close process techniques:

> For example, if a patient complains about the hostile and threatening attitudes of his fellow workers, the therapist is interested to know more about this difficult situation and to hear from the patient specific and detailed accounts of how fellow workers have demonstrated this hostility and their intentions to do harm to the patient. If the therapist's attitude in seeking such information is not confrontative or challenging, the patient is usually willing to present the details of his predicament and to present his story to the therapist.
>
> > [Close process methods assume the continuous and continuing task of free association. If patients can use such a method, therapists would tend to avoid becoming an authority who sets headings for or suggests a direction for the treatment. Patients are given every opportunity to say whatever they will next or to rebel against the therapist and not want to comply.]
>
> The very process of reconstructing the account for a sympathetic and noncritical listener begins the therapeutic process in the patient's own awareness. In telling the story and elaborating on its specifics, the patient is beginning the process of objectification that allows both the therapist and the patient himself to express, in an inchoatively distancing fashion, the facts, perceptions, and interpretations, and most particularly the emotional reactions, that constitute the material basis of the patient's projective system and his pathological reaction.
>
> > [Close process methods favor objects or surfaces of attention from within the session, meaning occurring in the act of talking to the therapist. Again, if patients can use such a method, therapists will focus less on "the facts, perceptions, and interpretations . . . and emotional reactions" as these supposed occurred "out there" (back then) and more on immediate experiences with the therapist.]
>
> In this detailed and objectifying recounting, it is almost inevitable that the patient's account not only presents elements from the projective system itself but also includes data deriving either directly or indirectly from the introjective level. If the patient is describing the malicious and hostile actions of his persecutors, there is an implication of his own sense of vulnerability and victimization. As the therapist listens to the account of these persecutors' hostility, he can usefully respond with empathic comments that convey to the patient a sense of his awareness of the patient's sense of threat, of the intensity and torment of his anxiety, and of how difficult it must have been and must be for the patient to be the object of such enmity and hostility. By the same token, and particularly where the elements of trust have found a sufficient footing, the therapist is also liable to hear more direct representations from the level of the patient's introjective organization. These will usually come in terms of descriptions of how threatened, anxious, and fearful the patient may have felt, or how vulnerable, weak, and helpless he may have felt, in the face of the threat of his adversaries. (1986, p. 244)

[Again, close process attention would focus less on "how difficult it must have been" and more on developing a shared awareness that "attempting spontaneity" is difficult and probably for reasons not unlike those that could be imagined might have occurred at the time of the events being reported. Reasonable therapists continue to differ about the wisdom and effectiveness of taking up paranoid and negative transference issues directly within the relationship with the therapist as opposed to in a current outside context. Close process work would tend to continue to help patients also look in even as they mainly focus out.]

CLOSE PROCESS ATTENTION IN PSYCHOTHERAPY

Although Gray's writings focused mainly on the use of close process attention in psychoanalysis, many of his followers have found that his way of thinking about the clinical situation has relevance to psychotherapy. As close process analysts turned their attention from analyses to psychotherapy and often as well to somewhat different kinds of patients, they encountered a variety of new issues and problems. Which patients can make use of and benefit from treatment using close process attention? Are modifications needed and, if so, of what type? How does an analyst test out and determine whether and when close process methods are efficacious?

Consider Hutchinson's (1996) chapter titled "Use of the Close Process Attention Technique in Patients with Impulse Disorders" in *Danger and Defense: The Technique of Close Process Attention* (Goldberger, 1996). In a kind of index to his paper, Hutchinson lists eight areas he selects for emphasis as he tries to bring close process insights to the treatment of impulsive, action-oriented patients:

The application of Gray's approach to impulsive patients can be considered in eight parts:

1. Analytic responses to powerful drive states.
2. Using words to replace action.
3. Analytic responses to the transference in those subject to primitive mental states.
4. Understanding the symbolic meanings of action.
5. Analyzing ego tendencies (defenses and regressions) that promote or permit impulsive action.
6. Ego splinting.
7. Modifying the harshness of the superego without weakening its necessary role in control of the drives and self-protection.
8. Establishing needed auxiliary modalities of treatment with a minimum of disruption to insight-oriented work. (Hutchinson, 1996, p. 144)

As many of Hutchinson's headings show, a fundamental issue in these treatments involves the analyst's selection of an analytic surface (a sequence for retrospective attention) now seen not so much in terms of shifts detectable within the "verbal stream" but in terms of often rapid and even disturbing shifts between various forms of action and enactment and from attitudes of self-observation and self-reflection to apparent absorption in action. The point selected for intervention must be "experience near" in the sense that it must include what such patients *can* observe about their experiences *in* the therapy. Gray's advice to maintain "a close and even focus on the audible flow of words and affects" (1994, p. 176) must be extended to include close attention to the flow of "action."

As we reflect on the analyst's trying to select an aspect of the surface for intervention, we have to accept that analytic perception is not just registration of what is there. As Schafer notes in a discussion of enactment in psychoanalysis:

> As soon as one reflects on what is being enacted, one comes face-to-face with the recognition that what seems to be a simple matter of perception is controlled, even if not fully determined, by preferred interpretive story lines (Schafer, 1992, 1997). These story lines, derived from master narratives, tell us how to conceive of unconscious mental functioning and unconscious intersubjectivity. For example, we may prefer to think in the traditional metapsychological manner of defenses struggling to ward off impulses and ending up in compromise formations; we may prefer to think of shifts between paranoid-schizoid and depressive positions (Segal, 1964), of fluctuations in the states of cohesiveness of the self (Kohut, 1977), or of changes in the "representational world" of self, objects, and their relationships that the ego, as one of its functions, builds up and then uses in constructing all new emotional-cognitive experience (Sandler & Rosenblatt, 1962). When we do confront this recognition, we realize that we must give up the assumption that what we do when we analyze is *un*cover or *dis*cover or *re*cover what is already there in fully developed form. (1997, pp. 124–125)

Schafer (1992, 1997), who like Gray is writing about analytic perception, reminds us that it's not just perception, but construction. The importance of the distinction may emerge as we begin to attempt to employ close process techniques and styles of perception to a wider scope of clinical problems and situations. In naïve or positivistic perceptual theories, we might imagine extending Gray's work by evolving lists such as Hutchinson's previously discussed for *all* clinical disorders in an attempt to correlate types of drive-derivative-defense moments with overall personality types and clinical presentations. However, Schafer's reminder that we are not finding these analytic objects but constructing them helps prepare us to look again at the issue of analytic observation.

There has been a tendency in psychoanalysis for clinical approaches to splinter into schools. Paul Gray's "ego psychological" methods, for example, might be seen as useful and appropriate for "neurotic" patients. Kohut's (1977) work leading to self-psychology initially was seen as particularly suited for work with narcissistic patients. Kernberg (1989) and object relations theory became associated with the treatment of patients with more severe personality disorders. Gabbard (1997) and Bram and Gabbard (2001) have argued for approaches that combine or incorporate "apparently dichotomous" (Gabbard, 1997, p. 15) positions. A split has occurred, for example, in modern psychoanalytic techniques between analysts such as Gray or classical structural analysts such as Brenner on one side and intersubjective analysts on the other. This split has sometimes been referred to as between "one-person" and "two-person" psychologies, but such summarizations can reduce and distort as much as they clarify. Bram and Gabbard (2001), in an attempted "conceptual clarification" of the concepts *potential space* and *reflective functioning*, introduce many of the challenges that face therapists hoping to move forward along a clinical developmental line highlighted by Gray. Their observations, like the close process attention literature, considers means of psychotherapeutic action via attention to and treatment of the ego's self-observational capacities. Drawing on work by Winnicott (1971), Fonagy and Target (1996), Target and Fonagy (1996), and others, Bram and Gabbard bring our clinical focus of attention to the therapeutic pair of minds, patient and therapist, as they attempt together to open a space and a cognitive process in which it is really possible to oscillate from experiencing to reflection and even to creativity. Such would be Hutchinson's goal, for example, because he recommends finding words for actions and Kernberg's because he attends first to whatever might threaten the treatment itself. Said metaphorically, if the whole atmosphere of treatment is agreed to be not safe, an analyst works to open a space or some spaces somewhere within it, in which patient and therapist can *think* and especially in which they can think about the treatment experience itself. Considered in its broadest meanings, such space may eventually serve to integrate the multiple "story lines" referred to by Schafer. "It" may become a place where patients and therapists can imagine and reflect on their experiences together from multiple observational perspectives. Close process attention may serve especially to highlight observing processes themselves, their inherent problems, and conflictual nature.

We know that most modern psychotherapies have moved away from the use of free association as a central task for the patient. The question we now should ask is whether such moves (or turns) to techniques based on "free communication" but not free association were true advances in technique or whether an updated approach, such as Gray's, to introducing the method of free association and working with resistances to it would make abandoning free association unnecessary and unwise. Seen from the perspectives of patient and therapist about to undertake a psychotherapy, free association can seem an alien, if not intolerable, task. Speaking of patients at the beginning of treatment, Gray (1994) remarks: "Analysands are not familiar with the nature of the activities in which the mind-at-surface quietly engages while they are speaking. Indeed, they are barely even aware of the existence of these activities" (p. 76).

What remains to be seen is whether psychoanalytic psychotherapists who are more interested in and knowledgeable about these mind-at-surface activities can learn to base psychotherapies there. And, we still don't understand enough about which psychotherapy patients will do best if treated with close process methods. Does the necessary level of patient-therapist cooperation have to be reasonably high early on and throughout the therapy, or can the struggles on the way to cooperation provide a useful enough base from which to work and progress? In object relations terms, Gray's technique assumes a certain level both of self- and object representation and stability so that an analyst could rely enough on the patient's observing ego and constructive, cooperative capacities to ally with similar capacities in the analyst allowing for mutual cooperative work. In treatments in which both self-observation and therapeutic cooperation are too infused with primitive and destructive processes (especially primitive aggression), primary attention has to be on just these threats to the treatment (see, for example, Kernberg, 1989, concerning his recommendation that the treatment focus follow a "hierarchy of thematic priority," p. 55) so that first attention is given to those developments in the treatment posing maximal threat to lives or to the treatment. In developmental terms, we need to learn whether certain aspects of self-observation require developmental achievements during certain earlier crucial developmental periods or whether (and to what extent) problems of self-reflection are remediable by later favorable experiences.

The question of whether close process methods can work in any particular case needs to be kept genuinely open. As Davison et al. said:

> There are patients who can rarely use close process monitoring. We do not know why this is so. It is not entirely intelligence-dependent. We need more experience to answer that question. With such people we use it sparingly. (Davison et al., 1996, pp. 39–40)

Addressing questions as to how to assess suitability for psychoanalysis, Rothstein (1995), in his *Creation of Psychoanalytic Patients,* argued that our current predictive powers are not such that we can know at the time of assessment except in broad terms which patients will be suitable for and might benefit from psychoanalysis. He argued that often analysts' reluctances to undertake treatment of certain patients may reflect countertransference issues that have not been sufficiently recognized and worked through rather than reliable prediction that the patient could not benefit from or tolerate analysis. Rothstein contends that a better predictor is an actual trial of analysis. I believe in an analogous way that many more patients can benefit from struggling with a free association-based psychotherapy than are currently offered such an approach. And as with Rothstein's trial analyses, it is likely that the most reliable way to come to know peoples' capacities to talk freely and spontaneously and to learn to observe their own minds in action at this task is to let them try it. Gray's emphases on the collaborative nature of the investigation and on the mutual goal of learning about how a particular individual experiences threats and copes with them are especially important in therapies that begin with patients who seem to come to the therapeutic situation with the expectation that they will be guided through the therapy process. Those attempting to use close process techniques in psychodynamic psychotherapies will have to learn how to blend enough attention to educating their patients in key aspects of a free-associative approach with enough analytic abstinence and restraint to open the space for these patients to free associate and attempt spontaneity.

SUMMARY AND CONCLUSIONS

Some central concepts of the close process attention method of psychoanalysis, as originally developed by Gray and colleagues, have been described and illustrated by extended excerpts from a week of such a clinical psychoanalysis reported by Davison et al. (1996). As a way of considering the potential applicability of such techniques to psychotherapies of patients with various personality disorders, Horowitz's approach to patients with Histrionic Personality Disorder and Meissner's approach to patients with paranoid disorders are discussed, and I highlight similarities and differences between close process and other psychoanalytic techniques as these address issues of personality.

It may be that, concerning therapeutic action, "all roads lead to Rome" in the sense that many clinical methods, when applied with the most skill and concern and in the right cases, show benefits. It seems too early to tell where close process attention will fit into the broad field of psychotherapies, whether it will mainly be used as a discrete method of treatment, or whether therapists will learn to integrate its wisdom and effectiveness into non-close-process clinical approaches. It would not be surprising if close process attention techniques came to play a leading role in particular in the understanding and treatment of those aspects of human problems that seem especially to hinge on difficulties with and deficits in the self-observing function.

REFERENCES

Bram, A. D., & Gabbard, G. O. (2001). Potential space and reflective functioning toward conceptual clarification and preliminary clinical implications. *International Journal of Psychoanalysis, 82*, 685–699.

Brenner, C. (1982). *The mind in conflict*. New York: International Universities Press.

Brenner, C. (1987). A structural theory perspective. *Psychoanalytic Inquiry, 7*, 167–171.

Davison, W. T., Pray, M., Bristol, C., & Welker, R. (1996). Defense analysis and mutative interpretation. In M. Goldberger (Ed.), *Danger and defense: The technique of close process attention a festschrift in honor of Paul Gray*. Northvale, NJ: Aronson.

Fonagy, P., & Target, M. (1996). Playing with reality: I. Theory of mind and the normal development of psychic reality. *International Journal of Psychoanalysis, 77*, 217–233.

Foucault, M. (1972). *The archaeology of knowledge*. New York: Pantheon Books.

Freud, A. (1966). *The ego and the mechanisms of defense: The writings of Anna Freud* (Vol. 2). New York: International Universities Press. (Original work published 1936)

Freud, S. (1926). Inhibitions, symptoms and anxiety. In J. Strachey (Ed.), *The standard edition of the complete psychological works of Sigmund Freud* (Vol. 20, pp. 75–175). London: Hogarth Press.

Gabbard, G. O. (1997). A reconsideration of objectivity in the analyst. *International Journal of Psychoanalysis, 78*, 15–26.

Goldberger, M. (Ed.). (1996). *Danger and defense: The technique of close process attention a festschrift in honor of Paul Gray*. Northvale, NJ: Aronson.

Gray, P. (1973). Psychoanalytic technique and the ego's capacity for viewing intrapsychic conflict. *Journal of the American Psychoanalytic Association, 21*, 474–494.

Gray, P. (1982). "Developmental lag" in the evolution of technique for psychoanalysis of neurotic conflict. *Journal of the American Psychoanalytic Association, 30*, 621–655.

Gray, P. (1994). *The ego and analysis of defense*. Northvale, NJ: Aronson.

Horowitz, M. J. (1991). *Hysterical personality style and the histrionic personality disorder*. Northvale, NJ: Aronson.

Hutchinson, J. H. (1996). Use of the close process attention technique in patients with impulse disorders. In M. Goldberger (Ed.), *Danger and defense: The technique of close process attention a festschrift in honor of Paul Gray* (pp. 131–172). Northvale, NJ: Aronson.

Kernberg, O. F. (1989). *Psychodynamic psychotherapy of borderline patients*. New York: Basic Books.

Kohut, H. (1977). *The restoration of the self*. New York: International Universities Press.

Levenson, L. (2003). *The patient's resistance to awareness of the analyst's presence*. (Unpublished manuscript).

Meissner, W. W. (1986). *Psychotherapy and the paranoid process*. Northvale, NJ: Aronson.

Pray, M. (1996). Two different methods of analyzing defense. In M. Goldberger (Ed.), *Danger and defense: The technique of close process attention a festschrift in honor of Paul Gray* (pp. 53–106). Northvale, NJ: Aronson.

Reik, T. (1948). *Listening with the third ear*. New York: Farrar, Straus.

Ritvo, S. (in press). *Conflicts of aggression in coming of age*.

Rothstein, A. (1995). *Psychoanalytic technique and the creation of analytic patients.* Madison, CT: International Universities Press.

Sandler, J., & Rosenblatt, B. (1962). The concept of the representational world. *Psychoanalytic Study of the Child, 17,* 128–145.

Schafer, R. (1992). *Retelling a life.* New York: Basic Books.

Schafer, R. (1997). *Tradition and change in psychoanalysis.* Madison, CT: International Universities Press.

Segal, H. (1964). *Introduction to the work of Melanie Klein.* New York: Basic Books.

Silverman, M. (1987). Clinical material. *Psychoanalytic Inquiry, 7*(2), 147–165.

Target, M., & Fonagy, P. (1996). Playing with Reality II. *International Journal of Psychoanalysis, 77* 459–480.

Winnicott, D. W. (1971). *Playing and reality.* New York: Routledge.

CHAPTER 14

Application of Eye Movement Desensitization and Reprocessing (EMDR) to Personality Disorders

Philip Manfield and Francine Shapiro

SINCE ITS INFCEPTION in 1987, EMDR has evolved into an integrated approach to psychotherapy that synthesizes aspects of the major psychological orientations. As such, its comprehensive treatment effects span cognitive, somatic, and affective domains (Shapiro, 2002). Although most widely used to process single or multiple incident traumatic memories, it can be used effectively to treat many conditions. In this chapter, we describe the theoretical foundations of this approach and how it is used to treat personality disorders.

THEORETICAL COMPONENTS OF THE MODEL

The development of EMDR began with the discovery that certain types of eye movements had a direct effect on cognitive processes and contributed to the resolution of troubling memories (Shapiro, 1989, 2001). Soon, other forms of stimulation were identified that produced the same effects (referred to collectively in this chapter as *EMs*; Shapiro, 1991, 1994).

To explain the clinical phenomena and patterns of memory that rapidly and consistently emerged during treatment sessions, an information processing model was developed. The resulting Adaptive Information Processing Model (Shapiro, 1995, 2001), which guides EMDR clinical practice, considers the psyche to be generally capable of self-healing, unless impeded in some way. It is believed that an intrinsic information processing mechanism functions to take disturbance to a level of mental health. That is, what is useful is learned, stored with appropriate affect, and available to effectively guide the person in the future. However, disturbing events can disrupt the brain's normal integrative process and cause experiences to be stored only partially processed, cut off from the rest of the memory system. A sign of dysfunctional storage is that memories include vivid aspects (e.g., affects, sensations) of the perceptions experienced at the time of the event. From the vantage point of the information processing model, any event that has a lasting negative effect on self or psyche is termed a *trauma*. Events of the type required for a diagnosis of Posttraumatic Stress Disorder (PTSD) are termed *large T traumas*. Those ubiquitous events that permeate childhood, such as accidents and humiliations, are termed *small t traumas*. Regardless of origins, these unprocessed events are viewed as the potential source of present dysfunction due to the incorporation of the earlier images, thoughts, sounds, emotions, physical sensations, or beliefs.

> These earlier perceptions may be accurate depictions of reality, or they may be intrinsically distorted because of the engendered affect, or an interaction of the experience and previously encoded dysfunction. Regardless, inappropriate fears of abandonment, lack of love, fear of failure, and all the ubiquitous psychic pains that mar a person's present existence can generally be traced to early childhood experiences physically stored in the brain. (Shapiro, 2002, pp. 10–11)

A tenet of the Adaptive Information Processing Model is that initial memories underlying current symptoms can be located and processed and that even characterological issues can be resolved when the underlying events have been successfully addressed.

RANGE OF PSYCHOPATHOLOGY AND PERSONALITY DISORDERS WITHIN SCOPE OF TREATMENT

Eye movement desensitization and reprocessing is used to address the experiential contributors to disorders and gaps in personal development. As such, it can be successfully applied to a wide range of psychopathology. It is believed that specific diagnoses offer important information about case management and the types of symptoms and characteristics that need to be addressed. In all cases, after appropriate stabilization, the memories that have set the symptoms in motion are directly processed. Personality disorders are viewed as a combination of characteristics that individually are based on early life experiences. These habitual responses are addressed by the EMDR processing of stored memories and incorporation of positive experiences needed to overcome the developmental deficits that have resulted in inappropriate intrapsychic and interpersonal patterns. Individual types of personality disorders are addressed with different case management strategies, depending on the particular types of early experiences and developmental deficits that are involved and the defensive patterns that result. Special care is taken to determine each client's readiness for processing of historical events.

TREATMENT METHODS AND TECHNICAL ASPECTS AND INTERVENTIONS

Eye movement desensitization and reprocessing treatment methods are intended to simultaneously attend to client management and information processing. In each of the interventions, the client-centered approach is geared to assist the client to maintain a state of equilibrium, manage negative affects that may emerge, and attain a state of personal empowerment. All interventions simultaneously are geared to enhance the targeting and reprocessing of information. *Reprocessing* is defined as the structured elicitation of a rapid learning state in which clients gain new insights and appropriate affects as experiences are assimilated into larger memory networks. The eight-phase approach used to identify and process relevant experiences is described next.

Eye Movement Desensitization and Reprocessing Eight-Phase Approach

Reprocessing is accomplished using an eight-phase approach. Each phase contains procedures to both help contain clients and facilitate rapid processing. These phases are the building blocks for EMDR treatment. The choice of targets for relatively straightforward conditions such as single incident traumas, phobias, or excessive grief is guided by a unique protocol particular to each condition, usually involving the earliest or source event related to the condition, the most recent related event or situation that elicits distress, and, finally, an imagined future event, or future template, which incorporates the affective and cognitive patterns the client will need to respond to in a new way. *Positive templates* involve the use of EMDR to enable a client to assimilate or solidify new skills and behaviors. The basic three-pronged protocol is used to determine the targets of processing during the eight phases.

Phase I: History   A careful history is taken to identify potential *targets* for processing, which include (1) past experiences that have become the foundation for dysfunction, (2) present situations that trigger disturbance, and (3) skills and behaviors needed for optimal functioning in the future. *Target* refers to a disturbing issue, situation, feeling, or memory used as an initial focus for EMDR processing. Special attention is given to memories for which the client still carries an emotional charge, either negative or positive. These include fearful or dangerous situations experienced or witnessed, sudden losses, experiences of humiliation or shame, significant successes, peak experiences, and moments of pride, confidence, or well-being. Maladaptive beliefs are also identified, and an overall treatment plan is discussed.

When the client has a personality disorder, this first phase is greatly extended. Because people with personality disorders often do not remember important formative childhood experiences, it is usually necessary to collect historical information in more creative ways. For instance, some therapists make extensive genograms or timelines to elaborate the client's history. Therapists may discuss movies and books that impacted emotionally on the client to try to identify themes that carry emotional charge. With EMDR, it is often not necessary to identify an actual experience when a fantasy image, cinematic image, or dream can be targeted in its place and achieve the same result. Even if the substitute image does not lead the client through associations to the actual source memories, the disturbing emotional content coupled with the maladaptive cognitions can often be resolved.

Phase II: Client Preparation   In the second phase, a groundwork is laid using specific metaphors and instructions to enhance client equilibrium and prepare them for disturbing affects that may arise during processing. Before beginning EMDR for the first time, it is recommended that the client identify a *safe place,* an image or memory that elicits comfortable feelings and a positive sense of self. This safe place can be used later to bring closure to an incomplete session, to help a client tolerate a particularly upsetting session, and to serve as a self-control technique for the client between sessions. Also helpful is to identify someone the client thinks of as a loving and well-intentioned person whose realistic mature positive perspective can be called into consciousness at times when the client may be having difficulty thinking of a memory from any point of view other than the maladaptive one established at the time the event first occurred.

Like the history-taking phase, this phase is also greatly extended and elaborated when the client has a personality disorder. More often than not, there is a flow back and forth between the preparation phase and the processing of events. In the preparation phase for personality disorders, the safe place exercise is enormously expanded. Real safe places can be difficult or sometimes impossible to find for clients with borderline, schizoid, and other personality disorders. When a safe place cannot be found in the real world, it must be constructed in the world of imagination.

Clients with personality disorders have limited access to their emotional resources. A set of procedures known as *EMDR Resource Development and Installation* (Korn & Leeds, in press; Leeds, 1998; Leeds & Shapiro, 2000; Phillips, 2001; Shapiro, 2001) can be used to increase their access to positive affects. Clients who do not tolerate affect well usually have difficulty accessing both negative and positive affect-laden memories. When a positive memory is held in mind, short sets of EMs allow positive affect to increase, vivifying the memory and allowing it to become more readily accessed. This process strengthens clients' access to positive affects in a relatively nonthreatening way. It can, for instance, help to imbue in clients a sense of safety or confidence through focusing on real or imagined experiences of self-efficacy or through identification with personally meaningful symbols of these quantities. In addition, the exercises developed by Linehan (1993) in her dialectic behavioral therapy for teaching borderline clients the practical skills necessary for functioning in the world without being self-destructive or creating crises are appropriate for the preparation phase and can be enhanced with EMs.

Clients with personality disorders, who may have friends for whom EMDR treatment involved a total of three sessions for treatment of simple PTSD, often seek EMDR expecting a three-session resolution of characterologically based issues. During the assessment phase, clients are oriented to the EMDR process and given information to help them fashion realistic expectations for their EMDR treatment.

Phase III: Assessment   During the third phase, the therapist helps the client to select a memory for processing and to identify an image that represents that memory. As in other treatments, choosing a memory when the client has a personality disorder resembles peeling an onion; the therapist cannot focus initially on the core memories because they are not sufficiently accessible to the client, so he or she works with the layers that are accessible and gradually moves deeper as the client becomes more stable and able to tolerate more intense work. Together, they also identify a negative self-statement that expresses the distortion in self-image (negative cognition) that arose from the targeted experience and a positive cognition that the client would like to replace it with. For example, a woman who is processing a childhood molestation felt guilty that she "let it happen," despite the fact that she was a child at the time and the perpetrator was a grown man much bigger and stronger than she. Her negative cognition was, "I'm a slut." Her positive cognition was, "It wasn't my fault. I did the best I could." Subjective measurements are solicited from the client of the currently felt validity of the positive cognition (VOC) as measured on a scale from one to seven (Shapiro, 1989, 1995) and the intensity of disturbance experienced when the memory is recalled as measured by Wolpe's (1958) Subjective Units of Disturbance Scale (SUDS). This phase also includes the identification of the emotions that arise when the client focuses on the selected memory and the location of the physical sensations in the client's body that correlate to the memory. All of these components, the image, the negative cognition, and the related dysphoric affect help to focus the client on the specific target material being processed.

Phase IV: Desensitization   In the fourth phase, reprocessing is inaugurated. The byproducts of this reprocessing are a desensitization of negative affects, elicitation of insights and awareness of associative links, and shifts to positive somatic states. Initially, the therapist asks the client to focus simultaneously on the image, the negative cognition, and the attendant disturbing body sensations. While the client is doing this, the therapist applies an alternating bilateral stimulation (EMs), which may take the form of moving a pointer from side to side for the client to follow with his or her eyes, playing a series of tones that alternate bilaterally, or physically tapping the client in an alternating bilateral fashion. The salutary effect of the EMs is discussed later in the section on mechanisms of change. After a set of EMs, the client is asked to report *briefly* on what has come up; this may be a thought, a feeling, a physical sensation, an image, a memory, or a change in any one of the previous. In the initial instructions to the client, the therapist also encourages the client to feel free to say there is nothing new to report.

Typically, after clients describe their experience and associations from the previous set of EMs, the therapist asks them to focus on the material they just described and begins a new set of EMs. This aspect of EMDR resembles classical free association. However, according to certain prescribed procedures, the therapist may also direct the client to focus on the original target memory or on some other image, thought, feeling, fantasy, physical sensation, or memory.

Although reprocessing is generally very straightforward and rapid in cases of uncomplicated trauma, there are many instances, particularly with personality disorders, where the clinician must be more active. The *cognitive interweave* (Shapiro, 1995, 2001) is an intervention used in certain situations when the processing seems to be stalled in which the therapist provides some direction or information designed to restart the processing.

One of the central principles of the Adaptive Information Processing Model is that, like the body, the psyche will heal itself unless blocked in some way. By observing the healing process as it normally occurs, therapists can recognize what needs to happen for clients whose healing process is blocked. For instance, sometimes clients get stuck in frightening memories. It was observed (Shapiro, 1995) during successful processing of traumatic memories with many clients that the issues of responsibility, safety, and choice would spontaneously emerge, usually in that order. As the memory was being processed, clients would recognize that what happened was not their responsibility, releasing them from the feelings of guilt that the experience had engendered. As processing continued, they would realize that they were not in current danger. Finally, they would recognize that, although when they had originally been trapped in a child's body, there was no way to escape the perpetrator, they were now adult with many new resources; their sense of helplessness would be replaced by the recognition that they now have choices.

With the observation of this sequence of issues involving responsibility, safety, and choice, it was realized that if a client became stuck, the process could be jump started by suggesting the missing piece in this sequence: "Whose responsibility was it that this happened?" "Where is he now? Can he still hurt you?" "Can you prevent that from happening to you as an adult?" The therapist mimics the resolution pattern observed in successful treatments to supply the missing piece necessary for processing to continue. Once the process is restarted, it tends to resume its spontaneous course to resolution. In general, the cognitive interweave involves asking a question, giving directions, or offering a missing piece of information in a manner intended to mimic spontaneous processing. Different interweaves are used depending on the type of block observed in the client.

Regardless of whether a cognitive interweave was used, the client's own associative process is encouraged throughout this phase. The overarching goal is to allow the targeted memory to arrive at an adaptive resolution, which often involves recognizing how the experience is connected with other life events and present concerns. The desensitization phase ends when the SUDS has reached a value of zero or one on a scale from zero to 10. At this point, the client has generally achieved significant insight and understanding in addition to the elimination of negative affect.

Clients with personality disorders require extensive preparation and careful selection of targets, especially in the early stages of treatment. In addition, these clients require careful monitoring and intervention by the therapist to ensure that the client's defenses do not sabotage the session by changing, distorting, or broadening the EMDR target. Despite a thorough preparation phase, it is often necessary to do further preparation as new deeper targets emerge.

Phase V: Installation   When the therapist judges that the desensitization is complete or as complete as can be hoped for given the client's current life condition, the client is asked to simultaneously hold in his or her mind the remainder of the original memory and the appropriate positive cognition, something that would not have been possible until the desensitization had been accomplished. This resolution of two initially conflicting phenomena is reinforced by a short set of EMs. During this *installation*, the client usually also experiences a feeling of well-being and a sense of accomplishment.

For clients with personality disorders, reaching the installation phase represents a significant achievement. They are being asked to hold the originally disturbing memory and, at the same time, the positive cognition. To do this, they cannot continue to split with respect to this memory; they must hold what was once a very negative memory and simultaneously a positive orientation in relation to this memory. With this population, it is generally not possible to attain this stage within one session. The processing of pivotal memories may proceed over a period of weeks before adaptive resolution is achieved. When the disturbance level is not especially high, but the target is not yet completely processed, the therapist can help the client to focus on some small shift that has occurred during the processing as a substitute for installation. A question such as, "What is the most important thing you learned today?" can often elicit suitable content. Progress with these clients occurs in very small increments, and it is useful to underscore what progress has occurred to help ensure that it is retained.

Phase VI: Body Scan   To verify whether the target has in fact been completely processed, clients are asked to scan their bodies for any remaining disturbing sensations. Usually, if an aspect of the target was not fully processed, clients report some uncomfortable sensation in their bodies. If a disturbing sensation is located, it becomes the focus of a few sets of eye movements to see if there is more material related to the original target or if, as is most often the case, the body sensation will disappear.

Phase VII: Closure   As the session is brought to a close, clients are instructed that the processing they have just done may continue after the session and to keep an informal log of whatever they notice between sessions that might be useful to target in the future. If the disturbance associated with the target has not been sufficiently eliminated, the therapist can use various techniques to help clients contain any remaining affect and leave the session feeling comfortable and with an appreciation of what has been accomplished.

Even neurotic clients are often resistant to maintaining a log between sessions, but clients with personality disorders are even more so, probably because keeping a log requires that they think about the therapy between sessions and maintain awareness of the issue being processed. Clients whose primary defense is splitting try to retain the positive part of the split in their conscious awareness, while keeping out of conscious awareness the negative part. Until a strong therapeutic alliance has been established, clients with personality disorders will not cooperate in maintaining a log that would represent a continual reminder of the very material they try to avoid.

Phase VIII: Reevaluation   The therapist normally begins the following session with a reevaluation of the results of the previous session. The therapist checks the subjective disturbance rating of the target from the previous session and asks whether the progress achieved has been sustained. Continuity between sessions is very important, especially with clients with personality disorders. By checking the level of disturbance remaining on the previous session's target, the therapist finds out how well the work of the previous session has held and conveys the message that each session is part of an ongoing process. In addition, beginning a session in this way helps to keep the session focused, preventing the client from opening a plethora of issues that will dilute or dissipate the treatment process.

The reevaluation phase leads the clinician to identify what targets need to be processed. Although many protocols have been written to address various disorders, it is important to address the early memories that set the foundation for the dysfunction, the present situations that trigger the disturbance, and *positive templates* for appropriate future action. For the positive template, also referred to as a *future template,* clients mentally rehearse making new choices in a situation resembling the original target to enable them to assimilate or solidify their new skills and behaviors. The imagined event is processed using the standard procedures just as a past event would be. If the original event was thoroughly addressed, the positive template will usually process very quickly.

PROCESS OF THERAPEUTIC APPROACH

The basic eight-phase approach can often be used straightforwardly with clients with personality disorders, as long as the target is relatively insulated from characterological issues. For instance, a narcissistic man is arrested in a police sting operation for soliciting a police officer posing as a prostitute. He spends a night in jail, pays a large fine, and is put on three years' probation. Feeling humiliated, he fragments, isolates himself from family and friends, and is unable to function effectively at work. For him, the worst moment was standing before the judge in court and feeling like a delinquent adolescent. This experience has no direct correlates in his past. In childhood, he had always succeeded in being looked on favorably by parents and authorities. Targeting his worst moment and using the simple eight-step process, he was able to resolve his feelings of humiliation and feel again like an adult, recognizing that he had received a very clear societal prohibition through the legal system about soliciting prostitutes.

When processing the actual character disorder, the process is obviously much longer and more complex. It can be roughly conceptualized as (1) stabilization, (2) working in the past, (3) working in the present, and (4) working in the future.

1. Stabilization   Like most other treatment approaches, much time is spent in EMDR treatment stabilizing the client. Clients are prepared for processing through the building of a therapeutic alliance and the use of the previously mentioned safe place and resource development techniques. Only after the client is able to tolerate negative affects and access positive affects is the processing of memories attempted.

2. Working in the Past   When the client seems ready and a target is identified that is accessible and appropriate for the client, EMDR processing is used to reprocess it. As clients succeed in processing memories, typically they feel stronger, explore new feelings, and experiment with new behaviors, which are sometimes successful and sometimes not. The therapist uses future templates to assist clients in preparing for these new experiences. The reevaluation phase is important because failures uncover new issues and new targets that the client needs to address. So, periods of appropriate targeting of memories are separated by periods of consolidation and experimentation, which lead to more resource building and new targets. As in other therapies, the EMDR therapist can jump ahead conceptually and guess at the nature of the client's underlying issues and targets, but readiness is essential, and the therapist must wait for clients to come along at their own pace as each layer of the onion is peeled.

3. Working in the Present   As the intense targets from the past become scarcer and as the client experiments with new skills and new behaviors, new targets continue to be identified. These targets, however, are usually relatively straightforward and easily processed; they are not related to deep or characterological issues, but to present stimuli that elicit disturbance. Clients' experience of this phase is one of discovery, realizing how behaviors that they have not even thought to identify as problems are actually related to early memories.

4. Working in the Future   During the final phase of treatment leading up to termination, feelings of loss, separation, independence, and abandonment associated with termination generate still more targets. Processing with EMs becomes more effective and rapid as the client becomes more whole and can more easily self-reference. There is additional focus on new choices the client will need to make in the future; anticipatory fears are targeted as well as positive templates that incorporate appropriate future behaviors.

CLINICAL CASE EXAMPLES

Background and History of Mr. A

Mr. A, a male in his early 40s, came to treatment (with the first author, P. M.) for severe depression and suicidal ideation after the breakup of a seven-year romantic relationship. Due to the constraints of managed care, he was seen once weekly. He described his childhood as one in which he excelled for the benefit of his parents. He felt unnoticed as a person by his parents but valued for his superior academic and athletic performance, which they bragged about to friends. Both parents appeared narcissistic and blaming, devaluing Mr. A whenever he disappointed them in the slightest. They both worked and he spent a fair amount of time with his mother's mother. There were many examples of unexplainable cruelty directed specifically at Mr. A on the part of the grandmother, which she justified by saying that he was not worthy of better treatment. He had been successful in college and landed a high profile job but was unable to retain it because of his social awkwardness and his lofty ideals, combined with uncompromising rigidity.

Clinical Presentation

Mr. A appeared to be highly motivated. He spoke carefully and without emotion, although during discussion of painful subjects, a barely discernable tightness in his throat betrayed emotion just below the surface. He lived alone and was profoundly isolated. He had no friends except an ex-girlfriend and shared his thoughts and feelings with no one; when asked about it, he stated that he believed that no one could be interested in anything personal that he might have to say. He not only felt this to be true but also believed it intellectually; he could find no data to contradict that belief. During the preparation phase when asked who in his life he had experienced as well-meaning and caring, he thought about the question and said that he believed no one had ever cared about him. When asked if he was religious, he said that he was a very religious man, and then, when asked if he thought that God loved him, he became sad and, avoiding a direct answer, said he thought that for some reason God was punishing him.

Diagnostic Formulation

Mr. A appeared to be in the schizoid-avoidant continuum, although a depressive personality disorder is not ruled out. His parents and his grandmother were narcissistic and extremely demanding. They tyrannized and berated him when he did not comply perfectly. The poignancy of his presentation, with emotion often just below the surface but never quite coming through, and his lack of relationships appeared schizoid or avoidant. He also had more access to childhood memories than is typical of other personality disorders (Manfield, 1992). Without outward affect, he was able to describe half a dozen specific memories that had been intensely emotionally painful for him.

TREATMENT PROCESS

The typical client with a personality disorder can describe a history of abusive treatment, but cannot recall specific examples. Mr. A's extensive recall of childhood memories, probably due to his ability to dissociate most of the affect from the factual memories of these events, made treatment easier. The initial sessions involved a careful review of his history with considerable attention paid to finding nurturing relationships that could later serve as a foundation for cathecting positive affects. A wide range of potential relationships was explored including romantic interests, relatives, friends, teachers, and ministers. None were found, except his ex-girlfriend, who was not useful for the purposes of EMDR because, although he was still friendly with her and she was the only person he would talk to at all, she still represented loss and rejection.

After reviewing his history, it was clear that he felt too isolated and vulnerable to process his painful memories of rejection and devaluation and that it would be necessary to develop internalized nurturing objects. In traditional therapies, the client's relationship with the therapist often serves as a central relationship resource, requiring a fair amount of treatment time before reaching a level of strength necessary for it to function in this role. In EMDR, less treatment time is required for this purpose because the therapeutic relationship is only one among other relationship resources and usually plays a less important role, although during abreactions the therapist's reassuring comments provide important emotional support and serve to help maintain the client's connection to the present therapeutic context. In the quest for nurturing objects for Mr. A, attention was turned to his other acquaintances, his job, and how he spent his free time, with the dual purpose of learning more about Mr. A and continuing to search for emotional resources. By the eighth session, the closest to a nurturing figure that had been found were some superficial relationships with coworkers. When no real relationship can be found, it is often necessary to turn to imagined relationships (Manfield, 1998; Shapiro, 1995, 2001). (In the transcripts that follow, the symbols ◇◇ represent a short set of eye movements. Although not specifically stated, it can be assumed that before the set began, the therapist said something akin to "think of that" and, after a set, the therapist asked Mr. A what he noticed or what was coming up.)

THERAPIST: Can you think of any public figures that you feel connected to?
CLIENT: No, I don't read the newspaper, and I try not to get involved in politics.
THERAPIST: I'm thinking of maybe actors, characters in movies that you liked or identified with.
CLIENT: Not really. To me, they're just stories.
THERAPIST: Well, stories can be meaningful. They can have characters whom you respect or admire. Heroes. What about fables or mythology, are there any characters from mythology you admire?
CLIENT: They're just not real to me. Oh, I just thought of someone I admire, Leo Bascalia. Do you know who he is?

THERAPIST: Yes, I've heard him on some specials on PBS. What do you admire about him?

CLIENT: Well, he seems like a good person. He seems to want to help people.

THERAPIST: Can you visualize him?

CLIENT: Yes, he's standing in front of an audience.

THERAPIST: Close your eyes and concentrate on that image. ◇◇ What came up for you when you did that?

CLIENT: I can see his face; he has a friendly face.

THERAPIST: Good, think of that. ◇◇

Comment on process and technique: The client is visually oriented. The therapist is making the memory of Mr. Bascalia more vivid by encouraging Mr. A to look at the image rather than think about it.

Technical intervention: Require the client to look at his image rather than generalize or conceptualize. Use EMs to make the image more vivid.

CLIENT: Nothing different. I still see his face.

THERAPIST: Can you imagine him with his family?

CLIENT: Yes. ◇◇ I think he is probably a good father. Loving. He probably grew up in a warm, healthy family himself.

THERAPIST: Can you picture his family?

CLIENT: Yes.

THERAPIST: What do you see that tells you he's a good father? ◇◇

CLIENT: Well, I'm imagining his family. I don't know how many kids he has, but I think of him as having two, and he has one hand on each of their shoulders, like they're posing for a picture.

Comment on process and technique: The therapist continues to make the memory of Mr. Bascalia more vivid. The purpose of this process is to create a felt sense in Mr. A's mind of a supportive, caring figure. The client's description of specific visual details is an indication of progress in making the image more real.

Technical intervention: Encourage focusing on the nurturing supportive qualities of Mr. Bascalia.

THERAPIST: Girls or boys?

CLIENT: One of each, a boy and a girl.

THERAPIST: What other details do you notice? ◇◇

CLIENT: Well, they're happy.

THERAPIST: How do you know?

CLIENT: They're smiling.

THERAPIST: So you think of Leo Bascalia as a caring person?

CLIENT: Yes, I do. ◇◇ Yes.

THERAPIST: Close your eyes and imagine being with Leo Bascalia. Think of where the two of you might be and how it would be for you. ◇◇

CLIENT: I like that. ◇◇ He's a nice man.

Comment on process and technique: The therapist continues to make the memory of Mr. Bascalia more vivid. The focus now is shifted to imagining a relationship with Mr. Bascalia in which his supportive qualities can be experienced by Mr. A.

Technical intervention: Encourage the client to close his eyes and imagine an interaction with the nurturing figure. Use EMs to strengthen the experience.

THERAPIST: Do you think if he knew you, he might have some caring feelings for you?

CLIENT: I think he just cares about people.

THERAPIST: Do you think he might care about you?

CLIENT: [pause] Yes. ◇◇

The session ended with Mr. A able to feel a caring bond with Mr. Bascalia.

In the following session, more work was done on this imagined relationship. With the help of EMs, Mr. A explored fantasies of having discussions with Mr. Bascalia, of telling Mr. Bascalia about himself, and of finding that Mr. Bascalia was interested and empathic. Mr. A was asked to identify body sensations associated with these pleasurable experiences, and these were reinforced with EMs. Mr. A was asked to feel these sensations and let his mind float back through his life to an experience involving similar feelings. This "float back" technique is usually successful in identifying antecedent events related to both positive and negative body sensations and feelings, but in this instance it yielded nothing.

In the following session, Mr. A described having gone to a bookstore during the week and browsed. He had found a book by a woman who had been extremely depressed; she had swallowed a bottle of pills, woken up the next morning still alive, decided that her life had been spared for a reason, found a new connection to God, and written the book about it. Mr. A had felt a strong connection to the woman's story and had read the book twice. After telling me this story, he looked up and in an emotion-choked voice said, "You know, I think God does love me." These three sessions represented a turning point in the treatment.

In subsequent sessions, some of Mr. A's earlier memories were targeted using the standard EMDR protocol. For example, he recalled that when he was with his grandmother and his cousins were visiting, she would give each of them, except Mr. A, some coins to buy ice cream from the ice cream truck. At the time, Mr. A internalized these experiences as meaning that there was something wrong with him or that he was bad, although he couldn't figure out why he would deserve this treatment. The image he thought of was of his cousins standing around the ice cream truck excitedly buying their ice cream pops and him standing by himself watching. His negative cognition was, "I'm not loveable," and the positive cognition was, "I'm okay." The VOC on "I'm okay" was between a one and a two. The positive cognition of "I deserve love" would have been a natural choice, but Mr. A described it as below a one on a VOC scale from one to seven.

Between reprocessing sessions, there was further discussion about relationships. One of Mr. A's coworkers had reached out to him, and Mr. A had spent several evenings with him and his wife, but he had not expressed any opinions or said anything personal to these people. Mr. A and I discussed what might happen if he were to say something of a personal nature and if, as he expected, they were not interested. He decided there was a possibility that they might respond in a positive way. I asked him to imagine saying something of a personal nature to these people and to imagine both a negative and a positive reaction; however, he had great difficulty imagining saying something personal and having a positive outcome. Accordingly, I asked him to imagine interacting with Leo Bascalia and imagine both a negative and a positive reaction. He was able to do this with EMs fairly easily, except he reported that the negative reaction was really just a misunderstanding that he was able to clear up with Mr. Bascalia right away. He was then successful at the original task of imagining saying something personal to his friends. With the EMs, the negative outcome lost its charge quickly and he decided that even if they did react as he expected they would, he would not lose their friendship entirely. After processing further with EMs, the positive outcome became more of a possibility.

A requirement of the successful treatment of a schizoid or avoidant personality disorder is that there be a balance of risk-taking within the treatment hour and in the client's behavior outside treatment (Manfield, 1992). In a subsequent session, Mr. A reported that he had forced himself to experiment with expressing a personal opinion to the couple. He said that they had not ignored him and had, in fact, responded to what he had said; he was enormously relieved. In the months that followed, Mr. A experimented further with minor forms of self-disclosure with generally good results. He was spending more time with the coworker and his wife and had begun to spend some time outside work with another coworker. He was finding these relationships gratifying. Some of his early memories were successfully targeted using EMDR processing as he reconnected with the dissociated affect. His increased vulnerability in social relationships became a focus of discussion and exploration, and a few disappointments in his experimentation with self-disclosure yielded additional targets.

After 15 months, his managed care insurance cut off his benefits. His depression having lifted and his social functioning much improved, he decided to stop treatment. Had he continued, he would have benefited from further treatment; as each level of openness and intimacy was attempted, deeper feelings of vulnerability would have emerged and new historical events would have become available for targeting.

This case is a good example of the interplay between building adult resources and the ability to address emotional conflict and process dysphoric affect, a central theme in the treatment of personality disorders. It also illustrates how the relationship with the therapist can be supplemented by the use of substitute objects to build emotional strength and resources. Although Mr. A was able to identify many specific historical targets, they were not fully available for EMDR targeting until he could access their emotional components. For clients without personality disorders, the missing components can surface spontaneously during EMDR processing; for this client, as for most clients with personality disorders, accessing the dysphoric affect productively became increasingly possible as the client's perceived sense of safety and self-efficacy grew.

Had Mr. A stayed in treatment longer, the pattern of reaching out into the world and using EMDR processing to handle the dysphoric material generated would no doubt have continued. The nature of the processing, however, would have become gradually easier and more rapid.

The following case offers an illustration of both mid-treatment and final phase processing.

Background and History of Mr. B

Mr. B originally came for treatment because of job performance issues. Although he had a college degree, he worked in a Fortune 500 company at an entry-level position that required only a high school education. He explained that he had been getting into trouble for repeatedly putting important papers in the drawer of his desk and leaving them there until his supervisor received complaints about them.

He had grown up in a religious fundamentalist home where his sensitivity and lack of athletic skill were extremely threatening to his father, a macho construction worker, leading to intense emotional abuse. In the face of his father's fierce intimidation and demands for perfection, Mr. B began stuttering at the age of 5, which became a source of humiliation and shame throughout his life. School work came easy and school served as one of his main sources of positive feelings about himself. He began to drink alcohol early and by the time he came to see me, he was drinking himself to sleep every night.

CLINICAL PRESENTATION

Mr. B began treatment in 1986 at the age of 32. He presented as cocky and superficial, with little ability to introspect. He could not explain his procrastinating behavior at work. All his relationships, including romantic involvements, were either extremely distant or brief. He had little involvement with any members of his family.

DIAGNOSTIC FORMULATION

Mr. B's abuse of alcohol was not at first obvious because he concealed it, but the seriousness of his addiction became increasingly apparent over time. His symptoms fit those of a closet narcissist. He felt covertly superior to everyone around him and was unable to form meaningful attachments. He was extremely reactive to even minor criticism and was obsessive in his efforts to avoid making mistakes. His stuttering seemed to be at least partially a result of the enormous anxiety he experienced at being seen as flawed.

TREATMENT PROCESS

Mr. B responded positively to psychotherapy. He seemed to enjoy the opportunity to talk about himself and have an attentive audience, and he rapidly developed a twinship transference. Because this treatment began five years before the therapist began using EMDR, it was conducted with a traditional self-psychology orientation for the first six years. By the time EMDR was begun, Mr. B had achieved a relatively balanced view of himself. He had received four promotions at work, acquiring a position more appropriate to his skills, and his responsibilities included supervising other people. His procrastination was no longer a problem, he related in a relatively genuine way to other people, and he had been in a stable romantic relationship for four years.

Mr. B's history of emotional abuse from his father and the repeated experiences of humiliation as classmates laughed at his stuttering provided plentiful targets for EMDR. His memories of humiliation in school during fits of stuttering were specific and vivid, although initially his memories of abuse at home were not. The former provided an ideal set of initial EMDR targets. The memories of humiliation in school were distinct enough from the abuse at home that they could be processed without bleeding into the latter memories. He was successful at processing individual memories of being laughed at, of hiding in dread behind the student seated in front of him so that the teacher wouldn't see him and call on him, and of specific teachers who were particularly insensitive. These successes were followed by successful processing of current situations in which he felt humiliation, such as talking on the telephone or talking in groups and "blocking." The emphasis of treatment was on his becoming comfortable with being a stutterer, not on eliminating blocking. EMDR future templates were used to enhance and cement his progress. As his anxiety about blocking dwindled, he blocked less, and stuttering eventually ceased to be a concern for him, even when leading meetings. Over time, the memories of being laughed at as a child gradually fed into memories of feeling different and isolated, and these memories also processed well. Memories related to being taunted for being sensitive and different came up next and were processed. The more intense memories of being condemned at church for refusing to give testimony in front of the congregation and of being taunted and humiliated by his father were not processed with EMDR until he was more comfortable with himself and more confident of his ability to process and resolve painful memories.

In the following transcript, he processes some of his feelings of isolation using EMDR.

CLIENT: Our friend Silvia, who is dying of cancer, has become good friends with Stella (Mr. B's partner), and I feel jealous. They have a lot in common and Silvia needs to talk. I've begun to feel hurt and left out; it's strange, because I can tell that I'm probably not going to become real good friends with Silvia and I should be happy about the connection that they have, but this other reaction has a life of its own sometimes. . . . I often get little pangs that there is something special going on and that I'm not included. But I manage it very well.

THERAPIST: Do you have an earlier memory that you associate with this experience of feeling left out?

CLIENT: Nothing specific. (Pause) Well, yes. I've seldom had a large number of friends at one time. I've had one or two people that I monopolized and felt like they were my territory. I don't know how far back that goes. Probably to the first time I felt that anyone liked me at all, because way back I used to think I was a hopeless case, and nobody could like me at all.

Comment on process and technique: In the interchange that followed, Mr. B attempted at first to shift the focus away from the disturbing material he had just accessed but was then able to focus specifically on a memory, identifying a time in high school when he had felt left out. The negative cognition was, "There is something intrinsically wrong with me." The positive cognition was, "I'm okay." VOC is 3. Initial SUDS was 5. The transcript takes up again near the beginning of the desensitization phase after several sets of EMs:

CLIENT: ◇◇ I almost choked in the beginning when you asked me to hold onto all that. There is a big distance between Stella and Silvia and me. ◇◇ I just got a real strong image of a high school girlfriend named Linda. She was the first girl I got a crush on, but she was enormously popular so I couldn't have her all to myself. ◇◇ I'm bouncing around. I have an extreme reaction in movies if there's been a schism or disruption in the family and then there is a reunion. I've been known to get up and leave theaters. I usually lie about why I left.

Comment on process and technique: Mr. B's associations at first do not make sense to him; describing himself as "bouncing around," he is implying that he is failing to do EMDR properly. In fact, the EMs are facilitating spontaneous free association.

CLIENT: ◇◇ I'm stuck on the same images, except that with Stella, she starts blubbering in movies at the same time as I get pissed off at the movie, at the situation. ◇◇ Those scenes are not a part of my reality and I'm real jealous. It's just not in the cards for me and I know that. I'm getting real strong images of my mother's face with a benign smile but without feeling; she's generally been very nice to me. ◇◇ There he is, my father yelling at Mother that I'll never turn out to be anything and that I'm crazy. ◇◇ To him, I was just an embarrassment. I wasn't even competent to know what foods tasted good, and I was told that all the time. Anything I said I was interested in or showed talent for, the reaction was "Are you going to do that for a living?" ◇◇ What's there now is that stunned feeling that I get as if you were hit real hard from the inside.

THERAPIST: Where do you feel that?

Comment on process and technique: Focusing on the associated physical sensation often helps the client process affect.

Technical intervention: Calls his attention to the present experience of the physical sensation related to affect.

CLIENT: Here (sternum) ◇◇ I've connected the loop. I have the same reaction when Stella and Silvia go off and talk by themselves as I did when my father yelled at me and I had no control. It's the same kind of hurt powerless reaction, only the two situations are worlds apart. ◇◇ It's a reaction I had a lot actually when I felt I've just been stung by criticism.

Comment on process and technique: Mr. B proceeds to recall his father's heavy criticism of him and to realize that it was not he who was defective, but his father. As the hour closes, Mr. B appears calm. The therapist checks the SUDS, which is 0, and the VOC, which is 7, and does a short installation.

The quality of EMDR targets during the last phase of treatment tends to be less intense. For instance, Mr. B comes to the session during this phase reporting that he has been filling out government forms all day at work and feels a bit dizzy. When asked if this reaction is typical, he says he always feels disoriented when he has to fill out official forms. He says he was sitting at his desk for a long time that day with papers in front of him and accomplished little. The therapist suggests that this might be a good target for EMDR and asks when the first time was that Mr. B could recall feeling this way. He immediately says, "Oh, I knew what it was the moment you asked. When I was young, my parents would always fight at tax time. My mother would berate my father for not keeping good enough records of his expenditures, and my father would yell at my mother to shut up and get off his back. I could hear them all the way from the other end of the house. My dad was real scary when he was angry. Every day for weeks I would wake up to yelling. It was so loud, I could hear it clearly through several closed doors."

After this association, the target is easily fleshed out. The image is of the closed door with the sounds of his parents' conflict heard clearly through it. The negative cognition is "I'm not safe." The positive cognition is "I can take care of myself."

VOC is 2 or 3 and SUDS is 7. The affect, anxiety, is felt in his stomach, where he also feels a slight nausea. The reprocessing is straightforward, lasting approximately 20 minutes and resulting in a complete resolution of the memory. Mr. B comes back to the following session reporting a different feeling about filling out government forms.

HOW THERAPEUTIC CHALLENGES ARE CONCEPTUALIZED AND MANAGED

The challenges of working with clients with personality disorders using EMDR are similar to those of any approach working with this population. Individuals with personality disorders exhibit the following:

- They are emotionally unstable and prone to acting out in destructive ways.
- They do not tolerate affect well, so they resist exploring uncomfortable or painful events and avoid dysphoric affect.
- They lack self-referencing skills and lean on the therapist for direction.
- They are prone to distorted perceptions of relationships, not the least of which is their relationship with the therapist.

EMOTIONAL INSTABILITY AND ACTING OUT

The tendency of clients with personality disorders to act out is always an issue in all approaches. Acting out results from clients' being flooded with more dysphoric affect than they are able to manage internally, so they attempt to manage it through manipulation of the world around them (Manfield, 1992). Preventing acting out is necessary to stabilize clients and bring some order to their life so that they can begin to look inward. In EMDR, the degree of dysphoric affect experienced by the client is modulated in a variety of ways including desensitizing through reprocessing the sources of dysphoric affect, carefully titrating the intensity of dysphoric affect through structure and choice of targets, resource development and installation, teaching affect containment and social skills (Linehan, 1993), and future templates.

LOW TOLERANCE FOR AFFECT

Avoidance defenses represent an obstacle to any attempt at treating a personality disorder. They cannot be managed through modulation of disturbance levels alone, because for someone with a lifelong pattern of avoidance, it has become automatic. In EMDR, avoidance becomes most noticeable during reprocessing in the quality of the client's associations. During successful EMDR processing, associations tend to bring underlying conflicts and events into increasingly clearer focus; when the client is avoiding, the emotional energy generated by the processing dissipates and the target loses focus. This can happen when associations detour into peripheral less charged memories or stories or when associations broaden into larger complaints for which the affective connection is weak.

As in most therapeutic approaches, the EMDR therapist must track clients' associations and continually evaluate if they are on track with their work or retreating into avoidance. Because avoidance can be automatic, simply asking clients if they have moved on from their previous focus because they felt finished with it or because it was uncomfortable is often enough to make them aware of their dynamic and allow them to resume productive work. If the original target was vivid enough, the therapist can also bring clients back into productive work by directing them to focus again on the original target and asking what about it remains disturbing. When the avoidance is a result of the intensity of the disturbing affect the work is engendering rather than a habitual response to disturbing affect, the therapist can use cognitive interweaves or dissociative techniques commonly used in hypnosis to help the client to modulate the level of affect (Shapiro, 1995, 2001, 2002).

LACK OF SELF-REFERENCING SKILLS

Clients with personality disorders have difficulty self-referencing; their senses of themselves are dictated by the responses they receive from the world around them. They usually begin treatment believing the primary source of their problems is located outside themselves, and they have little sense of the part they themselves play (Manfield, 1992; Masterson, 1981). In sessions, they describe the events that have occurred during the week with little sense of how these events reflect on their own inner processes. In EMDR, as in other approaches, the therapist helps clients to understand the relationship between the events they describe and their internal processes. This can be done through interpretation or Socratic exploration but is done most effectively by suggesting a target for EMDR processing. In this way, the EMDR therapist can work collaboratively with the client, whereas the primary insights and resolution come from the client rather than the therapist.

DISTORTED PERCEPTIONS OF RELATIONSHIPS

Transference issues play a lesser role in EMDR than in most other approaches. The client feels less dependent on the therapist because the treatment is more rapid and because of use of a wider range of emotional resources, including real or imagined nurturing figures other than the therapist. Negative transference occurs less often because there is less perceived dependency on the therapist and because the therapist and the client work collaboratively. The EMDR therapist does not require the client to unilaterally initiate and direct the focus of the treatment session as in nondirective therapies, a task which is normally frustrating for clients with personality disorders and can lead to a perception of the therapist as withholding. Also, when issues and events are targeted, the client is perceived as the source of potentially painful associations, not the therapist.

MECHANISMS OF CHANGE AND THERAPEUTIC ACTION

When traumatic memories are accessed, clients often revert to a dissociated child state in which all the powerlessness of childhood is reexperienced as if still valid for the adult; the mind-set through which the event was perceived and the meaning attached to it are replicated in its recall:

> Anything that happens to us in the present has to physiologically link up in the memory network with past events to be understood or recognized. The perceptions

of observing a cup in the present link up with our previous "cup" experiences in order to know what do with it. If the appearance is too dissimilar, its function will not be realized. Furthermore, if a person's childhood included experiences of being hit on the head with a cup, then the past childhood fear may be presently associated with the current perception of the cup. The fear may arise in the mind and body without the person knowing why, but it would be real and palpable in the present. Rather than (or, in certain instances, in addition to) simple conditioning, the information-processing paradigm posits that it is the early perceptions of the events that are stored and triggered. (Shapiro, 2002, p. 11)

Clinicians using other models might describe the client as operating from a child ego state when recalling an early traumatic memory; others might describe the memory as triggering splitting, in which the client is accessing a distorted view of self and object with associated disturbing affect. Whatever the language used to describe it, most clinicians would agree that these memories must somehow be linked up to a more mature reality-based adult perspective to be metabolized. Indeed, it appears that a significant salutary role played by therapists is to act as a tether to a healthy adult perspective when the client begins to dissociate into the memory of a formative childhood experience. One theory explaining the observed accelerating effect produced by EMs in processing of these memories (Shapiro, 2001; van der Kolk, 2002; Wachtel, 2002) is that the client is being asked to perform a task in present time while recalling the past, and this dual awareness causes a rapid oscillation of attention and awareness between the present and past perspectives, allowing for the swift integration of the two.

In addition, the EMs seem to make dysphoric affect more tolerable during desensitization. Perhaps the EMs provide a series of momentary distractions, a constant reminder of the present context that prevents the client from fully dissociating into the memory. For most people, the response to just a few sets of EMs, while holding in mind a disturbing image, is described as a loss of clarity of the image. People variously report that it seems like a veil has fallen between themselves and the image or that the image seems farther away, that it has become hazy, or that it is seeming as though the event being recalled actually happened to someone else, as if the holder of the memory were not there when it happened. Four controlled studies testing a variety of hypotheses (Andrade, Kavanagh, & Baddeley, 1997; Kavanagh, Freese, Andrade, & May, 2001; Sharpley, Montgomery, & Scalzo, 1996; van den Hout, Muris, Salemink, & Kindt, 2001) have reported that EMs decrease the vividness of memory images and the associated emotion.

Although the exact mechanisms are still being researched, we know that EMDR processing is able to bring about a rapid resolution of a dysfunctionally held memory, impacting both the dysphoric affect triggered by the memory and its associated maladaptive cognitions (see research section). The Adaptive Information Processing Model posits that all present experience is filtered through memories of past events, attaching to it associated affect and cognitions, which may or may not be adaptive. These affects and cognitions shape the meaning that we attach to our present experience, which then motivates our responses. The dysfunctional storage of the memories keeps us from spontaneously reprocessing these memories. Using the EMDR approach, when clients are ready, the early events at the core or their present distress are processed, the distressing affect is eliminated, and the maladaptive cognitions are replaced with adaptive ones, so that clients feel better about themselves and exercise new responses to present situations.

RESEARCH AND EMPIRICAL SUPPORT

Although there is little empirical research on the use of EMDR with personality disorders (Heber, Kellner, & Yehuda, in press; Korn & Leeds, in press) and few published reports (Fensterheim, 1996; Manfield, 1998), there is substantial evidence that it may be an effective treatment for them. In the short time since the first paper describing EMDR (then EMD), there has been a plethora of controlled studies establishing the effectiveness of EMDR in the treatment of trauma (Carlson, Chemtob, Rusnak, Hedlund, & Muraoka, 1998; Ironson, Freund, Strauss, & Williams, 2002; Lee, Gavriel, Drummond, Richards, & Greenwald, in press; Marcus, Marquis, & Sakai, 1997; Rothbaum, 1997; Scheck, Schaeffer, & Gillette, 1998; Wilson, Becker, & Tinker, 1995, 1997; contemporary reviews include Chemtob, Tolin, van der Kolk, & Pitman, 2000; Maxfield & Hyer, 2002; Perkins & Rouanzoin, 2002). In addition to PTSD, these studies establish the basis for EMDR's use with a range of conditions. Together with data-based case reports (Lazrove, Triffleman, Kite, McGlashan, & Rounsaville, 1998; Levin, Lazrove, & van der Kolk, 1999), they have evidenced substantial changes in anxiety, depression, and dimensions of personality on a wide range of clinical measures. A recent controlled study established the effect of EMDR in improving positive memory recall after the traumatic loss of a loved one (Sprang, 2001). Several of the studies compared their results on conditions resulting from traumatic events to those with a full PTSD diagnosis and found them comparable (Scheck et al., 1998; Wilson et al., 1995, 1997).

As noted by Azrin (1996), although research with EMDR on conditions other than PTSD has been limited, the information processing model presents a reasonable theoretical basis for the therapeutic use of EMDR in a wider range of conditions (see also Perkins & Rouanzoin, 2002; Rogers & Silver, 2002; Siegel, 2002; Stickgold, 2002; van der Kolk, 2002). In the standard EMDR protocol, memories are targeted along with associated cognitions and affect; clinical reports (Greenwald, 1999; Levin et al., 1999; Lipke, 2000; Lovett, 1999; Manfield, 1998; Shapiro, 2001, 2002; Silver & Rogers, 2002; Tinker & Wilson, 1999) have verified that as the memory is processed using EMDR, the cognitions and affect are adaptively modified as well as associated behavior.

Clients who suffer from single event trauma or a single class of events are relatively easy to treat with EMDR. Controlled research has found that approximately 85% to 90% of those with this class of civilian PTSD can be treated in the equivalent of three 90-minute sessions (Ironson et al., 2002; Marcus et al., 1997; Rothbaum, 1997; Wilson et al., 1997). As with all psychotherapy treatments, there have been no controlled studies of clients with personality disorders. There is, however, a fair amount of anecdotal evidence of EMDR used effectively with this population. Many of the published reports (Manfield, 1998) were begun before the therapist began using EMDR, so they involve a mixture of approaches; however, therapists report acceleration of the treatment once EMDR is introduced.

Research involving potential underlying mechanisms is essentially speculative. As noted previously, four studies have investigated the effects of eye movements on the vividness of memory images and the associated affect (Andrade et al., 1997; Kavanagh et al., 2001; Sharpley et al., 1996; van den Hout et al., 2001).

Teicher et al. (1997) compared EEG and MRI brain scans of adults who had experienced chronic neglect or physical, emotional, or sexual abuse as children to adults who had not. They found that interhemispheric communication in the brain was profoundly impaired in the group with abuse histories. When these subjects were asked to think of their most positive memory, brain scans showed that the right hemisphere of their brains became silent, and only the left hemisphere was active. Conversely, when the instruction was to think of their most unpleasant memory, the left hemisphere shut down and only the right hemisphere was active. In the control group of subjects with relatively nontraumatic childhoods but present-day problems, both instructions resulted in simultaneous activation of both hemispheres of the brain.

The left hemisphere of the brain is responsible for many of the functions necessary for psychotherapy, language, and the ability to use it to gain distance from the source of distress, organizing and problem-solving skills, the ability to analyze an experience, to orient it in time, and the ability to translate experience into meaning. The right brain has at best a minimal ability to communicate analytically or to reason. It is responsible for intuition, emotion, and artistic expression.

Teicher's research confirms clinical experiences with this population. People with histories of chronic abuse appear to experience normal life through the left hemisphere of their brains. They process life cognitively and are unable to be empathic or intimate. At these times, they do not have access to normal emotions, including sadness, anger, love, or joy. When they encounter a stimulus related to their traumatic past, their left brain shuts down and their right brain takes over, causing them to become flooded with emotion, which they are unable to think about rationally, to talk about, analyze or process; they are unable to modulate the affect or sooth themselves (Schore, 2002).

The implication of this study is that, although most psychotherapists encourage their clients to verbalize and analyze their early painful memories, for clients with histories of chronic abuse, their capacity to do this is extremely limited. In their 1997 study, Teicher et al. also found that childhood sexual abuse and chronic childhood neglect both correlate highly with abnormal physical maturation of the brain, resulting in particular in a significantly smaller corpus callosum, the part of the brain whose purpose is interhemispheric communication.

The population consisting of adults chronically abused as children and the population of adults with personality disorders have substantial overlap (Schore, 2001). The proportion of personality-disordered clients who have, in fact, been physically or sexually abused is high. Reports by Stone (1981) and others (Bryer, Nelson, Miller, & Krol, 1987) suggest that more than 75% of borderline clients have been sexually abused as children. Herman (1992a, 1992b) challenges the practice of diagnosing personality disorders in patients with a history of severe trauma, suggesting that they should be diagnosed as "complex PTSD" to take into account the effect on personality and future interpersonal relationships of repeated trauma. Referencing Joseph (1988) and Muller (1992), Teicher et al. (1997) conclude, "Muller theorized that borderline personality disorder may be the result of deficient hemispheric integration. . . . Deficient right and left hemisphere integration could result in the misperception of affect and foster a situation in which the right and left cerebral cortex may act in an uncooperative manner, giving rise to intrapsychic conflict and splitting." A more recent study used SPECT to look at lateralization of brain activity of six patients pre- and post-EMDR treatment;

consistent with Teicher et al.'s paper, it showed a significant increase in posttreatment activity in the left frontal lobe during recall of the trauma (Levin et al., 1999).

EMDR allows the nonverbal processing of traumatic memories, which is so important for a client whose left brain, the verbal part, is unavailable when recalling traumatic childhood memories (see also Siegel, 2002; Stickgold, 2002; van der Kolk, 2002). Brain imaging has shown that EMDR stimulates the activity of the corpus callosum (van der Kolk, 1997), the part that Teicher et al. found to be inadequately developed in their study. It is conjectured that this effect of the EMDR processing may be partially responsible for EMDR's efficacy with this population in making it possible for them to process disturbing memories.

SUMMARY AND CONCLUSIONS

A fundamental principle of the Adaptive Information Processing Model is that present disturbance and dysfunctional characteristics have their origins in past events; these antecedents, whether identified or not, can be processed to an adaptive resolution using EMDR. In treating personality disorders, the EMDR approach integrates procedures from many other orientations to stabilize clients and equip them to address their source memories. The accelerated processing of disturbing memories that takes place during EMDR makes it possible for clients to address and resolve their issues relatively rapidly.

REFERENCES

Andrade, J., Kavanagh, D., & Baddeley, A. (1997). Eye-movements and visual imagery: A working memory approach to the treatment of posttraumatic stress disorder. *British Journal of Clinical Psychology, 36*, 209–223.

Azrin, N. (1996). Book review of eye movement desensitization and reprocessing. *Private Practice, 12*, 82–84.

Bryer, J. B., Nelson, B. A., Miller, J. B., & Krol, P. A. (1987). Childhood sexual and physical abuse as factors in adult psychiatric illness. *American Journal of Psychiatry, 144*, 1426–1430.

Carlson, J. G., Chemtob, C. M., Rusnak, K., Hedlund, N. L., & Muraoka, M. Y. (1998). Eye movement desensitization and reprocessing for combat-related posttraumatic stress disorder. *Journal of Traumatic Stress, 11*, 3–24.

Chemtob, C. M., Tolin, D. F., van der Kolk, B. A., & Pitman, R. K. (2000). Eye movement desensitization and reprocessing. In E. B. Foa, T. M. Keane, & M. J. Friedman (Eds.), *Effective treatments for PTSD: Practice guidelines from the International Society for Traumatic Stress Studies* (pp. 139–154). New York: Guilford Press.

Fensterheim, H. (1996). Eye movement desensitization and reprocessing with complex personality pathology: An integrative therapy. *Journal of Psychotherapy Integration, 6*, 27–38.

Greenwald, R. (1999). *Eye movement desensitization reprocessing (EMDR) in child and adolescent psychotherapy.* New York: Aronson.

Heber, R., Kellner, M., & Yehuda, R. (2002). Salivary cortisol levels and the cortisol response to dexamethasone before and after EMDR: A case report. *Journal of Clinical Psychology, 58*, 1521–1530.

Herman, J. L. (1992a). Complex PTSD: A syndrome in survivors of prolonged and repeated trauma. *Journal of Traumatic Stress, 5*, 377–391.

Herman, J. L. (1992b). *Trauma and recovery.* New York: Basic Books.

Ironson, G., Freund, B., Strauss, J. L., & Williams, J. (2002). A comparison of two treatments for traumatic stress: A pilot study of EMDR and prolonged exposure. *Journal of Clinical Psychology, 58,* 113–128.

Joseph, R. (1988). The right cerebral hemisphere: Emotion, music, visual-spacial skills, body image, dreams, and awareness. *Journal of Clinical Psychology, 44,* 630–673.

Kavanagh, D. J., Freese, S., Andrade, J., & May, J. (2001). Effects of visuospatial tasks on desensitization to emotive memories. *British Journal of Clinical Psychology, 40,* 267–280.

Korn, D. L., & Leeds, A. M. (2002). Preliminary evidence of efficacy for EMDR resource development and installation in the stabilization phase of treatment of complex posttraumatic stress disorder. *Journal of Clinical Psychology, 58,* 1465–1487.

Lazrove, S., Triffleman, E., Kite, L., McGlashan, T., & Rounsaville, B. (1998). An open trial of EMDR as treatment for chronic PTSD. *American Journal of Orthopsychiatry, 69,* 601–608.

Lee, C., Gavriel, H., Drummond, P., Richards, J., & Greenwald, R. (2002). Treatment of posttraumatic stress disorder: A comparison of stress inoculation training with prolonged exposure and eye movement desensitization and reprocessing. *Journal of Clinical Psychology, 58,* 1071–1089.

Leeds, A. M. (1998). Lifting the burden of shame: Using EMDR resource installation to resolve a therapeutic impasse. In P. Manfield (Ed.), *Extending EMDR: A casebook of innovative applications* (pp. 256–282). New York: Norton.

Leeds, A. M., & Shapiro, F. (2000). EMDR and resource installation: Principles and procedures for enhancing current functioning and resolving traumatic experiences. In J. Carlson & L. Sperry (Eds.), *Brief therapy strategies with individuals and couples* (pp. 469–534). Phoenix, AZ: Zeig, Tucker.

Levin, P., Lazrove, S., & van der Kolk, B. A. (1999). What psychological testing and neuroimaging tell us about the treatment of posttraumatic stress disorder (PTSD) by eye movement desensitization and reprocessing (EMDR). *Journal of Anxiety Disorders, 13,* 159–172.

Linehan, M. M. (1993). *Cognitive-behavioral treatment of borderline personality disorder.* New York: Guilford Press.

Lipke, H. (2000). *EMDR and psychotherapy integration.* Boca Raton, FL: CRC Press.

Lovett, J. (1999). *Small wonders: Healing childhood trauma with EMDR.* New York: Free Press.

Manfield, P. (1992). *Split self/split object: Understanding and treating borderline, narcissistic and schizoid disorders.* Northvale, NJ: Aronson.

Manfield, P. (Ed.). (1998). *Extending EMDR: A casebook of innovative applications.* New York: Norton.

Marcus, S. V., Marquis, P., & Sakai, C. (1997). Controlled study of treatment of PTSD using EMDR in an HMO setting. *Psychotherapy, 34,* 307–315.

Masterson, J. F. (1981). *The narcissistic and borderline disorders: An integrated developmental approach.* New York: Brunner/Mazel.

Maxfield, L., & Hyer, L. A. (2002). The relationship between efficacy and methodology in studies investigating EMDR treatment of PTSD. *Journal of Clinical Psychology, 58,* 23–41.

Muller, R. J. (1992). Is there a neural basis for borderline splitting? *Comprehensive Psychiatry, 33,* 92–104.

Perkins, B., & Rouanzoin, C. (2002). A critical examination of current views regarding eye movement desensitization and reprocessing (EMDR): Clarifying points of confusion. *Journal of Clinical Psychology, 58,* 77–97.

Phillips, M. (2001). Potential contributions of hypnosis to ego-strengthening procedures in EMDR. *American Journal of Clinical Hypnosis, 43,* 247–262.

Rogers, S., & Silver, S. M. (2002). Is EMDR an exposure therapy? A review of trauma protocols. *Journal of Clinical Psychology, 58,* 43–59.

Rothbaum, B. O. (1997). A controlled study of eye movement desensitization and reprocessing for posttraumatic stress disordered sexual assault victims. *Bulletin of the Menninger Clinic, 61,* 317–334.

Scheck, M. M., Schaeffer, J. A., & Gillette, C. S. (1998). Brief psychological intervention with traumatized young women: The efficacy of eye movement desensitization and reprocessing. *Journal of Traumatic Stress, 11,* 25–44.

Schore, A. N. (2001). The effects of relational trauma on right brain development, affect regulation, and infant mental health. *Infant Mental Health Journal, 22,* 201–269.

Schore, A. N. (2002). Dysregulation of the right brain: A fundamental mechanism of traumatic attachment and the psychopathogenesis of posttraumatic stress disorders. *Australian and New Zealand Journal of Psychiatry, 36,* 9–30.

Shapiro, F. (1989). Efficacy of the eye movement desensitization procedure in the treatment of traumatic memories. *Journal of Traumatic Stress Studies, 2,* 199–223.

Shapiro, F. (1991). Stray thoughts. *EMDR Network Newsletter, 1,* 1–3.

Shapiro, F. (1994). Alternative stimuli in the use of EMD(R). *Journal of Behavior Therapy and Experimental Psychiatry, 25,* 89.

Shapiro, F. (1995). *Eye movement desensitization and reprocessing: Basic principles, protocols and procedures.* New York: Guilford Press.

Shapiro, F. (2001). *Eye movement desensitization and reprocessing: Basic principles, protocols and procedures* (2nd ed.). New York: Guilford Press.

Shapiro, F. (2002). *EMDR as an integrative psychotherapy approach: Experts of diverse orientations explore the paradigm prism.* Washington, DC: American Psychological Association.

Sharpley, C. F., Montgomery, I. M., & Scalzo, L. A. (1996). Comparative efficacy of EMDR and alternative procedures in reducing the vividness of mental images. *Scandinavian Journal of Behavior Therapy, 25,* 37–42.

Siegel, D. J. (2002). The developing mind and the resolution of trauma: Some ideas about information processing and an interpersonal neurobiology of psychotherapy. In F. Shapiro (Ed.), *EMDR as an integrative psychotherapy approach: Experts of diverse orientations explore the paradigm prism* (pp. 85–122). Washington, DC: American Psychological Association.

Silver, S. M., & Rogers, S. (2001). *Light in the heart of darkness: EMDR and the treatment of war and terrorism survivors.* New York: Norton.

Sprang, G. (2001). The use of eye movement desensitization and reprocessing (EMDR) in the treatment of traumatic stress and complicated mourning: Psychological and behavioral outcomes. *Research on Social Work Practice, 11,* 300–320.

Stickgold, R. (2002). EMDR: A putative neurobiological mechanism of action. *Journal of Clinical Psychology, 58,* 61–75.

Stone, M. H. (1981). Psychiatrically ill relatives of borderline patients: A family study. *Psychiatric Quarterly, 58,* 71–83.

Teicher, M., Ito, Y., Glod, C., Anderson, S., Dumont, N., & Ackerman, E. (1997). Preliminary evidence for abnormal cortical development in physically and sexually abused children, using EEG coherence and MRI. *Annals of the New York Academy of Sciences, 821,* 160–175.

Tinker, R. H., & Wilson, S. A. (1999). *Through the eyes of a child: EMDR with children.* New York: Norton.

van den Hout, M., Muris, P., Salemink, E., & Kindt, M. (2001). Autobiographical memories become less vivid and emotional after eye movements. *British Journal of Clinical Psychology, 40,* 121–130.

van der Kolk, B. A. (1997). The psychobiology of posttraumatic stress disorder. *Journal of Clinical Psychology, 58*(Suppl. 9), 16–24.

van der Kolk, B. A. (2002). Beyond the talking cure: Somatic experience and subcortical imprints in the treatment of trauma. In F. Shapiro (Ed.), *EMDR as an integrative psychotherapy approach: Experts of diverse orientations explore the paradigm prism* (pp. 57–84). Washington, DC: American Psychological Association.

Wachtel, P. L. (2002). EMDR and psychoanalysis. In F. Shapiro (Ed.), *EMDR as an integrative psychotherapy approach: Experts of diverse orientations explore the paradigm prism* (pp. 123–150). Washington, DC: American Psychological Association.

Wilson, S. A., Becker, L. A., & Tinker, R. H. (1995). Eye movement desensitization and reprocessing (EMDR) treatment for psychologically traumatized individuals. *Journal of Consulting and Clinical Psychology, 63,* 928–937.

Wilson, S. A., Becker, L. A., & Tinker, R. H. (1997). Fifteen-month follow-up of eye movement desensitization and reprocessing (EMDR) treatment for PTSD and psychological trauma. *Journal of Consulting and Clinical Psychology, 65,* 1047–1056.

Wolpe, J. (1958). *Psychotherapy by reciprocal inhibition.* Stanford, CA: Stanford University Press.

BROADENING THE SCOPE OF TREATMENT: SPECIAL POPULATIONS AND SETTINGS

CHAPTER 15

Pharmacotherapy of Personality Disorders

Robert Grossman

T HE PHARMACOTHERAPY OF patients with personality disorders (PDs) is currently one of the most challenging areas in psychiatry. A number of factors make this so, particularly the relative dearth of well-controlled and successful pharmacological trials in these patients as opposed to disorders such as Schizophrenia or Major Depression. In these and many other disorders, clinicians are able to prescribe a medication based on controlled trials in hundreds to thousands of subjects. Among the personality disorders, a fair number of promising medications are prescribed based on results in fewer than 20 subjects. There is no medication with a Food and Drug Administration indication for treatment of any of the personality disorders, nor are there any medications approved for treatment of applicable spectrum traits such as impulsivity, paranoia, or mood lability. Nonetheless, pharmacological treatment of personality-disordered patients is common practice, and a considerable amount of scientific data and clinical experience indicate that significant symptom reduction and functional improvement can occur with proper pharmacotherapy. In personality-disordered individuals, pharmacotherapy should usually be viewed not as the only component of treatment, but instead combined with any number of psychotherapy modalities. Numerous studies in many Axis I disorders have demonstrated the mutually complementary aspects of such an approach.

This chapter first details particular considerations for the pharmacotherapy of personality-disordered individuals. Each of the three personality disorder clusters and the specific disorders in each cluster are then individually discussed. Relevant information drawn on includes controlled studies, open-label studies, and clinical experience in treating both individual disorders and particular spectrum traits.

PRACTICAL AND THEORETICAL PERSPECTIVES

State versus Trait (Transient versus Chronic)

A young man whom you have treated for the past year has been relatively stable but walks into your office for his monthly appointment in a very distressed condition. He is tearful, disheveled, looks depressed, and tells you he feels like life is not worth living. Does he need a different antidepressant? Maybe, but one of the most important things is to inquire whether anything recently has happened in his life that might be associated with these feelings. He tells you his girlfriend left him. Almost by definition, the personality-disordered patient will have poor social support and stressed relationships in conjunction with primitive and often maladaptive defenses. This, combined with factors such as rejection sensitivity or mood lability heightens the degree to which an environmental event will impact the patient.

Paradoxically, one of the most problematic things you could do as a medication prescriber is to merely ask about symptoms such as sleep, appetite, sex drive, and conclude an antidepressant change is in order. This sends a number of potentially harmful messages to the patient: (1) It is possible for a medication to prevent me from ever feeling bad, (2) understanding why I am feeling certain ways is not important, and (3) this doctor cannot hear or is not really interested in my feelings. In Borderline Personality-disordered patients, such conclusions are even more likely because of their inherent lability and the strong transference and countertransference that may arise. A longitudinal sense of the individual's presentation is necessary in differentiating state versus trait symptoms. This perspective, shared by the patient and psychopharmacologist, may help prevent being inadvertently steered toward changing medications in a misdirected attempt to validate the patient's distress rather than verbally empathizing and helping the patient through what may be a transient event. Educating the patient as to what symptoms may be responsive to medications and to what degree is empowering and can greatly diminish distortions and unreasonable expectations about somatic treatments are essential aspects of the process. Keeping a log of mood or selected behaviors can aid both the patient and psychopharmacologist in assessing chronicity and severity of symptoms, triggering events, and response to pharmacological interventions.

Heterogeneity

As to making a diagnosis of Borderline or other PD, for example, the requirement of having five of nine symptoms results in 126 possible combinations. Many of these individuals are very different from one another as to psychodynamics, neurobiology, and suitable medication choice. Hence, it is not enough to know what PD an individual has, but specifics as to which traits are present greatly facilitate medication selection.

In most studies, the average number of PDs met by an individual with at least one PD is approximately 2.5. There is significant overlap of diagnostic criteria among personality disorders, particularly within clusters. Many *DSM-IV* criteria for the personality disorders are descriptions of behaviors, symptoms, or life situations that may hold a superficial similarity, but whose psychodynamic and neurobiological correlates, and medication management, are markedly different. For example, it is true of individuals with both Schizoid PD and Avoidant PD that they may have poor eye contact, give brief and superficial responses to questions, and have few, if any, close friends. However, the simple question, "Would you want to have more friends?" may lead the Schizoid patient to ask, "What for?" and the Avoidant patient to state, "Yes, but I'm scared they won't like me." The first answer may steer us toward an atypical antipsychotic for improvement of negative symptoms, whereas the second response suggests that a selective serotonin reuptake inhibitor (SSRI) may be efficacious for reduction of social anxiety and rejection sensitivity.

All this goes to say that the prescriber of medications to personality-disordered patients must be attuned to psychodynamics to not act out countertransference issues, not unknowingly promote distorted views of the role of medication treatment, and to differentiate between similar presentations that have very different underlying causes and neurobiologies.

NATURE VERSUS NURTURE

Traits that have proven to be substantially genetically heritable and related to measurable neurobiological alterations, such as impulsive aggression, clearly tie together neurobiology and behavior. As such, it is readily apparent that a medication may ameliorate the symptom or behavior by directly affecting the relevant neurobiology. With nonheritable traits or behaviors, the extent to which there is a corresponding neurobiology is less fixed and the issue is twofold. Certain environmental experiences such as severe physical abuse may result in particular brain changes such as decreased serotonergic function, which, in turn, may be pharmacologically addressable. Other environmental experiences, such as a very critical parent, may contribute to the schema "Whatever I do must be perfect" yet may not be accompanied by a measurable neurobiological alteration. In order not to create a brain-mind dichotomy, it is necessary to posit that all behaviors and attitudes are directly associated with a *particular* neurobiology and neurofunctional state, but you must differentiate how particular or unique or pervasive this state is. Hence, many views of yourself and the world that develop solely as a product of experience may not be effectively addressed pharmacologically.

BEHAVIORAL INERTIA

Personality-disordered patients often have to struggle in their lives and in therapy to make positive changes to grow. Change may involve learning new skills or seeing themselves and the world differently and then acting differently. A medication may improve mood, decrease mood lability, decrease anxiety, or some similar effect in a few weeks. Someone's personality likely arose from years of experiencing the world and themselves through these colored lenses and both understanding and acting accordingly. Hence, changing the underlying *cause* may be relatively simple and rapid, but changing the *habitual* manifestations may take months or years, even with appropriate complementary psychotherapy.

An example from a pharmacological treatment study in Posttraumatic Stress Disorder (PTSD) provides an appropriate analogy. Following initiation of SSRI treatment, patients with PTSD were found to show significant improvement in irritability, anhedonia, response to triggers, feelings of detachment, and hypervigilance in the first month of treatment. However, psychological and behavioral manifestations, such as the sense of a foreshortened future and avoidance of feared places and situations, took 2.5 months for a significant improvement to occur (Davidson, Rothbaum, van der Kolk, Sikes, & Farfel, 2001). Hence, it is important to have some understanding of the relative rate of time that various symptoms or behaviors typically take to change.

STRATEGIES FOR CHOOSING A MEDICATION

There are a number of ways to arrive at a reasonable medication choice for the personality-disordered patient. The most straightforward is prescribing a medication based on controlled or clinical information of the drug's efficacy in treatment of individuals with a particular personality disorder. This is a valid approach, but due to heterogeneity within personality disorders, may not address the symptoms that are of primary difficulty to the individual patient being treated. A complementary approach is to cluster various symptoms and view them on a spectrum, at times continuous with Axis I disorders.

SPECTRUM TRAITS

The personality disorders are clustered according to shared core features, and theorists have pointed out phenomenological and biological similarities between each of the clusters and corresponding Axis I disorders (Siever & Davis, 1991) and how these similarities can be used as a rationale for medication choice (Soloff, 1998).

Cluster A is characterized by quasi-psychotic symptoms including mild thought disorder, perceptual alterations, odd behaviors, and negative symptoms such as blunted affect and amotivation. Although not *DSM-IV* criteria, impaired neuropsychological functions such as attention, learning, and working memory certainly contribute to their impairments. It is reasonable to posit that because these individuals share (but often to a lesser extent) many of the neurobiological, neuroanatomic, and neuropsychological findings in Schizophrenia, antipsychotic agents would show some degree of efficacy in Cluster A personality-disordered individuals. Cluster B is characterized by often intense emotional states and mood lability and may be related to Axis I diagnoses of Unipolar and Bipolar Affective Disorders. Accordingly, antidepressant medications and mood-stabilizing medications may address these symptoms. Cluster C individuals tend to be chronically anxious and worried about a number of real or imagined fears. Medications that primarily act to decrease anxiety would be most logical from this perspective.

COMORBIDITY

Many times, personality-disordered patients seek psychotherapy or medication treatment, not because of their personality disorder symptoms themselves (which often are ego-syntonic), but because of a comorbid Axis I condition such as Major Depression, Panic Disorder, Generalized Anxiety Disorder, or one of many other disorders that may have a lifetime prevalence of up to 80% in these individuals. The Axis I condition may be not only causing more dysphoria, but also exacerbating Axis II symptomatology. As such, pharmacological treatment can be more parsimonious if an agent treats both the Axis I condition and core features of that patient's Axis II pathology. Further, it is important to know of comorbid conditions that may lead to a relative contraindication for prescribing a typical medication for the Axis II presentation (for example, not prescribing benzodiazepines for the Avoidant PD patient who is alcohol dependent).

For each personality disorder, medications are discussed in order of their relative applicability in treating core features of that personality disorder.

CLUSTER A (ODD/ECCENTRIC)

Schizotypal Personality Disorder

Of the Cluster A PDs, Schizotypal PD has been the most studied from perspectives of both neurobiology and psychopharmacological treatment. Neuropsychological testing in Schizotypal PD subjects has revealed deficits, similar but to a lesser degree than in Schizophrenia, in attention, working memory, and learning.

Most of the initial studies from which information on treating Schizotypal patients pharmacologically can be gleaned were done in primarily Borderline Personality-disordered subjects, and Schizotypal PD was a comorbid condition. This calls into question if results of the medication trials were due to benefits to core aspects of Schizotypal PD or whether improvement in Borderline PD symptomatology was the more direct cause.

Atypical Antipsychotics (D_2/5HT_2 Antagonists)   Although results from trials with *typical* antipsychotic medications are not particularly encouraging, the *atypical* agents are marked by better tolerability secondary to fewer side effects and greater efficacy for both positive and especially negative symptoms. One open-label olanzapine and one placebo-controlled risperidone study provides information on atypical antipsychotic agents in Schizotypal PD. Olanzapine (average dose 7.73 mg/day) was used in the treatment of 11 patients with Borderline PD and comorbid Dysthymia, seven of whom had comorbid Schizotypal PD (Schulz, Camlin, Berry, & Jesberger, 1999). Significant improvement was noted on scales of psychoticism, suspiciousness, phobic anxiety, and thought disturbance. However, lack of a placebo control and inability to determine whether improvements were due to the medication's effect on Borderline PD or Dysthymia temper the results.

A recent double-blind placebo-controlled study addressed these methodological problems by studying 23 subjects who all had primary Schizotypal PD, and only 20% of the subjects had comorbid Borderline PD, but in none of these cases was the Borderline PD primary (Koenigsberg et al., in press). After three weeks, the risperidone group showed significantly greater levels of improvement on negative symptom scales (and on average dose of 0.5 mg risperidone/day), and after seven weeks, there was a significant decrease in positive symptoms (on average dose of 1.5 mg risperidone/day). Hamilton Depression Scale (HAM-D) scores and clinical global impression (CGI) scores were not significantly different between groups at the study's conclusion, yet these scores were relatively low to begin with and a floor effect was possible. The medication was well tolerated, and there was not a greater dropout rate from the medication as opposed to the placebo group. This relatively small study performed in an 80% male group requires replication with more subjects and of both genders but seems to confirm the efficacy of an atypical antipsychotic agent in treatment of Schizotypal PD. The authors thought that due to the somatic preoccupation of Schizotypal PD patients, starting at a low dose and titrating gradually is preferable to minimize side effects.

Typical Antipsychotics (Primary D₁ Antagonists) Two placebo-controlled studies are available for these agents. In the first study, all subjects had to have at least one psychotic symptom for inclusion and subjects met *DSM-III* criteria for Borderline PD, Schizotypal PD, or both. On average, subjects received 8.7 mg/day of thiothixene. Schizotypal PD subjects were not separately analyzed, but the authors reported that delusions and ideas of reference showed greater improvement in the thiothixene-treated group (Goldberg et al., 1986). However, significant differences between drug and placebo were not found when standard psychological tests were used, and there was a high rate of side effects reported. The authors concluded that thiothixene showed minimal efficacy and should be considered only for treatment of PD patients with marked psychotic symptoms.

Another study compared the efficacy of haloperidol, amitriptyline, and placebo in acutely decompensated inpatients with Borderline PD, approximately a third of whom may have also met current diagnostic criteria for Schizotypal PD. The initial impression of these researchers was that haloperidol (at an average dose of 4.8 mg/day) resulted in an improvement in Schizotypal symptoms (Soloff, George, et al., 1986). In their final analysis of the data, it was concluded that treatment with haloperidol in this population was poorly tolerated and efficacy was not demonstrated (Soloff et al., 1989).

Selective Serotonin Reuptake Inhibitors (SSRIs)/Tricyclic Antidepressants (TCAs) Only one study is available in which to extrapolate information on SSRI use in Schizotypal PD. Twenty-two patients with Borderline PD and/or Schizotypal PD (only four had Schizotypal PD only) were treated with open-label fluoxetine (Markovitz, Calabrese, Schulz, & Meltzer, 1991). Improvement was noted on measures of psychoticism, depression, anxiety, interpersonal anxiety, and interpersonal sensitivity. In a study of mixed Schizotypal and Borderline PD subjects, the TCA imipramine resulted in an exacerbation of Schizotypal symptoms in two-thirds of the subjects (Parsons et al., 1989).

SCHIZOID PERSONALITY DISORDER

Pharmacotherapy of Schizoid PD is essentially unstudied. Only one open-label study provides some data. Four nonpsychotic relatives of Schizophrenic patients having negative symptoms, no positive symptoms, and neuropsychological deficits were treated with risperidone over a range of 1 to 2 mg/day (Tsuang, Stone, Tarbox, & Faraone, 2002). The authors did not diagnose these subjects, but they state that none were Schizotypal and the case descriptions of these subjects portray them as individuals rather typical of Schizoid PD. With risperidone treatment, all subjects were reported to show clinically significant improvements in negative symptoms resulting in their being more calm, enthusiastic, socially at ease, and interested in socializing. Meaningful improvement was noted in all cases on measures of attention and working memory.

PARANOID PERSONALITY DISORDER

There is no published data. If paranoia is viewed as a spectrum trait psychotic symptom, it is reasonable to consider treatment with an atypical antipsychotic medication. This requires controlled study.

CLUSTER A SUMMARY

Evidence is steadily gathering for the efficacy of atypical antipsychotic agents for treating this group. This is of relevance to not only positive symptoms, but also negative symptoms and accompanying neuropsychological deficits in attention, learning, and working memory. These deficits may be ameliorated through normalization of cortical dopaminergic function as a result of D_2 and $5HT_{2A}$ receptor antagonism (Ichikawa et al., 2001).

A recent meta-analysis of the neurocognitive effects of clozapine, olanzapine, risperidone, and haloperidol on Schizophrenic and Schizoaffective subjects gives some indication that various agents may show differing profiles in their relative ability to improve: (1) general executive and perceptual organization, (2) declarative verbal learning memory, and (3) processing speed and attention. Haloperidol did not result in improvement; the three atypical agents improved processing speed and attention. Both olanzapine and risperidone improved both general executive function and verbal learning/memory. Anticholinergic effects of concomitant benztropine in the haloperidol-treated group and the inherent anticholinergic effects of both clozaril and olanzapine were thought to impair performance (Bilder et al., 2002).

Atypical antipsychotics are the first-line medications for the treatment of most individuals with primarily cognitive-perceptual spectrum difficulties. There is no systematically-gathered data, but in patients not responding to atypical antipsychotics for negative symptoms or discomfort in social situations, a trial of an SSRI or benzodiazepine may be warranted. Medications with anticholinergic activity should be particularly avoided in personality-disordered patients with cognitive deficits, the majority of which, by definition, fall into the Cluster A group.

CLUSTER B (DRAMATIC/ERRATIC)

BORDERLINE PERSONALITY DISORDER

As to pharmacotherapy, Borderline PD has been the most studied of all the personality disorders, and it is the only personality disorder for which the American Psychiatric Association has released treatment guidelines (American Psychiatric Association [APA], 2001). Pharmacological treatment of the Borderline PD patient, however, remains challenging because although relatively well-studied compared to the other personality disorders, many questions remain unanswered. In addition, the typical life of the Borderline PD patient is full of chaos, crises, marked mood swings, and impulsive behaviors.

In this population, particular attention must be paid to state versus trait issues, suicidality, and transference/countertransference phenomena. Approximately 75% of Borderline PD patients will make a suicide attempt during their lives, and many times they will use their medications in this attempt. In general, medications that are lethal either alone or with other medications the patient is taking are relatively contraindicated and should be considered only if the patient is able to contract for safety, and adequate trials with other agents have not been successful. If treatment is split between a prescribing physician and therapist, it is of critical importance that the two communicate frequently because each provider may be seeing a very different presentation of the individual. With the tendency of the patient to fluctuate between idealization and devaluation, it is not uncommon for the medication prescriber to one week be "the doctor who is really helping me more than the pointless talking" and the next week be the "doctor who doesn't really give a shit about my problems and just wants to throw medications at me."

Patients with Borderline PD typically have difficulties in a number of areas, and looking at symptoms from a spectrum or cluster viewpoint is helpful in medication choice (APA, 2001). The three symptom clusters amenable to pharmacological treatment are:

1. Affective dysregulation (depression, mood lability, rejection sensitivity, intense inappropriate anger, environmental reactivity).
2. Impulsive-behavioral dyscontrol (impulsive aggression, self-injurious behavior, binge eating, risk-taking/sensation seeking, substance abuse/dependence).
3. Cognitive-perceptual (paranoia, illusions, suspiciousness, derealization, depersonalization, micropsychotic episodes).

See Figures 15.1 through 15.3 for medication algorithms for the different Borderline PD symptom clusters.

Substantial data validates that the first-line medications for both impulsive-behavioral dyscontrol and affective dysregulation symptom clusters are the SSRIs. Antipsychotic medications appear to be the most effective treatment for the cognitive-perceptual symptom cluster, with the atypical agents being much better tolerated (with associated higher compliance rates) and more effective (particularly for negative symptoms) than the typical antipsychotic agents.

Selective Serotonin Reuptake Inhibitors (SSRIs)   The SSRIs are probably the best-studied medications in the treatment of Borderline PD. Three double-blind placebo-controlled trials have been reported. A group of patients with mild and subthreshold Borderline PD (13 met full diagnostic criteria) were treated with fluoxetine (20 to 60 mg/day). The authors decreased the stringency of significance in their statistical analyses because of a large placebo effect and found that independent ratings for anger, depression, and global functioning showed significant improvement (Salzman et al., 1995). Although the relatively mild symptoms in these subjects limit the generalizability of the findings to the more symptomatic patients, it is important to recognize that people with these traits, not having full-symptom Borderline PD, can also be meaningfully helped by an SSRI.

More typical Borderline PD patients (more severe symptoms and greater Axis I comorbidity) were treated with fluoxetine at doses of up to 80 mg/day. In the 17 subjects studied, depression, anxiety, and global symptom measures showed significant improvement (Markovitz et al., 1991). Impulsive-aggressive behaviors are the number one cause for emergency room visits and hospitalization in Borderline PD subjects. The aforementioned study did not evaluate this parameter, but salient information is available from a study that sought to analyze efficacy of fluoxetine (20 to 60 mg/day), not for a specific personality disorder, but for treatment of the impulsive-aggressive behaviors (Coccaro & Kavoussi, 1997). Of the 40 patients studied, a third met full diagnostic criteria for Borderline PD. Patients with comorbid Bipolar Disorder or Major Depression were excluded. Verbal aggression and destruction of property were found to be significantly reduced by treatment with fluoxetine.

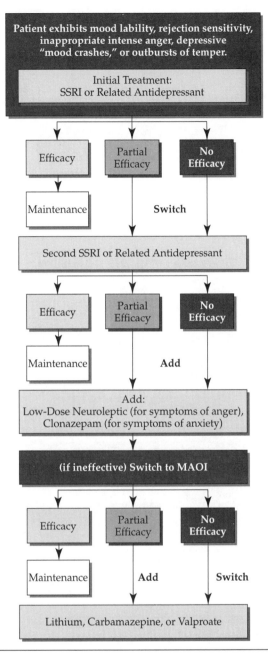

Figure 15.1 Psychopharmacological Treatment of Affective Dysregulation Symptoms in Patients with Borderline Personality Disorder. Algorithm based on clinical judgment that uses evidence currently in the literature, following the format of the International Psychopharmacology Algorithm Project (2). The first step in the algorithm is generally supported by the best empirical evidence. Recommendations may not be applicable to all patients or take individual needs into account. The empirical research studies on which these recommendations are based may be "first trials" involving previously untreated patients and may not take into account previous patient nonresponse to one, two, or even three levels of the algorithm (i.e., patients who, by definition, have more refractory disorders). There are no empirical trials of the complete algorithm. [*Source:* From "Practice Guideline for the Treatment of Patients with Borderline Personality Disorder," by American Psychiatric Association, October 2001, *American Journal of Psychiatry, 158*(Suppl. 10), pp. 1–52. Reprinted by permission.]

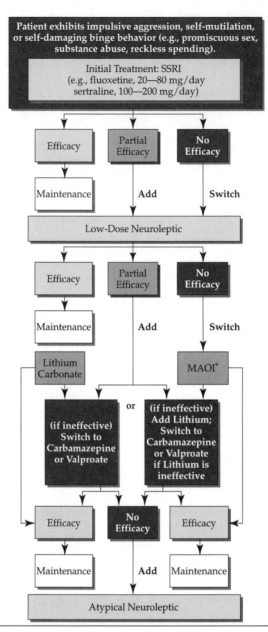

* SSRI treatment must be discontinued and followed with an adequate washout period before initiating treatment with an MAOI.

Figure 15.2   Psychopharmacological Treatment of Impulsive-Behavioral Dyscontrol Symptoms in Patients with Borderline Personality Disorder. Algorithm based on clinical judgment that uses evidence currently in the literature, following the format of the International Psychopharmacology Algorithm Project (2). The first step in the algorithm is generally supported by the best empirical evidence. Recommendations may not be applicable to all patients or take individual needs into account. The empirical research studies on which these recommendations are based may be "first trials" involving previously untreated patients and may not take into account previous patient nonresponse to one, two, or even three levels of the algorithm (i.e., patients who, by definition, have more refractory disorders). There are no empirical trials of the complete algorithm. [*Source:* From "Practice Guideline for the Treatment of Patients with Borderline Personality Disorder," by American Psychiatric Association, October 2001, *American Journal of Psychiatry, 158*(Suppl. 10), pp. 1–52. Reprinted by permission.]

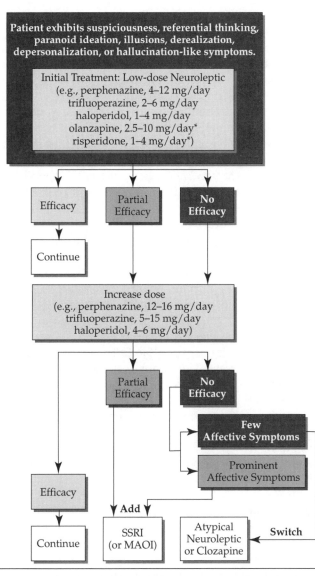

*The generally favorable side effect profiles of the newer atypical neuroleptic medications compared with those of conventional neuroleptics underscore the need for careful empirical trials of these newer medications in the treatment of patients with Borderline Personality Disorder.

Figure 15.3 Psychopharmacological Treatment of Cognitive-Perceptual Symptoms in Patients with Borderline Personality Disorder. Algorithm based on clinical judgment that uses evidence currently in the literature, following the format of the International Psychopharmacology Algorithm Project (2). The first step in the algorithm is generally supported by the best empirical evidence. Recommendations may not be applicable to all patients or take individual needs into account. The empirical research studies on which these recommendations are based may be "first trials" involving previously untreated patients and may not take into account previous patient nonresponse to one, two, or even three levels of the algorithm (i.e., patients who, by definition, have more refractory disorders). There are no empirical trials of the complete algorithm. [*Source:* From "Practice Guideline for the Treatment of Patients with Borderline Personality Disorder," by American Psychiatric Association, October 2001, *American Journal of Psychiatry, 158*(Suppl. 10), pp. 1–52. Reprinted by permission.]

An additional study of interest is an open-label study of fluoxetine (80 mg/day) in 12 Borderline PD patients who each were engaging in at least four self-injurious episodes per week (such as superficial cutting or burning). Remarkably, by the 12th and final week of the study, only two patients were still engaging in self-injury, and the other 10 had completely stopped (for a review of the pharmacotherapy of impulsive self-injurious behaviors, see Grossman & Siever, 2001).

The effects of SSRIs, however, can be broader, for a number of studies have reported improvement in cognitive-perceptual symptoms with SSRI treatment. It is relatively commonplace that an individual will not respond to one SSRI, but another will be effective (Markovitz, 1995). The current recommendation is to try a second SSRI and not to switch to a different class of medications in the case where the first SSRI was not effective.

In general, SSRIs are well tolerated, but significant numbers of patients have marked side effects, which can include symptoms such as increased anxiety, depersonalization, and derealization. In patients with marked anxiety or dissociative symptoms, it is advisable to begin treatment at a lower starting dose than usual and gradually titrate based on clinical observations. Differentiating between diagnoses of Borderline PD and Cyclothymia is important. Most controlled studies have not found a high comorbidity. However, those subjects who do have Cyclothymia or comorbid Bipolar Disorder are more susceptible to an iatrogenic hypomania or mania with the introduction of any antidepressant and should be closely monitored for the occurrence of such symptoms. In such cases, a mood stabilizer or atypical antipsychotic would be a better first choice.

In summary, flouxetine and sertraline have most clearly demonstrated efficacy in decreasing specific symptoms of depression, anxiety, anger, verbal aggression, physical aggression against objects, self-injurious behavior, and global level of function. Theoretically, other SSRIs should share these properties, but this has not been studied.

Monoamine Oxidase Inhibitors (MAOIs) Of applicability to Borderline PD, MAOIs were first reported to be effective in small open-label trials in patients with "hysteroid" or "rejection-sensitive dysphoria" (Liebowitz & Klein, 1979, 1981). Side effects of the MAOIs phenelzine and tranlycypromine are not inconsequential and include orthostatic hypotension (common), weight gain, sedation, and insomnia. MAOIs also carry the risk of a hypertensive crisis if patients eat certain tyramine-containing foods or various amine preparations (such as those for congestion) that are common in over-the-counter medications. Patients who are not able to be responsible in adhering to dietary restrictions, those who abuse stimulants, and those not able to endure a two-week washout period for other antidepressants they are on, should not be treated with an MAOI.

The three available placebo-controlled trials showed mixed results and have methodological problems of brevity of trial length, small sample sizes, medication carryover effects, and inadequate correction in the outcome analyses for multiple statistical comparisons. In an inpatient four-medication crossover study, 12 patients with comorbid hysteroid dysphoria were treated with tranylcypromine (40 mg/day). Significant decrease in anxiety, rage, impulsivity, and suicidality, in conjunction with an "increased capacity for pleasure," was reported (Cowdry & Gardner, 1988). Another study selected patients with primary atypical depression and comorbid Borderline PD. The authors reported that significant global improvement was seen in 92% of these outpatients treated with phenelzine (Parsons et al., 1989). These positive findings may relate more to improvement in mild depression, rather than core Borderline PD symptoms, and this study is best contrasted with a very well-controlled inpatient study of 34 subjects with a primary diagnosis of Borderline PD not selected for a comorbid depressive disorder. The treatment with phenelzine was not found to be effective (Soloff et al., 1993). Currently, MAOIs are viewed as third- or fourth-line medications in the treatment of the impulsive-behavioral dyscontrol and affective dysregulation symptom clusters.

Tricyclic Antidepressants (TCAs)   The primary mechanism of all the TCAs (except clomipramine) is inhibition of norepinepherine reuptake. In animals, increased norepinepherine makes the organism more reactive to environmental stimuli. This appears to be problematic in Borderline PD patients who are already overly reactive to environmental stressors and have poor behavioral or cognitive means to modulate this reactivity. Indeed, in two separate double-blind placebo-controlled studies, one with amytriptyline (Soloff, Anselm, Nathan, Schulz, & Perel, 1986) and another with imiprimine (Links, Steiner, Boiago, & Irwin, 1990), the Borderline PD subjects became worse with TCA treatment on measures of hostile depression, schizotypal factors, anxiety, hostility, agitation, dissociation, behavioral impulsivity, irritability, and suicidality. In short, adverse iatrogenic reactions, marked side effects, and lethality in overdose make TCAs relatively contraindicated in the treatment of Borderline patients.

Other Antidepressants   There are no reports of controlled trials using other antidepressants. Other than scattered case reports, the only published data is on an open-label trial of the mixed norepinepherine and serotonin reuptake inhibitor, venlafaxine. Thirty-nine outpatients meeting *DSM-III-R* criteria for Borderline PD, with a score of 60 or greater on the SCL-90, were treated with 100 to 200 mg venlafaxine bid. Two-thirds of the patients were on other psychotropic medications. The authors reported broad clinical efficacy with an approximate 40% reduction in each of the 10 SCL-90 subscales and cessation of self-injurious behaviors in five of the seven subjects who had been engaging in such acts. Of note, all but five of the study subjects also met criteria for current Major Depression, further confounding whether venlafaxine has specific efficacy for core Borderline PD symptoms (Markovitz & Wagner, 1995). Nonetheless, this medication, and virtually all of the other newer antidepressants not falling into classes already discussed (nefazadone, mirtazipine, buproprion), deserve further investigation.

Atypical Antipsychotics (D_2/5HT$_2$ Antagonists)   These agents have a remarkably better side effect profile than their classic D_1 antagonist progenitors, carry a lower risk for tardive dyskinesia, and patients feel better and are, therefore, more compliant with treatment on these as opposed to the typical antipsychotic medications. The first atypical antipsychotic approved for use in the United States was clozapine. Two open-label studies explored the efficacy of clozapine in patients with Borderline PD. In the first study (Frankenburg & Zanarini, 1993), 15 patients with Borderline PD and comorbid Psychotic Disorder NOS were treated with an average dose of 253 mg/day. These subjects were chosen based on their having been refractory or intolerant of other antipsychotic medications. Improvement, although modest, was seen for both positive and negative psychotic symptoms and global level of functioning. It is impossible, however, to extrapolate whether this medication would have been effective for cognitive-perceptual disturbances in a Borderline PD group not having a comorbid Axis I psychotic disorder.

This latter issue was addressed by a study in which only Borderline PD subjects without Axis I psychotic disorders were included, yet these patients also had been refractory to prior psychotherapy and medication treatment. The authors reported improvement in all of the three symptom clusters in Borderline PD (cognitive-perceptual, affective dysregulation, and impulsive behavioral dyscontrol) on a relatively low average dose of 44 mg/day (Benedetti, Sforzini, Colombo, Maffei, & Smeraldi, 1998). Clozapine, however, frequently causes weight gain, orthostasis, and sedation. In addition, the significant risk of agranulocytosis necessitates frequent and ongoing blood monitoring. Further, anticholinergic effects of this medication may exacerbate cognitive impairments.

The newer atypical agents have much more favorable side effect profiles, do not require frequent blood monitoring, and are better tolerated by patients. Unfortunately, only limited controlled data is available on use of these medications in patients with Borderline PD. One of the most favorable studies was a double-blind placebo-controlled (2:1 olanzapine to placebo) design in which 28 female Borderline PD patients were treated for six months. Statistically significant improvement occurred in subjects' interpersonal functioning, as well as the three core symptom clusters (Zanarini & Frankenburg, 2001). Another open-label case series reported on treatment of 11 subjects with Borderline PD and comorbid Dysthymia for eight weeks on an average dose of 7.5 mg/day. Seven of these subjects also met criteria for Schizotypal PD, so significant cognitive-perceptual symptoms were present in this group. Improvement was reported in areas of anger, depression, anxiety, interpersonal sensitivity, and psychoticism (Schulz, Camlin, Berry, & Jesberger, 1999).

Preliminary data on risperidone was published from a double-blind placebo-controlled trial at an average dose of 2.5 mg/day. The authors reported that the risperidone-treated group did not show statistically significant differences from the placebo-treated group. However, as additional subjects were added, the active medication group was starting to look as though they were improving more on measures of paranoia, psychoticism, interpersonal sensitivity, and phobic anxiety (Schulz, Camlin, Berry, & Friedman, 1999). An open-label trial reported reduction in aggression, depressive symptoms, and improved global functioning in 13 Borderline PD subjects treated with an average dose of 3.27 mg/day of risperidol (Rocca, Marchiaro, Cocuzza, & Bogetto, 2002). More controlled trials are needed for the atypical agents in treatment of Borderline PD. Atypical antipsychotics (excluding clozapine secondary to side effects) are considered to be first-line medications for the treatment of the cognitive-perceptual symptom cluster in Borderline PD patients. They are also useful as an augmentation agent to SSRIs or mood stabilizers for the treatment of severe anger or hostility (see Figure 15.2).

Typical Antipsychotics (Primary D_1 Antagonists)   This class of medications is being steadily replaced by the atypical antipsychotic agents. In general, a number of double-blind and placebo-controlled studies have found 8.7 mg/day thiothixene (Goldberg et al., 1986), 7.8 mg/day trifluoperazine (Cowdry & Gardner, 1988), 4.8 mg/day haloperidol (Soloff, George, et al., 1986; Soloff et al., 1989), and 3.9 mg/day haloperidol (Soloff et al., 1993) to have slight but significant positive effects on phobic anxiety, psychotic thinking, rejection sensitivity, suicidality, depression, hostility, and impulsive aggression. However, compliance with these medications was very low, and dropout rates for medication were up to 88%. Using a more conservative last observation carried forward (which does not bias the results by excluding those who dropped out secondary to active medication side effects), most of these studies either did not find significant improvement or the improvement was so slight and compliance such a problem that they recommended typical antipsychotic medication use only in patients with marked psychotic (cognitive perceptual) symptoms. These studies were all performed before atypical antipsychotics were available.

Lithium and Anticonvulsant Mood Stabilizers   A hallmark of Borderline PD is unstable mood. Some researchers have hypothesized that Borderline PD is essentially a variant of Bipolar Disorder (Akiskal, 1981). This is not the prevalent view at this time, and in the best controlled study exploring this, less than 10% of the 379 Borderline PD patients met diagnostic criteria for Bipolar II (Zanarini et al., 1998). Nonetheless, lithium and the anticonvulsant mood stabilizers have demonstrated efficacy for core Borderline PD symptoms.

Data from two double-blind placebo-controlled trials of lithium in Borderline PD are available. The first was carried out in a *DSM-I* precursor of Borderline PD, Emotionally Unstable Character Disorder. After six weeks of treatment, significant improvement was noted in global functioning and mood lability in 14 of the 21 subjects (Rifkin, Quitkin, & Curillo, 1972). A later study, also six weeks in duration, treated 17 subjects with an average dose of 1,000 mg/day in a crossover design. Ten subjects completed both the lithium and placebo phases, and significant improvement was seen globally and specifically in areas of impulsivity, anger, and suicidality (Links et al., 1990). The low therapeutic index of lithium means there is a narrow margin between an effective dose and one that causes toxicity. Lithium can be lethal when overdosed and often is associated with significant weight gain, tremor, acne, and hypothyroidism.

The best-studied of the anticonvulsant mood stabilizers in Borderline PD is divalproex sodium. In a recent double-blind placebo-controlled study, 30 subjects with Borderline PD and comorbid Bipolar II disorder were treated with divalproex sodium or placebo (2:1 ratio) at an average dose of 850 mg/day (Frankenburg & Zanarini, 2002). Using the last observation carried forward, divalproex sodium was significantly more effective than placebo in diminishing interpersonal sensitivity and anger/hostility as measured by the SCL-90. Another instrument found overall aggression to have also been significantly reduced by treatment with divalproex sodium. It is unclear to what extent improvement in these subjects was secondary to improvement in their bipolar-spectrum condition and whether the majority of Borderline PD patients who are not comorbid for Bipolar II (~90%) would have improved at all.

The only other data available from a placebo-controlled trial is preliminary and reflects results in only six subjects who completed the 10-week treatment. Five of the subjects showed significant improvement globally, with trend-level improvement in depressive symptoms (Hollander et al., 2001). This study is underpowered, and further studies with more subjects are required. The largest open-label trial was in 30 Borderline PD inpatients who were treated with divalproex sodium, titrated to a blood level of 100 µg/ml. Improvement was noted in anxiety, tension, global symptoms, and time spent in seclusion (Wilcox, 1994). Two other smaller open-label studies reported improvements in mood instability, impulsivity, anxiety, anger, rejection sensitivity (Stein, Simeon, Frenkel, Islam, & Hollander, 1995), aggression, and irritability (Kavoussi & Coccaro, 1998). A blood level of approximately 100 μg/ml valproate seems appropriate, but this has not been systematically studied.

The second most investigated anticonvulsant in the treatment of Borderline PD is carbamazepine. In the previously mentioned inpatient placebo-controlled crossover study (Cowdry & Gardner, 1988), it was reported that in Borderline PD patients with a history of behavioral dyscontrol, an average dose of 820 mg/day carbamazepine resulted in a decrease in both frequency and severity of such episodes. Improvement was also noted in areas of mood, anxiety, and anger. Although encouraging, treatment with carbamazepine was not without problems. Of the 17 patients treated, six developed allergic reactions to the medication, and three developed melancholic depression, which remitted on discontinuation of the carbamazepine (Gardner & Cowdry, 1986). In a second study of a similar number of Borderline PD subjects but in whom there was not significant behavioral dyscontrol, carbamazepine was not more effective than placebo (De la Fuente & Lotstra, 1994). Carbamazepine carries risks of aplastic anemia, rash, and induces its own metabolism, necessitating rather frequent level monitoring (in addition to blood counts), particularly in the first months of treatment. It may not cause melancholic depression, but seems not to prevent it. Current evidence ranks carbamazepine behind divalproex sodium when a mood stabilizer is indicated.

A number of newer anticonvulsant agents are available, many of which could likely show efficacy in adequately powered controlled trials. Lamotrigine, although it carries the risk of life-threatening rash, has significant antidepressant and mood-stabilizing properties. In eight antidepressant-resistant Borderline PD patients without apparent comorbid Bipolar Disorder or variants, three were reported to have shown a doubling of global functioning score and a decrease in impulsive behavior while treated with this medication (Pinto & Akiskal, 1998).

Anxiolytics Anxiety is not one of the *DSM* criteria for Borderline PD; however, many patients with Borderline PD struggle with chronic anxiety in the form of Generalized Anxiety Disorder, Social Phobia, Panic Attacks, and Posttraumatic Stress Disorder. In fact, the remarkably high comorbidity of anxiety disorders best differentiates Borderline PD patients from patients with other personality disorders (Zanarini et al., 1998). The novel anxiolytic, buspirone (a $5HT1_A$ agonist), has not been studied, and data on alprazolam is available from one controlled study and one small case series.

The aforementioned inpatient placebo-controlled crossover study (Cowdry & Gardner, 1988) had an alprazolam arm under which 12 patients were treated at an average dose of 4.7 mg/day. Seven of these inherently behaviorally dyscontrolled subjects demonstrated increased suicidality and dyscontrol as evidenced by drug overdosing, self-mutilation, and physical aggression. These behaviors were present in only one of the subjects while on placebo. Benzodiazepines, similar to alcohol, may lead to dysinhibition of aggressive behavior in individuals who are impulsive and who have strong aggressive urges. Alprazolam's rapid onset of action and short half life may contribute to problems with abuse and risks for addiction.

Prescribing these medications only to less impulsive-aggressive individuals may mitigate some of the risks, as demonstrated by an open-label series of three

Borderline PD patients who were nonresponsive to other medications. These patients, treated with alprazolam, were reported to show significant improvement (Faltus, 1984). Benzodiazepines are not absolutely contraindicated in Borderline PD patients, but impulsivity, aggression, and problems with substance or alcohol abuse or dependence are strong negative indications. There are some patients whose anxiety responds only to a benzodiazepine, in which case the medications with a slower onset of action and longer duration (such as clonazepam or diazepam) may be less destabilizing and carry a lower risk for abuse or causing dysinhibition.

Opioid Antagonists   Lack of pain during self-injurious behavior (SIB) in about half of Borderline PD patients and the "addictive" nature of the behavior has lead some researchers to hypothesize involvement of the endogenous opioid system. Endogenous opioids have also been hypothesized to play a role in certain dissociative states. Only open-label treatment reports are available for opioid receptor antagonists. In one case series, seven subjects with Borderline PD who engaged in SIB with accompanying analgesia and dysphoria reduction were treated with daily doses of naltrexone 50 mg/day. The authors reported that six of the subjects completely stopped the SIB, and the seventh greatly decreased the frequency and severity of the episodes (Roth, Ostroff, & Hoffman, 1996). Two other single case reports with positive outcomes have also been published (Griengl, Sendera, & Dantendorfer, 2001; McGee, 1997).

From the perspective of dissociation, naltrexone at doses up to 400 mg/day was used to treat 13 patients with Borderline PD, chosen for participation in the study based on histories of severe psychological trauma and marked dissociative symptoms. Two-thirds of the patients reported a decrease in dissociative symptoms of flashbacks and tonic immobility (Bohus et al., 1999). Dissociation often serves to protect the individual from overwhelming affect. Hence, successful medication treatment may eliminate dissociation as a coping mechanism, without adding any new means for an individual to deal with the tormenting thoughts, images, or feelings. The authors now stress the importance of a safe setting, in conjunction with behavioral skills training in relaxation and other self-soothing techniques before a trial with an opioid antagonist for dissociation is undertaken (M. J. Bohus, personal communication, July 2001). Findings for opioid antagonists in the treatment of SIB or dissociation are preliminary and require closer study under controlled conditions.

NARCISSISTIC PERSONALITY DISORDER

The personality disorders were classified on a separate axis because the initial theoretical perspective was that these disorders were developmental in origin, arising from various conflicts unsuccessfully navigated by the individual during their maturation. In prior chapters on the biology of personality, we have seen how numerous personality disorders or spectrum traits are associated with replicable altered biological, neuropsychological, or brain structure findings. These findings do not exist for Narcissistic PD, and, perhaps more than any other personality disorder, Narcissistic PD centers around an attitude about self and others, rather than odd behaviors, perceptions, mood changes, impulsivity, or anxiety. Narcissism and the accompanying nondelusional grandiosity are typically viewed as a façade, protecting a fragile and negative sense of self. As is true of any personality-disordered individual, stressors such as a comorbid anxiety disorder or depressive episodes often lead the individual to greater use of their maladaptive defense mechanisms and a concomitant exacerbation of their characterological pathology. Accordingly, particular attention should be paid to evaluation for frequently co-morbid anxiety and depressive disorders that can be pharmacologically treated and indirectly improve Narcissistic PD symptoms. Pharmacological treatment of Narcissistic PD without Axis I comorbidity has not been studied.

HISTRIONIC PERSONALITY DISORDER

There are also no pharmacological trials that have been reported for Histrionic PD. In *Neurotic Styles,* Shapiro (1965) presents the idea that an individual's personality and preferred defense/coping mechanisms arise from how they view and react to the world. We now know that aside from experiences that can change neurobiology, what we call *temperament* in the infant is highly heritable (biological). A central deficit in Histrionic PD is rapidly shifting and intense emotional reactions, in conjunction with favoring and acting on this information as opposed to reasoning and logic. From this perspective, medications that tend to decrease emotional reactivity and allow an individual to "step back and think" before acting, such as the SSRIs and possibly the anticonvulsant mood stabilizers, deserve consideration and study.

ANTISOCIAL PERSONALITY DISORDER

Core features of adult Antisocial PD are resistant to treatment with psychotherapy and pharmacotherapy. However, aggression, which is one of the most problematic behaviors of Antisocial individuals, can be effectively treated with a variety of medications, depending on the underlying pathophysiology. The type of violence or aggression most amenable to pharmacological treatment in this population is the explosive, impulsive variety, as opposed to premeditated affectively detached violence (Barratt, Stanford, Felthous, & Kent, 1997). Borderline PD is frequently comorbid with Antisocial PD, and pharmacotherapy of core Borderline PD features, as previously discussed, should be an integral part of treatment. The algorithm for treatment of impulsive aggression in Borderline PD is also applicable to Antisocial PD patients with this same spectrum trait. What can greatly aid in choice of a medication is to consider what the pathophysiology of the aggression is. Possible causes and first-line treatments can then be organized into groupings of low serotonergic function (treat with SSRIs), temporal lobe epilepsy (treat with anticonvulsants), mental retardation/organic dysfunction (treat with beta blockers), or psychosis/mania (treat with antipsychotic agents/mood stabilizers).

Antipsychotic Medications   Traditionally, the use of antipsychotic medications has been discouraged for the treatment of aggression in individuals whose aggression was not the direct result of their psychosis (Yudofsky, Silver, & Hales, 1995). However, the main reasons for this was that typical neuroleptics often caused akisthisia, which worsened agitation or aggression; and executive function was often further impaired. Atypical antipsychotics are less likely to cause these problems, and studies of their usefulness in impulsive aggression in patients with Borderline PD is encouraging. Only one case study has been reported of use of an atypical antipsychotic (risperidone) in an Antisocial patient, and marked reduction in aggression was noted (Hirose, 2001). (See the Atypical Antipsychotics section under Borderline PD for additional studies.)

Lithium and Anticonvulsant Mood Stabilizers   Some of the first successful medication studies for treatment of aggression were conducted using lithium in prison inmates. In both short-term (Sheard, 1971) and long-term (up to 1.5 years) open-label treatment (Tupin et al., 1973), lithium decreased violent behaviors and time spent in solitary confinement or other disciplinary actions. These were a mixed group of inmates, with more than half having a comorbid psychotic condition. All subjects had been treated with phenothiazines, but their violence had not decreased. The benefits of lithium were not limited to prisoners without EEG abnormalities. A later double-blind study of lithium at serum levels between 0.6 and 1.0 mEq/L found greater superiority of lithium over placebo for reduction of aggression among prisoners (Sheard, Marini, Bridges, & Wagner, 1976). Improvement was not secondary to amelioration of a manic or hypomanic state. Caution is indicated, however, because individuals with brain injury are more prone to lithium toxicity, and lithium may also lower the seizure threshold, thereby exacerbating temporal lobe epileptic activity-associated aggression (Schiff, Sabin, Geller, Alexander, & Mark, 1982).

Phenytoin was used in a double-blind placebo-crossover design in 60 prison inmates whose aggression was divided into premeditated versus impulsive. On a dose of 200 mg q am and 100 mg q pm, phenytoin significantly reduced impulsive-aggressive acts but not premeditated aggressive acts (Barratt et al., 1997). In approximately one-third of cases, impulsive-aggressive behaviors of the "low serotonin etiology" do not respond to treatment with SSRIs but do respond to treatment with an anticonvulsant mood stabilizer such as divalproex sodium (Kavoussi & Coccaro, 1998) or carbamazepine (Mattes, 1990).

In patients with outbursts of rage in conjunction with abnormal EEG findings, anticonvulsant mood stabilizers such as phenytoin, divalproex sodium, and carbamazepine (Stone, McDaniel, Hughes, & Hermann, 1986) are the treatment of choice. These agents are also effective for impulsive aggression not associated with EEG abnormalities. (See section under Borderline PD for additional studies.)

Selective Serotonin Reuptake Inhibitors (SSRIs)   Numerous biological studies involving serotonergic probes and neuroendocrine assessment, serotonergic probes and neuroimaging, serotonin receptor radioligands, radioiummunoassay of brain from autopsy specimens, and CSF 5-hydroxy-indole-acetic acid assays have found altered serotonergic functioning as associated with impulsive-aggressive behaviors. From this perspective, SSRIs are a logical medication choice (see section under Borderline PD for applicable studies) but have not been studied in Antisocial PD.

Beta Blockers   Most of the solid evidence for the efficacy of beta blockers in the treatment of aggression is in patients with dementia, mental retardation, psychosis, or brain injury. Abnormally high levels of frontal noradrenergic activation are believed to be the cause of aggression in many of these cases. In various controlled studies, propranolol at doses up to 800 mg per day (Silver et al., 1999), nadolol up to 80 mg per day (Ratey et al., 1992), and pindolol at doses up to 100 mg per day (Greendyke & Kanter, 1986) were effective. A caveat, however, is that none of these studies were conducted in individuals with primary personality disorders. There is need to do so. Although not part of the algorithm for impulsive aggression in Borderline PD (Figure 15.2), strong consideration of beta blockers should be entertained if the SSRIs, atypical antipsychotic agents, and lithium/mood stabilizers (alone and in combination) are not effective. Patients with asthma, chronic obstructive pulmonary disease, insulin dependent diabetes, CHF/angina, hyperthyroidism, and peripheral vascular disease are not appropriate for treatment with a beta blocker. Doses should be gradually titrated and stopped if the patient's pulse falls under 50 beats per minute, systolic BP drops below 90 mm Hg, or reduced/discontinued if wheezing, ataxia, or dizziness occurs.

CLUSTER C (ANXIOUS/FEARFUL)

Deficiencies in serotonergic function have been associated with impulsive aggression, whereas enhancing serotonin function has been shown to promote social status, decrease interpersonal sensitivity, and increase affiliative behavior in both primates and humans.

AVOIDANT PERSONALITY DISORDER

The pharmacotherapy of Avoidant PD has been minimally studied. However, Social Phobia or Social Anxiety Disorder (generalized type) has been rather extensively studied. Diagnostic criteria between Avoidant PD and Generalized Social Phobia grossly overlap, and there is greater than 90% comorbidity between these disorders. Further, structured psychological testing indicates they may be a single disorder (Noyes, Woodman, Holt, Reich, & Zimmerman, 1995). At present, the first-line treatment for Social Phobia is the SSRIs, based on their efficacy, safety, and tolerability (for review, see Blanco, Antia, & Liebowitz, 2002). Second-line agents that appear effective, but for which there is less data, include gabapentin, bupropion, and various benzodiazepines. MAOIs (primarily phenelzine) appear to be equal in efficacy to SSRIs, but they are not medications of first choice because of associated side effects and risks.

The MAOIs and SSRIs seem to ameliorate a core symptom of Avoidant PD, namely, interpersonal hypersensitivity. Responders in these studies had a decrease in social and performance anxiety, with a concomitant increase in social and work function. In fact, there is evidence that maladaptive personality traits of Avoidant PD/Generalized Social Phobia may even be more responsive to pharmacotherapy than these individuals' circumscribed social anxiety response (Fahlen, 1995). With medication treatment, typically one-third of patients will be very much improved, and an additional third will be much improved. There is evidence that patients who are successfully treated with a medication and then expose themselves to previously feared social situations derive a behavioral benefit that prevents return of symptoms even after discontinuation of the medication.

DEPENDENT PERSONALITY DISORDER

There are no pharmacological treatment studies of Dependent PD. Dependent PD may be viewed as a type of attachment disorder. Frequently, the patient reports high degrees of separation anxiety as a child, and, as adults, these patients have an increased prevalence of panic attacks. Whereas Social Phobics tend to have primarily Avoidant Personality traits, structured testing has found that Panic Disorder patients tend to have primarily Dependent traits (Noyes et al., 1995). Effective pharmacological treatments for Panic Disorder include SSRIs, tricyclic antidepressants, MAOIs, and benzodiazepines (Feighner, 1999). Of note, the most robust predictor of nonresponse to medication in a Panic Disorder patient is the presence of comorbid personality disorder (Slaap & den Boer, 2001).

OBSESSIVE-COMPULSIVE PERSONALITY DISORDER

There are no controlled pharmacological studies in Obsessive-Compulsive PD, and it is again necessary to extrapolate to get some indication of medications worthy of trial and controlled study. One of the central dynamic issues for individuals with Obsessive-Compulsive PD is a stubborn rigidity, which leads to great difficulty in cooperating with others, often in conjunction with difficulties controlling anger. In a neuroendocrine challenge study with the serotonergic probe fenfluramine, the group of subjects with Obsessive-Compulsive PD, as compared to personality-disordered subjects without Obsessive-Compulsive PD, had a blunting of the prolactin response (decreased serotonergic function), and the total number of Obsessive-Compulsive personality traits showed a positive correlation with degree of impulsive-aggressive behaviors (Stein et al., 1996).

Two very interesting placebo-controlled studies found that even among healthy volunteers, the SSRIs citalopram at 20 mg/day (Tse & Bond, 2002) and paroxetine at 20 mg/day (Allgulander, Cloninger, Przybeck, & Brandt, 1998) resulted in a significant increase in cooperative and affiliative behaviors, in conjunction with a decrease in hostility and aggressive behaviors. Serotonergic deficits in Obsessive-Compulsive PD, in conjunction with SSRIs' ability to increase affiliative behavior and decrease aggressive behavior, support SSRIs as a first-line medication in attempts to pharmacologically treat Obsessive-Compulsive PD. Controlled trials of these and other agents are certainly required.

SUMMARY AND CONCLUSION

Understanding both the individual psychodynamics of the patient along with the psychodynamics of your interaction with them is an important aspect in pharmacological treatment of the personality-disordered patient. Choice of medications is facilitated by considering whether that patient's symptoms are state or trait and what their core symptoms are (rather than just the particular personality disorder diagnosis). Grouping symptoms into the three categories of (1) affective dysregulation (depression, mood lability, rejection sensitivity, intense inappropriate anger, environmental reactivity), (2) impulsive-behavioral dyscontrol (impulsive aggression, self-injurious behavior, binge eating, risk-taking/sensation seeking, substance abuse/dependence), and (3) cognitive-perceptual (paranoia, illusions, suspiciousness, derealization, depersonalization, micropsychotic episodes) can direct you to first-line medication choices, not only for Borderline PD patients, but among all PD patients.

In general, atypical antipsychotic medications should usually be tried first in the Cluster A personality disorders, and SSRIs in the Cluster B and C personality disorders. It should be recalled that behavioral patterns arising from years of experiencing certain biological predispositions (such as mood lability, impulsivity, or paranoia) may take months or years to improve, even after the underlying neurobiology has been pharmacologically addressed. Prescribing medications for the treatment of the personality disorders is complex and challenging. However, the psychiatrist who is able to integrate diverse considerations and remain attuned to dynamic principles has a great advantage toward a successful outcome in such treatments.

REFERENCES

Akiskal, H. S. (1981). Subaffective disorders: Dysthymic, cyclothymic and bipolar II disorders in the "borderline" realm. *Psychiatric Clinics of North America, 4,* 25–46.

Allgulander, C., Cloninger, C. R., Przybeck, T. R., & Brandt, L. (1998). Changes on the Temperament and Character Inventory after paroxetine treatment in volunteers with generalized anxiety disorder. *Psychopharmacology Bulletin, 34*(2), 165–166.

American Psychiatric Association. (2001). Practice guideline for the treatment of patients with borderline personality disorder. *American Journal of Psychiatry, 158*(Suppl. 10), 1–52.

Barratt, E. S., Stanford, M. S., Felthous, A. R., & Kent, T. A. (1997). The effects of phenytoin on impulsive and premeditated aggression: A controlled study. *Journal of Clinical Psychopharmacology, 17*(5), 341–349.

Benedetti, F., Sforzini, L., Colombo, C., Maffei, C., & Smeraldi, E. (1998). Low-dose clozapine in acute and continuation treatment of severe borderline personality disorder. *Journal of Clinical Psychiatry, 59,* 103–107.

Bilder, R. M., Goldman, R. S., Volavka, J., Czobor, P., Hoptman, M., Sheitman, B., et al. (2002). Neurocognitive effects of clozapine, olanzapine, risperidone, and haloperidol in patients with chronic schizophrenia or schizoaffective disorder. *American Journal of Psychiatry, 159*(6), 1018–1028.

Blanco, C., Antia, S. X., & Liebowitz, M. R. (2002). Pharmacotherapy of social anxiety disorder [Review]. *Biological Psychiatry, 51*(1), 109–120.

Bohus, M. J., Landwehrmeyer, G. B., Stiglmayr, C. E., Limberger, M. F., Bohme, R., & Schmahl, C. G. (1999). Naltrexone in the treatment of dissociative symptoms in patients with borderline personality disorder: An open-label trial. *Journal of Clinical Psychiatry, 60*(9), 598–603.

Coccaro, E. F., & Kavoussi, R. J. (1997). Fluoxetine and impulsive aggressive behavior in personality-disordered subjects. *Archives of General Psychiatry, 54,* 1081–1088.

Cowdry, R. W., & Gardner, D. L. (1988). Pharmacotherapy of borderline personality disorder: Alprazolam, carbamazepine, trifluoperazine, and tranylcypromine. *Archives of General Psychiatry, 45,* 111–119.

Davidson, J. R., Rothbaum, B. O., van der Kolk, B. A., Sikes, C. R., & Farfel, G. M. (2001). Multicenter, double-blind comparison of sertraline and placebo in the treatment of posttraumatic stress disorder. *Archives of General Psychiatry, 58*(5), 485–492.

De la Fuente, J., & Lotstra, F. (1994). A trial of carbamazepine in borderline personality disorder. *European Neuropsychopharmacology, 4,* 479–486.

Fahlen, T. (1995). Personality traits in social phobia, II: Changes during drug treatment. *Journal of Clinical Psychiatry, 56*(12), 569–573.

Faltus, F. J. (1984). The positive effect of alprazolam in the treatment of three patients with borderline personality disorder. *American Journal of Psychiatry, 141,* 802–803.

Feighner, J. P. (1999). Overview of antidepressants currently used to treat anxiety disorders. *Journal of Clinical Psychiatry, 22,* 18–22.

Frankenburg, F. R., & Zanarini, M. C. (1993). Clozapine treatment of borderline patients: A preliminary study. *Comprehensive Psychiatry, 34,* 402–405.

Frankenburg, F. R., & Zanarini, M. C. (2002). Divalproex sodium treatment of women with borderline personality disorder and bipolar II disorder: A double-blind placebo-controlled pilot study. *Journal of Clinical Psychiatry, 63*(5), 442–446.

Gardner, D. L., & Cowdry, R. W. (1986). Development of melancholia during carbamazepine treatment in borderline personality disorder. *Journal of Clinical Psychopharmacology, 6,* 236–239.

Goldberg, S. C., Schulz, S. C., Schulz, P. M., Resnick, R. J., Hamer, R. M., & Friedel, R. O. (1986). Borderline and schizotypal personality disorders treated with low-dose thiothixene vs placebo. *Archives of General Psychiatry, 43,* 680–686.

Greendyke, R. M., & Kanter, D. R. (1986). Therapeutic effects of pindolol on behavioral disturbances associated with organic brain disease: A double-blind study. *Journal of Clinical Psychiatry, 47*(8), 423–426.

Griengl, H., Sendera, A., & Dantendorfer, K. (2001). Naltrexone as a treatment of self-injurious behavior: A case report. *Acta Psychiatrica Scandinavica, 103*(3), 234–236.

Grossman, R., & Siever, L. (2001). Impulsive self-injurious behaviors: Phenomenology, neurobiology and treatment. In D. Simeon & E. Hollander (Eds.), *Self-injurious behaviors* (pp. 117–148). Washington, DC: American Psychiatric Press.

Hirose, S. (2001). Effective treatment of aggression and impulsivity in antisocial personality disorder with risperidone. *Psychiatry and Clinical Neurosciences, 55*(2), 161–162.

Hollander, E., Allen, A., Lopez, R. P., Bienstock, C. A., Grossman, R., Siever, L. J., et al. (2001). A preliminary double-blind, placebo-controlled trial of divalproex sodium in borderline personality disorder. *Journal of Clinical Psychiatry, 62*(3), 199–203.

Ichikawa, J., Ishii, H., Bonaccorso, S., Fowler, W. L., O'Laughlin, I. A., & Meltzer, H. Y. (2001). 5-HT(2A) and D(2) receptor blockade increases cortical DA release via 5-HT(1A) receptor activation: A possible mechanism of atypical antipsychotic-induced cortical dopamine release. *Journal of Neurochemistry, 76*(5), 1521–1531.

Kavoussi, R. J., & Coccaro, E. F. (1998). Divalproex sodium for impulsive aggressive behavior in patients with personality disorder. *Journal of Clinical Psychiatry, 59,* 676–680.

Koenigsberg, H. W., Reynolds, D., Goodman, M., New, A., Mitropoulou, V., Treatment, R., et al. (in press). Risperidone in the treatment of schizotypal personality disorder. *Journal of Clinical Psychiatry.*

Liebowitz, M. R., & Klein, D. F. (1979). Hysteroid dysphoria. *Psychiatric Clinic of North America, 2,* 555–575.

Liebowitz, M. R., & Klein, D. F. (1981). Interrelationship of hysteroid dysphoria and borderline personality disorder. *Psychiatric Clinic of North America, 4,* 67–87.

Links, P. S., Steiner, M., Boiago, I., & Irwin, D. (1990). Lithium therapy for borderline patients: Preliminary findings. *Journal of Clinical Psychopharmacology, 4,* 173–181.

Markovitz, P. J. (1995). Pharmacotherapy of impulsivity, aggression, and related disorders. In E. Hollander & D. Stein (Eds.), *Impulsivity and aggression* (pp. 260–280). New York: Wiley.

Markovitz, P. J., Calabrese, J. R., Schulz, S. C., & Meltzer, H. Y. (1991). Fluoxetine treatment of borderline and schizotypal personality disorder. *American Journal of Psychiatry, 148,* 1064–1067.

Markovitz, P. J., & Wagner, S. (1995). Venlafaxine in the treatment of borderline personality disorder. *Psychopharmocology Bulletin, 31,* 773–777.

Mattes, J. A. (1990). Comparative effectiveness of carbamazepine and propranolol for rage outbursts. *Journal of Neuropsychiatry and Clinical Neurosciences, 2*(2), 159–164.

McGee, M. D. (1997). Cessation of self-mutilation in a patient with borderline personality disorder treated with naltrexone. *Journal of Clinical Psychiatry, 58*(1), 32–33.

Noyes, R., Jr., Woodman, C. L., Holt, C. S., Reich, J. H., & Zimmerman, M. B. (1995). Avoidant personality traits distinguish social phobic and panic disorder. *Journal of Nervous and Mental Diseases, 183*(3), 145–153.

Parsons, B., Quitkin, F. M., McGrath, P. J., Stewart, J. W., Tricamo, E., Ocepek-Welikson, K., et al. (1989). Phenelzine, imipramine, and placebo in borderline patients meeting criteria for atypical depression. *Psychopharmacology Bulletin, 25,* 524–534.

Pinto, O. C., & Akiskal, H. S. (1998). Lamotrigine as a promising approach to borderline personality: An open case series without concurrent *DSM-IV* major mood disorder. *Journal of Affective Disorders, 51,* 333–343.

Ratey, J. J., Sorgi, P., O'Driscoll, G. A., Sands, S., Daehler, M. L., Fletcher, J. R., et al. (1992). Nadolol to treat aggression and psychiatric symptomatology in chronic psychiatric inpatients: A double-blind, placebo-controlled study. *Journal of Clinical Psychiatry, 53*(2), 41–46.

Rifkin, A., Quitkin, F., & Curillo, C. (1972). Lithium carbonate in emotionally unstable character disorder. *Archives of General Psychiatry, 27,* 519–523.

Rocca, P., Marchiaro, L., Cocuzza, E., & Bogetto, F. (2002). Treatment of borderline personality disorder with risperidone. *Journal of Clinical Psychiatry, 63*(3), 241–244.

Roth, A. S., Ostroff, R. B., & Hoffman, R. E. (1996). Naltrexone as a treatment for repetitive self-injurious behavior: An open-label trial. *Journal of Clinical Psychiatry, 57*(6), 233–237.

Salzman, C., Wolfson, A. N., Schatzberg, A., Looper, J., Henke, R., Albanese, M., et al. (1995). Effect of fluoxetine on anger in symptomatic volunteers with borderline personality disorder. *Journal of Clinical Psychopharmacology, 15,* 23–29.

Schiff, H. B., Sabin, T. D., Geller, A., Alexander, L., & Mark, V. (1982). Lithium in aggressive behavior. *American Journal of Psychiatry, 139,* 1346–1348.

Schulz, S. C., Camlin, K. L., Berry, S. A., & Friedman, L. (1999). *Risperidone for borderline personality disorder: A double blind study.* Poster presented at the annual meeting of the American College of Neuropsychopharmacology, Puerto Rico.

Schulz, S. C., Camlin, K. L., Berry, S. A., & Jesberger, J. A. (1999). Olanzapine safety and efficacy in patients with borderline personality disorder and comorbid dysthymia. *Biological Psychiatry, 46,* 1429–1435.

Shapiro, D. (1965). *Neurotic styles.* New York: Basic Books.

Sheard, M. (1971). Effect of lithium on human aggression. *Nature, 230,* 113–114.

Sheard, M., Marini, J., Bridges, C., & Wagner, L. (1976). The effect of lithium on impulsive aggressive behavior in man. *American Journal of Psychiatry, 133,* 1409–1413.

Siever, L. J., & Davis, K. L. (1991). A psychobiological perspective on the personality disorders. *American Journal of Psychiatry, 148,* 1647–1658.

Silver, J. M., Yudofsky, S. C., Slater, J. A., Gold, R. K., Stryer, B. L., Williams, D. T., et al. (1999). Propranolol treatment of chronically hospitalized aggressive patients. *Journal of Neuropsychiatry and Clinical Neurosciences, 11*(3), 328–335.

Slaap, B. R., & den Boer, J. A. (2001). The prediction of nonresponse to pharmacotherapy in panic disorder: A review. *Depression and Anxiety, 14,* 112–122.

Soloff, P. H. (1998). Algorithms for pharmacological treatment of personality dimensions: Symptoms specific treatments for cognitive-perceptual, affective, and impulsive-behavioral dysregulation. *Bulletin of the Menninger Clinic, 62*(2), 195–214.

Soloff, P. H., Anselm, G., Nathan, R. S., Schulz, P. M., & Perel, J. M. (1986). Paradoxical effects of amitriptyline on borderline patients. *American Journal of Psychiatry, 143,* 1603–1605.

Soloff, P. H., Cornelius, J., George, A., Nathan, S., Perel, J. M., & Ulrich, R. F. (1993). Efficacy of phenelzine and haloperidol in borderline personality disorder. *Archives of General Psychiatry, 50,* 377–385.

Soloff, P. H., George, A., Nathan, R. S., Schulz, P. M., Cornelius, J. R., Herring, J., et al. (1989). Amitriptyline versus haloperidol in borderlines: Final outcomes and predictors of response. *Journal of Clinical Psychopharmacology, 9,* 238–246.

Soloff, P. H., George, A., Nathan, R. S., Schulz, P. M., Ulrich, R. F., & Perel, J. M. (1986). Progress in pharmacotherapy of borderline disorders: A double-blind study of amitriptyline, haloperidol, and placebo. *Archives of General Psychiatry, 43,* 691–697.

Stein, D. J., Simeon, D., Frenkel, M., Islam, M. N., & Hollander, E. (1995). An open label trial of valproate in borderline personality disorder. *Journal of Clinical Psychiatry, 56,* 506–510.

Stein, D. J., Trestman, R. L., Mitropoulou, V., Coccaro, E. F., Hollander, E., & Siever, L. J. (1996). Impulsivity and serotonergic function in compulsive personality disorder. *Journal of Neuropsychiatry and Clinical Neurosciences, 8*(4), 393–398.

Stone, J. L., McDaniel, K. D., Hughes, J. R., & Hermann, B. P. (1986). Episodic dyscontrol disorder and paroxysmal EEG abnormalities: Successful treatment with carbamazepine. *Biological Psychiatry, 21*(2), 208–212.

Tse, W. S., & Bond, A. J. (2002). Serotonergic intervention affects both social dominance and affiliative behavior. *Psychopharmacology, 161*(3), 324–330.

Tsuang, M. T., Stone, W. S., Tarbox, S. I., & Faraone, S. V. (2002). Treatment of nonpsychotic relatives of patients with schizophrenia: Six case studies. *American Journal of Medical Genetics, 114*(8), 943–948.

Tupin, J. P., Smith, D. B., Clanon, T. L., Kim, L. I., Nugent, A., & Groupe, A. (1973). The long-term use of lithium in aggressive prisoners. *Comprehensive Psychiatry, 14*(4), 311–317.

Wilcox, J. (1994). Divalproex sodium in the treatment of aggressive behavior. *Annals of Clinical Psychiatry, 6,* 17–20.

Yudofsky, S. C., Silver, J. M., & Hales, R. E. (1995). Treatment of aggressive disorders. In *The American Psychiatric Press textbook of psychopharmacology* (pp. 735–751). Washington, DC: American Psychiatric Press.

Zanarini, M. C., & Frankenburg, F. R. (2001). Olanzapine treatment of female borderline personality disorder patients: A double-blind, placebo-controlled pilot study. *Journal of Clinical Psychiatry, 62*(11), 849–854.

Zanarini, M. C., Frankenburg, F. R., Dubo, E. D., Sickel, A. E., Trikha, A., Levin, A., et al. (1998). Axis I comorbidity of borderline personality disorder. *American Journal of Psychiatry, 155*(12), 1733–1739.

CHAPTER 16

Day Treatment of
Personality Disorders

John S. Ogrodniczuk and William E. Piper

PERSONALITY DISORDERS (PDs) are regarded as one of the most important sources of long-term impairment in both treated and untreated psychiatric populations (Merikangas & Weissman, 1986). The chronic functional impairment of PDs creates substantial costs for society. The costs are associated with high levels of unemployment, substance abuse, hospitalization, marital difficulties, and suicide (Pilkonis, Neighbors, & Corbitt, 1999). As well, individuals with PDs are frequent users of health and social services (Bender et al., 2001). The costs involve not only the patients themselves, but also the many people (e.g., family, friends, work associates) whose lives they affect.

Given the characteristics of PDs (e.g., stable, resistant to change, difficult to treat), powerful treatments are required to achieve improvement. No single intervention is likely to meet the diverse needs of patients with PDs. Within each disorder, the patient may have a number of affective, cognitive, and behavioral impairments. Furthermore, most patients who receive an Axis II diagnosis meet criteria for between three and six PDs (Dolan, Evans, & Norton, 1995). These patients need diverse and intensive interventions to address their various problems. In the case of psychotherapy, this may mean frequent sessions over a long period of time and/or combined treatment approaches. Less intensive interventions (e.g., brief supportive counseling) might help patients adjust to periodic crises, but are unlikely to have a significant long-term impact. Full hospitalization is often not an appropriate treatment option for patients with PDs because it may be too restrictive and may promote dependency. Weekly outpatient psychotherapy is often not adequate because it may not provide enough holding and support. Partial hospitalization can be viewed as offering a more appropriate level of intensiveness and containment, thus facilitating treatment of the chronic emotional and behavioral difficulties experienced by these patients (Melson, 1995).

This chapter reviews the use of a particular form of partial hospitalization, known as day treatment, for individuals with PDs. First, we provide a description of day treatment, as well as an overview of features that make it an attractive treatment alternative for patients with PDs. An example of a particular day treatment program at the University of Alberta in Edmonton, Canada, is provided to illustrate how a day treatment program is organized. A case example of a patient who participated in this program follows. Current research pertaining to the effectiveness and selection of patients for day treatment is reviewed, and practical implications of the research findings are considered. Finally, we provide a concise summary of our knowledge concerning the use of day treatment for individuals with PDs.

DESCRIPTION OF DAY TREATMENT

Day treatment, day hospital, and day care, all forms of partial hospitalization, can be helpful for patients who do not require inpatient care but may benefit from more intensive care than is possible on an outpatient basis. Day treatment differs from day hospital and day care in the amount of emphasis that it gives to the treatment and rehabilitation of patients (Piper, Rosie, Joyce, & Azim, 1996). Treatment is concerned with the optimal recovery of the individual and aims to alleviate symptoms, promote recovery from illness, or facilitate insight and intrapsychic integration. Rehabilitation focuses on assisting the individual in accommodating to disability and seeking an optimal level of adaptive functioning in the community. Patients with PDs are believed to be good candidates for day treatment programs.

In contrast to day treatment, day hospital programs are concerned primarily with the treatment of acute illness. They focus on helping patients adjust to periodic crises. Day hospital is appropriate for individuals who would otherwise be treated as inpatients (e.g., a decompensated patient with Borderline PD). It is also used for the treatment or rehabilitation of patients who are in transition from inpatient to outpatient care.

Also in contrast to day treatment, day care programs are concerned primarily with maintaining patients with chronic debilitating mental disorders. Expectations for rehabilitation and adjustment are modest. Treatment is likely to have only a minor role in day care programs. Patients with Schizophrenia are major consumers of day care services.

Day treatment programs differ from the other two forms of partial hospitalization in emphasizing both intensive treatment and rehabilitation of patients. Day treatment appears to have unique advantages for the treatment of patients with PDs. It is an ambulatory approach that offers intensive and structured clinical services within a stable therapeutic milieu. Programs may or may not be time-limited. They often use a treatment approach based on group psychotherapy, biological psychiatry, milieu principles, and a systems orientation. They may or may not use individual therapy. Patients typically participate in a variety of therapy groups several hours each weekday for several months. The therapy groups draw from different technical orientations. For example, behavioral and cognitive interventions can be used in structured, skills-oriented groups, whereas dynamic interventions are used in unstructured, insight-oriented groups. Family and couple interventions may also be used. Day treatment programs share a number of goals that include reduction of problematic behaviors, modification of maladaptive character traits, symptom relief, and facilitation of psychological maturation.

FEATURES OF DAY TREATMENT THAT MAKE IT A POWERFUL TREATMENT FOR PERSONALITY DISORDERS

There are a number of features of day treatment that tend to make it an effective treatment for PDs (Piper & Rosie, 1998). First, there is the intensity of the group experience. Patients spend a considerable amount of time participating in a number of different groups each day. Second, the groups vary in size, structure, objectives, and processes. Such diversity provides a comprehensive approach to treatment. Third, the system of groups is integrated and synergistic. Patients are expected to bring up important material and events that occurred in previous groups during current groups. In this way, they are encouraged to think in terms of the total system. Fourth, patients benefit from working with multiple staff and a large number of other patients. Emotionally inhibited patients can benefit from observing emotionally expressive patients and vice versa. Time-limited programs provide an additional beneficial feature. From the beginning, there is a clear sense that much needs to be done in a limited and relatively short period of time. This puts pressure on patients (as well as staff) to work hard.

Day treatment programs create an intensive therapeutic community for patients (Piper et al., 1996). Underlying the therapeutic community approach is the understanding that an individual's social milieu can not only contribute to the individual's dysfunctional behavior, but also be used to correct it. Thus, a therapeutic community can be created to help individuals identify and modify dysfunctional patterns of behavior. An entire community of patients and staff forms continuous and sustained relationships throughout the duration of the treatment, through which patients have the opportunity to engage in responsible behavior. Ideally, this generalizes to the larger community in which the patient lives. Day treatment capitalizes on the traditional characteristics of a therapeutic community (democratization, permissiveness, communalism, reality confrontation):

1. *Democratization* refers to the deliberate flattening of the hierarchy among the staff and between the staff and patients.
2. *Permissiveness* refers to the therapeutic tolerance for the expression of affects, thoughts, and actions considered to be deviant by society.
3. *Communalism* refers to the highly integrated nature of the patients and groups in the program.
4. *Reality confrontation* refers to an environment of inquiry and sharing of feedback.

These four principles combine to produce a community that provides maximum opportunity for examination and understanding of patients' behaviors in relationship to one another and toward authority figures and institutions. The community fosters patients' experimentation with more responsible behaviors. It also provides therapeutic factors that are unique to group forms of treatment. These include universality (normalizing the patient's complaints or difficulties), interpersonal learning (demonstration of problems, feedback), altruistic opportunities (learning the value of and benefiting from helping others), and group cohesion (positive sense of working with others toward a common goal).

There are other benefits of day treatment. The structure of day treatment programs encourages patients to be responsible, engenders mutual respect between patients and staff, and facilitates patients' participation in the treatment of their peers. The group format of day treatment offers a number of advantages over individual therapy, such as dilution of intense transference feelings toward the therapist, provision of more controlled therapeutic regression, and increased opportunity for feedback. Patients in a group setting observe and take on many social roles that lead to increased opportunity for change. In addition, treating patients in a group, rather than individually, is appealing for economic reasons.

AN EXAMPLE: THE EDMONTON DAY TREATMENT PROGRAM

The Edmonton program is an 18-week, time-limited, intensive milieu treatment for patients with PDs. Mood and anxiety disorders are also prevalent. Treatment and rehabilitation in a variety of different groups constitute the total experience of the program for all patients. The pervasive treatment philosophy is psychodynamic, which is bolstered considerably by systems theory, group theory, and a modification of ideals formulated for the administration of therapeutic communities (Piper et al., 1996).

Consideration of the program as a total system that supports the application of group therapy is central. The organization and culture of the total system facilitate a highly intensive group therapy with many patients who would typically be unsuitable for intensive outpatient group or individual psychotherapy. The organization and culture promote, but also contain, sufficient regression of PD patients, thus allowing personal change to be initiated.

The treatment team consists of five therapists (from the disciplines of nursing, social work, occupational therapy, psychology), a teacher, a psychiatrist, and a secretary. The psychiatrist shares leadership of the program with one of the therapists who is an occupational therapist. The whole team meets daily from Monday to Friday.

All patients are expected to attend all day, five days a week, for 18 weeks. Approximately three-quarters of the patients who begin the program complete it. The average daily census is 30 to 35 patients. Two or three patients are admitted and a similar number are discharged each week. The new patients enter ongoing groups in the program. Treatment consists of a variety of small and large groups and psychopharmacology. Groups are divided into two broad categories: psychotherapeutic insight-oriented groups and rehabilitative sociotherapy groups. No individual therapy is offered. It is possible to calculate the amount of individual therapy that patients in the program would receive if the staff offered individual therapy instead of day treatment. Each patient would receive the individual therapy equivalent of approximately one hour of therapy per week for a year. Consent by the patient for at least one family assessment is a precondition for admission to the program. When appropriate, this is followed by family therapy or couple therapy.

The program is conceptualized as consisting of three six-week phases through which each patient progresses: beginning, middle, and termination. The schedule for groups is organized so that each patient is in a group with every other patient in the program at least once a day. All patients and all staff attend the daily large psychotherapy group, which is the patients' first group of the day. Following the large group, patients typically attend three other groups during the day. The specific nature of the groups is determined in part by the phase of the program.

PHASE I

Phase I is, in many respects, a preparatory phase. The groups of this phase are geared toward enhancing the patients' ability to utilize the other groups throughout the remainder of the program. Phase I groups include a communications group, a self-awareness group, a projectives group, an action-oriented group, and a daily living seminar. The communications group consists of exercises to promote improved communication skills. Didactic teaching on effective communication is followed by opportunities for patients to practice communicating with one another, with the support of their fellow patients and their therapists as coaches. For example, patients are taught how to express anger without attacking others.

The self-awareness group is an introduction to individual insight-oriented work in the context of a small group. The therapist gently encourages individual patients to explore perceptions of themselves and of others, while paying particular attention to emotions that may surface in the process. A patient talking about how a therapist reminds her of her mother might be asked to talk about the tears that are showing as she is reminded of her past experiences.

The projectives group also introduces patients to insight-oriented work in the context of a small group. The central exercise of this group is to explore possible meanings of drawings produced by the patients. Each session begins with the patients drawing pictures to represent a theme presented by the therapist. The remainder of the session involves the patients discussing the meaning of their own pictures and those of others.

The action group introduces the patients to psychodrama and gestalt techniques. This prepares patients for more advanced use of those techniques in the action groups of Phase II and Phase III. The daily living seminar encourages the patients to develop practical goals with appropriate tasks for activities in their daily lives. In each weekly session, individual patients identify a current problem area in their lives. Then they formulate a goal and task for the problem area. The task is to be accomplished in the ensuing week and the results reported back to the group in the next session.

PHASE II

Groups specific to Phase II include a TV group and a more advanced action group. The TV group sessions consist of two parts. The first 30 minutes of each 90-minute session constitute a small psychodynamic group that is videorecorded. During the remaining time in the session, the group observes and discusses video playback of parts of the session. There are three objectives for using the video playback. The first is for patients to have a second chance to address material that has been raised during the recorded part of the session. The second is for patients to further develop their capacity for self-observation. The third is for patients and staff to have further opportunity to observe and comment on interpersonal and group-as-a-whole interaction.

Patients who have experienced extreme humiliation and shame as children are intimidated by this group. Typically, they refuse to observe the video playback initially. Eventually, with the support of the group, they can learn to observe themselves with less discomfort. This improved capacity for self-observation serves them well in other groups in the program. It is also a fundamental social skill that they may retain lifelong.

PHASE III

The specific groups involved in Phase III include a reentry group and a vocational group. The reentry group provides an opportunity to address the return of symptoms, which is a common phenomenon for patients facing termination of treatment. Much of the difficult emotional work associated with saying goodbye is promoted in this group. Fears about living independently, without the daily support of the program, drive the return of symptoms. In this context, patients often explore their mixed feelings about ending treatment. There may be relief, sadness, anger, guilt, or feelings of being abandoned. Patients often come to understand that, although the return of symptoms is unpleasant, the familiarity of the old symptoms can be a source of comfort. Giving up the symptoms then becomes another part of the task of saying goodbye in the group.

The vocational group focuses on the practical tasks of reentering the work force. Patients are taught to examine their work and school history with a view to knowing their strengths and weaknesses. They prepare resumés and undergo mock job interviews. For about 20% of the patients, the vocational group is preparation for entering a six-week, supervised work placement, which is available following completion of the program.

GROUPS THAT ARE NOT PHASE-SPECIFIC

In addition to phase-specific groups, there are several groups that all patients attend throughout the 18 weeks. The daily large psychotherapy group is one example. Others include a weekly patient evaluation group, an exercise group, a relaxation-training group, a weekly social outing, a weekly government group in which patients plan and organize the social outings, and a weekly recreation group. On moving to Phase II, all patients enter one of two small psychodynamic groups in which they remain throughout the program.

ORGANIZATIONAL FEATURES

The organizational features of the program include mixing patients from different phases of treatment in the various small groups as well as the daily large group. For example, Phase II patients are divided between two concurrent small dynamic groups along with Phase III patients. However, Phase II patients all attend the TV group together, which does not include Phase III patients. This type of organization is consistent with the traditional therapeutic community concept of communalism, which refers to intercommunicative, tight-knit, and intimate sets of relationships. The interpersonal closeness inherent in this type of organization is effective in eliciting patients' pathological behavior that can be examined in the context of various groups. It is also argued that such a highly integrated system provides an opportunity for a corrective emotional experience for patients who have learned to be intolerant of closeness in relationships.

In the program, there is maximum opportunity for a patient to interact with a variety of other patients and staff members. Reflective of these multiple interactions between individuals is the interactive effect between groups. No single group can be considered in isolation. For example, emotions and conflicts generated in a job interview exercise in the vocational group may provide material for discussion about conflicts with authority in the large psychotherapy group. Initial exploration of these conflicts in the large group may be continued in greater depth in the small dynamic group or may foster discussion among Phase I patients concerning anxiety in relation to staff members in the self-awareness group and so on. A predominant theme often can be recognized throughout the program. Such themes typically last for days, sometimes weeks.

Given the interdependent roles of all the groups, it is perhaps presumptive to designate certain groups as more important than others. However, there are three groups that play key roles. The first is not a therapy group. It comprises staff only and is called the "staff relations group." The other two groups are the large psychotherapy group and the small psychodynamic group. We consider each in turn.

STAFF RELATIONS GROUP

O'Kelly and Azim (1993) have defined three purposes for the staff relations group. First, it provides a safe and open forum for staff members to work out interstaff, on-the-job conflicts. Second, it provides an opportunity for staff to offer feedback and support to one another about their performance as therapists. Third, it provides an opportunity to address how staff members' personal reactions may interfere with their effectiveness. In our experience, the staff relations group is a central mechanism for reducing the frequency and intensity of collective disturbances, which occur in all institutions. In the day treatment program, with the pressure-cooker effect of communalism of PD patients, the staff relations group is a sine qua non.

The group meets weekly for one hour during a lunch period. It is led by the psychiatrist and is the most difficult group to lead. The staff members' primary task is to support the patients in insight-oriented work; it is not to engage in personal therapy. Thus, the psychiatrist has to keep in mind that the purpose of the group is to explore day-to-day staff members' relations and feelings that are relevant to their work with the patients. Staff members' personal conflicts outside work are not a topic of focus. Occasionally, staff members inform one another about personal difficulties that might affect their work performance. Beyond these brief disclosures, however, the focus is on the here and now of their feelings and conflicts, which is the most difficult area for open discussion. Staff members' conflicts in the workplace are common, but talking about them openly in a group is rare.

The other inherent challenge for this group is that the leader is the staff members' boss. The leader has authority for hiring and terminating. For this reason, there is inevitably some anxiety about a therapist confronting the leader with feelings of anger. The degree to which the staff are able to confront the leader openly is probably an index of general safety in the group and an index of the group's effectiveness. For example, the psychiatrist had commented in a post-large group discussion that one of the therapists could appear harsh in her interactions with patients at times. He had been contrasting her approach with his own tendency to be unduly gentle with patients. The therapist was deeply hurt by the psychiatrist's comments and, with the staff's support, voiced her anger to him in the subsequent staff relations group. Through ongoing discussion in staff relations groups and through the staff's experience in other groups, it emerged that all the staff had been grappling with feelings of powerlessness over that time period. The continuing staff relations group provided opportunities to address these feelings openly while minimizing the destructive effects of potential power struggles.

LARGE PSYCHOTHERAPY GROUP

The second key group is the large psychotherapy group. This daily group complements the staff relations group's role in reducing and resolving collective disturbances in the total treatment system. This daily meeting of all patients and staff is a crucial stimulus for open confrontation of conflicts between group members.

The large group has several other important functions. A primary one is the facilitation of personal insight of individual patients. The patients talk about deeply personal issues in the context of others sharing personal information. With the assistance of therapists and fellow patients, they develop insight about interpersonal conflict and painful feelings. Another function of the large group is the opportunity for new patients to learn how to "do therapy" by observing their seasoned peers working in the group. It is also a meeting where new patients are introduced to the group as a whole and a meeting in which departing patients may say goodbye.

The group meets at the beginning of each day for one hour. The psychiatrist is the designated leader. The staff have to be alert to prevailing group themes that necessarily influence the timing and focus of their interventions. A common error of staff members is to enter the large group with an agenda, which often is the result of discussion in the staff meeting that precedes the large group. The result is empathic failure by the staff. In such situations, the staff members, and ultimately the staff leader, have to be open to receiving the anger of the patients.

In general, however, the staff are attuned to the topics that the group believes are important to deal with on any given day. The group is characterized by intense, effectively laden, insight-oriented work by individual patients. Some patients' anxiety interferes with their ability to interact in the large group. It is striking, however, how comfortable most patients become, thus facilitating their use of this forum for intensive psychotherapy. When this happens, there is ample opportunity for patients to learn how their perceptions in the group are affected by past experiences. They also learn how these perceptions influence their behavior toward others and how their behavior affects others' responses.

SMALL PSYCHODYNAMIC GROUP

The third group that deserves special mention is the small psychodynamic group. Each patient enters one of two such groups when moving to Phase II and remains in that group for the remainder of their stay in the program. Each group meets twice a week for 90-minute sessions. This group is viewed as a central treatment group of the program, the group for which other groups are preparatory. Many of the patients attending the program would not have been treatable in a traditional, intensive, small psychotherapy group in an outpatient setting. The structure and nature of the program allows patients with profound difficulties in their interpersonal relationships to approach insight-oriented work while receiving sufficient support and containment to mitigate against destructive behavior.

Each small psychodynamic group is led by a psychiatrist and a therapist. There is a strong emphasis on patients working to gain insight in the context of group support. Although the interpersonal aspects of group therapy, as emphasized by Yalom (1995), are valued, there is a strong emphasis on individual work. The work in the small group inevitably reflects themes operating throughout the program. An advantage of the small group, compared with the large psychotherapy group, is the greater time available for several individuals to talk in depth on a given issue. The leaders have to ensure, however, that material raised in the small group is not barred from discussion in the large group. During collective disturbances, divisive behavior is often demonstrated through idealization of one of the small groups and devaluation of the other.

CLINICAL CASE EXAMPLE

Having outlined the principles, organization, and function of specific groups in the Edmonton Day Treatment Program, we now present an example of a patient who successfully completed the program.

PRESENTING PROBLEM AND PATIENT DESCRIPTION

Peter was a 32-year-old, single, unemployed man who lived with his older brother in Edmonton. He was referred to the program by his psychiatrist of two years. His presenting complaints included low self-esteem, irregular sleep, loneliness, poor social skills, uncertainty about his career, and difficulty coming to terms with a recently diagnosed learning disability. He had struggled throughout adulthood with most of these symptoms. He received individual therapy for four years before entering day treatment. The first two years of individual therapy had been with a goal-oriented, supportive therapist. The second two years had been with a cognitive-behavior therapist who had also focused on assertiveness training. Despite these attempts at treatment, Peter's self-esteem remained low and, after failing university several months before admission to day treatment, he had become even more self-doubting, leading to disturbed sleep and extreme uncertainty about his future.

At the time of admission, Peter was given the *DSM-III-R* diagnosis of Dysthymia (primary type, early onset) and Dependent Personality Disorder with Obsessive-Compulsive Traits. Two years previously, he had been treated for Major Depression with an antidepressant for several months. This disorder was thought to be in remission at the time of admission. He was on a nighttime dose of clonazepam as treatment for nocturnal myoclonus, the only medication he received throughout his stay in the day treatment program.

CASE FORMULATION

Peter grew up in a high-achieving family of five children in Edmonton. He was the middle child, with three brothers and one sister. His sister was a school principal, two of his brothers were physicians, and the other brother was a lawyer. His mother had been the dominant figure in the family. She was a teacher who had had high expectations for academic achievement in all her children. His mother had been very ill throughout her pregnancy with Peter. Repeated respiratory problems in the first year of Peter's life had required several hospital admissions. These factors, plus the fact that he had great difficulty with reading and mathematics (Peter had a learning disability that remained undiagnosed until adulthood), served to throw his mother and himself into a deeply conflictual relationship from an early age. His mother's criticism and shouting, while trying to help Peter with his schoolwork, only served to frighten him and undermine his self-confidence. At times, he reached a compromise with his mother by assuming the role of house-keeper, while his more academically gifted siblings pursued their studies. His taking on more than his fair share of household chores seemed to partially appease his mother. However, even for this he experienced absence of criticism rather than praise. It also served to emphasize his differences from his siblings and, in his own mind, his inferiority to them. His enuresis, which persisted until age 18, served to contribute to low self-esteem.

His father was of little help. He was dominated by his wife and coped by watching television. The only expression of emotion between Peter's parents was during their frequent angry outbursts. When Peter was 16, his parents finally separated. Despite pervasive unhappiness in his home before the parental separation, Peter remembered experiencing shock and sadness. He stayed with his mother until his late teens, eventually leaving to live with his older brother because of continued battles with his mother.

Despite his learning disability, Peter managed to complete high school. For several years, he intermittently attended the arts faculty of his local university. Four years before his admission to day treatment, the diagnosis of learning disorder was made by a psychologist. Problems in the areas of logical reasoning, organization skills, and visual-motor and auditory-visual integration were noted. However, Peter persisted with his studies until the summer before his admission to day treatment. At that time, the university required him to withdraw permanently after repeated failures in several subjects. He found himself, therefore, at the age of 32 without any postsecondary qualification or career.

Socially, he was somewhat isolated during his childhood. He was shy and awkward among his peers. As an adult, he made some friends through playing badminton and attending church. However, there was a dependent quality to these relationships. The focus of conversations tended to center on his problems. A platonic friendship with a married woman ended abruptly with her accidental death a year before his admission. Peter's sexual activity during his teens was limited to masturbation. When he was 17, a male friend suggested having a sexual experience together. Peter passively acquiesced to an experience that involved anal intercourse. He was subsequently filled with remorse and shame, and the incident was never repeated. Although sexually attracted to women, he never dated a woman more than three times in his adult life and never experienced sexual intercourse with a woman.

In summary, Peter was a dependent man who suffered from low self-esteem throughout his life. His conflictual, dependent relationship with his intrusive mother had contributed to his failure to achieve intimacy with a woman as an adult and his unhelpful persistence in academic pursuits for which he was handicapped intellectually. Although desiring intimacy with a woman, he feared a repeat of the domination he had experienced with his mother. However, he found himself driven to prove himself, in his mother's eyes, through academic achievement. His rather passive experiment with sexuality with a man had served to enhance his low self-respect and shame. The model of his father's passivity probably added to his sense of hopelessness about achieving an equal relationship with a woman. The one woman with whom he had managed to maintain a friendship, despite his interpersonal difficulties, had been killed. This loss, the recent loss of his dream of academic success, being faced with unemployment, and having no career qualifications at the age of 32, precipitated his request for intensive treatment at the day program.

Course of Treatment

Within the first week of his admission to the program, his designated therapist clarified the following goals of treatment:

1. Exploration of anger toward his mother.
2. Emotional separation from his mother.
3. Exploration of his relationship with his father and how he had come to repeat his father's passive and dependent behavior.
4. Modification of his role as the "outsider" with his siblings.
5. Assertion in group and with family members.
6. Improved self-esteem.
7. Establishment of realistic goals as to career, friends, and living arrangements.
8. Social skills practice in the groups.
9. Exploration of his sexual identity and the influence of his parental models.

The issues that emerged for Peter during the program proved to be close to the original goals of treatment. Early on, he began to talk about his relationship with his mother. He talked of her controlling ways and how, as a child, he would try to appease her by doing housework. From the beginning of treatment, he was sexually attracted to a female therapist. He talked about this in the daily large group. Later on in the program, he was also able to explore his anger toward her for not engaging in a friendship with him. Fellow patients, however, noted that his expression of feelings appeared very controlled and he was encouraged to be more spontaneous.

In the first few weeks, he talked frankly to his mother for the first time about his disappointment with her. Two of his brothers subsequently criticized him for upsetting his mother. In the required family interview, which occurred after two months of treatment, Peter was rather passive, as was his father, in the presence of his mother. However, Peter did let his mother know that, although he appreciated her advice, he would appreciate it also if she would respect his decision not to follow it all the time. One of his brothers and his mother were openly critical of the program and questioned its validity. In the patient evaluation meeting that followed the family interview, the female therapist to whom he was attracted commented about Peter's passivity in the face of his mother. In a subsequent large group, he confronted her with his anger about her comment.

About halfway through the program, Peter began to talk about his habit of picking at his skin, which he had developed in his teen years. This was an issue of great shame for him. Over the subsequent weeks in several groups, he explored the meaning of this behavior. In his own mind, it was a way of self-punishment, as well as an indirect angry statement toward his mother in particular. He talked of the debt he felt toward her as a result of her difficult pregnancy with him and of his neediness as a young child because of his own illness. And yet she failed to recognize his different needs in schooling and instead had become frustrated with him and had encouraged his siblings to be critical of his mediocre performance at school.

While exploring themes of conflict with his family members throughout the program, he practiced addressing parallel conflicts with group members. He was supported in this by fellow patients, who encouraged spontaneity and abandonment of his typically passive stance in relationships. Some patients confronted him early on with their fear that he would explode because of the unexpressed anger that they perceived in him. He was also confronted for trying to be the perfect patient in a way that also interfered with spontaneity. His passivity in the face of his family was again highlighted in a psychodrama when it was noted that instead of moving toward or away from patients playing the roles of his family members, he waited for them to move toward him. In different groups throughout the program, he was able to reverse his passive tendency by confronting several significant group members: the female therapist to whom he felt strongly attached, a male therapist whom he perceived as "slamming a door in my face," the male psychiatrist whose own passivity was a reminder of the patient's father's inaction, and a female patient who had advised Peter that it was all right not to have negative feelings about his homosexual encounter in his teens if it had felt good to him.

Paradoxically, this last interaction allowed him to explore, for the first time, feelings that had eluded him about his homosexual experimentation as a teen. The anger that he mobilized toward the fellow patient seemed to surmount the overwhelming shame that had prevented him from exploring the mixed feelings of anger, guilt, and sexual pleasure associated with his experience. Shame is a common problem for many patients in the program, and Peter's experience of talking through shameful issues, in the presence of others who truly understood and were able to share similar experiences, was thought to be fundamental to the effectiveness of treatment. The shameful issues included his homosexual encounter, his self-mutilation, and his failure to separate from "Mom."

During the final weeks of the program, as is typical, themes of loss emerged for Peter. He began to talk about the death of his female friend who had been killed a year before his admission to the program. Initially, when he started talking about this in the small dynamic group, it was without affect. However, in subsequent large groups, he was able to return to the issue and wept while talking of the loss of this woman, the friendship that had existed with her husband before her death, and the anger he was now experiencing toward the drunken driver who had been responsible for her demise.

In the final phase of the program, his anger toward women in general was highlighted when he engaged in a sarcastic interchange with a female patient who had commented that she did not like him. He began to realize his high expectations of the group to give him support. When the group failed to live up to his expectations, his disappointment emerged in sarcasm toward female patients. Perhaps the group had come to symbolize "mother" in his own mind.

In one of the small groups, near the end of the program, he further explored his feelings of attraction to the female therapist. He realized that by having talked about his feelings toward her without negative consequence, he had engaged in a new kind of relationship with an attractive woman. Before the program, he had thought "something would have to happen" if he experienced sexual feelings toward a woman. As a result of his new experience, he felt less burdened by his sexual thoughts and more open to support from this woman whom he liked.

In parallel with his increased assertiveness in the program, he began to conduct himself differently outside the program. He refused to engage further in discussions with his father about his father's resentment toward his mother. At the same time, his father became more openly friendly with Peter. Peter made plans to move out of his brother's home and made arrangements to enter a computer programmer training course. He also consolidated plans to spend a vacation with a female friend in British Columbia. He thought that this relationship could become a romantic one but had been delaying pursuit of the woman for over a year.

Outcome and Prognosis

At the end of treatment, his therapist summarized that there appeared to be progress in the course of Peter's therapy. He had learned to be assertive with patients, staff, and family. Although still learning to recognize and express his feelings in relationships, he had been able to progress to a point of being more open in this respect and of being more tolerant of support from others. In his own mind, support was no longer confused with domination. His self-confidence and self-esteem appeared much improved at discharge.

Peter reported high satisfaction with the program and with his progress. He believed the program had helped improve his emotional well-being and his relationships. The three most important things he had learned were (1) to be more aware of his feelings, (2) the link between feelings and emotional health, and (3) the need to risk expressing his emotions more often. He listed the three most important treatment experiences as his experience of anger when being confronted by the female therapist about his passivity in the family interview, his expression of anger when he perceived the male therapist as slamming a door in his face, and his experience of being cared for when being asked once by the female therapist if he had needed a prescription. Peter also demonstrated considerable improvement on several outcome measures. Most of his gains were maintained at the time of an eight-month follow-up assessment.

This clinical example reported a positive outcome for a patient who participated in the Edmonton Day Treatment Program and described how different aspects of the program facilitated the patient's improvement. An obvious question to follow is whether similar positive gains are typically experienced by patients who receive day treatment. Another issue is whether there are important variables to consider when providing day treatment that may significantly influence patient benefit. These questions are most appropriately addressed through research, which we review next.

EMPIRICAL STUDIES OF DAY TREATMENT FOR PERSONALITY DISORDERS

Although a number of authors have written about the appropriateness of treating patients with PDs in day treatment, research in this area has been slow to accumulate. This has been changing over the past decade. However, the literature is still composed primarily of uncontrolled descriptive studies. Few controlled studies have been conducted. Most research on day treatment involves diagnostically mixed samples of patients that include patients with PDs. Only a small number of studies have examined day treatment specifically for this patient population. Because research on day treatment for individuals with PDs is limited, we review empirical studies of day treatment if PD patients are among the subjects. The studies can be divided into two categories: treatment outcome studies and predictor studies. Treatment outcome studies have the primary objective of examining change in outcome following treatment. Predictor studies have the primary objective of identifying variables that are predictive of important clinical events such as outcome or dropping out. We review recent studies in each of these two categories.

DAY TREATMENT OUTCOME STUDIES

One of the earlier studies to examine the effectiveness of day treatment for PDs was conducted by Vaglum et al. (1990). Their study examined treatment response for 97 consecutively admitted patients, 75 of whom had a PD. The most frequent diagnosis provided was Borderline PD. Nearly all (94) patients also received an Axis I diagnosis, the most frequent being Depression, Anxiety, or Substance Abuse. The day treatment program was psychodynamically oriented and included both group and individual therapy. The program was five days per week, seven hours per day and consisted of elements such as daily community meetings, psychotherapy, art therapy, and body awareness group therapy. It was designed to accommodate 16 patients at any one time. Patients were expected to attend the program for four to eight months.

Response to treatment was represented by frequency of irregular discharge, change in self-reported symptom level, and overall psychopathology. Treatment response at discharge was compared for three groups of patients: (1) those with severe PDs (Borderline, Schizotypal), (2) those with other, nonsevere PDs, and (3) those with no PD.

At discharge, there was no significant difference in length of stay among the three groups. The average time spent in the program was approximately four months. Twenty-three percent of the sample dropped out or were discharged from the program because of rule violations. Of these patients, 77% had a severe PD. All patients who completed the program improved significantly on the Global Severity Index (GSI) of the Symptom Checklist-90. There were no significant differences between the groups in amount of change at discharge. In addition, all patients improved on the Health Sickness Rating Scale (HSRS), although change for the severe group was modest.

Follow-up of these patients at an average of three years postadmission revealed that discharge levels of global symptomatology (GSI) were maintained (Mehlum et al., 1991). In addition, patients increased their HSRS scores from admission to follow-up. Ratings on the Social Adjustment Scale were also made at admission and at follow-up. Only Borderline and Schizotypal patients failed to show improvement in social functioning.

Our research group conducted a controlled trial of the Edmonton Day Treatment Program (Piper, Rosie, Azim, & Joyce, 1993), one of the very few controlled trials reported in the literature. The study attempted to avoid the problems associated with previous studies of day treatment, for example, small sample size, lack of randomization, minimal control of variables such as diagnosis or medication, lack of standard outcome measures, and poorly defined programs. The sample included psychiatric outpatients with affective and personality disorders. The prospective trial used a randomized treatment-versus-control (delayed treatment) design. In our study, 29% of the patients who began the program dropped out.

Sixty matched pairs of patients ($N = 120$) completed the treatment and control conditions. Sixty percent of the sample of 120 had a personality disorder. The most frequent *DSM-III-R* Axis II diagnoses were Dependent and Borderline. Half of the sample received diagnoses of both affective and personality disorders. Treatment outcome was assessed in a number of areas. These included interpersonal functioning, psychiatric symptomatology, self-esteem, life satisfaction, defensive functioning, and personalized target objectives. Outcome in these areas was assessed at pretherapy, posttherapy, and follow-up.

Findings from the study showed that treated patients evidenced significantly better outcome than control patients on several outcome variables: social dysfunction, family dysfunction, interpersonal behavior, mood level, life satisfaction, self-esteem, and severity of disturbance associated with individual goals of treatment. These findings could not be accounted for by use of medication. Benefits were maintained over the follow-up period.

Krawitz (1997) conducted a small, uncontrolled outcome study of day treatment for PDs. The treatment was an unusual day and semiresidential program. Because of its rural setting, some patients came great distances to attend. Thus, a temporary residence was established for these patients. Treatment was psychodynamically informed and group-oriented. The program was set up to accommodate eight patients at a time. Patients attended the program for eight hours per day, 3.5 days per week. The average length of stay was about four months.

The most frequent *DSM-III-R* Axis II diagnoses were Dependent, Borderline, and PD Not Otherwise Specified. The study involved examining outcome in general symptoms, goal attainment, and global functioning at pretherapy, posttherapy, and at 4-, 12-, and 24-month follow-up. Measures of health resource usage were also completed at these assessment times.

The findings indicated large, statistically significant improvements on all outcome scales following treatment, which were sustained over a two-year follow-up period. The study also provided important health economic data. The average decrease in measured costs to the health system after therapy was NZ$3,082 (U.S. $1,220) per patient per year. There was a significant reduction of general practitioner visits per patient per year at 4 and 24 months. Hours spent in therapy also decreased significantly at 4, 12, and 24 months. The number of patients who were unemployed and who received government funded benefits, however, did not change markedly.

Wilberg and colleagues conducted a comprehensive study of day treatment for patients diagnosed with PDs (Wilberg, Karterud, Urnes, Pedersen, & Friis, 1998). The study was a naturalistic prospective study of 183 patients admitted to their day treatment program. Eighty-seven percent of the patients received a diagnosis of a PD, most frequently, Borderline and Avoidant. Nearly all patients (98%) had a current Axis I diagnosis, with Social Phobia and Dysthymia being the most common. The 18-week program could accommodate 24 patients. It consisted of a combination of analytically oriented groups and cognitive-behavioral groups.

Patients attended the program for five hours per day, five days per week. The day treatment program is followed by outpatient analytic group therapy, 1.5 hours weekly, with a time limit of 3.5 years.

Patients with Borderline PD and Antisocial PD had the highest rates of irregular discharge. A total of 138 patients (75% of the sample) completed the program. Complications (e.g., threatening behavior, self-mutilation, decompensation) were experienced by 17% of the sample. Outcome, assessed on several measures, was positive for the group of treatment completers. Effect sizes were in the medium to high range for patients in each of the three PD clusters, indicating a substantial level of improvement. A one-year follow-up of these patients (Wilberg et al., 1999) indicated that improvements were maintained during the follow-up period. Sixty-four percent of the treatment completers continued in the outpatient group therapy.

Most recently, Bateman and Fonagy (1999) reported on a randomized clinical trial study of a day treatment program for patients with Borderline PD. Their study compared the effectiveness of a psychoanalytically oriented day treatment program with standard psychiatric care for Borderline patients. Day treatment consisted of (1) once-weekly, psychoanalytically oriented individual psychotherapy, (2) thrice-weekly group analytic psychotherapy, (3) once-weekly expressive psychotherapy oriented toward psychodrama techniques, and (4) a weekly community meeting. Patients attended the program five days per week for a maximum of 18 months. The day program was able to accommodate 30 patients. Standard care consisted of (1) twice-monthly meetings with a psychiatrist (when necessary); (2) inpatient admission, if necessary (admission rate = 90%, average stay = 11.6 days) with discharge to nonpsychoanalytic, psychiatric partial hospitalization focusing on problem-solving (65% of the sample were partially hospitalized, average stay = 6 months); followed by (3) outpatient and community follow-up (every two weeks). The authors reported that standard care group patients received no formal psychotherapy.

Forty-four patients were randomly assigned to either day treatment or standard care. Outcome measures included the frequency of suicide attempts and acts of self-mutilation, the number and duration of inpatient admissions, use of psychotropic medication (i.e., need for medication), and self-report measures of depression, anxiety, general symptomatic distress, interpersonal function, and social adjustment.

Patients who participated in day treatment showed a significant decrease on all measures, in contrast to the standard care group, which showed limited change and even deterioration over the same period. They found that much of the improvement for those in the day program began after six months in treatment and continued until the end of treatment at 18 months. Patients who completed day treatment not only maintained these gains, but also showed continued improvement during an 18-month follow-up period, whereas those treated with standard care showed little change (Bateman & Fonagy, 2001).

We have reviewed several studies that provide convincing support for the effectiveness of day treatment for patients with PDs. In addition to outcome studies of day treatment, a number of studies have been conducted to identify predictors of important clinical events such as whether patients remain, work, and benefit from therapy. The practical value of such studies lies in being able to provide clinicians with information that will allow them to direct the most appropriate patients into day treatment and identify those patients who are less likely to succeed. We review such studies next.

Day Treatment Predictor Studies

Perhaps the most comprehensive examination of predictors of day treatment success was conducted by our research group in Edmonton, Canada. A series of three studies evolved from our controlled clinical trial of day treatment that was described earlier in this chapter. In the first of these studies, we were interested in discovering whether pretreatment characteristics of the patients were predictive of remaining in the program and achieving a favorable outcome (Piper, Joyce, Azim, & Rosie, 1994). Five predictor variables (age, marital status, previous psychiatric hospitalization, presence of a personality disorder, initial disturbance) were chosen on the basis of significant findings from previous research. Two predictor variables, quality of object relations (QOR) and psychological mindedness (PM), were chosen on the basis of theory. QOR is defined as a person's enduring tendency to establish certain kinds of relationships with others. PM is defined as the ability to identify dynamic (intrapsychic) components and relate them to a person's difficulties. Overall, PM and QOR were the strongest single predictors of remaining and benefiting. The ability to identify conflictual components and relate them to a person's difficulties (reflecting high PM) represents a valuable skill in the day treatment program. As well, the ability to establish mature, give-and-take relationships (reflecting high QOR) allows patients to tolerate the daily interpersonal demands and stresses of the program.

An additional means of increasing understanding of treatment effectiveness is identifying processes of the treatment or the patient that are associated with improvement. Our second predictor study involved investigating a process variable, the patient's tendency to work in therapy, as a predictor of outcome (Piper, Joyce, Rosie, & Azim, 1994). The study examined whether PM was associated with work in therapy, whether work in therapy was associated with outcome, and whether PM and outcome in therapy combined to predict outcome. Thus, the study attempted to understand *why* day treatment was effective with certain types of patients.

The study revealed a direct relation between PM and work. PM represents a skill that was relevant to performing work in the day treatment groups. The study also found a direct relation between work in therapy and outcome. Patients who work harder should be expected to experience greater benefit from treatment. Evidence of a direct relation between PM and work in therapy was also found. The presence of significant, direct relationships among PM, work, and outcome provides confirmation of a meaningful predictor-process-outcome pattern.

The third study examined whether perceptions of the psychosocial environment of the day treatment program were predictive of outcome (Joyce, Piper, Rosie, & Azim, 1994). We used the Community-Oriented Programs Environment Scale (COPES) to assess the perceived environment of the day program. Patient ratings clearly reflected their experience of a milieu oriented to intensive psychodynamic group treatment—in other words, perceptions of a high degree of spontaneous involvement and tolerance for the intensity of anger expression.

Positive therapeutic climate was related directly to outcome. The findings suggested that perceiving the treatment program as a "good enough" parental object (positive therapeutic environment) may allow the patient to progress toward an improved equilibrium. In addition, perceived opportunities for catharsis (perception that the program encouraged expression of anger) may also be an important aspect of change.

Wilberg and colleagues also explored predictors of outcome (Wilberg, Friis, et al., 1998). Patients were clustered into four groups representing different courses of outcome. These were labeled good, fair, late improvement, and poor. Predictors of the various courses were examined. For the prediction analyses, patients were dichotomized into two groups based on their Axis II diagnosis. The two groups were: no PD/Cluster C versus Cluster A/B. This dichotomy was a significant predictor of outcome course. Patients in the Cluster A/B group (who were primarily Borderline patients) were more likely to be in the fair improvement group. In addition, work status at admission and irregular discharge from the day treatment program predicted a poor or late improvement course versus a fair course. Patients in the poor and late improvement groups were more often discharged on an irregular basis from day treatment and were more likely to not be working at admission to the program.

A study by Dazord, Gerin, Seulin, Duclos, and Amar (1997) examined a number of variables as potential predictors of day treatment outcome. Their program is composed of a large group forum; smaller psychodrama, discussion, molding, photography, relaxation, and swimming pool groups; physical expression and drawing groups; and pastry groups. Patients attend either mornings or afternoons, Monday through Friday.

The study included all patients ($N = 121$) who stayed in the program for at least 15 days. Twenty-five percent of the sample received a PD diagnosis. Outcome was evaluated using the Health Sickness Rating Scale (HSRS) and the Clinical Evaluation Profile (CEP). Predictor variables were: patient motivation, initial clinical state, helping alliance, and patient's commitment to the different elements of the day program.

Dazord et al. (1997) examined the relation between each of the predictors and outcome for the PD group. They found that patient commitment to the large group forum was directly associated with favorable change on the HSRS variables. In addition, the authors found that a stronger helping alliance was associated with favorable outcome on the HSRS variables, although the magnitude of the correlations was modest. The authors suggested that PD patients tend to have positive outcome via the large group forum because it is there that they may find support in expressing themselves and their needs to members of the clinical team and to other patients.

A study conducted by Gillis, Russell, and Busby (1997) evaluated the adequacy of sociodemographic and clinical descriptors as predictors of unplanned discharge from and completion of day treatment. They completed a chart review of all patients ($N = 327$) who attended one of three day treatment programs. The authors indicate that 15% of the total sample were diagnosed with Borderline PD, whereas another 24% were diagnosed with PD Not Otherwise Specified. The findings indicated that factors associated with program completion were diagnoses of Major Depression or Posttraumatic Stress Disorder, a history of completing a prior day treatment program, and higher education levels. Active substance abuse and a history of three or more inpatient admissions were associated with unplanned discharge.

In an effort to examine more conceptually relevant predictors of completion status, Tasca et al. (1999) conducted a study that examined psychological minded-ness (PM), interpersonal functioning, and chronicity of psychiatric problems as predictors. The study included 102 patients consecutively admitted to a day treat-ment program. Seventy-two percent of the sample was diagnosed with a PD.

The findings revealed that PM and chronicity of problems were each signifi-cantly associated with completion status. Completers had higher levels of PM than noncompleters. As well, completers tended to have less chronic psychiatric prob-lems. Chronicity was the stronger predictor of the two and was the only variable that significantly increased the probability of classifying completers and noncom-pleters. The interaction between PM and chronicity was also significant, although the interaction did not greatly increase the accuracy of classifying completers. The interaction suggested that those with a higher number of years of psychiatric problems were more likely to complete day treatment if they had higher levels of PM. This can be interpreted to suggest that for those with more chronic problems, completion of an intensive day treatment program may require a higher level of PM. Psychological mindedness may act as a buffer or moderator of the overall neg-ative impact of years of psychiatric problems.

SUMMARY OF FINDINGS

Existing empirical studies on the effectiveness of day treatment for patients with PDs reveal consistent positive findings. Day treatment programs of varying lengths and orientation were investigated by five different research groups. All found that day treatment led to significant reductions in psychiatric symptoma-tology and improvements in social and interpersonal functioning and life satis-faction. The fact that the findings were consistent across studies of different methodologies is encouraging. Furthermore, significant benefits were seen in studies in which patients from the three PD clusters were represented, suggest-ing that day treatment may be beneficial for different types of PDs. Particularly notable were the significant improvements evidenced by Borderline patients in many of the studies. This patient group is often very difficult to treat. Although most investigations were uncontrolled descriptive studies, which limits confi-dence in their findings, more carefully controlled studies also found that day treatment was effective. The study by Bateman and Fonagy demonstrated that day treatment is more effective than the standard treatment that PD patients often receive (i.e., medication, brief counseling, inpatient admissions, day care). Preliminary evidence provided by the Krawitz study also suggests that day treat-ment may lead to a reduction of future health services costs. Supportive evidence for this also comes from the Bateman and Fonagy study, where it was found that the number and duration of inpatient admissions was reduced, as well as the need for psychotropic medication, for patients who participated in a day treat-ment program.

Studies of day treatment have also identified significant predictors of patient success (remaining, benefiting). The findings revealed that remaining in day treat-ment may be dependent on a number of variables. They suggest that patients who are more likely to remain in day treatment are more psychologically minded, have more mature interpersonal relationships, are older and married, have diagnoses of Major Depression or Posttraumatic Stress Disorder, have previously completed a day treatment program, are more educated, and have fewer years of experiencing psychiatric difficulties. A wide variety of variables that represent characteristics of the patient, the therapy process, and the treatment milieu have also been found to be predictive of favorable outcome. These findings suggest that better outcome is dependent on the patient's being more psychologically minded, having a history of mature interpersonal relationships, being employed, remaining in treatment, and being committed to the day treatment group. Other findings indicated that greater work on the patient's behalf is likely to increase benefit from treatment. Finally, other findings suggest that a treatment milieu that is characterized by a high degree of spontaneous involvement and tolerance for the expression of anger is facilitative of favorable treatment outcome.

PRACTICAL IMPLICATIONS OF RESEARCH FINDINGS

The primary implication of the findings from the effectiveness studies is that day treatment should be considered an effective treatment for PD patients, including Borderline patients. There are a number of guiding principles for the successful implementation of a day treatment program. These principles are elaborated on with greater detail and examples in Piper et al. (1996). We believe that programs should:

1. Attend carefully to referral sources.
2. Select patients with attention to optimal patient-treatment matching.
3. Encourage personal responsibility in the patients.
4. Facilitate patient participation in one another's treatment.
5. Conduct multiple groups throughout the treatment system.
6. Foster mutual respect between patients and staff members.
7. Implement the judicious use of authority by staff members.
8. Provide stable leadership that supports a consistent treatment philosophy.
9. Collaborate with higher order systems, for example, forming links with other psychiatric services, keeping administrators informed.

Successful implementation also involves avoiding certain pitfalls that historically have plagued many programs. In general, violations of these nine principles cover the majority of the pitfalls. However, some errors have been particularly problematic, even in well-established programs. These merit highlighting:

1. Attempting to treat inappropriate patients in day treatment—for example, those who are too acutely disturbed or those who are too chronically disabled to engage in therapeutic tasks. Day hospital or day care, respectively, may be more appropriate for these patients.
2. Attempting to treat a mixture of patients with conflicting needs in the same program—for example, those who would benefit from intensive treatment and those who require support and management.
3. Alternating between leadership phases characterized by abdication of authority and abuse of power. Here, authority refers to control in the service of the collective goals of the treatment program. Power is control in the service of personal goals of the leader.

No program can continuously adhere to all of these principles and completely avoid difficult problems. What is essential is that there are ongoing opportunities for staff members to reflect on the multilevel processes of the program and make adjustments that support the principles and attempt to overcome the difficulties. Staff members must be willing to examine their own interactions with patients and with one another. This may be done in a staff member-to-staff member relations group. Essential staff member qualities appear to include humility, containment of narcissistic needs, capacity to contain the projections of patients, and, above all, a willingness to learn. These qualities require time to develop, which underscores the importance of maintaining a stable staff over time.

The practical implications of the findings from the predictor studies are less obvious. Although the availability of a large number of predictors may appear advantageous, it creates a particular problem: uncertainty about the validity of the predictors because they may represent chance findings. When studies conduct a large number of statistical tests to identify significant predictors, some of the tests will emerge significant by chance. Those results represent error. If only a few of a large number of tests are significant, little confidence can be placed in their validity. One means of reducing the large number of predictors reviewed in this article to a more manageable set is to select only those variables that were found to be significant in more than one study. Another, more meaningful approach to choosing predictors that can be used as selection criteria is to choose variables on the basis of theory. That is, clinicians may choose variables as selection criteria that for theoretical reasons should be related to success in day treatment. Two variables that stand out as important for theoretical reasons and were found to be significantly associated with remaining and benefiting from day treatment are the patient personality characteristics: quality of object relations and psychological mindedness. The findings suggest that patients with low psychological mindedness and a history of primitive relationships are at a greater risk of dropping out and benefiting less from day treatment.

Prediction, however, is never perfect. Some patients who are regarded as high risk, based on their selection criteria scores, inevitably surprise us and do well. Excluding all patients who do not meet the selection criteria means that such patients would be prevented from receiving a beneficial treatment. We do not want to deprive all high-risk patients of an opportunity to benefit, even though we know a number of such patients will not. Researchers can inform clinicians about risk or selection factors, and then clinicians can make decisions about how much risk or how many high-risk patients to accept for their program. Having a few high-risk patients in a day treatment program is far different from having many.

SUMMARY AND CONCLUSIONS

Personality disorders are serious long-term conditions that are resistant to change and difficult to treat. Day treatment, a form of partial hospitalization, may have unique advantages for the treatment of patients with PDs. It offers an optimal level of intensiveness and containment, thus facilitating treatment of the chronic emotional and behavioral difficulties experienced by these patients. We have described a particular day treatment program that has treated patients with PDs for more than 30 years. A case example illustrated how the program is capable of bringing about important changes. Findings of several studies have indicated that day treatment is effective for this patient population. In addition, researchers have begun to identify predictors of success in day treatment, thus contributing to proper patient selection. Additional research will help confirm that day treatment is an effective and efficient intervention for individuals suffering from severe PDs.

REFERENCES

Bateman, A., & Fonagy, P. (1999). Effectiveness of partial hospitalization in the treatment of borderline personality disorder: A randomized controlled trial. *American Journal of Psychiatry, 156,* 1563–1569.

Bateman, A., & Fonagy, P. (2001). Treatment of borderline personality disorder with psychoanalytically oriented partial hospitalization: An 18-month follow-up. *American Journal of Psychiatry, 158,* 36–42.

Bender, D. S., Dolan, R. T., Skodol, A. E., Sanislow, C. A., Dyck, I. R., McGlashan, T. H., et al. (2001). Treatment utilization by patients with personality disorders. *American Journal of Psychiatry, 158,* 295–302.

Dazord, A., Gerin, P., Seulin, C., Duclos, A., & Amar, A. (1997). Day treatment evaluation: Therapeutic outcome after a treatment in a psychiatric day-treatment center: Another look at the Outcome Equivalence Paradox. *Psychotherapy Research, 7,* 57–69.

Dolan, B., Evans, C., & Norton, K. (1995). Multiple Axis-II diagnoses of personality disorder. *British Journal of Psychiatry, 166,* 107–112.

Gillis, K., Russell, R., & Busby, K. (1997). Factors associated with unplanned discharge from psychiatric day treatment programs. *General Hospital Psychiatry, 19,* 355–361.

Joyce, A. S., Piper, W. E., Rosie, J. S., & Azim, H. F. A. (1994). The psychosocial environment of an intensive day treatment program. *Continuum: Developments in Ambulatory Mental Health Care, 1,* 219–237.

Krawitz, R. (1997). A prospective psychotherapy outcome study. *Australian and New Zealand Journal of Psychiatry, 31,* 465–473.

Mehlum, L., Friis, S., Irion, T., Johns, S., Karterud, S., Vaglum, P., et al. (1991). Personality disorders 2–5 years after treatment: A prospective study. *Acta Psychiatrica Scandinavica, 84,* 72–77.

Melson, S. J. (1995). Brief day treatment for nonpsychotic patients. In K. R. MacKenzie (Ed.), *Effective use of group therapy in managed care* (pp. 113–128). Washington, DC: American Psychiatric Press.

Merikangas, K. R., & Weissman, M. M. (1986). Epidemiology of *DSM-III* Axis II personality disorders. In A. J. Frances & R. E. Hales (Eds.), *Psychiatry update: American Psychiatric Association annual review* (Vol. 5, pp. 258–278). Washington, DC: American Psychiatric Press.

O'Kelly, J. G., & Azim, H. F. A. (1993). Staff-staff relations group. *International Journal of Group Psychotherapy, 43,* 469–483.

Pilkonis, P. A., Neighbors, B. D., & Corbitt, E. M. (1999). Personality disorders. In N. E. Miller & K. M. Magruder (Eds.), *Cost-effectiveness of psychotherapy* (pp. 279–290). New York: Oxford University Press.

Piper, W. E., Joyce, A. S., Azim, H. F. A., & Rosie, J. S. (1994). Patient characteristics and success in day treatment. *Journal of Nervous and Mental Diseases, 182,* 381–386.

Piper, W. E., Joyce, A. S., Rosie, A. S., & Azim, H. F. A. (1994). Psychological mindedness, work, and outcome in day treatment. *International Journal of Group Psychotherapy, 44,* 291–311.

Piper, W. E., & Rosie, J. S. (1998). Group treatment of personality disorder: The power of the group in the intensive treatment of personality disorders. *In Session: Psychotherapy in Practice, 4,* 19–34.

Piper, W. E., Rosie, J. S., Azim, H. F. A., & Joyce, A. S. (1993). A randomized trial of psychiatric day treatment for patients with affective and personality disorders. *Hospital and Community Psychiatry, 44,* 757–763.

Piper, W. E., Rosie, J. S., Joyce, A. S., & Azim, H. F. A. (1996). *Time-limited day treatment for personality disorders.* Washington, DC: American Psychological Association.

Tasca, G. A., Balfour, L., Bissada, H., Busby, K., Conrad, G., Cameron, P., et al. (1999). Treatment completion and outcome in a partial hospitalization program: Interactions among patient variables. *Psychotherapy Research, 9,* 232–247.

Vaglum, P., Friis, S., Irion, T., Johns, S., Karterud, S., Larsen, F., et al. (1990). Treatment response of severe and nonsevere personality disorders in a therapeutic community day unit. *Journal of Personality Disorders, 4,* 161–172.

Wilberg, T., Friis, S., Karterud, S., Mehlum, L., Urnes, Ø., & Vaglum, P. (1998). Patterns of short-term course in patients treated in a day unit for personality disorders. *Comprehensive Psychiatry, 39,* 75–84.

Wilberg, T., Karterud, S., Urnes, Ø., Pedersen, G., & Friis, S. (1998). Outcomes of poorly functioning patients with personality disorders in a day treatment program. *Psychiatric Services, 49,* 1462–1467.

Wilberg, T., Urnes, Ø., Friis, S., Irion, T., Pedersen, G., & Karterud, S. (1999). One-year follow-up of day treatment for poorly functioning patients with personality disorders. *Psychiatric Services, 50,* 1326–1330.

Yalom, I. D. (1995). *The theory and practice of group psychotherapy* (4th ed.). New York: Basic Books.

CHAPTER 17

Residential Treatment of Personality Disorders: The Containing Function

Barri Belnap, Cuneyt Iscan, and Eric M. Plakun

RESIDENTIAL TREATMENT, EXTENDED hospitalization, and long-term inpatient treatment are interchangeable names for a treatment modality that has become less available in today's mental health environment. Economic, political, and societal pressures and forces in psychiatry drive the trend toward brief hospitalizations and crisis intervention (Higgitt & Fonagy, 1992). Despite the current climate, extended treatment programs remain necessary for "difficult-to-treat" or "treatment refractory" illnesses that do not respond to brief intervention, short-term treatment, or outpatient treatment (Menninger, 2000). The vast majority of patients who are in the category of "difficult-to-treat" or "treatment resistant" suffer from comorbid personality disorders besides their Axis I pathologies (Chiesa & Fonagy, 2000; Plakun, 2003). These patients use, and sometimes are felt to abuse, medical and psychiatric resources. When they do not improve or even deteriorate in spite of treatment, they may be referred to inpatient or residential treatment centers. This chapter focuses on the way the *containing* or *holding* function offered by residential treatment centers can allow a subgroup of these patients with personality disorders to make gains that could not be achieved in outpatient treatment or short-term hospitalization. The term *holding* is usually employed to refer to Winnicott's ideas about the environmental conditions best suited to meeting certain human developmental needs (1965c), whereas *containment* typically refers to Bion's (1962) ideas about projective identification. The terms are used interchangeably in this discussion because the therapeutic environment we are describing inevitably involves both functions.

CLINICAL CHARACTERISTICS

Many of the personality disorder patients who wind up in residential treatment have Borderline Personality Disorder, usually comorbid with multiple other Axis I or II disorders (Plakun, 2003). In the "Practice Guidelines for Borderline

Personality Disorder" (APA, 2001), the American Psychiatric Association recognizes that in certain situations, extended inpatient or residential treatment may be indicated. They suggest that outpatient treatment may no longer be viable at times of significant threat to the patient or to the frame of the treatment. Such threats might include impulsive behavior associated with danger to self and others, poor compliance with the treatment plan, and symptoms that interfere with the patient's capacity to function in interpersonal, familial, work, or other life roles. Other clinical characteristics of the subset of personality disorder patients who are candidates for residential treatment may include:

1. Patients who present with multiple comorbid psychiatric disorders, including substance abuse and psychotic episodes.
2. Patients who, because of impulsive/self-destructive behaviors or overwhelming affect states, cannot manage between sessions or who make suicidal gestures that reduce the therapeutic work to management and control of behavior.
3. Patients whose symptoms routinely are not engaged in the outpatient setting. These patients deprive treaters of the information necessary to make treatment viable. This may occur through splitting, displacement into action outside the therapy, severe difficulties managing affect states, or avoidance of key issues. Treaters of these patients find their therapeutic efforts repeatedly stymied by what the patient is not or cannot bring into the therapy session.
4. Patients whose dynamics frequently lead to such degrees of acting out or splitting that a high degree of integration and collaboration among treaters is required to hold the patient in relation to symptoms, so that they can be translated into words and addressed therapeutically.
5. Patients whose current life circumstances are either so unstable or so dangerous that they are exposed to unacceptable risk of harm.
6. Impasse in the outpatient treatment. Impasses may result for many reasons, including a tendency to evoke unbearable countertransference in treaters. Other causes may include the repeated development of a psychotic transference, malignant regression, or enactments involving mutual projective identification between therapist and patient (Plakun, 2001; Shapiro & Carr, 1991).
7. Severe personality disorder in combination with one or more Axis I disorders that requires greater containment than can be provided in the outpatient setting.

We now consider what makes patients with personality disorders difficult to treat and why it is that some outpatient treatments fail. Patients with personality disorders present to their treaters in complex and often difficult-to-understand ways. Their symptoms derive from problems in areas of affect, impulse control, identity, the capacity for interpersonal relationships, and deficits in the social understanding necessary to function adequately in basic life roles. The capacity for these individuals to learn from their experience seems severely constricted. In general, these individuals seem unwittingly to repeat traumatic and painful experience as if they have no choice. Often, they repeat things in action for which they neither understand nor remember the experiential origins, motivations, and significance. The sense of mastery and confidence that individuals without personality disorders gain from active engagement of life problems is unavailable to the personality-disordered patient, who experiences neither choice nor understanding of how to master the problems being repeated. Their experience is of inefficacy. For all of these reasons, these patients challenge clinicians' therapeutic ambitions. The difficulty of working with these patients and the time required to see change has led some to become cynical about the possibility of effective treatments. And yet, there is data (see later discussion) that some of these individuals are able to make use of treatment.

In his 1965b paper on the "Psychotherapy of Character Disorders," Winnicott provides important insights into personality disorders. He suggests it is useful to think of personality or character disorder as a "hidden illness" in an otherwise "intact" personality. This hidden illness is the result of a "distortion" of the personality—a distortion that arose in response to a "significant deprivation" in the person's early life. By *deprivation,* he refers to repeated and problematic experiences that are highly emotionally charged or traumatic in the individual's relationship with those on whom he or she most depended. The deprivation and the resulting distortion it fosters interfere with normal developmental processes. Individuals become "stunted" emotionally and compensate through problematic adaptations that hide but do not resolve the deprivation. In the interpersonal realm, the effect of the distorted adaptation on others may promote the collaboration of others in recreating in the present the experience of the original deprivation. This robs the personality disorder patient of the possibility of new learning and leaves him or her demoralized by repetitions of the same trouble. In another paper (1965a), Winnicott included some of these notions in his theorizing about false self-organization.

Because the trouble these patients struggle with arose in relationship to others, resolution requires interpersonal relationships to see and resolve the problem; or in Winnicott's terms, it has a "social" origin and "social" resolution. Winnicott names the symptoms or difficult interpersonal postures of these patients their "antisocial tendency." Here "antisocial" refers not to sociopathy, but to the form of the repeated interpersonal problems. Winnicott suggests the antisocial tendency is actually unconsciously motivated to engage others' help to clarify and resolve the initial deprivation and the resulting distortion (e.g., problematic adaptation) in the personality. The usual social response to this request tends to be to the acting out, that is, to the distortion, and usually fails to recognize the underlying request for help. The consequences of repeated symptomatic acting out are destroyed relationships and failures in roles. This leaves personality disordered patients with an exaggerated impression of their destructiveness and of the vulnerability of those they seek to engage. Just as personality-disordered patients may have had a role in the family of origin as the carrier of the family's difficulties, they may unwittingly be used or scapegoated by society as the carrier of the unwanted parts of the social group. In these ways, society may promote the consolidation of the personality disorder by tolerating failure to fully contribute "in" the society to which they belong and by exploiting or attempting to repress the distortions of patients' character. Social avoidance of the underlying request for help is understandable because the request is often voiced in the form of a complaint or an accusation of wrongdoing to which the personality-disordered individual feels subjected. In the logic of the distortion, this complaint becomes the justification for the problematic and often aggressive acting-out behaviors.

If we accept Winnicott's notion that personality-disordered patients have successfully hidden the trouble, engaging that trouble in a treatment process that leads to conscious knowing and understanding means that patients will likely become more manifestly "ill." They have to give up the defenses that hid the problem and prevented its resolution. In other language from Winnicott (1965a), treatment asks the patient to give up the false self and take the risk of exposing the true self, complete with its deprivations and often ambivalently expressed angry complaints. This requires an environment, whether outpatient, inpatient, or residential, that is prepared to embrace the apparent worsening of the patient and view it as a necessary collaborative engagement in treatment. The patient will need support to deal with the shame and dependency that must of necessity accompany such opening up. In treatment, aggressive attacks on authority or self-destructiveness need to be met in a manner that facilitates uncovering the "hidden illness" and revealing the dynamics from whence it derives, rather than punishing the patient and thereby misunderstanding the symptom's developmental value and meaning.

THE CONTAINING FUNCTION IN THE TREATMENT OF PERSONALITY DISORDERS

Treatment for the personality-disordered patient requires an environment that can *hold* or *contain* the patient's unconscious and unintegrated parts along with their behavioral expressions. This environment has been called by Winnicott (1965c) the "holding environment" or "facilitating environment" and serves a containing function that holds patients in relation to their symptoms. This holding or containment allows patients to expose the hidden illness in a treatment context that does not respond the way the larger world does. The therapeutic containment is intended to foster learning and development rather than suppress symptoms. This containing function is part of treatment of personality disorders in all settings whether outpatient, inpatient, or residential (Kernberg, 1984). Society provides other forms of containment for personality disorder patients who do not find their way into treatment settings. This containment ranges from family, to community structures such as therapeutic community programs for delinquents, to prisons.

In outpatient treatment, patients are responsible for managing their behavior between the sessions in a manner that allows the therapy to progress safely. Problematic behaviors are ideally contained within the transference relationship with the therapist. If acting out can be confined to the transference and if the affective states mobilized in the transference-countertransference relationship are not so primitive and intense that it is hard for a therapist alone to bear them, a personality-disordered patient can be treated as an outpatient. Similarly, when a patient can adequately symbolize or mentalize (Fonagy, Gergely, Jurist, & Target, 2002) experience, rather than live it out in extreme split and displaced forms, outpatient treatment is usually a viable option. When splitting, dissociation, reality distortion, regression, depersonalization, or other primitive defenses make the patient's symptomatic expressions unusable or unavailable to the therapist, the specific and unique containing function provided by an inpatient or residential treatment center may be indicated. If periods of high risk or shifts to crisis management are brief, short-term inpatient treatment may contain temporary symptomatic exacerbations. The control *over* behavior provided in these settings, through locked doors, the capacity for intensive observation, and rapid adjustment-stabilization of psychotropic medications may be sufficient to return the patient to an otherwise viable outpatient treatment that has temporarily become dangerous or unworkable. Similarly, brief partial hospital programs sometimes provide the added support necessary to sustain a working outpatient treatment through a difficult phase. However, there are also instances when either the degree of acting out, the intensity of the affects mobilized in the transference, or the lack of integration of the overall treatment calls for additional structures that can provide ongoing containment necessary to allow the treatment to go beyond chronic crisis management. This additional containment is what we have referred to as *holding* and may be required to stabilize the treatment and support the patient, the family, and/or the staff. Residential treatment centers provide additional structures and resources to the treatment enterprise that make this holding possible under circumstances that are otherwise too difficult, dangerous, or unstable.

For outpatient treatment to work, a patient, in spite of the difficulties of a personality disorder, must have the capacity to form a stable attachment to the therapist. The relationship must be secure enough to sustain the therapeutic effort in spite of disruptions between sessions and the conflicts that inevitably arise as a necessary part of the patient's development. Challenges to the stability of the patient's therapeutic attachment sometimes arise in the form of temporary regressions in the treatment to painful states during which the patient's past "problems" with significant others seem to be happening in the present with the therapist. In addition to a stable therapeutic attachment, outpatient treatment requires that the patient have the ego strength required to switch on and switch off the process of therapeutic regression in sessions. That is, on entering the session, the patient switches on the capacity to regress, to remember painful experiences and their associated affects, to mobilize powerful negative transferences, and to work collaboratively with these in the service of the therapeutic task. When the hour ends, an outpatient is asked, in effect, to switch off the disorganizing here-and-now aspects of this complicated intrapsychic and interpersonal work so as to function adaptively until the next session. This is not a trivial request to make of a personality disorder patient. For patients who cannot do this, the implicit goal of residential treatment may be achievement of this capacity to switch off that which has been mobilized in sessions and to manage adaptively between sessions. Embedded in the notion of switching off at the end of the session is a great deal of complicated work. There is a need to develop ego functioning adequate to allow mobilized affects and acting out to be contained within the transference, rather than spilling out into the rest of the patient's life. In fact, one way to think of the task of extended residential treatment is to create an opportunity for patients to develop this specific capacity.

RESIDENTIAL TREATMENT OF PERSONALITY DISORDERS

Residential treatment centers are more than just a place for patients to live under close supervision. From a behavioral perspective, they are places where experiential learning is fostered and prioritized. These programs are based on a belief that patients learn through experience to change perspectives of themselves and their environment so that they feel agency and responsibility for what happens to them. When patients develop new perspectives on significant deprivations and the ways they have been affected by them, patients can then choose to act differently. The specific structures and therapeutic values that are now considered characteristic of residential treatments were developed over the years in an effort to provide the necessary structures within which such therapeutic change for personality-disordered patients becomes possible.

In general, residential treatments may be modeled after a therapeutic community model, whether psychoanalytic or not, a token economy (or other behavioral treatment models), or a moral treatment custodial care model (Menninger, 2000). During the twentieth century, one idea of how to create an environment that would facilitate the treatment of patients developed into the notion of the "therapeutic community." This treatment modality was introduced in England by Thomas Main and popularized by Maxwell Jones. In his paper "The Hospital As a Therapeutic Institution," Main (1989) took the perspective that the hospital, as a *social system*, could be employed therapeutically as an agent of change. It could be a therapeutic community. This notion represented a radical change from how hospitals were previously thought to work. He states, "It is doubtful whether the hospital can usefully remain a building within which individual treatment is practiced. Perhaps it must become a therapeutic institution" (p. 8). Main focused on the ways the structures and relationships that make up institutional life are of significance to the patient and to the therapeutic task. He writes, "The daily life of the community must be related to real tasks, truly relevant both to the needs and aspirations of the small society of the hospital, and the larger society" (p. 8). Both Main and Jones valued democratizing treatment processes as a way of enhancing patient responsibility and learning.

Kernberg (1984) has also theorized about the therapeutic community. His summary of assumptions about treatment in a therapeutic community includes:

1. It is assumed that the patients as individuals and as a group are able to help one another.
2. Patients functioning in a group setting may react in appropriate and responsible ways as a group.
3. Staff as a group may function pathologically and antitherapeutically at times.
4. Authoritarianism is antitherapeutic, and decisions made on the basis of *power* rather than *reason* mitigate against patients' development and may contribute to regression.
5. Democratization increases the patient's self-esteem, the effectiveness of his or her social functioning, encourages the honesty of his or her communications, and promotes individual development and therapeutic goals of differentiation, responsibility, and an understanding of social and interpersonal consequences of choices.
6. Collective participation in decision making at public meetings is assumed to be therapeutic.
7. Patients are assumed to be able to help one another as individuals to develop interpersonal skills and creativity as well as ego strength.

These assumptions are not simply about patients and what they need to do to get better; they also recognize the participation of the staff in therapeutic and antitherapeutic processes.

What hospitals and residential treatment centers offer patients are opportunities for containment and holding within a community. Treatment settings may organize themselves differently around priorities for how the containing function is to be accomplished, but all seek to hold the patient in relation to his or her symptoms in a way that promotes their resolution while attending to the safety of the patient. Problems of pathological dependency or malignant regression may occur in inpatient or residential settings when the containing *structure* (e.g., use of restraints, locked wards) is confused with the containing *function* (e.g., human relationships or community membership). Emphasis on the containing structure leads to efforts to suppress symptomatology, whereas emphasis on the containing function implies a need for the provision of those resources necessary to engage symptoms in ways that promote personal development and self-understanding.

The containing function of therapeutic communities is, in part, provided by the ways in which patient choice, responsibility, and strengths are actively engaged. When the patient experiences himself or herself as choosing treatment and participates in a treatment that is structured to acknowledge and depend on patient agency and competencies, the risk of malignant regression or pathological dependency is minimized. The therapeutic community formally recognizes patient agency by expecting that the patient for whom this treatment approach is a reasonable risk will function competently. Deviations from competent functioning are what is taken up in various ways by staff and other members of the patient community. For outpatients, the therapist expects the patient to collaborate with the treatment frame and relies on the patient to choose to do so. In hospital and residential contexts, but particularly in the open setting framework of programs such as that of the Austen Riggs Center, an explicit negotiation of the working alliance and of each party's responsibilities in the therapeutic work is an essential antecedent to the patient's entry into treatment (Plakun, 1994, 2001). It represents one structural way to engage the patient's choice and agency and make explicit expectations of competence. The open setting has no locked doors and no compulsory interventions, except membership in the community. It functions by asking patients to make a choice to be in treatment and to honor the responsibilities that follow—to the treatment, to the therapeutic community, and to themselves.

DOES IT WORK?

Empirical data and clinical observations suggest that residential treatment is effective for some patients. Plakun (2003) has published preliminary findings from a prospective, longitudinal study of patients in treatment at the Austen Riggs Center, an inpatient-residential continuum of care that specializes in such treatment. The Riggs continuum of care adds to general psychiatric treatment four-times-weekly individual psychodynamic therapy and a sophisticated milieu program in a completely open setting. Treatment averages eight months. Led by J. Christopher Perry, Riggs is conducting an ongoing, naturalistic, longitudinal follow-along study of patients during and after treatment at Riggs. The study uses reliable measures of symptom change, but also reliable measures of psychodynamic constructs such as defenses and conflicts.

Data on the first 57 study patients with three to five years of follow-up reveals 86% had personality disorders, usually Borderline Personality Disorder, whereas

80% had reliably diagnosed mood disorders. The patients were a disturbed group, with 40% having six or more self-destructive episodes, 50% having made at least one serious suicide attempt, and 60% having had three or more previous hospitalizations. Nearly half had histories of childhood trauma. Preliminary findings suggest significant improvement over three to five years of follow-up, with most of the change occurring after the first two years following admission. Conservatively estimated effect sizes ranged from 0.4 (for self-report measures) to 0.5 to 1.0 (for employment, defenses, and the Hamilton anxiety and depression scales) to 1.5 (for Global Assessment of Functioning [GAF]). These are large changes in a disturbed and previously treatment refractory group of patients.

PHASES OF TREATMENT IN A PSYCHODYNAMIC THERAPEUTIC COMMUNITY

Treatment of personality disorders in all settings requires understanding and then integration of the personal and experiential origins of illness. Personality disorders are assumed to have a substantial part of their origin in the patterns that evolved as patients encountered difficulties in negotiating subjective experiences of early, generally intrafamilial, failures, deprivations, and traumas. In residential settings, patients come to understand these origins and the motivations for current behaviors as they live out their original traumas in the present in an environment that allows the difficulties to be noticed and interpreted. This process provides opportunities for patients to learn how those original experiences have come to determine perceptions and choices in the present. They learn to recognize repetitions in the here and now and sometimes to relate in new and more mature ways to aspects of the original problematic relationships. That being accomplished, patients are provided with capacities that allow them to respond differently to the pressures that led to the original distortions in their developmental response.

How do these treatments work and what is their goal? As noted previously, the goal of inpatient-residential treatment is generally to return the patient to a viable outpatient treatment. Patients who enter these treatment centers have for one or several reasons not been successful at this. The entrance into the inpatient-residential treatment setting is an important opportunity to review, and sometimes relive in the here and now, what went wrong in the outpatient treatment and what has gone wrong in life. The stable and more concrete boundaries of these institutions sometimes provide the structures around which patients will repeat those very same problems that stymied the outpatient work. A careful delineation of problems that occurred in relation to the framework of the outpatient treatment can prepare and guide the patient and hospital-residential treatment staff through the important learning that occurs during the entrance phase, to the extent that it can be expected that the same troubles are likely to be repeated in the inpatient-residential treatment.

The next phase of treatment involves the consolidation and integration of that learning into a way of living and interacting with people. As developmental impasses and the distortions they fostered are understood, the holding environment of a therapeutic community provides opportunities for practice and experimentation. This process in turn promotes and requires reoperationalizing maturational processes. In this phase, the patient needs support, mirroring, and the option to "get it wrong" repeatedly in the service of learning without provoking unduly stifling social consequences that could disrupt his or her developmental efforts. This is hard to achieve in an outpatient treatment and is the focus of the residential treatment effort in a therapeutic community model.

For the individual therapist working in a therapeutic milieu, engaging in this work means being the one with whom the patient seeks to evoke the past traumatic relationships. Therefore, therapist "failures" will occur and are expected in the treatment. As patterns are repeated, therapists are required to acknowledge their own real failures in the here-and-now relation to the patient and make the link to the transference. This work asks a great deal of therapists—at times, perhaps too much. Some patients have powerful transferences that induce intense countertransference responses in treaters. At times, these may become too much for any one treater to bear working alone. Sometimes, even when distributed over an entire institution, the countertransference can be difficult to bear.

CASE ILLUSTRATION

Sheila was admitted to a psychiatric residential treatment facility after one of what had become nearly daily alcohol binges. When she did not show up for work, a colleague found her intoxicated in her apartment. Her alcohol use was a problem that she had kept hidden from her therapist despite the intensity and frequency of their work together over the prior six years. Sheila carried diagnoses of Borderline Personality Disorder, recurrent Major Depressive Disorder, PTSD, Alcohol Dependence, and suffered from a chronic pain syndrome. She struggled with intrusive memories of severe physical as well as sexual childhood abuse and neglect. She demonstrated trouble with interpersonal relationships that left her isolated, depressed, and passively suicidal. This difficulty relating to people interfered with her capacity to work. She complained that she did not "feel real." She described feeling tossed back and forth from shame and self-hatred to heroic expectations of herself to "learn the right way" to be so as to "make everything okay." Her tendency to anticipate that others would respond to her needs in undependable and brutal ways probably derived from early childhood experiences of poverty and cruelty at the hands of parents whom she depended on. Her defensive, avoidant, and counterdependent ways made sense in that context. She grew up in a world where basic trust could not be taken for granted, not even in relation to parents, and in a context in which the community "stood by" and acted as if they did not see the trouble she was in. Teachers, doctors, or social workers did not intervene to protect her even when it was their mandate to do so. She experienced the absence of responsiveness to her needs from neighbors and judges to be evidence that either they did not believe her experience was "real" or, as she described it in her own words, that she herself "did not exist" in some very real way.

As a child, and even as an adult, she found herself unable, ashamed, and afraid to say explicitly what happened behind the walls of her home. What happened to her was too threatening. She felt neglected and abandoned. Yet, something in her found hope in her observation that others lived better. Sheila believed she could live better, if only she could understand the "rules" so that she could change her life. The tension between these hopes for the future and catastrophic expectations of being neglected and humiliated that came from her early family experience were reflected in the split and divergent ways she experienced herself and the world around her.

In her present life, Sheila's way of engaging people (including her doctor) repeated early traumatic experiences. She approached others with a manner that ensured their misunderstanding and/or abandonment of her, instead of putting them in a position to give her the help she so desperately needed and wanted. She then would interpret the "abandoning" reaction to her that she unconsciously expected and set up as confirmation that she was "bad" and deserving of the unfair and cruel punishments that she received. She did not experience herself as having choices in these recurring patterns. In general, she felt damaged and hopeless. The only evidence that she felt entitled to or hopeful for something better could be found in moments when she acted out angrily and impulsively at some injustice she perceived in what was happening to her. Ironically, her angry complaints and attacks were efforts to change things. They represented a tentative and perhaps unconscious hope that she could induce a different response in those around her.

Depression and suicidal ideation were prominent expressions of her anger and hopelessness. Both symptoms offered a chance for someone to see the problem and help. In a habitual expression of cynicism, she most directly focused her anger toward herself in the form of shame and self-hatred at not being able to do better. The immediacy and forcefulness of her wish for things to be different were reflected in her desire to "not be alive." She tried to hide these feelings from herself and others through "heroic" efforts to be "good" and "normal." Consciously, she believed that she had survived as well as she had in life because she was successful at "pretending" to be normal. She believed her life to be bad and abnormal at the same time that she watched with envy and imitative hope the way others lived. The difference between her life and theirs left her feeling unreal, dissociated, and contributed to her difficulties relating interpersonally. She fought to make her life "normal" by copying theirs, but, not believing she deserved it, she repeatedly undermined her efforts in a seemingly self-defeating process. *Ironically, that self-defeat was protective of her potential for psychological growth because it prevented her from rigidifying the "false self" organization. Copying others "normal" solutions without acknowledging her own emotional experience would likely lead to such "false self" organization. Her self-defeating failures brought her back to face earlier dilemmas that demanded resolution before she would be able to go on to take up her life in a more developmentally appropriate and less conflicted way.*

Despite her work in outpatient therapy, Sheila lived a marginal and emotionally stunted life. Her capacity to function at the most basic level and to care for herself were severely limited. In the context of current stressors, her previous way of making do in the world by "pretending to be normal" failed her. Her mind as well as her home was marked by signs of chaos and despair. Her bills had not been paid for months and lay around the apartment in general disarray, along with dirty dishes and empty vodka bottles. There were burns on the carpet where cigarettes had fallen when she lapsed into drunken sleep. Her health and ability to move around were compromised by poor nutrition and by a chronic pain syndrome and the prescribed narcotics she used to subdue it. Her narcotic use had reached such high levels that she was left cognitively, affectively, and functionally impaired. Her internist and pain consultant despaired that she would ever be able to relinquish narcotics and continued to prescribe opiate analgesics despite the debilitation they caused.

Significantly, even her outpatient therapist, with whom she had done great work in the past and to whom she was very attached, was not aware of the severity of her difficulties. He had no way of knowing because she split out the troubled aspect of her experience and showed him only her bravery, while secretly hating him for not seeing through her attempts to be "good." He participated in the enactment by joining her wish for a heroic cure that he felt himself to be a part of and supported her "good efforts" without recognizing the troubles they hid and suppressed, most especially her anger.

The therapist was reluctant to know about or how her unstated hatred might be directed at him. He was in a collusive unconscious agreement with the patient to "not know" what he and she might otherwise have noticed. This enactment, based on mutual projective identification (Plakun, 2001), led him to support her heroism and unwittingly become an "unseeing bystander" to her trouble. Later, Sheila was able to reflect back on that time in treatment with her outpatient therapist, recognizing that she had been angry at his absences. Linking this observation to her family life, she realized that his absences had taken on particular significance because her mother's failing health confronted her with the memory of maternal neglect and abandonment as a child. Her mother, in addition to teachers and social workers, had stood by as a collusive bystander when Sheila was beaten and then sexually abused by her father. Her experience had shown Sheila repeatedly that the people and institutions mandated to support and protect her stood by doing nothing as if they didn't see what was happening, or they betrayed her. She learned to respond to such disappointments or abandonments with one of two extreme expressions of avoidance and anger: "Fuck you, I'll kill myself" or "Fuck you, I'll take care of everything myself." Her therapist had unwittingly become another significant onlooker who "should have known" what she did not, could not, say in words. Her use of alcohol, which she rationalized as intended to "save her life" by "taking care" of feelings she could not bear "by herself," became the means to kill herself right under his nose.

There were multiple determinants of the self-defeating process by which she undermined her therapy and forced her outpatient therapist, on learning of her predicament, to end their work together and refer her to a residential treatment program. On the one hand, Sheila was showing in action what she could not say in words. Later in her treatment, she reflected back on the state she was in before admission to the residential treatment setting. She said, "It [had] to do with wanting something even if I am not asking for [it] directly. Before I came here, there was something that I wanted that I just couldn't ask for, and I felt ungrateful because I had seemingly everything, except that I couldn't have relationships that I could feel inside. I would have been dead in two days if someone had not stopped me." She felt dead inside, and killing herself was a way of finding coherence, a way of resolving the split created by pretending to be "good" and acting as if things were okay. She went on to say, "I think that most of the times, it has to do with disappointing people and that the secrets, whatever they might be, are an effort to try and be whatever I should be, and I think that's connected with my inability to feel [my] connection with people."

Sheila repeated a version of the experience of being neglected and abandoned with her new therapist/psychopharmacologist during the first weeks of her stay at the residential treatment center. He experienced her as difficult to understand and, as a result, found himself disbelieving or not listening to her. She fostered the impression he had formed of her by claiming a "learning disability" that she held responsible for her trouble feeling understood. He experienced her stance as defensive and not genuine. He discounted her efforts to speak to him because he felt she used them to disavow responsibility and to compel him into action rather than to communicate. Sheila's expectation was that therapy would teach her the "right way" to be and that he had the answers that would "make her okay" if only he would listen and give them to her. He felt angry at what he felt she was doing to him and at her seeming unwillingness to collaborate with his wish for her to speak differently so that he could understand her. This dynamic pattern was simultaneously being enacted with the consultant in internal medicine at the treatment center. The patient also accused this consultant of "not listening" and "not believing" that her bodily pain was "real." She complained angrily that the doctor had and was withholding the medications that would "make things okay."

In this first section of the vignette, we see problems found in a patient who cannot be contained in an outpatient treatment: serious and at times life-threatening trouble with self-care, suicidal ideation, an enactment of her trouble in relation to the frame of the treatment (hiding information from her therapist, causing him to abandon her in confirmation of her expectations), and multiple comorbid diagnoses. As an outpatient, her secret alcohol abuse represented an attack on the frame of the outpatient treatment and, as a result, on her therapist's authority to define and provide a containing structure for their therapeutic work. In the transference, her "attack" had multiple and layered meanings. It was an attempt to locate in the here and now of the therapy the original deprivation, which was similarly a situation in which her pain was "not seen," "not listened to," and "not considered real." Additionally, her attack on him was an acknowledgment of her anger at his absences, a recognition of her dependence on him, and an experience of crisis she experienced when her adaptations of "Fuck you, I'll do it myself" and "Fuck you, I'll kill myself" were mobilized. It rekindled her experience of betrayal and shame at sadness at what she could not say about her trouble and need for help.

Attacks on the frame or authority of the treatment are common in outpatient treatments that become unworkable. In her case, the secret undisclosed attacks on the authority of the treatment were a transference recreation of early experiences of maternal neglect and abandonment and of paternal abuse. It was hard to interpret this in the transference because her therapist was blinded by her efforts to keep it secret, by his reluctance to recognize her anger at him, and by his difficulty admitting to himself that he was frustrated with her. Sheila's initial interactions with her therapist in the residential setting engaged these same issues. It is sometimes the case that only after acting out significant but unconscious relationships and interpreting them in relation to the transference can certain key memories of important early experiences be brought into awareness. These memories may be the experiential referent for assumptions and expectations that drive the repetition. Enactments and acting out provide opportunities for some forms of unconscious experience to be translated into conscious memories. Reexamination of these memories from the perspective of the patient in the present, characterized by greater maturity and resources, may provide important clues about the patient's core difficulties and problematic patterns of response.

On entering the residential treatment setting, Sheila immediately engaged the staff around the issues that had plagued her outpatient work. Suicidal impulses, alcoholic binges, and abandoning her treatment (by either not showing up to therapy sessions or by taking drugs for pain relief that left her cognitively and emotionally unavailable to do the work of therapy) evoked an experience of hopelessness and despair in the staff. Sheila reacted to the multiple examples of abandonment and neglect she perceived in staff behavior with rage and entitled demands for immediate action. The staff split into those who would "not listen" and those who evidenced their acceptance of the reality of her physical pain by advocating for her right to pain relief through angry confrontations with her doctors for being "negligent."

Sheila possessed a similar split intrapsychically, which was demonstrated in the way she spoke about her emotional pain in psychotherapy. She insisted her emotional pain was not a problem and attacked her therapist for not believing her. The problem, she claimed, was physical pain in her body and staff's refusal to satisfy her "right" to be given "pain relievers" that would make it go away. The space in the therapy to reflect or explore psychological meaning was collapsed by the intrusion of physical symptoms and the demand for relief. Initially, her therapist took the position of "not knowing" for sure where Sheila's pain was located, but suggested that patient and therapist together might begin to observe their experience in the therapy to eventually draw their own conclusions about what seemed to be the case. Over time, her therapist observed that, as the therapeutic work deepened, Sheila's complaints of physical pain and her use of narcotics increased. Her therapist formed the opinion that Sheila's experience of physical pain intruded into the therapy sessions in a way that effectively cut off exploration of potentially painful memories and affects. It also became evident that the pain medication was beginning to seriously impair the patient's cognition and alertness and, thus, her capacity to work in psychotherapy. Initial attempts to discuss these observations with Sheila led to fights, but fights that indicated something was changing for Sheila in that, over time, she became increasingly able to fight about her complaints in a manner that was emotionally connected and communicative. This was particularly true concerning hostile affects. To accomplish this, Sheila had to relinquish a bit of her "goodness" and to learn that both she and her therapist could survive this. When her therapist pointed this pattern out to her, Sheila associated to the childhood memory of going to neighbors and a local judge to ask to be taken away from her parents, but being "not believed" because the damage could not be seen. She remembered inferring at that time that she either "did not exist" or was not good enough to make them want to take care of her. Hence, to give up "goodness" felt very risky to her.

Sheila's experience was divided between mind and body. On one hand, she defensively denied the emotional reality of the abusive experiences that had happened to her and to her body. On the other, she believed that others did not take seriously the reality of any psychological experience that did not show itself concretely in the body. This was perhaps another reference to the experience of neighbors and a judge sending her back to her home to be abused because they could see nothing wrong. Sheila's dilemma was complicated by the conviction that she could not ask for what she wanted but could only demand what she needed on the basis of the only entitlement she felt she possessed, which was her "illness." In her mind, the illness was the product of her mother's neglect and her father's sexual abuse of her.

After entry into a residential treatment setting, both patient and staff are actively engaged in the mutual experience of observing patterns of behavior and the recording of feelings about their implications. These are the basis for later observation, reflection, and interpretation. This phase is full of hypothesis building and reflections on the quality of data that both staff and patient are gathering. Specific treatment goals are shaped that include identification of core problems that are salient to the place the patient currently occupies in his or her development (characterized by resources as well as sources of impasse). Once the patterns are identified, the patient can begin to explore their motivations and meanings. The experience of having choices in life results, in part, from understanding and contextualizing symptomatic or unconsciously driven patterns of behavior. After patients make the choice to change, a period follows of practicing the change and learning about the implications of the choice to do things differently.

Treatment is integrated by a dynamic formulation that allows symptomatic patterns to be translated into language. Eventually, it is hoped that the patient will speak in words about the significant relationships and life events of which he or she is a product. To the extent that the dynamic formulation affirms the meaningfulness and interpretability of symptomatic experience, it creates the possibility for patients to learn from their current experience instead of feeling trapped in old patterns. The dynamic formulation integrates and guides the treatment team's work and creates the possibility of finding meaning in the previously endless repetition of self-defeating patterns. In summary, the treatment goal is to shift the patient's experience from the bewildering one characterized by intrusive, repetitive symptoms, interpretable only by experts, to motivated behaviors arising naturally and understandably from a context in which they have a particular function. The development of the capacity to understand the connection among stimuli, their associated emotional responses, and the choices patients make about how to respond allows patients, over time, to develop a sense of personal consistency, control, competence, and connection.

Sheila's admission to a residential treatment setting was followed by observation of patterns of behavior by nursing, other clinicians, and peers in the therapeutic community. As they communicated to her how they saw her, Sheila began to gain perspective on painful experiences and her characteristic responses to them, including her suicidal self-destructiveness and attacks on institutions and representatives of abandoning authority figures. This learning led to a greater understanding of how she tended to respond to disappointments and limitations in general. The first function of the containing environment was to help her safely manage destructive behaviors so that she could observe patterns and their repetition. The second function of her work in treatment was more difficult and involved learning about why and how these patterns repeated, especially as she felt helpless and demoralized in relation to them. She began to repeat the experience of perceived abandonment leading to violent self-attack in response to the nurses and physicians at the residential treatment center. She practiced the cycle of perceived injury followed by repair, with the effect of slowly improving her capacity to trust others. This allowed her to hear others differently. She understood them better as a result of giving more credence to what they were saying. This ability reflected an increased capacity to trust experience that was not hers. At the same time, she felt less often misunderstood because she was more aware of her own tendency to presume that wanting something from another person inevitably led to getting hurt and then feeling self-destructive.

This increased self-awareness put her more consciously in touch with large but hidden stores of emotional pain in herself. This caused Sheila to develop more physical pain and to escalate her demands for narcotics.

Sheila's psychotherapist and other members of the treatment team worked with a notion that one goal of treatment was to understand how feelings were linked to the events that contextualized them. However, they noticed that, instead of linking one to the other, both insight and emotion led to more pain and more demand for narcotics. The patient did not see this pattern despite input from nurses, clinicians, and peers, who reacted to her increasing sedation and cognitive impairment with alarm. At one point in a psychotherapy session, the emotionally laden recollection of a painful event was followed abruptly by painful bodily sensation. Sheila denied this connection at first, but, as the experience was repeated in the therapy with staff and with peers, it became hard to deny that something was happening inside her that caused painful emotions to be annihilated by and translated into painful body sensations. It took repeated tracking of the conversion of emotions elicited in therapy to bodily pain to convince Sheila that there was a connection. The work in this area became severely compromised by the patient's demand for narcotics that left her emotionally unavailable and cognitively impaired.

Sheila met with her treatment team to discuss the pattern. Her therapist said that he could not continue to work this way. If the patient wanted what therapy could offer, namely, the ability to have an emotional experience that she could understand and put into words, the confounding effects of narcotic use would have to be eliminated. The team's effort was aided by reliance on a previously negotiated dynamic formulation suggesting that the patient was relying on physical pain to make her distress heard. It was as if she assumed that staff would judge her emotional pain to be illegitimate, just as she felt her emotional experience to have been discounted in the past by family and others. Sheila had developed sufficient experience of her own and trust in her treatment team and experience of her own to accept the team's interpretation that she had the ability to replace narcotics with alternative treatments, including acupuncture and myofascial release therapy. In agreeing to this plan, Sheila anticipated that at times she would feel like undoing it when the pain felt unbearable. She asked staff to refuse to give into her demands at those times. This became very helpful when the anticipated attacks and rage occurred. In those moments, staff felt authorized by the patient to refuse her. They reminded Sheila of her request to help her remain true to her resolve by saying no to her demands. She, on her part, was able to listen.

It is not uncommon for the treatment to nearly founder around a treatment issue in a residential setting, just as may have been the case in the outpatient treatment. In this case, the "faith" that the patient had to find in her treatment team, and, through them, in herself, represented a different kind of "courage" than she had been accustomed to and shifted the nature of her dependency from one based on "perfect" control and entitled demand to one based on trust in people in the context of limitations. This also meant Sheila had begun to experience herself in relation to another person whom she could "trust in." This represented a departure from her previous pattern of finding all objects of her dependency to be corrupt, betraying, and untrustworthy. It also allowed Sheila to give up bodily pain as the only genuine and credible representation of pain. Through the insistence that she stop taking narcotics so that her thoughts and feelings could be fully engaged, Sheila's treatment had advanced far enough that her thoughts and emotional experience could now be accepted as real and valuable.

Once off narcotics, Sheila's rages dissipated. The bodily pains initially worsened but then improved dramatically. She became more functional and less emotionally irritable. Previously, she had only the strength of her emotions and the compelling nature of her memories to rely on as evidence of the reality of her experience. Sheila now found that people listened to her. She began to listen, too, and to regard her own painful experience as valid and meaningful. She began to feel "real" for the first time in her life. Sheila reflected on how, for most of her life, she had "disappeared" herself so that she felt alone and unreal even when embraced in the arms of friends. Now, feeling the warmth of connection, she felt sadness at what she had missed in her life and rage at the conditions of her life that she held responsible for making it that way.

As this shift occurred, Sheila's focus switched from internal conflicts about whether her experience was real to the interpersonal arena. As she came to desire things from others, she began to notice how unreal and depersonalized she felt. She began to use the mirroring capacities of her relationships with peers and staff to explore how her inability to connect with and depend on others led to her isolating "fuck you" solutions. She noticed her impulses to suicide, dissociate, or self-destruct (at times physically, at others psychically) followed severely punitive and degrading self-dialogues that she initiated when feeling as though she needed something. She had in the past relied on her illness to demand and expect that her needs be satisfied. Without its defensive use, she began to experience the vulnerability of asking something from someone while allowing the possibility that they could choose to say no.

At this stage in the treatment, Sheila had acquired not only self-knowledge, but, importantly, the knowledge that self-understanding was possible and some sense of how to go about getting it. She had understood and worked through a significant part of the dynamics that led her to attack the frame of her treatment at the residential treatment center and in her outpatient therapy. She had identified resources in herself and others on which she could rely to avoid repeating old patterns and to deal with new problems that would inevitably arise. The question of termination of the residential treatment became salient, and the therapeutic focus shifted to the ending boundary.

When the resolution of symptoms of depression led Sheila's insurance company to refuse to support further treatment, the extent to which Sheila's sense of self and of security depended on her connection to others became apparent. As part of considering the end of her treatment, Sheila was asked whether she could imagine not being ill. This caused a crisis. Sheila felt rage. Not to be ill meant to her that she would lose the connections to clinicians that had become so valuable. She became aware that she was enraged at society for the way she perceived it to have been a complicit bystander to her experiences of abuse and neglect. These were injuries that she felt could never be healed and for which she should always be entitled to treatment. When she made conscious the link between her illness and the injuries she had experienced, Sheila was able to begin to let go of her attachment to it. The entitlements she demanded from hospitals and insurers, as representatives of the society that stood by and watched, were partly informed by a vengeful wish to "make them pay" for her and for all children who were so abandoned. Coming up against the boundary of her illness (as reflected by the insurer's refusal to continue to recognize her claims of medical necessity at this point) in the context of her wish to continue to work on issues in treatment brought Sheila face to face with unexamined issues. She realized she had come to see herself primarily as a trauma victim (as if that were all that was real about her) and, thus, a person entitled only to need and to feel by virtue of the trauma done to her and the recompense she was owed. The insurer's refusal to pay remained a firm boundary in relation to which she explored her wish for someone heroically to turn the tables and reinstate her in the "normal" life she felt had been denied her, namely, one in which a powerful mother was able to provide for and protect her children. Mourning the loss and absence of such a maternal presence in her life, through confrontation of her therapist's refusal to live out the role, she began to have the vulnerable but freer experience of asking for what she wanted as opposed to demanding what she felt entitled to.

It is worth noting the stance Sheila's therapist took in response to the insurer's determination that there was no longer medical necessity for residential treatment. Rather than join the patient's invitation to project badness into the insurer, as another example of a depriving and abusive parent, the therapist noted the invitation and interpreted the patient's wish for an endlessly funded treatment as equivalent to the wish for an endlessly loving parental figure who dispensed resources without limitations. This led to the emergence in the transference relationship of rage at the therapist for not gratifying Sheila's wishes or at least for not siding with them. The negative transference intensified and was survived as Sheila was able to rage and to grieve around the end of treatment and the limitations of resources as both a reality and a metaphor for other limitations in her life (Plakun, 1996, 2002).

At the end of her treatment, Sheila reflected on the significance of the moment when her treatment team believed in her ability to give up narcotic analgesics in the service of preserving the cognitive resources she needed for treatment by asking her to choose between treatment and narcotics. She felt that the belief in her demonstrated by the team had become a belief in herself that gave her the courage to face the unknown challenges following discharge.

SUMMARY AND CONCLUSIONS

The previous clinical vignette describes a patient seeking treatment for troubles deriving primarily from a personality disorder, but requiring more than outpatient treatment can provide. The needs she demonstrates illustrate issues frequently encountered in the treatment of patients with personality disorders in residential settings. The containing function of these settings is conceptualized here as the critical element. The structural component of the containing function provides resources to both the patient and staff. The closed setting of the locked unit or the rules, norms, and social accountability of the open therapeutic community provide safety and containment of the patient's impulsiveness through mirroring of the dilemmas or problems that are a core part of his or her pathology. These settings provide an opportunity for patients to engage in the expectable struggles characteristic of their disorder in a way that promotes learning. To do this, contexts are provided in which behaviors (from motivation to consequence) are reflected back to patients in a manner that enables them to appreciate how and why they make choices that repeatedly lead to the distress for which they seek treatment. The staff must provide itself with resources to create the possibility for the kind of direct observation and interaction with patients that is essential to support (1) the mirroring function of the environment patients will rely on as they come to understand the nature of their difficulties and (2) the provision of opportunities to practice and test learning with the support of staff and interpretation of the meaning of staff. Because staff, in its empathic and mirroring functions, can become very involved in and with the patient's difficulties, to the extent of sometimes joining the repetition of pathological patterns, it is essential that forums be provided to work through countertransference and parallel process enactments. A higher degree of staff collaboration and integration is required than can be provided in outpatient settings. Staff works in an integrated way to apprehend, comprehend, and represent to the patient information about problematic behaviors in ways that support the patient's efforts to tolerate the affects related to them, while translating acting-out behaviors into words.

From this perspective, the containing function does not prevent the expression of symptomatology as much as provide resources that allow patients to understand how their symptoms are an outgrowth of their experience and are maintained by choices occurring in the contexts of triggers that may or may not be conscious. Change is not done *to* patients, but is the product of the choice to change and the provision of a treatment context that holds the patient in relation to symptoms, their causes, and consequences in a way that can allow them to be understood and learned from. Residential therapeutic environments provide an opportunity for the patient to engage with staff around the expectable problems and struggles that constitute the core of the patient's pathology. In other words, patients are expected to bring their problems to the setting so they can be engaged in a manner that creates opportunities for new learning, personal development, and change.

Treatment of personality disorder demands an essential recognition of the interpersonal origins and consequences of patients' symptoms. Residential treatment centers address this interpersonal component directly by providing a context in which patients can learn how behaviors are interpersonally motivated, by offering opportunities for practice and development of interpersonal skills and for testing the reality of fears about social processes, and for gaining an understanding of the barriers that prevent patients from taking up personally meaningful social roles.

REFERENCES

American Psychiatric Association. (2001, October). Practice guideline for the treatment of patients with borderline personality disorder. *American Journal of Psychiatry, 158* (Suppl. 10), 1–52.

Bion, W. (1962). *Learning from experience.* New York: Basic Books.

Chiesa, M., & Fonagy, P. (2000). Cassel personality disorder study. *British Journal of Psychiatry, 176,* 485–491.

Fonagy, P., Gergely, G., Jurist, E. L., & Target, M. (2002). *Affect regulation, mentalization and the development of the self.* New York: Other Press.

Higgitt, A., & Fonagy, P. (1992). Psychotherapy in borderline and narcissistic disorder. *British Journal of Psychiatry, 161,* 23–43.

Kernberg, O. F. (1984). *Severe personality disorders: Psychotherapeutic strategies.* New Haven, CT: Yale University Press.

Main, T. (1989). *The ailment and other psychoanalytic essays.* London: Free Associations Books.

Menninger, W. W. (2000). Role of the psychiatric hospital in the treatment of mental illness. In B. J. Sadock & V. A. Sadock (Eds.), *Kaplan and Sadock's comprehensive textbook of psychiatry* (pp. 3210–3218). Philadelphia: Lippincott, Williams, & Wilkins.

Plakun, E. M. (1994). Principles in the psychotherapy of self-destructive borderline patients. *Journal of Psychotherapy Practice and Research, 3,* 138–148.

Plakun, E. M. (1996). Economic grand rounds: Treatment of personality disorders in an era of resource limitation. *Psychiatric Services, 47,* 128–130.

Plakun, E. M. (2001). Making the alliance and taking the transference in work with suicidal borderline patients. *Journal of Psychotherapy Practice and Research, 10,* 269–276.

Plakun, E. M. (2002). Jihad McWorld and enactment in the postmodern mental health world. *Journal of the American Academy of Psychoanalysis, 30,* 341–353.

Plakun, E. M. (2003). Treatment refractory mood disorders: A psychodynamic perspective. *Journal of Psychiatric Practice, 9*(3), 209–218.

Shapiro, E. R., & Carr, A. W. (1991). *Lost in familiar places.* New Haven, CT: Yale University Press.

Winnicott, D. W. (Ed.). (1965a). Ego distortion in terms of true and false self. In *The maturational processes and the facilitating environment* (pp. 140–152). New York: International Universities Press.

Winnicott, D. W. (Ed.). (1965b). Psychotherapy of character disorders. In *The maturational processes and the facilitating environment* (pp. 203–216). New York: International Universities Press.

Winnicott, D. W. (Ed.). (1965c). The theory of the parent-infant relationship. In *The maturational processes and the facilitating environment* (pp. 37–55). New York: International Universities Press.

CHAPTER 18

Treatment of Personality Disorders with Co-occurring Substance Dependence: Dual Focus Schema Therapy

Samuel A. Ball

THE SPECIFICATION OF PSYCHOTHERAPY MODELS FOR PERSONALITY DISORDER

RECENT REVIEWS OF the empirical literature (Perry, Banon, & Ianni, 1999; Sanislow & McGlashan, 1998) indicate that individuals with personality disorders improve over time and benefit substantially from intensive psychosocial interventions. Clinical reports and uncontrolled study designs suggest that cognitive-behavioral therapy may be effective for some personality disorders, but controlled outcome studies are very limited (Shea, 1993). Several cognitive-behavioral therapy models have been described (A. T. Beck, Freeman, & Associates,

Some sections of this chapter are abstracted or reprinted from previously published work and reprinted by permission of the publishers: Ball and Young (2000), copyright by the Association for Advancement of Behavior Therapy; Ball (1998), copyright by Elsevier Science; Ball and Cecero (2001), copyright by Guilford Press. Research summarized in this chapter was supported by a National Institute on Drug Abuse behavioral therapy development grant (R01 DA10012) to me and diagnostic (R01 DA05592) and psychotherapy center grants (P50-DA09241) to Bruce Rounsaville. I acknowledge the mentoring I have received in diagnostic and psychotherapy research by Bruce Rounsaville and Kathleen Carroll, specifically as to therapist training procedures and the development of treatment manuals and adherence/competence rating systems. I also acknowledge the invaluable guidance and encouragement of the originator of the schema therapy model, Jeffrey Young, who also trained all therapists in the research to date and consulted on my adaptation, development, and implementation of the Dual Focus Schema Therapy manual. Correspondence concerning this article should be addressed to me at: Yale University School of Medicine, VA CT Healthcare (151D), 950 Campbell Avenue, West Haven, CT 06516 or by electronic mail (samuel.ball@yale.edu).

1990; J. S. Beck, 1998; Young, 1994) that focus specifically on the problematic beliefs, assumptions, or schemas that underlie the symptoms of personality disorder. As with most approaches described in this volume, these treatment models have been developed and actively disseminated but have never been subjected to the rigors of a controlled, empirical study of their efficacy, and none have developed detailed, time-limited treatment manuals necessary for such an investigation.

Treatment manuals and training programs have become a virtual requirement in the technology of psychotherapy research (Carroll, 1997) because they allow for the specification of therapeutic ingredients, therapist behaviors, and intervention strategies so therapists can deliver treatments as intended by the developer. By far, the most developed, promising, and popular manual-guided approach has been dialectical behavioral therapy (DBT) for Borderline Personality Disorder by Linehan (1993). However, no well-specified treatment manuals exist for the wider range of personality disorders, and no individual therapy has been fully articulated that integrates a dual focus on the diverse personality disorders and their commonly co-occurring Axis I disorders, such as Substance Abuse and Dependence. This is an important limitation because personality-disordered individuals rarely seek psychotherapy specifically for their personality disorder. Typically, it is a co-occurring Axis I disorder or strong environmental pressure that provides the motivation to seek help.

This chapter describes dual focus schema therapy (DFST; Ball, 1998; Ball & Young, 1998, 2000), a manual-guided individual cognitive-behavioral therapy that integrates a schema-focused approach (Young, 1994) with symptom-focused relapse prevention coping skills interventions (Kadden et al., 1992; Marlatt & Gordon, 1985; Monti, Abram, Kadden, & Cooney, 1989) to treat the interrelated symptoms of substance abuse and personality disorders. After providing background on the important link between personality disorder and substance abuse, the treatment model is summarized, ongoing research is reviewed, and important training and dissemination issues are considered.

THE PERSONALITY DISORDER-SUBSTANCE ABUSE CONNECTION

Over the past 50 to 60 years, theoreticians have attempted to conceptualize the complex association between personality disorder and substance dependence. Psychoanalytic conceptualizations of addiction influenced the first and second editions of the *Diagnostic and Statistical Manual of Mental Disorders* (*DSM*; American Psychiatric Association [APA], 1952, 1968) and classified drug addiction and alcoholism under the category of "sociopathic personality disturbance" or the broader category of "personality disorders." Substance use disorders achieved differentiation from antisocial and other personality disorders only with the shift to a multiaxial system in the last three *DSM* revisions (APA, 1980, 1987, 1994). Once this diagnostic distinction occurred, it became meaningful to evaluate the co-occurrence of these disorders.

RATES OF CO-OCCURRENCE

As a broad diagnostic group, the Axis II personality disorders are the most common co-occurring disorders in treated substance abusers. Median prevalence rates of Axis II are especially high among treated opiate- (79%) and cocaine- (70%) dependent patients and somewhat lower in alcohol-dependent samples (44%; see reviews by DeJong, van den Brink, Harteveld, & van der Wielen, 1993; Verheul, Ball, & van den Brink, 1998). Although studies that evaluate all Axis II disorders indicate that Cluster B disorders are the most prevalent (Antisocial, Borderline, and, less often, Narcissistic and Histrionic), both Cluster C (Avoidant and Dependent and, less often, Obsessive-Compulsive) and Cluster A (Paranoid and, less often, Schizoid and Schizotypal) disorders also seem to be highly prevalent among substance abusers. The wide range of prevalence rates seen in more than 100 comorbidity studies seems to be related to differences in the substance abused, the setting, and the method of assessment.

An important feature of the program of research on personality disorders and substance abuse at Yale Medical School's Division of Substance Abuse has been the simultaneous attention to characterizing this substantial, complex dually disordered group of patients and developing and testing a promising treatment approach. Early work (Kosten, Kosten, & Rounsaville, 1989; Rounsaville, Kosten, Weissman, & Kleber, 1986) determined high rates of *DSM-III* personality disorders and their association with worse prognosis among methadone-maintained patients. More recently, the prevalence, reliability, and validity of *DSM-III-R* and *DSM-IV* personality disorders and the major dimensions of personality were evaluated in a sample of 370 opiate, cocaine, and alcohol-dependent outpatients and inpatients and 187 community controls. The majority of substance abusers (70%) met criteria for one or more personality disorders. Cluster B disorders were the most prevalent (61%) followed by Cluster C (34%) and Cluster A (22%). Antisocial (46%), Borderline (30%), and Avoidant (20%) were the most common specific personality disorders (Rounsaville et al., 1998).

In addition to finding substantial rates of personality disorders in the treatment samples of substance abusers, Rounsaville et al. (1998) established guidelines for distinguishing between personality disorder symptoms that are related to substance abuse versus symptoms independent from substance abuse. This diagnostic approach helps identify individuals whose Axis II conditions may be more likely to endure even when the substance use disorder is in remission and thus require additional intervention for better long-term outcome. The interview method involves allowing a two- to three-week stabilization period following treatment entry and then inquiring into each positive personality disorder symptom to determine whether it should be considered independent from the acute or chronic effects of substance abuse (e.g., intoxication, withdrawal, drug craving or seeking behavior). Symptoms are counted as positive only if they persist during drug-free periods. This more conservative diagnostic approach resulted in a 13% decrease in the rates of overall personality disorders (i.e., from 70% to 57%). Cluster B disorder prevalence was particularly reduced by the exclusion of substance-related symptoms (from 61% to 46%). Of the specific personality disorders, Antisocial (from 46% to 27%) and Borderline (from 30% to 18%) were more affected than Avoidant (from 20% to 18%).

SYMPTOM SEVERITY AND OUTCOME

As to treatment response, the impact of reduction of substance abuse was evaluated on baseline-to-one-year follow-up remission rates of mood, anxiety, and personality disorders (Verheul et al., 2000). Reduction in substance abuse was associated with improvement and recovery from mood and anxiety disorders, but not with significant changes in personality disorder symptoms. The failure of Axis II pathology to diminish with abstinence from drugs and alcohol suggests that personality disorders are independent entities requiring additional therapeutic intervention. Other investigators have found that the co-occurrence of substance abuse and personality disorders is associated with greater substance abuse and psychiatric symptom severity (Brooner, King, Kidorf, Schmidt, & Bigelow, 1997; Rounsaville et al., 1986; Rutherford, Cacciola, & Alterman, 1994) and increased risk for suicide, hospitalization, repeated treatment admissions, overuse of medical care, employment and legal problems, victimization or perpetration of abuse, and HIV infection (Links, 1998; Target, 1998). These dual-disordered patients appear to be more susceptible to relapse in the presence of craving, negative physical and emotional states, and interpersonal conflict (Kruedelbach, McCormick, Schulz, & Grueneich, 1993; Nace, Davis, & Gaspari, 1991; Smyth & Washousky, 1995).

Studies have found that personality disorders are usually associated with worse outcomes when provided routine or less intensive addiction treatment (DeJong et al., 1993; Griggs & Tyrer, 1981; Kofoed, Kania, Walsh, & Atkinson, 1986; Kosten et al., 1989; Nace & Davis, 1993; Rounsaville et al., 1986). At one year following standard inpatient treatment, 94% of patients with personality disorders relapsed in comparison to 56% of those without personality disorder (Thomas, Melchert, & Banken, 1999). However, Borderline Personality Disorder patients benefit at least as much as non-Borderline patients when provided an intensive, psychiatrically oriented inpatient alcoholism treatment (Nace & Davis, 1993; Nace, Saxon, & Shore, 1986). Although Antisocial Personality Disorder (ASPD) is widely considered to be a robust predictor of negative outcome, several studies find little evidence of worse prognosis when psychotherapy, potent behavioral incentive contingencies, or at least moderately intensive psychosocial treatments are provided (Alterman & Cacciola, 1991; Brooner, Kidorf, King, & Stoller, 1998; Cacciola, Alterman, & Rutherford, 1995; Cacciola, Rutherford, Alterman, McKay, & Snider, 1996). Alcohol-dependent individuals with greater sociopathy tend to have better outcomes with cognitive-behavioral coping skills treatment than with an interactional group therapy (Kadden, Cooney, Getter, & Litt, 1989; Longabaugh et al., 1994). Woody, McLellan, Luborsky, and O'Brien (1985) have shown that methadone patients with ASPD and a lifetime diagnosis of Major Depression were able to benefit as much from individual psychotherapy as patients without ASPD.

TYPE A AND B SUBSTANCE ABUSERS

Research evaluating the validity of multidimensional addiction typologies has integrated personality traits and disorders with other dimensions relevant to the etiology, symptom presentation, and prognosis of substance use disorders. Type B substance abusers are characterized as having an earlier age of onset of substance abuse and greater family history, childhood conduct problems, impulsivity or sensation seeking, addiction symptom severity, polysubstance use, and co-occurring psychiatric disorders (especially depression and Antisocial Personality Disorder; Ball, 1996; Ball, Carroll, Babor, & Rounsaville, 1995). Type As have a later onset and less severe form of substance abuse. Type B substance abusers also have higher rates of diagnosed personality disorders than Type As and seem to exhibit general personality pathology and secondary psychopathy (Ball, Kranzler, Tennen, Poling, & Rounsaville, 1997). This finding has relevance to the treatment development process because Type B (i.e., personality-disordered) substance abusers have more severe problems, higher psychological distress, relapse faster, and seem to benefit more from a cognitive-behavioral coping skills approach (Litt, Babor, DelBoca, Kadden, & Cooney, 1992). These subtypes are strongly related to outcome and to the major dimensions of normal personality that contribute significantly to the prediction of personality disorder severity above and beyond substance abuse and depression symptoms (Ball, Rounsaville, Tennen, & Kranzler, 2001; Ball, Tennen, Poling, Kranzler, & Rounsaville, 1997; Ball, Young, Rounsaville, & Carroll, 1999). Through this work, a psychotherapeutic focus on personality trait dimensions (temperament and coping) was conceptualized that has informed the developing treatment approach (Ball, 2001; Ball & Schottenfeld, 1997; Ball & Young, 2000; Verheul et al., 1998).

TREATMENT CONSTRUCTS AND MODEL

Dual Focus Schema Therapy hypotheses that two broad cognitive-behavioral constructs interact and form the core pathology observed in personality disordered individuals. These two constructs (early maladaptive schemas and maladaptive coping styles) are the primary targets for a series of interventions designed to lessen the intensity of the schemas and develop more adaptive coping strategies. The overarching goal of DFST is to help individuals achieve behavioral control and fulfil their core human needs. Various psychoeducational, cognitive, experiential, behavioral, and relational techniques are employed to accomplish these goals via Axis I and II symptom reduction.

EARLY MALADAPTIVE SCHEMAS

A. T. Beck et al. (1990) and Young (1994) have defined maladaptive or dysfunctional schemas as enduring, unconditional, negative beliefs about oneself, others, and the environment that organize an individual's experiences and behaviors. These schemas are very broad, pervasive themes that are learned early in life and then reinforced, elaborated, and perpetuated in adulthood. Over time, these mental structures become dysfunctional to a significant degree and highly resistant to change in persons with personality disorders (Young, 1994; Young, Klosko, & Weishaar, 2003). Early maladaptive schemas share the following characteristics:

- Develop from the interaction between temperament and repeated early negative experiences with parents, siblings, and peers.
- Generate high levels of affect, self-defeating consequences, or harm to others.
- Interfere with meeting core needs for autonomy, connection, and self-expression.
- Are deeply entrenched, central to self, self-perpetuating, and difficult to change.
- Are triggered by everyday schema-relevant events or mood states (Young, 1994; Young et al., 2003).

In contrast to Beck's approach, Young (1994) does not connect specific schemas to each *DSM-IV* personality disorder but rather describes 18 core schemas, one or more of which is present in personality-disordered patients. The 18 early maladaptive schemas (listed in parentheses) are grouped into five broader domains of:

1. Disconnection and rejection (abandonment/instability, mistrust/abuse, emotional deprivation, defectiveness/shame, social isolation/alienation).
2. Impaired autonomy and performance (dependence/incompetence, vulnerability to danger, enmeshment/undeveloped self, failure to achieve).
3. Impaired limits (entitlement/domination, insufficient self-control/self-discipline).
4. Other directedness (subjugation, self-sacrifice, approval-seeking).
5. Overvigilance and inhibition (vulnerability to error/negativity, overcontrol/emotional inhibition, unrelenting standards, punitiveness (Schmidt, Joiner, Young, & Telch, 1995; Young, 1994; Young et al., 2003).

MALADAPTIVE COPING STYLES

Because the thoughts, feelings, impulses, and memories associated with early maladaptive schemas are distressing to the individual or others, the individual typically develops strategies to cope. These long-standing, overlearned, usually unrecognized, cognitive, affective, interpersonal, and behavioral responses to the triggering of a schema are called *maladaptive coping styles*. Although these behaviors may effectively reduce the negative affect associated with schema activation, they are self-defeating and impede the meeting of basic needs and the change process (Young, 1994; Young et al., 2003).

Coping styles are categorized as schema surrender, schema avoidance, or schema compensation. Schema surrender represents a complying or giving in to the person or situation (or the associated affect) that evokes the schema. Schema avoidance includes various forms of escape or avoidance from people, situations, or mood states that activate the schema, for example, social withdrawal, excessive autonomy, compulsive stimulation-seeking, addictive self-soothing, and psychological withdrawal. Schema compensation involves different forms of fighting off or counterattacking the schema-triggering stimuli and includes aggression or hostility, dominance, excessive self-assertion, recognition or status-seeking, manipulation, exploitation, passive-aggressive rebellion, and excessive orderliness (Young, 1994; Young et al., 2003).

Dual focus schema therapy (Ball, 1998; Ball & Young, 1998, 2000) recognizes active addiction as a primary disorder, but also conceptualizes schema activation and maladaptive avoidance as heightening the ongoing risk for relapse among individuals with significant personality problems. The model hypothesizes that substance use can occur as a direct behavioral expression of the activation of impaired limits schemas (entitlement, insufficient self-control) or when an other-directedness schema (subjugation, self-sacrifice, approval-seeking) gets triggered within a substance-abusing or otherwise dysfunctional relationship. Another potent relapse risk factor is the patient's overreliance on avoidance as a maladaptive means of coping with the affect or conflict associated with the activation of schemas (and associated memories) around themes of disconnection and rejection (abandonment, mistrust/abuse, emotional deprivation, defectiveness, social isolation) or impaired autonomy/performance (dependence/incompetence, vulnerability to danger, enmeshment, failure to achieve).

DUAL FOCUS SCHEMA THERAPY (DFST) MODEL AND MANUAL

As described in this chapter, DFST (Ball, 1998; Ball & Young, 1998, 2000) is a 24-week, manual-guided individual therapy consisting of a set of core topics, the specific content and delivery of which are determined by an assessment and conceptualization of the individual's early maladaptive schemas and coping styles. Session topics are shown in Table 18.1. DFST includes symptom-focused relapse prevention coping skills techniques for interpersonal, affective, and craving experiences (Kadden et al., 1992; Marlatt & Gordon, 1985; Monti et al., 1989) and schema-focused techniques for the maladaptive schemas and coping styles (Young, 1994; Young et al., 2003). Cognitive-behavioral therapy appears to be an excellent choice for developing an integrated treatment strategy that has a dual focus on substance abuse and personality disorders. It was developed initially and found to be effective for the treatment of depression and, later, substance abuse, which are the two most common Axis I disorders in personality-disordered patients. DFST interventions are focused on addictive behaviors and personality disorder symptoms through an integrated series of core techniques. For example, functional analysis is used to understand recent episodes of substance use and craving as well as maladaptive schemas and coping and their triggering events. Self-monitoring, problem-solving, and coping skills training occur similarly for both the addiction and personality problems.

ASSUMPTION OF DUAL FOCUS SCHEMA THERAPY

Dual focus schema therapy hypothesizes that a broad range of the patient's difficulties can be subsumed by a single or few early maladaptive schemas and coping styles. Targeted change in substance use and core schemas can have a significant impact on a broader range of behaviors by disrupting some of the behavioral and interpersonal chain of events that perpetuate the dual disorder in adulthood. DFST does not have the unrealistic goal of curing a chronic, life-defining personality disorder through a 24-week manual-guided treatment. Realistic goals are extremely important, such as improving self-esteem, relationships, work, and symptoms through improved retention and exposure to a substance abuse treatment that explicitly addresses the personality functioning of the patient. The model assumes that the treatment of personality disorders is best viewed ultimately as a long-term process of controlling substance use and other coexisting Axis I disorders through the combined approaches of psychotherapeutic, psychosocial, pharmacological, and self-help experiences.

Another important assumption of the treatment model is that a therapist's ability to promote cognitive-behavioral change and symptom reduction depends on his or her empathic understanding of the origins and reasons for maladaptivity, the confrontation of the patient's addiction and personality (schemas, coping) problems, and the quality of the therapeutic relationship (Linehan, 1993; Young, 1994). Attempts at cognitive disputes or rapid behavior change will be ineffective if they fail to appreciate the historical origins of these problems, the

Table 18.1
List of Core and Elective Topics for the
Dual Focus Schema Therapy Manual

Core Topics

Topic A	Identification and analysis of current problems.
Topic B	Understanding historical patterns.
Topic C	Defining personality, schemas, and coping.
Topic D	Schemas education.
Topic E	Schema assessment through imagery.
Topic F	Early origins.
Topic G	Maladaptive behavioral and coping patterns.
Topic H	Problem conceptualization and focus.
Topic I	Schema evidence and coping pros and cons.
Topic J	Schema confrontation and disputes.
Topic K	Flashcards.
Topic L	Confronting past/parents through imagery.
Topic M	Schema reattribution through imagery.
Topic N	Writing letters.
Topic O	Changing relationships.
Topic P	Skill building and behavior change.
Topic Q	Termination and continuing change.

Elective Module Topics—Axis I Relapse

Topic 1	Internal and external triggers.
Topic 2	Coping with high risk situations.
Topic 3	Coping with craving.
Topic 4	Activity planning.

Elective Module Topics—Mode Work

Topic 5	Schema modes.
Topic 6	Vulnerable child and detached protector.
Topic 7	Confronting the punitive parent.
Topic 8	Coping with the angry or impulsive child.

Elective Module Topics—Therapy Interference

Topic 9	Therapeutic relationship.
Topic 10	Traumatic memories of abuse.
Topic 11	Self-injury.
Topic 12	Managing boundaries and limits.

Elective Module Topics—Community Adaptation

Topic 13	Introduction: Upsetting and uplifting situations.
Topic 14	Understanding current and historical problems and patterns.
Topic 15	Problem solving.
Topic 16	Personality: Conflicts and opportunity within a new community.

reasons certain coping styles developed, and the rationality of the self-defeating behavioral cycle that forms the core of personality pathology and the resistance to change. A therapist can push for significant behavior change and recovery after the patient feels that his or her resistance to change is empathically understood.

Stages of Dual Focus Schema Therapy

In the first stage of DFST, the therapist integrates early relapse prevention work with an identification and education about early maladaptive schemas and coping styles and their association with substance use and other presenting life problems. This educational stage is meant to accomplish at least three important goals:

1. Initiating abstinence or significantly reduced substance use.
2. Establishing a strong therapeutic alliance.
3. Developing a detailed case conceptualization.

The development of a strong therapeutic alliance is dependent on both the patient's experience of the therapist's limit setting and focused attention on addictive behaviors as well as the therapist's interest in understanding the patient's personality (temperament, schemas, coping style) and its origins (reactions and behaviors of significant others).

The first few months of therapy include a discussion and analysis of the patient's presenting problems and life patterns, particularly as they are related to substance dependence. Maladaptive schemas and coping styles are assessed through the completion of four questionnaires developed by Young and associates to measure: (1) schemas; (2) parental origins; (3) avoidant coping; and (4) compensatory coping. Reactions to homework readings, in-session behaviors and discussions of schemas, imagery exercises, and the nature of the therapy relationship provide additional information to identify those schemas and coping styles that are central to the patient. As such, the assessment process is complex and relies on several different sources of data. Patients develop a sense of trust and collaboration through the therapist's interest in obtaining and providing information and personality feedback and developing a highly individualized conceptualization of their past and current problems.

Once the therapist completes this detailed assessment and develops an empathic appreciation and conceptualization of the history of the patient's current life problems, the stage is set for changing the maladaptive schemas and coping styles that contribute to the personality and addiction problems. The individualized case conceptualization guides the development of a technically eclectic, but theoretically integrated, series of change strategies for the schemas and coping styles (Young, 1994):

1. Cognitive (schema validity, disputes, and dialogues, flash cards for healthier internal voice, reframe past to create distance, identify and confront validity of schemas and usefulness of coping style, substance abuse as avoidant coping).
2. Experiential (imagery and inner child work, role play, ventilation about past and toward caregivers, work on schema origins, letter writing).
3. Behavioral (change self-defeating behaviors maintaining the schemas, identify life change and overcoming avoidance, in-session rehearsal, graded task

assignment, individualized schema relevant coping skills training, empathic confrontation).

4. Therapy relationship (confront in-session schemas and coping styles, limited re-parenting).

During either the first (assessment or education) or second (change) stage of treatment, other elective module session topics may be used to address persistent, treatment-interfering substance use; extreme avoidance; boundary violations and limit setting in the therapeutic relationship; working with traumatic memories of abuse; managing suicidal crises and self-injurious behavior; and working with schema modes. Although the focus on initiating or maintaining abstinence from substances is continually integrated within the framework of DFST, therapists may shift to a primary focus on relapse prevention when clinically indicated. This work includes identification of intrapersonal and interpersonal relapse precipitants, coping skills training for high-risk situations, resisting social pressures to use, assertive communication, coping with cravings, and developing pleasurable activities. Over the course of treatment, the depth of focus and relative emphasis (i.e., substance use versus maladaptive schemas and coping) in any single therapy session are guided by clinical judgment, supervision, and an ongoing evaluation of substance use.

Other special problems frequently occur in the treatment of personality-disordered patients. When intractable avoidance of the therapeutic work is encountered, the therapist may shift to a focus on schema modes. A mode may consist of several linked early maladaptive schemas combined with a predominant affect and coping style and is experienced and expressed as broader (typically unintegrated) components or sides of the patient's personality (i.e., similar to an ego state). In mode work, these various sides or states of the patient are identified and labeled (e.g., detached protector, vulnerable child, punitive parent), and their origin and functions are explored and targeted for change through cognitive disputes, empathic confrontation, imagery, and empty chair techniques. Mode work appears to be especially useful when working with borderline or highly avoidant, overcompensating, or self-critical patients. The concept of modes seems to be easily grasped by substance abusers who may have split off an "addictive, antisocial, acting-out" personality from their "recovering, vulnerable, emotional" identity.

DUAL FOCUS SCHEMA THERAPY FOR PERSONALITY-DISORDERED OPIATE ABUSERS

Through the collaborative effort of several individuals, most notably Jeffrey Young who created the original schema therapy model, we have successfully developed a detailed treatment manual and are in the process of evaluating its efficacy in four different projects and a planned fifth project. Much of this treatment development and evaluation work has been funded through the National Institutes of Health.

Manual Development Pilot Project

Ten individuals participated in the pilot-testing phase of a behavioral therapy development project funded by the National Institute on Drug Abuse (NIDA), which focused on the development and refinement of a treatment manual for personality-disordered substance abusers. Study inclusion criteria were: (1) *DSM-IV* diagnosis of opioid dependence, (2) receiving a stable dose of methadone for at least one month, (3) not participating in additional psychotherapy other than drug abuse counseling at the methadone clinic, and (4) no evidence of acute psychosis or suicidality/homicidality. Outpatients were recruited from The APT Foundation's Orchard, Park Hill, and Women in Treatment methadone programs in New Haven, Connecticut.

Two patients dropped out after four months of therapy, and two were highly symptomatic and chaotic at baseline and dropped out after one appointment. The two patients with the best attendance were both employed full time. It is interesting that the three patients with the lowest retention or attendance all had a primary Axis II diagnosis of Avoidant Personality Disorder (with secondary Antisocial). Because the two patients who dropped out after one appointment were discharged soon thereafter from the methadone treatment program and could not be located, these monthly follow-up assessments could not be completed. Although the monthly assessment results are biased because they exclude the two poor outcome patients, they do provide a gross estimate of the effect of the psychotherapy being developed on those eight who received an adequate "dose." An inspection of the aggregate data indicated that patients had decreases in the frequency of their substance use, the severity of their psychiatric symptoms, and ratings of dysphoria. An observed increase in primary substance use frequency at six months was accounted for primarily by one of the patients who dropped out of the study after four months and had resumed daily benzodiazepine use by the time of the termination assessment. Ratings of dysphoria (depression, anxiety, hostility) decreased by the fourth month to the point of equaling positive affect ratings (which remained fairly stable across the study). Finally, although subjective in nature, all eight patients reported at study termination that they found the therapy very useful and were disappointed that it could not continue.

RANDOMIZED CONTROLLED PILOT TRIAL

Through this NIDA funding, a group of therapists were trained and a randomized pilot study was completed involving 30 methadone-maintained patients comparing individual manual-guided DFST to 12-step facilitation therapy (12FT; Nowinski, Baker, & Carroll, 1992). Urines and self-reports of substance use were collected weekly. Measures of addiction-related psychosocial impairment, psychiatric symptoms, affect states, and the therapeutic alliance were assessed monthly, and various personality indicators assessed at baseline were repeated at treatment termination.

Study Sample Characteristics   The trial sample was predominantly Caucasian (85%; 13% African American; 2% Hispanic) men (46%) and women (54%) with a mean age of 37.4 (*SD* = 5.9). Patients were mostly single (46%; 32% separated or divorced; 22% married or cohabitating) and high school educated. Patients met structured interview criteria for an average of 3.3 personality disorders with Antisocial Personality Disorder present in more than 70% of the cases, and Borderline and Avoidant Personality Disorders present in more than half of the cases. Paranoid and Dependent were present in more than 10% of the cases, and the remainder of the Axis II disorders were less prevalent (Ball et al., 1999; Ball & Cecero, 2001). At the time of screening for study eligibility, approximately one-third of the sample self-reported significant symptoms of depression, anxiety, violent behavior, suicidal ideation or attempts in the past 30 days, and the majority had experienced these symptoms in their lifetime. One-half of the sample reported engaging in at least one HIV-related risky behavior in the past three months, and 15% reported being HIV positive. The majority (85%) reported experiencing emotional abuse as children, and a significant number reported past physical (49%) and sexual (27%) abuse.

As to their addiction, patients averaged more than 10 years of substance abuse, with polydrug abuse common. The length of patients' current methadone treatment episode was varied with a mean of 23.1 ($SD = 42.1$; range 1 to 180) months in treatment. Patients were mostly injection drug users by history (71%; intranasal 27%; oral 2%), and 47% of the sample reported using heroin in the 30 days before assessment (37% used alcohol, 34% cocaine, 27% tranquilizers, 6% cannabis in the prior 30 days). Multiple treatments in substance abuse (Mean = 7.5) and psychiatric (Mean = 5.0) programs and criminal arrests (Mean = 16.2) and incarcerations (Mean = 25.2 months) during adulthood provided further evidence for considering this a chronic, difficult-to-treat sample of dual-disordered individuals.

As to the assessment of maladaptive schemas and coping styles, avoidant coping was highly common, and the mistrust/abuse schema was related to 8 of the 12 personality disorders assessed and seemed to be common to all except the Cluster C disorders, which often had subjugation and self-sacrifice schemas (Ball & Cecero, 2001). Personality and trait affect dimensions and specific interpersonal problems (e.g., vindictiveness, domineering, nonassertiveness, exploitable) provided further differentiation of the personality disorders. Neuroticism or negative affect appears to serve as a common risk factor for most Axis II disorders whereas the traits of extraversion, agreeableness, conscientiousness, and sensation-seeking differentiate specific disorders (see also Ball, 2001; Ball, Kranzler, et al., 1997).

Treatment Outcomes   The principal analyses for the effects of study treatments were: (1) analysis of variance for continuous summary variables at termination (e.g., retention measures, urines, abstinence) and (2) random effects regression for continuous outcome variables, which were measured monthly. Significant Treatment (12FT versus DFST) × Time (six monthly assessments) effects were found for the percent of days per week of primary substance use, dysphoria ratings, and strength of the therapeutic alliance. Patients assigned to DFST reduced substance use frequency more rapidly over the 24-week treatment than did patients assigned to 12FT. Further inspection of the data suggested a difference beginning to emerge at the third month, which corresponds to a point in the manual where the treatment is shifting from an assessment and education focus to an active change focus (Ball et al., 1999).

Analyses of the dysphoria ratings favored the 12FT condition in which patients exhibited steady decreases in this summary measure of negative mood (as distinct from psychiatric symptoms) over time in comparison to DFST patients who showed no change in dysphoria. As it turned out, however, this sustained dysphoric mood was not related to relapse or drop out. In fact, the reverse seemed to be true, that is, substance abuse symptoms decreased and the working alliance strengthened despite the lack of change in negative mood over time. This very preliminary finding was consistent with a long-standing clinical belief that mobilizing negative affect may be critical to sustain productive work and effect change in personality-disordered patients.

As stated, DFST patients reported an increase from a good early therapeutic alliance to a very strong alliance over the subsequent months of treatment whereas 12FT patients demonstrated no such increase. Consistent with this finding, DFST therapists reported feeling as though they had a stronger working alliance with patients than did 12FT therapists. There were no treatment-related adverse events involving the randomized pilot patients, and there were no retention differences between the treatment conditions. The mean number of weeks completed was 13.5 for DFST and 14.7 for 12FT (nonsignificant), suggesting that any outcome differences could not be attributed to the confounding influence of one group receiving more treatment.

Proposed Stage II Study in Methadone-Maintained Patients

Having accomplished all of the major goals for a behavioral therapy development project (see Rounsaville, Carroll, & Onken, 2001), a more ambitious randomized clinical trial of this promising psychotherapy for personality-disordered drug abusers has been proposed, specifically to: (1) conduct a definitive comparison of the efficacy of the two 24-week manual-guided individual therapies (DFST versus 12FT) in 120 methadone-maintained patients with personality disorders; (2) evaluate changes in primary and secondary outcomes from baseline, monthly during treatment, at treatment termination, and 3, 6, 12, and 18 months posttreatment. Secondary analyses will: (1) evaluate post hoc whether the presence or absence of the more common personality disorder categories (Borderline, Antisocial, Avoidant) are related to differential response to the two treatment conditions and (2) evaluate process dimensions related to discriminability of treatments and treatment-specific changes. Primary outcomes will be: (1) frequency and severity of substance use (cocaine, alcohol, marijuana, benzodiazepines) as measured by both self-report and urine testing and (2) severity of psychiatric symptoms as measured by the self-report and interview assessments. Secondary outcomes include: (1) changes in personality dimensions that may be associated with changes in personality disorder (personality traits, affective states, interpersonal problems, HIV risk behaviors) and (2) general (therapeutic alliance) and treatment-specific (schemas or coping styles, 12-step meeting attendance) measures of therapy process.

Although most of the manual development work occurred with the first 10 pilot patients of the earlier study, several minor changes were incorporated based on experience with the subsequent 30 methadone patients. Several of the DFST experiential and relational change techniques seemed to heighten affective distress (self-reported sadness, anger, anxiety) and the use of avoidant coping (i.e., missed appointments, resistance to imagery or role play) by several patients. These reactions were not a complete surprise given the theory that DFST would work by targeting painful past and current emotional and relational themes while also trying to remove substance abuse as the patient's dominant method of avoidant coping. However, several adjustments were made because of concerns about heightening risk for relapse or decompensation:

1. Shifting the more affect mobilizing techniques to later in the manual and implemented only after several months of abstinence.

2. Movement of coping skills sessions earlier into the manual during treatment and incorporating a 5- to 10-minute "decompression" period into the more affectively charged sessions.

3. Development of the special problem modules for the manual discussed previously.

DUAL FOCUS SCHEMA THERAPY IN A DRUG-FREE THERAPEUTIC COMMUNITY

Premature dropout remains the major problem undercutting the effectiveness of drug-free residential therapeutic community (TC) treatment, and this problem has been exacerbated as TCs have admitted individuals with higher levels of psychopathology. Personality disorders are the most common psychiatric conditions in inpatient addiction programs, and TCs view significant personality disturbance as common to all patients and a core component of addiction. In this ongoing study, I hypothesize that retention in a TC (The APT Foundation's Residential Services Division in Bridgeport, Connecticut) will be enhanced by the application of DFST because it targets the maladaptive cognitive, behavioral, interpersonal, and emotional processes that interfere with the accommodation and assimilation of the patient to the processes and core elements of a TC.

In a therapy model adapted to the controlled residential environment of a TC, DFST first focuses on improving engagement in a therapeutic process through psychoeducation on the patient's personality (symptoms, traits, schemas, coping) and the suitability, relevance, and utility of a TC for addressing these individual differences and needs. Early dropout risk is assumed to be high because the TC immediately expects behaviors (e.g., self-disclosure, delay of gratification, rule-following, accepting strong feedback, sociability, cooperativeness) that are contrary to the patient's personality style and addictive behavior. The patient's reaction to this stressful experience is normalized, coping with this challenging treatment environment is emphasized, and potentially problematic personality traits are identified. Thus, this first stage of DFST treatment provides a form of psychological inoculation for why the TC may be a difficult form of treatment (given the interaction of the patient's core issues and themes with the program's confrontational atmosphere). In such a situation, the impulse to escape, avoid, or act out can be viewed as normal but must be restrained to achieve benefits from the TC model.

The behavior change techniques used in the second phase of DFST (two to six months) are conceptualized as working synergistically with the TC methods, processes, or elements. For example, schemas and maladaptive coping are triggered through job (adult patients) or school (adolescent patients) responsibilities, community incidents, rules, consequences, and groups, and the TC is a specialized, safe, and therapeutic learning laboratory in which this can be worked through more adaptively. Enhanced by such a psychotherapeutic context, a TC can be viewed as a milieu in which the patient's personality problems can be expressed, contained, and confronted by the peer community, but with acceptance and support of the person-as-a-whole. Patient acting out can be viewed as an expected method of communicating internal conflicts that can be addressed with firm support and confrontation. Reactions to the TC rules, techniques, group experiences, or structure are used as opportunities for observation, discussion, understanding, and confrontation. Here-and-now confrontation of patient's maladaptive patterns of coping and relating to others is considered one of the cornerstones of the TC resocialization and rehabilitation process (Chiesa, 2000) and are consistent with DFST.

The purpose of this recently funded NIDA study is to: (1) compare the efficacy of two manual-guided individual behavioral therapies (DFST versus individual drug counseling [IDC]) delivered to 100 adult and adolescent substance abusers as an enhancement to the first 24 weeks of the standard TC treatment program; (2) evaluate differences in retention on a monthly basis as the primary outcome of interest; and (3) evaluate changes in psychological indicators related to personality disturbance (personality disorder symptoms, Axis I psychiatric symptoms, interpersonal conflict, negative affect, HIV risk, maladaptive schemas, and coping styles) and treatment processes related to the TC (therapeutic alliance, perceived TC suitability, value of TC core elements, treatment atmosphere) as secondary outcomes at 6 (therapy termination), 12, 18, and 24 months postenrollment. In addition, exploratory analyses will evaluate several Attribute (patient characteristics) × Treatment (DFST versus IDC) interactions. For example, there will be an evaluation of whether baseline severity of Axis I and Axis II symptoms predicts differential response to the two treatment conditions concerning both primary (retention) and secondary (psychological and treatment process indicators) outcomes. It is hypothesized that severe personality disturbance causes significant problems with an individual's initial adjustment and effective utilization of TC processes and techniques and that a therapy that targets personality pathology will result in better early retention, engagement, and symptom reduction than will the more general or standard addiction counseling approach.

DUAL FOCUS SCHEMA THERAPY FOR HOMELESS PERSONALITY-DISORDERED SUBSTANCE ABUSERS

In another randomized clinical trial currently underway, DFST is being compared to a standard drug counseling group for homeless drop-in center clients with substance abuse and personality disorders (Langeloth Foundation; Patricia Cobb-Richardson). Like many urban homeless social services program, the Neighborhood Coalition for Shelter in New York City historically has been unable to engage a large number of individuals who constitute their long-term homeless population. This population has a history of substance abuse and psychiatric symptoms that significantly impede their ability to access social services. Members of this population also appear to have lower success rates in housing and vocational placements because their personality disorders compromise their ability to develop positive living and working relationships with peers, coworkers, and supervisors and, consequently, significantly hinder the development of functional independent living skills.

Sixty homeless clients meeting structured diagnostic interview criteria for substance abuse and personality disorder at the drop-in center are being randomly assigned to one of two on-site 24-week treatment conditions: (1) substance abuse counseling (SAC) group and (2) individual DFST. It is predicted that this population will experience improved outcomes when a targeted psychotherapeutic intervention is combined with case management, vocational training, and educational services. It is predicted that therapeutic attention to the symptoms of personality disorder will reduce behaviors such as relapse, depression, anxiety, and disruptive behaviors that lead to drop out or removal from homeless programs and substance abuse treatment. It is also predicted that clients who participate in DFST will be more likely to remain in treatment and increase their ability to follow through successfully with other social services referrals than clients who participate in the SAC group. Substance abuse, attendance, retention, psychiatric symptoms, employment, housing eligibility, and interpersonal problems will be assessed at baseline, throughout 24 weeks of treatment, and at a three-month posttermination assessment.

Both therapy conditions are delivered by licensed social workers with more than 10 years' experience in the field of substance abuse. The DFST therapist received two weeks (beginner, advanced) of training in the schema therapy model by Jeffrey Young and is employed at Young's Schema Therapy Center in New York. In addition, he receives weekly supervision facilitated by my weekly review of session audiotapes. Although outcomes of these two trials are not yet available, preliminary impressions confirm impressions from the prior methadone study. Although DFST is not a standard form of treatment in these settings, clients report finding it acceptable and comprehensible. In fact, many of these chronic, treatment refractory patients report that it is the first of many therapeutic experiences they have found relevant to their specific struggles related to addiction.

DUAL FOCUS SCHEMA THERAPY FOR DEPRESSED WOMEN WITH CHILDHOOD SEXUAL ABUSE HISTORIES

There are a number of effective pharmacological and psychosocial treatments for major depression, but a substantial number of patients do not respond to these treatments either through insufficient response, noncompliance, or frequent relapse. Research suggests that depressed individuals with poor treatment response are most often those with histories of childhood sexual abuse, posttraumatic stress, and personality disorders. Childhood sexual abuse is significantly associated with major depression in adulthood, especially in women, and is believed to be associated with a more chronic course of depression (Brown & Moran, 1994), including lower initial recovery rates and higher subsequent relapse rates (Brown, Harris, Hepworth, & Robinson, 1994; Zlotnick, Ryan, Miller, & Keitner, 1995).

In an exploratory treatment research project, DFST is being modified for depressed women with histories of childhood sexual abuse and compared to pharmacotherapy and clinical management (National Institute of Mental Health; C. Zlotnick). The major goals of this outpatient study conducted at Butler Hospital in Providence, Rhode Island, are to:

1. Modify the DFST manual for patients with current major depression and histories of sexual abuse and pilot its use on 11 women.
2. Implement a therapist training program.
3. Conduct a randomized controlled pilot study of the efficacy, feasibility, and acceptability of schema therapy plus clinical management/pharmacotherapy in comparison to clinical management/pharmacotherapy alone in a sample of 24 women.

Primary outcomes are treatment retention and depression symptoms.

A schema-focused therapy is hypothesized to be useful for this population because of its careful use of exposure techniques (i.e., controlled activation of schemas and childhood events through imagery), emphasis on coping skills, and targeting of the maladaptive schemas believed to underlie the depressive symptoms. It also targets for change cognitive and affective avoidance as defenses against overwhelming memory-driven affects and specifically addresses schemas of mistrust/abuse and vulnerability to harm and their reenactment in current relationships. It focuses on dysfunctional cognitions originating in traumatic childhood experiences; emphasizes safety and stability within the therapeutic relationship; and emphasizes the development of self-care, affect stabilization, and stress management skills. Zlotnick has developed an affect management module that is integrated into the early stage treatment process. Rather than using experiential techniques to elicit intensely painful affects and memories, early emphasis is placed on the management of negative affect (e.g., through distraction, self-soothing, distress tolerance, crisis planning skills) without resorting to maladaptive behaviors such as self-harm or dissociation.

TRAINING AND IMPLEMENTATION ISSUES

Attendance at schema therapy workshops conducted by Dr. Young and requests for the DFST manual suggests that there is significant interest among clinicians in the field. Most practitioners appear to be attracted to the approach because of its integration of different therapeutic techniques, its skill sets for managing and treating complex psychopathology, and its coherent theory of personality disorder which clinicians appear to grasp more readily than some other models. However, there is a big difference between understanding an approach through workshop participation or manual reading and delivering the therapy with skill and fidelity to the model. At this point in the development of DFST, I recommend that it be delivered within the context of another treatment modality (e.g., pharmacotherapy, partial hospital, and inpatient/residential) by a skilled clinician who has received intensive training and supervision.

Dual Focus Schema Therapy as a Treatment Enhancement

Unlike many of the psychotherapy models described in this volume, DFST has not been conceptualized as a stand-alone therapy. Undoubtedly, this reflects the obvious differences between the patients from the series of studies discussed here and those seen in the office-based practices of other personality disorder therapy models. Given the complicated, severe, and long-standing problems associated with personality disorders and co-occurring Axis I conditions, the optimal delivery of this manual-guided psychotherapy may be within the context of a structured, longer term or open-ended treatment experience. In all studies conducted or being conducted, DFST is being added as an enhancement to standard services that range from moderate to intensive. In New York City, DFST is being added to a drop-in center that provides meals, emergency housing, case management, psychiatric consultation, and vocational and educational activities. In New Haven, DFST is added to methadone programs, which provide this highly effective agonist medication in addition to group counseling, primary medical care, case management, and psychiatric consultation. In Bridgeport, DFST is added to a residential therapeutic community that provides this powerful milieu treatment in combination with group counseling, education, vocational training, case management, and medical and psychiatric care. In Providence, the model is being adapted and integrated with clinical management and pharmacotherapy provided by a psychiatrist. All of these treatment programs are conceptualized along a long-term or chronic care model for the presenting Axis I condition.

Implicit in this model is the assumption that a certain level of psychological containment and psychiatric symptom stabilization is optimal for DFST to be administered with a level of efficacy and fidelity to the original schema therapy model as developed by Young (1994; Young et al., 2003). The background treatment helps provide this as well as the ostensible reason for treatment for a personality disorder for which the patient would be unlikely to seek treatment if not so distressed. From a research integrity perspective, this level of standard treatment platform also helps retain patients in treatment and reduces the likelihood of differential attrition between the treatment conditions that might confound the interpretations of findings. The receipt of these concurrent services by all patients does represent a potential confound for determining specific treatment efficacy. However, regular individual psychotherapy is rarely provided in these settings so that the addition of this service can be evaluated and the receipt of other services can be controlled for in analyses.

APPROPRIATE COMPARISON CONDITIONS FOR CLINICAL TRIALS

A critically important issue when evaluating psychotherapy for personality disorders is the treatment condition to which it will be compared in a clinical trial. Given the number of competing treatments now being marketed for these disorders, it is no longer sufficient to present a model with a few illustrative cases. Instead, the treatment needs to be specified in a manner in which it can be evaluated against another credible form of treatment. In all of the previously described studies, the use of placebo or delayed treatment controls was considered unethical because of the level of acute problems these patients experience. In addition, the empirical question of whether (any) treatment is better than no treatment has been answered, and the field should now compare innovative treatments to some standard form of care. Such comparisons are also important because they control for nonspecific factors (e.g., general support, empathy, advice, attention) that contribute to positive outcome and must be controlled to conclude that a treatment being developed provides some specific (and added) benefit.

Another option considered was to compare DFST to treatment-as-usual however the patient chose to pursue this. This was the approach used by Linehan in her original DBT study, but it has some serious problems, not the least of which is that the powerful effects of one condition receiving significantly more treatment can never be ruled out. It is no longer considered a contribution to the literature to find that treatment is better than no treatment or that intensive treatment is better than minimal treatment. The standard now should be higher than what has been used in DBT studies, and newer treatment models should have the burden of proving themselves superior to some standard active reference treatment either in the management of the primary (e.g., substance abuse) or secondary (e.g., depression) Axis I symptoms or in the management of these problems in patients with more severe personality pathology. Ultimately, a complex psychotherapy model for complex patients should not be adopted in standard clinical practice unless it demonstrates its superiority over more easily trainable or already popular models. This is obviously a fairly stringent test of DFST.

For this reason, DFST is being compared to standard forms of counseling (individual or group drug counseling, 12-step facilitation, psychiatric case management) to evaluate whether an individual therapy that targets personality problems leads to better outcomes for personality-disordered drug abusers than a standard, active reference therapy. For example, individual drug counseling (Mercer, 2000; Mercer & Woody, 1999) is a common synthesis of many recovery topics used in standard inpatient and outpatient addiction treatment programs across the country, and its manualized version is one of the first three treatment manuals in the NIDA "Clinician Toolbox" series. Thus, IDC provides a credible psychotherapy control and allows an evaluation of the efficacy of adding DFST therapeutic content to the standard treatment content while controlling for time and attention provided by individual sessions. In comparison to the equal emphasis DFST places on personality dysfunction and addiction, IDC remains more narrowly focused on addiction as a disease and views personality dysfunction as secondary manifestation and not a major focus of treatment. The primary role of the IDC therapist is to help patients admit their addiction, teach recovery tools, motivate patients, encourage the development of drug-free social supports, promote abstinence, review self-help philosophy, and encourage meeting attendance. Likewise, DFST has been compared to 12-step facilitation treatment because this is a standard form of counseling with little theoretical or technical overlap with DFST. Some of the other manualized comparison treatments considered (e.g., standard cognitive-behavioral coping skills, interpersonal psychotherapy, supportive-expressive therapy) have too many areas of overlap with DFST.

The studies in Providence and New York City also make use of a comparison condition employing a standard reference therapy. In the drop-in center study, DFST is being compared to a substance abuse counseling group available on-site several times per week that includes addiction psychoeducation, 12-step principles, and relapse prevention concepts. In the study of depressed women with childhood histories of sexual abuse, the comparison is to regular clinical management provided by a psychiatrist who is prescribing an antidepressant. Thus, DFST is being evaluated as an enhancement to what has become the standard form of psychiatric treatment for depression in the United States.

THERAPIST SELECTION AND TRAINING PROCEDURES

Although therapist training for Axis I disorders requires time and effort, effective training for a personality disorder psychotherapy such as DFST and the other treatment models developed by many of the contributors to this volume is best described as burdensome. Developing treatment manuals greatly facilitates the process of working with very challenging patients, but it cannot substitute for an intensive training period followed by close supervision of some ongoing cases. DFST therapists typically receive two to three full days of training by Jeffrey Young for schema therapy; then I provide an additional day of training specifically in the use of the DFST manual. The training material and procedures have been developed through Young's extensive training series and through the original DFST study. Didactic material is integrated with videotaped case demonstrations and role plays. The review of the therapy manual is intended to allow therapists to understand the demarcation between the internal and external boundaries of the treatment approach and specific therapist behaviors that are prescribed and proscribed as a means of reducing overlap between approaches. After the training workshop, therapists treat one or more pilot patients, and videotapes of these sessions are reviewed and rated. I provide detailed guidance and feedback as well as evaluate the therapist's adherence, competence, and readiness to participate as a therapist. In addition to supervising the DFST therapists in the NIDA methadone study, I have served as a consultant to the other studies described in this chapter, listen to and rate audiotapes, and hold phone or in-person supervision sessions weekly.

Another important issue is the training criteria for selecting who is qualified to deliver DFST. Regardless of level of education, therapists must be highly competent because the training and treatment manuals are not designed to teach basic skills to novice therapists, but rather to augment existing skills for the treatment of this specific dual-disordered population. The treatment development study used a more select group of doctoral-level clinical psychologists specializing in therapy with substance abusers with advanced training in cognitive-behavioral or psychodynamic therapies. It was believed that highly trained clinicians were needed to provide therapy because of the complex, challenging psychopathology that is often found in this population and the negative reactions these patients often elicit in clinicians without advanced training in psychotherapy and exposure to theories of psychopathology and personality. Adherence or competence measures indicated that the training and ongoing supervision plan was effective in transmitting the skills and techniques to therapists who were able to both adhere to the DFST manual as well as perform it with adequate skill.

The degree to which less educated or experienced clinicians can provide this approach with the fidelity necessary for a clinical trial is an empirical question currently being addressed. All three ongoing studies are using masters-level clinicians, but in all cases these are individuals with substantial clinical experience working with their respective target populations. A more sophisticated question is whether clinicians of diverse professional backgrounds and levels of education and experience are able to provide all components of the treatment model with equal fidelity or whether only some components can be delivered by a broad range of clinicians (e.g., psychoeducational material, but not cognitive or experiential change strategies). Until research can answer these questions, it is recommended that clinicians considering use of this model have formal education and advanced training in theories of psychopathology, psychotherapeutic techniques, and, specifically, experience in treating the commonly co-occurring Axis I conditions. Clinicians should have several years of experience treating individuals with substance abuse, severe mental illness, or dual diagnosis. Clinicians should be familiar with cognitive-behavioral approaches, willing to learn and follow a manual-guided approach, and participate in an intensive training and supervisory process.

SUMMARY AND CONCLUSIONS

Patients with co-occurring personality disorders and substance abuse are frequently seen in treatment programs (Verheul et al., 1998), consume a disproportionate amount of staff time, and may be less likely to respond favorably to standard substance abuse treatment interventions (Griggs & Tyrer, 1981; Kosten et al., 1989; Nace & Davis, 1993). This chapter summarizes a new program of research that has focused over the past five years on the assessment and treatment implications of personality disorders in substance abusers. During this time, our research team has developed considerable expertise in the complexities of diagnosing personality disorders in substance abusers, particularly the ability to separate drug-related behaviors from personality disorders and to evaluate the reliability and validity of personality disorder diagnoses. A diagnostic procedure has been established that minimizes the likelihood of finding spurious changes in personality disorder symptom severity. Diagnostic research has mapped out the association between categorical personality disorders and underlying personality trait, cognitive, affective, and interpersonal dimensions. These dimensional constructs, and especially maladaptive schemas and coping styles, are thought to translate better into more specific interventions for personality-related problems than the Axis II categorical constructs.

Through both diagnostic and therapy development research, the ability to recruit sufficient numbers of patients with personality disorders has been established. A cognitive-behavioral approach has excellent potential for integrating the treatment for substance abuse and the diverse range of personality disorders, and a NIDA-funded treatment development study has:

- Determined the feasibility, safety, and acceptability of DFST.
- Developed a detailed session-by-session treatment manual with prescribed and proscribed techniques.
- Developed comprehensive, effective training packages for therapists.
- Conducted a small randomized pilot trial demonstrating the promise of DFST.
- Developed adherence/competence scales and a rater guide and established treatment discriminability.

The success of this project has led to three (and, it is hoped, a fourth) separately funded clinical trials evaluating DFST in different clinical populations.

The individual therapy model described in this chapter and elsewhere (Ball, 1998; Ball & Young, 2000) is only one of a growing number of promising, time-limited treatment approaches for personality disorders. The field of personality disorder treatment has been separated historically into groups that questioned the existence of personality and its disordered expression (behavioral), had developed short-term, symptom-focused techniques that seemed ineffective for "difficult-to-treat" patients (cognitive), or had viewed treatment as a very long-term process with unclear outcomes for a fairly narrow functional range of character disturbance (psychoanalytic). Limited clinical success combined with major shifts in the delivery of psychotherapy under managed care stimulated each of these major individual therapy models to adapt their traditional methods to respond better to the needs of this complex population in a challenging health care environment. Shorter term psychodynamic approaches were developed, which focused increasingly on conscious thought processes, core conflicts or relational themes, and confrontive techniques, whereas longer term cognitive-behavioral approaches began to focus on the origins of maladaptive behavioral patterns and cognitive themes, their expression in the therapeutic relationship, and the importance of empathic understanding. These are major theoretical and technical changes. Although the language used to describe psychopathology and psychotherapy remains different, the underlying similarities of constructs and approaches is evident in the different theoretical and clinical writing and videotaped demonstrations of cases.

Although there is now some excitement about conducting personality disorder treatment research, it is not a time for unrealistic optimism. Although many approaches appear promising, empirical support for their efficacy is almost nonexistent. The major exception to this is Linehan's (1993) DBT, which shows targeted effects on reducing parasuicidality and hospitalization (Linehan, Armstrong, Suarez, Allmon, & Heard, 1991; Linehan, Heard, & Armstrong, 1993) and for which there are few efficacy studies. For the field to continue to advance, it will need to value these improvements in focal life areas rather than expect deeper, structural change as the major outcome of interest. Realistic goals are necessary when treating severe personality disorders and substance dependence (e.g., improving self-esteem, emotional functioning, relationships, psychiatric symptoms) through improved retention and outcome in a treatment that explicitly addresses the Axis I and II problems of the patient. For an empirically supported treatment literature to develop, clinicians and theoreticians will need to articulate their approaches in ways that permit independent investigators to replicate promising single case studies through controlled clinical trials.

As previously discussed (Ball, 1998), research in this area struggles with a number of practical problems, including:

- Diagnostic reliability and stability of *DSM-IV* personality disorders.
- Recruitment of sufficient sample sizes.
- Need to address the Axis I symptoms that typically motivate the individual to seek treatment.
- Controlling for additional treatments.
- Training therapists in a complex psychotherapeutic approach.
- Treatment time frame.

As to the last point, six months is probably an inappropriately short period within which to expect change in this population, yet it stretches the duration beyond that of most clinical research and managed care plans. It is hoped that relatively short-term approaches such as DFST will show enough promise that a more extended course of therapy may be justified on the basis of longer term cost-effectiveness or as an effective means to prevent relapse of a presenting Axis I disorder. From the standpoint of personality disorder treatment, even one year is probably an unrealistically short time for addressing longstanding, maladaptive patterns of viewing self and relating to others and severe addiction. Meta-analytic (Perry et al., 1999) and literature reviews (Sanislow & McGlashan, 1998) suggest that symptomatic improvements must be measured over a long follow-up period when evaluating change in a chronic condition such as personality disorders (and drug dependence).

The originator of cognitive-behavioral therapy for personality disorders (A. T. Beck et al., 1990), the theorist and investigator of the only empirically supported treatment for a specific personality disorder (Linehan, 1993), and the author of a meta-analysis (Perry et al., 1999) all argue that separate treatments are needed for the different *DSM-IV* personality disorders. In fact, the developer of schema therapy (Young) now believes that the original model may be less appropriate for some personality disorders (especially Borderline, Narcissistic, and Avoidant patients) than a mode-focused approach. However, the evaluation of separate manuals for each disorder is impractical in clinical trials and in clinical practice, especially because the number of mixed, "not otherwise specified," or co-occurring cases of personality disorders greatly outnumbers the "pure cases." Such approaches also afford these categorical diagnoses a status that is unjustified based on reliability and validity research. Rather than using a different approach for each of the 10 personality disorders, DFST consists of a series of core topics, the specific content and delivery of which are determined by an assessment and conceptualization of the individual's maladaptive schemas and coping styles.

DFST focuses on theoretical constructs with treatment implications that cut across and below the surface of the syndrome- and symptom-focused *DSM* system. Although the clinical conceptualization (e.g., schemas, coping styles) necessarily varies from case to case, use of a common core of cognitive, experiential, relational, and behavioral techniques for all disorders should facilitate a more efficient evaluation of the therapy's effectiveness by other investigators in the substance abuse field as well as for other Axis I disorders commonly seen in personality-disordered individuals (e.g., depressive, anxiety, eating, somatoform, trauma-related disorders). Nonetheless, the issue of treatment-specific focus (i.e., categories or dimensions) may be resolved only through empirical study. Although results using a single, integrative DFST manual were promising, such small-scale studies do not permit an analysis of outcome for patients who meet different categorical personality disorders. In the larger scale study proposed in the methadone program, exploratory analyses will be conducted on the basis of the presence or absence of Borderline, Antisocial, and Avoidant Personality Disorder.

Because this group of individuals rarely present for treatment for their personality disorders per se, researchers invariably study and treat these disorders in the context of alleviating a presenting Axis I disorder or significant pressure in the patient's environment. For this reason, a treatment manual for personality disorders should be integrated with an Axis I symptom-focused approach. One advantage of DFST is that it targets both overt symptoms (e.g., substance use, depressed mood, interpersonal problems) and underlying themes (e.g., schemas, coping styles) and transitions from behavioral symptoms to internal and external determinants of psychopathology in a manner that is theoretically consistent for the therapist and, more importantly, comprehensible to the patient and responsive to his or her needs.

Several factors may limit the adoption in clinical practice of many of the innovative psychotherapy models that have been developed for the personality disorders. First, with rare exception (Linehan's DBT being the best known), none have been evaluated in a clinical trial and are many years away from achieving recognition as an empirically supported treatment. In fact, many either do not hold this as a goal or are conceptualized at a level of complexity that makes such a goal unachievable. Second, and again with DBT as the exception, few if any of these approaches have developed a sufficiently detailed treatment manual to facilitate effective training and dissemination. Third, most models are based on work with Borderline, Narcissistic, and, occasionally, Avoidant patients, and the techniques used for these individuals may not always be relevant to the broader range of specific or mixed/unspecified personality disorders or their co-occurring Axis I conditions encountered in clinical practice. DFST is a promising approach on all three counts. Although research support is still preliminary, ongoing or planned randomized clinical trials should have an answer to the efficacy question in five years. DFST has a highly detailed therapy manual, and the feedback by providers who have reviewed it after completing an intensive training has been very positive. In addition, the approach cuts across the current Axis II categories (and thus would not be affected by inevitable changes to the *DSM* nomenclature) and is flexible in its ability to incorporate a treatment focus on the common presenting Axis I conditions.

Stone (2001) has raised the important related concern that very little has been written about the multiply disadvantaged borderline and other personality-disordered patients existing on the margins of society—for example, the poorly educated, unemployed, substance abusing, traumatized, homeless individuals with histories of repeated hospitalization and incarceration. Although the higher functioning personality-disordered patients on whom most current models were developed are certainly troubled and deserving of treatment, they are not necessarily representative of the kinds of chronic patients that most practitioners encounter in mental health clinics, hospitals, or another nonpsychiatric settings (addiction treatment programs, social service agencies, shelters, vocational programs). The growing number of professional and lay books for personality disorders may be less relevant to lower functioning patients because they fail to account for the significant additional Axis I, case management, and ancillary service needs that must be integrated with the personality disorder therapy. In contrast, DFST (like DBT) has been developed, initially tested, and is currently being evaluated on a variety of lower functioning patients with difficult-to-treat Axis I and II disorders and often severe problems with daily living.

REFERENCES

Alterman, A. I., & Cacciola, J. S. (1991). The antisocial personality disorder diagnosis in substance abusers: Problems and issues. *Journal of Nervous and Mental Diseases, 179,* 401–409.

American Psychiatric Association. (1952). *Diagnostic and statistical manual of mental disorders.* Washington, DC: Author.

American Psychiatric Association. (1968). *Diagnostic and statistical manual of mental disorders* (2nd ed.). Washington, DC: Author.

American Psychiatric Association. (1980). *Diagnostic and statistical manual of mental disorders* (3rd ed.). Washington, DC: Author.

American Psychiatric Association. (1987). *Diagnostic and statistical manual of mental disorders* (3rd ed., rev.). Washington, DC: Author.

American Psychiatric Association. (1994). *Diagnostic and statistical manual of mental disorders* (4th ed.). Washington, DC: Author.

Ball, S. A. (1996). Type A and B alcoholism: Applicability across subpopulations and treatment settings. *Alcohol Health and Research World, 20,* 30–35.

Ball, S. A. (1998). Manualized treatment for substance abusers with personality disorders: Dual Focus Schema Therapy. *Addictive Behaviors, 23,* 883–891.

Ball, S. A. (2001). Big five, alternative five, and seven personality dimensions: Validity in substance dependent patients. In P. T. Costa Jr. & T. A. Widiger (Eds.), *Personality disorders and the five-factor model of personality* (2nd ed., pp. 177–201). Washington, DC: American Psychological Association.

Ball, S. A., Carroll, K. M., Babor, T. F., & Rounsaville, B. J. (1995). Subtypes of cocaine abusers: Support for a Type A-Type B distinction. *Journal of Consulting and Clinical Psychology, 63,* 115–124.

Ball, S. A., & Cecero, J. J. (2001). Addicted patients with personality disorders: Symptoms, schema, and traits. *Journal of Personality Disorders, 15,* 72–83.

Ball, S. A., Kranzler, H. R., Tennen, H., Poling, J. C., & Rounsaville, B. J. (1997). Personality disorder and dimension differences between Type A and Type B substance abusers. *Journal of Personality Disorders, 12,* 1–12.

Ball, S. A., Rounsaville, B. J., Tennen, H., & Kranzler, H. R. (2001). Reliability of personality disorder symptoms and personality traits in substance dependent inpatients. *Journal of Abnormal Psychology, 110,* 341–352.

Ball, S. A., & Schottenfeld, R. S. (1997). A five-factor model of personality and addiction, psychiatric, and AIDS risk severity in pregnant and postpartum cocaine misusers. *Substance Use and Misuse, 32,* 25–41.

Ball, S. A., Tennen, H., Poling, J. C., Kranzler, H. R., & Rounsaville, B. J. (1997). Personality, temperament, and character dimensions and the *DSM-IV* personality disorders in substance abusers. *Journal of Abnormal Psychology, 106,* 545–553.

Ball, S. A., & Young, J. E. (1998). *Dual focus schema therapy: A treatment manual for personality disorder and addiction.* Unpublished treatment manual.

Ball, S. A., & Young, J. E. (2000). Dual focus schema therapy for personality disorders and substance dependence: Case study results. *Cognitive and Behavioral Practice, 7,* 270–281.

Ball, S. A., Young, J. E., Rounsaville, B. J., & Carroll, K. M. (1999, September). *Dual focus schema therapy vs. 12-step drug counseling for personality disorders and addiction: Randomized pilot study.* Paper presented at the 6th International Congress of the Disorders of Personality, Geneva, Switzerland.

Beck, A. T., Freeman, A., & Associates. (1990). *Cognitive therapy of personality disorders.* New York: Guilford Press.

Beck, J. S. (1998). Complex cognitive therapy treatment for personality disorder patients. *Bulletin of the Menninger Clinic, 62,* 170–194.

Brooner, R. K., Kidorf, M., King, V. L., & Stoller, K. (1998). Preliminary evidence of good treatment response in antisocial drug abusers. *Drug and Alcohol Dependence, 49,* 249–260.

Brooner, R. K., King, V. L., Kidorf, M., Schmidt, C. W., & Bigelow, G. E. (1997). Psychiatric and substance use comorbidity among treatment-seeking opioid abusers. *Archives of General Psychiatry, 54,* 71–80.

Brown, G. W., Harris, T. O., Hepworth, C., & Robinson, R. (1994). Clinical and psychosocial origins of chronic depressive episodes. II: A patient enquiry. *British Journal of Psychiatry, 164,* 457–465.

Brown, G. W., & Moran, P. (1994). Clinical and psychosocial origins of chronic depressive episodes. I: A community survey. *British Journal of Psychiatry, 165,* 447–456.

Cacciola, J. S., Alterman, A. I., & Rutherford, M. J. (1995). Treatment response and problem severity of antisocial substance abusers. *Journal of Nervous and Mental Diseases, 183,* 166–171.

Cacciola, J. S., Rutherford, M. J., Alterman, A. I., McKay, J. R., & Snider, E. C. (1996). Personality disorders and treatment outcome in methadone maintenance patients. *Journal of Nervous and Mental Diseases, 184,* 234–239.

Carroll, K. M. (1997). Manual guided psychosocial treatment: A new virtual requirement for pharmacotherapy trials. *Archives of General Psychiatry, 54,* 923–928.

Chiesa, M. (2000). Hospital adjustment in personality disorder patients admitted to a therapeutic community milieu. *British Journal of Medical Psychology, 73,* 259–267.

DeJong, C., van den Brink, W., Harteveld, F. M., & van der Wielen, G. M. (1993). Personality disorders in alcoholics and drug addicts. *Comprehensive Psychiatry, 34,* 87–94.

Griggs, S. M., & Tyrer, P. J. (1981). Personality disorder, social adjustment and treatment outcome in alcoholics. *Journal of Studies on Alcohol, 42,* 802–805.

Kadden, R. M., Carroll, K. M., Donovan, D., Cooney, N. L., Monti, P., Abram, D., et al. (1992). Cognitive-behavioral coping skills therapy manual: A clinical research guide for therapists treating individuals with alcohol abuse and dependence. In M. E. Mattson (Ed.), *NIAAA Project MATCH Monograph Series* (Vol. 3, DHHS Publication No. ADM 92–1895). Washington, DC: U.S. Government Printing Office.

Kadden, R. M., Cooney, N. L., Getter, H., & Litt, M. D. (1989). Matching alcoholics to coping skills or interactional therapies: Posttreatment results. *Journal of Consulting and Clinical Psychology, 57,* 698–704.

Kofoed, L., Kania, J., Walsh, T., & Atkinson, R. (1986). Outpatient treatment of patients with substance abuse and co-existing psychiatric disorders. *American Journal of Psychiatry, 143,* 867–872.

Kosten, T. A., Kosten, T. R., & Rounsaville, B. J. (1989). Personality disorders in opiate addicts show prognostic specificity. *Journal of Substance Abuse Treatment, 6,* 163–168.

Kruedelbach, N., McCormick, R. A., Schulz, S. C., & Grueneich, R. (1993). Impulsivity, coping styles, and triggers for craving in substance abusers with borderline personality disorder. *Journal of Personality Disorders, 7,* 214–222.

Linehan, M. M. (1993). *Cognitive behavior therapy for borderline personality disorder.* New York: Guilford Press.

Linehan, M. M., Armstrong, H. E., Suarez, A., Allmon, D., & Heard, H. L. (1991). Cognitive-behavioral treatment of chronically parasuicidal borderline patients. *Archives of General Psychiatry, 48,* 1060–1064.

Linehan, M. M., Heard, H. L., & Armstrong, H. E. (1993). Naturalistic follow-up of a behavioral treatment for chronically parasuicidal borderline patients. *Archives of General Psychiatry, 50,* 971–974.

Links, P. S. (1998). Developing effective services for patients with personality disorders. *Canadian Journal of Psychiatry, 43,* 251–259.

Litt, M. D., Babor, T. F., DelBoca, F. K., Kadden, R. M., & Cooney, N. L. (1992). Types of alcoholics. II: Application of an empirically derived typology to treatment matching. *Archives of General Psychiatry, 49,* 609–614.

Longabaugh, R., Rubin, A., Malloy, P., Beattie, M., Clifford, P. R., & Noel, N. (1994). Drinking outcome of alcohol abusers diagnosed as antisocial personality disorder. *Alcoholism: Clinical and Experimental Research, 18,* 410–416.

Marlatt, G. A., & Gordon, J. R. (1985). *Relapse prevention.* New York: Guilford Press.

Mercer, D. E. (2000). Description of an addiction counseling approach. In J. J. Boren, L. S. Onken, & K. M. Carroll (Eds.), *Approaches to drug abuse counseling.* Bethesda, MD: National Institute on Drug Abuse.

Mercer, D. E., & Woody, G. E. (1999). *An individual counseling approach to treat cocaine addiction: The collaborative cocaine treatment study model. Therapy Manuals for Addiction* (manual 3). Bethesda, MD: National Institute on Drug Abuse.

Monti, P. M., Abram, D. B., Kadden, R. M., & Cooney, N. L. (1989). *Treating alcohol dependence: A coping skills training guide.* New York: Guilford Press.

Nace, E. P., & Davis, C. W. (1993). Treatment outcome in substance abusing patients with a personality disorder. *American Journal of Addictions, 2,* 26–33.

Nace, E. P., Davis, C. W., & Gaspari, J. P. (1991). Axis II comorbidity in substance abusers. *American Journal of Psychiatry, 148,* 118–120.

Nace, E. P., Saxon, J. J., & Shore, N. (1986). Borderline personality disorder and alcoholism treatment: A one-year follow-up study. *Journal of Studies on Alcohol, 47,* 196–200.

Nowinski, J., Baker, S., & Carroll, K. M. (1992). Twelve-step facilitation therapy manual: A clinical research guide for therapists treating individuals with alcohol abuse and dependence. *NIAAA Project MATCH Monograph Series* (Vol. 1, DHHS Publication No. ADM 92–1893). Washington, DC: U.S. Government Printing Office.

Perry, J. C., Banon, E., & Ianni, F. (1999). Effectiveness of psychotherapy for personality disorders. *American Journal of Psychiatry, 156,* 1312–1321.

Rounsaville, B. J., Carroll, K. M., & Onken, L. S. (2001). NIDA's stage model of behavioral therapies research: Getting started and moving on from Stage 1. *Clinical Psychology: Science and Practice, 8,* 133–142.

Rounsaville, B. J., Kosten, T. R., Weissman, M. M., & Kleber, H. D. (1986). Prognostic significance of psychopathology in treated opiate addicts. *Archives of General Psychiatry, 43,* 739–745.

Rounsaville, B. J., Kranzler, H. R., Ball, S. A., Tennen, H., Poling, J., & Triffleman, E. (1998). Personality disorders in substance abusers: Relation to substance abuse. *Journal of Nervous and Mental Diseases, 186,* 87–95.

Rutherford, M. J., Cacciola, J. S., & Alterman, A. I. (1994). Relationship of personality disorders with problem severity in methadone patients. *Drug and Alcohol Dependence, 35,* 69–76.

Sanislow, C. A., & McGlashan, T. H. (1998). Treatment outcome of personality disorders. *Canadian Journal of Psychiatry, 43,* 237–250.

Schmidt, N. B., Joiner, T. E., Young, J. E., & Telch, M. J. (1995). The Schema Questionnaire: Investigation of psychometric properties and hierarchical structure of a measure of maladaptive schemas. *Cognitive Therapy and Research, 19,* 295–321.

Shea, M. T. (1993). Psychosocial treatment of personality disorders. *Journal of Personality Disorders* (Special Suppl.), 167–180.

Smyth, N. J., & Washousky, R. C. (1995). The coping styles of alcoholics with Axis II disorders. *Journal of Substance Abuse, 7,* 425–435.

Stone, M. (2001). Natural history and long-term outcome. In W. J. Livesley (Ed.), *Handbook of personality disorders* (pp. 259–273). New York: Guilford Press.

Target, M. (1998). Outcome research on the psychosocial treatment of personality disorders. *Bulletin of the Menninger Clinic, 62,* 215–230.

Thomas, V. H., Melchert, T. P., & Banken, J. A. (1999). Substance dependence and personality disorders: Comorbidity and treatment outcome in an inpatient treatment population. *Journal of Studies on Alcohol, 60,* 271–277.

Verheul, R., Ball, S. A., & van den Brink, W. (1998). Substance abuse and personality disorders. In H. R. Kranzler & B. J. Rounsaville (Eds.), *Dual diagnosis and treatment: Substance abuse and comorbid medical and psychiatric disorders* (pp. 317–363). New York: Marcel Dekker.

Verheul, R., Kranzler, H. R., Poling, J., Tennen, H., Ball, A., & Rounsaville, B. J. (2000). Axis I and Axis II disorders in alcoholics and drug addicts: Fact or artifact? *Journal of Studies on Alcohol, 61,* 101–110.

Woody, G., McLellan, A. T., Luborsky, L., & O'Brien, C. P. (1985). Sociopathy and psychotherapy outcome. *Archives of General Psychiatry, 42,* 1081–1086.

Young, J. E. (1994). *Cognitive therapy for personality disorders: A schema-focused approach.* Sarasota, FL: Professional Resource Exchange.

Young, J. E., Klosko, J. S., & Weishaar, M. E. (2003). *Schema therapy: A practitioner's guide.* New York: Guilford Press.

Zlotnick, C., Ryan, C. E., Miller, I. W., & Keitner, G. I. (1995). Childhood abuse and recovery from major depression. *Child Abuse and Neglect, 19,* 1513–1516.

CHAPTER 19

Personality-Guided Therapy for Treating Medical Patients

Ellen A. Dornelas

AN APPRECIATION OF personality theory by medical caregivers would advance the treatment of medical patients, but the topic is sufficiently complex such that the majority of mental health professionals focus on Axis I symptoms, rather than personality organization. The *Diagnostic and Statistical Manual* (*DSM-IV-TR;* American Psychiatric Association [APA], 2000) does have a multiaxial approach, but it is essentially an atheoretical, pathology-based, typological model. Each category of Axis II diagnosis describes a distinct disorder; this categorization can be useful but is not comprehensive. The benefits of using *DSM* descriptions of personality are greater reliability and validity in making diagnoses. Diagnostic precision is highly valued in medicine, but the trade-off is a blanket disregard of virtually all that is known about personality, in large part because of the difficulties in making operational definitions. Clinical diagnosis of personality is an emotionally charged and controversial issue because many mental health professionals believe that rendering a judgment about personality organization is pejorative and stigmatizing. The result is that the fields of psychology and psychiatry have spent a century gridlocked, unable to reach consensus on what constitutes personality and thus marginalizing a topic that is highly relevant to health care.

Though *mind-body* medicine enjoyed increased attention and study in the past two decades, scant attention has been paid to incorporating personality theory into this burgeoning field. The interaction between physical health and personality organization is indirect, and the complexity of the task is daunting. This chapter makes the argument that personality factors should be assessed and considered when treating medical patients. To make this case, an operational definition of personality is described briefly in the following section.

Many clinically derived theories of personality (Johnson, 1994; McWilliams, 1994; Millon, 1999) have argued that it is useful to construe personality as having multiple dimensions. For the present discussion, the dimensions of temperament,

426

self-image, interpersonal relationships, and cognition are included. This conceptualization is offered for its heuristic value and potential relevance to medicine. *Temperament* refers to biological or genetically derived tendencies to react to the environment in particular ways. For example, among the variety of temperament traits that have been studied, extroversion and neuroticism have the highest degrees of heritability (Loehlin, 1982), and Eysenck and Eysenck (1983) have referred to them accordingly as "supertraits." *Self-image* refers to perceptions of an individual's own distinct, unique identity (Millon, 1999). *Interpersonal relationships* are defined as a person's social ties with others (spouse, children, siblings, parents, bosses, and peers at work) and provide information about the quality and quantity of attachments to important others in the individual's daily life. *Cognition* refers to "thought content (what we think), thought processes (how we think), and self-schemas (what structures our thinking)" (Winston & Winston, 2002, p. 20).

People with medical problems (eventually this includes everyone) vary widely in their personality organization (innate temperament, capacity to feel, think, and relate to other people). Personality plays a role in whether we develop or prevent some types of illness and disability through risky versus health-promoting behaviors. Personality shapes whether we avoid or overuse the health care system and how we react to medical caregivers. Personality drives our psychological defensive system and defines how we cope with a diagnosis of physical illness. And in exchange, our physical vulnerabilities and knowledge (or denial) of our own mortality shape our personality. Medical caregivers are no different from psychotherapists in being truly stymied by the complex ways in which personality can impact on development of and recovery from physical illness. The challenge for psychotherapists who work with medical patients is to broaden their scope beyond simply helping addressing the needs of people adjusting to major medical illness or treating the comorbid Axis I disorders and symptomatic distress that can accompany health problems. Personality theorists are challenged to help both medical caregivers and medical patients understand the multidirectional process by which personality and physical well-being influence each other. Personality-guided interventions may offer the best hope for changing complex health behaviors (Dornelas & Magnavita, 2001). Distress created by medical problems has traditionally been viewed as an "adjustment issue" by psychotherapists. However, a medical crisis presents a unique opportunity for personality maturation. More than 25 years ago, Engel (1977) predicted that a crisis in medicine would occur because of reliance on a narrow biomedical model for conceptualizing patient care. As predicted, the health care crisis has been well underway for some time now, though there is currently a greater acceptance of social and psychological factors (biopsychosocial model) in medicine. In the decades to come, the biopsychosocial model will evolve to include greater use of personality theory to guide the treatment of medical patients.

THE MULTIDIRECTIONAL RELATIONSHIP BETWEEN PERSONALITY AND PHYSICAL HEALTH

There are many areas of medicine where patients have maladaptive personality traits that impact health and vex the primary care physician. This chapter focuses on three: health risk behaviors, somatoform disorders, and psychological adjustment to illness. In the first category, there are many behaviors that endanger health, for example, smoking, substance abuse, unsafe sex, and driving while intoxicated. Risky health behaviors place individuals at increased probability of preventable illness such as lung cancer, heart disease, HIV, and traumatic brain injury. In the second category, anxiety-related physical symptoms are extremely common among medical patients. Many medical patients suffer from somatic symptoms that are completely or partially attributable to personality organization. The last category focuses on the ways in which personality deficits and strengths define how people cope with illness. The role that personality plays in helping people cope with serious illness has been largely unstudied but is important to those clinicians who attempt to help patients identify issues related to meaning and purpose in life.

HEALTH RISK BEHAVIORS

Personality structure seems to coalesce during early adulthood, a juncture of life when risky health behaviors are more likely displayed. Most people, however, do not continue to practice unsafe sex, abuse alcohol and drugs, or smoke cigarettes into their 30s and beyond. Risk-taking individuals are more likely to be extraverted, anticonformist, rebellious, impulsive, sensation seeking, antagonistic, and hostile (Lipkus, Barefoot, Williams, & Siegler, 1994). Using our operational definition of personality, it is not difficult to make an argument that health risk behaviors are personality-driven. Some variance in these traits is attributable to temperamental differences, an important foundation of personality, as noted in the introduction of this chapter. Parenting behaviors, early developmental experiences, and constitutional differences also play a role in how people regulate mood. Affect regulation and stabilization of self-image, in turn, are important functions of risk-taking health behaviors, such as cigarette smoking and drug or alcohol abuse (Miller & Brown, 1997). For example, sadness, anxiety, low self-esteem, and anger are consistently associated with cigarette smoking and predict failure to quit (Hall, Munoz, Reus, & Sees, 1993). Significant cognitive differences exist in perceptions of what constitutes health risk, and these perceptions, in turn, are influenced by a multitude of social-environmental factors (e.g., education, socioeconomic status, cultural norms). Last, there is a well-documented, robust, bidirectional relationship between health risk behaviors and interpersonal relationships indicating that poor interpersonal relationships and social isolation correlate with risk-taking health behaviors (Sarafino, 1994). Social support can *buffer* individuals against the deleterious effects of stress, making them less likely to use alcohol and drugs when their coping abilities are overwhelmed (Cohen & Wills, 1985). In the reverse direction, an individual's social network may encourage (or inhibit) use of alcohol, cigarettes, or other drugs as a function of acceptance. Among pregnant smokers, the support of the marital or live-in partner is an important predictor of long-term abstinence (Fingerhut, Kleinman, & Kendrick, 1990). Many primary care physicians do recognize that a complex constellation of personality factors are related to behaviors such as cigarette smoking, alcohol abuse, and unsafe sex—they simply don't know how to effectively intervene until after the patient has already become ill. Though there are no simple solutions, primary care doctors could do a better job at motivating patients to become curious about the link between their personality and their health risk behavior.

SOMATOFORM DISORDERS

Somatoform disorders are a "group of problems characterized by persistent bodily symptoms or concerns that cannot be fully accounted for by diagnosable disease" (Looper & Kirmayer, 2002, p. 810). Included in this grouping are Hypochondriasis, Body Dysmorphic Disorder, Conversion Disorder, Chronic Fatigue Syndrome, Pain Disorder (pain with no medical explanation), and Noncardiac Chest Pain. It is difficult to devise interventions for the health care setting that are effective for such complex syndromes but attempts have been made. For example, using a model of physician-delivered intervention, primary care physicians were trained in a three-stage reattribution model to treat somatizing patients (Blankenstein et al., 2002). During Stage 1, the goal was to help the patient to feel understood by taking a complete history of symptoms and careful listening for emotional, social, and family factors as well as health beliefs. In Stage 2, the physician broadened the agenda by feeding back results from the examination and introducing the use of a symptom diary. In Stage 3, the physician used the diary to help patients to make a link among psychological distress, physiological changes, and somatic symptoms. The authors suggest that such a model might have particular relevance in a stepped-care approach. A physician-delivered reattribution intervention might help patients with less severe somatoform disorders. Patients with more severe somatoform disorders might then be referred to mental health professionals.

There is some evidence that somatoform disorders are associated with the spectrum of personality disorders that fall into Clusters B and C (Tyrer, Gunderson, Lyons, & Tohen, 1997). It might seem intuitively obvious that the pathways to somatization are as varied as the unique constellations of traits that comprise an individual's personality. In broad terms, people approach their body and doctor in the same way that they approach other facets of their life. Obsessive individuals channel their anxiety into hypersensitivity to the physiology of their body. Obsessive personalities with somatoform disorders are highly responsive to internal physical sensations and external and internal stimuli. Heightened sensitivity can create difficulty in interpreting internal stimuli; for example, a common somatic complaint is an individual's perception that his or her heart is skipping beats, even when cardiac examination has ruled out this possibility.

Narcissistic and histrionic patients go doctor shopping, initially idealizing and then devaluing the physician who cannot help them. Millon has referred to the narcissists who "become the 'household tyrants', not only creating guilt in others for failure to attend to the needs of the 'sick person' but by demanding that their claims for special status be instituted" (1999, p. 223). Histrionic personalities use dramatic, attention-getting physical complaints, consistent with their style, designed to solicit attention and care. The overexaggerating style used by histrionic personalities can result in a plethora of uncomfortable medical tests, designed to pinpoint a physiological basis for the complaint. For example, a woman with a long history of varied physical complaints was bothered by a headache. When asked about routine symptoms designed to rule out meningitis, she immediately endorsed and amplified other symptoms not previously reported ("a really terribly stiff neck and the worst fever I ever remember") though in fact she had not taken her temperature and the physician could massage her neck without causing any discomfort. People with dependent personality disorders often take a helpless stance and look for a cure, conceptualizing the body as though it were an automobile that needs replacement parts (DeGood, 1983). A 53-year-old woman with dependent traits complained of numbness in her hands. Her physician recommended a four-week course of physical therapy to which she replied, "Isn't there some type of surgery you could do instead?" As shown from this example, viewing health care as something external often leads to unnecessary procedures when patients are unwilling to engage themselves in rehabilitative or preventive behaviors. Passive-aggressive individuals can be help-rejecting complainers with medical professionals and may act out their anger toward family members by ensuring that family life revolves around their illness. For example, a 42-year-old woman diagnosed with Chronic Fatigue Syndrome was advised by her physician to continue to work because inactivity seemed to worsen her symptoms and mood. She disregarded his advice, leaving her job of 15 years, and crippling the family finances. Millon (1999) has suggested that somatization, hypochondriasis, and pain disorders all reflect the same psychic process of transforming ambivalent, conflicted feelings—often anger—into bodily symptoms. The influence of the somatizing patient's physical symptoms on his or her interpersonal relationships is undeniable. Physical complaints can effectively control the behavior of a loved one and induce guilt in others. A significant number of medical patients with somatization disorders have few social ties (this is particularly true if they are elderly), thus the relationship with the physician assumes a high degree of importance, and medical attention serves to substitute for relationships with family and friends.

In the era of managed health care, somatoform disorders are ultimately a public health problem, in that excessive amounts of money are spent for medical procedures, examinations, and laboratory tests in an effort to find the elusive medical explanation for a patient's somatic complaints. The function of medical attention-seeking is typically the feeling of being cared for, receiving attention, and/or reducing anxiety. The difficulty for the physician is that many somatic complaints have some degree of physiological basis, but personality factors exaggerate or exacerbate the organic pathology. Many medical patients who don't meet diagnostic criteria for somatoform disorders still have subthreshold symptoms that cause significant distress. Successful treatment of such patients by a psychotherapist has the goal of helping a patient "increase awareness of the interplay between behavior, mood, and physical distress and, in turn, the relationship of these dimensions to one's social and physical environment" (DeGood, 1983, p. 577). Ultimately, successful treatment of somatoform disorders depends on the physician's ability to help the patient think more broadly about how to interpret his or her symptoms and accept a referral to a mental health professional if the problem does not remit.

COPING WITH ILLNESS

The majority of psychotherapy work done with medical patients has focused on helping people with adjustment and end-of-life issues, particular in the field of cancer treatment. *Diathesis,* a term often used in the medical literature, refers to a vulnerability or predisposition to disease. Diathesis-stress models (Coyne & Whiffen, 1995), in which personality is the diathesis and medical illness is the stress, are useful in explaining the wide variability in ability to cope with disease. In some individuals, a diagnosis of cancer or heart disease may weaken a vulnerable personality organization, causing the person to become cognitively and emotionally overwhelmed. In other people, a life-threatening medical diagnosis serves to provide sufficient emotional arousal such that they are able to conquer longstanding behavior patterns, such as reluctance to exercise, that were heretofore resistant to change. All personality traits can become more exaggerated with the stress of a medical illness. Depressive individuals may become more withdrawn; obsessives, more anxious; patients with disorders of the self will be more vulnerable to fragmentation. The following is an example of a patient with dependent, depressive, and passive-aggressive personality traits, who was diagnosed with cancer.

The patient, who was in her late 50s, was accompanied by her husband, who spoke for her during the clinical interview. She had no significant psychiatric history, and her oncologist had reassured her that her medical condition was stable, with no metastases or evidence of cancer. She was very depressed and had stopped eating. Her husband was preoccupied with his wife's eating patterns and managing her medical treatment. At an earlier point in the acute phase of her treatment, his style was appropriate and appreciated by the patient, but at this stage he was controlling and extremely anxious. She took a passive approach to his overinvolvement, expressing her anger by refusing to eat. She recounted a 23-year marriage with numerous examples of not asserting herself, repressing her anger, and a lifelong struggle with depression. The medical staff threatened to give her a feeding tube and referred her for psychiatric evaluation. A combination of pharmacotherapy, individual therapy, and marital therapy were employed concurrently to treat the patient's depressed mood, anorexia, and marital issues. Individual therapy focused on building self-esteem and helping the patient to express her anger toward her husband directly, rather than by refusing to eat. Marital therapy focused on the couple's mutual difficulties in expressing anger, the patient's fear of dying, and the husband's fear of being left alone.

Supportive psychotherapy designed to help the patient regain psychological equilibrium after medical diagnosis may miss an opportunity, especially when the patient has had a longstanding self-defeating personality pattern. A life-threatening health crisis can serve as a catalyst, forcing the person's immature coping strategies against an onslaught of stressors such as medical procedures, office visits, interruptions to work, pain, and existential anxiety. The experience of anxiety is essential for behavior change, yet too much anxiety inevitably gives rise to psychological defenses at the cost of more adaptive functioning. Too little anxiety allows the person to maintain a homeostatic balance but provides no motivation for behavior change. For example, a 49-year-old man with a longstanding weight problem was diagnosed with diabetes, hypertension, and, eventually, congestive heart disease. Though his weight increased over a 15-year period to more than 400 pounds, he was hospitalized for three weeks, and his physician noted that he could not return to work, he had difficulty thinking of himself as "a person who is sick." On further exploration, the patient revealed that he had always believed he was going to die at a young age (his older brother had died in his 20s). The patient's unconscious anxiety about dying young perpetuated his denial about his deteriorating physical health. In addition, though this patient often sought out the advice of his cardiologist, he had a lifelong, ego-syntonic pattern of defying authority figures. Psychotherapy used a psychodynamically oriented emphasis on conflict resolution (coming to terms with the death of the brother and the patient's place in his family of origin), behavioral change techniques (exercise, joining Weight Watchers, and dietary counseling), and interviewing techniques designed to assist the patient in exploring a longstanding pattern of defying authority figures and his fear of dying prematurely. In hindsight, multiple modalities (cardiologist, group support from Weight Watchers, dietician, and psychotherapist) had a synergistic effect and provided the patient with many opportunities to test new ways of relating to authority figures and food.

With enough stress, each of us could be reduced to our lowest level of functioning. Yet in some instances, severe health problems can transfigure some individuals to achieve a new level of emotional well-being and stability. Helping restore patients to a previous level of functioning sets the therapeutic bar too low in many instances. The challenge for the psychotherapist is to use a medical crisis as a window of opportunity to help patients make personality change.

The case example that follows illustrates how one individual's personality organization is linked to each of the areas outlined previously: health risk behaviors, somatic complaints, and adjustment to heart attack. Over a two-year period, multiple factors contributed to a reorganization of his personality and improvement in his physical well-being. The patient was treated with psychotherapy by me, and my office is located in the department of cardiology at the same hospital where he was treated for his cardiac problems.

CLINICAL CASE EXAMPLE

Paul was a 49-year-old patient who had a heart attack 15 months before seeking therapy. On first presentation, he looked to me like a corpse. He was thin to the point of being skeletal, and his forehead was etched in a permanent scowl. His hands moved expressively as he spoke, often punching the air to make a point. He was wary and mistrustful. He had stopped drinking and smoking cigarettes immediately after the heart attack 15 months prior. I asked him to elaborate on this.

There was a moment, he reported, of clarity. It wasn't quite an epiphany, but it felt like a moment of revelation, where he understood, without a doubt, for him, there would be no next time. He visualized his friends, who he said were more like fellow drunks, ensconced on their bar stools, chain-smoking. The moment of clarity occurred to him while lying on the table undergoing cardiac catheterization (also called coronary angiography), a process in which dye is injected into the coronary arteries via a catheter inserted through the femoral artery in the groin. The angiographer is able to locate the precise site of any coronary artery narrowing or obstructions as the patient lies awake on the table. In Paul's case, three atherosclerotic plaques, the genesis of future heart attacks, were revealed. He had suffered a myocardial infarction (heart attack) the day before, but his cardiologist assured him minimal damage was done to the heart muscle.

From Paul's perspective, the outcome of his life, previously unknown and uncontemplated, was evident. When asked to elaborate, he described his future with certainty. He would feel crushing chest pain and death would come quickly. His wife, he fantasized, would be shocked, but she had nagged him for decades to quit drinking and smoking. She would be distraught but still capable of mentally calculating his life insurance proceeds. While being prodded by a tense angiographer, whom he felt sure blamed him for his own illness, Paul decided to stop drinking and smoking. He had little will to live and no hope for the future, but a sense of defiance motivated him to put death off a while longer.

CLINICAL PRESENTATION

Fifteen months after the heart attack, Paul wondered aloud what the point was of quitting drinking and smoking. He was sober, nicotine-free, and had trimmed his fat intake to less than 25%. His cardiologist pronounced him healthy and took him off all but two of his medicines. Yet, as more time went on, he felt chest pain with no organic cause. On two occasions, he had driven to the emergency room, only to be humiliated in finding out that he wasn't having a heart attack. Subsequently, his cardiologist sent him to me for stress management.

Paul was an outwardly angry patient who scowled and made sarcastic remarks to the therapist. His day-to-day existence consisted of rising early each day to oversee a business he owned in partnership with his father. Before the day began, he felt a familiar tightening of the chest and gut, as he contemplated how his father might provoke him. He had worked in businesses owned by his father since he dropped out of high school at age 17. Over time, he assumed all of the responsibility of running the business but never owned the majority of it. He referred to his father as the "Old Man."

In his 30s, Paul had married a successful businesswoman who urged him to get out from under the "Old Man." But he endured, hoping that, as promised, his father would retire at age 60. His father's 60th and 70th birthdays passed, and although he gave over all day-to-day responsibilities to Paul, he retained the majority share of the business. As Paul himself approached 50 and his father showed no sign of letting go, the patient's bitterness was impossible to contain. Getting drunk each night for close to 30 years had helped him suppress his resentment. But with one heart attack behind him and no alcohol or nicotine to diffuse his rage, he felt ready to explode. Daily, his chest pain worsened. Getting drunk had served as a defense against Paul's rage for all of his adult life before the heart attack. Without the defensive shield provided by alcohol, Paul's anger gave rise to anxiety, which expressed itself somatically with chest pain.

The "Old Man," according to Paul, was a "controlling, manipulative, son-of-a-bitch." He was verbally and physically abusive to Paul and his four younger siblings during their childhood. With a look of self-contempt, Paul described the pattern, "Just when I'm ready to cut him off forever, he sucks up to me and says what I want to hear, and I live for that compliment. I mean, I really live for him to say something nice to me. It happens maybe once every three years." Each time Paul reached a breaking point, his father would, with sadistic precision, find the exact words to validate his son and keep him entrapped.

Paul and his wife were inseparable but fought bitterly. "We both," he said sadly, "have horrible fathers and so we have a lot of bad dad days." During any given skirmish, curses were exchanged, doors slammed, and each partner tried to destroy the other's self-esteem. Paul's mother was a self-sacrificing woman who enabled her husband. She endured the brunt of his wrath, but minimized the abuse to her children.

DIAGNOSTIC FORMULATION

At first presentation, Paul had symptoms of anxiety and longstanding depression on Axis I, meeting criteria for Dysthymia. He had endorsed some of the items on the somatization subscale of the *Brief Symptom Inventory* (Deragotis, 1993) and met Axis I criteria for Pain Disorder associated with both psychological factors and a general medical condition. On Axis II, Paul had passive-aggressive, depressive, and narcissistic traits. Hostility and dominance, both pathological elements of the Type A behavior pattern, were evident during the initial clinical interview. Hostility is a construct involving the repression or suppression of anger manifested as contempt and scorn; behaviors that are verbally or physically aggressive; and cognitions of cynicism, mistrust, and perceiving others to be aggressive (Smith & Ruiz, 2002). Hostile people have lower social support and are more susceptible to cardiovascular and neuroendocrine reactivity in a variety of stressful situations (Smith & Ruiz, 2002). Paul readily admitted to feeling angry most of the time, having frequent verbally abusive fights with his wife and father, and the belief that most people were really out for themselves. Initially, Paul, like most people, equated arguing and yelling with anger. In reality, he was unable to experience his anger without building up so much tension that he would discharge it in an explosive manner. Paul's core pathology was expressed by the belief that trusting others would lead to exploitation, anger that could be quickly triggered by narcissistic injury, and addictive behaviors that served to defend against his rage.

In the initial interview, Paul attempted to take a dominant position by questioning the need to complete the *Brief Symptom Inventory* and assuming an oppositional stance. He interrupted and talked over the therapist when he wanted to express a point. In the original Western Collaborative Group studies of Type A behavior, dominance was identified as an element of Type A behavior that is distinct from hostility and independently predicts coronary heart disease (Houston, Babyak, Chesney, Black, & Ragland, 1997). Several studies suggest that dominance is linked to the development of coronary heart disease. Dominance involves efforts to exert interpersonal control over others. Paul struggled between oppositional defiance and submission in his relationships with his father, wife, and medical caregivers. His struggles with interpersonal control seemed linked to the degree of control that his father exerted over him. As a child, he hated his "phony" teachers who, he felt sure, got their kicks by controlling him. In his business, he portrayed himself as an exacting but fair boss, who wanted an honest day's work from his employees. Managing staff provided one outlet for Paul's wish to dominate. But he perceived his father and, to a lesser degree, his wife, as figures to be outsmarted. In his encounters with his father, he had perfected the passive-aggressive personality style. The better part of a morning might be spent planning "dummy errands" on which to send the "Old Man" and efforts to thwart his control of the finances. At home, he would deliberately ignore his wife's request to take care of household chores. This style provoked her resentment and exacerbated the couple's pattern of building up anger and discharging it with loud, argumentative exchanges.

Paul's self-destructive personality pattern was partially expressed throughout most of his adult life with his drinking and smoking. There is abundant literature describing the comorbid personality pathology of people with addictive disorders (Miller & Brown, 1997). The drinking and smoking in turn contributed to the development of heart disease. Chronically elevated blood pressure combined with an unrelenting hostile mood may also have played a contributing role in the disease progression.

TREATMENT PROCESS

The focus of Paul's therapy, eleven 45-minute sessions in eight months, was on his anger toward his father. When his anger was contacted, it felt to him like a murderous rage. From the second session of therapy, he was able to freely fantasize pummeling his father to death. He felt sickened by the guilt afterward and would remark, "I bet you are thinking I'm one sick pup." Davanloo (1980), as well as later generations of writers (McCullough Vaillant, 1997), have described the guilt associated with sadistic, murderous rage as crippling. The adaptive, evolutionary nature of guilt is clear: It acts as an internal warning system to alert the self that an action or impulse is wrong and serves an inhibitory function (Lewis, 1992). Guilt is an important cause of self-destructive personality patterns (Magnavita, 1997). In Paul's case, it seemed likely that massive guilt contributed to his need to keep punishing himself by drinking, smoking, and continuing to keep himself yoked to his father in the business. Contacting Paul's unconscious guilt was a painful but necessary step in the psychotherapeutic process. The experience of such guilt is critical to affective restructuring and improved tolerance for anger.

Interventions with Paul most often consisted of defensive restructuring as described in *Short-Term Dynamic Therapy* (Davanloo, 1980). *Defensive restructuring* refers to efforts by the therapist to bring maladaptive coping patterns (defenses) to the patient's attention to allow the patient full expression of warded-off emotion. Defensive restructuring is grounded in the theoretical principle that the psyche seeks to maintain a homeostatic balance among anxiety, defense, and feeling (or impulse, when the feeling is so sudden and fleeting that it can't be described as such). David Malan (1976) has described impulse/feeling, defense, and anxiety as the three corners of the "Triangle of Conflict." Though the "Triangle of Conflict" is rooted in a psychodynamically oriented conflict-resolution model, the construct can actually integrate multiple therapeutic modalities (McCullough Vaillant, 1997). For example, gestalt techniques are often used in short-term dynamic therapy to help patients to describe the physiological experience of the impulse or feeling. A therapist might say, "You just made a fist. What do you feel in your arm right now?" Cognitive techniques are useful in refuting anxiety-driven maladaptive beliefs. The therapist might ask, "What do you think would happen if you allowed yourself to cry?" This is often followed with the response, "I wouldn't be able to stop," from patients who have been previously unable to contact sadness or grief. In Paul's case, many interventions were aimed at interrupting him to clarify the nature of his defenses and the hostile feelings, behaviors, and thoughts he expressed. Interruptions had the effect of generating more intense anger toward the therapist, which was then identified and linked to his other experiences with authority figures. In the initial therapy session, it was pointed out that Paul had a habit of talking over the therapist and attempting to dominate the session. When repeatedly brought to his awareness, he responded positively and was able to develop and continue a strong collaborative alliance throughout the course of his treatment.

Between sessions, Paul worked hard to extricate himself from his father's partnership. Having invested more than 30 years, he wasn't willing to simply walk away from the business. His father wouldn't allow himself to be bought out. He enlisted a lawyer and accountant and eventually succeeded in mediating a deal that would leave Paul free of his father's day-to-day presence. His father demanded exorbitant sums of money until Paul threatened to sell out his own share. His father put up quite a fight and tried without success to insert legal clauses into the contract designed to guarantee himself daily contact with Paul.

Identifying Paul's sadism and passive-aggressive interpersonal style by continuing to bring it to his awareness was painful but ultimately liberating for him. The therapist also made extensive use of interventions aimed at improving his poor self-esteem and strengthening his positive attachments. Integrated therapy approaches usually try to balance interventions designed to resolve intrapsychic conflict (e.g., defense analysis) with interventions designed to resolve deficits of the self (e.g., supportive affirmation; McCullough Vaillant, 1997). Over time, Paul began to express positive and negative feelings to his wife in a more direct manner. Fortified by the backup of the accountant, the lawyer, the therapist, and the cardiologist, he began to express his feelings toward his father. He vacillated for several months between intense anger and pity toward his father.

Paul's chest pain remitted by the second session of therapy as the therapist focused on his anger. In contrast to a patient with somatization disorder, Paul did not have a longstanding history of many physical symptoms in various parts of the body. He had developed chest pain only after he quit smoking and drinking and was left with no effective method of coping with anger and guilt toward his father. His memory of the trauma of the recent heart attack made it likely that his anxiety would get channeled through somatic pathways and experienced as chest pain. It would be unlikely that a patient with somatization disorder would experience a comprehensive, long-lasting improvement in physical complaints so quickly in the psychotherapeutic process. Patients with somatization disorder are often resistant to the notion that psychological factors cause or exacerbate their medical condition. They may also have an unconscious need to seek attention or caregiving. Paul was open to the idea that his chest pain was "stress-related" though he initially showed little curiosity about his own inner world. In addition, his mistrust of authority figures, including medical professionals, made them unlikely targets for solicitation of attention. Paul showed a great hunger for information on the physiology of the heart. While waiting for the therapist, he always chose to read one of the medical cardiology journals on the bookshelf in the waiting area, rather than the wide array of newspapers and magazines available for patients. Before therapy, Paul had viewed his life as meaningless and hopeless, but early on in the process he reported a new sense of productivity and purpose. His wife was already in individual therapy and was supportive of his efforts. Their communication and conflict resolution skills improved.

Paul's mother died suddenly of cancer attributable to cigarette smoking toward the end of his treatment. He was able to grieve her death. Initially, he was shocked that the time from diagnosis to death was only a few weeks. He expressed anger that his father made little effort to acknowledge his mother's dying by spending time with her or helping to make hospice arrangements. At the same time, he experienced some positive memories of his mother's caretaking as well as a deep sadness that her whole life had been "under the thumb" of his father. In particular, Paul was enraged that while his mother was dying, his father was openly seeing a woman with whom he had a longstanding extramarital affair. Paul initially blamed his father for his mother's death but later came to blame her cigarette smoking. He empathized with her tobacco addiction, and his grief motivated him to remain abstinent from smoking. Paul's tenacity was evident during therapy. The shadowy ghost of a younger, softer, more vulnerable Paul occasionally surfaced, along with his sadness at having spent so many years in misery.

MECHANISMS OF CHANGE

A heightened awareness of Paul's own mortality with the emergence of existential or death anxiety was the most critical element that laid the foundation for personality change. His heart attack led to an emotional crisis, motivating him to quit smoking and drinking. Both of these addictive behaviors had helped him to cope with negative emotions throughout his life. Without smoking and drinking, Paul was left with inadequate coping mechanisms that led him to express his distress partially through somatic channels.

THE IMPORTANCE OF A TEAM APPROACH

Patient care is inevitably improved when multiple caregivers deliver the same message. In his emergency room visits, Paul received feedback from both nurses and physicians that was echoed by his own cardiologist. After all potential medical causes have been ruled out, his cardiologist, a diplomatic and psychologically astute caregiver, helped Paul to consider the possibility that his chest pain was "stress-related" and referred him to the therapist. For patients to consider the possibility that psychological factors contribute to physical complaints, the medical system must change and educate itself in this regard as well. Too often, it is difficult for health care providers to present a unified team approach because of the time commitment involved with communicating with other disciplines. Moreover, the psychological-mindedness of the medical provider, in large part, dictates whether psychological factors are considered in formulating a diagnosis or treatment plan. Medical providers who have had a positive experience with mental health professionals are more likely to make referrals for psychotherapy. Yet even when medical providers want to refer patients for psychotherapy, there are significant economic, insurance, and other logistical barriers to overcome. Despite these hurdles, medical schools currently give more physicians training about psychological issues than in previous decades. As personality theory continues to become more integrated into mainstream psychotherapeutic approaches, awareness will likely carry over to the medical professions as well.

Paul's treatment was limited to just 11 sessions but was, by his report and therapist observation in the follow-up interview, highly effective. Paul's symptoms of anxiety, depression, and chest pain were not evident at follow-up. He was able to express anger and affection freely toward his wife and in therapy sessions. His relationship with his wife was more emotionally intimate, and he reported that their sexual relationship was very satisfying. At work, Paul felt a greater sense of confidence and happiness in owning the entire business. His relationships with his staff at work also improved, and he took pains not to repeat personnel management mistakes that he had observed in his father. Paul made several business decisions that rendered him financially very well off. He and his wife took pleasure in building a new home. Paul quit drinking and smoking on his own before coming to therapy and did not relapse at all. Paul's relationship with his father improved once they severed the business relationship. His father "dropped in" at work about once a week, but Paul reported not feeling bothered by this and sometimes enjoying his company. Factors that promoted change during therapy included:

- Early formation of a strong positive therapeutic alliance.
- Intense focus on repressed anger manifested as hostile disturbance from the first session of therapy.
- The presence of a supportive spouse.
- Intermittent psychotherapy sessions, which were agreed on by both therapist and patient and stretched out over eight months.
- Working through of three major current conflicts during therapy:
    1. Freeing himself from the entrapment of an enmeshed use-abuse relationship with his father, which allowed him to negotiate a business agreement to purchase the business.
    2. Existential crisis brought on by the heart attack.
    3. Grief over the death of his mother and sadness at never having a close relationship with either parent.

As this case illustrates, there is a multidirectional, multidimensional relationship between physical well-being and personality organization. When the stress of a health problem exceeds the capacity of the individual to cope effectively, it creates an untenable intrapsychic condition that can lead to somatic reactivity. Though self-destructive, Paul's drinking and smoking had a great adaptive function throughout all of his adult life in helping him to dissociate from his feelings toward his father. The combination of removing these two important defensive ways of dealing with his negative feelings, plus the acute awareness of his own mortality brought on by his heart attack, left Paul with levels of anxiety that exceeded his coping abilities. Though speculative, it seems likely that continued experience of such anxiety without psychological intervention would have eventually led to relapse to drinking, smoking, or both because addictive behaviors serve an important anxiety-regulating function (Dornelas & Thompson, 2002).

The breakdown of physical health creates a condition where human beings must either accept or deny the eventuality of death. In this heightened state of awareness or repression of our own mortality, we move up or down on the continuum of psychological differentiation outlined by Bowen (1978). David Schnarch (1991) uses the Bowenian concept of differentiation to treat sexual and marital dysfunction in a model he has termed the "sexual crucible." A crucible is a vessel in which raw material is transformed into a different final product. An external pressure (e.g., heat) is applied to the vessel, which must be sufficiently nonreactive so as to contain the catalytic process. This conceptual model also has some relevance to personality and illness. When people with maladaptive personality patterns experience a breakdown in their physical well-being, accompanied by an acute awareness of the finiteness of their life, they will either experience a strengthened personality organization or fragmentation. In the most optimal outcome, health problems can create an external pressure whereby the person experiences the paradoxical duality of "the acute experience of self as the center of one's phenomenological universe, and the equally acute experience of self as finite, inextricably separate, and on the periphery of a much larger whole" (p. 216). This acute existential awareness can precipitate permanent personality change, affecting the dimensions of self-image, cognition, and interpersonal relationships.

THERAPEUTIC CHALLENGES

The challenges of trying to address characterological issues with medical patients are numerous. It is difficult for physicians working in conventional third-party reimbursement systems to abandon the biomedical model that relies on diagnosed pathology, because diagnosis is essential for payment. Biopsychosocial models exist in the theoretical realm but are not truly incorporated into mainstream medicine. Holistic, multifaceted models incorporating psychological, medical, and lifestyle interventions have been evaluated (Billings, Scherwitz, Sullivan, Sparler, & Ornish, 1996), but there has been little integration of such models into the delivery of routine primary care.

Medical providers' impressions of the patient's personality undoubtedly impact communication with the patient. Yet, there is no good method for health care providers to incorporate information about personality into their diagnosis. Although the *DSM* (APA, 2000) does have a multiaxial assessment system, utilization of the *DSM* requires mental health training. Even mental health providers rarely diagnose medical patients on Axis II. There are areas of health care that routinely employ mental health professionals (i.e., consultation-liaison psychiatry, neurology, and rehabilitation), but those specialty providers rarely diagnose personality disorders. The current *DSM* is helpful but inadequate for use in the primary care setting.

There are many valid reasons that personality is not assessed with medical patients, including: limitations of the *DSM*, lack of formal training in personality theory, insufficient time to formulate a diagnosis, and stigma associated with a diagnosis of personality pathology. In addition, health care professionals have different epistemological stances from mental health providers; that is, those in the medical setting are trained in problem-oriented interventions whereas those in the mental health field are typically trained in process-oriented therapies (Pace, Chaney, Mullins, & Olson, 1995). Quick solutions are rarely forthcoming from mental health professionals. The 5 to 15 minutes allotted for medical office visits would be insufficient for even the most clinically astute of psychotherapists to render a diagnosis on Axis II. Yet, because personality pathology is by definition a *historical* diagnosis, health care professionals who have a unique opportunity to observe patients in multiple visits over time often do draw conclusions about the patient's personality. The language used by the physician may have little advantage over the layman's verbiage (e.g., "crazy," "demanding," "hypochondriacal") and does little to guide intervention. An integrated approach that incorporates personality factors into diagnostic formulation might help to guide more effective interventions for health promotion, treating somatoform disorders, and aiding medical patients in adjusting to illness.

SUMMARY AND CONCLUSIONS

We are challenged to help people with medical problems examine the interplay between their personality organization and physical health. However, it is evident that personality pathology is expressed in the medical arena through risky health practices, somatic complaints, and psychological sequelae of medical illness. The medical care system offers more opportunity for personality-guided interventions than the mental health system, simply because it is more accessible to people. Regardless of what mental health providers do to raise awareness and reduce the stigma, patients are far more likely to visit their primary care physician rather than a mental health professional for problems that are psychological in nature (Magill & Garrett, 1988).

The medical care system already has considerable difficulty in helping the disproportionate numbers of medical patients who visit their primary care physician for anxiety and depression. Patients who meet criteria for Axis I disorders are not typically given optimal treatment in the primary care setting; thus, you might well ask: Why complicate the picture further by suggesting that personality ought to be considered? The natural evolution of medical treatment will eventually bring more attention to the impact of personality on physical health for several reasons:

1. Personality pathology is a cause of high medical service utilization, and escalating health care costs will eventually precipitate a demand for cost effectiveness studies of this area.
2. Including personality factors in diagnostic formulation is synonymous with the practice of holistic medicine, an area that has developed exponentially during the past 20 years in Western health care systems.
3. It is virtually impossible to produce longstanding change in risky health behaviors without patient awareness of the personality traits that jeopardize his or her health. Because the leading causes of disease are largely preventable and attributable to behavior, methods of changing health risk behaviors will assume an even greater priority to policymakers in the future.

Most psychotherapists fall between two extremes on the continuum of belief about whether personality can change. At one end, there is the perspective that personality is relatively immutable and true personality change is rare indeed. At the other end of the continuum, proponents have argued that *all* psychotherapy is about personality change, and major life events (e.g., a heart attack) can cause permanent character restructuring. It is my perspective that personality can change, and most psychotherapy patients would be better served if they had therapists who helped them try to change their personalities. The therapist who is most successful at assisting patients in making character change does so by restructuring psychological defenses and ability to process affect (Magnavita, 1997; McCullough Vaillant, 1997). Personality change can be viewed from many dimensions (e.g., interpersonal relationships, cognitions, self-image), and it is reasonable to assume that improved physical health is another aspect of well-being that could be improved through a personality-guided intervention. Greater ability to directly express emotion without defensive responding decreases the need to cope with anxiety through addictive behaviors or via somatic channels. Character change is achieved when "defensive responding is not only increased (when deficient) or reduced (when excessive) but also qualitatively changed from a more maladaptive, immature level of response to a more adaptive, mature response" (McCullough Vaillant, 1997, p. 45). The same personality-guided interventions that have been developed primarily for mental health outpatients and are well articulated in this book have great relevance to medical patients. We are challenged to apply personality-guided therapies to address a problem often untouched in traditional psychotherapy—the physical health and illness of our patients.

REFERENCES

American Psychiatric Association. (2000). *Diagnostic and statistical manual of mental disorders* (4th ed., text rev.). Washington, DC: Author.

Billings, J. H., Scherwitz, L. W., Sullivan, R., Sparler, S., & Ornish, D. M. (1996). The Lifestyle Heart Trial: Comprehensive treatment and group support therapy. In R. Allan & S. Scheidt (Eds.), *Heart and mind: The practice of cardiac psychology* (pp. 233–253). Washington, DC: American Psychological Association.

Blankenstein, A. H., van der Horst, H. E., Schilte, A. F., de Vries, D., Zaat, J. O. M., Knottnerus, A., et al. (2002). Development and feasibility of a modified reattribution model for somatising patients, applied by their own general practitioners. *Patient Education and Counseling, 47,* 229–235.

Bowen, M. (1978). *Family therapy in clinical practice.* New York: Aronson.

Cohen, S., & Wills, T. A. (1985). Stress, social support and the buffering hypothesis. *Psychological Bulletin, 98,* 310–357.

Coyne, J. C., & Whiffen, V. E. (1995). Issues in personality as diathesis for depression: The case of sociotropy-dependency and autonomy-self-criticism. *Psychological Bulletin, 118,* 358–378.

Davanloo, H. (1980). *Short-term dynamic psychotherapy.* Northvale, NJ: Aronson.

DeGood, D. E. (1983). Reducing medical patients' reluctance to participate in psychological therapies: The initial session. *Professional Psychology: Research and Practice, 14,* 570–579.

Deragotis, L. R. (1993). *BSI: Brief Symptom Inventory Administration, Scoring and Procedures Manual.* Minneapolis, MN: National Computer Systems.

Dornelas, E. A., & Magnavita, J. J. (2001). High impact therapy for smoking cessation. *Journal of Clinical Psychology, 57,* 1311–1322.

Dornelas, E. A., & Thompson, P. D. (2002). Perspectives from health psychology: Psychodynamic treatment for cardiac patients. In J. J. Magnavita (Ed.), *Comprehensive handbook of psychotherapy: Psychodynamic/object relations* (Vol. 1, pp. 549–564). Hoboken, NJ: Wiley.

Engel, G. L. (1977). The need for a new medical model: A challenge for biomedicine. *Science, 196,* 129–136.

Eysenck, H. J., & Eysenck, S. B. (1983). Recent advances: The cross-cultural study of personality. In J. N. Butcher & C. D. Spielberger (Eds.), *Advances in personality assessment* (Vol. 2, pp. 41–72). Hillsdale, NJ: Erlbaum.

Fingerhut, L. A., Kleinman, J. C., & Kendrick, J. S. (1990). Smoking before, during and after pregnancy. *American Journal of Public Health, 80,* 541–544.

Hall, S. M., Munoz, R. F., Reus, V. I., & Sees, K. L. (1993). Nicotine, negative affect and depression. *Journal of Consulting and Clinical Psychology, 61,* 761–767.

Houston, B. K., Babyak, M. A., Chesney, M. A., Black, G., & Ragland, D. R. (1997). Social dominance and 22-year all cause mortality in men. *Psychosomatic Medicine, 59,* 5–12.

Johnson, S. M. (1994). *Character styles.* New York: Norton.

Lewis, M. (1992). *Shame: The exposed self.* New York: Free Press.

Lipkus, I. M., Barefoot, J. C., Williams, R. B., & Siegler, I. C. (1994). Personality measures as predictors of smoking initiation and cessation in the UNC Alumni Heart Study. *Health Psychology, 13,* 149–155.

Loehlin, J. C. (1982). Are personality traits differentially heritable? *Behavior Genetics, 12,* 417–428.

Looper, K. J., & Kirmayer, L. J. (2002). Behavioral medicine approaches to somatoform disorders. *Journal of Counseling and Clinical Psychology, 70,* 810–827.

Magill, M. K., & Garrett, R. W. (1988). Behavioral and psychiatric problems. In R. B. Taylor (Ed.), *Family medicine* (3rd ed., pp. 534–562). New York: Springer-Verlag.

Magnavita, J. J. (1997). *Restructuring personality disorders: A short-term dynamic approach.* New York: Guilford Press.

Malan, D. H. (1976). *The frontier of brief psychotherapy: An example of the convergence of research and clinical practice.* New York: Plenum Medical.

Miller, W. R., & Brown, S. A. (1997). Why psychologists should treat alcohol and drug problems. *American Psychologist, 52,* 1269–1279.

Millon, T. (1999). *Personality-guided therapy.* New York: Wiley.

McCullough Vaillant, L. (1997). *Changing character: Short-term anxiety-regulating psychotherapy for restructuring defenses, affects, and attachment.* New York: Basic Books.

McWilliams, N. (1994). *Psychoanalytical diagnosis: Understanding personality structure in the clinical process.* New York: Guilford Press.

Pace, T. M., Chaney, J. M., Mullins, L. L., & Olson, R. A. (1995). Psychological consultation with primary care physicians: Obstacles and opportunities in the medical setting. *Professional Psychology: Research and Practice, 26*(2), 123–131.

Sarafino, E. P. (1994). *Health psychology: Biopsychosocial interactions* (2nd ed.). New York: Wiley.

Schnarch, D. (1991). *Constructing the sexual crucible: An integration of sexual and marital therapy.* New York: Norton.

Smith, T. W., & Ruiz, J. M. (2002). Psychosocial influences on the development and course of coronary heart disease: Current status and implications for research and practice. *Journal of Consulting and Clinical Psychology, 70,* 548–568.

Tyrer, P., Gunderson, J., Lyons, M., & Tohen, M. (1997). Extent of comorbidity between mental states and personality disorders. *Journal of Personality Disorders, 11,* 242–259.

Winston, A., & Winston, B. (2002). *Handbook of integrated short-term psychotherapy.* Washington, DC: American Psychiatric Press.

CHAPTER 20

The Role of Trauma, Memory, Neurobiology, and the Self in the Formation of Personality Disorders

Mark R. Elin

Memory brought madness with it, and when I thought of what had passed, a real insanity possessed me; sometimes I was furious and burned with rage; sometimes low and despondent.

—Spoken by the monster Frankenstein. (Shelley, 1978, p. 181)

MEMORY IS AT the heart of personality. This chapter presents a theory for understanding personality disorders based on my previously described ideas about self-memory, a deeply imbedded meaning-making system that works with the cognitive and affective systems to memorialize the self and give it a sense of existence (Elin, in Appelbaum, Uyehara, & Elin, 1997). Under normal developmental conditions, self-memory works with a person's cognitive and affective systems to make meaning of the world. During trauma, this meaning-making process can be disrupted. Self-memory can separate from cognition and/or affect during trauma, causing a range of dissociative symptoms. Over time, dissociation can result in a disordered personality, a developmental process highlighted in this chapter through actual case studies, examples from film and literature, and a discussion of the neurobiology of trauma.

Without self-memory, there would be no I, it, or other. In the immortal words of Popeye the Sailor Man, "I am what I am and that's all that I am." In a more serious vein, God alluded to the concept of self-memory when he said to Moses, "I am who I am." Self-memory is so magnetic a force that writers, artists, and philosophers have for centuries speculated about the relationships among the self, cognition, and affect. In *The Divine Comedy,* Dante explores the relationship among memory, cognition, and affect: "For when our intellect draws near its goal, and fathoms to the depths of its desires, the memory is powerless to follow" (Alighieri, 1984, p. 1). In

443

his attempt to explain the powerful relationship between cognition and the self, the French philosopher Rene Descartes penned the famous line, "Cognito ergo sum (I think therefore I am)."

Holocaust survivors, in their autobiographical accounts, talk about how they were forced to separate their self and cognitive systems from each other to survive the severe traumas they experienced. Charlotte Delbo, a survivor of Auschwitz, wrote: "[I] can talk to you about Auschwitz without exhibiting or registering any anxiety or emotion. Because when I talk to you about Auschwitz, it is not from deep memory that my words issue. They come from external memory, if I may put it that way, from intellectual memory, the memory connected with the thinking process" (Delbo, 1990, p. 1).

A DESCRIPTION OF SELF-MEMORY

The self-memory system can be located within deep levels of time and space. It has its own neurobiology, which is described later in the chapter. There are an almost infinite number of memory systems (parallel information distributive systems) contained within self-memory. These memory systems range from moral, linguistic, and gastronomic memories to movement and sensory memories. We all have art and music memories, love and attunement memories, media and technological memories, and familial and cultural memories. We have aesthetic memories. We have math and language memories, visual and auditory memories, and pain and illness memories. We have affective memories. We have memories of our dreams and fantasies; we even have memories of our memories.

During the Holocaust, a group of Jewish women in a concentration camp used their gastronomic and sensory memories as a survival mechanism; starved almost to death, they spent hours recalling their traditional and religious recipes, which they wrote down on scraps of paper. Unable to nourish their bodies, they nourished their memories about food and taste. Many years later, the scraps of paper were recovered and the women's recipes gathered into a cookbook. Because of the traumatic conditions under which they lived, some of the women's memories were dissociated from cognitive memory: Many of the recipes in the cookbook lack key ingredients (De Silva, 1996).

All that enters the self-memory system from birth to death is memorialized. Self-memory's lifelong task is integration: all memory systems within the container of self-memory to make meaning of the world. Adult personality is the culmination and expression of self-memory's meaning-making system. In other words, each person's personality is a unique display of where and how dissociations have occurred over the course of development. By disrupting meaning-making processes during crucial developmental benchmarks, trauma and dissociation can create severely disordered personalities. Whether a personality disorder will develop in a certain individual is the result of numerous factors, including the trauma victim's stage of development, genetics, personal resilience, family dynamics, support systems, cultural norms, and the timing and nature of the trauma.

This chapter provides examples from art, film, literature, and actual case studies to show how the development of personality disorders is related to the integrity of the self-memory system. Case studies of Borderline, Sociopathic, and Obsessive-Compulsive Disorder (OCD) patients; the short stories of horror writer Edgar Allen Poe; and fictional characters from film and television are used to illustrate the model. Cultural, familial, and psychological factors that led Michael Corleone (Al Pacino) to develop a severe psychopathic personality disorder in the *Godfather* film trilogy is analyzed.

Ideas presented in this chapter about self-memory draw from Freud's (1915/1957, 1925) idea of the unconscious, Kohut's ideas of the self (1977), Kielstrom's (1987) writings about the cognitive unconscious, and existential ideas about the soul (Moore, 1994). The theory advanced in this chapter places self-memory neurobiologically and psychodynamically on an equal footing with all other information processing systems. Building on the ideas of Epstein (1973, 1985, 1994) and others, I have previously described self-memory as a meaning-making system, which memorializes the self and gives it a sense of existence and meaning (Elin, in Appelbaum et al., 1997).

Self-memory craves relationships. Its natural impulse is to form relationships with itself, with the outside world, and with the cognitive and affective systems. Its job is to organize, working with the cognitive and affective systems to evaluate everything that enters the person on a nonverbal level, including spatial and sensory information. A news segment that aired on January 20, 2003, on ABC shows the driving force of self-memory even in cases of severe autism. A technique known as facilitated communication is allowing autistic people to communicate by typing on a keyboard. The typing is prompted by a touch on the shoulder. An autistic young woman, Lucy, 26, wrote, "I am like everyone else inside my body." Lucy's mother was quoted on the show as saying, "And she is in there, two feet away from us and we didn't know she was there" (abc.news.com). Certain types of strokes can create similar locked-in syndromes. A number of stroke patients of mine, when asked to blink if "you are in there," responded by blinking, showing that self-memory exists independent of cognition.

Self-memory is a driving force for survival. The language of self-memory is nonverbal, but it responds to the tonality and prosody of language; it has its own lexicon of nonverbal sounds, symbols, and representations. Patterns are innate to its existence. These patterns can be expressed through music, dance, poetic metaphor, art, color, shading, forms, ambiance, and rhythm. The nuances of an individual's self-memory can be seen through the Rorschach Inkblot Test as the patient responds to color, space, transparencies, form, patterns, and shapes. Under normal development, these aspects of self-memory work with cognition to make meaning of the world. The movie *A Beautiful Mind* is an example of how self-memory is at home with complex patterns. The mathematician, John Nash (Russell Crowe), was blessed with a genius-level ability to discern patterns and shapes. He was able to come up with a new mathematical theory by integrating his pattern-rich self-memory with his cognition. This was a very rich and healthy part of his personality. However, when he began to experience delusions, his self-memory dissociated from his cognition. He was alone with a complex and frightening array of patterns as well as the associated affects. His self-memory coped by trying to make meaning of the patterns. But because it did this while separated from his cognition, he saw bizarre codes in magazine clippings and had delusions about working with government agents on a decoding project.

One of self-memory's most important functions is reality testing. In his short story, *The Pit and the Pendulum*, horror writer Edgar Allen Poe vividly shows his unnamed protagonist employing this reality testing system in an effort to survive an episode of extreme trauma. *The Pit and the Pendulum* illustrates psychological time and space while describing the desperate attempts of a traumatized prisoner to bring together the self and cognitive systems to test the reality of his situation. It is interesting that this story was written decades before Freud's theories were popularized. As the story opens, Poe's unnamed protagonist has been thrown into a pitch-black dungeon. Here the protagonist speaks to us in the first person to describe how, in his effort to make sense of the horror that was happening to him, he bounced between times of pure terror (self) and rational thinking (cognition):

> Then the mere consciousness of existence, without thought—a condition which lasted long. Then, very suddenly, *thought,* and shuddering terror, and earnest endeavor to comprehend my true state. Then a strong desire to lapse into insensibility. (Poe, 1940, p. 298)

While exploring the space in which he was imprisoned, Poe's hero discovers a giant pit in the center of the dungeon. This abyss, into which the hero almost tumbles, is an apt metaphor for the gaping chasm between self-memory and cognition that can occur during and after severe trauma. The protagonist, after suffering a series of horrors and indignities, is able to save himself because he manages to integrate his self and cognitive systems to probe his situation. The dungeon is totally dark but he uses his hands to survey the space, estimating its size, shape, and dimensions. He develops a strategy to avoid falling into the pit. He also uses the tools of self-memory to soothe himself by sleeping, remembering, using fantasy, and summoning up feelings of hope. During moments of absolute hopelessness, the prisoner relies on his creative spirit—a major force of self-memory—by using his innate sense of curiosity to continue exploring the dungeon. "Amid frequent and thoughtful endeavors to remember, amid earnest struggles to regather some token of the state of seeming nothingness into which my soul (read: self) had lapsed, there have been moments when I have dreamed of success; there have been brief, very brief periods when I have conjured up remembrances which the lucid reason of a later epoch assures me could have had reference only to that condition of seeming unconsciousness" (Poe, 1940, p. 298).

Because he was presumably a psychologically healthy adult with an integrated personality at the time of his trauma, Poe's protagonist was able to cognitively test the realities of his situation despite the feelings of horror that flooded him again and again. Keep in mind that young children who are traumatized do not always have these cognitive integrative capacities or mature-enough neurological systems to cope as well as Poe's protagonist. Poe's unnamed hero was even able to gather information about the abyss, tossing a rock into the hole to estimate its watery depths.

The story is an apt metaphor of how trauma can trigger severe dissociation even in a healthy adult. Chronic trauma during childhood will affect personality development. Personality disorders can develop whenever there are severe and numerous gaps in a person's reality testing system because of multiple memory dissociations. Depending on the extent and developmental timing of a trauma, the gulf between a person's self-memory and cognitive systems can be huge, making it difficult for the person to integrate the two systems. Sometimes the dissociative abyss can be too wide to cross and meaning making is impossible.

The Pit and the Pendulum explores the relationships among psychological time, space, and memory. The dungeon—a damp, dark, foul-smelling room—functions in the story as a physical and metaphorical space that the hero cognitively probes in a desperate attempt to save himself. He tries to figure out the size and shape of the cell. He throws a rock down the deep abyss that yawns in the center of his dungeon. Time is also metaphorically represented in *The Pit and the Pendulum*—the giant swinging pendulum that threatens to slice him in two is part of a ticking clock that hangs above his head. The ticking clock symbolizes the fact that Poe's hero is in a timeless state. He sleeps, but does not know for how long. He wakes up, inching along the ground. His spatial frames of reference are also distorted. The dark space changes constantly because the walls have been mechanically rigged to close in on him; this horrifies the prisoner and is an apt metaphor for how the psychospatial distortions of trauma can generate feelings of fear and powerless in the victim.

Other components of self-memory symbolized in Poe's story include sound and movement. Poe's hero refers repeatedly to the sounds and movements around him. "Then again, sound. And motion and touch—a tingling sensation pervading my frame"(Poe, 1940, p. 298). It is interesting that the prisoner's reassociation begins at the moment when a faint light appears, illuminating the dungeon.

LIGHT AND MEMORY

Light is critical to my ideas about self-memory. The brain is illuminated from within; for example, our memories and dreams can be well lit and colorful under normal development. In trauma, what is seen and remembered is more opaque and shadowy and always available for the kind of reflection necessary for healing. Self-reflection requires light. The brain throws light on itself to allow a person to go deeper and deeper into his or her crevices of self-memory, the process portrayed so beautifully in *The Pit and the Pendulum*. Light—in both a real and metaphorical sense—was used for integrating the hero's self- and cognitive systems.

Writers and scholars have explored this connection between light and self-memory for centuries. In his final canto of *El Paradiso*, Dante, in the thirteenth century, wrote:

> Oh Eternal Light fixed in Self-alone
> Known only to Yourself, and knowing self
> You love and glow, knowing and being known! (Alighieri, 1984, p. 393)

Therapy illuminates self-memory, beaming light on images, impressions, fantasy, dreams, and imagination. Think of working memory (cognitive memory) as a beam of light. Retrieving memories is a function of the frontal lobes, which metaphorically beam light on lower and deeper structures located in the hippocampus and amygdala. When first imprisoned, Poe's prisoner was literally and cognitively in total darkness. As he adjusted to the situation, however, he was able to create a map of his own surroundings that he could visualize as though viewing it in the light. When the actual light from the outer world came into his reality, he knew that he was going to survive. He had achieved a full integration with himself and the outer world. This restored a sense of hope, which is always vital to therapy and to healing. He was able to see himself in "a different light"—as a person who might be able to survive his ordeal. With disordered personalities, however, shadowy areas exist where light should be. A borderline patient with Dissociative Identity Disorder (DID) features recently reinforced this idea when she described to me her DID states as seeing the world "through gauze."

During trauma, as described so vividly in *The Pit and the Pendulum,* time slows down. Over the course of development, especially under conditions of prolonged trauma, a person's concept of time can become severely warped. This warping of time is metaphorically seen in the paintings of the surrealist Salvador Dali, famous for his bent and twisted watches. I believe that Dali lived in the world of his self-memory; his work is a wonderful visual display of how time, space, and self-memory can be made into artistic images and shared with the world. His artistic talent allowed him to project his difficult life experiences into the external world. His self-memory was made conscious through his images. Personality disorders can be seen as outward displays of self-memory.

We know that traumatic memories can become encapsulated; these encapsulations can be seen as units of time that contain behavioral and affective features of various development stages. Life serves up trauma and hardship to everyone; we all have small areas of encapsulated time and space as a result of the small and large traumas of daily living. Each encapsulation, or unit of time, represents an area of dissociation: an area where self-memory and affect are separated from cognition. These encapsulations move through psychological time and space (i.e., the course of development). In a normal person, there are relatively few encapsulations; thus, the meaning-making links among self-memory, affect, and cognition remain relatively intact over time. Disordered personalities develop when numerous and rigid encapsulations hinder communication among the individual's self-memory and other information processing systems.

ENCAPSULATION OF TRAUMATIC MEMORIES

We know that people with personality disorders often have difficulties with temporality in interpersonal relationships—for example, understanding the nuances and timing of interpersonal communication. They may miss normal timing cues in their verbal and nonverbal communications—as well as to what is going on in the outer world—to the point that they may appear to have nonverbal learning disabilities (Johnson & Myklebust, 1967). They may misperceive the temporal and spatial aspects of their own body, as illustrated in anorexics or borderline people who cut themselves and, in its most severe form, in people who attempt suicide.

DEVELOPMENT AS MOVEMENT THROUGH TIME

Self-memory is a natural choreographer. Dance—stylized movement set to music—is a universal form of cultural expression because it springs directly from self-memory. Movement is crucial to how self-memory operates. Psychological movement occurs whenever the self reacts to danger and trauma as well as to intimacy and attunement. Development can be described as movement through time. Personality problems can develop when internal movement—development—is arrested. Francesca, a patient with an Avoidant Personality Disorder, reported in therapy that she did not dream. Dreaming is an important type of internal movement. Without psychological movement, including the internal movement of dreams, personalities can become rigidified and depressed. Francesca had been asked to leave her job and was living alone with her daughter. She had few friends. She came to therapy feeling very depressed and unsatisfied. She had recently experienced the death of an important family member.

She displayed very little affective, cognitive, and interpersonal movement. It took a year of therapy before Francesca reported her first dream. It is interesting that her first dream reflected the early trauma of her mother's mental illness and the subsequent lack of movement in Francesca's own development.

Repression is the opposite of forward movement as material is shoved to the background of self-memory. A person's psychological movement can be seen as the self reacts to the Rorschach Inkblot Test. Morris, an elderly patient, is a Holocaust survivor who experienced severe and prolonged horrors. He was a young husband and father when the Nazis invaded his village and forced him to watch his children being killed. His wife died in the Bergen Belsen concentration camp. When responding to card No. 6, Morris revealed for the first time the horrors that had befallen "my first family, my real family." The intrusive quality of the card caused him to remember the violent actions of the Nazis. Rapid and intense psychological movement occurred when Morris's deeply encapsulated memories broke open—50-plus years after they occurred—and moved into the present time in the safety of my office.

Rapid and intense psychological movement, in fact, characterizes some personality disorders. Patients with Borderline Personality Disorders are known for moving psychodynamically with lightning speed; they vacillate rapidly from idealization to devaluation. Avoidant personalities, on the other hand, try to remain hidden and passive within themselves and avoid movement and interaction with the outside world. Humor—like trauma—represents a rapid and unexpected movement into self-memory. We all know that humor is based on timing. The lightning speed of humor gives immediate access to self-memory by bypassing normal defense mechanisms. People with disordered personalities are often described as humorless—their rigid and unmoving defensive mechanisms block the meaning and affects associated with a joke. People with disordered personalities often don't "get the joke" because of their use of projective identification to ward off feelings of shame, guilt, embarrassment, or humiliation.

People with disordered personalities often avoid intimacy, which can be seen as a forward movement to connect with others in reciprocity. Learning about the self—especially in a therapeutic setting—requires emotional, cognitive, intrapsychic, and even neurobiological/chemical movement. Jack, a Borderline patient who was also extremely obese, was repeatedly abused and beaten by his nanny when he was a child. Jack was unable to have affective and meaningful reciprocity with others. When he received a higher educational degree, he was unable to perform the activities of that profession and went on to something else. Because he was so tied to his traumatic past, his cognitive, neurobiological, and self-memory systems formed a template for stagnation, which blocked him from forward professional movement. Jack's self-memory contained numerous somatic memories of being hurt and inactive. While making a major transition from one job to another, Jack injured his spine playing basketball and required dozens of surgeries, which immobilized him physically. His physical limitation mirrored the lack of movement in his emotional, psychological, and self-systems. His obesity also demonstrated his lack of movement and can be seen as a literal physical encapsulation.

Sound—because it is the carrier of spoken language—is an important component of self-memory. Our earliest sounds are our mother's heartbeat, internal functions, and voice. Under normal conditions, the infant responds positively to these noises as well as to the myriad sounds of nature and normal domestic life. Attunement may be highly based on sounds, including the harmonics of language. An example is hearing Hebrew prayers and moving rhythmically to these sounds even if the words are not understood. Opera is another wonderful example of being emotionally moved (possibly to tears) even though the actual words may not be cognitively understood. The sounds of opera are beautiful and rhythmic as are the sounds of poetry and prayer; the sounds of trauma, however, are threatening and intrusive. This auditory intrusiveness can occur even before the child can understand spoken language. In some cases—as, for example, a young Hungarian-speaking child who was transported to a German concentration camp, the threatening words are bellowed out in a foreign language. In this situation, there is no way to understand the words on a cognitive (verbal) level even though it is clear to the victim that the words are threatening. These traumatic "sound bites" can become encapsulated in the same way as light, time, and movement can become encapsulated. I propose that this happens via an inner language process, including symbolic thought, as described by Critchley (1953). This inner language process permits "the transformation of information into symbols," in other words, into encapsulations.

Luke, a patient, is an example of how a sound bite can become encapsulated during trauma. Luke was sitting on a "bag of rounds" during the war in Grenada when he heard a sniper's bullet explode. The bullet entered Luke's neck, traversed his heart, and came out his lung. He was hospitalized in Grenada, requiring three months of treatment. Twenty years later, Luke was in a car crash and, even though he escaped with just a broken arm, he sustained anterograde and retrograde amnesia. He dissociated neurobiologically. Luke was unable to return to work even though he was physically capable of doing so. He came to therapy to discuss the lack of movement in his life. As he was telling the story of his car accident, he initially said he was sleeping at the time of the accident while his friend was driving. The car veered off the road and crashed into a ravine. Luke climbed out of the car and was treated for his broken arm. I asked him if he remembered anything before the accident. At first, he failed to recall anything. In a subsequent session, however, he remembered hearing a crashing sound and then waking up in the ravine. This sound reminded him of his trauma in Grenada. On hearing the sound of the car crash, he dissociated. The traumatic sound of the ammunition exploding was encapsulated in Luke's self-memory, causing a split between his cognition and self-memory. Luke did not have a personality disorder. Because he was a psychologically healthy adult at the time of his initial trauma, he was able to encapsulate the experience in a way that allowed him to function in his role as husband, father, and provider; it wasn't until the car accident that the encapsulation split open and caused his amnesia.

Prosody of language may be important during severe trauma. A victim of trauma may dissociate so completely from his or her cognitive functions that the meaning of what is being said is lost. The victim of abuse may no longer trust tone or word meaning. An example is a parent who says to a child in a sweet tone, "I am whipping you because I love you." The meaning of that sentence does not make cognitive sense. The tonality and prosody of that sentence, however, will be encoded in self-memory without cognitive meaning. These kinds of language events can become encapsulated bits of sound memory. The two aspects of language—verbal and nonverbal—are split. For some trauma victims, words as carriers of emotion and meaning making can no longer be trusted. This can help to explain the results of Bremner et al. (1995), who found short-term verbal memory loss in victims of childhood abuse. Self-memory was trying to protect itself from the fearful word utterings associated with the abuse. This process also helps to explain why people with personality disorders misinterpret social nuances, linguistic utterances, and their affective linkages. Some encapsulations contain bits of light, sound, and movement and thus have multiple permutations, which add to the color and complexity of an individual's personality. This is why it is so important to look at personality disorders not as a classification system but as a dynamic developmental process.

The trauma victim's developmental stage is key to how any kind of encapsulation will be expressed. Children are most vulnerable to trauma because their brains are still developing. Recent research has shown that the development of the frontal lobes lasts until young adulthood. During adolescence, teenagers display a type of behavioral-personality style, which resembles a dysexecutive syndrome. Trauma during the teenage years is variable in terms of how information is going to be encoded. Some adolescent trauma victims might do well and some might not, depending on a variety of factors including genetics, neurohormones, and support systems. For example, an adolescent patient named Jake received a double amputation of his arms after being struck by lightning at age 16. He failed to seek shelter during a thunderstorm and did not foresee the consequences of his behavior. Jake saw himself as emotionally defective in his character because of the loss of his previous lifestyle. His character changed from an extroverted style to an introversive one that manifested his new and fragile sense of himself. Despite these changes, Jake was willing, on a limited basis, to reengage himself interpersonally and academically. His self-memory now contains a deep understanding of how dangerous it is to exist in the world and how the self can subject a person to danger and annihilation. The events of September 11, 2001, forced Americans on a political and social level to think about the fragility of life. While running around in the storm, Jake was unaware he was placing himself in danger. In the same way, many Americans were unaware of how our policies were affecting people around the world. Countries, like people, have self-memories. We, like Jake, were disconnected in many ways. His subsequent inability to trust himself, which became embedded in the deepest level of his self-memory, may linger to some extent all his life; the implications for his future personality development are serious. He may find the necessary compensatory features in his personality to mature over time, but his true sense of himself has been seriously wounded. It is interesting that this young man is succeeding academically, a testimony to the fact that self-memory and cognition can split during trauma and later reassociate.

William is a 79-year-old patient who was adopted at birth by a Christian couple. He always knew he was adopted. William lived a life of luxury with his adopted parents, earned an Ivy League education, and became a successful businessman. He came to therapy following life-threatening surgery. His physical illness exacerbated his longstanding depression, anxiety, and Narcissistic Character Disorder. At about age 14, he learned that his biological father was involved in a profession sought out by many Jewish men in his generation. I queried about his biological father's last name. He told me the name, which turned out to be a surname that could very well have identified the patient as being of Jewish descent. He initially resisted this idea because of his adopted background and culture as well as his active involvement in a church.

During a recent session, William looked around my office and saw a figurine of a rabbi reading from the Torah. This figure had sat for years on the same coffee table. In one choreographed movement, William touched the holy book with his left hand and then proceeded to kiss his hand. This symbolic act is one way in which Jewish people give reverence to God and the holy teachings of the Talmud and the Torah. For various reasons, I did not interpret this very rich gesture to him. This was a moving moment in which William's self-memory was engaged and visibly made its presence known. It will always remain a mystery as to whether his father was actually Jewish and whether this gesture represented his actual genetic and ancestral roots and the need for self-memory to be seen during a moment of reassociation. Moments before William touched the rabbi figurine, he was reporting to me that he would be going to a meeting at his church following our session. He made a humorous reference to the possibility of his Jewish roots. Humor is often a direct portal into self-memory. The joke lowered his defenses by alleviating anxiety and tension and allowed him to create a nonverbal metaphor for reassociation.

In William's case, adoption made him feel special, but this sense of being chosen may have been a defense for an underlying sense of low self-esteem and short physical stature. William always felt disconnected from his biological roots. One way he sought to solve these problems on his own was through drinking alcohol as a teenager and later as a middle-age man. Characteristically, alcohol may take the place of a nurturing experience because its effects are warm and soothing. Using alcohol, however, retards affective and neuropsychological development. This is especially true during adolescence because the brain is still developing. William began to drink again during middle age because of marital and business pressures. He always saw himself as unable to take care of himself and his family despite his financial success. He continues to have mild drinking problems during his elder years.

AGING AND PERSONALITY

It is important to discuss aging during any discussion of personality development. When the brain is undergoing age-related changes because of conditions such as vascular disease or Alzheimer's, personality disorders can become exacerbated. Older patients who are experiencing memory disorders may also display significant changes in their characterological styles. These changes may include increasing levels of anger, irritability, and depression, which can lead to further confusion, disorientation, and lack of participation with caregivers. This is why it is so important to evaluate an older person's characterological style because changes may be a prodromal feature of a dementing process. For example, Alice, age 75, has experienced symptoms of depression, anxiety, and panic for the past three years. She also exhibits mild cognitive deficits, which appear to be age-related. Recently, her husband became concerned about Alice's characterological changes and brought these to the attention of her physician. She was disoriented at times for names, dates, and reasons that she was looking for objects in rooms. Her behaviors became more complicated over time with increasingly rigid defenses and stilted memories. During her most recent evaluation, she was found to have both a vascular and Alzheimer's dementia associated with motor, verbal and nonverbal memory, and executive and sensory-perceptual deficits. Her neuroimaging studies confirmed these neuropsychological findings. Alice's self has not lost its capacity to know that she exists. She can relate to past memories, but more importantly, she exists in relationship to her self and to others.

In another example, a 76-year-old woman, Gladys, was referred to me. She had a depression beginning when her children were little. She had about 15 rounds of electroconvulsive shock therapy (ECT) as a young woman. Her psychological history is complex. Her family as a young child and into her adulthood coveted her. She developed high skills academically and just fell short of reaching a graduate degree before she married a physician. She had highly developed intellectual capacities and identified herself as a scholar. She worked during her adult years as a professional but once again, never felt satisfied with her accomplishments, which took second seat to her parental and spousal responsibilities. Several of her family members had mental illness when she was growing up and during her adult years. Gladys had a Narcissistic Character Disorder with Borderline features, which often revealed itself by devaluing others while inflating her own self-worth. In therapy, Gladys was able to analyze her depressions as becoming more debilitating when other people received more praise, success, or attention. On her neuropsychological testing, she revealed a vascular-type dementia. As her symptoms of narcissism have developed over time, she has become more rigid, reactive, and less defensive against these perceived personal injuries and wounds. In fact, recently, she reentered the hospital following the birth of a grandchild, who received a lot of attention, presents, and became the gratification of other family members. The focus of staff and group interactions helped to shift her defensive posture to a more resilient position. However, I anticipate that because of her changing brain status, it will take less and less of an insult for Alice's personality to decompensate. Ironically, as seen here, the aging process can sometimes make a person more rigid and more open at the same time.

THE DISSOCIATIVE ABYSS

Recall the dissociative abyss that Poe so aptly described in *The Pit and the Pendulum.* Sometimes, these abysses between self-memory and cognition may be too wide to cross. Emotions—especially shame, humiliation, and fear—can become encapsulated under trauma. Anger that is repressed during early childhood can remain in its primitive state and lead to acting out in its most extreme and dangerous form: sociopathic behavior. Tony Soprano (James Gandolfini), a character on HBO's hit series *The Sopranos,* is a brilliant fictional example of how primitive feelings of shame, guilt, and humiliation can become encapsulated in a child. Tony is a 40-something mobster who suffers from frequent anxiety attacks. Tony—whose outward persona is that of a cold-hearted mob boss—has developed a habit of fainting whenever he sees meat being cooked. But as a mob boss, Tony cannot afford to be seen as weak or ill. The pressure to put on a constant show of violent macho strength makes him more and more anxious. His fainting spells become so troublesome that he is forced to defy his cultural and gender expectations and seek out therapy. Each weekly episode is built around scenes of Tony undergoing therapy with his psychiatrist, Dr. Jennifer Malfi (Lorraine Bracco).

After several years of therapy, Tony is able to connect his fainting spells with an encapsulated childhood traumatic memory. He shifts nervously in his chair and roars out swear words as he describes the memory to Dr. Malfi. When he was 10 or 11 years old, Tony's father told him to remain in the car while he ran inside the butcher's shop to buy some meat. His father was gone for what seemed to Tony like a long time. Bored and restless, young Tony disobeyed his father by getting out of the car and going inside the butcher shop. What he saw was horrific: His father was in the act of chopping off the butcher's finger as retribution for a gambling debt. Young Tony shrank in horror as the butcher screamed. The scene was messy and violent. Tony's father then raided the butcher's freezer and helped himself to a roast. Young Tony was stunned and horrified at his father's brutality.

Later that night, young Tony could not make cognitive sense of the event even though his father sat him down for a father-son chat in which he tried to explain his actions. His father told young Tony that he brutalized the butcher as a way to financially support Tony and his sister. Tony, thus, felt responsible for what happened to the butcher and was flooded with feelings of guilt and shame. He also felt guilty for disobeying his father by not staying in the car.

Young Tony, unable to make cognitive or emotional sense of the event, encapsulated the memories. These encapsulations contained primitive forms of shame, guilt, horror, fear, and moral confusion. Later that night, Tony's mother, Olivia (Nancy Marchand), prepared a meal for the family with the stolen roast. Tony watched as his mother stood at the stove and engaged in a seductive dance with his father. The scene is disturbing: Olivia gyrates at the stove, licking the meat and pressing herself against the husband who has provided her with the delicious culinary treat. Young Tony is confused and embarrassed by his parent's inappropriate display of sexuality. Sexual shame is now added to his encapsulated memories of guilt and horror. The eating of the dinner is a metaphorical representation of self-memory literally ingesting the emotional horror of the day's event. He sees that his mother not only is colluding with his father in violence but also is sexualizing the horror, thus blending female sexuality and male aggression.

Tony's adult personality is a dramatic display of these encapsulated moral and emotional contradictions. He is a loving father who attends his children's recitals; he is also a mob boss who orders the violent death of his enemies. He has a very strong sexual transference with his therapist. His sexual fantasies show the deep split between his self-memory and cognition that occurred when his father injured the butcher and his mother sexualized the event. He showers his wife with jewels and furs but he cheats on her with a series of mistresses. When he suspects that his best friend is working as an FBI informant, he takes the friend out on a yacht and, in a scene of heartless cruelty, kills the friend and dumps the body in the ocean.

Many factors—including the degree of trauma, the developmental stage of the victim, familial and interpersonal dynamics, their primary care-giving relationships, genetic and neurobiological redispositions, and even luck—help to determine the depth of and spaces between an individual's *dissociative abyss*. A patient named Mary experienced severe developmental trauma because her family was involved in the drug wars. She came to therapy with numerous and rigid encapsulations. She was diagnosed with Borderline and Narcissistic Personality Disorders. She was raped as a young adolescent. She experienced both personal and family abuse over the course of her development. As a young child, Mary experienced severe separation anxiety from her mother. Her early-encapsulated self-memories—which contain deep fears and annihilation—are sometimes rigid and isolated from each other; at other times, they are in dynamic relationship to each other. As an example of how her encapsulated self-memories can sometimes operate separately from her cognition, Mary recently left her infant son alone in his crib while she ran an errand. This irresponsible action, which happened during a dissociative state, can be seen as the breaking open of early encapsulated memories of how her own mother abandoned her. The ruptured encapsulation caused her to dissociate. At this moment in collapsed time, Mary was experiencing the feelings of being an abandoned little girl. In deciding to leave the baby in his crib instead of taking him with her on the errand, Mary was using the cognitive tools of a child and not an adult. When, on the other hand, her encapsulated self-memories act dynamically, crashing into each other, she acts explosively, yelling and screaming.

Rosemary, a patient with Anorexia Nervosa, is a tragic example of how the brain can distort spatial information and create splits or deep dissociative abysses on many functional levels. Rosemary's brain did not know that she was killing her own body through starvation. Her brain was in effect disconnected from its own neurobiolological cues. Rosemary's story is horrific. She was raised, from birth, inside a Mexican prison because her mother had been convicted of smuggling drugs. Inside the prison, Rosemary was sexually abused on a regular basis. Her mother used Rosemary as a bargaining chip for favors. Rosemary and her mother were released from prison when Rosemary was in early adolescence. By the time she was 16, Rosemary was hospitalized for severe Anorexia. Rosemary's spatial, linguistic, affective, and social boundaries had been repeatedly broken under the extreme conditions in prison. Linguistically, she had no words to link her affective and cognitive systems to meaning-making efforts on her self-memory level. In therapy, she volunteered few words and mostly used hand gestures to communicate.

Because her dissociative abysses were so deep and numerous, Rosemary's hunger was neuropsychologically separated from her autonomic nervous system. She could not psychologically receive gustatorial and gastronomic information from her body. In contrast, the Jewish women mentioned at the beginning of the chapter were able to use their gastronomic and gustatorial memories to survive the concentration camp; they were assumedly healthy and normal adults at the time of the Holocaust and were able to use their cognitive resources and to engage their positive self-memories in a productive way. Writing down their traditional recipes allowed them to survive.

Rosemary never grew up because she suffered huge and numerous time and space encapsulations during her development. Her language functions were so regressed that her grammatical skills were on a level of a 7-year-old. She could not engage with other people in reciprocal play. She always felt as though she was locked in psychologically and felt comfortable only when she was locked into an inpatient psychiatric unit. Her dissociative abyss was so wide that she experienced life as a prison within a prison. She saw people as automatons with no connections to her on the self, cognitive, or affective level.

MORAL ASPECTS OF SELF-MEMORY

Self-memory is a kind of working memory (Baddeley, 1986; Goldman-Rakic, 1984) that constantly scans and focuses on the internal environment from the physical to the psychological. It is always poised to react to real or imagined danger—internal as well as external. I maintain that morality is an important component of self-memory. Personality disorders are also outward displays of moral engagement. People with Narcissistic Personality Disorders, for example, are more morally engaged with themselves than with the outside world. The Antisocial Personality or Psychopath, however, moves away from moral attunement with others and toward its own fantasy life. A psychopathic person cannot tell the difference between fantasy or myth and reality.

Self-memory is a natural mythmaker—it makes and interprets its own history. Under normal development, these self-memorialized myths are more or less grounded in healthy fantasies. By separating this myth-making system from cognition, trauma can create the kinds of distorted myths that characterize personality disorders. I believe that self-memory is intergenerational—part of its own mythology can be passed on from generation to generation. An example of how this intergenerational quality of self-memory can create psychopathic family members is beautifully illustrated in the *Godfather* cinematic trilogy. Moral disengagement is a crucial part of this intergenerational tale. A series of cinematic flashbacks in *Godfather Part II* shows the early life of the future Godfather (Marlon Brando). The first flashback takes place in a small Sicilian village. Vito, the future Godfather, marches sadly in the funeral procession of his father, who was killed by the village mob boss. At the gravesite, Vito's brother is shot dead. A few days later, Vito sees his mother shot at close range as she begs the mob boss to spare Vito's life. The mother flies through the air like a large bird as the bullet smashes into her chest. Vito goes into hiding. With his life in danger, Vito immigrates to America. He spends several months in isolation at Ellis Island because of an illness. He does not talk during this time but sits alone in his room. He sings a folk song to soothe himself. Vito is linguistically disconnected—not only from the English that is being spoken around him but from his native Sicilian tongue as well. His lullabies are haunting to the viewer, which represents the depths of self-memory. He is recapitulating his development while waiting to transcend into a more complex personality.

Within a few years, Vito becomes a thief and mobster. He shoots his enemies, replaying the shooting of his father again and again. His encapsulated moral coda has become so distorted that he is able to rationalize shooting and stealing and gun running. Vito's favorite son, Michael (Al Pacino), tries hard to resist the magnetic pull to crime but after Vito is shot during a gang war, Michael retaliates. He shoots a policeman in the head at close range in the famous restaurant scene. He has his own brother, Fredo, shot and killed. In *Godfather Part III,* the cycle is completed when Michael's daughter, Mary, is shot and killed on the steps of an opera house in Sicily.

As the *Godfather* trilogy shows, the force pulling the self to self-memory is magnetic on an individual, familial, and cultural level. A Borderline patient, Susan, described this magnetic pull during therapy. Susan grew up in a highly educated Jewish family and is now a professor of music. As a young child, she was sexually abused by a neighbor and subjected to intense anti-Semitism. Her parents were ex-hippies who tried to minimize the prejudices she faced. They were aloof during Susan's childhood and heavily involved in their own activities. Because of this very poor parenting, Susan never felt supported psychologically and developed a fragmented personality. As a result of this split between cognition and self-memory, she describes herself today as being torn apart by the force of her own self-memory system. "I feel that my bones, my heart, my skin are being torn and ripped apart with the intensity of an object being sucked into a black hole." This magnetic force separated her self-memory into the polar personality fragments that are characteristic of the Borderline personality.

THE NEUROBIOLOGY OF PERSONALITY DISORDERS

As my theory about self-memory emphasizes, whatever enters the system can be hidden but never taken away. Everything that enters the brain is metabolized psychologically via self-memory and is encoded neurobiologically as well. This process begins at birth and continues throughout life. We are just now beginning to understand the neurobiological basis of this encoding process.

In a study of rats injected with a corticotropin-releasing hormone (CRH), Brunson, Eghbal-Ahmadi, Bender, Chen, and Baran (2001) speculate the memory loss and impaired cognitive abilities that occur in abused and neglected infants may be caused by the same hormone. Even though the rats were injected only once with CRH, cell death occurred in the hippocampus and memory problems continued to worsen with age.

The neurobiological encoding process creates a lifelong template for conscious and unconscious behavior, in other words, for personality. Personality can be seen as the outward display of the lifelong encoding process. This template is one reason that personality disorders can be so rigid, inflexible, and hard to change. In adults, this deeply embedded template—and its associated self-memories—are very resistant to change on a neurobiological, cognitive, and psychological level. Brain plasticity allows for some change in this template to occur, especially during childhood. The extent of change depends on numerous factors including genetics, gender, uterine and birth history, developmental stage, environment, primary caregiver relationships, and psychological and neurobiological insults such as injury, disease, or trauma.

The following case study illustrates how a severe brain injury neurobiologically affected a patient's personality over the course of his development. An 11-year-old boy named Nick suffered brain damage and temporary cortical blindness after a mild stroke. Nick's trauma occurred during a developmentally important transition from preadolescence to adolescence, a period of plasticity in brain functioning. His trauma had a significant effect on his personality because he had to rehabilitate himself on both a cognitive and self-memory level. It's taken a 12-year course of psychotherapy (still ongoing) to address the injuries to his psychological, neurobiological, cognitive, and self-systems.

Nick's trauma created numerous encapsulations. He bypassed critical stages in his development. For example, he did not experience a normal puberty process. This may be because of the injury to his frontal, temporal, and parietal lobes as well as to his limbic and neurohormonal systems. He has a hard time filtering out exogenous and endogenous stimuli. Any disruption to the frontal lobe region will cause disruptions in affective regulation and cognitive processing. This is exactly what happened to Nick.

There are numerous connections between the frontal lobes and limbic systems. The pathway for this, although it has yet to be proven through research, may be through the uncus. We know that the lower brain centers have direct access and influence on the frontal lobe systems and vice versa. Nick's cognitive, self-memory, and affective systems were all severely impaired. Ten years after the stroke, he still has significant difficulty reading interpersonal cues and nuances. Exacerbating this condition is impairment to his right hemisphere. Neuropsychological testing showed visuospatial, constructional, and memory problems following his injury. This problem, as well as ataxia and apraxia, cleared up about a year after his injury. Affectively, however, at age 23, Nick continues to have aprosodia (monotone quality) and mistiming between affects and social cues.

All of these problems have had a direct effect on his personality development. Cognitively, he still has difficulty organizing, sequencing, and planning information. He has problems shifting from one changing set of demands to another. The frontal lobes, in conjunction with the right hemisphere, assist in organizing information including language that comes into the central nervous system. Any disruption to these organizing functions, as in Nick's case, can distort information coming from the self and from the outside world. For Nick, this disruption widened the dissociative split between self-memory and cognition.

On a deeper level, Nick's self-memory was imbued with (and still contains) feelings of grave injury. He felt shame over not being able to protect himself from the devastating effects of the stroke. As he developed into an adult, he felt strong feelings of mourning and grief. He longed for his lost childhood. He mourned what he had lost as a young man, that is, independence, normal peer relationships, dating, feeling the integrity of his body, and being able to drive.

After the stroke, he suffered from severe learning disabilities and was ridiculed by his peer group. This contributed to his isolation because he could not participate in sports or school. In terms of his self-memory, he sometimes felt defective and exiled by friends. His neurological injury, coupled with the social isolation and ridicule, caused his self-memory to partially separate from his cognition. He experienced most of the symptoms of Posttraumatic Stress Disorder (PTSD). There has been a dissociative quality to his personality since his stroke. He felt frightened and panicky for years. He has a proclivity for poor judgment, breech of reality testing, and dissociative episodes.

Nick's sexual development did not follow a normal adolescent course. Today, at 23, he is primarily interested in prepubescent girls and actively seeks out pedophilic Internet sites. Nick was 11 when the injury occurred, providing an example of how self-memories can become encoded psychologically, neurobiologically, and even hormonally.

In van der Kolk's words (1994), "His body kept the score." Because Nick's trauma occurred during early adolescence, it is not surprising that his sexual interests are fixated at the level of preadolescent and early adolescent girls. His self-memory relied on immature sexual fantasies to help make meaning of his experience. He suffers from a Personality Disorder Not Otherwise Specified that includes Borderline features, Avoidant, and Paranoid tendencies. He has displayed suicidal gestures; his moods have fluctuated. His negative personality features are most prominent under stressful conditions. In some structured settings, such as work, he is better able to function. His negative personality features are rarely expressed in his work as a veterinary assistant because they remain sequestered and split off from self-memory. At work, he can operate in a goal-oriented manner within a very structured setting.

In therapy, Nick has become more and more aware of his self-memory system. We have set up a computer safeguard, which prohibits him from accessing the pedophilic material on the Internet. This intervention helps to control his impulses by integrating his cognitive and self-systems.

TIME, SPACE, AND LIGHT

Recall the previous section on time, space, and light. Nick's vivid dreams during moments of darkness represent the brain's capacity to light up his internal life to handle the many stressors that were taking place. Because his development was halted at age 11, numerous developmental encapsulations formed both in terms of time and space. He still suffers from numerous misperceptions of time and space. For example, he views himself as a younger person. He has impaired visual perception, which prohibits him from driving or operating machinery.

Nick's thoughts and feelings are in disequilibrium with each other. In a temporal sense, he is negatively influenced by stimuli competing for his attention. His timing between his thoughts and affects is also in disequilibrium. Because of problems with timing on a perceptual, structural, and neurohormonal level, he often appears to be awkward and confused. During these episodes, the information he is receiving from the outside world does not coincide with his internal experience. Recall that he suffered lesions to his right hemisphere, which is responsible for spatial relationships and for organizing cognitive and personality functions.

GENDER ROLE SOCIALIZATION

It seems evident that hormones and gender role socialization play major roles in the expression of self-memory and personality disorders. Because of space limitations, the following discussion is by necessity limited in scope; however, the role of gender in the development of personality disorders can provide a fruitful area for further study. Women tend to suffer more frequently with Borderline Personality Disorders whereas men tend to suffer from Antisocial Personality Disorders.

Gender-specific hormones are critical in the development of personality because they strongly influence inner and outer directed behaviors. MRI studies have shown structural differences between male and female brains. For example, women tend to have richer corpus colossal fibers, larger left temporal lobes, and larger limbic systems (Seeley, Tate, & Stephens, 2000), suggesting another rich area for future research on personality. One of the most prominent character differences between men and women is how aggression is handled and expressed. Consider the recent events surrounding the Beltway Sniper in the Washington, DC area. It is hard to imagine a woman setting up a car as a sniper's nest and shooting people at random. The overwhelming majority of serial killers and violent criminals such as kidnappers are men. Social and cultural norms may gradually change the way men and women express conflicts in their personalities. For example, several Palestine teenage girls have recently blown themselves up in what has typically been male, suicide-bomber style.

The symptoms of women with personality disorders tend to be inner directed, that is, they involve an intense focus on the self-memory system, which may contain annihilation fantasies, feelings of abandonment, extreme psychological pain, and isolation. For example, Borderline victims tend to exhibit more suicidal and self-destructive tendencies and self-mutilating behaviors. Although female puberty may not carry many positive social reinforcements in many cultures because of gender role biases, I propose that it contains many self-affirming qualities such as nurturance and generative power on the self-memory level. Again, further research in needed in this area.

We are only now beginning to learn about some of the specific neurobiological aspects of personality disorders. These can be interpreted in light of the previous ideas about gender and trauma. For example, a recent neuroimaging study by Driessen et al. (2000) found that women with Borderline Personality Disorders had hippocampuses that were 16% smaller than a control group. They also found an 8% reduction in amygdala volume. The authors suggest that stress plays a significant role in these neuroanatomical changes. We know that many people with Borderline Personality Disorders may have suffered physical and sexual abuse when they were children. Bremner et al. (1995) found that children who experienced physical and sexual abuse had long-term deficits in verbal short-term memory. There may be lacunae of memory deficits occurring across development, a possible explanation for the occurrence of learning disabilities and other communication deficits in abused children. Similar deficits were found in patients with combat-related PTSD.

These kinds of anatomical brain changes may be linked to neuropsychological findings. Voglmaier et al. (2000) found that male patients with Schizotypal Personality Disorders showed a mild to moderate reduction in performance on verbal measures of persistence and short-term retention. Their verbal learning was more severely impaired than their nonverbal analogs.

Trauma affects not only structural but also neuropsychological correlates. Self-memories can become embedded at different stages throughout development on different neurological and neurocognitive levels. Downhill et al. (2000) found that the size of the corpus callosum was smaller in people with Schizotypal Personality Disorders and smallest in Schizophrenic subjects compared to a group of controls. Reduction in the corpus callosum may impair connections between the two hemispheres, causing uneven communication of language and spatial information. The transfer of information—both verbal and nonverbal—is less effective. Metaphorically, this is a neuropsychological description of Poe's dissociative abyss. Because of the inefficient information transfer from one hemisphere to another, self-memory may be fragmented and dissociated from cognition. This shows the importance of brain function to an integrated personality system.

Anxiety is a major fuel for developing personality disorders. In people with personality disorders, anxiety over the long term is disassociated from cognition and self-memory. It can be said that they do not "know" or experience their anxiety. This occurs neurobiologically as well as psychologically and accounts for what seems at first glance to be contradictory results in a study by Yehuda, Kahana, et al. (1996). They found lower levels of cortisol in Holocaust survivors with PTSD symptoms compared to a control group of Holocaust survivors without PTSD. I believe that these results demonstrate the affective dissociation between cognition and self-memory. The survivors with PTSD may be more dissociated, accounting for the lower cortisol levels. The group without PTSD symptoms had higher levels of cortisol because they were more cognitively and psychologically aware of their trauma. Another Yehuda, Elkin, et al. (1996) study found that Holocaust survivors with PTSD manifested more dissociative symptoms than survivors without PTSD. Yehuda, Halligan, and Bierer (2001) also found that Holocaust survivors with PTSD tended to pass these symptoms on to their children. This finding is very important in understanding personality. Trauma, via familial and cultural self-memory, has the capacity to be intergenerational.

Studies of trauma make this point repeatedly. In a study of rape victims, Resnick, Yehuda, Pitman, and Foy (1995) found that women with an assault had lower mean acute cortisol levels after a rape but a higher probability of subsequently developing PTSD. Kellner, Yehuda, Arlt, and Wiedemann (2002), in a two-year study of a patient with chronic PTSD, found that the level of cortisol decreased dramatically three months after the traumatic event.

Southwick, Bremner, Krystal, and Charney (1994) reported that PTSD could affect nearly all areas of a person's life. Trauma can alter the neurobiological response to stress even years after the event. Increased sensitivity of the noradrenergic system may leave the victim hyperaroused, vigilant, and sleep-deprived. Catecholamine depletion has been seen in individuals with PTSD.

An important area of the brain, which has been associated with panic attacks, is the locus coeruleus. This structure is located in the pons and contains more than 50% of all afferent projections to the brain including the hippocampus, amygdala, limbic lobe, and cerebral cortex. Charney, Deutch, Krystal, Southwick, and Davis (1993) found a similar neurobiological reaction to trauma including fear conditioning, extinction, and sensitization. Charney suggests that the noradrenergic, dopaminergic, opiate, and HPA neuronal systems and the locus coeruleus, amygdala, hypothalamus, hippocampus, and prefrontal cortex are important mediators of the stress response. Grillon, Southwick, and Charney (1996) describe "a dysfunctional multiple psychobiological system" that develops with exposure to trauma. The amygdala, which plays a crucial role in the encoding and retrieval of fear memories, may be especially affected by trauma.

Bremner and Narayan (1998) found decreased hippocampus volume in individuals with PTSD. Gurvits et al.'s (1996) research supports these findings, as does Pitman, Shin, and Rauch's (2001) research with MRI and PET scans. Structural abnormalities in PTSD were found on MRIs, including nonspecific white matter lesions and decreased hippocampal volume. These abnormalities may reflect pretrauma vulnerability to develop PTSD or they may be the result of traumatic exposure or PTSD.

SUMMARY AND CONCLUSIONS

Personality disorders are really trauma disorders. Trauma causes varying degrees of neurobiological dissociations among cognition, affect, and self-memory. This occurs neurobiologically as well as psychologically. Cultural and social factors play an important part in how personality disorders will be expressed. Other factors include genetic, environmental, and parental influences. Personality disorders are not static; they are not just a list of symptoms in the *DSM-IV* but are dynamic and multidimensional. The nature of personality disorders may change in the future. Technology is making the unconscious conscious through avenues such as the Internet. People, including young children, can download images of death and gore or child sexual abuse material that was not easily accessed just a decade ago. Viewing this kind of information is both a trauma and a source of gratification, especially for children. Children do not have the skills to handle this kind of information. Many will dissociate while viewing it. These explicit fantasies will bypass children's cognitive systems and head straight for the self-memory system. Recall that the self-memory system works to make meaning of the world. It will immediately identify the explicit images as a threat; a child's self-memory system will try to contain or repress the material. A healthy child will be able to manage viewing such images once or twice; long-term viewing of these images may cause children to become more and more absorbed in their own world. Part of the problem is the instantaneous and infinite nature of these images; this is the first time in human history that children have had immediate and unlimited access to these unconscious adult fantasies. This access to the adult world is creating a dangerous sense of control in children. Even adults are creating their own reality—a good example of this is the fantasy bookkeeping that characterized the Enron scandal. A secure personality requires that the developing individual come to understand the boundaries between fantasy and reality, a task that is becoming harder and harder to do.

Technology is replacing human contact. Individuals no longer have to repress their impulses or peculiar idiosyncratic needs such as a desire for violence or child pornography. Community controls, which worked to some extent on the village level, are no longer able to safeguard society. Therefore, boundaries between fantasy and reality have become so permeable that people, including children, can act out and gratify their fantasies and desires instantaneously. A healthy fantasy life is important for the development of a healthy personality. As more and more children tap into adult-level fantasies, they will be unable to process them psychologically and neurobiologically. I believe that this will create an evolution in personality disorders. We will see expanded definitions and, by necessity, will become more tolerant of mild and extreme forms of personality disorders. This will have a profound impact on the self-memory system.

The nature of relationships, even marriage, is changing. People are no longer connected with one another on the neighborhood and community level. Our children's defense mechanisms are developing differently. As they grow up now, their immature brains have to cope with adult stressors such as school shootings, the images of which are beamed continuously into their homes. Coping with a pornographic web site is a far different psychodynamic challenge for children than dealing with a difficult event such as the shared experience of living through the Depression. A child who accidentally logs onto a porn site is confronted by fantasy material that breaks down the barrier between fantasy and reality. That which was once forbidden is now normal. This will affect children's neurohormonal systems as they have instant access to more and more explicit material. Predators on the Internet and in person are attacking children's reality and safety. People are not necessarily who they say they are or appear to be. This is going to create some extreme narcissistic defenses and other acting-out behaviors such as difficulty in intimate relationships.

This has grave implications for the field of psychotherapy. Understanding self-memory and its role in personality development will be an important tool for therapists in the future. Teaching patients about self-memory may help them to better understand their inner life. The model can help patients with personality disorders to understand their misperceptions in time and space. This can help them to reassociate their cognitive, affective, and self-memory systems. This reassociative process may become even more important in the future because we are living in a world that is more and more dissociated from reality through technology. Technology may help to create new and scary types of memories, especially in children. As the character Frankenstein pointed out more than 200 years ago, "Memory brought madness with it" (Shelley, 1978). The reality is that technology is here to stay. We will need to find new ways to reassociate ourselves with others and our communities to restore a healthier balance between fantasy and reality.

REFERENCES

ABC.news.com. Retrieved January 23, 2003.

Alighieri, D. (1984). *The divine comedy* (M. Musa, Trans.). Bloomington: Indiana University Press.

Appelbaum, P. S., Uyehara, L. A., & Elin, M. R. (1997). *Trauma and memory: Clinical and legal controversies.* New York: Oxford University Press.

Baddeley, A. (1986). *Working memory.* Oxford, England: Oxford University Press.

Bremner, J. D., & Narayan, M. (1998). The effects of stress on memory and the hippocampus throughout the life cycle: Implications for childhood development and aging. *Development and Psychopathology, 10*(4), 871–885.

Bremner, J. D., Randall, P., Scott, T. M., Capelli, S., Delaney, R., McCarthy, G., et al. (1995). Deficits in short-term memory in adult survivors of childhood abuse. *Psychiatry Research, 59*(1/2), 97–107.

Brunson, K., Eghbal-Ahmadi, M., Bender, R., Chen, Y., & Baran, T. Z. (2001). Long-term, progressive hippocampal cell loss and dysfunction induced by early-life administration of corticotropin-releasing hormone reproduce the effects of early-life stress. *Proceedings of the National Academy of Sciences, USA, 98,* 8856–8861.

Charney, D. S., Deutch, A. Y., Krystal, J. H., Southwick, S. M., & Davis, M. (1993). Psychobiological mechanisms of post traumatic stress disorder. *Archives of General Psychiatry, 50,* 294–305.

Chase, D. (Producer). (1999). *The Sopranos* [Television series]. New York: Home Box Office.

Coppola, F. F. (Director). (1972). *Godfather* [Motion picture]. United States: Paramount Films.

Coppola, F. F. (Director). (1974). *Godfather Part II* [Motion picture]. United States: Paramount Films.

Coppola, F. F. (Director). (1990). *Godfather Part III* [Motion picture]. United States: Paramount Films.

Critchley, M. (1953). *The parietal lobes* (pp. 36–37). London: Edward Arnold.

Delbo, C. (1990). *Days and memories* (R. Lamont, Trans.; p. 3). Marlboro, VT: Marlboro Press.

De Silva, C. (Ed.). (1996). *In memory's kitchen* (B. S. Brown, Trans.). Northvale, NJ: Aronson.

Downhill, J. E., Jr., Buchsbaum, M. S., Wei, T., Spiegel-Cohen, J., Hazlett, E. A., Haznedar, M. M., et al. (2000). Shape and size of the corpus callosum in schizophrenia and schizotypal personality disorder. *Schizophrenia Research, 42*(3), 193–208.

Driessen, M., Herrmann, J., Stahl, K., de Zwaan, M., Meier, S., Hill, A., et al. (2000). Magnetic resonance imaging volumes of the hippocampus and amygdala in women with borderline personality disorder and early traumatization. *Archives of General Psychiatry, 57*(12), 1115–1122.

Epstein, S. (1973). The self concept revisited or a theory of a theory. *American Psychologist, 29,* 404–416.

Epstein, S. (1985). The implications of cognitive experiential self-theory for research and social psychology and personality. *Theory of Social Behavior, 15,* 283–310.

Epstein, S. (1994). Integration of the cognitive and psychodynamic unconsciousness. *American Psychologist, 49,* 709–724.

Freud, S. (1925). On negation. *International Journal of Psycho-Analysis, 19,* 235.

Freud, S. (1957). The unconscious. In J. Strachey (Ed.), *The standard edition of the complete psychological works of Sigmund Freud* (Vol. 14, pp. 159–215). London: Hogarth Press. (Original work published 1915)

Goldman-Rakic, P. S. (1984). Modular organization of prefrontal cortex. *Trends in Neurosciences, 7,* 419–429.

Grillon, C., Southwick, S. M., & Charney, D. S. (1996). The psychobiological basis of posttraumatic stress disorder. *Molecular Psychiatry, 1*(4), 278–297.

Gurvits, T. V., Shenton, M. E., Hokama, H., Ohta, H., Lasko, N. B., Gilbertson, M. W., et al. (1996). Magnetic resonance imaging study of hippocampal volume in chronic, combat-related posttraumatic stress disorder. *Biological Psychiatry, 40*(11), 1091–1099.

Howard, Ron. (Director). (2001). *A Beautiful Mind* [Motion picture]. United States: Universal Films.

Johnson, D. J., & Myklebust, H. R. (1967). *Learning disabilities: Educational principles and practices.* New York: Grune & Stratton.

Kellner, M., Yehuda, R., Arlt, J., & Wiedemann, K. (2002). Longitudinal course of salivary cortisol in post-traumatic stress disorder. *Acta Psychiatrica Scandinavica, 105*(2), 153–155.

Kihlstrom, S. F. (1987). The cognitive unconscious. *Science, 237,* 1145–1451.

Kohut, H. (1977). *The restoration of the self.* New York: International Universities Press.

Moore, T. (1994). *Care of the soul.* New York: HarperCollins.

Pitman, R. K., Shin, L. M., & Rauch, S. L. (2001). Investigating the pathogenesis of posttraumatic stress disorder with neuroimaging. *Journal of Clinical Psychiatry, 17,* 47–54.

Poe, E. A. (1940). *Great tales and poems of Edgar Allan Poe.* New York: Washington Square Press.

Resnick, H. S., Yehuda, R., Pitman, R. K., & Foy, D. W. (1995). Effect of previous trauma on acute plasma cortisol level following rape. *American Journal of Psychiatry, 152*(11), 1675–1677.

Seeley, R., Tate, P., & Stephens, T. (2000). *Essentials of anatomy and physiology* (5th ed.). New York: McGraw-Hill.

Shelley, M. (1978). Frankenstein. In *Frankenstein, Dracula, Dr. Jekyll and Mr. Hyde.* New York: New America Library.

Southwick, S. M., Bremner, D., Krystal, J. H., & Charney, D. S. (1994). Psychobiologic research in posttraumatic stress disorder. *Psychiatric Clinics of North America, 17*(2), 251–264.

van der Kolk, B. A. (1994). The body keeps the score: Memory and the evolving psychobiology of posttraumatic stress. *Harvard Review of Psychiatry, 1*(5), 253–265.

Voglmaier, M. M., Seidman, L. J., Niznikiewicz, M. A., Dickey, C. C., Shenton, M. E., & McCarley, R. W. (2000). Verbal and nonverbal neuropsychological test performance in subjects with schizotypal personality disorder. *American Journal of Psychiatry, 157*(5), 787–793.

Yehuda, R., Elkin, A., Binder-Brynes, K., Kahana, B., Southwick, S. M., Schmeidler, J., et al. (1996). Dissociation in aging Holocaust survivors. *American Journal of Psychiatry, 153*(7), 935–940.

Yehuda, R., Halligan, S. L., & Bierer, L. M. (2001). Relationship of parental trauma exposure and PTSD to PTSD, depressive and anxiety disorders in offspring. *Journal of Psychiatric Research, 35*(5), 261–270.

Yehuda, R., Kahana, B., Binder-Brynes, K., Southwick, S. M., Mason, J. W., & Giller, E. L. (1996). Low urinary cortisol excretion in Holocaust survivors with posttraumatic stress disorder. *American Journal of Psychiatry, 153*(6), 846.

EXPANDING THE RANGE OF TREATMENT: CHILD, ADOLESCENT, AND ELDERLY MODELS

Treatment of Dramatic Personality Disorders in Children and Adolescents

Efrain Bleiberg

HILDREN IN THE process of developing a dramatic (Cluster B) personality disorder—an Antisocial, Narcissistic, Histrionic, or Borderline Personality Disorder—confront clinicians with unique challenges to their skill, sensitivity, and capacity to manage their own emotional reactions. The coping strategies these children employ to ensure a sense of safety, control, identity, and human connection evoke responses in others that often destroy the efforts to help them and reinforce, instead, these children's maladjustment (Bleiberg, 2001; Kernberg, Weiner, & Bardenstein, 2000). This chapter presents a treatment model that integrates individual psychotherapy, family treatment, and pharmacotherapy and aims at addressing key processes that generate, maintain, and reinforce the development of dramatic personality disorders in children and adolescents.

Studies of individuals with fully developed dramatic personality disorder (Gunderson, Zanarini, & Kisiel, 1991; Paris & Zweig-Frank, 1992; Zanarini & Frankenburg, 1997) document that their developmental trajectory was shaped by an array of biopsychosocial risk factors, including neurobiological vulnerabilities and adverse childhood experiences. Some of these individuals' minds and bodies have been traumatized by the destructive intrusions of physical and/or sexual abuse. Others are burdened by neuropsychiatric vulnerabilities, such as mood disorders, Attention Deficit/Hyperactivity Disorder (ADHD), and learning disorders. Yet, regardless of the degree of environmental adversity or neurobiological handicap, children in the process of organizing a dramatic personality disorder share a striking incongruity: an uncanny sensitivity and reactivity to other people's mental states, incongruously coexisting with remarkable self-centeredness and utter disregard for other people's feelings. One moment they can be engaging and appealing, the next moment, however, their rage, demandingness, manipulativeness, and destructiveness become overwhelming to parents, teachers, and clinicians.

Equally incongruous is the coexistence of a sense of extraordinary power and invincibility verging on omnipotence with utter helplessness and lack of sense of agency. The power and the helplessness are more or less overt and more or less secret: The Antisocial and Narcissistic individuals are typically overtly omnipotent while secretly feeling helpless, whereas the Borderline person characteristically feels overtly helpless and secretly powerful. The paradoxical coexistence of mysterious sensitivity and brutal lack of concern and of power and helplessness offers clues about the developmental disruptions underlying these children's paths to dramatic personality disorders—and serve to guide a treatment model tailored to the developmental and contextual issues generating and perpetuating these children's maladjustment.

At the heart of this treatment model is the concept of mentalization or reflective function. *Mentalization* refers to the biologically prepared capacity to interpret, represent, and respond to human behavior (that of self and others) in human, meaningful terms. As Fonagy's (Fonagy, Gergely, Jurist, & Target, 2002) research demonstrates, this capacity emerges in the interactive processes of the attachment system. Mentalization enables children to read other people's minds and grasp the feelings, beliefs, thoughts, and intentions underlying human behavior—their own and that of others. The development of mentalization promotes four essential developmental achievements:

1. The achievement of a sense of self-agency and the construction of an autobiographical narrative.
2. The capacity for social reciprocity, empathy, and the flexible activation of mental representations in response to social context.
3. The ability for self-regulating limit-setting, affect-modulating, and direction-giving functions.
4. The capacity to symbolize, play, fantasize, and use humor.

The developmental trajectory leading to severe personality disorders reaches a critical milestone when children adapt to an unusual disposition to mind reading—reinforced by an environment that responds to signals of distress with terrified and/or terrifying responses and intermittent misattunement—often coupled with other genetic vulnerabilities and unusual sensitivities, such as dysregulations of mood, arousal, or cognition. The crucial adaptation is a coping strategy that relies on hypervigilance to the internal and interpersonal cues that normally trigger an intensification of the need for proximity and human connection and is followed by the inhibition of mentalization in response to such internal and interpersonal cues. The prototype of such adaptation is the disorganized pattern of attachment (Main & Solomon, 1990).

A consequence of the intermittent inhibition of mentalization in attachment contexts is the *fractionation* of psychological functioning (Fischer, Kenny, & Pipp, 1990). Fractionation refers to the state-dependent development and organization of mental experience. It leads to the construction of some subsets of experience that are organized in a mentalizing mode whereas other subsets are organized in a nonmentalizing mode. The activation of nonmentalizing modes of experience leads to coercive behavior designed to evoke interpersonal responses that perfectly match the person's mental state. Coercive strategies, in turn, trigger a parallel protective inhibition of mentalization in others, including the parents. As a consequence, children and parents—and later other significant adults, such as teachers and treaters—become entrapped in coercive cycles of relatedness that greatly increase the odds of neglect and maltreatment and powerfully reinforce maladaptive patterns of experiencing, coping, and relating.

BEGINNING TREATMENT: CREATING A SECURE BASE AND A REPRESENTATIONAL MISMATCH

Clinical experience suggests that meaningful engagement in treatment by children with dramatic personality disorders is unlikely unless there is movement in their interpersonal context in a direction that creates what Horowitz (1987) called a *representational mismatch*. In Horowitz's formulation, a representational mismatch is created when external reality challenges the expectations embedded in internal representational models (Bleiberg, 2001). In the case of youngsters with dramatic personality disorders, a representational mismatch arises when parents and treaters demonstrate effectiveness and consistency in providing children with limit-setting, nurturance and support, generational boundaries, and encouragement for mastery and autonomy. For Narcissistic and Narcissistic-Antisocial children, a representational mismatch results from a challenge to their omnipotence and their insistence that others are worthless, weak, and incompetent. For Borderline youngsters, a mismatch is produced when parents are able to protect their children from maladaptive behavior, such as promiscuous sex or drugs that give these youngsters a momentary sense of well-being, control, and connection with others. Thwarting children's self-defeating and self-destructive behavior challenges these children's view of their parents and other adults as unreliable, ineffectual, or indifferent—or as brutal and exploitative.

Youngsters with a dramatic personality disorder respond to a representational mismatch with desperate and often destructive efforts to recreate the patterns of interaction that, although maladaptive, also provided them with a sense of safety, control, and attachment. Such efforts can be so destructive that they exceed the capacity for containment of most parents. Treatment in specialized residential centers or day treatment with high or moderate management combined with school-based and after-school services can effectively support a representational mismatch (Bleiberg, 2001). Contrasting, however, with earlier models of residential treatment (Bettelheim & Sylvester, 1948; Rinsley, 1980a, 1980b) that conceptualized the residential milieu as *the* site of treatment in effect, taking over the parenting role, contemporary residential treatment (Leichtman & Leichtman, 1996a, 1996b, 1996c) for dramatic personality disorders consists of more focused interventions. In this paradigm, residential treatment generally lasts one to six months, rather than two to five years; is conceived as part of a continuum of services (Behar, 1996; Sharfstein & Kent, 1997); and is designed to support rather than replace parental competence. The goals of residential treatment are to help break coercive cycles, to stabilize symptomatology, and to facilitate the use of outpatient interventions and social supports to continue treatment (Bleiberg, 2001).

Regardless of whether residential treatment becomes necessary or not, the key to a representational mismatch, however, is the efforts to enhance parents' competence and establish an alliance between parents and clinicians. To facilitate the creation of a treatment alliance with the parents, the clinicians must first share with the parents a common understanding of the children's problems. This assessment examines the retreat from mentalization as a coping strategy to perceived threats to the continuity and safety of attachments. Parents are thus introduced to a perspective on coercive patterns of interaction driven by inhibited mentalization. Such a perspective is essential to shift the discussion from behavior that needs to be managed or eliminated to relationships and internal states that can change by being shared and by becoming meaningful. *Implicitly,* the parents are invited to consider their own roles in maintaining and reinforcing cycles of nonmentalizing interactions. Treaters make clear to the parents that their competence and well-being are essential to their children's adjustment. Minimizing parental deficiencies is crucial and can be aided by formulations that point out the active role that children's behavior plays in shaping family interactions. Parents find it particularly helpful when clinicians recognize the significance of neurobiological vulnerabilities such as Attention Deficit Disorder, Mood Disorder, and unusual sensitivities to human responses, which shape the family's emotional and interpersonal patterns of interaction.

Helping parents to see their youngsters' difficulties as an expression of disruptions in attachment and mentalization sets the stage for two important steps. First, clinicians present the formulation that mutually reinforcing patterns of nonmentalizing experience and coercive behavior are at the heart of the unrewarding cycles of anger, despair, and helplessness in which parents and children find themselves stuck. From this perspective, the central therapeutic task is to promote a shift from coercive and nonmentalizing exchanges—for example, the "dialogue of the deaf" (Liddle & Hogue, 2000) between parents who bemoan their children's "out of control" behavior, while the children bristle and reject their parents' efforts to control them—to a genuinely reflective, mentalizing dialogue that enables all family members to grasp one another's point of view and convey their own experience.

Second, treaters and parents can together examine how particular experiences or interpersonal transactions in the developmental history of the family become signals of danger and triggers of a defensive retreat from mentalization. These experiences typically concern issues of safety and trust, commitment and loyalty, protection and love as well as betrayal, abuse, abandonment, neglect, and misattunement. The ensuing readiness to respond rigidly and unreflectively to specific cues and perceived threats create circular, self-reinforcing cycles of nonmentalizing that render families less able to respond adequately to developmental pressures for change.

Breaking the cycle of coercion and nonmentalization ultimately rekindles empathy, mutuality, and a sense of agency in children and parents. But empathy does not preclude limit-setting. An attachment framework recognizes that mentalization is built on the foundation of *effective* and *responsive* parenting. As Diamond and Liddle (1999) point out, family members must have "a fundamental basis of trust and attachment before they are willing to learn communication skills and seek mutually supportive solutions to problems" (pp. 7–8). Such trust, in turn, grows out of children's repeated experiences with strong, reliable, and responsive parents who are capable of regulating their children's distress and overarousal, of nurturing them, and of ensuring their safety. For children and adolescents with dramatic personality disorders, competent parenting entails combining continued connection and support with containment of destructive, self-destructive, or otherwise maladaptive behavior—a combination associated empirically with a decrease in adolescent deviance and substance abuse (Fletcher, Darling, & Steinberg, 1995; Schmidt, Liddle, & Dakof, 1996).

Framing the goals of treatment along these lines focuses the therapeutic process on first assisting the parents in achieving the skills they need to remain calm and in control when facing the internal and interpersonal cues that have signaled a retreat from mentalization.

ROLE OF PHARMACOTHERAPY AS AN ADJUNCT TO MENTALIZATION AND SUPPORT OF PARENT'S COMPETENCE

The use of medications can powerfully support the parents' competence—and the alliance between parents and treaters. The rationale for pharmacological interventions with children and adolescents in the process of developing a dramatic personality disorder is based on clinical studies and research with adults with dramatic personality disorder (Coccaro & Kavoussi, 1997; Coccaro et al., 1989; Gunderson & Links, 1995; Kapfhammer & Hippius, 1998; Soloff, 1998). It is also grounded in clinical experience with these youngsters (Bleiberg, 2001) and in studies documenting the effectiveness of pharmacotherapy in a range of related or comorbid child and adolescent problems. The role of pharmacotherapy in the treatment of youngsters with dramatic personality disorders is to target dysregulations of arousal, cognition, affect, and impulse that promote the inhibition of mentalization in at least four ways:

1. They generate in the youngsters a heightened need for attuned responses to restore psychophysiological regulation.
2. The dysregulations evoke distress, frustration, and inhibition of mentalization in the parents.
3. They increase the intensity of distress, anxiety, or hyperarousal that leads to fight or flight reactions of sufficient intensity to block the exercise of mentalization.
4. They decrease the availability of symbolic capacities, energy level, or concentration necessary for mentalization.

Pharmacotherapy targets both the symptoms that emerge during episodes of acute psychobiological decompensation and the trait vulnerabilities that represent an enduring diathesis to dysfunction. No one-to-one correspondence has been identified between specific neurobiological vulnerabilities and types of personality disorder. Thus, given the current level of knowledge, pharmacotherapy targets personality dimensions, such as affective dysregulation and impulsive-behavior dysregulation (Bleiberg, 2001; Soloff, 1998) and Axis I disorders (*Diagnostic and Statistical Manual of Mental Disorders*, American Psychiatric Association [APA], 1994), such as depression, anxiety disorders, ADHD, and mood disorders. By impacting the neurobiological underpinnings of arousal, cognition, affect, and impulse, pharmacotherapy creates more optimal conditions for psychotherapy, and family treatment youngsters can more readily restore their inhibited capacity to mentalize. They are less buffeted by subjective distress, anxiety, or hyperarousal or when their depressed energy level and reduced capacity for concentration have improved. Parents place themselves in the prescription, and administration of effective medication places the adults in the position of helping children gain control and self-regulation when they collaborate with the treaters in administering effective medication.

A collaborative relationship with the parents is thus built around an effort to enhance the parents' competence, comfort, and sense of control. In so doing, parents and treaters create an interpersonal context that implicitly challenges the children's nonmentalizing mode of experiencing, coping, and relating. By producing an implicit representational mismatch, the alliance between parents and treaters generates a creative crisis that, in the words of Minuchin and Fishman (1981), takes a family "stuck along the developmental spiral . . . and pushes it in the direction of its own evolution" (p. 26). To summarize: Treatment of children with a dramatic personality disorder requires the "secure base" (Bowlby, 1980) of a collaborative relationship between parents and treaters. Such alliance can be optimally achieved by the following:

1. Minimizing the parents' experience of shame, blame, guilt, helplessness, and incompetence by emphasizing the nonmentalizing, coercive transactions and cycles in which youngsters and parents are stuck.
2. Defining as a crucial task of treatment the breaking up of coercive cycles that prevent secure attachments and a substantial mentalizing perspective.
3. Redirecting the discussion with the parents from children's behavioral problems to relationship concerns tied to internal states in an effort to begin promoting the parents' capacity to mentalize.
4. Introducing the goal of building the parents' sense of competence and control as a prerequisite for helping children mentalize.
5. Providing targeted pharmacotherapy to address dysregulation of arousal, cognition, affect, and/or impulse.
6. Recognizing that treatment can proceed only when parents agree with each other and with the treaters on their understanding of the problem, the goals of treatment, and the approaches to achieve such goals.
7. Anticipating problematic areas, including, in particular, the parents' experience that treatment will take control away or threaten the connections between family members. Treatment should be defined, instead, as an effort to find the optimal distance between protecting personal space and maintaining sustaining attachments.

EARLY STAGES OF TREATMENTS: FORMING AN ALLIANCE AND ENHANCING MENTALIZATION

Evidence of collaboration between parents and treaters (e.g., support for the treatment plan, agreement with giving medications, or a concerted effort by parents to set limits, provide structure, and maintain generational boundaries) creates a mismatch with the youngsters' expectations about parents' incompetence and unreliability. This mismatch disrupts coercive patterns of interaction and challenges the youngsters' maladaptive coping mechanisms, thus promoting anxiety and creating the conditions that will make an individual psychotherapy process possible. Treaters can then sort out whether they will conduct simultaneously the individual and family aspects of the treatment or refer the individual process to another clinician, a practice often preferable with adolescents. The division of labor, however, creates the necessity of ongoing communication and coordination between the treaters. The goals of the initial phase of psychotherapy are: (1) to form a collaborative relationship with these youngsters in which they can explore sharing some aspects of their experience as a vehicle to get help by understanding the internal states underlying their behavior and (2) to enhance self-control through the use of mentalization. However, faced with even a hint of collaboration between treaters and parents, youngsters with dramatic personality disorders typically react with efforts, either blatant or subtle, to sabotage adult competence and undermine their collaboration. Open defiance and contempt, threats, assaults, or attempts to run away are the most obvious expressions of these children's attempts to instigate chaos in their environment, ultimately in the service of preserving the status quo.

Narcissistic and Narcissistic-Antisocial youngsters often present themselves in the initial therapy sessions as hotshots filled with bravado and pretentious self-sufficiency, bent on demeaning the therapist. Yet, they may also appear grateful and seemingly compliant, brimming with intellectual insights or seductively conveying to the therapists that they find them exceptionally sensitive, brilliant, and helpful. Borderline youngsters can fall madly in love with their therapists and are eager to praise their good fortune in having found the "perfect" person to love—and to be loved by them. The youngsters' initial gambit provides a window into the range of interpersonal experiences and internal states that trigger an inhibition of mentalization. The fundamental goal of the initial phase of treatment is to transform the sterility of coercive and unreflective interactions into at least a modest sense of mutuality. Contracting with the patients and parents is generally helpful but fraught with problems: Most parents, let alone most youngsters with dramatic personality disorders, are in no position to negotiate a meaningful contract. Contracts that define a priori the conditions that will bring treatment to an end set the stage for testing limits and active efforts to destroy treatment.

A more useful clinical stance is described by Gunderson (2000), who proposes to limit the contracting to an agreement about practical issues, such as fees and frequency of sessions, and to add a few simple statements about the therapists' role and the nature of the treatment process. The purpose of these statements is to make explicit that the way to address problems in therapy is by "making sense" of what underlies behavior. It is useful to also underscore what seems to trouble the patient and point out that these problems are amenable to change. Stressing confidentiality helps build an alliance—with the only exception being information about the patient's behavior that endangers them or others.

On the basis of clinical experience, it appears that generally two or more sessions of individual therapy per week, typically extending for one to three years, are required to transform disorganized attachments into secure relationships guided by mentalization. Clinical experience suggests that psychotherapy processes carried out at a frequency of one session a week or less generally revolve around providing advice, education, limits, and crisis management rather than creating the conditions that allow youngsters to regain the capacity to mentalize. If residential treatment is necessary, psychotherapy is optimally initiated while the youngster is still in residential treatment. Psychotherapy thus provides continuity of attachments and planning after the residential treatment is completed.

Even at an optimal frequency of sessions, the difficulties in creating such conditions are formidable, as illustrated in the following case.

CASE ILLUSTRATION—ROBERT

A 15-year-old adolescent in a residential treatment unit, Robert began therapy with a superficial eagerness to solve his problems. Such therapeutic zeal soon gave way to rather flamboyant expressions of contempt for the residential center, its staff, and the therapist. He had expected that "a famous clinic" would provide him with a therapist perfectly suited to treat him—a "perfect match." Robert had some hope when he first met me because he noticed that we both had blond hair and blue eyes. He was quickly disappointed, however, when he heard my obviously foreign accent. He could not understand why he had been subjected to the ignominy of having a "spic" for a therapist.

I commented that—if I heard him right—he seemed to experience my accent as a putdown that would embarrass him by association. "Not bad for a spic," Robert replied, quickly turning to his doubts about whether "spics" could understand the concerns of someone of obvious Nordic descent. I said that, if I heard him correctly, he seemed to be saying that if we were not identical, not only in looks but also in background, I would not be able to understand and appreciate him. "Not bad for a spic" was again his response. Yet, I could detect a budding relatedness in his mocking compliment.

Such relatedness was only tentative. Nonetheless, in a subsequent session, Robert confided that if he trusted me, I might find a way to sabotage his plans to "behave appropriately" and maintain "a positive attitude" to convince his parents and the treatment team that he was ready to return to his beautiful northern state instead of rotting in dreadful Kansas. This comment was meant to show me how clever and in control he really was, as well as how little he valued my home state and anything Kansas had to offer him. It might also, however, betray his own questions about how effectively manipulation and pretense could solve his problems. Not picking up on any of these issues, I commented instead that, if I heard him right, he was concerned about what would happen if, indeed, I heard him right and he got to trust me even a bit. Would it help him or derail his plans and get him to lose control?

This vignette illustrates the principle of creating a context of safety (where children can share some aspects of their subjective experience) by focusing initial interventions on clarifying the patient's intended communication, perceptions, and feelings of the moment ("Let me see if I understand what you are saying—am I hearing you correctly?"). This stance only makes explicit the therapist's assumption that all of the patient's behaviors convey meanings based on internal states that give such behavior purpose—including a communicative purpose. In so doing, the therapist seeks to strike a careful balance between "too much" empathy, which these children experience as overwhelming (because it threatens to expose to themselves, as well as others, their hidden vulnerabilities), and "too little" empathy, which promotes despair and reinforces the conviction that relationships lead only to frustration, hurt, and misattunement.

What the therapist avoids doing is at least as important. At no point during the initial phase will the therapist point out the patient's envy, sadness, vulnerability, or rage, nor the related defenses of grandiosity, dissociation, denial, or projective identification. Linking the patient's current feelings and thoughts to events or feelings in the past is bound to create the same response as that given to a premature confrontation of vulnerability or defensiveness: an exacerbation of maladaptive defenses and an increase in the need for distance, control, or devaluation of the treatment and the therapist.

An indication that an area of tentative attachment is being established occurs when the child eagerly uses the therapist as an audience. Robert, for example, proceeded to fill our sessions with lengthy dissertations about his multiple areas of expertise, namely, nautical history, gourmet food (he prided himself on his culinary skills and wished to become a famous chef), and old movie stars (he fancied himself a connoisseur of classic films). In a cautious way, he seemed to invite me to share at least some aspects of his life.

INTERVENTIONS TO ENHANCE MENTALIZATION, STRENGTHEN IMPULSE CONTROL, AND CREATE AWARENESS OF OTHER'S MENTAL STATE

Interventions that help these youngsters save face pave the way for a therapeutic alliance, that is, the budding conviction that they stand to gain something from collaborating with the therapist. Face-saving interventions help youngsters with dramatic personality disorders maintain a sense of control and attachment when confronted with the representational mismatch created by the parents' efforts to set limits and form an alliance with the treaters. Therapeutic face-saving—as opposed to maladaptive efforts to maintain an illusion of power and control—involve a delicate balance between fostering more adaptive responses to social demands while allowing the youngsters to maintain a semblance of control. At this stage of treatment, three categories of interventions are particularly critical:

1. Interventions designed to enhance mentalization in general.
2. Interventions designed to strengthen children's impulse control and self-regulation by using mentalizing capacities.
3. Interventions designed to help children become aware of others' mental states.

These sets of interventions are used simultaneously during the early stage of therapy and tend to reinforce one another.

1. ENHANCING MENTALIZATION

How does a therapist go about enhancing children's capacity to mentalize? They first need to learn to observe their own emotions and feel safe doing so. Therapists can suggest that they can retain a sense of control even when those around them fail to follow the expected ways of responding and interacting. They can achieve such sense of control by understanding their own reactions, for instance, the relationship between feeling frustrated and becoming anxious. As part of this process, therapists help children observe, label, and understand their emotional states, including the associated physiological reactions. Therapists thus introduce a mentalizing perspective that links behavior to underlying mental states.

During the initial stage of therapy, therapists keep the focus on simple mental states, such as belief and desire, rather than on more complex ones, such as conflict or ambivalence. Alvarez (1992) noted how Borderline children respond to anxiety with a loss of reflectiveness. With a young Borderline girl, terrified of separations, Alvarez realized that instead of saying that the girl seemed to believe that something terrible would happen during separation, the therapist had to turn the idea around and talk to the girl about her difficulty in believing that both of them might make it through a separation. Alvarez's comments point out the importance of refraining from linking children's feelings to dissociated or repressed experiences or to past events. Working with current, moment-to-moment changes in a child's mental state within the sessions, the therapist can focus the child's attention on the circumstances that lead, for example, to aggression in situations in which the child feels misunderstood, blocked, confused, or made anxious by others. At the same time, the therapist can point out how gaining control over automatic reactions may actually help these children feel more in charge of their own lives and behavior.

In this respect, the approach recommended during the beginning stage of psychotherapy requires a reversal of classic psychoanalytic techniques. Child—and adult—analysis opens paths to children's experience of repudiated affect. In contrast, children with severe personality disorders are likely to inhibit mentalization and thus require help in the opposite direction (cognitive restructuring): to learn how to use their ideational capacity to modulate their emotional experience. Such children need help understanding which thoughts, ideas, and circumstances—both internal and environmental—make them feel certain things. Likewise, they need help learning to recognize what they say to themselves that aggravates or modulates their emotional experience. The parallels here with cognitive therapy techniques for children and with dialectic behavior therapy (Linehan, 1993) are obvious.

Robert, the boy described earlier in this chapter, followed my clarifications— "Let me see if I hear right what you are saying"—of his disparaging remarks about me, my heritage, the Menninger Clinic, and the state of Kansas, with an acknowledgment that he found it utterly demeaning to be "incarcerated" and in an abject state of deprivation of control and dignity and in a hick town such as Topeka to boot. He could only imagine what his friends back home would be thinking of him. He blushed as he said this. With this statement, he seemed to demonstrate a capacity to respond to a therapeutic stance aimed at recognizing him as an intentional being who communicated his mental states through his behavior. I proceeded to remark that, if I heard him right, it was an image in his mind of his friends looking on disapprovingly, perhaps mockingly, that seemed to trigger painful and angry feelings in him.

This inhibition of mentalization turns children's experience of thoughts and feelings into something akin to bodily states (McDougall, 1989; Sifneos, Apfel-Savitz, & Frankel, 1977). In another case, Megan, an 8-year-old girl, was totally overwhelmed by the rage and anxiety she experienced when her mother left her. In the early sessions with Megan, I drew attention to her flushed face and wide-open eyes and then wondered aloud if she found me threatening. Several sessions later, as she had become more comfortable expressing and verbalizing simple mental states, she confided that when her mother was not around, she was overcome with anger and dread fueled by thoughts that her mother was going to be abducted or dismembered in a horrible car wreck. I was careful not to suggest any links between Megan's own anger at losing control of her mother and the thoughts about something horrible happening to her mother. We focused instead on devising ways to chart her worry and anger to identify the point at which she lost the capacity to think clearly and feel that she had control over her own mind. Megan discovered a method to accomplish this task by posting on the refrigerator door—in proximity of both a "cooling" presence and nurturing supplies—a "worry chart" and an "anger thermometer," where she could record the extent of her angry feelings or worrisome thoughts.

In summary, the therapist aims to enhance the reflective process by encouraging children to observe and label their somatic and psychological experiences. Key aspects of this intervention involve helping children focus on states felt in the immediate therapy situation and encouraging verbalization as a way to increase children's sense of control and lessen their feelings of vulnerability and shame.

2. STRENGTHENING IMPULSE CONTROL AND ENHANCING SELF-REGULATION

Children with dramatic personality disorders, particularly Borderline youngsters, require considerable help in curbing their impulsivity. Rosenfeld and Sprince (1963) described a 6-year-old Borderline child, Pedro, who frequently urinated on the therapist and her possessions. Other features of this child's behavior led the therapist to understand his urination as a crude attempt to coerce her into maintaining a connection to him in the form of a victim-victimizer mutuality. Neither interpretations nor physical restraint proved successful in reducing this misbehavior. The therapist then devised a way to address Pedro's need to stay connected (and avoid a disruption of attachment): She told him that she would continue whatever activity in which they were jointly engaged while he went to the restroom and that she would give him a running commentary of what she was doing while he was in there. Because he seemingly felt able to maintain contact with the therapist through her voice, Pedro stopped urinating in the treatment room.

Mayes and Cohen (1993) pointed out that, for some children, the very process of developing imaginative play—or fantasy, pretending, and humor with adolescents—is the most helpful aspect of treatment. A good deal of the work, according to these authors, centers on helping children address the issues that create obstacles to entering the imaginary world. Appreciating the difference between internal experience and directly perceivable experience paves the way for enhanced symbolic thinking and, along with that, imagery, guessing, hoping, experimenting, planning, revising, and working through.

Indeed, the capacity to take a playful, humorous, or "as if" stance may be a critical step in the development—or the ability to maintain—mentalization, because it requires simultaneously holding in mind two realities, the pretend and the actual, in synchronicity with a moment-to-moment reading of the other person's state of mind. Therapists often need to create a context in which an attitude of pretense or humor is possible. For example, they may exaggerate their actions to mark for children the pretend nature of interactions, or they may choose objects that are clearly incapable of adopting an intentional stance (e.g., crude toys) in a way similar to how caregivers "mark" (Gergely & Watson, 1999) their attuned responses to their children's internal states. Children who are confronted with intolerable anxiety when they genuinely try to take on the point of view of others may find it acceptable to imagine pieces of wood (or finger people) thinking and feeling. Under the section on becoming aware of others' mental states, I discuss the implications (beyond strengthening impulse control) of learning to play with objects and persons. During the beginning of therapy, however, the central message is that play, fantasy, and humor offer a way to step back from overwhelming or unmanageable experiences and help break them down into more manageable, easier-to-master bits.

Tooley's (1973) *Playing It Right* is a beautiful account of how therapists can attempt to align the behavior and play of impulsive children with the constraints of reality. Children are nudged to introduce small modifications gradually in their play or behavior so that it better encompasses the complexities, limitations, and frustrations of reality. Borderline youngsters, in particular, create such elaborately vivid and absorbing play themes that they—and, at times, their therapists—can no longer differentiate between fantasy and reality. In their play and fantasy life, these youngsters literally come to life, and they fight mightily against reality intruding and questioning the arbitrariness they impose on their life and relationships. In the magic of play—and in the fantasy world they inhabit—these children create an illusion of perfect relationships, while safely keeping away threatening aspects of themselves and others.

By playing it right, therapists can introduce children to the very idea of control. Pedro took on the role of a powerful but uncontrolled mechanical object—the most awesome train engine in the world. He proved his strength by climbing and jumping on the windowsill, whistling like a train, pulling the curtains down, and threatening to jump out the window. His therapist suggested that really powerful vehicles have brakes and that a true demonstration of strength consists of the ability to start and stop at will. Pedro took eagerly to the game of stopping and starting, allowing more space for the therapist to speak. She subsequently brought up the idea of a very clever mechanic who understood how the train worked and what could go wrong and was thus able to figure out how to prevent breakdowns and damage. Pedro was able to use this bridge between psychological and physical reality to gain greater recognition and control of his feelings.

Play, fantasy, and humor offer a bridge between automatic, unreflective, and coercive models of self and others and the world of mentalized subjectivity. But before those bridges can be built, as these youngsters' attachment to their therapist grows, their impulsivity—at least during the sessions—will actually be exacerbated, because attachment brings about the very internal states of vulnerability, fear of abandonment, and dependency that trigger for them a retreat from mentalization. In the throes of nonmentalizing models, Borderline youngsters often require help to manage suicidal, parasuicidal, and other self-harming behavior, such as substance abuse or binge eating. The use of an addiction model involving groups and psychoeducation is helpful and effective (Chu, 1998).

Improved self-care and symptom control can be supported in the individual sessions with psychoeducational approaches and "grounding" strategies (Chu, 1998). Psychoeducational interventions emphasize communicating to the patient that symptoms such as flashbacks, dysphoric mood states, or overwhelming anxiety or panic—which contribute to feeling out of control and to hurtful, impulsive responses to blot them out—can in fact be controlled. Helping patients achieve improved self-control is indeed a key goal of treatment. For youngsters with a history of physical or sexual abuse, it is often helpful during the beginning phase of treatment to acknowledge the effects of early traumatization, including the adaptive function of their symptomatology, as crucial attempts to stay in control and maintain attachment. But this acknowledgment should be made without embarking on a detailed exploration of the traumatic events or the feelings associated with them.

Grounding techniques are approaches that seek to identify concretely both the moments when these youngsters feel unsafe during the sessions and the actions they can take to counter such unsafe feelings (e.g., maintaining eye contact). In addition, the therapist helps them define the concrete circumstances when they are more prone to feel overwhelmed, such as when they are tired or alone at night. Then, the therapist helps the patients design a *crisis plan* to deal with these moments when they feel unsafe or out of control.

Parents provide therapists with information about potentially disruptive events (e.g., divorces, hospitalizations, loss of employment). Anticipating how the parents are likely to feel promotes a mentalizing stance and introduces the idea that, in the face of certain internal or environmental events, they "lose" the capacity to mentalize and, with it, the ability to stay in control of themselves.

Sharing information about neuropsychiatric vulnerabilities (e.g., attention deficit, hyperactivity, mood, or reading disorders) provides a way to explain problems in self-control and opens the possibility for planning therapeutic responses to address these vulnerabilities. Such responses include medications, educational remediation, and cognitive strategies to compensate for deficits in attention or organization. Just as important, such discussion introduces the possibility of examining how these children experience their deficits and the implications of those deficits for their life, identity, adjustment, and self-esteem. This discussion is generally left to the middle phase of treatment, because it requires the protection of a more secure attachment to the therapist and a greater readiness on the part of the patient to explore areas of personal vulnerability.

To summarize, during the beginning stage of therapy, the therapist looks for strategies that children can learn for channeling impulsive behavior into socially acceptable forms of conduct, with increasing control over the expression of feelings in actions. Only later do therapists examine the specific cues generated in the attachment relationship between patient and therapist that trigger an intensification of impulsivity.

3. Creating Awareness of Others' Mental States

The therapeutic situation pushes children to become aware of the mental states of others. The aim is to show them that all may not be as it seems. Thus, the children begin to learn that their habitual thoughts and feelings are not the only way of seeing the world—or even, necessarily, the way that others see the world. Children with dramatic personality disorders, however, actively resist such awareness. They find the mental states of adults confusing or frightening and oftentimes the trigger of threatening or overwhelming internal states. Clinical experience has shown that these children are best helped via interventions focused on their perceptions of the therapist's mental states as a precursor to mentalization. The therapist thus seeks to create a relatively safe environment where children can get to know how they are seen by others, mirroring the normal developmental process whereby mentalization and the sense of self and others arise from grasping how others experience them as intentional beings. Therapists do not necessarily reveal to these children what they actually experience; rather, they share with the children their perception of how the children might be experiencing the therapist's state of mind. Some therapists have used guessing games along these lines. George Moran (1984) offered an illustration of this approach that serves also to show the limitation of a traditional interpretive technique.

Aggressive youngsters benefit from social skills and anger coping skills training (Bierman, 1989; Lochman & Wells, 1996) and particularly from problem-solving skills training (Spivak & Shure, 1978). Problem-solving skills training (PSST), the most systematically researched approach to the behavioral treatment of conduct difficulties, has demonstrated effectiveness in rigorously conducted studies, particularly in combination with parent training (Kazdin, 1996b; Kazdin, Siegel, & Bass, 1992; Webster-Stratton & Hammond, 1997). In this program, the therapist examines the habitual ways children address interpersonal situations, then encourages a step-by-step approach to solving interpersonal problems that includes "self-talk" to direct attention to aspects of the problem that may lead to effective and adaptive solutions. Modeling and reinforcing prosocial behavior are used, as are practice, feedback, homework assignments, and role playing in the context of structured tasks based on relevant, real-life situations.

Individual therapy can take advantage of these approaches and reinforce their applicability in the context of discussing with these youngsters ways to focus on their distorted appraisal of social events and other people's internal states. Finally, the attachments cultivated in individual and family work with the youngsters and their parents seek to address the key limitation of cognitive-behavioral programs of known effectiveness, mainly the high risk of premature termination (Kazdin, 1996a).

MANAGING COUNTERTRANSFERENCE EXPERIENCES

Not just the patient's reactions require careful attention, however. Perhaps the greatest challenge clinicians face when treating youngsters with dramatic personality disorders is their own emotional response. There is now considerable agreement in the psychoanalytic literature (Gabbard, 1995; Ogden, 1994) that the transference-countertransference relationship is a joint construction between patient and therapist rather than the product of the patient's projections alone. The countertransference responses evoked by youngsters with dramatic personality disorders, however, place unique demands on the emotional resources, technical skills, boundaries, professional ethics, and personal integrity of treaters.

Therapists grow wary of the repeated alternation between reflective and unreflective modes of relatedness. As treaters, we enter into lives often marked by unspeakable despair and terror and find ourselves responding to the sheer determination to survive that so many of these youngsters exude. Yet, the very process of developing an attachment triggers in the patients a retreat from mentalization and the activation of coercive, unreflective modes of experiencing and relating. As Gabbard (1995) points out, a common thread in contemporary psychoanalytic thinking about countertransference is that the mental contents of the patient are not somewhat mystically transported from patient to clinician. Rather, argues Gabbard, "interpersonal pressure is applied by specific patient behaviors that evoke specific clinician responses" (p. 7). The unreflective and coercive nature of the interpersonal pressures applied by youngsters with dramatic personality disorders is not only difficult to resist but also tends to evoke a predictable response in all people, including therapists: the momentary loss of the capacity to maintain mentalization.

The result of the activation of nonmentalizing modes of operation in the therapist is an experience of an alien force disrupting an individual's sense of self and others. Certain patterns of response embody the therapist's efforts to contain and defend against this alien presence or, alternatively, result from the clinician's being "taken over" by coercive pressures and responding in kind with unreflectiveness. Therapists often grow to dread the sessions, anticipating the "loss" of the key personal and professional attributes that form the basis of their practice: a capacity to listen empathically to patients and then to respond flexibly, thoughtfully, and ethically. Instead, therapists feel "fooled" by Borderline youngsters' pleas for relatedness that alternate with their coercive tyranny. Narcissistic and Antisocial youngsters, bent on producing helplessness and vulnerability in the therapist, often evoke boredom, irritation, or rage when they deny dependence or turn the therapist into an admiring audience. Therapists' defensive reactions against being subjugated and victimized throw them into a fight-or-flight mode that translates into open rage or pressure to demonstrate power and control. Alternatively, the unremitting devaluation and disparagement of attachment by Narcissistic and Antisocial youngsters paralyze therapists who feel as drained, defeated, worthless, and helpless as these patients would feel without their defensive grandiosity and projected vulnerability.

Borderline and Histrionic youngsters seduce therapists by attributing to them perfect empathy, extraordinary power, or unique wisdom. Therapists are vulnerable to experiencing the coercive pressure to become an idealized rescuer (i.e., one who can heal the patient's wounds). The compelling notion of such unreflective models plays a significant role in leading to the destructive outcome of violations of professional boundaries—including therapists' professing love for or engaging in sexual relations with their patients—with tragic consequences for all involved.

Borderline youngsters who threaten suicide, who injure themselves, frequently without intending to die, and who make serious suicide attempts from time to time stir up powerful reactions in those who treat them. These patients often threaten their therapists with the implicit message: "If I die, it will be because of your failure." The "failures" in question involve feelings that the therapist has in fact been coerced to experience—but against which he or she typically struggles. These feelings include "not giving a damn anymore," hatefulness, loss of hope, and the secret—or not so secret—desire for the patient to die.

Countertransference reactions to youngsters with dramatic personality disorders are not shaped just by therapist-patient interactions. The therapist's responses shape and are shaped by the entire system of family transactions in which the patient's life—and the treatment relationship—is embedded. Thus, therapists find themselves reacting to the parents' behavior toward the patient and the treaters themselves, as well as to the responses of the patient to their caregivers' experience of the treatment. Two patterns of countertransference entrapment are common:

1. Therapists who unthinkingly seek to rescue parents from the cruelty and disruption inflicted on them by their children.
2. Therapists who compete with the parents, devalue them in overt or subtle ways, and find themselves compelled to "adopt" the patient and save him or her from abusive, unfeeling, exploitive, or self-centered caregivers.

Although the enactment of one of these nonmentalizing patterns of countertransference can derail the treatment, anticipating their emergence also opens new opportunities for therapeutic intervention. Carpy (1989) argues that the patient's observation of the therapist's ability to contain, tolerate, and reflect on intense feelings experienced in the therapeutic relationship is mutative in and of itself. Arguably, therapists' capacity to manage in a mentalizing way the patient's barrage of coercive messages and feelings conveys that the feelings themselves are potentially manageable. Thus, the patient is offered a model of how to break the cycle of coercion and unreflectiveness, which can be demonstrated *in vivo* when the therapists follow—and comment on—a sequence of internal activities, not only focusing on diagnosing the patient's internal relations but also conducting self-examination and internal supervision (Gabbard & Wilkinson, 1994).

In summary, during the initial phase of individual psychotherapy with children and adolescents with dramatic personality disorders, the goal is to develop a working alliance. Children must be convinced that they can benefit from collaborating and forming a relationship with the therapist that will lead to enhanced self-control and adaptation. To this end:

1. Therapists must avoid confronting vulnerabilities and defenses by linking past and present or addressing repressed or dissociated experience. By minimizing regression, therapists can seek to balance *too much* with *too little* empathy.

2. Therapists can promote verbalization of internal states and differentiation of feelings—and implicitly convey their conception of the patient as an intentional being—by clarifying children's communication ("Let me see if I hear you right").

3. Therapists can build a working alliance by helping the patient save face. Interventions designed to help patients save face minimize feelings of shame and being out of control and being disconnected from others, all of which are brought about by the representational mismatch created by changes in the parents' competence.

4. Therapists can help their patients save face, regain control, and establish a sense of greater safety and connection by enhancing mentalization, strengthening impulse control and self-regulation, increasing awareness of others, and using countertransference:

    a. Enhancing mentalization can be achieved by helping children observe, label, and understand their internal states—initially, the relatively simple states that arise on a moment-to-moment basis in the sessions—and the circumstances that lead to automatic reactions as a way to feel more in charge of their behavior.

    b. Helping to strengthen impulse control and self-regulation occurs by introducing a playful, humorous, or "as if" perspective as a way to step back from overwhelming or unmanageable experiences. Such distancing facilitates breaking down experiences into more manageable bits that children can master. *Playing it right* is one strategy for channeling a patient's impulsive behavior into socially acceptable conduct, with increasing control over the expression of feelings in action. When indicated, psychoeducational approaches, grounding strategies, and discussion of neuropsychiatric vulnerabilities can enhance self-control in highly impulsive youngsters.

c. Increasing patients' awareness of others can be achieved by helping them focus on understanding the mental states of their therapists and other people. In particular, it can be helpful for young patients to understand how therapists conceptualize the internal states that facilitate cause-and-effect relationships and establish reciprocity in the therapeutic relationship. In turn, reciprocity forms the basis for a mentalizing stance in the face of threatening internal cues. These approaches support structured programs designed to enhance problem solving.

d. Using countertransference becomes possible when therapists experience their own unreflectiveness as a window into the internal and intersubjective conditions that evoke inhibition of the patient's mentalization—and subsequently activate coercive models of relatedness.

MIDDLE AND LATE STAGES OF TREATMENT: USING CONNECTION TO MOVE TOWARD INTEGRATION

Youngsters signal their readiness to enter a more advanced phase of treatment by their capacity to use the therapeutic relationship as a trial base for more adaptive responses to environmental challenges. This capacity is demonstrated by how much youngsters can use the help of therapists to improve self-care, lessen self-destructive impulsivity, or, more generally, save face, that is, respond to the enhanced limit setting of parents—the "representational mismatch"—without an exacerbation of maladaptive defensive mechanisms. A child's ability to enter into pretend play without demanding that the therapist totally submit to a rigid script suggests a growing security of attachment to the therapist. Security of attachment is also implied by the capacity of adolescent patients to banter or enter into give-and-take exchanges with humor and playfulness. These indicators of attachment security may be subtle, but they point to the children's desire for closeness with their therapist and the dawning conviction—fraught with uncertainty and fear of being abused, subjugated, abandoned, destroyed, or humiliated—that hope and help can be derived from this collaborative relationship. Therapists need to test the readiness of children to enter this state of treatment by following the steps described here. Clinical experience suggests that 3 to 12 months of treatment are needed before reaching this stage.

The presence of an embryonic collaboration allows therapists to gently encourage youngsters to consider an expansion in the range of "shareable" experiences. Narcissistic youngsters are invited to share their experiences of vulnerability. Borderline youngsters are introduced to the notion of a continuity of self in relationships, including an opening for the exploration of traumatic events that disrupt such continuity.

For example, as Jimmy, a 10-year-old boy, gradually shifted from his initial efforts to exercise absolute control over his therapy sessions, various concerns began to creep into the therapy. He made a clay figure of a woman with large breasts, which he attempted to jam into the therapist's mouth. He also staged a game consisting of a gang led by a wicked woman, the "mother of the gang," whom he instructed the therapist to capture and kill.

The therapist, invariably the persecutor, commented how, in the pretend play, everyone seemed to have trouble getting what they wanted. Even mothers were involved in leading others into stealing. Jimmy then created a play theme involving his father, a role that he assigned to the therapist, who was to be the president of the United States. This president, however, turned out to be a rather pathetic figure who could barely function without Jimmy's direction. The boy delighted in ordering his father-therapist-president around, while shouting directives for the country. The therapist began to point out how this play offered Jimmy a chance to share in the power of an exalted, yet secretly diminished, ruler. If he could be the real power behind the president, maybe he would not have to feel little or vulnerable or afraid that others, envious of his power, might attack him. Perhaps, noted the therapist questioningly, Jimmy's insistence on placing himself in the position of the ultimate, yet secret, ruler betrayed how vulnerable he felt sometimes?

Although the relationship between patient and therapist is clearly the central therapeutic arena, work with these youngsters is not aimed at *interpreting* the transference in the classic sense of expecting and commenting on how thoughts, feelings, wishes, and conflicts about caregivers are transferred to the therapist. Instead, the relationship with the therapist is central, because it is, first and foremost, the most effective route toward acquiring and sustaining a mentalizing capacity in the context of a significant attachment.

But the very stirrings of a growing attachment also trigger increased anxiety and defensiveness. Jimmy, indeed, became extremely anxious when his therapist pointed out his defensive need to cover up his fear of exposing his vulnerability. Similarly, the case of Joe, an 11-year-old boy with a history of brutal physical and sexual abuse at the hands of an alcoholic father, shows dramatically how unbearable it was for Joe to experience desires for closeness with me. Almost in spite of himself, Joe—spurred by face-saving therapeutic assistance with his challenging math homework—began to feel more comfortable in the sessions, but as he did so, he found himself hating his liking for me. He thus began to look for "mistakes" that would demonstrate how much I was a pedantic "know-it-all" who really knew little, if anything, about real life. According to Joe, I had learned everything I had in my "fucking rich shrink" collection of books, a source of knowledge that left me obviously unable to survive the mean streets of the big city, let alone able to help someone hardened by life on those streets. No longer willing to put up with me, Joe then declared his intention to run away from his residential treatment unit, locate my house, and set it on fire after raping my wife and murdering my children with intravenous injections of cocaine.

Joe's tirade spoke loudly of what his sense of a growing attachment to me had stirred in him: an intense fear of painful invasion of his house-body; the penetration of his self, his body, and his bloodstream, leading to an initial rush of excitement followed by inner feelings of deadness; and the envy of my possessions and relationships and his desire to deprive me of them all, hoping perhaps that he could more easily feel attached to me if we were both equally deprived, locked in a tight embrace of shared hatred, loneliness, and deprivation—once he had eliminated all rivals for my affection.

A check of an individual's emotional reactivity can also provide helpful clues to guide interventions. While attempting to weather the storm of Joe's threats, I felt neither threatened nor cut off from him—the telltale signs of the activation of a fight-or-flight response in the presence of an unmodulated threat. I silently wondered if Joe wished to let me know that any more explicit discussion of our relationship was more than he could handle. He seemed to be provoking a change in our interaction from its focus on what gets in the way of greater closeness to more familiar, and thus safer, territory. Sensing his desire to maintain a relationship with me while overtly disowning it, I commented on the meanness and cruelty of his imagery—without referring to either one of us or our relationship. He looked at me with mixed contempt and amusement and proceeded to describe, in a wildly exaggerated fashion, the toughness of the neighborhood and the brutal gang he had survived. He was certain that a wimpy nerd like me had been sheltered from such roughness and would perish in such an environment in a matter of minutes.

Although his statement was richly seasoned with contempt and devaluation, I detected a distinctly teasing, playful invitation to join him in his account of gang adventures. In effect, I knew—and he knew that I knew—that he had grown up in the far more sedate environment of an upper-middle-class community in New England. His interest in, and knowledge of, gangs had been acquired mostly through extensive reading. In earlier sessions, Joe had brought in magazines and tapes glorifying gangs.

I picked up (perhaps with more hope than conviction) on the implied teasing and replied with an even more fantastic account of my own heroic battles as a gang kingpin—a secret identity hidden behind my deceptively mild appearance. Joe seemed to enjoy this gambit and responded with mock disparagement. Over the next few sessions, we engaged in a good deal of increasingly good-natured bantering about the relative merits of his gang and mine. Only after this bantering had gone on for about two weeks was he able to initiate—between denunciations of my Latin Kings—a more serious discussion of how gangs helped by providing a sense of belonging and powerful protection. He asked me: "What do you do when you are upset?" I replied that his question was an excellent and very tough one to ask or answer. I added that I would only tell him some of the things I do; I said that I try to bring to my memories of times when I have been similarly upset, ways I have managed to feel better, and people who have soothed me and provided comfort. Joe seemed puzzled by my answer and, after a moment of hesitation, said: "But I don't have any memories like that." After thinking a bit more, however, he corrected himself: "No wait . . . ," he said, and proceeded to relate, for the first time, how, when he was 6 or 7, he and his father would dance to the mellow tunes of soft rock music. These were the times when he had been sexually abused.

This vignette illustrates several principles that guide interventions in the middle stage of therapy with youngsters who have dramatic personality disorders; in particular, it points to the importance of pacing and the use of transitional experiences to face traumatic attachments and explore an alternative mode of relationships. Youngsters with dramatic personality disorders have fractionated their sense of relatedness. They carry forward an internal model of a cycle of interactions that involves emotionally intense, close relationships in the context of physical and sexual abuse or in the guilty, overinvolved aftermath of maltreatment. The alternative to this intense relatedness entails moments of painful neglect and emotional disconnection. The prospect of a benign, attuned, caring relationship fills them with panic. As Joe's case illustrates, connection happens for them only in intense, violent, abusive relationships. But such abuse also increases their need for comfort, security, and soothing, thus heightening their need to cling to the only model of attachment available to them.

However, internal states in these youngsters that are associated with attachment also signal danger, because they indicate that parents may be driven to frightened or frightening responses, resulting in traumatic experiences. Thus, the youngsters retreat from mentalization—from awareness of their own and their parents' internal states—and cling instead in a nonreflective, procedural fashion to coercive, rigid models of self-other interaction. Rather than simply acknowledging how much the patient has been abused, the therapist can gradually help flush out the many reasons for clinging to abusive models of relationships. Discussing traumatic experiences such as sexual or physical abuse is helpful when such experiences can be placed in a relational context. Such a context gives meaning to the patient's understandable reluctance to give up patterns of coping and relating that cause pain and maladaptation, yet are the only known sources of safety and connection.

Abreaction of traumatic experiences requires a careful, ongoing assessment of a youngster's security of attachment to the therapist and capacity to envision the self as someone other than a victim or victimizer. Without such capacities, these youngsters cannot be expected to give up a model of relatedness that evolved around trauma and detachment. Instead, they experience this possibility as a challenge to plunge into a total void, without their only source of identity, security, and attachment. Therapists find themselves struggling with the urge to cajole the patient into abandoning obviously self-destructive and maladaptive modes of coping, relating, and experiencing. Such a stance by the therapist only increases the patient's anxiety, suspicion of the therapist, and need to defeat the treatment.

At this juncture, youngsters in treatment often require a transitional area of relatedness, akin to Winnicott's (1953) transitional experience, as a safe place to test the possibility of secure attachments, mutuality, and reflective function. Play, fantasy, and humor offer just such transition space. With Joe, the tall tales we exchanged about "our gangs" provided the threads that wove a jointly created story in which Joe could both own and disown feelings of dependence, belonging, security, and vulnerability. At the same time, he was testing out my attunement, respect, and responsiveness to the vulnerable, attachment-seeking aspects of his self.

Some young Narcissistic children, such as Jimmy, introduce an imaginary twin as a transitional relationship. This "twin" typically embodies the weak, helpless, dependent experiences that such children find unbearable. Somatic complaints or somatic crises, such as the ones engineered by David, offer another version of a transitional experience of sharing feelings of pain and vulnerability while also asking for help without explicitly acknowledging such feelings. The transitional sphere of shared play, fantasy, or humor, which can be structured as games (e.g., see Moran's, 1984, "What I think you think I am thinking about you"), provides a safe arena in which to create an illusion of secure attachment with the therapist. At the same time, threatening aspects of the self and others, and of reality constraints, can be kept at a safe distance.

The transitional space of shared play, humor, or fantasy offers a stage on which to explore new ways of being in the world. It allows patients to relate to others—in Joe's case, this form of relating permitted him to ask openly for advice and help; it tested behavior that may promise greater mastery, pleasure, and adaptation; and it explored the bringing together of the split-off or fractionated aspects of Joe's internal world. Thus, Joe could examine his longing for security and belonging in the space provided by our shared construction of the "gang's" world. The magic of anonymity afforded by the transitional space is a function of an implicit agreement to treat these constructions as if they are real, yet clearly knowing that they are all—or almost all—pretend. Thus, in a transitional space, children can be invited to consider that a whole region of their experience stands unlived, so to speak (i.e., never processed in the reflective mode that allows for sharing, ownership, and integration). Such exchanges offer the opportunity to explore the advantages of—as well as the price exacted by—split or fractionated ways of experiencing, coping, and relating in different contexts.

To summarize:

1. Readiness to enter a more advanced stage of therapy is signaled by evidence of a collaborative relationship between patient and therapist. At this point, children demonstrate that they can use their therapist's help to enhance their adaptation.
2. The first set of interventions in the middle stage of treatment should be designed to address the anxieties and defenses that these children mobilize against a closer attachment with their therapist. The possibility of a closer attachment intensifies anxiety and thus triggers an exacerbation of maladaptive defense mechanisms—particularly evident in the relationship with the therapist.
3. Therapists must resist the urge to cajole their patients to relinquish maladaptive defenses and patterns of attachment, recognizing instead that these are the only source of identity, security, and connection available to these youngsters.
4. Patients can benefit from a transitional space provided by shared play, fantasy, and humor. This space allows them to explore more safely issues of attachment, the possibility of integrating aspects of their internal world, and the use of alternative modes of coping and relating.

FACILITATING INTERVENTIONS AND
THE THERAPEUTIC BARGAIN

The transitional space provides a relatively safe haven for beginning to examine systematically not only youngsters' maladaptive patterns of coping and relating but also the motives that underlie the perpetuation of such patterns. Not surprisingly, intense anxiety and intensified reliance on maladaptive coping mechanisms accompany every move in this process, as Joe's case illustrates.

Therapists can expect to be turned into transitional objects (Winnicott, 1953) by their patients' efforts to buffer the emotional storms that buffet them. Gunderson (1996) proposes a hierarchy of transitional options that therapists can offer patients with dramatic personality disorder to help them deal, in particular, with the panic, rage, and dysregulation brought about by interruptions in the treatment or other disruptions in their attachment with the therapist. At the end of the hierarchy, therapists make themselves accessible by telephone either as needed or on a prescheduled basis. In the middle part of the hierarchy, the therapist provides therapist-associated transitional objects such as handwritten notes that the patient can use for comfort and reassurance, cognitive directives to follow at times of distress, or items from the therapist's office to remind the patient of the support offered by the therapist.

The use of these transitional activities offers a buffer that allows the youngster to tolerate a range of internal and interpersonal experiences without entering into fight or flight and inhibiting mentalization, thus permitting the active exploration of the youngster's inner world. The therapist's acknowledgment of the utter terror that children must feel as they enter unexplored areas of self-other relatedness is often useful in preventing a therapeutic stalemate. Facilitating comments at this juncture may provide a needed therapeutic push. Only in the later stages of therapy can therapists use less-reality-distorting options in the hierarchy of transitional activities, namely, self-initiated options such as planning increased contact with friends or accessing other supports during therapists' absences, as examples of a more adaptive way to anticipate and cope with stress and vulnerability.

Pointing out the courage required to venture further into this unfamiliar territory—for example, Joe's question about how to deal with distress—aligns the therapist with the patient's "proximal area of development" (Vygotsky, 1962, 1978), that is, with what Friedman (1982) calls "the person he is about to become" (p. 12).

In fact, as described earlier, such alignment is generally more effective when therapists point out the price—in greater anxiety and exposure to unfamiliar dangers and vulnerability—of giving up the maladaptive mechanisms that these children have found as their only source of identity, security, control, and attachment. Thus, after Joe related his experience of abuse, I pointed out how understandable it was that he would want to dismiss any possibility of closeness with anyone, including a "fucking rich shrink" like me, and the tremendous amount of guts it would take for him to venture into exploring closeness. On the other hand, keeping people at a distance and afraid of him helped Joe feel safe and in control.

Such a stance can free these youngsters to examine the price they pay for relying on maladaptive patterns of coping, experiencing, and relating. At this point in treatment, therapists present to their patients in more explicit fashion the therapeutic bargain that the treatment represents: The patients can choose, if they are able, to relinquish pathological, maladaptive defenses and coercive patterns of relatedness—and the illusion and control, safety, and connection they derive from them—but such relinquishment requires the laborious and at times painful process of attempting real mastery and meaningful relationships. Youngsters call into play strong compensatory mechanisms in response to the "offer" of a therapeutic bargain. If both the therapist and the patient can withstand the onslaught of unreflective coercion that usually follows, themes of dependence, safety, autonomy, vulnerability, body integrity, envy, and competition become available for exploration. Intermixed with these issues are the real joy, renewed hope, and genuine pride these youngsters experience as a result of their increasing capacity to conceive of themselves and others as genuine human beings. The crucial milestones at this stage in the treatment process are:

1. Patients give evidence of a capacity to be aware of the implications of their thoughts, feelings, and intentions toward another person from the point of view of a third person, that is, a capacity to maintain a mentalizing stance that simultaneously encompasses several psychic realities.

2. Patients give evidence that they can respond to stress, anxiety, and conflict with the development of defensive adaptations based on repression, thus not necessitating the suspension of mentalization and the loss of the capacity to consider various levels of meaning simultaneously.
3. Patients give evidence of restored hope—or "remoralization" (Bateman & Fonagy, 1999)—that is manifested by a resistance to the inclination to reject offers of help at moments of anxiety or conflict.

These milestones indicate youngsters' readiness to embark on the construction—more accurately, a co-construction in which the therapists participate—of a narrative of their lives and experience that offers them meaning and identity.

To summarize, the use of facilitating interventions enables the therapist to explore the motives behind maladaptive patterns of coping, experiencing, and relating in the following ways:

1. By acknowledging the terror associated with changing and the advantages of not changing—and the courage required to entertain the therapeutic bargain of substituting illusory control for the effort to achieve real mastery and genuine attachments.
2. By freeing youngsters to acknowledge the price they pay for relying on maladaptive patterns of coping, relating, and experiencing. Such acknowledgment opens the path to a more systematic exploration of core beliefs and experiences that are at the root of maladaptive coping. In turn, this exploration allows for a shift from interventions designed to promote mentalization to the examination of defensive maneuvers against specific mental states.

FAMILY TREATMENT: ENHANCING CAREGIVERS' COMPETENCE AND SENSITIVITY

Enduring changes in mentalizing capacities and the readiness to relinquish rigidly held coping and relationship patterns are unlikely unless such changes are syntonic with changes in children's interpersonal context. Without an alignment of individual and family treatment, the therapeutic bargain offered by the therapist is unlikely to prove appealing.

The alignment begins with parents' capacity to support and promote their children's mentalization in the face of danger signals. Such a capacity, in turn, is predicated on the parents' receiving help to become more competent and feel more in control, rather than feeling buffeted by the emotional and behavioral turmoil that they and their children generate. The first order of business is to assist parents in becoming more effective and consistent at setting limits, more capable of maintaining generational boundaries, and more invested in extricating their children from the roles they play in perpetuating the family's and the children's own maladjustment. Such roles may include deflecting one parent's hostility against the other; holding the parents' relationship together; or maintaining parental self-esteem while relieving the parents' own traumatic memories of pain, vulnerability, and helplessness.

There is strong empirical evidence that a number of structured approaches designed to help parents improve their parental effectiveness can also alter the destructive and self-destructive behavior of children and adolescents. Although the literature about the effectiveness of parent training is compelling, for a substantial number of families (particularly for the most dysfunctional ones with the least support and the greatest disadvantages), the demands of structured parent training prove overwhelming. In addition to attending sessions, these demands include reviewing educational material, systematically observing children's behavior, implementing reinforcement procedures, and maintaining telephone contact with the treaters. Not surprisingly, a large percentage of families prematurely discontinue the treatment.

Arguably, the dropout range can be reduced if therapists first build a collaborative relationship. Such collaboration is fostered when treaters and parents assess together whether every aspect of the treatment makes sense to the parents. Treaters' consistent stance is that nothing that undermines parents' sense of comfort and control—or does not make sense to them—is likely to benefit the youngsters who are the primary focus of treatment.

Structured approaches to parent training, such as "Helping the Non-Compliant Child" (Forehand & Long, 1988; Long, Forehand, Wierson, & Morgan, 1994), videotape modeling group discussion (Webster-Stratton, 1996), the Oregon Social Learning Center Program (Patterson & Chamberlin, 1988; Patterson & Forgatch, 1995), and the Parent-Child Interaction Therapy (Eyberg, Boggs, & Algina, 1995), can be incorporated into the treatment to help parents increase their competence.

Helping parents increase their parenting competence, however, is rarely a straightforward proposition. The very fact of being in treatment, and of being offered help, is often as much a signal of danger to the parents and other family members as it is to the identified patient. Thus, involvement in treatment and evidence of the youngsters' formation of a collaborative relationship with the treater characteristically mobilize parents' efforts, often not conscious, to undermine the treatment and the youngsters' engagement in it. The unreflective patterns of interaction triggered by the cues of therapeutic engagement are powerfully coercive and carry the strongest affective load: guilt, anxiety, shame, and vague but overwhelming dread of ridicule, banishment, damnation, abandonment, and destruction of the self and the family. Treaters can assist parents in regaining a mentalizing stance by exploring the historical and multigenerational context in which dysfunctional patterns of interaction have emerged.

To promote the parents' mentalization requires an acknowledgment that they are generally under enormous strain from a variety of sources. Many are single parents with other children and are entangled in bitter battles with the other parent or deeply resent his or her abandonment. Others struggle with relationships or are themselves riddled with depression or trapped in lives marked by despair, substance abuse, and/or financial hardship. Stressors on the caregivers precipitate coercive cycles in the family and symptoms resulting from the youngsters' inhibition of mentalization.

A significant focus of the work with the parents is thus devoted, as Liddle and Hogue (2000) recommended, to (1) identifying how these stressors affect their caregiving capability and the caregiving environment in the family; (2) determining how the children may be better protected from their impact; and (3) helping parents access supportive resources, including psychiatric assistance for themselves and other family members.

In focusing on these issues, it is helpful to examine the history of how the parents attempted to raise their troubled youngster while also coping with multiple stressors. The narrative that emerges from this account serves to point out how, under certain conditions, mentalization—and narrative coherence—are lost, undermining the parents' best efforts to be effective and helpful to their children. Parents often, either spontaneously or with the assistance of the treaters, place their parenting efforts against the background of the parenting they received in their family of origin. Developing these narratives allows for detailed discussion of the parents' unspoken or not fully conscious attributions that underlie their parenting as a preamble to focusing on parenting practices related to how to set and enforce rules, monitor behavior, and provide support, guidance, and recognition of the children's individuality.

These discussions are carried out only with the parents alone and precede sessions that include the parents, the youngsters, and other siblings. These sessions are designed to create an interactional context in which families develop the motivation, skills, and experience to break coercive cycles, promote security of attachment, and interact in a mentalizing mode. As Liddle and Hogue (2000) suggest, parents and their children are asked explicitly to "evaluate their attachment bonds and the balance they achieved between autonomy and connectedness" (p. 273). The therapist's crucial goal is to find the optimal point at which specific family members can both be themselves and feel connected to one another.

The main approach to achieve this goal is to review interactions that either occur spontaneously during the sessions or are promoted by the therapist or family—specific care themes. The therapist first observes how caregivers and children communicate, how they recognize or ignore each other's individuality and intentionality. The therapist then proposes new modes of interaction in an attempt to interrupt coercive cycles and promote mentalization. This may require "translating" one person to another, ascribing meaning to an interaction as it unfolds—particularly, by pointing out when specific interactions trigger a loss of mentalization or by heightening or lowering the intensity of the discussion.

Often, both the youngster and the parents need considerable individual coaching before they can engage in reflective interactions concerning particularly emotionally loaded or conflictual topics. The coaching is carried out in sessions designed to help family members—whether the parent or the child—with "the content and style of what is to be said, prepare for potential reactions by other participants, and solidify a minicontract that challenges the participants to follow through as planned once the interaction begins" (Liddle & Hogue, 2000, p. 274).

The preparatory coaching often focuses on enabling family members to appreciate others' points of view and to become clear about their own perspective and motivation, which encourages less extreme and rigid positions. By processing in advance interactions that habitually result in the loss of mentalization, family members can take a first step toward restoring it. The therapists can help the family recognize what a reflective interaction feels like by pointing out when it takes place either spontaneously or in a planned exchange.

A useful approach that promotes parents' mentalization is to encourage one or both parents to tell their children stories about times when they themselves felt distressed, in circumstances comparable to those now faced by the children, and how they coped with such distress. I could, for example, point out to Joe's father, when, after years of estrangement he indicated a desire to reconnect with his son and share with him his success in conquering alcoholism and turning his life around, Joe was courageously asking, "What do you do when you get upset?" because he did not know how to grow up as a man facing distress, pain, and vulnerability. Could Joe's father help by sharing stories not only about his successes but also about his struggles? Storytelling serves to connect parents with their own vulnerability in the process of helping their children and collaborating with the therapist in a way that avoids the "patient" role.

Paradoxically, interventions that help parents attain a mentalizing stance and empathize with their children—and themselves—free them to "fire" their children from the role of functioning to maintain the family's equilibrium.

Children observe, question, and test the encouragement and assurances offered by their parents. But changes in family interaction patterns and the growing capacity of the parents to sustain mentalization allow all family members to experiment with previously restricted behavior and modes of relationship. Not only do children find greater developmental opportunities but also they receive "permission" to bring to their individual therapy a host of important issues, with greater freedom from the binds of loyalty and concern about the implied rules of family life.

In summary, by doing the following, therapists involved in family treatment strive to enhance caregivers' competence and sensitivity:

1. Aligning the youngster's interpersonal context with the individual psychotherapy. The first step in helping parents retain mentalization involves enhancing parental competence. Several structured parent training approaches that can boost parental competence also place substantial demands on the most vulnerable families.
2. Recognizing that parents will mobilize coercive patterns in response to their children and to their own involvement in treatment.
3. Exploring historical and multigenerational interactive patterns associated with an inhibition of mentalization, thereby promoting parents' ability to retain a reflective perspective.
4. Acknowledging the stressors impinging on the parents and identifying how these stressors affect the caregiving environment.
5. Determining ways to protect the children from the impact of stressors that affect the parents.
6. Helping the parents access support and, if necessary, treatment for themselves and other family members.
7. Focusing on parental practices for setting rules, monitoring behavior, and providing support, guidance, and recognition of individuality.
8. Evaluating explicitly the family's attachment bonds and the balance between autonomy and connectedness.
9. Reviewing interactions around specific core themes and planning new modes of interaction designed to break coercive cycles and promote mentalization. Individual coaching is often required before these interactions can take place.
10. Enhancing parents' mentalizing capacity by encouraging them to share stories about their own experiences of vulnerability.

11. Increasing parents' empathy, which enables them to "fire" the patient from the special role he or she plays in the family's dysfunction, and giving the youngster permission to connect with the other parent.

TERMINATION: MOURNING AND RESUMING DEVELOPMENT

The harbingers of termination are found both inside and outside the treatment process. Naturally, a sustained amelioration of symptomatic and maladaptive behavior is an important sign. Perhaps even more significant is the achievement of nondelinquent peer relationships and interests. Changes in family interaction and school functioning are also particularly important. A child's growing ability to use parents and other nondelinquent adults as sources of protection, comfort, and regulation and as models of identification signals the end of the therapeutic process. When the youngster can approach parents and teachers for help in solving problems in reality, the beginning of termination is in view.

Within the treatment process, therapists recognize the other clues of impending termination: youngsters' open acknowledgment of missing their therapists during interruptions and vacations, expressions of gratitude for help received, youngsters' accounts of how they use outside the sessions what they learned in treatment, and—perhaps the most sensitive clue—patients' reports in treatment of their sense of loss about missed or botched opportunities.

The final stage of therapy generally begins after one to three years of treatment and offers a chance to test children's readiness to relinquish pathological defenses. Discussing possible termination dates with patients and parents fuels anxiety and often brings about both a reactivation of symptoms in the patient and a resurgence of dysfunctional interaction patterns in the parents. Mourning the anticipated loss of the therapy and the therapist is an essential task of the termination phase. Just as important is the opportunity for children to work through their disappointments in their own shortcomings, in the adults who never measured up to their expectations, in everything they could not achieve in therapy, and in the therapist's limitations.

Regardless of apparent regression and symptomatic reactivations, the termination phase requires a relaxation of supervision and the provision of expanded responsibilities and increased privileges. Naturally, such a stance is not without risk. The following vignette illustrates the vicissitudes that can be encountered during termination.

Adam, a 12-year-old boy, found himself in the state's custody after his mother repeatedly deserted him. His unremitting destructiveness and defiance landed him in a residential treatment center. There he explained to his therapist, in the metaphor of his play, the reasons for his hatred: The therapist, the leader of the "Irams"—the treatment occurred at the time of the Teheran embassy hostage crisis—had kidnapped his mother. Adam naturally was bent on revenge and fully intended to rob all the banks in the world and kill people until his mother was released. Much work went into turning this play theme slowly around, until it could encompass the possibilities of maternal abandonment, Adam's rage at his mother, and the notion that his badness, greed, and neediness had damaged his mother and driven her away.

When discharge to a group home became a realistic possibility, Adam ran away. However, he returned on his own a few days later. He had traveled more than 100 miles and located his mother (a feat that had eluded the investigative power of child protective services). Having found her, he said, he had made peace with this distraught and rather limited woman. Soberly, Adam told his mother that "he knew what she had done" and no matter what happened between them, he still loved her and would go on with his life. Anna Freud herself could not have stated more eloquently the criteria for termination: the child's experience of reinstatement on the path of growth and development, a reinstatement built on a renewed capacity to access human attachments.

SUMMARY AND CONCLUSION

This chapter presents a treatment approach based on the premise that disruptions in attachment and in the exercise of mentalization are at the heart of the developmental trajectory leading to dramatic personality disorders. This treatment model seeks to create the conditions, both in the child and in the family, under which disorganized attachments, coercive cycles, and inhibited mentalization can evolve into healing and sustaining connections supported by an enhanced capacity for mentalization.

REFERENCES

Alvarez, A. (1992). *Live company: Psychoanalytic psychotherapy with autistic, borderline, deprived, and abused children.* New York: Routledge.

American Psychiatric Association. (1994). *Diagnostic and statistical manual of mental disorders* (4th ed.). Washington, DC: Author.

Bateman, A., & Fonagy, P. (1999). Effectiveness of partial hospitalization in the treatment of borderline personality disorder: A randomized controlled trial. *American Journal of Psychiatry, 156,* 1563–1569.

Behar, L. (1990). Financing mental health services for children and adolescents. *Bulletin of the Menninger Clinic, 54,* 127–139.

Bettelheim, B., & Sylvester, E. (1948). A therapeutic milieu. *American Journal of Orthopsychiatry, 18,* 191–206.

Bierman, K. L. (1989). Improving the peer relationships of rejected children. In B. B. Lahey & A. E. Kazdin (Eds.), *Advances in clinical child psychology* (Vol. 12, pp. 53–84). New York: Plenum Press.

Bleiberg, E. (2001). *Treating personality disorders in children and adolescents: A relational approach.* New York: Guilford Press.

Bowlby, J. (1980). *Attachment and loss. Volume III: Loss: Sadness and depression.* New York: Basic Books.

Carpy, D. V. (1989). Tolerating the countertransference: A mutative process. *International Journal of Psycho-Analysis, 70,* 287–294.

Chu, J. A. (1998). *Rebuilding shattered lives: The responsible treatment of complex posttraumatic and dissociative disorders.* New York: Wiley.

Coccaro, E. F., & Kavoussi, R. J. (1997). Fluoxetine and impulsive-aggressive behavior in personality-disordered subjects. *Archives of General Psychiatry, 54,* 1081–1088.

Coccaro, E. F., Siever, L. J., Klar, H. M., Maurer, G., Cochrane, K., Cooper, T. B., et al. (1989). Serotonergic studies in patients with affective and personality disorders:

Correlates with suicidal and impulsive aggressive behavior. *Archives of General Psychiatry, 46,* 587–599.

Diamond, G. S., & Liddle, H. A. (1999). Transforming negative parent-adolescent interactions: From impasse to dialogue. *Family Process, 38,* 5–26.

Eyberg, S. M., Boggs, S. R., & Algina, J. (1995). Parent-child interaction therapy: A psychosocial model for the treatment of young children with conduct problem behavior and their families. *Psychopharmacology Bulletin, 31,* 83–91.

Fischer, K. W., Kenny, S. L., & Pipp, S. L. (1990). How cognitive processes and environmental conditions organize discontinuities in the develop of abstractions. In C. N. Alexander & E. J. Langer (Eds.), *Higher stages of human development: Perspectives on adult growth* (pp. 162–187). New York: Oxford University Press.

Fletcher, A. C., Darling, N., & Steinberg, L. (1995). Parental monitoring and peer influences on adolescent substance use. In J. McCord (Ed.), *Coercion and punishment in long-term perspectives* (pp. 259–271). New York: Cambridge University Press.

Fonagy, P., Gergely, G., Jurist, E. L., & Target, M. (2002). *Affect regulation, mentalization and the development of the self.* New York: Other Press.

Forehand, R., & Long, N. (1988). Outpatient treatment of the acting out child: Procedures, long-term follow-up data, and clinical problems. *Advances in Behavior Research and Therapy, 10,* 129–177.

Friedman, L. (1982). The humanistic trend in recent psychoanalytic theory. *Psychoanalytic Quarterly, 51,* 353–371.

Gabbard, G. O. (1995). Countertransference: The emerging common ground. *International Journal of Psycho-Analysis, 76,* 475–485.

Gabbard, G. O., & Wilkinson, S. M. (1994). *Management of countertransference with borderline patients.* Washington, DC: American Psychiatric Press.

Gergely, G., & Watson, J. S. (1999). Early socioemotional development: Contingency perception and the social-biofeedback model. In P. Rochat (Ed.), *Early social cognition: Understanding others in the first months of life* (pp. 101–136). Hillsdale, NJ: Erlbaum.

Gunderson, J. G. (1996). The borderline patient's intolerance of aloneness: Insecure attachments and therapist availability. *American Journal of Psychiatry, 153,* 752–758.

Gunderson, J. G. (2000). Psychodynamic psychotherapy for borderline personality disorder. In J. G. Gunderson & G. O. Gabbard (Eds.), *Psychotherapy for personality disorders* (pp. 33–64). Washington, DC: American Psychiatric Press.

Gunderson, J. G., & Links, P. S. (1995). Borderline personality disorder. In G. O. Gabbard (Ed.), *Treatments of psychiatric disorders* (2nd ed., Vol. 2, pp. 2291–2310). Washington, DC: American Psychiatric Press.

Gunderson, J. G., Zanarini, M. C., & Kisiel, C. L. (1991). Borderline personality disorder: A review of data on *DSM-III-R* descriptions. *Journal of Personality Disorders, 5,* 340–352.

Horowitz, M. J. (1987). *States of mind: Configurational analysis of individual psychology* (2nd ed.). New York: Plenum Press.

Kapfhammer, H. P., & Hippius, H. (1998). Pharmacotherapy in personality disorders. *Journal of Personality Disorders, 12,* 277–288.

Kazdin, A. E. (1996a). Dropping out of child psychotherapy: Issues for research and implications for practice. *Clinical Child Psychology and Psychiatry, 1,* 133–156.

Kazdin, A. E. (1996b). Problem solving and parent management in treating aggressive and antisocial behavior. In E. D. Hibbs & P. S. Jensen (Eds.), *Psychosocial treatments for child and adolescent disorder: Empirically based strategies for clinical practice* (pp. 377–408). Washington, DC: American Psychological Association.

Kazdin, A. E., Siegel, T. C., & Bass, D. (1992). Cognitive problem-solving skills training and parent management training in the treatment of antisocial behavior in children. *Journal of Consulting and Clinical Psychology, 60,* 733–747.

Kernberg, P. F., Weiner, A. S., & Bardenstein, K. K. (2000). *Personality disorders in children and adolescents.* New York: Basic Books.

Leichtman, M., & Leichtman, M. L. (1996a). A model of psychodynamic short-term residential treatment: I. The nature of the challenge. In C. Waller (Ed.), *Contributions to residential treatment, 1996* (pp. 85–92). Alexandria, VA: American Association of Children's Residential Centers.

Leichtman, M., & Leichtman, M. L. (1996b). A model of psychodynamic short-term residential treatment: II. General principles. In C. Waller (Ed.), *Contributions to residential treatment, 1996* (pp. 93–102). Alexandria, VA: American Association of Children's Residential Centers.

Leichtman, M., & Leichtman, M. L. (1996c). A model of psychodynamic short-term residential treatment: III. Changing roles. In C. Waller (Ed.), *Contributions to residential treatment, 1996* (pp. 103–109). Alexandria, VA: American Association of Children's Residential Centers.

Liddle, H. A., & Hogue, A. (2000). A family-based, developmental-ecological preventive intervention for high-risk adolescents. *Journal of Marital and Family Therapy, 26,* 265–279.

Linehan, M. M. (1993). *Skills training manual for treating borderline personality disorder.* New York: Guilford Press.

Lochman, J. E., & Wells, K. C. (1996). A social-cognitive intervention with aggressive children: Prevention effects and contextual implementation issues. In R. D. Peters & R. J. McMahon (Eds.), *Preventing childhood disorders, substance abuse, and delinquency* (pp. 111–143). Thousand Oaks, CA: Sage.

Long, P., Forehand, R., Wierson, M., & Morgan, A. (1994). Does parent training with young noncompliant children have long-term effects? *Behavior Research and Therapy, 32,* 101–107.

Main, M., & Solomon, J. (1990). Procedures for identifying infants as disorganized/disoriented during the Ainsworth Strange Situation. In M. T. Greenberg, D. Cicchetti, & E. M. Cummings (Eds.), *Attachment in the preschool years: Theory, research and intervention* (pp. 121–160). Chicago: University of Chicago Press.

Mayes, L. C., & Cohen, D. J. (1993). Playing and therapeutic action in child analysis. *International Journal of Psycho-Analysis, 74,* 1235–1244.

McDougall, J. (1989). *Theaters of the body: A psychoanalytic approach to psychosomatic illness.* New York: Norton.

Minuchin, S., & Fishman, H. C. (1981). *Family therapy techniques.* Cambridge, MA: Harvard University Press.

Moran, G. S. (1984). Psychoanalytic treatment of diabetic children. *Psychoanalytic Study of the Child, 28,* 407–447.

Ogden, T. H. (1994). *Subjects of analysis.* Northvale, NJ: Aronson.

Paris, J., & Zweig-Frank, H. (1992). A critical review of the role of childhood sexual abuse in the etiology of borderline personality disorder. *Canadian Journal of Psychiatry, 37,* 125–128.

Patterson, G. R., & Chamberlin, P. (1988). Treatment process: A problem at three levels. In L. C. Wynne (Ed.), *The state of the art in family therapy research: Controversies and recommendations* (pp. 189–223). New York: Family Process Press.

Patterson, G. R., & Forgatch, M. S. (1995). Predicting future clinical adjustment from treatment outcome and process variables. *Psychological Assessment, 7,* 275–285.

Rinsley, D. B. (1980a). The developmental etiology of borderline and narcissistic disorders. *Bulletin of the Menninger Clinic, 44,* 127–134.

Rinsley, D. B. (1980b). Principles of therapeutic milieu with children. In G. G. Sholevar, R. M. Benson, & B. J. Blinder (Eds.), *Emotional disorders in children and adolescents: Medical and psychological approaches to treatment* (pp. 191–208). New York: Spectrum.

Rosenfeld, S. K., & Sprince, M. P. (1963). An attempt to formulate the meaning of the concept "borderline." *Psychoanalytic Study of the Child, 18,* 603–635.

Schmidt, S. E., Liddle, H. A., & Dakof, G. A. (1996). Changes in parenting practices and adolescent drug abuse during multidimensional family therapy. *Journal of Family Psychology, 10,* 12–27.

Sharfstein, S. S., & Kent, J. J., Jr. (1997). Restructuring for survival: The Sheppard Pratt transformation. In R. K. Schreter, S. S. Sharfstein, & C. A. Schreter (Eds.), *Managing care, not dollars: The continuum of mental health services* (pp. 281–298). Washington, DC: American Psychiatric Press.

Sifneos, P. E., Apfel-Savitz, R., & Frankel, F. H. (1997). The phenomenon of "alexithymia": Observations in neurotic and psychosomatic patients. *Psychotherapy and Psychosomatics, 28,* 47–57.

Soloff, P. H. (1998). Algorithms for pharmacological treatment of personality dimensions: Symptom-specific treatments for cognitive-perceptual, affective, and impulsive-behavioral dysregulation. *Bulletin of the Menninger Clinic, 62,* 195–214.

Spivak, G., & Shure, M. B. (1978). *Problem solving techniques in child-rearing.* San Francisco: Jossey-Bass.

Tooley, K. (1973). Playing it right: A technique for the treatment of borderline children. *Journal of the American Academy of Child Psychiatry, 12,* 615–631.

Vygotsky, L. S. (1962). *Thought and language* (E. Hanfmann & G. Vakar, Eds. & Trans.). Cambridge, MA: MIT Press.

Vygotsky, L. S. (1978). *Mind in society: The development of higher psychological processes.* Cambridge, MA: Harvard University Press.

Webster-Stratton, C. (1996). Early interventions with videotape modeling: Programs for families of children with oppositional defiant disorder or conduct disorder. In E. D. Hibbs & P. S. Jensen (Eds.), *Psychosocial treatments for child and adolescent disorders: Empirically based strategies for clinical practice* (pp. 435–474). Washington, DC: American Psychological Association.

Webster-Stratton, C., & Hammond, M. (1997). Treating children with early-onset conduct problems: A comparison of child and parent training interventions. *Journal of Consulting and Clinical Psychology, 65,* 93–109.

Winnicott, D. W. (1953). Transitional objects and transitional phenomena: A study of the first not-me possession. *International Journal of Psycho-Analysis, 34,* 89–97.

Zanarini, M. C., & Frankenburg, F. R. (1997). Pathways to the development of borderline personality disorder. *Journal of Personality Disorders, 11,* 93–104.

CHAPTER 22

Treatment of Personality Disorders in Older Adults: A Community Mental Health Model

Rosemary Snapp Kean, Kathleen M. Hoey, and Stephen L. Pinals

FORMULATING AN EFFECTIVE treatment plan for an older adult with a personality disorder requires looking at a complex array of clinical and social information. Age-related losses are known to compromise the stability and function of healthy older adults, as well as those with more fragile coping strategies, limited attachments, or poor self-image. This chapter examines the ways in which diagnosis and treatment present unique issues in this age group. It also considers how older adults with personality disorders typically present to treatment, the settings where treatment occurs, and the importance of working with the broader health care and social networks. A prototype case is presented to illustrate how these differences in assessment and treatment affect both the development of the therapeutic alliance and the tailoring of an integrated treatment model.

A broad range of prevalence rates is reported for personality disorders in older adults among studies examining both community and inpatient samples. Kunik et al. (1994) estimated that 6% to 7% of elderly outpatients met criteria for a primary diagnosis of personality disorder. Abrams and Horowitz (1999) described a range of 6% to 33% for Axis II disorders in adults over age 50, with an average prevalence rate of 10%. Some studies of older adults with personality disorders and comorbid Major Depression or dementia suggest similar prevalence rates between 6% and 24% (Kunik et al., 1994). However, one retrospective review found that older adults with a diagnosis of Major Depression had a significantly lower rate of *DSM-III* Axis II diagnoses (Fogel & Westlake, 1990). One explanation for this finding is that personality disorders are often difficult to diagnose in older adults with Major Depression because of a substantial overlap of symptom and diagnostic criteria (Agronin, 1994). Furthermore, health care providers are more likely to diagnose *DSM-IV* Axis I disorders because they are easier to recognize, accept, and treat (Lynch & Aspnes, 2001). There may be a tendency for clinicians to soften criteria required to make an Axis I diagnosis in older adults, while choosing to "defer" on the decision to diagnose a personality disorder. Reaching the diagnosis of a personality disorder can be challenging given the long history of adult experiences to review and the difficulty accessing information from the past. Increasing medical problems, cognitive decline, and behavior patterns that naturally change over time also serve to complicate the diagnostic process and compromise the accuracy of any Axis II diagnosis.

Although many personality traits may remain relatively stable over time, others will be subject to the effects of age and environment, physical and social decline. Solomon (1981) suggested that individuals with personality disorders characterized by prominent affective symptoms and behavioral lability may improve with aging because older adults are less likely to be impulsive or aggressive. It is hypothesized that prevalence rates for this group may actually decline in late life because of greater mortality due to risk-taking behavior in earlier life (Fishbain, 1991). Some researchers believe that personality disorders seem to be less prevalent among older adults as compared to young adults (Ames & Molinari, 1994; Solomon, 1981), while others cite mounting evidence that personality disorders may be equally prevalent in late life (Morse & Lynch, 2000). Although reliable estimates of prevalence rates in this population are difficult to achieve, overall trends suggest that personality disorders are lifelong chronic conditions whose particular manifestations may change as the individual ages (Sadavoy, 1987).

PRESENTING TO TREATMENT

Self-referral for psychotherapy is not a common occurrence for older adults. According to the U.S. Department of Health and Human Services, Administration on Aging (AOA; DHHS, 1999), many older adults have had little or no contact with mental health providers. The stigma associated with mental illness often contributes to the denial of mental health problems and avoidance of appropriate treatment. The stereotype and ageist perception of elders as less than fully functioning human beings with minimal chance for improvement creates yet another layer of resistance to the possibility for seeking and receiving adequate care (Butler, Lewis, & Sutherland, 1991). For these reasons and many others, older adults who are in need of mental health services may find their way to treatment in a manner very distinct from that of younger adults.

Age-related physiologic events and environmental factors often influence or precipitate the time when evaluation and treatment are deemed necessary. Potential stressors particularly associated with old age include:

1. Physiologic changes, for example, declining strength and energy, declining vision, changes in appearance of skin and hair, declines in cardiac and pulmonary function.
2. Losses of important supportive relationships due to death of family and friends.
3. Role changes and losses due to retirement, giving up of volunteer work, loss of roles of spouse or sibling, loss of roles of homemaker or homeowner.
4. Loss of health and resulting loss of function.
5. Anticipation of dying and loss of life.

Life events such as these typically challenge attitudes and postures maintained over a lifetime and may lead to the reluctant acceptance of a mental health referral from a primary health care provider, a social service agency, housing manager, or family member.

The AOA report on community mental health services notes that community mental health programs generally underserve the older adult population. One reason for this problem is simply that older adults are not comfortable with "traditional mental health settings or services" (DHHS, 1999). For the subgroup of older adults who have personality disorders, rigid behavior patterns, suspiciousness, negativity, and poor self-care skills present further obstacles to seeking essential mental health or social services. The additional burden of debilitating medical problems and physical decline leaves the patient with a personality disorder in a dependent and vulnerable position. Outreach via home visits is identified as a significant way to increase access for older people to mental health care (DHHS, 1999).

Maintaining a sense of autonomy while adopting some form of increasing dependence is a developmental task associated with old age (Greenberg, 1994). Allowing for the emergence of dependence on others, whether gradual or acute in onset, is often perceived as a loss of independence rather than a normal variation on the continuum of dependence that is planned for and expected (Lowry, 1989). For the older person with inflexible and impaired social functioning, relying on family members or caregivers for their access to professional care may lead to increasing interpersonal conflict as well as intense expressions of emotion. The limitations and potential burnout of caregivers increase anxiety and fear of abandonment, which can lead to growing frustration, anger, and mutual feelings of resentment.

When a referral is suggested for mental health intervention, it may be perceived as punitive, demeaning, or threatening. Patients who are brought to treatment by any form of coercion will likely be ambivalent, negative, or hostile at the outset of treatment. The multitude of factors leading to the referral creates the context of the initial sessions and influences the course and outcome of treatment.

ROLE OF THE PRIMARY CARE PHYSICIAN

Older adults with personality disorders are likely to seek assistance from their general medical practitioner before consulting mental health clinicians. Generational bias may determine preference for the culturally normative experience of the physical examination as opposed to the potentially stigmatizing and burdensome label of mental illness that might result from a visit to a therapist. The psychiatric evaluation of any older adult, and particularly one with a suspected personality disorder, must include a routine physical exam and laboratory studies. Acute or new onset conditions, including common infections, metabolic disturbances, and endocrine abnormalities such as thyroid dysfunction, must be excluded as potential complications to chronic underlying conditions.

Physicians may comprise the front line of evaluation and treatment and typically first seek physiologic explanations for personality-driven complaints before considering psychological roots. Medical screening and testing may indefinitely deter an older adult from receiving appropriate treatment. This problem is further intensified by the growing demands placed on internists to see increasing numbers of patients for briefer periods of time. As a result, internists may be more inclined to prescribe psychotropic medications for symptomatic relief and perhaps be less likely to suggest psychotherapy as an alternative mode of treatment.

If a patient becomes particularly difficult by demanding excessive services or attention or if the internist is psychologically minded and comfortable seeking consultation, a referral to a mental health specialist is more likely to occur. During this process, it is crucial that regular communication exist between the physician and consultant, with careful attention to the boundaries of each relationship. The internist may often continue to be perceived as the central focus of care, allowing for this positive transference to be extended to other caregivers. Many older adults find the close collaboration of internists and mental health consultants to be reassuring and acceptable.

ASSESSMENT AND COMORBID DIAGNOSIS

Evaluating and treating older adults with personality disorders and comorbid Axis I illness are exceptionally complex and a great challenge to many clinicians. Dependent, Compulsive, and Avoidant Personality Disorders appear to be most likely to accompany Major Depression, suggesting an overlap of these diagnostic entities (Agronin, 1994). Many symptoms of Major Depression may mimic, influence, or distort the expression of underlying personality traits, further complicating an accurate diagnosis. A parallel interaction also exists for those who may be predisposed to depressive symptoms from sudden losses, physical disability, or other life changes described previously. These issues become particularly significant because older adults with personality disorders may have limited social supports and a decline in global functioning and quality of life (Abrams, Alexopoulos, Spielman, Klausner, & Kakuma, 2001). Thus, it comes as no surprise that older adults with personality disorders and a comorbid diagnosis of late-life depression may have a poorer response to psychotherapy (Thompson, Gallagher, & Czirr, 1988).

A study of older adults with Generalized Anxiety revealed higher rates of Dependent and Avoidant Personality Disorders when compared with nonanxious older adults (Coolidge, Segal, Hook, & Stewart, 2000). Prominent symptoms of anxiety are a common presentation for older adults, which may mask or energize underlying personality traits. Anxious older adults with Dependent Personality may seek the submissive comfort and familiarity of the doctor-patient relationship, with repeated pharmacological interventions to temporarily gratify the need for nurturance and support. Those with Avoidant Personality will find the brief and structured evaluations of their primary care physician to be more tolerable than an encounter with a mental health provider. Likewise, the prospect of receiving medications to treat anxiety symptoms without close follow-up or supervision is preferable but unlikely to address underlying concerns. Physicians may find that typical medical treatment is less effective for this population, and medication trials will serve to delay the initiation of other therapeutic techniques.

Personality changes also commonly occur in patients with dementia (Aitken, Simpson, & Burns, 1999) and are at times more prominent than the cognitive decline found in initial stages of the disease (De Leo, Scocco, & Meneghel, 1999). Family members and caregivers of Alzheimer's patients often describe the alterations of personality that occurred during early stages of the disease. Symptoms of apathy, irritability, poor energy, or agitation may appear before any significant cognitive changes occur (Petry, Cummings, Hill, & Shapira, 1988) and are typically mistaken for symptoms of primary depression or anxiety. These personality changes can be distinguished from symptoms of personality disorders by the family report of a recent change in behavior and personality.

The occurrence of acute or chronic medical illnesses in addition to a personality disorder will considerably affect the course and treatment of both conditions. One example of this is found in older adults with Avoidant Personality who become medically ill, feel unappealing and inadequate, refuse interpersonal contact, and limit the possibility of receiving adequate care. Likewise, medically ill older adults with Dependent Personality may seek physicians to take responsibility for their health care decisions, be unable to disagree with their providers for fear of losing their support, and seem increasingly helpless in the context of their physical decline. In either case, physicians who are unaware of these characterological complexities often find great difficulty in treating the medical illness alone. A poor or unexpected response to various treatments may finally lead to a mental health referral.

Somatic preoccupation is another common symptom described by older adults presenting to treatment in medical and psychiatric facilities. The aging body allows for the communication of unlimited messages to family, friends, and caregivers alike. Increasing frailty and physical decline create a fertile environment for somatization (Sadavoy, 1987). Physicians are given the difficult responsibility of determining how deeply to explore each new emerging symptom. Health care providers are often unable to determine the influence of anxiety, depression, psychosis, and personality disorders. These patients are typically passed around to various consultants or specialists with poor communication between providers and limited collaboration. The ideal modality of treatment for this population proceeds from a multidisciplinary mental health team working in partnership with medical care providers.

THE MULTIDISCIPLINARY TREATMENT TEAM

A multidisciplinary community mental health team is most effective when able to work with older adults with personality disorders in a variety of settings, that is, at home, in nursing homes or other residential care settings, in hospitals, and in traditional outpatient settings. This team ideally consists of at least the four primary mental health disciplines of psychiatric nursing, psychiatry, psychology, and social work and may also include case managers and mental health workers. Each discipline brings a unique perspective to treatment planning meetings. All team members are aware of the necessity of clarifying health problems. An initial evaluation by the psychiatrist is preferred and is essential when medical or neurologic issues are primary. Clinical social work expertise, which includes working with families and larger systems, is key in providing community-based care. A wide variety of perspectives are contributed by psychology, including assessment via neuropsychological testing. The psychiatric nursing knowledge base, which combines medical and mental health problems and treatments, can be ideally suited to working with older adults.

MEDICATION TREATMENT

Psychiatrists are often called on to prescribe psychotropic medications for older adults suffering from Axis II disorders. Whereas careful attention is warranted in considering the potential risk for toxicity, interactions, and adverse side effects, psychiatrists must also be aware of subtle differences in prescribing medications to an older population. Young adults are more likely to seek independent verification of appropriate medical diagnoses and treatment, sometimes checking references and Internet sites for information about new medications. Older adults may present with a more dependent and submissive stance ("well, you are the doctor"), accepting the prescribed treatment without seeking further information or consultation. Alternatively, older adults may be more suspicious of the many new medications now available, leading to quick rejection or possibly the acceptance of a prescription with subsequent poor compliance. Passive-aggressive individuals are likely to report the forgetting of doses or describe numerous side effects that thwart treatment. Older adults with Paranoid Personality Disorder typically avoid and distrust any physician attempting to make a diagnosis and offer pharmacological treatment. Those with personalities in the dramatic cluster (Antisocial, Borderline, and Narcissistic) are more susceptible to medication abuse, polypharmacy, and possibly self-injurious use (Agronin, 1994). Anticipating these types of reactions to medical recommendations may allow the physician and patient to openly discuss their mutual concerns and possibly improve compliance or facilitate greater communication.

TREATMENT SETTING

Historically, receiving a visit from a nurse or social worker at home is an accepted form of health service to older adults with little, if any, stigma attached. The assessment broadens to include a wealth of data the therapist can observe in the home setting, including, for example, the patient's ability to organize tasks of daily living, the home environment as a reflection of the patient's internal state, and relationship dynamics if family members or friends are present.

Another advantage to choosing the patient's home as the setting for psychotherapy is the fact that treatment at home can support a sense of identity and autonomy. The therapist encounters many opportunities for validation, and patients' sense of self is fostered in a setting where they are surrounded by their own belongings. Photographs may give evidence of meaningful past relationships, and books, plants, or a sewing machine may speak to avocations or interests. The therapeutic alliance is then founded on recognition of who the patient is and respect for individuality. This has been characterized as a narcissistic alliance, that is, an alliance focused on maintaining self-esteem (Mehlman, 1977). From this base, the therapy is able to move toward establishing a "coherent narrative," connecting the patient's life story to current problems and symptoms (Viederman, 1983).

A characteristic of a therapist who can be effective in the home setting is that he or she is able to give up, to some extent, the professional's authority figure role. The therapist is a guest in the patient's home, and the patient controls the environment to a large degree. The therapist must be flexible enough to adapt the structure and work of therapy to the patient's turf, incorporating distractions and interruptions into the therapy hour, while at the same time maintaining professional boundaries.

The therapist's role goes back and forth between the workplace dictum of "Don't just sit there, do something!" and the psychotherapy reminder to "Don't just do something, sit there!" Sometimes the concrete issues identified as problems by the referral source—for example, housing, the threat of eviction, health problems, conflicts with family or neighbors—require the therapist to take on a case manager or service coordinator role at the outset of treatment if no one else is assuming these functions. The therapist may be the only person or one of very few people to enter the client's home each week. The balance between maintaining an alliance with the patient and involving other needed community services can be achieved when at least one problem is identified by the patient and one goal held in common by patient and therapist. This initial phase of treatment has been thought of as crisis intervention (Solomon, 1981).

TREATMENT APPROACHES AND TECHNIQUES

Although it is necessary to have a psychodynamic understanding of human development to assess the nature of the mental health issues affecting an older adult, it is not necessary and may be contraindicated to provide a traditional course of psychodynamic psychotherapy. Focusing on transference issues and offering interpretations are culture-bound interventions and may well act as blocks to the establishment of an effective therapeutic alliance. This idea that interpretation is not always the most helpful therapeutic intervention goes back at least 50 years in the literature of psychotherapy (Bibring, 1947). Supportive psychotherapy can be an acceptable approach to older adult patients.

As the crisis situation is dealt with and the Axis I symptoms are ameliorated, entrenched maladaptive behaviors become apparent. However, treatment goals do not focus directly on changing the patient's personality structure (Morse & Lynch, 2000). Instead, initial concrete goals acknowledged as worthwhile by the patient might include seeing a doctor or accepting help with personal care. As the positive transference develops and the therapeutic alliance is strengthened by the therapist's attention to concrete needs and advocacy where appropriate, outcomes of this supportive treatment can include modulated affect, less intense interpersonal conflicts, decreasing social isolation, and decreasing somatic preoccupation.

Achieving these goals and seeing these changes in functioning can easily take a year or more, given the entrenched nature of the patient's maladaptive coping behaviors and the slower pace sometimes needed in working with older people. Visual and hearing losses can exacerbate perceptual and relational difficulties, and energy drained by medical illness may delay progress in therapy.

It is also possible that the older patient with a personality disorder may have increased motivation to engage in psychotherapy stemming from increasing awareness of mortality (Solomon, 1981). The therapist watches for signs that the patient may be able to process, in part or in whole, regrets or losses and assists in recognizing achievements as well. In his groundbreaking article on the life review process in old age, Robert Butler quotes Erik Erikson, "identity formation neither begins nor ends with adolescence: it is a lifelong development largely unconscious to the individual and to his society" (Butler, 1963).

Older adults with personality disorders may act out their emotional responses to loss and be incapable of directly processing their feelings and thoughts. The patient can become unstable, labile, intense, and regressed. Addressing the behavioral manifestations of the grief concentrating on basic needs, personal self-care, safety, and firm, compassionate limit setting may be the first or only avenue of treatment. Tolerating strong feelings associated with loss can be extremely difficult, especially when old, unresolved wounds are retriggered. Self-soothing techniques, using distractions as well as displacement, may be useful coping strategies.

Cognitive-behavioral therapy (CBT) techniques may be employed to address symptoms of anxiety, depression, affect lability, and interpersonal conflicts. Target symptoms, rather than underlying problems, are the focus of CBT, and CBT does not emphasize interpretation. Focusing on patient strengths as evidenced in past achievements and examining how to use and generalize these strengths are interventions that support the therapeutic alliance based on maintaining and enhancing self-esteem (Goisman, 1999). For example, a brief intervention with a nursing home resident, who put off asking for needed help with toileting until it was almost too late and then was angry and critical of staff slowness, consisted of writing down the statement It's okay to ask for help when I need it. Over time and with reenforcement and practice, the patient's interactions with staff began to improve.

Additionally, the optimistic CBT belief that people can make changes in thoughts, feelings, and behaviors at any point in life can be instrumental in instilling hope in both the therapist and patient. The spirit of collaboration and learning something together (Goisman, 1999) may make CBT culturally acceptable to older adults.

COUNTERTRANSFERENCE REACTIONS

Countertransference responses to the older adult patient with a personality disorder may have nothing to do with the patient's age. For example, when the therapist's desire to help is frustrated by repeated procrastination or forgetting by the patient, anger is likely to be generated in the therapist whether the patient is 35 or 70. In the same way, the patient who demands increasingly more time and attention may produce a desire in the therapist to withdraw and distance himself from a patient of any age.

However, the therapist's beliefs about old age can influence the development of countertransference. Negative countertransference occurs when old age is seen only as an inevitable decline leading to death (Malamud, 1996). Illness and loss of function are seen as inherently a part of aging and old age. This negative view of old age can combine with the widely held understanding that personality disorders are very resistant to treatment (Millon & Davis, 2001, p. 87). The resulting sense of hopelessness produces therapeutic nihilism in the therapist, which, in turn, leads to inadequate assessment and treatment.

Another kind of countertransference can be suspected when the therapist is more active and helpful than needed. This countertransference fosters inappropriate dependency. It can serve to move the therapy away from a focus on painful issues of loss and grief and create a therapy described as too gentle, that is, the patient is not helped to address conflicts or achieve personal growth (Solomon, 1981). Effective therapy for older adults requires that the therapist has dealt with his or her own issues of loss and fears of illness and death.

Regular supervision is the primary mechanism for recognizing and managing countertransference and, as such, is essential in providing high-quality mental health care to older adults with personality disorders. Therapists can also be alerted to the presence of a personality disorder and developing countertransference when they observe changes in their own behavior about a particular patient, for example, unnecessary advocacy, changing the length or frequency of sessions, excessive thinking about the patient, worry, changing how supervision is used, talking to people not involved in the patient's care about the patient, or closing down emotionally when with the patient (Rosowsky & Dougherty, 1998).

Both positive and negative countertransference issues need to be examined. A particular countertransference issue sometimes arises when the therapy setting is the patient's home. The therapist's desire to help the patient to continue living at home can interfere with making an accurate assessment of the patient's ability or motivation to do this in the face of declining health and function. Therapists may find themselves in conflict with other health or social service agencies. Again, therapists can make use of supervision to identify situations where advocacy is or is not therapeutic.

Health care workers in hospital, nursing home, assisted living, or day treatment settings experience highly emotional countertransference responses to the older adult who engages in sabotaging staff efforts at care or who disrupts the treatment setting with angry, dramatic outbursts. Many older personality-disordered patients have learned adaptive coping strategies to maintain daily living in the community. With the crisis of nursing home placement and the stressors of illness, disability, and dependency, the patient's dysfunctional patterns become predominant and challenging. Problem behaviors may include acting out, refusing to cooperate, denial that interferes with care, or staff splitting.

Often the patient is unable to use therapy to grieve losses or to change behavior patterns. The mental health consultant may be most effective by helping staff to put the patient's behavior in the context of his or her developmental history of coping with problems and illness. Creating a narrative that addresses the patient as a whole person with a history and unique identity can enable staff to see beyond the frustrations of the moment and maintain a therapeutic response (Friedman, 1993). Case conferences help staff ventilate anger, frustration, and confusion. They are then able to adjust the treatment plan, recognizing the patient's need for control or inability to change an entrenched behavior pattern. Systems assessment and systems intervention are key to defusing negative countertransference responses in the treatment or residential setting.

The following composite case study of patient A.B. looks at the treatment of an older adult with Obsessive-Compulsive Personality and demonstrates general issues of working with the older adult population.

CASE STUDY

A.B. was referred at age 70 by her case manager from the local Elder Service agency, who had been addressing concerns about housing and home repair with her and suspected she was depressed. At this time, A.B. weighed 72 pounds and was recovering from an ankle fracture. Additional health concerns included COPD, osteoporosis, and chronic constipation that became so severe that she had made repeated emergency room visits with sharp abdominal pain. A.B. denied symptoms of anorexia or bulimia. Her internist had done extensive testing and found no medical problems to explain her low weight. At the time of her initial mental health evaluation, the patient was critical of her internist and had recently missed several appointments without canceling them.

A.B. had no prior history of mental illness or treatment and denied any family history. She had lived in her family home since birth, had an eighth-grade education, worked briefly doing factory work, and then stopped working to care for her parents who had since died, her father most recently 10 years before she entered treatment. A.B. had never married and reported no serious relationships. She had two older siblings, sisters, who had moved away. Both had died in the past six years.

At the time of referral, A.B. had little social contact or support. A year earlier, she had stopped attending the senior center because of a conflict with a friend there with whom she had been close for several years, including spending holidays with her. She reported having no other friends but maintained contact with out-of-state relatives by mail and occasional phone calls.

A.B. denied feeling depressed despite having symptoms of depression including anhedonia, hopelessness, social isolation, fatigue, difficulty falling asleep, and depressed mood. She refused an antidepressant trial and refused to come for outpatient treatment but accepted social work visits at home, although frequently "forgot" appointments or was not home during the first six months of treatment. The first year of treatment focused on establishing a therapeutic alliance, supporting and assisting A.B. in coping with health and housing problems, and providing education concerning symptoms of depression and treatment options.

Twice during the first year of treatment, A.B. verbalized suicidal thoughts without a plan or intention to act. At these times, mental health treatment options were reviewed, including taking an antidepressant medicine, hospitalization, or partial hospital care. A.B. wished to avoid all of these treatments and continued to ask if the therapist really thought she was depressed. A.B. acknowledged the therapist's observation of her denial of problems between emergencies: "I hide from the problem." Therapist and patient agreed that this coping style didn't seem to be working. A.B.'s ambivalence about moving seemed unending and perhaps would have been so if not for a nephew who became more involved. A.B., the therapist, and the nephew met together to consider the housing problem. A.B. eventually decided to move to elder housing, and her nephew facilitated the move.

Sometime after the first year of treatment was completed, A.B. began referring to a calendar at the beginning of sessions to review the past week. She claimed to have a poor memory and to rely on the calendar to remind her of recent events. In fact, she scored 30 of 30 on the Mini Mental Status Exam but did evidence selective recall. Using the calendar to bring order to the session correlated with A.B.'s beginning to use the therapy hour less for managing a crisis and more for addressing less emergent issues. She agreed to a low dose SSRI trial. Over the coming year, A.B. stopped the medication three times without mentioning she was stopping it. A.B.'s pattern of alternating between asking the therapist to tell her what to do and then, in a few weeks, not following through on a clear, agreed on plan became apparent. The third time this happened, A.B. recalled the therapist's asking earlier if A.B. felt rebellious about taking medication and stated "I guess I am a rebel."

An agreement was made to count her pills every week as a way to be sure that she was taking them. This idea was offered by the therapist and welcomed by A.B. The idea had originated in the therapist's supervision where she had been venting frustration and confusion about not being able to get A.B. to stick with her medicine long enough to tell if it might help. The therapist used supervision regularly to ventilate worry about A.B., whose health continued precarious, with regular COPD exacerbations and dangerously low weight.

A.B.'s conflict with her primary physician ended when he retired. At this time, A.B. looked to the therapist for help in choosing a new doctor and made her initial visit with the therapist. Her worries about her health and fears of health care procedures became more clear as she used sessions to talk about these issues.

When asked about her early history, A.B. had little to say other than to describe her childhood as happy. She reported that her mother was her best friend, they attended bingo games together, and A.B.'s friends were women in her mother's age group. A.B. described her father as a good man who worked as a shoe salesman. She rarely referred to him over a four-year therapy and, in fact, shared no detailed memories of her life. A.B. demonstrated the isolation of affect and shriveled memories associated with Obsessive-Compulsive Personality, which severely limited history gathering. Over time, her preoccupation with details and order, perfectionism, miserly spending, and rigidity and stubbornness became more apparent. In addition to these Obsessive-Compulsive Personality Disorder behaviors, A.B. demonstrated characteristics of the negativistic personality. These included the pattern of ignoring recommendations of her internist and finding fault with him and focusing on complaints about others instead of her own role in the problem at hand. In this way, A.B. could fill a session with a detailed discussion of the irrelevant and say little about the main issue (Millon & Davis, 2001). Maintaining a supportive, empathic connection while also keeping a focus on treatment issues and goals became a careful balancing act in the therapy hour.

The next time A.B. stopped her antidepressant, she externalized responsibility for this action saying: "Well, no one told me to keep taking it" and by claiming no knowledge of the therapy contract to discuss before changing the dose or stopping medication. She did acknowledge for the first time a pattern of stopping or cutting back on medicine, food, or social contact when stressed. This acknowledgment of the connection between maladaptive behaviors and feelings of anxiety opened a discussion of what thoughts and circumstances produced anxiety for A.B. Teaching about the relationship between thoughts and feelings was met with skepticism.

At this point, A.B. began attending Mass and bingo games in her apartment building. When her mood became more depressed at the holiday season, a cognitive therapy intervention was introduced. At first, A.B. was unable to identify her strengths. Gradually, a list of strengths was developed and used by A.B. to stabilize her mood.

She continued procrastinating and forgetting to act on ideas generated during sessions, for example, returning to the senior center, telling her internist about a vision problem, and exploring a smoking cessation program. Identifying a shared treatment goal around issues such as seeing a nutritionist or accepting a consultation with behavioral medicine around eating and low weight proved difficult. At this time, supervision focused on the transference as it related to A.B.'s experience of being overinvolved with her mother. The therapy relationship continued at times to be one that A.B. valued and depended on but also rebelled against by sabotaging her health or health care.

Into the third year of treatment, A.B. began establishing relationships with several other residents in her elder housing site, visiting "my friend" in the friend's apartment during the holiday season. She acknowledged feeling less lonely, and depressive mood episodes became less intense and less frequent. She reported improved nutrition but did not gain weight. A.B. had no severe episodes of constipation and no broken bones. She remained emotionally restricted and unable to grieve losses.

A.B.'s treatment demonstrates many of the issues that characterize the treatment of personality disorders in old age. A.B. presented to treatment via a social service referral with an array of behavioral symptoms as well as health and housing problems. A.B., like many older adults, refused outpatient psychotherapy but engaged in treatment offered at home. The therapist's role was an active one when assisting A.B. to meet a new primary care provider and when facilitating communication with her nephew. The therapist saw herself as a liaison to the wider health care team including A.B.'s internist, nutritionist, and a behavioral medicine consultant. The therapeutic alliance developed around the mutually agreed-on goal of addressing problems directly, that is, the concrete health and housing issues initially and, later on, her depressed mood and difficulty with self-care and establishing an effective support system. Progress in treatment was seen in mood improvement, fewer health problems, and an increase in self-care behaviors such as keeping medical appointments and initiating social contact.

SUMMARY AND CONCLUSION

Treatment of an older adult with a personality disorder highlights the usefulness of the *DSM* multiaxial diagnostic framework. The effect of psychosocial stressors and acute and chronic health problems on rigid behavior patterns often leads to the development of an Axis I disorder, most frequently a depressive or anxiety disorder. The complex nature of these social and clinical issues is best addressed by a multidisciplinary community-based treatment team, which works in partnership with a range of social and health care programs.

REFERENCES

Abrams, R. C., Alexopoulos, G. S., Spielman, L. A., Klausner, E., & Kakuma, T. (2001). Personality disorder symptoms predict declines in global functioning and quality of life in elderly depressed patients. *American Journal of Geriatric Psychiatry, 9*, 67–71.

Abrams, R. C., & Horowitz, S. V. (1999). Personality disorders after age 50: A meta-analytic review of the literature. In E. Rosowsky, R. C. Abrams, & R. A. Zweig (Eds.), *Personality disorders in older adults: Emerging issues in diagnosis and treatment* (pp. 55–68). Mahwah, NJ: Erlbaum.

Agronin, M. E. (1994). Personality disorders in the elderly: An overview. *Journal of Geriatric Psychiatry, 27*, 151–191.

Aitken, L., Simpson, S., & Burns, A. (1999). Personality change in dementia. *International Psychogeriatrics, 11*(3), 263–271.

American Psychiatric Association. (1994). *Diagnostic and statistical manual of mental disorders* (4th ed.). Washington, DC: Author.

Ames, A., & Molinari, V. (1994). Prevalence of personality disorders in community-living elderly. *Journal of Geriatric Psychiatry and Neurology, 7*, 189–194.

Bibring, G. L. (1947). Psychiatry and social work. *Journal of Social Casework, 28*, 2, 3, 211.

Butler, R. N. (1963). The life review: An interpretation of reminiscence in the aged. *Psychiatry, 26*, 486–496.

Butler, R. N., Lewis, M., & Sutherland, T. (1991). *Aging and mental health: Positive psychosocial and biomedical approaches.* New York: Macmillan.

Coolidge, F. L., Segal, D. L., Hook, J. N., & Stewart, S. (2000). Personality disorders and coping among anxious older adults. *Journal of Anxiety Disorders, 14*(1), 157–172.

De Leo, D., Scocco, P., & Meneghel, G. (1999). Pharmacological and psychotherapeutic treatment of personality disorders in the elderly. *International Psychogeriatrics, 11*(2), 191–206.

Fishbain, D. A. (1991). Personality disorder diagnosis in old age. *Journal of Clinical Psychiatry, 52*(11), 477–478.

Fogel, B. S., & Westlake, R. (1990). Personality disorder and diagnosis and age in inpatients with major depression. *Journal of Clinical Psychiatry, 51,* 232–235.

Friedman, R. S. (1993). Aging of personality types. *Journal of Geriatric Psychiatry, 26*(2), 149–177.

Goisman, R. M. (1999). Cognitive-behavioral therapy, personality disorders, and the elderly: Clinical and theoretical considerations. In E. Rosowsky, R. C. Abrams, & R. A. Zweig (Eds.), *Personality disorders in older adults: Emerging issues in diagnosis and treatment.* Mahwah, NJ: Erlbaum.

Greenberg, S. (1994). Mutuality in families: A framework for continued growth in late life. *Journal of Geriatric Psychiatry, 27*(1), 79–95.

Kunik, M. E., Mulsant, B. H., Rifai, H., Sweet, R. A., Pasternak, R., Rosen, J., et al. (1994). Diagnostic rate of comorbid personality disorders in elderly psychiatric inpatients. *American Journal of Psychiatry, 151,* 603–605.

Lowry, L. (1989). Independence and dependence in aging: A new balance. *Journal Gerontological Social Work, 13,* 133–146.

Lynch, T. R., & Aspnes, A. (2001). Personality disorders in older adults: Diagnostic and theoretic issues. *Clinical Geriatrics, 9*(101), 64–68.

Malamud, W. I. (1996). Countertransferences issues with the elderly. *Journal of Geriatric Psychiatry, 29*(1), 33–60.

Mehlman, R. D. (1977). Normal psychology of the aging, process, revisited. *Journal of Geriatric Psychiatry, 10,* 53–60.

Millon, T., & Davis, R. (2001). *Personality disorders in modern life.* New York: Wiley.

Morse, J. Q., & Lynch, T. R. (2000). Personality disorders in late-life. *Current Psychiatry Reports, 2,* 24–31.

Petry, S., Cummings, J., Hill, M., & Shapira, J. (1988). Personality alterations in dementia of the Alzheimer's type. *Archives of Neurology, 45,* 1187–1190.

Rosowsky, E., & Dougherty, L. M. (1998). Personality disorders and clinician responses. *Clinical Gerontologist, 18*(4), 31–42.

Sadavoy, J. (1987). Character disorders in the elderly: An overview. In J. Sadavoy (Ed.), *Treating the elderly with psychotherapy* (pp. 175–229). Madison, CT: International University Press.

Solomon, K. (1981). Personality disorders in the elderly. In J. R. Lion (Ed.), *Personality disorders: Diagnosis and management* (pp. 310–338). Baltimore: Williams & Wilkins.

Thompson, L. W., Gallagher, D., & Czirr, R. (1988). Personality disorder and outcome in the treatment of late-life depression. *Journal of Geriatric Psychiatry, 21,* 133–146.

U.S. Department of Health and Human Services. (1999). *Mental health: A report of the Surgeon General.* Rockville, MD: Author.

Viederman, M. (1983). The psychodynamic life narrative: A psychotherapeutic intervention useful in crisis situations. *Psychiatry, 46,* 236–246.

RESEARCH FINDINGS AND FUTURE CHALLENGES

Empirical Research on the Treatment of Personality Disorders

Paul Crits-Christoph and Jacques P. Barber

THE TREATMENT OF severe personality problems as captured by the *DSM* personality disorders has long been discussed in the clinical psychotherapy literature, particularly from a psychoanalytic perspective (Kernberg, 1984; Kohut, 1984) and, more recently, a cognitive-behavioral (Linehan, 1993) perspective. Despite this vast clinical literature and the relatively high prevalence of Axis II disorders (Samuels, Nestadt, Romanoski, Folstein, & McHugh, 1994), there have been relatively few empirical studies of psychotherapy for personality disorders. In the past decade, however, there has been growing attention to research on the treatment of personality disorders, including studies of pharmacotherapy as well as psychotherapy.

In this chapter, we systematically review the available empirical literature on the treatment of personality disorders. Studies of psychotherapies are reviewed first, followed by studies of pharmacotherapy. In drawing conclusions from this literature, we place the greatest weight on controlled empirical studies, although such studies are rare. We review studies of each specific personality disorder, as well as studies of mixed samples. The relevance of personality disorders in the treatment of Axis I conditions is also reviewed.

PSYCHOTHERAPY FOR PERSONALITY DISORDERS

META-ANALYSIS OF THE TREATMENT OF PERSONALITY DISORDERS

A meta-analysis reviewing 15 studies of psychotherapy for personality disorders was reported by Perry, Banon, and Ianni (1999). Four of the studies focused on patients with Borderline Personality Disorder (Liberman & Eckman, 1981;

The preparation of this chapter was funded in part by National Institute of Mental Health grants P30-MH-45178, K02-MH00756, and RO1-MH40472. Address reprint requests to Paul Crits-Christoph, PhD, Room 650, 3535 Market St., Philadelphia, PA 19104.

Linehan, Tutek, Heard, & Armstrong, 1994; Munroe-Blum & Marziali, 1995; Stevenson & Meares, 1992), one on Borderline and Schizotypal Personality Disorders (Karterud et al., 1992), one on Avoidant Personality Disorder (Alden, 1989), and one on Antisocial (Woody, McLellan, Luborsky, & O'Brien, 1985). The remaining eight studies focused on mixed types of personality disorders (Budman, Demby, Soldz, & Merry, 1996; Diguer, Barber, & Luborsky, 1993; Fahy, Eisler, & Russell, 1993; Hardy et al., 1995; Hoglend, 1993; Monsen, Odland, Faugli, Daae, & Eilertsen, 1995; Rosenthal, Muran, Pinsker, Hellerstein, & Winston, 1999; Winston et al., 1994). Because most of these studies were not randomized trials, Perry et al. calculated an index of the size of the treatment effect within each treatment group (posttreatment mean minus pretreatment mean divided by pretreatment standard deviation). Averaged across studies, these "effect sizes" ranged from 1.1 to 1.3 depending on the outcome measure. A more clinically useful outcome was also examined by Perry et al.: the percentage of patients who no longer met Axis II criteria at the follow-up assessment. For four studies of Borderline Personality Disorder patients, Perry et al. showed that, in comparison to the natural history of Borderline Personality Disorder, patients who received psychotherapy had a sevenfold faster rate of recovery. However, the validity of this comparison is unclear because only half of the patients in the four studies had met diagnostic criteria for Borderline Personality Disorder. Individual studies from this meta-analysis are described in more detail in the following sections, which review investigations of specific personality disorders.

AVOIDANT PERSONALITY DISORDER

In a randomized controlled trial, Alden (1989) compared graded exposure, standard social skills training, intimacy-focused social skills training, and a wait-list control as treatment for Avoidant Personality Disorder. All of the behavioral treatments were administered in group format. The results indicated that all of the active treatments were better than the wait-list control. No differences among the active treatments were found at the end of the 10-week treatment period or at follow-up. Although patients improved over the course of treatment, at termination, patients were not functioning at the level of normative comparison samples. The sample size in this study (less than 20 patients per group) was relatively small, thereby limiting the statistical power for detecting differences among the treatments.

In a subsequent paper (Alden & Capreol, 1993), potential moderators of treatment response in the Alden (1989) study were examined. Specifically, the authors examined the hypothesis that different kinds of interpersonal problems would moderate the response to different treatments. Patients who had problems related to distrustful and angry behavior improved more in graded exposure therapy. Patients who had problems resisting others' demands benefited from both graded exposure and social skills training, but were especially responsive to intimacy-focused social skills training. These results indicate that assessment of interpersonal problems may be useful in planning what type of treatment intervention is most likely to be beneficial to patients with Avoidant Personality Disorder.

One noncontrolled evaluation of psychotherapy for Avoidant Personality Disorder has been reported (Renneberg, Goldstein, Phillips, & Chambless, 1990). In this study, an intensive (four full days) group behavioral treatment program was evaluated. Seventeen patients were treated with group systematic desensitization, behavioral rehearsal, and self-image work. Patients improved from baseline to posttreatment, especially in terms of fear of negative evaluation. Gains were maintained at the one-year follow-up.

Using a crossover design, Stravynski, Lesage, Marcouiller, and Elie (1989) compared social skills training with group discussion plus homework for patients with *DSM-III* Avoidant Personality Disorder. Improvements on most measures were evident, but no significant differences between the treatment modalities were found. The study, therefore, did not provide support for skills acquisition as the mechanism of action of social skills training. An important limitation of this study, however, was that treatment was very brief (five sessions). In another study, Stravynski, Belisle, Marcouiller, and Lavallee (1994) investigated whether in vivo skills training (real-life interactions with people in shopping malls, a cafeteria, etc.) enhanced the outcome of office-based social skills training for 28 patients with *DSM-III* Avoidant Personality Disorder. The authors found equivalent outcomes for the two treatments. The group with in vivo skills training, however, had a higher attrition rate.

Schema-focused cognitive therapy (CT) was examined as a treatment for Avoidant Personality Disorder in a case report by Coon (1994). Outcome measures suggested that positive outcomes were evident not only at termination but also at one-year follow-up.

One study has examined psychodynamic therapy for Avoidant Personality Disorder. Barber, Morse, Krakauer, Chittams, and Crits-Christoph (1997) assessed the outcomes of patients treated with one year of manual-based supportive-expressive dynamic therapy. At the end of treatment, 61% of patients no longer met criteria for Avoidant Personality Disorder diagnosis.

OBSESSIVE-COMPULSIVE PERSONALITY DISORDER

There has been only one published study on Obsessive-Compulsive Personality Disorder. In this study (Barber et al., 1997), 14 patients were treated with one year of supportive-expressive psychodynamic therapy. At the end of treatment, only 15% of patients continued to meet criteria for Obsessive-Compulsive Personality Disorder. In fact, most patients had lost their diagnoses by four months into treatment. Moreover, significant improvements across time on measures of personality disorders, depression, anxiety, general functioning, and interpersonal problems were found.

BORDERLINE PERSONALITY DISORDER

Over the past decade, there has been substantial clinical interest in Linehan's (1993) dialectical behavior therapy (DBT) for Borderline Personality Disorder (see chapter 11 for a description of DBT). Because of the refractory nature of Borderline Personality Disorder and the stress of providing treatment to such patients, who characteristically have chaotic interpersonal relationships and are prone to suicide attempts and other impulsive acts, clinicians have gravitated toward new approaches that appear promising in the management of Borderline Personality Disorder. The optimism concerning DBT was generated from the initial study (Linehan, Hubert, Suarez, Douglas, & Heard, 1991) of 44 women with Borderline

Personality Disorder who evidenced parasuicidal behavior. Patients were randomly assigned to either DBT or treatment as usual (TAU) in the community. The results indicated that DBT produced relatively fewer and less severe episodes of parasuicidal behavior and fewer days of hospitalization compared to TAU, but no differences in depression, hopelessness, or suicidal ideation were found. Fewer patients dropped out of DBT (16.7%) compared to TAU (58.3%). One-year follow-up data revealed that the superiority of DBT to TAU was maintained (Koerner & Linehan, 2000). To date, this study is one of the most important and influential studies of the treatment of Borderline Personality Disorder. Although the study has a number of notable strengths, one limitation is that the therapists in the TAU condition were not equated with the DBT therapists on experience in treating patients with Borderline Personality Disorder. In addition, 27% of the control patients never actually began therapy although they were referred to a therapist. These limitations raise questions about whether the differences found between DBT and the control group are a function of the active ingredients of DBT or other differences between the treatment groups. Nevertheless, the study documents the clinical promise of DBT.

Several additional studies have provided empirical support for the usefulness of DBT with Borderline Personality Disorder. One study found that DBT decreased the rates of incident reports of self-inflicted injuries and overdoses for inpatients with Borderline Personality Disorder (Barley et al., 1993). In a comparison of DBT to TAU for drug-dependent women with Borderline Personality Disorder (Linehan et al., 1999), it was found that DBT patients had significantly greater reductions in drug abuse during a one-year treatment period and also at follow-up than did TAU patients.

Psychodynamic therapy has been evaluated as a treatment for Borderline Personality Disorder in several studies. One controlled investigation (Bateman & Fonagy, 1999) randomized patients to either partial hospitalization ($n = 19$) or to standard care ($n = 19$). The partial hospitalization program involved individual and group psychoanalytic psychotherapy for up to 18 months. Standard care consisted of (1) regular psychiatric review with a senior psychiatrist when necessary (on average, twice per month); (2) inpatient admission as appropriate, with discharge to nonpsychoanalytic psychiatric partial hospitalization focusing on problem solving; followed by (3) outpatient and community follow-up. Members of the standard care group received no formal psychotherapy. The results indicated that patients who received the psychoanalytically based partial hospitalization treatment program improved significantly more than those who received standard care on measures of number of suicidal attempts, acts of self-harm, psychiatric symptoms, inpatient days, and social and interpersonal functioning. These differences were evident at both the 6-month and 18-month assessments.

Psychodynamic psychotherapy for Borderline Personality Disorder was also examined in a study by Munroe-Blum and Marziali (1995). These authors evaluated the outcomes of an open-ended individual psychodynamic therapy compared to 30 sessions of manualized interpersonal group therapy for 110 patients with Borderline Personality Disorder. Both treatments produced clinical benefits, but there were no differences between the treatments at either the one-year or two-year postbaseline assessments.

Stevenson and Meares (1992) assessed outcomes of a self-psychology-based dynamic therapy model for Borderline Personality Disorder. The goals of treatment were to help patients discover and elaborate their inner life, with attention to disruptions in empathy as a central aspect of the process of therapy (Meares, 1987). In the study, 30 patients with Borderline Personality Disorder were treated with twice-per-week therapy for one year, and outcome was assessed one year after termination of treatment. The results indicated that substantial reductions in violent behavior, drug use, medical visits, episodes of self-harm, time away from work, and symptoms occurred. In addition, 30% of the sample no longer met criteria for Borderline Personality Disorder. Follow-up assessments indicated that these improvements continued over five years with substantial savings in health care costs (Stevenson & Meares, 1999).

OTHER PERSONALITY DISORDERS

To date, there have been no controlled or uncontrolled (single group) outcome evaluations of treatments for Histrionic, Dependent, Schizotypal, Schizoid, Narcissistic, Passive-Aggressive, Antisocial, or Paranoid Personality Disorders. A quantitative single case study of cognitive therapy for Paranoid Personality Disorder reported positive outcomes (Williams, 1988).

MIXED AXIS II SAMPLES

A number of studies have used samples that included a mixture of personality disorders. Although such studies go against the trend in psychiatric treatment research to develop and test specific treatments for specific disorders, they have the advantage of potentially greater generalizability to clinical practice. In part, this is because many patients receive multiple personality disorder diagnoses. Thus, the utility of specific treatments for individual personality disorders may be limited if few patients actually have the single target disorder. Another important consideration is that the diagnostic boundaries between the personality disorders are strongly supported by research (reference), suggesting that focusing on a class of personality disorders may be more fruitful.

One controlled study examined treatments for mixed personality disorders (Winston et al., 1991, 1994). Eighty-one patients with personality disorders were randomly assigned to a wait-list control or one of two forms of brief dynamic therapy: brief adaptive therapy (a relatively less confrontational form of cognitively oriented brief dynamic therapy) or short-term dynamic therapy (a treatment oriented toward confronting defenses and eliciting affect based on Davanloo, 1980). Included in the sample were patients who had evidence of at least one close personal relationship and who were diagnosed with Cluster B (but excluding Borderline and Narcissistic) or C personality disorders or Personality Disorder Not Otherwise Specified (mostly with Cluster C features). The two active psychotherapies lasted on average 40 weeks, whereas the waitlist was on average 15 weeks long. Both forms of brief dynamic therapy produced substantial improvements in general psychiatric symptoms, social adjustment, and target complaints. Follow-up assessments, conducted one and a half years (on average) after termination, showed that the gains were maintained on target complaints (the only outcome measured).

In a subsequent study, the same research group also investigated supportive therapy ($n = 24$) compared to short-term dynamic psychotherapy ($n = 25$) for mixed personality disorders (Hellerstein et al., 1998). Each treatment was planned for 40 sessions. However, a relatively large proportion (35%) dropped out of treatment before the scheduled termination. Outcome comparisons revealed no significant differences between the treatment modalities at midphase (week 20), termination, or six-month follow-up. Substantial improvements were evident for both treatments on all outcome measures.

Some articles have reported outcome results for a subsample of patients with personality disorders who participated in a larger study of an Axis I disorder. For example, Hardy et al. (1995) describe the outcomes of 27 patients diagnosed with a Cluster C personality disorder. These patients were drawn from a larger sample of 114 with Major Depressive Disorder who participated in a comparison of cognitive therapy with interpersonal-psychodynamic therapy (Shapiro et al., 1994). At the end of treatment, Cluster C personality disorder patients continued to display significantly more severe symptoms than non-Cluster C personality disorder patients if they received dynamic therapy, but not if they received CT.

Karterud et al. (1992) examined the outcomes of 97 patients who received day hospital community treatment. Of the 97 patients, 74 had a personality disorder diagnosis (34 were Borderline Personality Disorder, 13 were Schizotypal Personality Disorder, and 27 were other personality disorders). The average length of stay in the program was 171 days. All of the patients with personality disorders, with the exception of those with Schizotypal Personality Disorder, improved significantly from baseline to discharge on measures of symptoms and overall functioning.

An investigation by Monsen et al. (1995) examined the outcomes of 25 patients, 23 of whom had an Axis II diagnosis, treated with psychodynamic therapy that lasted on average about two years. At termination of treatment, large improvements were evident on measures of symptoms, affect consciousness, and defenses. Moreover, 72% of the 23 patients who received an Axis II diagnosis at intake no longer met criteria for a personality disorder at the end of treatment. Improvements seen over the course of treatment were maintained at the five-year follow-up assessment.

One study (Hoglend, 1993) sought to examine the impact of treatment length on psychotherapy for patients with versus those without a personality disorder. Fifteen patients with a range of personality disorders (eight Avoidant or Dependent [Cluster C] and seven Histrionic, Narcissistic, or Borderline [Cluster B]) were compared to 30 patients without Axis II disorders. Treatment was psychodynamic therapy based on the approaches of Sifneos (1979) and Malan (1976) and lasted from 9 to 53 sessions. At the end of treatment, patients with a personality disorder showed less improvement than those without Axis II diagnoses, although this difference was not apparent at the four-year follow-up. The acquisition of insight and the achievement of psychodynamic change were significantly associated with positive outcome among those with a personality disorder. Thus, longer treatment appeared to be especially important for those with an Axis II diagnosis.

Relation of Axis II Diagnosis to the Outcome of Treatment for Axis I Disorders

Reich and Green (1991) reviewed 21 studies, and Reich and Vasile (1993) reviewed 17 additional studies that examined the relation of personality traits and Axis II disorders to the outcome of treatments (both psychosocial and psychopharmacological) that targeted Axis I disorders. The general trend in the studies reviewed by Reich and Green and Reich and Vasile, also found in further studies published since these reviews, has been for patients with an Axis II diagnosis to improve less than those without an Axis II diagnosis in brief treatments for Axis I disorders. A few studies, however, have not been consistent with this trend. Longabaugh et al. (1994), for example, explored the impact of Antisocial Personality Disorder on the outcome of treatments for alcohol abuse. In this study, one form of group cognitive-behavioral treatment (including stimulus control, rearranging consequences, restructuring cognitions, assertion training, problem solving for alternatives to drinking, and dealing with slips or relapses) was compared to another form of cognitive-behavioral therapy that emphasized relationship enhancement (enhancing reinforcements in relationships with partners, using partners' relationship to reinforce abstinence, and educational-didactic sessions for partners). Patients with Antisocial Personality Disorder had relatively good outcomes in the standard cognitive-behavioral treatment but relatively poor outcomes in the relationship enhancement treatment. Patients with a diagnosis of Antisocial Personality Disorder had intermediate outcomes in both treatment conditions. This interaction, however, was found for only one measure of alcohol use. At the follow-up assessment (13 to 18 months), a main affect for Antisocial Personality Disorder was evident rather than an interaction. Patients with Antisocial Personality Disorder reported more days abstinent compared to non-Antisocial Personality Disorder patients.

Matching specific type of personality disorder features to type of Axis I treatment was explored in a post hoc analysis conducted by Barber and Muenz (1996) using data from the NIMH Treatment of Depression Collaborative Study (Elkin et al., 1989). Interpersonal therapy (Klerman, Weissman, Rounsaville, & Chevron, 1984) was found to produce superior outcomes for depressed patients with features of Obsessive-Compulsive Personality Disorder, whereas cognitive therapy (Beck, Rush, Shaw, & Emery, 1979) yielded better outcomes with depressed patients who had features of Avoidant Personality Disorder. These findings were consistent with the subsequent study described earlier that found that patients with Obsessive-Compulsive Disorder, compared to those with Avoidant Personality Disorder, generally fared better in an interpersonal-oriented psychodynamic therapy (Barber et al., 1997).

Hofmann, Newman, Becker, Taylor, and Roth (1995) investigated presence of Avoidant Personality Disorder as a predictor of the outcome of treatment of public speaking anxiety among patients with social phobia. The results indicated that treatment was equally successful in those with and without Avoidant Personality Disorder.

PSYCHOPHARMACOLOGICAL TREATMENT OF PERSONALITY DISORDERS

Research and clinical trials are beginning to suggest that many personality characteristics, and thus to some extent personality disorders, are associated with neurochemical abnormalities (Coccaro, Berman, Kavoussi, & Hauger, 1996; Coccaro, Kavoussi, Hauger, Cooper, & Ferris, 1998; Markovitz, 2001), providing, therefore, the rationale for a biological treatment of personality disorder. However, relatively few double-blind randomized controlled studies have been conducted. One of the main problems in conducting and interpreting studies of pharmacotherapy of personality disorder is the fact that most personality disorder patients are also suffering from comorbid depressive, anxiety, psychotic, substance abuse, or other disorders (Koenigsberg, Woo-Ming, & Siever, 2002; Teusch, Bohme, Finke, & Gastpar, 2001).

Other studies have been conducted to examine the effect of combining psychotherapy with pharmacotherapy for personality disorders. A study of the effects of client centered therapy (CCT), both in combination with and versus antidepressant treatment for a sample of patients with a wide range of personality disorders, suggested that concurrent CCT and medication were no more effective than the CCT alone (Teusch et al., 2001). These results are countered by the claims of Gabbard (2000) and Cloninger, Svrakic, and Przybeck (1993), who posit that the combination of psychotherapy and pharmacotherapy could be very useful for patients suffering from personality disorders. Gabbard suggests a model whereby medication essentially eliminates the affective "background noise" associated with the disorder, allowing for the conduct of a more effective psychotherapy. More specifically, the three main roles played by medication are to:

1. Modify temperament.
2. Address specific target symptoms (taking the form of cognitive-perceptual symptoms, impulsive-behavioral symptoms, and affective symptoms).
3. Treat comorbid Axis I disorders (pp. 66–67).

Although this approach makes clinical sense, the evidence to support it has not yet been gathered.

An important emphasis of the efficacy research of pharmacotherapy for personality disorder has focused on the following disorders: Borderline Personality Disorder, Schizotypal Personality Disorder, and Avoidant Personality Disorder.

Borderline Personality Disorder   Symptoms of Borderline Personality Disorder such as impulsivity, mood lability, hostility, depression, and anxiety have been targeted by pharmacotherapists. Many drugs have been used to help patients with Borderline Personality Disorder. Among the most researched are antidepressants such as fluoxetine and nefazodone and both typical neuroleptics and atypical antipsychotics. Fluoxetine was shown to be effective in decreasing impulsive aggression and depression scores and improving a range of symptoms including rejection sensitivity, anxiety, psychoticism, and obsessive-compulsive symptoms in a placebo-controlled (Coccaro & Kavoussi, 1995) and an open trial (Markovitz, Calabrese, Schulz, & Meltzer, 1991). In another study, 63% of patients with Borderline Personality Disorder responded to nefazodone (Markovitz & Wagner, 1997; open trial). It has been speculated that the effect of these agents on Borderline Personality Disorder is resultant of the serotonin-2 (5-HT_2) antagonism properties of the medication. This speculation arises from the fact that the atypical antipsychotics have neuroleptic-like activity at the dopamine-2 (D_2) receptors and also antagonize the serotonin-2 (5-HT_2) receptors, yet show subtler effects on Borderline Personality Disorder than the aforementioned antidepressants, which likely mediate their effect through 5-HT_2 antagonism (Narayan et al., 1998; Taylor et al., 1995).

Schizotypal Personality Disorder   Because Schizotypal Personality Disorder is rarely presented as the primary cause for treatment, few studies of strictly Schizotypal

Personality Disorder patients have been conducted. The stereotypical symptoms of Schizotypal Personality Disorder cluster into three groups, which have, therefore, become the target of pharmacotherapy. Antipsychotic medications have been studied for their use in alleviating the psychotic-like symptoms (such as magical thinking, ideas of reference, and perceptual distortion). Dopaminergic agents have likewise been considered for their effects on deficit-like symptoms (such as poor interpersonal relatedness) and cognitive disorganization (attentional symptoms; Koenigsberg et al., 2002). However, dopaminergic agents such as amphetamine, which have been implicated in improvement of deficit-like symptoms, often aggravate and worsen the concurrent psychotic-like symptoms (Schulz, Cornelius, Schulz, & Soloff, 1988). In one study examining fluoxetine efficacy in Borderline Personality Disorder patients, a grouping of patients (with concurrent Schizotypal Personality Disorder such that the group was even more strongly Schizotypal Personality Disorder than Borderline Personality Disorder) showed meaningful improvement as a result of the fluoxetine treatment. Perhaps selective serotonin reuptake inhibitors should be further studied for their efficacy in treating Schizotypal Personality Disorder because Schizotypal Personality Disorder patients not only have a high rate of comorbid depressive disorders, but also may be viewed as exhibiting obsessive-compulsive behavior (Markovitz, 2001), which has been shown to respond to treatment with these medications.

Avoidant Personality Disorder   Because of its strong likeness to Social Anxiety Disorder and the rate of comorbidity among the two, it is reasonable to assume that treatments for Social Anxiety Disorder would be examined for patients with Avoidant Personality Disorder. Paroxetine, sertraline, fluoxetine, venlafaxine, and brofaromine have all shown efficacy in reducing social anxiety, but the results did not explicitly suggest any effect on Avoidant Personality Disorder. No trials looking specifically at Avoidant Personality Disorder have yet been published, but as Markovitz (2001) suggests, it would be logical to consider paroxetine, fluvoxamine, or venlafaxine for their relatively lower rates of agitation because Avoidant Personality Disorder patients typically exhibit a high level of anxiety. In addition, Avoidant Personality Disorder lends itself nicely to the combined treatment strategy offered by Gabbard (2000). As the flawed neurochemistry of the afflicted individual would conceivably result in a pathological learning model and, in turn, an abnormal behavior pattern, pharmacotherapy would be useful in restoring a normal biochemistry, whereas concurrent psychotherapy could help assist the individual in learning to respond in a more socially acceptable way (Markovitz, 2001).

SUMMARY OF RESEARCH LITERATURE

With the relative limited number of systematic controlled studies of treatments for personality disorders, it is difficult to draw any strong conclusions. For the treatment of Borderline Personality Disorder, two psychotherapeutic treatments look promising based on randomized trials:

1. Linehan's (1993) dialectical behavior therapy.
2. Psychodynamic treatment as a component of a partial hospitalization program as described by Bateman and Fonagy (1999).

Among medications, both fluoxetine and nefazodone appear efficacious for Borderline Personality Disorder. As to Avoidant Personality Disorder, behavior therapy has demonstrated efficacy, but the specific type of behavior therapy that is most useful may depend on the nature of patients' types of interpersonal problems, with graded exposure better when distrust is an issue and intimacy-focused social skills training preferable when resisting others' demands is the major interpersonal problem. For Antisocial Personality Disorder, a structured cognitive-behavioral treatment appears to be efficacious. Based on evidence from a controlled trial and two uncontrolled trials, psychodynamic therapy appears useful for the treatment of mixed personality disorders.

Perhaps the strongest conclusion that can be made from empirical studies is that brief treatment (either psychotherapy or medication) for Axis I disorders is often not successful when an Axis II disorder is present.

Research on the treatment of personality disorders should be a high priority. Personality disorders are common, are associated with significant impairments in functioning, and often lead to failure in the treatment of Axis I disorders. Thus, the treatment of personality disorders is a major future challenge for the mental health field.

It is not clear why there has been scant research attention to the treatment of these common and serious disorders. Perhaps the fact that *character* has traditionally not fit within the medical model conceptualization of mental illnesses as easily as Axis I disorders is a factor in the relative lack of attention to research on the treatment of personality disorders. Another issue might be the fact that most patients do not seek treatment for their Axis II disorder per se. In many areas of medicine, however, patients do not seek treatment for their disorder or syndrome; they seek treatment for the current set of symptoms they are experiencing. As with other medical disorders, it is the clinician's responsibility to accurately diagnose Axis II disorders and, in collaboration with the patient, formulate an appropriate treatment plan.

CLINICAL RECOMMENDATIONS BASED ON RESEARCH LITERATURE

The existing empirical literature on the treatment of personality disorders, although relatively underdeveloped, suggests a number of recommendations for practicing clinicians. As described, certain treatments have demonstrated efficacy in the treatment of personality disorders, and these treatments should be considered first-line treatment by clinicians unless there are important clinical concerns not addressed in these research studies that need to be considered (e.g., comorbid disorders that were excluded from the research studies).

Although the research literature for matching certain psychotherapies to certain personality disorders or traits is underdeveloped, there is some evidence that clinicians would be wise to take into account such personality disorders or features in their style of therapy if not the modality (Barber et al., 1997). Patients with Avoidant Personality Disorder, like those with anxiety disorders, can benefit from greater structure and behavioral tasks (exposure), whereas patients with Obsessive-Compulsive Disorder or features of the disorder appear to work better in a therapy context in which they are given greater control and autonomy, such as interpersonal therapy or psychodynamic therapy.

Beyond the choice of treatment modality for Axis II, another important clinical recommendation relates to treatments for Axis I disorders. We recommend that clinicians assess for Axis II disorders when conducting an initial intake evaluation and treatment plan. If brief treatment is initiated with patients with a personality disorder, the treatment plan should be reevaluated if progress is not made over the first four to eight weeks of treatment. Clinicians should also be aware that patients with characterological symptoms that are typical of personality disorders often do not show clinically significant change on such symptoms until approximately 52 treatment sessions (Kopta, Howard, Lowry, & Beutler, 1994). Thus, our strong clinical recommendation is that long-term therapy (one year or more) be considered as a treatment option for those patients with Axis II disorders who do not show improvement after a course of short-term treatment.

FUTURE DIRECTIONS FOR RESEARCH ON THE TREATMENT OF PERSONALITY DISORDERS

The studies we have reviewed suggest a number of promising directions for research on the treatment of personality disorders. One important issue is the modification of existing Axis I treatments to take into account Axis II pathology. Such modifications will likely include longer duration of treatment and greater attention to the core belief systems and maladaptive interpersonal patterns of Axis II patients, rather than a sole focus on symptoms or recent triggers. An alternative to modifying existing treatments is the search for fruitful matches between patient characteristics and treatment modalities. Matching can be examined in terms of personality disorder syndrome or other patient attributes that underlie the distinctions among personality disorders. Beutler, Mohr, Grawe, and Engle (1991) have suggested, for example, that impulsivity-external coping style is an important dimension for matching patients to treatments. Impulsivity and external coping style are seen as underlying features of Antisocial Personality Disorder. Patients with these features are suggested to fare better in a more structured treatment modality. Thus, the underlying dimensions of impulsivity and external coping style that characterize but do not uniquely define Antisocial Personality Disorder might be a more salient basis for treatment selection than the Axis II disorder per se.

A final likely influence on future research on personality disorders is the evolving movement toward psychotherapy integration. Linehan's (1993) dialectical behavior therapy designed for Borderline Personality Disorder is actually a complex treatment that integrates techniques from a variety of traditional approaches. Because of the diverse set of problems (i.e., impairments in social functioning, work functioning, and a variety of symptoms) that often occur with Axis II patients, a range of approaches might be necessary to effectively make progress in these domains. Combined psychotherapy and medication may be especially useful for many patients, particularly those with severe Axis II disorders and comorbid Axis I conditions. We look forward to potential advances in the treatment of personality disorders in the coming years. Such advances will not only have important public health implications, but also raise optimism among clinicians who encounter these difficult, often treatment-resistant individuals in their practices.

REFERENCES

Alden, L. E. (1989). Short-term structured treatment for avoidant personality disorder. *Journal of Consulting and Clinical Psychology, 57,* 756–764.

Alden, L. E., & Capreol, M. J. (1993). Avoidant personality disorder: Interpersonal problems as predictors of treatment response. *Behavior Therapy, 24,* 357–376.

Barber, J. P., Morse, J. Q., Krakauer, I., Chittams, J., & Crits-Christoph, K. (1997). Change in obsessive-compulsive and avoidant personality disorders following time-limited supportive-expressive therapy. *Psychotherapy, 34,* 133–143.

Barber, J. P., & Muenz, L. R. (1996). The role of avoidance and obsessiveness in matching patients to cognitive and interpersonal psychotherapy: Empirical findings from the Treatment for Depression Collaborative Research Program. *Journal of Consulting and Clinical Psychology, 64,* 951–958.

Bateman, A., & Fonagy, P. (1999). Effectiveness of partial hospitalization in the treatment of borderline personality disorder: A randomized controlled trial. *American Journal of Psychiatry, 156,* 1563–1569.

Beck, A. T., Rush, A. J., Shaw, B. F., & Emery, G. (1979). Cognitive therapy of depression. New York: Guilford.

Beutler, L. E., Mohr, D. C., Grawe, K., & Engle, D. (1991). Looking for differential treatment effects: Cross-cultural predictors of differential psychotherapy efficacy. *Journal of Psychotherapy Integration, 1,* 121–141.

Budman, S., Demby, A., Soldz, S., & Merry, J. (1996). Time-limited group psychotherapy for patients with personality disorders: Outcomes and drop-outs. *International Journal of Group Psychotherapy, 46,* 357–377.

Cloninger, C. R., Svrakic, D. M., & Przybeck, T. R. (1993). A psychobiological model of temperament and character. *Archives of General Psychiatry, 50,* 975–990.

Coccaro, E. F., Berman, M. E., Kavoussi, R. J., & Hauger, R. L. (1996). Relationship of prolactin response to d-fenfluramine to behavioral and questionnaire assessments of aggression in personality-disordered men. *Biological Psychiatry, 40,* 157–164.

Coccaro, E. F., & Kavoussi, R. J. (1995, May). *Fluoxetine in aggression in personality disorders.* Paper presented at the American Psychiatric Association 148th annual meeting, Miami, Florida.

Coccaro, E. F., Kavoussi, R. J., Hauger, R. L., Cooper, T. B., & Ferris, C. F. (1998). Cerebrospinal fluid vaspressin levels: Correlates with aggression and serotonin function in personality-disordered subjects. *Archives of General Psychiatry, 55,* 708–714.

Coon, D. W. (1994). Cognitive-behavioral interventions with avoidant personality: A single case study. *Journal of Cognitive Psychotherapy: An International Quarterly, 8,* 243–253.

Davanloo, H. (1980). *Short-term dynamic psychotherapy.* New York: Aronson.

Diguer, L., Barber, J. P., & Luborsky, L. (1993). Three concomitants: Personality disorders, psychiatric severity, and outcome of dynamic psychotherapy of major depression. *American Journal of Psychiatry, 150,* 1246–1248.

Elkin, I., Shea, M. T., Watkins, J. T., Imber, S. D., Sotsky, S. M., Collins, J. F., et al. (1989). NIMH Treatment of Depression Collaborative Research Program: General effectiveness of treatments. *Archives of General Psychiatry, 46,* 971–982.

Fahy, T. A., Eisler, I., & Russell, G. F. (1993). Personality disorder and treatment response in bulimia nervosa. *British Journal of Psychiatry, 162,* 765–770.

Gabbard, G. O. (2000). Combining medication with psychotherapy in the treatment of personality disorders. In J. G. Gunderson & G. O. Gabbard (Eds.), *Psychotherapy for personality disorders: Review of psychiatry* (Vol. 19, pp. 65–94). Washington, DC: American Psychiatric Press.

Hardy, G. E., Barkham, M., Shapiro, D. A., Stiles, W. B., Rees, A., & Reynolds, S. (1995). Impact of Cluster C personality disorders on outcomes of contrasting brief psychotherapies for depression. *Journal of Consulting and Clinical Psychology, 63,* 997–1004.

Hellerstein, D. J., Rosenthal, R. N., Pinsker, H., Samstag, L. W., Muran, J. C., & Winston, A. (1998). A randomized prospective study comparing supportive and dynamic therapies. *Journal of Psychotherapy Practice and Research, 7,* 261–271.

Hofmann, S. G., Newman, M. G., Becker, E., Taylor, C. B., & Roth, W. T. (1995). Social phobia with and without avoidant personality disorder: Preliminary behavior therapy outcome findings. *Journal of Anxiety Disorders, 9,* 427–438.

Hoglend, P. (1993). Personality disorders and long-term outcome after brief dynamic psychotherapy. *Journal of Personality Disorders, 7,* 168–181.

Karterud, S., Vaglum, S., Friis, S., Irion, T., Johns, S., & Vaglum, P. (1992). Day hospital therapeutic community treatment for patients with personality disorders: An empirical evaluation of the containment function. *Journal of Nervous and Mental Diseases, 180,* 238–43.

Kernberg, O. F. (1984). *Severe personality disorders: Psychotherapeutic strategies.* New Haven, CT: Yale University Press.

Klerman, G. L., Weissman, M. M., Rounsaville, B. J., & Chevron, E. (1984). *Interpersonal psychotherapy of depression.* New York: Basic Books.

Koenigsberg, H. W., Woo-Ming, A. M., & Siever, L. J. (2002). Pharmacological treatments for personality disorders. In P. E. Nathan & J. M. Gorman (Eds.), *A guide to treatments that work* (2nd ed., pp. 625–641). London: Oxford University Press.

Koerner, K., & Linehan, M. M. (2000). Research on dialectical behavior therapy for patients with borderline personality disorder. *Psychiatric Clinics of North America, 23,* 151–167.

Kohut, H. (1984). *How does analysis cure?* Chicago: University of Chicago Press.

Kopta, S. M., Howard, K. I., Lowry, J. L., & Beutler, L. E. (1994). Patterns of symptomatic recovery in psychotherapy. *Journal of Consulting and Clinical Psychology, 62,* 1009–1016.

Liberman, R. P., & Eckman, T. (1981). Behavior therapy vs. insight-oriented therapy for repeated suicide attempters. *Archives of General Psychiatry, 38,* 1126–1130.

Linehan, M. M. (1993). *Cognitive-behavioral treatment of borderline personality disorder.* New York: Guilford Press.

Linehan, M. M., Hubert, A. E., Suarez, A., Douglas, A., & Heard, H. L. (1991). Cognitive-behavioral treatment of chronically parasuicidal borderline patients. *Archives of General Psychiatry, 48,* 1060–1064.

Linehan, M. M., Schmidt, H., Dimeff, L. A., Craft, J. C., Kanter, J., & Comtois, K. A. (1999). Dialectical behavior therapy for patients with borderline personality disorder and drug-dependence. *American Journal on Addictions, 8,* 279–292.

Linehan, M. M., Tutek, D. A., Heard, H. L., & Armstrong, H. E. (1994). Interpersonal outcome of cognitive behavioral treatment for chronically suicidal borderline patients. *American Journal of Psychiatry, 151,* 1771–1776.

Longabaugh, R., Rubin, A., Malloy, P., Beattie, M., Clifford, P. R., & Noel, N. (1994). Drinking outcomes of alcohol abusers diagnosed as antisocial personality disorder. *Alcoholism: Clinical and Experimental Research, 18,* 778–785.

Malan, D. H. (1976). *The frontier of brief psychotherapy.* New York: Plenum Press.

Markovitz, P. (2001). Pharmacotherapy. In W. J. Livesley (Ed.), *Handbook of personality disorders: Theory, research, and treatment* (pp. 475–493). New York: Guilford Press.

Markovitz, P. J., Calabrese, J. R., Schulz, S. C., & Meltzer, H. Y. (1991). Fluoxetine treatment of borderline and schizotypal personality disorder. *American Journal of Psychiatry, 148,* 1064–1067.

Markovitz, P. J., & Wagner, S. (1997). *Pharmacotherapy of borderline personality disorders.* Paper presented at International Society for the Study of Personality Disorders, Vancouver, British Columbia, Canada.

Meares, R. (1987). The secret and the self: On a new direction in psychotherapy. *Australian and New Zealand Journal of Psychiatry, 21,* 545–559.

Monsen, J., Odland, T., Faugli, A., Daae, E., & Eilertsen, D. E. (1995). Personality disorders: Changes and stability after intensive psychotherapy focusing on affect consciousness. *Psychotherapy Research, 5,* 33–48.

Munroe-Blum, H., & Marziali, E. (1995). A controlled trial of short-term group treatment for borderline personality disorder. *Journal of Personality Disorders, 9,* 190–198.

Narayan, M., Anderson, G., Cellar, J., Mallison, R. T., Price, L. H., & Nielson, J. C. (1998). Serotonin transporter-blocking properties of nefazodone assessed by measurement of platelet serotonin. *Journal of Clinical Psychopharmacology, 18,* 67–71.

Perry, J. C., Banon, E., & Ianni, F. (1999). Effectiveness of psychotherapy for personality disorders. *American Journal of Psychiatry, 156,* 1312–1321.

Pilkonis, P. A., & Frank, E. L. (1988). Personality pathology in recurrent depression: Nature, prevalence, and relationship to treatment response. *American Journal of Psychiatry, 145,* 435–441.

Reich, J. H., & Green, A. I. (1991). Effect of personality disorders on outcome of treatment. *Journal of Nervous and Mental Diseases, 179,* 74–82.

Reich, J. H., & Vasile, R. G. (1993). Effect of personality disorders on the treatment outcome of Axis I conditions: An update. *Journal of Nervous and Mental Diseases, 181,* 475–484.

Renneberg, B., Goldstein, A. J., Phillips, D., & Chambless, D. L. (1990). Intensive behavioral group treatment of avoidant personality disorder. *Behavior Therapy, 21,* 363–377.

Rosenthal, R. N., Muran, J. C., Pinsker, H., Hellerstein, D., & Winston, A. (1999). Interpersonal change in brief supportive psychotherapy. *Journal of Psychotherapy Practice and Research, 8,* 55–63.

Samuels, J. F., Nestadt, G., Romanoski, A. J., Folstein, M. F., & McHugh, P. R. (1994). *DSM-III* personality disorders in the community. *American Journal of Psychiatry, 151,* 1055–1062.

Schulz, S. C., Cornelius, J., Schulz, P. M., & Soloff, P. H. (1988). The amphetamine challenge test in patients with borderline personality disorder. *American Journal of Psychiatry, 145,* 809–814.

Shapiro, D. A., Barkham, M., Rees, A., Hardy, G. E., Reynolds, S., & Startup, M. (1994). Effects of treatment duration and severity of depression on the effectiveness of cognitive-behavioral and psychodynamic-interpersonal psychotherapy. *Journal of Consulting and Clinical Psychology, 62,* 522–534.

Sifneos, P. E. (1979). *Short-term dynamic psychotherapy.* New York: Plenum Press.

Stevenson, J., & Meares, R. (1992). An outcome study of psychotherapy for patients with borderline personality disorder. *American Journal of Psychiatry, 149,* 358–362.

Stevenson, J., & Meares, R. (1999). Psychotherapy with borderline patients. II: A preliminary cost benefit study. *Australian and New Zealand Journal of Psychiatry, 33,* 473–477.

Stravynski, A., Belisle, M., Marcouiller, M., & Lavallee, Y. (1994). The treatment of avoidant personality disorder by social skills training in the clinic or in real-life settings. *Canadian Journal of Psychiatry, 39,* 377–383.

Stravynski, A., Lesage, A., Marcouiller, M., & Elie, R. (1989). A test of the therapeutic mechanism in social skills training with avoidant personality disorder. *Journal of Nervous and Mental Diseases, 177,* 739–744.

Taylor, D., Carter, R., Eison, A., Mullins, U., Smith, H., Torrente, J., et al. (1995). Pharmacology and neurochemistry of nefazodone, a novel antidepressant drug. *Journal of Clinical Psychiatry, 56*(Suppl. 6), 3–11.

Teusch, L., Bohme, H., Finke, J., & Gastpar, M. (2001). Effects of client-centered psycho-therapy for personality disorders alone and in combination with psychopharmacolog-ical treatment. *Psychotherapy and Psychosomatics, 70,* 328–336.

Williams, J. G. (1988). Cognitive intervention for a paranoid personality disorder. *Psycho-therapy, 25,* 570–575.

Winston, A., Laikin, M., Pollack, J., Samstag, L. W., McCullough, L., & Muran, J. C. (1994). Short-term psychotherapy of personality disorders. *American Journal of Psychiatry, 151,* 190–194.

Winston, A., Pollack, J., McCullough, L., Flegenheimer, W., Kestenbaum, R., & Trujillo, M. (1991). Brief psychotherapy of personality disorders. *Journal of Nervous and Mental Diseases, 179,* 188–193.

Woody, G. E., McLellan, A. T., Luborsky, L., & O'Brien, C. P. (1985). Sociopathy and psycho-therapy outcome. *Archives of General Psychiatry, 42,* 1081–1086.

CHAPTER 24

Toward a Unified Model of Treatment for Personality Dysfunction

Jeffrey J. Magnavita

William James once commented on the "classic steps" in the life of theory. First it is attacked as utterly absurd. Then it gets accepted as obvious and insignificant. Finally, it is understood as so important that its opponents claim that they had said it all before.

—Strozier (2001, p. 227)

T HE MOVEMENT TOWARD a unified model of treating personality dysfunction is inevitable; the time for it has come. A unified model of personality systems offers an overarching, evolving, metapsychology that will enable clinicians to more effectively conceptualize and treat personality dysfunction. The quest for this unified model might be likened to the search for the human genome, something extraordinarily complex but within the reach of modern behavioral science. The unification of psychology is not a new idea. Almost since the beginning of modern psychology, great synthesizers such as William James (1890) foreshadowed this development. Gordon Allport (1968), during the mid-twentieth century, called for "systematic eclecticism," by which he meant "a system that seeks the solution of the fundamental problems by selecting and uniting what it regards as true in the specialized approaches to psychological sciences" (pp. 5–6). More recently, Sternberg and Grigorenko (2001) suggested a unification of psychology, a "multiparadigmatic, multidisciplinary, and integrated study of psychological phenomenon through converging operations" (p. 1069). Wilber (2000) also encouraged synthesizing knowledge in his proposal for a "holonic" model where reality is "neither wholes nor parts" composed of "whole/parts or holons" (p. 52). The biologist E. O. Wilson (1998) calls for a consilience of knowledge and writes: "The greatest challenge today not just in cell biology and ecology but in all of the science, is the

528

accurate and complete description of complex systems" (p. 85). Although the trend toward unified knowledge may seem somewhat grandiose, the challenge offered is to seek the interconnections among various bodies of knowledge and disciplines. On a somewhat more modest scale, it might be useful to apply this search to the treatment of personality dysfunction. Personality is a natural, complex organic system with multiple, interconnected domains; we can view its phenomena from the microscopic to the macroscopic levels of abstraction. This chapter presents one such unified model, which has been developed over a number of years from a clinical perspective, working with people suffering from poorly functioning personality systems, coming from many walks of life and of various ages.

A unified model for treating personality dysfunction allows a much greater conceptual reach than any single domain approach. All "effective" clinicians have a unified model of the mind and personality that guides their conceptualization and treatment interventions. Most clinicians use a model built on years of clinical experience and a layering of methods, techniques, and approaches acquired over the years. It appears that for most clinicians, the system they use is part of the procedural memory system and, therefore, is automatic and not easily articulated. For any system to have clinical utility, it must have face validity and make sense; otherwise, it will likely not be retained. In this chapter, one such system is presented. A more in-depth description of this model is presented in *Personality-Guided Relational Therapy* (Magnavita, in press). There are a number of advantages and disadvantages to a unified model for treating personality dysfunction, which is explored in the following section.

A BRIEF EXAMINATION OF THE ADVANTAGES AND DISADVANTAGES OF A UNIFIED MODEL FOR PERSONALITY

Before explicating a unified model for personality and the central challenge, treating personality dysfunction, we examine the advantages and disadvantages of developing a unified approach. It is beyond the scope of this chapter to present a comprehensive debate on the advantages and disadvantages to a unified model. However, it is important to highlight some of the central considerations.

ADVANTAGES OF A UNIFIED MODEL

Holistic Perspective to Human Functioning   A unified model for the treatment of personality dysfunction provides a framework that views personality function and dysfunction as part of an interrelated system and eschews Cartesian dualism. Human functioning, both adaptive and maladaptive, can be conceptualized using a holistic perspective. Even though it may be useful for research purposes to focus on one or more component domains of a unified system, there is less likelihood in a unified system that the other parts will be ignored in conceptualizing the whole. A unified model encourages us to maintain an awareness of the location of a particular domain within the system. Millon (1999) refers to a "holographic metaphor" where "each realm is a part of a unified whole" (p. 90). Trujillo (2002) uses a metaphor he terms the "psychodynamic hologram" to conceptualize the "global picture of the patient's functional problems, their dynamic sources, and the core genetic determinants of both" (p. 349). A unified model encourages the development of holographic maps of the personality system domains to gain a deeper understanding of the complex systems and representations that are expressed in various domains of personality.

More Closely Matches the Phenomenon   A unified model more closely resembles the phenomena we are concerned with: human personality adaptation and function and the central domains such as affect, cognition, defense, and relational systems that influence and shape personality. The reduction of personality to a compilation of traits or neurotransmitters does not provide an outcome that resembles the clinical phenomenon being mapped. A unified model allows us to track the undercurrents, currents, and cross currents that are part of the patient's total ecosystem, such as political, cultural, and socioeconomic forces.

A Common Domain-Based as Opposed to School-Based Language   Ideally, a unified model would offer domain-based language that would be common to all who use the model. The common domains such as neurobiological, affective, cognitive, defense, dyadic, and triadic systems can be described using specialized language that is easily communicated among clinicians, theorists, and researchers.

DISADVANTAGES OF A UNIFIED MODEL

Difficult to Research   A unified model does not have scientific precision; therefore, it may be difficult to establish its credibility as a scientific theory. This is true of all overarching constructs; it is difficult to prove or invalidate its processes and constructs. The complexity of such a theory might make it difficult to untangle and the processes difficult to verify.

Requirements for Advanced Training   Using a unified model requires a broad empirical, theoretical, and clinical knowledge base that might be unattainable for the average clinician. Most clinicians may feel more comfortable being grounded in one or maybe two approaches and incorporate one or two modalities. A unified model encourages the practitioner to struggle to conceptualize and map highly complex interrelated domains. Mastery of such a system might not be feasible; rather, continuous improvement is a more likely scenario.

Difficulty Merging Various Perspectives   It might be unrealistic to attempt to integrate divergent perspectives (Chao, 2002). In a critique of Sternberg and Grigorenko (2001), Chao writes: "Unified psychologists would specialize in converging many methods or disciplines and would develop technical language that is specific and exclusive to unified psychology" (p. 1128). Whether this would be a problem for a unified treatment for personality dysfunction is not clear. The danger is that it might be unreasonable to expect multiple perspectives and domains of knowledge to be "mastered" by most clinicians.

Difficulty Manualizing Treatment Model   Another disadvantage of a unified model is the difficulty manualizing the treatment procedures of such a broad theoretical system. The complexity of processes within multiple domains makes developing manuals a challenging task. Single-domain systems are much easier to operationalize, and the steps are easier to describe.

A SYSTEMICALLY BASED ECOLOGICAL MODEL

In the following section, a systemically based ecological model is offered, not as a final product, but an attempt to establish a starting point. There are two fundamental constructs and processes to any unified model: personality systemics and ecological domains.

PERSONALITY SYSTEMICS

It is essential that any unified model be based on an understanding of personality systemics (see chapter 1). *Systemics* seeks to establish the underlying processes within domains and among various domains of larger systems. *Personality systemics* is the application of this systemic approach to the personality system and subsystem. Lazarus (1991) describes the importance of understanding the system in the study of personality:

> Although personality, too, is said to be an organismic concept that encompasses adaptation, and indeed is so conceived traditionally, modern personality research had too often strayed from this ideal. Personality is seldom explored as a complex, integrated system—as a person struggling to manage transactions with the physical and social environment and being shaped and changed by this struggle. Instead, research in personality tends to be about one or a few traits with little or no attention paid to how they are organized within an individual. (p. 6)

Unification requires a systemic scaffold to begin to understand the complex operations that are involved in total personality functioning, from the microlevel to the macrolevel of abstraction. A unified model eschews a single-minded focus on any one domain without consideration of its relationship to other domains.

ECOLOGICAL DOMAINS

To understand the complex and abstract phenomena that determine personality functioning, we need to categorize the system levels and domains they encompass. Bronfenbrenner (1979) established various system levels in his conceptualization of human development. He describes his model and its emphasis:

> Different kinds of settings are also analyzed in terms of their structure. Here the approach departs in yet another respect from that of conventional research models': environments are not distinguished by reference to linear variables but are analyzed in systems terms. Beginning at the innermost level of the ecological schema, one of the basic units is the dyad, or two-person system. . . . For instance, from dyadic data it appears that if one member of the pair undergoes a process of development, the other does also. (p. 5)

Next he describes the triadic:

> In addition, a systems model of the immediate situation extends beyond the dyad and accords equal developmental importance to what are called *N + 2 systems*— triads, tetrads, and larger interpersonal structures. (p. 5)

Bronfenbrenner organizes the total ecological system of the individual from the microscopic to the total ecological containers. This theoretical approach seems eminently useful for the purposes of developing a unified personality model. What Bronfenbrenner underscores in his work is the fundamental importance of relational systems in human development and functioning.

In addition to the dyadic and triadic, the intrapsychic system must be represented in any unified model.

A Convergence of Evidence Linking Relationship or Attachment Experience to Brain Organization and Personality

Over the past century, there has been a convergence of various lines of empirical research and clinical evidence that supports considering the relational system as the main element of a unified treatment model for personality dysfunction. Much of this evidence, some of which is highlighted in the next section, supports the importance of the attachment-interpersonal or relational matrix on the development of the mind and the personality system. Conversely, we must also recognize the mutual influence of intrapsychic structures and schema on the relational system.

Attachment Theory, Love, and the Relational Matrix

It is hard to imagine that a little more than a half century ago, some of the major figures in psychology recommended that infants should be handled as little as possible (Watson, 1928) and suggested that raising a baby in a tender box was going to be the new wave in child care (Skinner, 1979). Parents were discouraged from touching their babies while they were hospitalized. Blum (2002) summarizes Watson's view at that time on child rearing:

> Watson wrote that he dreamed of a baby farm where hundreds of infants could be taken away from their parents and raised according to scientific principles. Ideally, he said, a mother would not even know which child was hers and therefore could not ruin it. Emotional responses to children should be controlled, Watson insisted, by using an enlightened scientific approach. Parents should participate in shaping their children by simple, objective conditioning techniques. And if parents chose affection and nurturing instead, ignoring his advice? In his own words, there are "serious rocks ahead for the over-kissed child." (p. 39)

Around the turn of the century, it became clear that something was radically wrong with child-rearing practices. Psychologists, pediatricians, and psychiatrists were amassing damning evidence that children left in foundling homes and orphanages, not an uncommon practice in the early twentieth century, led to a "failure to thrive" syndrome. These young children were dying at an unprecedented rate; in some institutions, up to 90% were dead within a year, in spite of being kept in perfectly sanitary conditions. Those who didn't die were likely to be severely impaired and incapable of sustaining relationships as they matured. The centrality of the relational matrix in the development of the personality system was demonstrated by a number of courageous and outspoken leaders. A number of converging forces turned those faulty notions about the need for affection upside down (Blum, 2002). Three major research trends emerged during the middle of the twentieth century, which turned the field of psychology and psychiatry upside down by demonstrating the extreme importance of attachment.

NATURALISTIC OBSERVATIONS OF INFANTS

Spitz (1947) made a film called *Grief: A Peril in Infancy,* which shocked viewers. It recorded the rapid onset of depression and apathy in an infant deprived of all but minimal human contact. It was becoming apparent to Spitz, and to many other pioneers, that failure to thrive was being caused by something other than infection and medical illness. Other researchers were struck by the powerful effect of parental separation on the mental health of children, even when the environment they were placed in was a secure one. In England during World War II, about 700,000 children were sent to the country to be out of harm's way during the bombing of the cities. These children demonstrated what appeared to be traumatic reactions to the separation from primary attachment figures (Blum, 2002).

ANIMAL MODELS OF ATTACHMENT AND SEPARATION

Another major revolution was taking place at this time in the primate research on love and attachment conducted by Harry Harlow at the University of Wisconsin (Blum, 2002). Although a controversial figure, his research remains a groundbreaking demonstration of the importance of attachment and love in the healthy development of primates. Harlow's research demonstrated that attachment is more important than food or conditioning for the development of healthy primates. In addition, he found that a balance between a secure attachment and well-timed encouragement to explore the world was necessary for optimal development. In other experiments, he demonstrated the severe impact that isolation has on development and was able to create animal models of depression and psychoses and what might now be described as severe personality dysfunction in these monkeys.

Neurobiological Findings and Brain Structure   The organization and structuralization of the brain develop through stimulation and experiences. Neurobiology and experience act in unison to determine who we are and whether we will develop dysfunction in our personality system. If the diathesis-stress is unfavorable, the pathway toward dysfunctional personality is initiated. Siegel (1999) describes the neurobiological effects of interpersonal experience:

> The mind develops at the interface of neurophysiological processes and interpersonal relationships. Relationship experiences have a dominant influence on the brain because the circuits responsible for social perception are the same as or tightly linked to those that integrate the important functions controlling the creation of meaning, the regulation of bodily states, the modulation of emotion, the organization of memory, and the capacity for interpersonal communication. Interpersonal experience thus plays a special organizing role in determining the development of brain structure early in life and the ongoing emergence of brain function throughout the lifespan. (p. 21)

Psychotherapists have been concerned with what occurs when the individual is subjected to trauma. Recent neuroscientific findings suggest that the impact of trauma on the brain may lead to scarring of the tissue.

Trauma Theory   Trauma theory, although controversial (Magnavita, 2002), has been robust in its ability to explain various aspects of development, especially pathological development. Severe and sustained traumatic experiences such as physical and sexual abuse have been fairly well documented as important etiological factors in the development of personality dysfunction, and there is accumulating evidence that the neurobiology of an individual is altered by the experience of trauma. In addition to traumatic sexual and physical abuse, which may have long-term impacts on personality functioning, Bernstein (2002) proposes two categories of nonphysical abuse: emotional abuse and emotional neglect. Emotional abuse and neglect may be less obvious but can be equally destructive. Dysfunction is often the result of trauma that is embedded in the personality system.

The Common Link—The Centrality of Relationships in Human Development   The centrality of relationships in the development of the personality is unequivocal. Almost every clinical theory of the mind, human behavior, psychotherapy, and personality converge on this point. Relationships are the container in which attachments are formed and lost and from which personality evolves and is consolidated as development proceeds. "In one sense, all therapeutic endeavors are broadly 'relational.' Behavior therapists, cognitive therapists, experiential therapists, psychodynamic therapists, and even pharmacotherapists all conduct the therapeutic transaction within the relational matrix" (Magnavita, 2000, p. 999). Psychotherapy is based on the premise that in our relationships the "genetic" structure of our personality is encoded and expressed through relational schema, reenactment patterns, repetition compulsion, cyclical maladaptive patterns, and so forth. Using a unified model, we can peer into the human personality system, using multiple lenses of magnification, and "read" or "map" the genetic code of various domains of the personality system to form a holographic representation. We can then determine which domains must be restructured to effect change in the system. Elements of this genetic code related to core trauma and developmental insult are expressed in interpersonal patterns, self-perception and belief, psychic organization, defensive structure, affective response systems, and so forth. Reading many components of a personality system enables us to understand the genetic code of the personality system and to understand why it is in a state of dysfunction.

ASPECTS OF A UNIFIED MODEL

A unified model must be capable of depicting active processes of personality systems, which are self-organizing and in continual motion. The self-organizing function pertains to the fact that all personality systems seek adaptation and equilibrium based on evolutionary principles. This is not meant to suggest that personality systems do not dysfunction and even self-destruct, but that they generally seek adaptation to environmental conditions to survive. A stagnant model will not serve: Individuals are constantly growing, differentiating, moving through developmental processes, and interacting with highly complex external environments and social systems.

USING TRIANGLES TO VISUALLY DEPICT THE MICROSYSTEM, MACROSYSTEM, AND MESOSYSTEM PROCESSES WITHIN THE TOTAL ECOLOGICAL MATRIX

Personality systems can be truly understood only when the holonic map of the entire system or total ecology of an individual is taken into consideration. Any attempt to understand one aspect of personality without an appreciation for the total system will not give satisfactory results. In a unified model, examining the essential domains from the microscopic to macroscopic levels of process can disentangle the multiple domains of personality. At the microscopic level, we concern ourselves with the intrapsychic processes, which include neurobiological, affective-cognitive systems, and defensive functions. These can be viewed in the physiological and nonverbal channels of expression; this is termed the *intrapsychic-biological triangle*. To use the metaphor of a microscope, if we decrease the magnification of our view, we can look at what occurs between individuals in dyadic configurations. This can be observed by tracking communication processes. This level of magnification is wider and is termed the *interpersonal-dyadic triangle*. Again, decreasing our level of magnification, we can view more complex configurations or what occurs in three-person systems (Bowen, 1976; Bronfenbrenner, 1979). This can be viewed as the communication process in the threesome. This level of magnification is termed the *relational-triadic configuration* (Guerin, Fogarty, Fay, & Kautto, 1996). If we minimize our level of magnification to the mesosystem, we can examine the interrelationship of the individual personality system, family system, and sociocultural system. This is termed the *sociocultural-family triangle*. Finally, levels of organization interact within the total ecological system with multiple interactive levels, such as the total universe, the world, nation, state, neighborhood, and so forth.

USE OF TRIANGULAR CONFIGURATIONS TO DEPICT PROCESS

Triangles are excellent symbols for depicting a system consisting of three main elements. Triangles suggest process and nonlinearity among the three corners. An impact on any corner of a triangle impacts the remaining corners. Thus, a triangle can denote synergism. The use of triangles in psychology and psychotherapy has an auspicious history. Modern psychology's classic triangle is the oedipal triangle, representing the forces that operate in a parental system as a child competes for the attention of the opposite sex parent. Many theorists have used the triangle to represent various elements of psychotherapy. Menninger (1958) presented his "triangle of insight" that depicted dyadic patterns among past relationships, current relationships, and the transference relationship. Ezriel (1952) coined the term "triangle of conflict," which describes intrapsychic process and the relationship among hidden feeling, anxiety, and defense patterns. Malan (1979) combined these two triangles into what has turned out to be a remarkable breakthrough in conceptualizing brief dynamic psychotherapy. Bowen (1976) made a significant leap when he used the triangle to represent relational patterns in triads. Bronfenbrenner (1979) also developed the concept of the triangle in his depiction of triadic processes. For example, in a traumatic event, the cognitive-affective corner of the intrapsychic-biological triangle becomes overwhelmed, increasing anxiety, and potentially disrupting defenses. Neurobiological effects might include scarring of the brain or sensitizing or "kindling" neural networks so that they are easily reactivated.

Intrapsychic-Biological Triangle (Individual System)   The *intrapsychic-biological trian-gle* depicts the interrelationship among the *affective-cognitive matrix* at the bottom, *anxiety* at the top right, and *defense* at the top left (see Figure 24.1).

This matrix of cognitive-affective-defensive components is linked to the neuro-biological system. A perturbation of any of the components of the system will alter the organization of the matrix and the way it functions. For example, a neg-ative thought may activate a complex of negative self-attributions and emotion. An alteration of the neurotransmitter system will have an impact on affective-defensive-cognitive activation and the reverse is also true. Lazarus (1991) de-scribes the centrality of emotion in this system:

> If we are to speak of an organismic concept, one that best expresses the adaptational wholeness or integrity of persons rather than merely separate functions, emotion is surely it. Emotions are complex, patterned, organismic reactions to how we think we are doing in our lifelong efforts to survive and flourish and to achieve what we wish for ourselves. Emotions are like no other psychobiological construct in that they express the intimate personal meaning of what is happening in our social lives and combine motivational, cognitive, adaptational, and physiological processes into a single complex state that involves several levels of analysis. (p. 6)

Interpersonal-Dyadic Triangle (Two-Person System)   The *interpersonal-dyadic triangle* depicts the dyadic configuration that is created when two individuals are in a re-lationship and reenacting aspects of past relational schema (see Figure 24.2). These interpersonal processes can be depicted in the dyadic in two ways.

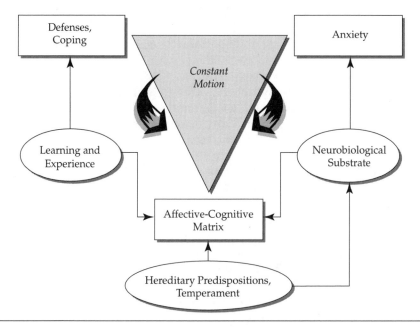

Figure 24.1   Intrapsychic-Biological Functions.

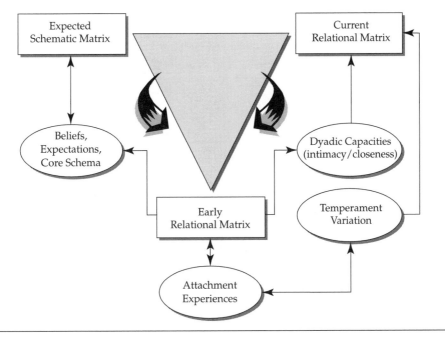

Figure 24.2   Interpersonal-Dyadic Triangle.

The bottom corner of the triangle, or the *early relational matrix,* includes attachment-dyadic experiences that form and shape the intrapsychic structure depicted in the intrapsychic-biological triangle. These dyads reflect the temperamental style (intrapsychic-biological triangle) and capacity of the primary caregivers to form a caregiving style. The upper right corner depicts the *current relational matrix.* This represents dyadic configurations that shape and reinforce personality patterns. Interpersonal patterns can be read in this corner. The upper left corner of the triangle represents the *expected relational matrix.* This represents the process by which an individual projects or transfers core schemata to a new person, usually the therapist. The expected relational matrix refers to the expectation of an individual that he or she will be received in an interpersonal transaction in a particular way regardless of the actual perception and reaction of the therapist.

Relational-Triadic Configuration (Three-Person Configurations)   The *relational-triadic configuration* represents the triangular relations that ensue when unstable dyads seek homeostasis by engaging a third, usually more vulnerable, individual (see Figure 24.3).

An unstable dyad is one that has more anxiety than it can manage. It may attempt to deflect the anxiety onto a third party. The lower level of differentiation of the two individuals, both emotional and self-other, determines the level at which triangulation will occur. The lower the level of differentiation that occurs, the more likely a dyad is to triangulate (Bowen, 1976). A frequently seen example of triangulation occurs when a child is symptomatic and where the symptoms

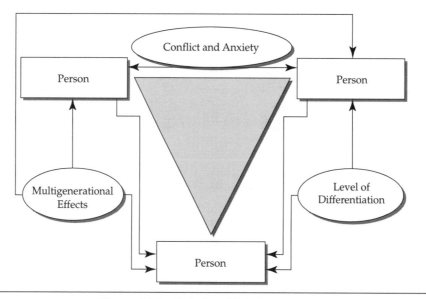

Figure 24.3   Relational-Triadic Triangle.

serve to distract a marital dyad from conflict and anxiety that they cannot contain within their own personality systems or within the dyadic system.

Sociocultural-Familial Triangle (Mesosystem)   The *sociocultural-family triangle* depicts the synergy among three corners, the individual personality system, the family system, and the cultural system (see Figure 24.4).

This system is termed the *mesosystem*. The interaction of these three corners has a major impact on the development of personality dysfunction. This triangular matrix accounts for the often-neglected sociocultural aspects of pathology. For example, a true understanding of eating disorders and other current culturally influenced disorders requires an understanding of the impact of popular culture on eating habits. Eating disorders are most common in Western middle-class adolescent females (Herscovici, 2002).

The importance of the mesosystem in the shaping of personality systems should be obvious to all observers of human behavior. The impact of political upheaval and war on human personality and the degradation of institutions is well documented. Hedges (2002) describes the meaning of war and the sociopolitical forces that result in the myths that develop around war allowing for atrocities to be committed on the demonized other. He illustrates the impact of the severe mesosystem disequilibrium that war creates:

> The reporters, diplomats, aid workers, and peacekeepers who travel into war zones, without the restraint of law and amid a sea of powerless people, often view themselves as entitled. They excuse immoral behavior because of the belief that the work they carry out is for a greater good—the rescue of those around them—which outweigh impropriety. They become giddy with admiration and social status that come with being protected and privileged. (p. 114)

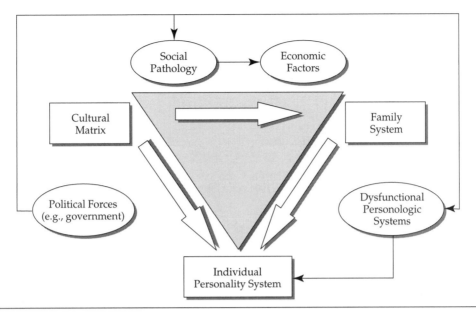

Figure 24.4   Sociocultural-Familial Triangle.

J. Reich (2002) and others have found preliminary evidence for a "stress-induced personality disorder." This concept may be used to understand the phenomenon of personality regression that occurs for all of those who are involved in war. These examples are suggestive of the malleability of personality functioning and the powerful effect of the mesosystem.

APPLICATION OF THEORY TO DYSFUNCTION OF THE PERSONALITY SYSTEM

The application of unified theory can be used to guide clinical practice. The disruption of the equilibrium of the various personality subsystems reverberates throughout the entire personality system. When individual, dyadic, triadic, familial, and cultural systems are chronically stressed, dysfunction will occur at the various diathesis points; for example, a vulnerability of the biological system might emerge as depression when a family loses its economic standing. Over the course of time, dysfunction in the family system might result in marital disturbance or child behavioral problems. Left untreated, there may be a cascading chain of events over the generations leading to greater dysfunction (Magnavita, 2000).

READING THE "GENETIC" CODE

In each personality system, the psychobiological genetic code that has influence in determining personality dysfunction must be read, just as scientists read physical genes. The genetic code is affected by nonmetabolized traumatic and relational experiences that alter personality development, such as the following (Magnavita, 1997):

- Insufficient attachment and responsiveness of early caretakers.
- Incidents of physical and/or sexual trauma.
- Patterns of neglect.
- Loss of attachment.
- Injuries sustained by emotional use.
- Exploitation.
- Dysfunctional family systems.
- Natural disasters.
- Socioeconomic upheaval.

The genetic code is embedded in personality systems. These reveal themselves in the various levels of the relational system in their diverse forms of expression.

METHODS OF TREATMENT OF A UNIFIED MODEL

When we examine the dominant methods developed by the major schools of psychotherapy, certain commonalties in methods are evident. A common cross-theoretical term often used to describe processes of psychotherapy is *restructuring.* We can organize the various methods of restructuring at the systemic level in which they operate. For example, intrapsychic is the microscopic level as it re-organizes internal affective-cognitive-defensive-biological systems. There are four major categories of restructuring using a unified model: (1) intrapsychic restructuring, (2) dyadic restructuring, (3) triadic restructuring, and (4) mesosystem restructuring. Each category of restructuring concerns itself primarily with processes that can be conceptualized at the microscopic to macroscopic levels of analysis (see Table 24.1).

INTRAPSYCHIC RESTRUCTURING

Intrapsychic restructuring (IR) refers to methods and techniques of treatment that are aimed at the individual personality system (Magnavita, 1997). The focus of action is on the neurobiological-affective-cognitive-defensive matrix and may include (1) defensive restructuring, (2) cognitive restructuring, (3) affective restructuring, (4) cognitive-behavioral restructuring, and (5) neurobiological restructuring.

DEFENSIVE RESTRUCTURING

Methods of defensive restructuring have been developed in the past century by a number of psychoanalytic clinicians (Davanloo, 1980; Fenichel, 1945; W. Reich, 1933). Defensive restructuring is a method whereby the individual's defensive patterns are elucidated and challenged and thus made conscious. The cataloguing of defenses, along with demonstration to the patient as to how they operate, increases awareness, disrupts the intrapsychic homeostasis, and allows for the development of new patterns (Magnavita, 1997). Defenses evolve in a process of maturation and reflect differential demands for adaptation. When defenses are no longer needed but are still retained, they impair healthy personality functioning. What once might have been an adaptive function ceases to be. Thus, disruption of defenses may be an essential method for some personality-disordered patients to begin to change. In an attempt to consolidate a neurodynamic model

Table 24.1
Main Categories of Restructuring, Methods, and Systemic Level Targeted

---

Intrapsychic Restructuring (IR)

System Level: *Intrapsychic-Biological Triangle*

1. Defensive restructuring: Focus on defensive operations.
2. Cognitive restructuring: Focus on cognitive schema and beliefs.
3. Affective restructuring: Focus on affective process and experience.
4. Cognitive-behavioral restructuring: Focus on affective experience and learning.
5. Neurobiological restructuring: Focus on neurotransmitter and biobehavioral systems.

Dyadic Restructuring (DR)

System Level: *Dyadic-Interpersonal Triangle*

1. Expected-transactive restructuring: Focus on expected relationship with therapist.
2. Self-other restructuring: Focus on real relationship with therapist.
3. Relational-dyadic restructuring: Focus on relationship with other.

Triadic Restructuring (TR)

System Level: *Triadic-Relational Configuration*

1. Relational-triadic restructuring: Focus on three-person relationships.
2. Symbolic-relational restructuring: Focus on symbolic representation.

Mesosystem Restructuring (MR)

System Level: *Sociocultural-Familial Triangle*

1. Ecosystem restructuring: Focus on altering components of mesosystem.

---

of personality, Grigsby and Stevens (2000) emphasize the centrality of memory and suggest that character reflects procedural knowledge. *Procedural* memory refers to the retention of habits, which are nonconscious. Memory can also be *declarative*; declarative memory "has to do with the retention of events and information" (p. 91) and can be further divided into *episodic* and *semantic* memory. Episodic memory refers to subjective events in an individual's life. Semantic memory refers to the recall of objective facts. Procedural memory improves or becomes increasingly automatic with repetition. The more automatic the behavior becomes, the less easily it is monitored. Grigsby and Stevens propose "that character—which is composed of those things that people do routinely, automatically, and nonconsciously, and which make us knowable and predictable—can be understood as a manifestation of procedural learning" (p. 102).

The early short-term dynamic psychotherapists, beginning with Ferenczi (Ferenczi & Rank, 1925), suggested that for personality to change, habitual patterns of behavior need to be disrupted, consistent with Grigsby and Stevens' neurodynamic model. Ferenczi pioneered active forms of psychotherapy primarily developed for the "difficult" patient. Many of his techniques remain vital in this regard. Grigsby and Stevens' (2000) findings are also relevant:

Often the first step in perturbing the operation of procedurally learned processes is to bring the nonconscious behavior into the patient's awareness. This has the effect of disrupting what ordinarily is an automatic process, and repeated disruptions of this sort further interfere with its automaticity. By increasing an individual's awareness of such behaviors, the procedural memories are modified somewhat over time, especially as they become increasingly likely to be associated with awareness. At first, the effort of the therapist is required in order to make the patient conscious of the manifestations of character. (p. 370)

Thus, they describe creating an intrapsychic disequilibrium. Defensive restructuring is probably one of the most controversial methods of psychotherapy, because it may appear harsh and nonempathic to the observer. The mastery of methods of defensive restructuring is challenging, but for many therapists the investment is worthwhile and the benefits to many patients quickly seen.

COGNITIVE RESTRUCTURING

Another major method of intrapsychic restructuring is cognitive restructuring. Cognitive restructuring is included in intrapsychic methods because "its roots are in psychoanalysis and the dynamic therapies. The intellectual parents of cognitive therapy are Freud and Melanie Klein, not Pavlov and Thorndike" (Groves, 1992, p. 43). More importantly, its mode of action is in the intrapsychic system. Cognitive restructuring was primarily developed by Beck (1976; Beck, Freeman, & Associates, 1990; Beck, Rush, Shaw, & Emery, 1979), who based his theories and methods on an information-processing model. *Cognitive restructuring* refers to a group of techniques that target the internalized primarily conscious schematic representations that influence and guide behavior. Schemas are scripts or frameworks based on an individual's experience, as described by Greenberg, Rice, and Elliott (1993): "The basic contribution of the schema concept is that it recognizes that humans internally represent objects or events by a configuration of features. Schemas include but go beyond purely propositional representations to encode regularities in categories that are both perceptual and conceptual" (pp. 46–47). Cognition is a fundamental domain of the intrapsychic system, which influences emotional reaction and defensive responding. When dysfunctional schemas are restructured, an individual's core organization shifts. Core beliefs about self exert powerful nonconscious influence on behavior and personality functions. For example, individuals who have endured neglect during childhood can easily develop the core belief that they are unworthy. This, then, can become a guiding principle that is applied to significant relationships, which further consolidates the nonmetabolized effect that has resulted from mistreatment. In therapy, as the cognitions are brought to awareness and explored, associated affective complexes emerge and can be processed. Beck and his associates (1976, 1990) have articulated a set of techniques whose aim is to restructure this dysfunctional or maladaptive schema. Young (1990) has also developed techniques to restructure early maladaptive schema. The techniques include challenging arbitrary inferences, selective abstraction, overgeneralization, magnification and minimization, personalization, and dichotomous thinking.

Most therapists are attentive to cognitive distortions that are offered without awareness. These dysfunctional beliefs can be highly toxic and, if not restructured, add to the continuation of maladaptive personality patterns, perpetuate negative self-perceptions, and cause ongoing disturbances in relationships. Substituting these dysfunctional beliefs with more adaptive ones is the goal of restructuring.

AFFECTIVE RESTRUCTURING

Another intrapsychic restructuring method is "emotion restructuring" emanating from the work of experiential therapy (Greenberg & Paivio, 1997), also called "affective restructuring," derived from short-term dynamic therapy (STDT; McCullough Vaillant, 1997), which emphasizes the centrality of emotion (Fosha, 2000). These techniques draw primarily from experiential-humanistic approaches to psychotherapy (Greenberg & Paivio, 1997; Greenberg et al., 1993). Affective restructuring techniques primarily aim to increase awareness of emotional process and differentiation. Two of the pioneers in this regard, Fritz Perls (1969) and Carl Rogers (1951), developed very different methods of affective restructuring. Rogers' approach was to elicit feeling through the process of closely monitoring affective response fluctuations, labeling, and offering reflection of nonverbal communication. Perls developed more confrontational techniques to intensify affect and assist the patient in "owning" or integrating split-off aspects of the emotional process. Perls encouraged patients to become acquainted with their emotions and to thereby undo projection, which is a common defense in patients who are "out of touch" with their emotion and their conflicts.

Contemporary workers have expanded on and identified the centrality of affective restructuring (Greenberg & Paivio, 1997; Greenberg et al., 1993). Greenberg et al. wrote: "Empathic attunement to clients' ongoing affective experience is a crucial aspect of the essential fabric of the therapist's involvement. Empathic attunement to clients' feelings helps clients to confirm and strengthen their own sense of themselves" (p. 20). Enhancing "emotional intelligence" by differentiation, labeling, and expression of feeling is the goal of affective restructuring (Goleman, 1994).

COGNITIVE-BEHAVIORAL RESTRUCTURING

Another type of intrapsychic restructuring is cognitive-behavioral restructuring, which modifies the internal contingencies and reinforcement patterns that are in operation in the intrapsychic domain. The two primary methods include classical and instrumental conditioning. Classical conditioning is the paradigm discovered by Pavlov (1927), who demonstrated the power of associative learning and its effect on autonomic system function. The second of these methodologies is instrumental or operant conditioning, which demonstrates how behavior can be shaped using principles of reinforcement (Skinner, 1953). For example, one approach used to reduce a phobic response is the relaxation technique (Barlow, 1988). Systematic desensitization is another technique that aims to restructure the intrapsychic matrix by altering the conditioned responses that have been shaped by faulty learning experiences. Innovative approaches include eye movement desensitization and reprocessing (EMDR; Shapiro, 1995) and many of the techniques of dialectical behavioral therapy (DBT; Linehan, 1993). Cognitive-behavioral restructuring seeks to extinguish cognitive-affective-behavioral associative pairings that are maladaptive.

NEUROBIOLOGICAL RESTRUCTURING

The final method of intrapsychic restructuring is neurobiological restructuring, which aims to directly alter the neurobiological system of the individual. This includes the application of psychopharmacological agents to enhance, mend, or improve the functioning of this system. Kramer (1993) describes the use of pharmacotherapy and the impact on the personality of many of the patients he has treated. According to Kramer's observation, an alteration of neural networks in some individuals appears to effect a transformation in personality. When the basic action of the neurobiological system is altered, affective-cognitive systems are also restructured.

DYADIC RESTRUCTURING

Dyadic restructuring (DR) is a method whose roots are in the work of Murray Bowen (1976) and Harry Stack Sullivan (1953). The main goals of dyadic restructuring are increased emotional differentiation and self-differentiation, as well as an increased awareness of and alteration to the interpersonal patterns that are often nonconsciously recreated in significant relationships (Benjamin, 1993). The modes of dyadic restructuring can be portrayed by examining the various corners of the interpersonal-dyadic triangle (see Figure 24.2). Dyadic restructuring occurs between two individuals and is particularly concerned with boundary space or intersubjectivity (Safran & Muran, 2000) or with the projected or expected relational schema. If the focus of the restructuring emphasizes the "real" relationship between the patient and therapist, this is termed *self-other restructuring* (McCullough Vaillant, 1997). If the focus is on the process and mechanisms by which to alter the manner in which the patient expects and possibly encourages the therapist to be or behave in a particular fashion, this we call *expected-transactive restructuring*.

EXPECTED-TRANSACTIVE RESTRUCTURING

In the classic psychotherapy interviews where Rogers, Perls, and Ellis interview the now-famous Gloria, the viewer is often struck by how Gloria begins her interviews with Rogers and Perls. Gloria expects that Rogers and then Perls will be "harsh and critical" even before she has had an opportunity to interact. She even reports reading Rogers' works so that she would have a different picture. This is a good example of how a patient places his or her relational schema on the therapist and expects a certain treatment or reaction. This is one of the remarkable discoveries made by Freud more than a century ago, which he aptly termed *transference* and was the basis of psychoanalysis. In transference, his or her complexes onto the "neutral" and "blank" therapist, the analyst could then allow a transference neurosis to develop, which would be analyzed during the course of treatment. From many converging lines of evidence, we can see how robust this process is in therapy. Interpersonal theorists (Benjamin, 1993; chapter 8, this volume) and later analytic workers have shown how there is a transactive process. The transference pulls for countertransference. In expected-transactive restructuring, the therapist can use the interpersonal reenactments and expectancies that are activated in the relationship with the therapist and described in relationships with others to enhance awareness and link these to the primary attachment figures and offer more adaptive and mature ways of relating.

SELF-OTHER RESTRUCTURING

The focus of "self-other restructuring" (McCullough Vaillant, 1997) is the differentiation of self from the therapist. *"Restructuring or self-other representations* means that the therapist helps the patient regulate the degree of aversiveness or inhibition that has been associated with attachment, that is, experience of self, others, or both" (p. 36). Self-other restructuring was pioneered primarily by Rogers (1951) and Kohut (1971, 1977) and is especially concerned with empathic attunement to damaged zones of the self. Self-other restructuring is primarily concerned with the intersubjective space co-constructed between therapist and patient (Safran & Muran, 2000) and emphasizes identification of ruptures of the therapeutic alliance and mending these as they occur. As Muran and Safran (2002) describe it, "a central tenet of our relational perspective is the recognition that there is an ongoing reciprocal relationship between self-states of one person and those of the other in a dyadic interaction" (p. 255). They believe: "Change is essentially understood as involving the parallel processes of increasing immediate awareness of self and other and providing a new interpersonal experience" (p. 255). Jordan's (1997, 2000) relational model also primarily emphasizes connection and the role of mutual empathy as vital to the therapeutic process (also see chapter 6 in this volume).

Greenspan (1992, 1997) advanced a developmentally-oriented approach that is used with both children and adults that focuses on the attachment system. Greenspan (2002) describes a major component of this developmental psychotherapy approach as a process that "involves *the role of relationships and affective interactions* in facilitating a child's intellectual and emotional growth" (p. 15). A major component of his restructuring "is to help the child learn how to attend and to become engaged or connected, and to be calm and regulated at the same time" (p. 445).

RELATIONAL DYADIC RESTRUCTURING

The focus of dyadic restructuring can occur in current relationships between partners, parent-child dyads, and so on and is usually done in a couples modality or in a group setting when the dyadic relationship of two group members is the focus of the intervention. Dyadic restructuring emphasizes the use of adaptive communication skills, such as the ability to listen and respond to another without employing projection onto another. Solomon (1989) and Solomon and Lynn (2002) have developed relational restructuring techniques for couples that are especially useful for those with personality dysfunction. Magnavita (2000) presents various types of restructuring dyadic relationships. Much of relational restructuring emphasizes the intimacy-closeness dimension.

Meissner (1978) describe the balance necessary between fusion-intimacy and isolation-autonomy:

> As the person with a well-differentiated and individuated identity enters into a relationship as close and intimately interdependent as the marital relationship, he or she is able to enter into, share, and participate freely in the emotional life that takes place between and around the marital partners. The less the degree of individuation or of differentiation of self, however, the more emotion tends to spill over and be communicated to the other member. Within this complex of implicit and relatively

unconscious emotional influences, a pattern tends to establish itself in which one of the partners begins to function with a façade of exaggerated strength and assertion, while the other partner shifts to a position of compliance, submissiveness, and giving-in to the influence and domination of the more adequate partner. Within the emotional matrix there is a phenomenological shift in which one partner seems to attain a degree of hyperadequacy and the confirming of pseudoidentity, while the other partner seems to lose identity and become a relative nonentity. (p. 47)

During the course of dyadic restructuring, patterns of interpersonal behavior are brought to the awareness of the dyad and defensive operations may be pointed out. The goal is to increase the capacity for intimacy and closeness. This requires the concomitant increase in emotional differentiation, that is, the ability to acknowledge, label, and express feelings.

TRIADIC RESTRUCTURING

Triadic restructuring (TR) is a method primarily pioneered by Murray Bowen (1976) and Salvadore Minuchin (1974), which emphasizes alteration of the processes and structure that occur in a three-person system or multiple overlapping triangular configurations. Although generally carried out in a two-person + N system, triadic restructuring can be done in virtually any psychotherapeutic modality of treatment. In fact, therapists who are not aware of the manner in which triangular configurations or three-person systems function unwittingly carry out much of triadic restructuring. For example, a child therapist seeing a child for individual therapy may not be aware of his or her impact on the triangle of the parents and child. The closeness with the therapist might threaten the parental dyad, and they may unknowingly engage in subterfuge to keep the child from gaining distance, which might destabilize their relationship. There are two basic types of triadic restructuring: The first, which focuses on triadic configurations in vivo, is called *relational-triadic restructuring;* the other focuses on triadic configurations when the other members are unavailable or deceased in a symbolic manner and is termed *symbolic-relational restructuring.*

RELATIONAL-TRIADIC RESTRUCTURING

The ability to establish and maintain relationships is a critical element of healthy personality functioning. When dyadic configurations are unstable, a third party is used to stabilize the dyad. Relational-triadic restructuring attempts to alter or stop the mutigenerational transmission processes (Bowen, 1976). Minuchin (1974) developed many useful techniques of relational restructuring. Many of his interventions consisted of blocking transactions to restructure hierarchy in a family and actively rearranging family members to restructure their preferred relational patterns. Satir (1964) and Selvini Palazzoli, Boscolo, Cecchin, and Prata (1978) were also major innovators of restructuring techniques for larger systems.

SYMBOLIC-RELATIONAL RESTRUCTURING

When the therapist is working with triangular relationships wherein there are unavailable or deceased members or if the restructuring is occurring in individual therapy, the restructuring occurs at a symbolic level rather than with the participants.

MESOSYSTEM RESTRUCTURING

Mesosystem restructuring (MR) primarily occurs at the family system and sociocultural corners of the sociocultural. This is often overlooked by many theoretical systems of personality and psychotherapy as being beyond the realm of the clinician's purview. However, this is short sighted; implementing a unified model would improve the perspective on the mesosystem. The therapist may teach the patient about the nature of triangles and help understand how he or she may still be captive to this system and then offer symbolic actions to detriangulate the patient. In one case, the patient was said to be chained to his dead father and caught in a triangle with his unhappy mother, who continued to control his life. It was suggested that he go to his father's grave and begin to cut the chain by expressing how he felt. This activated many feelings that could be addressed with affective restructuring in the next session.

RESTRUCTURING DYSFUNCTIONAL FAMILY SYSTEMS

Modifying the ecological setting may restructure the mesosystem. For example, eliminating or reducing poverty and providing more opportunities for inner city youths may have a direct impact on their personality adaptation. Direct intervention with parent-child systems in high-risk families in the community is one example of an exciting use of this type of restructuring (Pawl & St. John, 2002). The authors write: "Home visiting has been an inherent component of and vehicle for the practice of infant-parent psychotherapy since its inception" (p. 86). The authors say that most of the families would not be treated if they were expected to go to a clinic. In this innovative approach, the parent-child dyads and triads are treated right in their community.

RESTRUCTURING MALADAPTIVE SOCIAL SYSTEMS

The last type of restructuring focuses on the alteration of social systems that are maladaptive or not operating well enough to enhance the functioning of its members. Programs that are able to address needs in a community are examples of this type of restructuring. These include programs that address societal issues such as teenage pregnancy, abusive family systems, socioeconomic disadvantage, juvenile delinquency, divorce, and drug and alcohol abuse and addiction. Programs or efforts to increase resiliency of vulnerable groups, provide quality daycare, and enhance emotional and social intelligence also are examples of mesosystem restructuring (Magnavita, 2000).

MODALITIES OF TREATMENT OF A UNIFIED MODEL

A unified model for treating personality dysfunction is necessarily multimodal. No single mode of treatment has proved to be superior at this time and is unlikely to be in the future. Clinical experience suggests that using various modalities of treatment during particular stages of treatment can be beneficial. Each modality has its advantage and range of efficacy. Some modalities offer more opportunity to incorporate multiple methods of restructuring such as couples, group, and family:

- *Individual psychotherapy* has been a mainstay of treatment for personality dysfunction, which primarily uses methods of intrapsychic restructuring. There are both long- and short-term individual therapy approaches that run the gamut from EMDR to psychodynamic psychotherapy, many of which are presented in this volume.
- *Couples therapy* is a recent newcomer to the treatment of personality dysfunction whose potency in the hands of a well-trained clinician can be remarkable. Couples therapy affords the clinician the opportunity to conduct dyadic restructuring.
- *Family therapy* is also a newcomer to the treatment of personality dysfunction whose application is only recently being explored by theorists and clinicians. Family therapy primarily uses methods of dyadic and triadic restructuring but can also employ intrapsychic restructuring methods; therefore, it is highly utilitarian. However, many therapists are not adequately trained in this modality and are intimidated by the thought of managing the multiple alliances and transference-countertransference enactments that occur, especially in the severely dysfunctional family system.
- *Multiple family therapy* is an excellent modality, particularly when children and adolescents are the focus of treatment. Modeling of more adaptive interaction styles and the use of the group as a support system can have a profound influence on family process.
- *Group therapy* for personality dysfunction is probably the second most used modality in the armamentarium of clinicians who treat personality disorders. Group therapy offers the option of many forms of restructuring and is a powerful modality when group composition is optimal. One of the challenges is to select members who can optimize the treatment experience for all participants.
- *Psychoeducational* intervention is being used more frequently as an adjunctive modality, especially for the more severe personality disorders. Self-help groups often provide useful information to those suffering from personality dysfunction and their family members. Excellent resources are now available for most personality disturbances and can be used to inform and educate.
- *Pharmacotherapy,* the use of psychotrophic medications for treating symptoms of personality dysfunction and comorbid conditions, is advancing rapidly. Medications that target affective dysregulation, impulse dyscontrol, anxiety, and psychotic symptoms are valuable additions to treatment packages offered to patients and families.
- *Milieu therapy* is another modality that has a long history of use in treating personality disorders. This modality is the most effective choice for some expressions of personality dysfunction such as antisocial conditions.

TREATMENT PACKAGES—SEQUENTIAL AND COMBINED TREATMENT APPLICATIONS

It is common in contemporary clinical practice to combine treatment modalities, especially for severe personality dysfunction. Although there is an absence of empirical literature, clinical observation and experience support the view that combining treatment modalities can have an additive value and lead to treatment "synergy" (Millon et al., 1999; Sperry, 1995). Understanding a unified system will enhance the ability of a clinician to develop treatment packages (TPs) and to offer them with a theoretically grounded explanation for potential effectiveness. TPs are informed attempts to organize and offer treatment with consideration of the full range of variables, including format, modality, and methods of restructuring. *Sequential* TPs incorporate various modalities in sequence whereas *combined* TPs offer multiple modalities simultaneously delivered (Magnavita, 1998b).

TREATMENT FORMATS, SPACING, AND LENGTH OF SESSIONS

A critical element of the TP is the treatment format, the manner in which the treatment is delivered. The basic formats are:

- *Long-term treatment:* The treatment tends to be open ended and does not set specific time frames but pays more attention to the process of recovery and the attainment of maximal health.
- *Short-term treatment:* This treatment is often the first format offered, especially to higher functioning patients. The time frame can be set beforehand or at least there is an explicit agreement that the treatment will be of a "short-term" type.
- *Intermittent life-cycle treatment:* Many patients use treatment intermittently throughout their lives, and this can be a useful format for many patients. As patients encounter stressful periods, they can seek treatment for themselves or their families.
- *Maintenance treatment:* Some patients will require lifelong treatment regardless of their efforts to live without it. This generally represents a small percentage of the patient population and is most commonly seen when comorbid psychiatric disturbances such as schizophrenia or bipolar disorders exist.
- *Spacing and length of sessions:* The spacing and length of sessions must be considered. Sessions can be spaced to maximize potency based on an assessment of needs and logistical considerations such as distance and availability of transportation. Offering extended sessions is another way the potency might be enhanced, although there is little empirical evidence to support this.

AVOIDING "PATHOLOGICAL" THEORETICAL CERTAINTY

Jordan (chapter 6) believes that psychotherapy requires of its practitioners the ability to deal with uncertainty and not retreat into theoretical certainty when feeling overwhelmed with the process. Patients have often expressed that they have to train clinicians how to treat them. This is not to be taken lightly. Each patient must be able to train clinicians in the approach that will best activate the change process. A unified theory eschews the position of theoretical certainty because it allows for many styles and approaches consistent with the overall model.

BROADENING THE TREATMENT RANGE

The following suggestions have been made in a previous publication for broadening the range of treatment and include:

- Emphasize a relational-oriented therapeutic stance.
- Observe the clinical phenomena from various levels of abstraction.
- Maintain a modulated level of therapeutic activity and engagement.
- Be flexible in shifting approaches and modalities.
- Mobilize change patterns in various systems.
- Use theory as a springboard to creative interventions.
- Use various modalities sequentially and in combination.
- Attempt a shorter-term approach first and shift format if warranted.
- Use a treatment team approach whenever possible (Magnavita, 1998a, p. 12).

EMPIRICAL SUPPORT AND EVIDENCE OF CONVERGENCE

The empirical support for a unified model for treating personality must come from the component systems involved. Many of these methods are presented in this volume and can be placed in a unified system. Many of the restructuring methods presented in this chapter have accumulated sound empirical support. There is evidence to support a move toward a unified theory (Magnavita, 1998a), as seen in the following trends: (1) theoretical convergence and technical blending, (2) psychopharmacotherapy and psychotherapy integration, and (3) multimodal treatment combinations. Psychotherapy research by and large has failed to document any model of treatment as superior to others. What the research does suggest is that the relational matrix is the essential ingredient of psychotherapy and, to a large degree, pharmacotherapy. "Concomitantly, there is an assumption that the therapeutic process relies most heavily not on the techniques but on the quality and mutual experience of these relationships" (p. 999). What unify all psychotherapy are the common factors, such as empathy, hope, caring, and understanding vital to all approaches. These common factors are the most important aspects of a relational model.

SUMMARY AND CONCLUSIONS

The time has come for developing a unified approach to the treatment of personality dysfunction that considers the entire ecological system of the individual, dyad, family, and culture in which the personality process occurs. Many of the cutting edge approaches presented in this volume can be understood using the framework of a unified system. The complexity of personality function and dysfunction requires a unification of the domains that have been identified over the past century as being essential to personality. Here at the beginning of the new millennium, a unified model is within our reach. The hope is to provide a multidisciplinary, component systems model that will leave out nothing of importance. Clinicians of the future may feel more empowered in their ability to address the pervasive and often difficult-to-treat dysfunctional systems. The model must be large enough to allow every patient, couple, and family to instruct us.

REFERENCES

Allport, G. W. (1968). *The person in psychology: Selected essays.* Boston: Beacon Press.
Barlow, D. H. (1988). *Anxiety and its disorders: The nature and treatment of anxiety and panic.* New York: Guilford Press.

Beck, A. T. (1976). *Cognitive therapy and emotional disorders.* New York: International Universities Press.

Beck, A. T., Freeman, A., & Associates. (1990). *Cognitive therapy of personality disorders.* New York: Guilford Press.

Beck, A. T., Rush, A. J., Shaw, B. F., & Emery, G. (1979). *Cognitive therapy of depression.* New York: Guilford Press.

Benjamin, L. S. (1993). *Interpersonal diagnosis and treatment of personality disorders.* New York: Guilford Press.

Bernstein, D. P. (2002). Cognitive therapy of personality disorders in patients with histories of emotional abuse or neglect. *Psychiatric Annals, 32*(10), 618–628.

Blum, D. (2002). *Love at Goon Park: Harry Harlow and the science of affection.* Cambridge, MA: Perseus.

Bowen, M. (1976). Theory and practice of family therapy. In P. J. Guerin Jr. (Ed.), *Family therapy: Theory and practice* (pp. 42–90). New York: Gardner Press.

Bronfenbrenner, U. (1979). *The ecology of human development: Experiments by nature and design.* Cambridge, MA: Harvard University Press.

Chao, R. (2002). Seeing the forest and seeing the trees in psychology. *American Psychologist, 57*(12), 1128–1129.

Davanloo, H. (Ed.). (1980). *Short-term dynamic psychotherapy.* New York: Aronson.

Ezriel, H. (1952). Notes on psychoanalytic group therapy: Interpretation and research. *Psychiatry, 15,* 119–126.

Fenichel, O. (1945). *The psychoanalytic theory of neurosis.* New York: Norton.

Ferenczi, S., & Rank, O. (1925). *The development of psychoanalysis.* New York: Nervous and Mental Diseases.

Fosha, D. (2000). *The transforming power of affect: A model for accelerated change.* New York: Basic Books.

Goleman, D. (1994). *Emotional intelligence.* New York: Bantam Books.

Greenberg, L. S., & Paivio, S. C. (1997). *Working with emotions in psychotherapy.* New York: Guilford Press.

Greenberg, L. S., Rice, L. N., & Elliott, R. (1993). *Facilitating emotional change: The moment-by-moment process.* New York: Guilford Press.

Greenspan, S. I. (1992). *Infancy and early childhood: The practice of clinical assessment and intervention with emotional and developmental challenges.* Madison, CT: International Universities Press.

Greenspan, S. I. (1997). *Developmentally based psychotherapy.* Madison, CT: International Universities Press.

Greenspan, S. I. (2002). The developmental basis of psychotherapeutic processes. In F. W. Kaslow (Editor-in-Chief) & J. J. Magnavita (Vol. Ed.), *Comprehensive handbook of psychotherapy: Psychodynamic/object relations* (Vol. 1, pp. 15–45). New York: Wiley.

Grigsby, J., & Stevens, D. (2000). *Neurodynamics of personality.* New York: Guilford Press.

Groves, J. E. (1992). The short-term dynamic psychotherapies: An overview. In J. S. Rutan (Ed.), *Psychotherapy for the 1990's* (pp. 35–59). New York: Guilford Press.

Guerin, P. J., Fogarty, T. F., Fay, L. F., & Kautto, J. G. (1996). *Working with relational triangles: The one-two-three of psychotherapy.* New York: Guilford Press.

Hedges, C. (2002). *War is a force that gives meaning.* Cambridge, MA: Perseus.

Herscovici, C. R. (2002). Eating disorders in adolescents. In F. W. Kaslow (Editor-in-Chief) & J. J. Magnavita (Vol. Ed.), *Comprehensive handbook of psychotherapy: Psychodynamic/object relations* (Vol. 1, pp. 133–159). New York: Wiley.

James, W. (1890). *The principles of psychology* (Vols. I & II). New York: Henry Holt.

Jordan, J. V. (Ed.). (1997). *Women's growth in diversity.* New York: Guilford Press.

Jordan, J. V. (2000). The role of mutual empathy in relational/cultural therapy. *Journal of Clinical Psychology/In Session: Psychotherapy in Practice, 56*(8), 1005–1016.

Kohut, H. (1971). *The analysis of the self.* New York: International Universities Press.

Kohut, H. (1977). *The restoration of the self.* New York: International Universities Press.

Kramer, P. D. (1993). *Listening to Prozac.* New York: Viking.

Lazarus, R. S. (1991). *Emotion and adaptation.* New York: Oxford University Press.

Linehan, M. M. (1993). *Cognitive-behavioral treatment of borderline personality disorder.* New York: Guilford Press.

Magnavita, J. J. (1997). *Restructuring personality disorders: A short-term dynamic approach.* New York: Guilford Press.

Magnavita, J. J. (1998a). Challenges in the treatment of personality disorders: When the disorder demands comprehensive integration. *Journal of Clinical Psychology/In Session: Psychotherapy in Practice, 4*(4), 5–17.

Magnavita, J. J. (1998b). Methods of restructuring personality disorders with comorbid syndromes. *Journal of Clinical Psychology/In Session: Psychotherapy in Practice, 4*(4), 73–89.

Magnavita, J. J. (2000). Introduction: The growth of relational therapy. *Journal of Clinical Psychology/In Session: Psychotherapy in Practice, 56*(8), 999–1994.

Magnavita, J. J. (2002). Psychodynamic approaches to psychotherapy: A century of innovations. In F. W. Kaslow (Editor-in-Chief) & J. J. Magnavita (Vol. Ed.), *Comprehensive handbook of psychotherapy: Psychodynamic/object relations* (Vol. 1, pp. 1–12). New York: Wiley.

Magnavita, J. J. (in press). *Personality-guided relational therapy: A component system model.* Washington, DC: American Psychological Association.

Malan, D. H. (1979). *Individual psychotherapy and the science of psychodynamics.* London: Butterworth.

McCullough Vaillant, L. (1997). *Changing character: Short-term anxiety-regulating psychotherapy for restructuring defenses, affects, and attachments.* New York: Basic Books.

Meissner, W. W. (1978). The conceptualization of marriage and family dynamics from a psychoanalytic perspective. In T. J. Paglino & B. S. McCrady (Eds.), *Marriage and marital therapy: Psychoanalytic, behavioral and systems theory perspectives* (pp. 25–101). New York: Brunner/Mazel.

Menninger, K. (1958). *Theory of psychoanalytic technique.* New York: Basic Books.

Millon, T. (with Grossman, S., Meagher, S., Millon, C., & Everly, G.). (1999). *Personality-guided therapy.* New York: Wiley.

Minuchin, S. (1974). *Families and family therapy.* Cambridge, MA: Harvard University Press.

Muran, J. C., & Safran, J. D. (2002). A relational approach to psychotherapy. In F. W. Kaslow (Editor-in-Chief) & J. J. Magnavita (Vol. Ed.), *Comprehensive handbook of psychotherapy: Psychodynamic/object relations* (Vol. 1, pp. 253–281). New York: Wiley.

Pavlov, I. P. (1927). *Conditioned reflexes: An investigation of the physiological activity of the cerebral cortex* (G. V. Anrep, Trans.). New York: Oxford University Press.

Pawl, J. H., & St. John, M. (2002). Infant mental health. In F. W. Kaslow (Editor-in-Chief) & J. J. Magnavita (Vol. Ed.), *Comprehensive handbook of psychotherapy: Psychodynamic/object relations* (Vol. 1, pp. 81–104). New York: Wiley.

Perls, F. S. (1969). *Gestalt therapy verbatim.* Lafayette, CA: Real People Press.

Reich, J. (2002). Clinical correlates of stress-induced personality disorder. *Psychiatric Annals, 32*(10), 581–588.

Reich, W. (1933). *Character analysis.* Leipzig, Germany: Verlag.

Rogers, C. (1951). *Client-centered therapy.* Boston: Houghton Mifflin.

Safran, J. D., & Muran, J. C. (Eds.). (2000). *Negotiating the therapeutic alliance: A relational treatment guide.* New York: Guilford Press.

Satir, V. (1964). *Conjoint family therapy.* Palo Alto, CA: Science and Behavior Books.

Selvini Palazzoli, M., Boscolo, L., Cecchin, G., & Prata, G. (1978). *Paradox and counterparadox.* New York: Guilford Press.

Shapiro, F. (1995). *Eye movement desensitization and reprocessing (EMDR): Basic principles, protocols and procedures.* New York: Guilford Press.

Siegel, D. J. (1999). *The developing mind: Toward a neurobiology of interpersonal experience.* New York: Guilford Press.

Skinner, B. F. (1953). *Science and human behavior.* New York: Bantam Books.

Skinner, B. F. (1979). *The shaping of a behaviorist.* New York: Alfred A. Knopf.

Solomon, M. F. (1989). *Narcissism and intimacy: Love and marriage in an age of confusion.* New York: Norton.

Solomon, M. F., & Lynn, R. E. (2002). Object-relations couples therapy. In F. W. Kaslow (Editor-in-Chief) & J. J. Magnavita (Vol. Ed.), *Comprehensive handbook of psychotherapy: Psychodynamic/object relations* (Vol. 1, pp. 387–405). New York: Wiley.

Sperry, L. (1995). *Handbook of diagnosis and treatment of the DSM-IV personality disorders.* New York: Brunner/Mazel.

Spitz, R. (1947). *Grief: A peril in infancy* [Silent film].

Sternberg, R. J., & Grigorenko, E. L. (2001). Unified psychology. *American Psychologist, 56*(12), 1069–1079.

Strozier, C. B. (2001). *Heinz Kohut: The making of a psychoanalyst.* New York: Farrar, Straus and Giroux.

Sullivan, H. S. (1953). *The interpersonal theory of psychiatry.* New York: Norton.

Trujillo, M. (2002). Short-term dynamic psychotherapy of narcissistic personality disorders. In F. W. Kaslow (Editor-in-Chief) & J. J. Magnavita (Vol. Ed.). *Comprehensive handbook of psychotherapy: Psychodynamic/object relations* (Vol. 1, pp. 345–364). New York: Wiley.

Watson, J. B. (1928). *The psychological care of the child and infant.* London: Allen.

Wilber, K. (2000). *A theory of everything: An integral vision for business, politics, and spirituality.* Boston: Shambhala.

Wilson, E. O. (1998). *Consilience: The unity of knowledge.* New York: Alfred A. Knopf.

Young, J. E. (1990). *Cognitive therapy for personality disorders. A schema-focused approach* (Rev. ed.). Sarasota, FL: Professional Resource Exchange.

Author Index

Abraham, K., 98
Abram, D., 399, 404
Abrams, R. C., 498, 501
Ackerman, E., 324
Adams, H. E., 19
Agras, W. S., 250, 251
Agronin, M. E., 498, 501, 503
Aitken, L., 501
Akhtar, S., 93
Akiskal, H. S., 345, 346
Albanese, M., 338
Alden, L. E., 514
Alexander, F., 3, 4, 259, 260
Alexander, L., 349
Alexopoulos, G. S., 501
Algina, J., 490
Alighieri, D., 443, 447
Allen, A., 345
Allgulander, C., 86, 351
Allmon, D., 189, 238, 250, 419
Allport, G. W., 7, 60, 62, 528
Alterman, A. I., 401
Alvarez, A., 475
Alvarez, W., 276
Amar, A., 373
Ames, A., 499
Anchin, J. C., 255
Anderson, G., 520
Anderson, S., 324
Anderson, T., 276
Andrade, J., 322, 323
Anselm, G., 343
Antia, S. X., 350
Apfel-Savitz, R., 476
Appelbaum, A., 105, 126
Appelbaum, P. S., 443, 445
Arinami, T., 86
Arlt, J., 461
Armstrong, H. E., 189, 238, 250, 419, 514
Arntz, A., 187
Aspnes, A., 498
Atkinson, R., 401
Auerbach, A., 189
Azim, H. F. A., 260, 357, 358, 359, 362, 369, 372, 375
Azrin, N., 323

Babor, T. F., 401, 402
Babyak, M. A., 434

Baddeley, A., 322, 323, 455
Bader, E., 217
Bailey, R., 218
Baker, S., 408
Balfour, L., 374
Ball, A., 401
Ball, E. M., 226
Ball, S. A., 86, 398, 399, 400, 401, 402, 403, 404, 408, 409, 417, 418, 419
Ballou, M., 124
Bandura, A., 49, 139
Banken, J. A., 401
Banks, A., 121
Banon, E., 139, 398, 419, 513
Baran, T. Z., 457
Barber, J. P., 514, 515, 519, 522
Bardenstein, K. K., 10, 12, 71, 144, 467
Barefoot, J. C., 428
Barenbaum, N. B., 15, 18
Barkham, M., 190, 514, 518
Barley, W. D., 226, 251
Barlow, D. H., 25, 543
Barratt, E. S., 348, 349
Barron, J. W., 26
Bartholomew, K., 17
Bass, D., 480
Bateman, A., 140, 371, 489, 516, 521
Baucom, D. H., 173
Bauman, K., 131
Bayon, C., 85, 86
Beach, S. R. H., 8
Bearman, P., 131
Beattie, M., 401, 519
Beck, A. T., 7, 41, 49, 63, 66, 139, 140, 169, 173, 175, 177, 178, 179, 180, 184, 187, 190, 398, 402, 419, 519, 542
Beck, J. S., 175, 177, 187, 399
Becker, E., 519
Becker, L. A., 323
Beckham, E., 190
Begin, A., 226
Behar, L., 469
Bein, E., 254, 275, 276
Beitman, B., 254
Belisle, M., 515
Bender, D. S., 135, 356
Bender, R., 457
Benderly, B. L., 16, 19
Benedetti, F., 344

Benjamin, L. S., 8, 49, 66, 151, 152, 153, 154, 156, 157, 160, 161, 163, 164, 165, 166, 167, 255, 274, 544
Ben-Porath, Y. S., 84
Bergin, A. E., 260
Bergman, A., 94
Berman, M. E., 519
Berne, E., 194, 202
Bernheim, H., 4
Bernstein, D., 10, 534
Berry, S. A., 335, 344
Bettelheim, B., 469
Beutler, L. E., 523
Bibring, G. L., 504
Bienstock, C. A., 345
Bienvenu, O. J., 135
Bierer, L. M., 460
Bierman, K. L., 480
Bigelow, G. E., 401
Bilder, R. M., 337
Billings, J. H., 439
Binder, J. L., 254, 255, 256, 258, 260, 261, 264, 274, 275, 276
Binder-Brynes, K., 460
Bion, W., 115, 116, 379
Bissada, H., 374
Black, G., 434
Blais, M. A., 88
Blanco, C., 350
Bland, R. C., 136, 138
Blaney, P. H., 19
Blankenstein, A. H., 429
Blatt, S. J., 26
Bleiberg, E., 71, 467, 469, 471
Bliwise, N. G., 274
Blum, D., 61, 63, 532, 533
Blum, R., 131
Bogetto, F., 344
Boggs, S. R., 490
Bohme, H., 520
Bohme, R., 226, 347
Bohus, M., 226, 347
Boiago, I., 343, 345
Bolter, K., 276
Bonaccorso, S., 337
Bond, A. J., 351
Boscolo, L., 546
Bowen, M., 8, 67, 438, 535, 537, 544, 546
Bowlby, J., 61, 151, 257, 472
Boyer, R., 138
Braendstroem, S., 86
Bram, A. D., 299
Brandt, L., 86, 351
Bremner, D., 461
Bremner, J. D., 450, 460, 461
Brenner, C., 284
Bridges, C., 349
Bristol, C., 281, 287, 301
Bronfenbrenner, U., 20, 531, 535
Brooner, R. K., 401
Brown, C. H., 135
Brown, G. K., 187
Brown, G. W., 413

Brown, L. S., 124
Brown, M. Z., 223
Brown, S. A., 428, 434
Brunson, K., 457
Bryer, J. B., 324
Buchsbaum, M. S., 460
Buchtel, H. A., 188
Budman, S., 276, 514
Buie, S. E., 226, 251
Burns, A., 501
Burns, B. D., 180, 190
Burnstein, E. D., 105
Busby, K., 373, 374
Buss, D. M., 16
Butcher, J. N., 135
Butler, A. C., 187
Butler, R. N., 499, 504
Butler, S. F., 254, 261, 264, 275, 276

Cacciola, J. S., 401
Cai, T., 135
Calabrese, J. R., 336, 338, 520
Cameron, P., 374
Camlin, K. L., 335, 344
Campbell, S. B., 19, 20
Capelli, S., 450, 460
Capers, H., 199
Capreol, M. J., 514
Carlson, J. G., 323
Carpy, D. V., 482
Carr, A., 126, 380
Carroll, K. M., 399, 401, 402, 404, 408, 409, 410
Carson, R. C., 29
Carter, R., 520
Caspi, A., 18, 137
Cassidy, J. R., 151
Cattell, R. B., 80
C'deBaca, J., 18
Cecchin, G., 546
Cecero, J. J., 398, 408, 409
Cellar, J., 520
Chamberlin, P., 490
Chambless, D. L., 514
Chaney, J. M., 439
Change, L. Y., 136
Chao, R., 530
Charcot, J. M., 3
Charney, D. S., 461
Chase, D., 463
Chemtob, C. M., 323
Chen, Y., 457
Chesney, M. A., 434
Chess, S., 16, 17
Chevron, E., 519
Chiesa, M., 379, 412
Chittams, J., 515, 519, 522
Chrzanowski, G., 61
Chu, J. A., 478
Clance, P. R., 255
Clanon, T. L., 349
Clark, L. A., 84, 88
Clarkin, J. F., 4, 62, 65, 69, 70, 84, 85, 111, 114, 116

Clifford, P. R., 401, 519
Cloninger, C. R., 16, 66, 85, 86, 92, 351, 520
Coccaro, E. F., 338, 346, 349, 351, 471, 519, 520
Cochrane, K., 471
Cocuzza, E., 344
Cohen, D. J., 477
Cohen, P., 10
Cohen, S., 428
Collins, J. F., 190, 519
Colombo, C., 344
Comtois, K. A., 223, 250, 516
Conrad, G., 374
Coolidge, F. L., 501
Coon, D. W., 515
Cooney, N. L., 399, 401, 402, 404
Cooper, T. B., 471, 519
Coppola, F. F., 463
Corbitt, E. M., 356
Cornelius, J., 336, 343, 344, 521
Costa, P. T., 7, 81, 82, 83, 84, 135, 139
Costello, E., 226
Cowdry, R. W., 342, 344, 346
Coyne, J. C., 430
Coyne, L., 105
Craft, J. C., 250, 516
Craighead, L. W., 47, 49
Craighead, W. E., 47, 49
Critchley, M., 450
Crits-Christoph, K., 515, 519, 522
Cummings, E. M., 19, 20
Cummings, J., 501
Cummings, N. A., 267
Curillo, C., 345
Czirr, R., 501
Czobor, P., 337

Daae, E., 514, 518
Daehler, M. L., 349
Dahlsgaard, K. K., 187
Dai, X., 135
Dakof, G. A., 471
Dammann, G. W., 70
Daniel, S. S., 188
Dantendorfer, K., 347
Darling, N., 471
Darwin, C. R., 63
Davanloo, H., 435, 517, 540
Davidson, J. R., 334
Davidson, R. J., 63
Davies, P. T., 19, 20
Davis, C. W., 401, 418
Davis, D. D., 173, 175, 179, 180, 184
Davis, K. L., 66, 138, 334
Davis, M., 61, 461
Davis, R., 4, 8, 9, 19, 25, 30, 35, 79, 80, 505, 508
Davison, G. C., 49
Davison, W. T., 281, 287, 301
Dazord, A., 373
DeFries, J. C., 139
DeGood, D. E., 430
DeJong, C., 400, 401

De la Fuente, J., 346
Delaney, R., 450, 460
Delbo, C., 444
DelBoca, F. K., 402
De Leo, D., 501
Demby, A., 514
den Boer, J. A., 351
Dennett, D. C., 63
Depue, R. A., 16, 101
Deragotis, L. R., 433
De Silva, C., 444
Deutch, A. Y., 461
deVegvar, M. L., 97
de Vries, D., 429
de Zwaan, M., 460
Diamond, G. S., 470
Dickey, C. C., 460
DiClemente, C. C., 155, 164
Dietzel, R., 187
Diguer, L., 514
Dimeff, L. A., 250, 516
Dolan, B., 356
Dolan, R. T., 356
Dolan-Sewell, R. T., 12
Dollard, J., 60
Donovan, D., 399, 404
Dornelas, E. A., 427, 438
Dougherty, L. M., 506
Douglas, A., 515
Downhill, J. E., Jr., 460
Dreesen, L., 187
Driessen, M., 460
Drummond, P., 323
Dubo, E. D., 345, 346
Duclos, A., 373
Dulit, R. A., 226
Dumont, N., 324
Dyck, I. R., 135, 356
Dyck, R. J., 136, 138

Eaton, W. W., 135
Eckman, T., 513
Edvardsen, J., 139, 222
Eghbal-Ahmadi, M., 457
Eilertsen, D. E., 514, 518
Eisler, I., 514
Eison, A., 520
Ekman, P., 63
Eldridge, N., 50
Elie, R., 515
Elin, M. R., 443, 445
Elkin, A., 460
Elkin, I., 190, 519
Elliott, G. R., 223
Elliott, R., 542, 543
Ellis, A., 41, 49, 160
Emery, G., 63, 169, 173, 175, 177, 178, 179, 180, 519, 542
Engel, G. L., 13, 427
Engle, D., 523
Epstein, N. B., 173
Epstein, S., 445
Erickson, E. H., 18

Erikson, E. H., 93
Eshelman, S., 137
Evans, C., 356
Everly, G., 13, 64, 70
Exner, J. E., 87
Eyberg, S. M., 490
Eysenck, H. J., 61, 135, 427
Eysenck, S. B., 427
Ezriel, H., 535

Fabrega, H., 12
Fadiman, J., 5
Fagan, J., 197
Fahlen, T., 350
Fahy, T. A., 514
Faltus, F. J., 347
Faraone, S. V., 336
Farfel, G. M., 334
Faugli, A., 514, 518
Fay, L. F., 535
Feighner, J. P., 351
Felthous, A. R., 348, 349
Fenichel, O., 98, 540
Fensterheim, H., 323
Ferenczi, S., 50, 59, 63, 541
Ferris, C. F., 519
Fingerhut, L. A., 428
Finke, J., 520
Fischer, K. W., 468
Fishbain, D. A., 499
Fisher, S., 260
Fishman, H. C., 472
Fisler, R. E., 97
Flegenheimer, W., 517
Fleming, B., 173, 175, 179, 180, 184, 185
Fletcher, A. C., 471
Fletcher, J. R., 349
Fogarty, T. F., 535
Fogel, B. S., 498
Folstein, M. F., 513
Fonagy, P., 71, 140, 300, 371, 379, 382, 468, 489, 516, 521
Forehand, R., 490
Forgatch, M. S., 490
Forsgren, T., 86
Fosha, D., 543
Foucault, M., 294
Fowler, J. C., 88
Fowler, W. L., 337
Foy, D. W., 461
Foyle, L. W., 188
Frager, R., 5
Frances, A. J., 4
Francis, A., 11
Frank, E. L., 526
Frankel, F. H., 476
Frankenburg, F. R., 343, 344, 345, 346, 467
Frankenburg, M. D., 221
Freeman, A., 7, 41, 49, 63, 66, 139, 140, 173, 175, 179, 180, 184, 185, 398, 402, 419, 542
Freese, S., 322, 323
French, T. M., 259, 260

Frenkel, M., 346
Freud, A., 281, 282, 283
Freud, S., 59, 78, 79, 97, 98, 120, 123, 162, 198, 282, 445
Freund, B., 323
Freyhan, F. A., 45
Friedel, R. O., 336, 344
Friedman, E. S., 154
Friedman, L., 335, 344, 488
Friedman, R. S., 506
Friis, S., 369, 370, 371, 373, 514, 518
Fruzzetti, A. E., 225
Fuller, R. D., 171
Furer, M., 94
Furstenberg, F. F., 136

Gabbard, G. O., 299, 480, 482, 520, 521
Galenson, E., 97
Gallagher, D., 501
Gardner, D. L., 342, 344, 346
Garfield, S. L., 260
Garrett, R. W., 440
Gaspari, J. P., 401
Gaston, L., 260
Gastpar, M., 520
Gavriel, H., 323
Geller, A., 349
George, A., 336, 343, 344
Gergely, G., 382, 468, 477
Gerin, P., 373
Getter, H., 401
Gilbert, M., 218
Gilbertson, M. W., 461
Gill, M. M., 263
Giller, E. L., 97, 460
Gillette, C. S., 323
Gilligan, C., 122
Gillis, K., 373
Glass, G. V., 61
Gleick, J., 15
Glickhauf-Hughes, C., 255
Glod, C., 324
Goisman, R. M., 505
Gold, R. K., 349
Goldberg, L. R., 81
Goldberg, S. C., 336, 344
Goldberger, M., 287, 293, 298
Goldfried, M. R., 49, 62, 75
Goldman, R. S., 337
Goldman-Rakic, P. S., 455
Goldstein, A. J., 514
Goldstein, K., 47
Goleman, D., 543
Gonzalez, A. M., 238, 250
Goodman, M., 335
Goodman, P., 195, 202
Gordon, J. M., 177
Gordon, J. R., 399, 404
Gould, S., 50
Goulding, M., 195, 197, 199
Goulding, R., 195, 197, 199
Grawe, K., 523
Gray, P., 281, 282, 284, 285, 286, 299, 300

Green, A. I., 518
Greenberg, D., 189
Greenberg, J. R., 255
Greenberg, L. S., 542, 543
Greenberg, R. P., 260
Greenberg, S., 500
Greenberger, D., 175
Greendyke, R. M., 349
Greenspan, S. I., 16, 19, 545
Greenwald, R., 323
Griengl, H., 347
Griggs, S. M., 401, 418
Grigorenko, E. L., 64, 528, 530
Grigsby, J., 19, 541
Grillon, C., 461
Griva, M., 226, 251
Grossman, R., 342, 345
Grossman, S., 13, 64, 68, 70
Grossman, W., 97
Groupe, A., 349
Groves, J. E., 542
Grueneich, R., 401
Grünbaum, A., 27
Grunberg, F., 138
Guerin, P. J., 535
Gunderson, J., 12, 69, 135, 223, 429, 467, 471, 473, 487
Gurman, A. S., 49
Gurvits, T. V., 461

Haaf, B., 226
Hales, R. E., 348
Hall, S. M., 428
Halligan, S. L., 460
Hamer, R. M., 336, 344
Hammond, M., 480
Hardy, G. E., 190, 514, 518
Hare, R. D., 85
Harlow, H., 151
Harlow, M., 151
Harmon, R., 188
Harpur, T. J., 85
Harris, K., 131
Harris, T. O., 413
Harrison, J. A., 84, 88
Harrist, R. S., 274
Hart, S. D., 17, 85
Harteveld, F. M., 400, 401
Hartling, L., 123
Hartmann, K., 275
Hauger, R. L., 519
Hazlett, E. A., 460
Haznedar, M. M., 460
Heagerty, P., 250
Heard, H. L., 189, 238, 250, 419, 514, 515
Heatherton, T. F., 18
Heber, R., 323
Hedges, C., 538
Hedlund, N. L., 323
Hefferline, R. F., 195, 202
Heine, R. W., 3
Hellerstein, D., 514, 518
Hempel, C. G., 29

Henke, R., 338
Hennen, J., 221
Henry, W. P., 260, 264, 274, 275, 276
Hepworth, C., 413
Herman, J., 17, 63, 97, 126, 324
Hermann, B. P., 349
Herring, J., 336, 344
Herrmann, J., 460
Herrnstein, R. J., 16
Herron, N., 97
Herscovici, C. R., 538
Hersen, M., 19
Heslegrave, R., 221
Hickerson, S. C., 226, 251
Higgitt, A., 379
Hill, A., 460
Hill, K., 86
Hill, M., 501
Hilsenroth, M. J., 88
Hippius, H., 471
Hirose, S., 349
Hirschfeld, R. M. A., 135
Hoffman, R. E., 347
Hofmann, S. G., 519
Hoglend, P., 514, 518
Hogue, A., 470, 490, 491
Hokama, H., 461
Holland, J. L., 82
Hollander, E., 345, 346, 351
Hollingsworth, A. S., 226, 251
Holt, C. S., 350, 351
Hook, J. N., 501
hooks, b., 124
Hoptman, M., 337
Horne-Moyer, H. L., 274
Horney, K., 36
Horowitz, L., 105
Horowitz, M. J., 293, 294, 295, 469
Horowitz, S. V., 498
Hostetler, A., 97
Houston, B. K., 434
Howard, K. I., 523
Howard, R., 464
Howland, R. H., 154
Hubert, A. E., 515
Hughes, J. R., 349
Hughes, M., 137
Hutchinson, J. H., 298
Hwu, H. G., 136
Hyer, L. A., 323

Ianni, F., 139, 398, 419, 513
Ichikawa, J., 337
Imber, S. D., 519
Irion, T., 369, 371, 514, 518
Ironson, G., 323
Irwin, D., 343, 345
Isen, A. M., 171
Ishii, H., 337
Islam, M. N., 346
Isogawa, K., 86
Ito, Y., 324
Ivanoff, A., 221, 226

Jackson, D. N., 135
Jackson, S. W., 4
Jacobson, E., 93, 95
Jacobwitz, D., 258
James, W., 58, 528
Jang, K., 135, 222
Jesberger, J. A., 344
Johns, S., 369, 514, 518
Johnson, D., 188, 448
Johnson, M. E., 275
Johnson, S. M., 68, 426
Joiner, T. E., 403
Joines, V., 195, 196, 220
Jones, J., 131
Jones, R. A., 255
Jordan, J. V., 120, 121, 123, 127, 128, 545
Joseph, R., 324
Joyce, A. S., 140, 260, 357, 358, 359, 369, 372, 375
Joyce, P. R., 86
Jurist, E. L., 382, 468

Kadden, R. M., 399, 401, 402, 404
Kadis, L. B., 195, 218
Kagan, J., 138
Kahana, B., 460
Kahler, T., 195, 196, 199
Kakuma, T., 501
Kania, J., 401
Kanter, D. R., 349
Kanter, J., 250, 516
Kapfhammer, H. P., 471
Kaplan, A. G., 120, 123
Karterud, S., 369, 370, 371, 373, 514, 518
Kaslow, F. W., 8
Katsuragi, S., 86
Kautto, J. G., 535
Kavanagh, D., 322, 323
Kavoussi, R. J., 338, 346, 349, 471, 519, 520
Kazdin, A. E., 47, 49, 480
Keitner, G. I., 413
Kellner, M., 323, 461
Kendrick, J. S., 428
Kenny, S. L., 468
Kent, J. J., Jr., 469
Kent, T. A., 348, 349
Kernberg, O. F., 8, 44, 70, 92, 93, 94, 95, 96, 98, 99, 100, 101, 103, 104, 105, 108, 109, 114, 116, 126, 142, 299, 300, 382, 384, 513
Kernberg, P. F., 10, 12, 71, 467
Kerr, M. E., 67
Kessler, R. C., 137
Kestenbaum, R., 517
Kidorf, M., 401
Kiesler, D. J., 38, 39, 49, 50, 255, 258
Kihlstrom, S. F., 445
Kim, L. I., 349
Kindt, M., 322, 323
King, V. L., 401
Kirmayer, L. J., 429
Kisiel, C. L., 467
Kite, L., 323
Kiyota, A., 86
Klar, H. M., 471

Klausner, E., 501
Kleber, H. D., 400, 401
Klein, D., 10, 66, 342
Klein, M., 120
Kleinman, A., 135
Kleinman, J. C., 428
Klerman, G. L., 519
Klosko, J. S., 402, 403, 404, 415
Kniskern, K., 49
Knottnerus, A., 429
Koenigsberg, H., 126, 335, 520, 521
Koerner, K., 516
Kofoed, L., 401
Kohlenberg, R. J., 255
Kohut, H., 120, 138, 143, 299, 445, 513, 545
Koons, C., 238, 249, 250
Kopta, S. M., 523
Korn, D. L., 307, 323
Kosten, T. A., 400, 401, 418
Kosten, T. R., 400, 401, 418
Kraepelin, E., 4
Krakauer, I., 515, 519, 522
Kramer, P. D., 62, 544
Kranzler, H. R., 86, 400, 401, 402, 409
Krause, R., 93, 96
Krawitz, R., 370
Krol, P. A., 324
Kruedelbach, N., 401
Krueger, R. F., 12
Krystal, J. H., 461
Kuhn, T. S., 58
Kunik, M. E., 498
Kwong, M. J., 17

Laikin, M., 7, 514, 517
Lambert, M. J., 276
Landwehrmeyer, G. B., 347
Lane, T. W., 264
Larsen, F., 369
Lasko, N. B., 461
Lavallee, Y., 515
Lazarus, A. A., 28
Lazarus, R. S., 531, 536
Lazrove, S., 323, 325
Leary, T., 8, 66
Lee, C., 323
Leeds, A. M., 307, 323
Leichtman, M., 469
Leichtman, M. L., 469
Lenzenweger, M. F., 16, 62, 65, 69
Lerman, H., 124
Lerner, D., 136
Lesage, A., 138, 515
Levensky, E. R., 225
Levenson, H., 254, 257, 261, 274, 275, 276
Levenson, L., 285
Levin, A., 345, 346
Levin, P., 323, 325
Levinson, H., 226
Levy, K. N., 26, 70
Lewin, K., 29
Lewinsohn, P., 10
Lewis, M., 435, 499

Liberman, M. A., 217
Liberman, R. P., 513
Liddle, H. A., 470, 471, 490, 491
Liebowitz, M. R., 342, 350
Liese, B. S., 173
Limberger, M. F., 347
Linehan, M. M., 66, 70, 138, 139, 140, 141, 142,
    165, 179, 184, 185, 189, 221, 222, 223, 225,
    226, 233, 236, 238, 239, 250, 307, 320, 399,
    404, 419, 476, 513, 514, 515, 516, 521, 523,
    543
Links, P. S., 221, 343, 345, 401, 471
Lipke, H., 323
Lipkus, I. M., 428
Litt, M. D., 401, 402
Livesley, W. J., 135, 222
Lochman, J. E., 480
Loehlin, J. C., 427
Loevinger, J., 29
Lohr, N. E., 188
Long, N., 490
Long, P., 490
Longabaugh, R., 401, 519
Looper, J., 338
Looper, K. J., 429
Lopez, R. P., 345
Loranger, A. W., 135
Lotstra, F., 346
Lovett, J., 323
Lowry, J. L., 523
Lowry, L., 500
Luborsky, L., 189, 190, 401, 514
Lundberg, M., 86
Lunnen, K. M., 276
Lutolf, P., 93
Lygren, S., 139, 222
Lynch, T. R., 238, 250, 251, 498, 499, 504
Lynn, R. E., 545
Lyons, M., 12, 429
Lyons-Ruth, K., 258

MacFarlane, M. M., 17, 67
MacKenzie, K. R., 85
MacLaren, C., 49
Maffei, C., 344
Magill, M. K., 440
Magnavita, J. J., 3, 4, 5, 6, 8, 12, 13, 17, 18, 19, 44,
    57, 58, 60, 61, 63, 65, 67, 68, 69, 427, 435,
    440, 529, 534, 539, 540, 545, 547, 549, 550
Mahler, M., 94
Mahoney, M. J., 47, 49
Main, M., 468
Main, T., 384
Maisto, S. A., 188
Malamud, W. I., 505
Malan, D. H., 435, 518, 535
Mallison, R. T., 520
Malloy, P., 401, 519
Manfield, P., 312, 313, 316, 320, 321, 323
Marchiaro, L., 344
Marcouiller, M., 515
Marcus, S. V., 323
Marini, J., 349

Mark, V., 349
Markovitz, P., 336, 338, 342, 343, 519, 520, 521
Marks, I., 189
Marlatt, G. A., 177, 399, 404
Marquis, P., 323
Marziali, E., 97, 514, 516
Mason, J. W., 460
Masterson, J. F., 71, 321
Mathews, A., 171
Matte-Blanco, I., 113
Mattes, J. A., 349
Mattia, J. I., 10
Maurer, G., 471
Maxfield, L., 323
May, J., 322, 323
Mayes, L. C., 477
Mays, D. T., 179, 185
McCallum, M., 260
McCann, R. A., 226
McCarley, R. W., 460
McCarthy, G., 450, 460
McClearn, G. E., 139
McClendon, R., 218
McCormick, R. A., 401
McCrae, R. R., 7, 81, 82, 83, 84, 135, 139
McCullough, L., 7, 514, 517
McCullough Vaillant, L., 435, 436, 440, 543, 544,
    545
McDaniel, K. D., 349
McDougall, J., 476
McFarlane, A. C., 17, 127
McGee, M. D., 347
McGinn, L. K., 173, 184, 190
McGlashan, T., 135, 141, 144, 323, 356, 398, 419
McGonagle, K. A., 137
McGorry, P. D., 173
McGrath, P. J., 336, 343
McHugh, P. R., 513
McIntosh, P., 124
McKay, J. R., 401
McLellan, A. T., 189, 190, 401, 514
McNeel, J., 217
McWilliams, N., 6, 7, 426
Meagher, S., 13, 64, 68, 70
Meara, N. M., 274
Meares, R., 514, 516, 517
Mehlman, R. D., 503
Mehlum, L., 369, 373
Meier, S., 460
Meissner, W. W., 296, 297, 545
Melchert, T. P., 401
Mellon, J., 275
Melson, S. J., 356
Meltzer, H. Y., 336, 337, 338, 520
Mendelson, T., 251
Meneghel, G., 501
Menninger, K., 260, 535
Menninger, W. W., 379, 384
Mercer, D. E., 416
Merikangas, K. R., 10, 356
Merry, J., 514
Messer, S. B., 255
Messich, J. E., 12

Miles, M. B., 217
Miller, A. L., 251
Miller, I. W., 413
Miller, J. B., 120, 121, 122, 123, 124, 324
Miller, N. E., 60
Miller, T. I., 61
Miller, W. R., 18, 428, 434
Millon, C., 13, 64, 70, 79
Millon, T., 4, 8, 9, 13, 19, 25, 27, 29, 30, 35, 36, 38, 41, 44, 47, 49, 64, 68, 70, 78, 79, 80, 136, 138, 426, 427, 429, 430, 505, 508, 529, 549
Minuchin, S., 472, 546
Mitchell, S. A., 255
Mitropoulou, V., 335, 351
Moffitt, T. E., 137
Mohr, D. C., 523
Molinari, V., 499
Monroe, S. M., 14
Monsen, J., 514, 518
Montgomery, I. M., 322, 323
Monti, P., 399, 404
Moore, T., 445
Moran, G. S., 479
Moran, P., 413
Morgan, A., 490
Morrisette, R., 138
Morse, J. Q., 238, 250, 251, 499, 504, 515, 519, 522
Muenz, L. R., 519
Mulberry, S., 226
Mulder, R. T., 86
Muller, R. J., 324
Mullins, L. L., 439
Mullins, U., 520
Mulsant, B. H., 498
Munoz, R. F., 135, 428
Munroe-Blum, H., 514, 516
Muran, C., 7
Muran, J. C., 514, 517, 518, 544, 545
Muraoka, M. Y., 323
Muris, P., 322, 323
Murray, C., 16
Murray, H. A., 5, 60
Myklebust, H. R., 448

Nace, E. P., 401, 418
Nagayama, H., 86
Narayan, M., 461, 520
Nathan, R. S., 336, 343, 344
Nathan, S., 343, 344
Neff, W. L., 276
Neighbors, B. D., 356
Nelson, B. A., 324
Nelson, C. B., 137
Nelson-Gray, R. O., 188
Nestadt, G., 135, 513
New, A., 335
Newman, C. F., 62, 75, 173, 187
Newman, D. L., 137
Newman, M. G., 519
Newman, S. C., 136, 138
Nielson, J. C., 520
Niznikiewicz, M. A., 460

Noel, N., 401, 519
Norcross, J. C., 62, 155, 164
Norton, K., 356
Nowak, A., 15
Nowinski, J., 408
Noyes, R., Jr., 350, 351
Nugent, A., 349

O'Brien, C. P., 189, 190, 401, 514
Ocepek-Welikson, K., 336, 343
Odbert, H. S., 7, 60
Odland, T., 514, 518
O'Driscoll, G. A., 349
Ogden, T. H., 480
Ohta, H., 461
Oien, P. A., 139, 222
O'Kelly, J. G., 362
O'Laughlin, I. A., 337
Olson, R. A., 439
Onken, L. S., 410
Onstad, S., 139, 222
Orn, H., 136, 138
Ornish, D. M., 439
Ostroff, R. B., 347
Ottaviani, R., 173, 175, 179, 180, 184
Overstreet, D., 275

Pace, T. M., 439
Padesky, C. A., 175, 179, 184, 185
Paivio, S. C., 543
Paris, J., 14, 17, 18, 136, 138, 140, 141, 467
Parsons, B., 336, 343
Pasternak, R., 498
Patterson, G. R., 490
Patterson, T., 66
Pavlov, I. P., 543
Pawl, J. H., 547
Pedersen, G., 370, 371
Perel, J. M., 336, 343, 344
Perkins, B., 323
Perlmutter, R. A., 67
Perloff, J. M., 180, 190
Perls, F. S., 195, 202, 543
Perris, C., 173
Perry, B. D., 97
Perry, J. C., 97, 139, 398, 419, 513
Perry, S., 4
Persons, J. B., 178, 180, 190
Peterson, E. W., 226, 251
Petry, S., 501
Phillips, D., 514
Phillips, M., 307
Piedmont, R. L., 81
Pilkonis, P., 12, 190, 356, 526
Pincus, A. L., 39
Pine, F., 94
Pinker, S., 63
Pinsker, H., 514, 518
Pinto, O. C., 346
Piper, W. E., 140, 260, 357, 358, 359, 369, 372, 375
Pipp, S. L., 468
Pistorello, J., 226

Pitman, R. K., 323, 461
Plakun, E. M., 379, 380, 385, 389, 395
Plomin, R., 18, 139
Poe, E. A., 446, 447
Pohl, U., 226
Poling, J., 86, 400, 401, 402, 409
Pollack, J., 7, 514, 517
Popp, C., 275
Powers, T., 254
Prata, G., 546
Pray, M., 281, 282, 283, 287, 301
Preston, J. D., 68
Pretzer, J. L., 173, 175, 179, 180, 184, 185
Price, L. H., 520
Prochaska, J. O., 155, 164
Przybeck, T. R., 85, 86, 92, 351, 520

Quine, W. V. O., 29
Quintana, S. M., 274
Quitkin, F., 336, 343, 345

Rachman, A. W., 63
Ragland, D. R., 434
Randall, P., 450, 460
Rank, O., 59, 63, 541
Ratey, J. J., 349
Rathus, J. H., 251
Rauch, S. L., 461
Rayner, E., 17
Raynor, R., 59
Rees, A., 190, 514, 518
Regier, D. A., 135, 137
Reich, J., 350, 351, 518, 539
Reich, W., 60, 540
Reik, T., 281
Renneberg, B., 514
Resnick, H. S., 461
Resnick, M., 131
Resnick, R. J., 336, 344
Reus, V. I., 428
Reviere, S. L., 255
Reynolds, D., 335
Reynolds, S., 190, 250, 514, 518
Rice, L. N., 542, 543
Richards, J., 323
Richter, J., 86
Rifai, H., 498
Rifkin, A., 345
Rilling, M., 59
Rinsley, D. B., 469
Ritvo, S., 287
Robins, C. J., 221, 222, 229, 238, 249, 250, 251
Robins, L. N., 137
Robinson, R., 413
Rocca, P., 344
Rogers, C., 42, 543, 545
Rogers, S., 323
Rohde, P., 10
Romanoski, A. J., 513
Root, M., 126
Rosen, J., 498
Rosenblatt, B., 299
Rosenbluth, M., 65

Rosenfeld, S. K., 477
Rosenthal, R. N., 514, 518
Rosie, J. S., 140, 357, 358, 359, 369, 372, 375
Rosowsky, E., 506
Roth, A. S., 347
Roth, W. T., 519
Rothbaum, B. O., 323, 334
Rothstein, A., 301
Rothstein, M. M., 173, 184
Rouanzoin, C., 323
Rounsaville, B. J., 86, 323, 400, 401, 402, 409,
    410, 418, 519
Rubin, A., 401, 519
Ruegg, R., 11
Ruiz, J. M., 434
Rush, A. J., 63, 169, 173, 175, 177, 178, 179, 180,
    519, 542
Rusnak, K., 323
Russell, D., 126
Russell, G. F., 514
Russell, R., 373
Rutherford, M. J., 401
Rutter, M., 136, 139
Ryan, C. E., 413
Rychlak, J. F., 57, 59, 68, 72

Sabin, T. D., 349
Sadavoy, J., 499, 502
Safer, D. L., 251
Safran, J. D., 255, 259, 544, 545
St. John, M., 547
Sakai, C., 323
Salemink, E., 322, 323
Salzman, C., 338
Sampson, H., 259
Samstag, L. W., 7, 514, 517, 518
Samuels, J., 135, 513
Sanderson, C., 84, 85, 222, 226
Sanderson, W. C., 190
Sandler, J., 258, 299
Sands, S., 349
Sanislow, C. A., 356, 398, 419
Sapolsky, R. M., 222
Sarafino, E. P., 428
Sartorius, N., 135
Satir, V., 546
Sato, T., 136
Saucier, G., 81
Saxon, J. J., 401
Scalzo, L. A., 322, 323
Schacht, T. E., 260, 264, 274, 275, 276
Schaeffer, J. A., 323
Schafer, R., 299
Schatzberg, A., 338
Scheck, M. M., 323
Scherwitz, L. W., 439
Schiff, H. B., 349
Schilte, A. F., 429
Schlette, P., 86
Schmahl, C. G., 347
Schmeidler, J., 460
Schmidt, C. W., 401
Schmidt, H., 250, 516

Schmidt, N. B., 403
Schmidt, S. E., 471
Schnarch, D., 438
Schore, A. N., 324
Schottenfeld, R. S., 402
Schroeder, M. L., 135
Schulz, P. M., 336, 343, 344, 521
Schulz, S. C., 335, 336, 338, 344, 401, 520, 521
Schwab-Stone, M., 10
Scocco, P., 501
Scott, T. M., 450, 460
Seeley, J., 10
Seeley, R., 459
Sees, K. L., 428
Segal, D. L., 501
Segal, H., 299
Segal, Z. V., 255, 259
Seidman, L. J., 460
Selesnick, S. T., 3, 4
Selvini Palazzoli, M., 546
Selzer, M. A., 111, 126
Sendera, A., 347
Seulin, C., 373
Sforzini, L., 344
Shapira, J., 501
Shapiro, D., 190, 348, 514, 518
Shapiro, E. R., 380
Shapiro, F., 304, 305, 307, 308, 313, 321, 322, 323, 543
Sharfstein, S. S., 469
Sharpley, C. F., 322, 323
Shaver, P. E., 151
Shaw, B. F., 63, 169, 173, 175, 177, 178, 179, 180, 519, 542
Shea, M. T., 12, 154, 190, 398, 519
Sheard, M., 349
Sheitman, B., 337
Shelley, M., 443, 463
Shenton, M. E., 460, 461
Shepherd, R., 61
Sheppard, I., 197
Sher, K. J., 84
Shin, L. M., 461
Shinsato, L., 10
Shore, N., 401
Shure, M. B., 480
Sickel, A. E., 345, 346
Siegel, D. J., 19, 255, 257, 260, 323, 325, 533
Siegel, T. C., 480
Siegler, I. C., 428
Siever, L., 10, 66, 97, 138, 334, 342, 345, 351, 471, 520, 521
Sifneos, P. E., 50, 476, 518
Sigvardsson, S., 86
Sikes, C. R., 334
Silk, K. R., 188, 221
Silva, P. A., 137
Silver, J. M., 348, 349
Silver, S. M., 323
Silverman, M., 283
Simeon, D., 346
Simon, K. M., 173, 175, 179, 180, 184, 185
Simons, A. D., 14

Simpson, E. B., 226
Simpson, S., 501
Singer, M. T., 69
Skinner, B. F., 532, 543
Skodol, A. E., 135, 356
Skre, I., 139, 222
Slaap, B. R., 351
Slater, J. A., 349
Slavson, S. R., 40
Smeraldi, E., 344
Smith, D. B., 349
Smith, D. J., 136
Smith, H., 520
Smith, M. L., 61
Smith, T. W., 434
Smyth, N. J., 401
Snider, E. C., 401
Soldz, S., 514
Soloff, P. H., 139, 334, 336, 343, 344, 471, 521
Solomon, J., 468
Solomon, K., 499, 504, 505
Solomon, M. F., 545
Sorgi, P., 349
Sotsky, S. M., 190, 519
Southwick, S. M., 97, 460, 461
Sparler, S., 439
Sperry, L., 62, 66, 68, 549
Spiegel-Cohen, J., 460
Spielman, L. A., 501
Spitz, R., 533
Spivak, G., 480
Sprang, G., 323
Sprince, M. P., 477
Springer, T., 188
Stahl, K., 460
Stanford, M. S., 348, 349
Startup, M., 518
Stein, D. J., 346, 351
Steinberg, L., 471
Steiner, J., 113, 114
Steiner, M., 343, 345
Stephens, T., 459
Stern, D., 255
Sternberg, R. J., 64, 528, 530
Stevens, D., 19, 541
Stevenson, J., 514, 516, 517
Stewart, I., 195, 220
Stewart, J. W., 336, 343
Stewart, S., 501
Stickgold, R., 323, 325
Stiglmayr, C., 226, 347
Stiles, W. B., 190, 514, 518
Stiver, I. P., 120, 121, 122, 123
Stoller, K., 401
Stone, J. L., 349
Stone, M., 93, 97, 126, 421
Stone, M. H., 324
Stone, M. M., 3
Stone, W. S., 336
Stout, R. L., 135
Strauss, J. L., 323
Stravynski, A., 189, 515
Strozier, C. B., 528

Strupp, H. H., 254, 255, 256, 258, 260, 261, 264, 274, 275, 276
Stryer, B. L., 349
Suarez, A., 189, 238, 250, 419, 515
Sullivan, H. S., 8, 61, 66, 255, 258, 544
Sullivan, R., 439
Surrey, J., 120, 123
Sutherland, T., 499
Sutker, P. B., 19
Svrakic, D. M., 85, 86, 92, 520
Sweet, R. A., 498
Swenson, C. R., 226
Sylvester, E., 469

Takeichi, M., 136
Tarbox, S. I., 336
Target, M., 71, 300, 382, 401, 468
Tasca, G. A., 374
Tate, P., 459
Taylor, C. B., 519
Taylor, D., 520
Teicher, M., 324
Telch, C. F., 250, 251
Telch, M. J., 403
Tennen, H., 86, 400, 401, 402, 409
Teusch, L., 520
Thase, M. E., 154
Thomas, A., 16, 17
Thomas, V. H., 401
Thompson, L. W., 501
Thompson, P. D., 438
Tinker, R. H., 323
Tohen, M., 12, 429
Tolin, D. F., 323
Tomkins, S. S., 63
Tooley, K., 478
Torgersen, A. M., 92
Torgersen, S., 139, 142, 222
Torrente, J., 520
Travis, L. A., 274
Treatment, R., 335
Trestman, R. L., 97, 351
Tricamo, E., 336, 343
Triffleman, E., 323, 400
Trikha, A., 345, 346
Trujillo, M., 517, 529
Trull, T. J., 84
Tsai, J. L., 135
Tsai, M., 255
Tse, W. S., 351
Tsuang, M. T., 336
Tsutsumi, T., 86
Tupin, J. P., 349
Turkat, I. D., 188
Turner, S. M., 19
Tutek, D. A., 189, 250, 514
Tweed, J. L., 238, 250
Tyrer, P., 12, 401, 418, 429

Ulrich, R., 12., 336, 343, 344
Urnes, Ø., 370, 371, 373
Useda, D. C., 84
Uyehara, L. A., 443, 445

Vaglum, P., 369, 373, 514, 518
Vaglum, S., 514, 518
Vallacher, R. R., 15
Vallis, T. M., 173, 184
van den Brink, W., 400, 401, 402, 417
van den Hout, M., 322, 323
van der Horst, H. E., 429
van der Kolk, B. A., 17, 97, 121, 125, 126, 127, 322, 323, 325, 334, 458
van der Wielen, G. M., 400, 401
Vanier, C., 138
van Reekum, R., 221
Vasile, R. G., 518
Velex, N., 10
Verheul, R., 400, 401, 402, 417
Vernon, P. A., 222
Viederman, M., 503
Vitousek, K., 135
Voglmaier, M. M., 460
Volavka, J., 337
Volkan, V., 93
von Bertalanffy, L., 14, 20, 61, 257
Voth, H., 105
Vygotsky, L. S., 488

Wachtel, P. L., 36, 68, 258, 261, 322
Wagner, L., 349
Wagner, S., 343, 520
Wakefield, J. C., 6
Waldinger, R. J., 69
Walker, M., 124
Waller, N. G., 84
Wallerstein, R., 94
Walsh, T., 401
Ware, P., 194, 196
Warren, C. S., 255
Washousky, R. C., 401
Watkins, J. T., 519
Watkins, P. C., 171
Watson, J. B., 59, 532
Watson, J. S., 477
Webster-Stratton, C., 480, 490
Wei, T., 460
Weinberger, J. L., 18
Weiner, A. S., 10, 12, 71, 467
Weisaeth, L., 17, 127
Weishaar, M. E., 402, 403, 404, 415
Weiss, J., 259
Weiss, L., 79
Weissman, M. M., 10, 135, 356, 400, 401, 519
Welch, S. S., 250
Welker, R., 281, 287, 301
Wells, K. C., 480
Wepman, J. M., 3
West, C., 11, 18
Westen, D., 25, 26
Westlake, R., 498
Whiffen, V. E., 430
Whitehead, C., 86
Widiger, T. A., 81, 84
Wiedemann, K., 461
Wierson, M., 490
Wiggins, J. S., 39

Wilber, K., 64, 528
Wilberg, T., 370, 371, 373
Wilcox, J., 346
Wilkinson, S. M., 482
Williams, D. T., 349
Williams, J., 323, 517
Williams, R. B., 428
Williamson, D. A., 171
Wills, T. A., 428
Wilson, E. O., 64, 528
Wilson, S. A., 323
Winnicott, C., 61
Winnicott, D., 115, 120, 300, 379, 381, 382, 486, 487
Winston, A., 7, 427, 514, 517, 518
Winston, B., 427
Winter, D. G., 15, 18
Wittchen, H. U., 137
Wolfson, A. N., 338
Wolpe, J., 308
Woodman, C. L., 350, 351

Woody, G., 189, 190, 401, 416, 514
Woo-Ming, A. M., 520, 521
Wright, F. D., 173
Wright, J. H., 179

Yalom, I. D., 49, 217, 364
Yang, J., 135
Yao, S., 135
Yeh, E. K., 136
Yehuda, R., 97, 323, 460, 461
Yeomans, F. E., 70, 111, 114, 116
Young, J. E., 68, 140, 173, 184, 398, 399, 402, 403, 404, 406, 409, 415, 418, 542
Yudofsky, S. C., 348, 349
Yule, W., 189

Zaat, J. O. M., 429
Zanarini, M. C., 221, 343, 344, 345, 346, 467
Zimmerman, M., 10, 350, 351
Zlotnick, C., 413
Zweig-Frank, H., 140, 141, 467

Subject Index

ABC (affect/behavior/cognition), 161
Active-passive polarity, 8, 30, 79, 80, 88
Adaptive Information Processing Model, 305
ADHD (Attention-Deficit Hyperactivity Disorder), 219, 467, 471
Adjustment disorders and personality adaptations, 201
Adolescents/youth:
  cultural differences, 136–137
  dramatic personality disorders in (*see* Children/adolescents, treatment of dramatic personality disorders in)
  treatment models, 70–71
Affect(s):
  ABC (affect/behavior/cognition), 161
  cognitive/subjective/subjective components, 103
  low tolerance for (EMDR), 320–321
  motivational aspects of personality organization, 96–99
  storms, transference-focused management of, 112–117
Affective restructuring, 543
Affective science, emergence of, 63
Aggression, 96–99
Aging. *See* Elderly, treatment of personality disorders in
Agreeableness, 7, 81, 82, 83, 88
Alliance building, 178–180, 472–473
Animal models of attachment and separation, 533–534
Anorexia Nervosa, 455
Anticonvulsant mood stabilizers, 345–346, 349
Antidepressants, 336, 343
Antipsychotic medications, 348–349
  atypical, 335, 343–344
  typical, 336, 344–345
Antisocial personality adaptations (promoters/charming-manipulators), 195, 196, 206–207
Antisocial Personality Disorder:
  adaptations, 201
  borderline personality organization and, 100
  cognitive therapy, 189
  day treatment, 371
  developmental factors, 103
  effectiveness of cognitive-behavioral treatment, 188, 189
  empirical research, psychotherapy, 517

  expression across domains of clinical science, 34
  medication, 348–350
  outcomes, 401
  social factors in, 137–138, 144
Anxiety disorders, 12
Anxiolytics, 346–347
Anxious/fearful personality disorders (Cluster C), 7, 8, 12, 144, 350–351, 400, 429
Arrogance, syndrome of, 116
Assessment. *See* Psychopathologic assessment
Attachment, 17, 61, 532–534
Attention-Deficit Hyperactivity Disorder (ADHD), 219, 467, 471
Avoidant Personality Disorder:
  adaptations, 196
  behavior therapy, 522
  clinical recommendations, 522
  cognitive conceptualizations/treatment, 187, 188, 189
  dreaming, 448
  elderly, 501
  expression across domains of clinical science, 34
  medications, 45, 332, 350, 521
  modality selection, 51
  movement, avoiding, 449
  noncompliance/resistance, 185–186
  polarity goals, 48
  psychotherapy, empirical research on, 514–515
  social factors in, 138–139
  social phobia and, 12
Axis I disorders, relation of Axis II diagnosis to the outcome of treatment for, 518–519

Behavior(s):
  ABC (affect/behavior/cognition), 161
  dysregulation, 223
  expressive (parallel therapies), 38
  quality-of-life interfering, 238–239
  therapy-interfering, 238
Behavioral analysis, 228
Behavioral experiments, 176
Behavioral inertia, 333–334
Behavioral therapy, 38, 522. *See also* Cognitive therapy
Behaviorism, rise of, 59–60
Beta blockers, 349–350

Big Five model, 80–85
Biopsychosocial model, 13–14
Biosocial-learning theory, 78–79
Biosocial theory of Borderline Personality Disorder, 222–223
Bipolar Disorder, 156
Borderline Personality Disorder, 92–117
  adaptations, 196
  biosocial theory of, 222–223
  case examples, 239–249, 454
  cognitive-behavioral model/treatment, 66, 184, 186, 187, 188, 189
  critique of (RCT perspective), 125–128
  day treatment, 369, 371
  depression and, 12
  dialectical behavior therapy (DBT) for, 221, 223, 515–516
  expression across domains of clinical science, 34
  interpersonal reconstructive therapy (IRT) and, 165
  medications, 337–347, 520, 522
  movement, 449
  neurotransmitters/neuroimaging study, 97, 460
  personality organization, 100
  psychotherapy for, 515–517
  recovery, 140
  residential treatment, 385
  self-psychology based dynamic therapy for, 516–517
  sexual abuse in etiology of, 126
  social factors in, 138
  social structures, role of (in treatment), 144
  trait modification therapy, 141–142
Borderline personality organization, 8, 69, 71, 99–100, 447
  developmental perspective, 71
  Dissociative Identity Disorder and, 447
  etiology and psychopathology, 101–104
  motivational aspects of personality organization: affects and drives, 96–99
  normal personality organization, 92–96
  personality disorders with, 100
  psychoanalytic model of nosology, 99–101
  suicidal risk management, 110–112
  therapeutic strategy (psychodynamic psychotherapy), 104–110
  transference-focused management of affect storms, 112–117
  youngsters, 477
Brief focused therapy. See Time-limited dynamic psychotherapy
Butterfly Effect, 15

Case management strategies, 227, 234–235
Castastrophizing, 170
Catalytic sequences, 51
Categorical classification of personality (DSM clusters), 6–7
Certainty, avoiding "pathological" theoretical, 549

Change:
  continuous, principle of, 225
  enabling will to, 163–164
  mechanisms of, 166, 186–187, 249–250, 321–323, 437
  natural, 234
  resistance to, 356
  theory of, 153
  therapeutic process (case example), 155–164
Channels, 106
Chaos and complexity theory, 14–15
Character, 60, 86, 92, 93
Children/adolescents, treatment of dramatic personality disorders in, 467–494. See also Adolescents/youth
  case illustration, 474–475
  facilitating interventions and the therapeutic bargain, 487–489
  family role/treatment, 470, 472, 489–493
  interventions to enhance mentalization, strengthen impulse control, and create awareness of other's mental state, 475–480
  pharmacotherapy as adjunct to mentalization and support of parent's competence, 471–472
  representational mismatch, 469–471
  stages of treatment, 469–471, 472–473, 483–487
  termination, 493–494
  transference/countertransference, 480–483, 484
Chronic Fatigue Syndrome, 430
Chronic illness, older adults, 502
Circumplex representation, 38–39
Classification of personality, 4–9
  categorical, 6–7
  dimensional, 7, 78–89
  prototypal, 8, 31, 32
  relational, 8
  structural-dynamic, 7–8, 92–96
  subtypes, 30–31, 80
Classification of personality disorders:
  application of, to therapeutic strategy, 35–36
  Cluster A (odd/eccentric) personality disorders, 7, 8, 12, 84, 144, 335–337, 400
  Cluster B (dramatic/erratic) personality disorders, 7, 8, 12, 84–85, 144, 337–350, 400, 429, 502 (see also Children/adolescents, treatment of dramatic personality disorders in)
  Cluster C (anxious/fearful) personality disorders, 7, 8, 12, 144, 350–351, 400, 429
  DSM criteria/clusters, 7, 8, 32–33, 62
    as barrier, 26
    development of, 62
    further study, appendixes of DSM-III-R and DSM-IV, 79, 80
    problems with, 7
    structural spectrum, overlay, 8
  utility of diagnostic classifications, 24–28
Client-centered therapy (CCT), 520

Clinical Evaluation Profile (CEP), 373
Clinical recommendations based on research
    literature, 522–523
Clinical utility:
    of diagnostic classifications, 24–28
    of theory, 72–73
Clinician as clinical theorist, 73
Close process attention method, in
        psychoanalytic psychotherapy, 280–302
    analysis of defense, 282–284
    analytic surface, 284–285
    clinical case example, 288–292
    close process monitoring in psychoanalysis,
        287–288
    defined, 281–282
    Histrionic Personality Disorder, treatment of,
        293–296
    inside focus, 282
    interpretation, four steps to mutative, 287
    paranoid process, treatment of, 296–298
    personality disorders and, 293
    psychoanalysis *vs.*, 298–301
    resistances, 285–286
    superego function, analyst's, 285–287
Cluster A (odd/eccentric) personality
        disorders, 7, 8, 12, 84, 144, 335–337, 400
Cluster B (dramatic/erratic) personality
        disorders, 7, 8, 12, 84–85, 144, 337–350, 400,
        429, 502. *See also* Children/adolescents,
        treatment of dramatic personality
        disorders in
Cluster C (anxious/fearful) personality
        disorders, 7, 8, 12, 144, 350–351, 400, 429
Cognition, 427
Cognitive assessment domains/parallel
        therapies, 40–41
Cognitive-behavioral models of personality
        disorders, 66
Cognitive-behavioral restructuring, 543
Cognitive dysregulation, 224
Cognitive-interpersonal cycle, 171
Cognitive modification, 228, 231–232
Cognitive restructuring, 542–543
Cognitive revolution, 63
Cognitive therapy, 40–41, 169–191, 505
    alliance building, 178–180
    assessment phase, 178
    case example, 181–184
    common cognitive distortions, 170
    effectiveness, 187–190
    general principles, 174
    how therapeutic challenges are
        conceptualized and managed, 184–186
    mechanisms of change and therapeutic
        action, 186–187
    older adults, 505
    process of therapeutic approach, 178–181
    range of psychopathology and personality
        disorders within scope of treatment, 173
    relapse prevention, 177–178
    research and empirical support, 187–190
    self-monitoring, 175
    termination, 180–181

theoretical components of model, 169–173
    treatment methods and technical aspects or
        interventions, 173–178
    validity of cognitive conceptualizations of
        personality disorder, 187
Communication style strategies, 227, 234
Comorbidity, 12
    medication choice and, 334–335
    older adults, 501–502
    substance abuse, 399–400
Compensatory subtype, 80
Complexity theory, 14–15
Complex syndromes, treatment goals, 36–45
Compulsive personalities, 34, 35, 45, 501. *See
        also* Obsessive-Compulsive Personality
        Disorder
Computer modeling, 15–16
Conditioning (operant/instrumental;
        respondent/classical), 224
Conflicted/deficient/imbalanced personality,
        79
Cons, confronting, 203
Conscientiousness (five-factor model of
        personality), 7, 81, 83
Consciousness, emergence of neuroscience and
        study of, 63
Consilience, concept of, 64
Contact, 202
Contact doors, 196
Containing/holding function, 115, 382–383. *See
        also* Residential treatment
Contingency management, 228, 230–231
Continuous change, principle of, 225
Continuum, personality pattern, 37
Contracting, 202–203
Cooperativeness (character dimension), 86,
        88
COPES (Community-Oriented Programs
        Environment Scale), 372
Coping styles, maladaptive, 403–404
Copy processes (identification/recapitulation/
        introjection), 152
Core beliefs, identifying/modifying, 177
Core conflictual relationship theme (CCRT)
        method, 275
Corrective emotional experience, 259–260
Counterinjunctions, 199
Counter-subjects, 32
Countertransference, 107, 258, 480–483,
        505–506. *See also* Transference
Couples therapy (modality of treatment,
        unified model), 548
Culture-bound, 135
Cyclical maladaptive pattern (CMP), 261, 275,
        276
Cyclical psychodynamic model, 68
Cyclothymic, 102

Dance, and self-memory, 448
Day treatment, 356–377, 521
    clinical case example, 364–368
    description, 357
    empirical studies, 368–374

Day treatment (*Continued*)
example (Edmonton Day Treatment
Program), 359–364
groups that are not phase-specific, 361
large psychotherapy group, 363
organizational features, 361–362
phases, 360–361
small psychodynamic group, 363–364
staff relations group, 362–363
features making it effective for personality
disorders, 358
practical implications of research findings,
375–376
DEAR MAN (acronym for skills), 230
Decontamination work, 203
Defense, analysis of, 282–284
Defense mechanisms, 43
Defensive restructuring, 435, 540–542
Deficient/imbalanced/conflicted personality,
79
Dementia in older adults, 501–502. *See also*
Elderly, treatment of personality
disorders in
Democratization, 358
Dependent Personality Disorder:
adaptations, 196, 201
cognitive-behavioral treatment, 188
cognitive conceptualizations, 187
day treatment, 370
developmental lines, 102
expression across domains of clinical
science, 34
medication, 350–351
modality selection, 51
older adults, 501
psychotherapy, empirical research on, 517
Depression:
cognitive therapy and, 189
comorbidity, 12, 501
Dual Focus Schema Therapy (DFST) for
depressed women with childhood sexual
abuse histories, 413–414
Depressive-Masochistic Personality Disorder,
98, 102
Depressive Personality Disorder, 12, 34, 80
Developmental personology/perspective, 19,
71, 94–96, 102, 103, 123–125
Devil's advocate strategy, 233
Dialectical behavior therapy of severe
personality disorders, 70, 221–251, 521
allowing natural change, 234
assessment, 234, 235–236
behavioral analysis, 228
biosocial theory of Borderline Personality
Disorder, 222–223
Borderline Personality Disorder, 239–249,
515–516
case management strategies, 227, 234–235
clinical case example, 239–249
cognitive modification, 228, 231–232
communication style strategies, 227, 234
consultation team meeting, 227
contingency management, 228, 230–231
core treatment principles:

dialectics, 225
learning theory, 224
principle of continuous change, 225
principle of interrelatedness and
wholeness, 225
principle of polarity, 225
Zen, 224–225
Devil's advocate technique, 233
entering the paradox, 233
environmental intervention, 235
exposure, 228, 231
extending, 233
generalizing learning: telephone coaching,
226–227
how therapeutic challenges are
conceptualized and managed, 249
"making lemonade out of lemons," 234
mechanisms of change and therapeutic
action, 249–250
metaphor technique, 233
problem-solving strategies, 226, 228
process of therapeutic approach, 235–239
range of psychopathology within scope of
treatment, 225–226
research and empirical support, 250–251, 521
skills training, 226, 228, 229, 239
stages of treatment, 236–239
strategies:
balancing, 227–232, 233
core, 227
dialectical, 227, 233–234
synthesis, 239
targets, 237–239, 243–244
theoretical components of model, 221–225
treatment methods and technical aspects
and interventions, 226–233
validation strategies, 232–233
wise mind, 233–234
Diathesis-stress model, 14, 430
Dichotomous thinking, 170
Dimensional classification of personality, 7,
78–89
evolutionary model (Millon), 78–80
Five-Factor Model, 80–85
Rorschach Descriptive Model, 87–88
Seven-Factor Model, 85–87
Disconfirmation, experiential, 259
Disconnection, relational. *See* Personality
disorder(s), *vs.* relational disconnection
Disqualifying the positive, 170
Dissociative abyss, 453–454
Distress tolerance skills, 229
Domain-based *vs.* school-based language, 530
Domain-oriented assessment (and parallel
therapeutic modalities), 34, 38–45
cognitive modes, 40–41
expression of personality disorders across
domains of clinical science, 34
expressive behaviors, 38
interpersonal/relational conduct, 38–40
intrapsychic assessment domains, 42–44
intrapsychic objects, 42
morphologic organization, 43–44
regulatory mechanisms, 42–43

mood/temperament, 44–45
self-image, 41–42
Dramatic personality disorders (Cluster B), 7, 8, 12, 84–85, 144, 337–350, 400, 429, 502. *See also* Children/adolescents, treatment of dramatic personality disorders in
Dreaming, 448
Drives, 96–99
D-score, 87
Dual Focus Schema Therapy (DFST), 398–421
connection between substance abuse and personality disorders, 399–402
rates of co-occurrence, 399–400
symptom severity and outcome, 400–401
Type A and Type B substance abusers, 401–402
for depressed women with childhood sexual abuse histories, 413–414
discussion, 417–421
in a drug-free therapeutic community, 411–412
for homeless personality-disordered substance abusers, 412–413
implementation issues, 414–417
manual development pilot project, 407–408
for personality-disordered opiate abusers, 407–414
proposed Stage II study in methadone-maintained patients, 410–411
randomized controlled pilot trial, 408–410
specification of psychotherapy for personality disorders, 398–399
study sample characteristics, 408–409
therapist selection and training procedures, 416–417
training issues, 414–417
treatment constructs and model, 402–407
as treatment enhancement, 414–415
treatment outcomes, 400–401, 409–410
Dyadic relationships (family system diagram), 69
Dyadic restructuring, 544–546
expected-transactive restructuring, 544
relational dyadic restructuring, 545–546
self-other restructuring, 545
Dynamic psychotherapy. *See* Time-limited dynamic psychotherapy
Dysthymia, 370

Early decisions, 200
Early scene work, 203–204
Eating disorders, 12
EB variable, 87
Eclecticism:
systematic, 528
technical, 28
Ecological model, systemically based, 531–534
Ego-adaptive capacity, 8
Ego development, 94
Ego identity, 93
Ego psychology, 65, 299
Ego states, 198

Elderly, treatment of personality disorders in, 71, 498–509
community mental health model for treatment of personality disorders in:
assessment and comorbid diagnosis, 501–502
case study, 506–509
cognitive-behavioral therapy (CBT), 505
countertransference reactions, 505–506
medication treatment, 502–503
presenting to treatment, 499–500
team, multidisciplinary, 502
treatment approaches and techniques, 504–505
treatment setting, 503–504
personality and aging, 452–453
prevalence rates, 498
primary care physician's role, 500–501
self-referral, 499
Elitist subtype, 80
Emotional reasoning, 170
Emotional stability/instability, 81, 320
Emotion regulation/dysregulation, 222–223, 229
Empathy, 132, 159–160
Escape hatches, 200–201
Etiology. *See* Personality disorder(s), etiology
Evolutionary model (Millon), 78–80
Evolution as natural framework, 29–32
Expectations of others' reactions, 262, 263
Expected-transactive restructuring, 544
Experiential disconfirmation, 259
Exposure, 228, 231
Expressive behaviors/therapies, 38
Extending, 233
Extraversion, 7, 81, 82, 83, 84, 85, 88
Eye Movement Desensitization and Reprocessing (EMDR), 65, 304–325
clinical case examples, 312–320
how therapeutic challenges are conceptualized and managed:
distorted perceptions of relationships, 321
emotional instability and acting out, 320
lack of self-referencing skills, 321
low tolerance for affect, 320–321
mechanisms of change and therapeutic action, 321–323
process of therapeutic approach, 311–312
range of psychopathology and personality disorders within scope of treatment, 305
research and empirical support, 323–325
stabilization, 311
target, 306
theoretical components, 304–305
treatment methods and technical aspects and interventions, 305–312
phase 1 history, 306
phase 2 client preparation, 306–307
phase 3 assessment, 307–308
phase 4 desensitization, 308–309
phase 5 installation, 309–310
phase 6 body scan, 310
phase 7 closure, 310
phase 8 reevaluation, 310

Eye Movement Desensitization and
    Reprocessing (EMDR) *(Continued)*
  working in the future, 311–312
  working in the past, 311
  working in the present, 311

Family:
  level of differentiation, 67
  models, 67, 69
  personality disorders, and
      constellation/dysfunction, 17–18
  restructuring dysfunctional systems, 547
  systems theory, 67
  therapy, 39, 489–493, 548
  triangles, 67
Fantasy, use of, 197
Five-factor model (FFM), 7, 80–85
Fortune-telling, 170
Fractionation, 468
Frame/framing, 105, 202
Free association, 300
Functional domains, 33

Games/game analysis, 198–199, 203
Gender role socialization, 459–461
General system theory, 14, 61
Genetic code, reading, 539–540
Genetic factors, 16–17, 69
Genuineness of therapist, 42
Gestalt techniques, 197–198
Gift of love (GOL), 153
Global Severity Index (GSI), 369
Goodness of fit (family system diagram), 69
Grandiosity, 142
Gregariousness, 82
Grounding techniques, 479
Group therapy, 40, 548
Growth collaborator (Green), 153, 160
Guided discovery, 175

Harm Avoidance, 85–86, 87, 88, 92
Health risk behaviors, 428
Health Sickness Rating Scale (HSRS), 373
Heterogeneity, 332–333
History. *See* Personology/psychotherapeutic
    approaches, history/trends/evolution
Histrionic adaptation (enthusiastic-
    overreactors), 196, 210
Histrionic Personality Disorder:
  adaptations, 201
  close process attention method, 280, 293–296
  cognitive-behavioral treatment, 188
  developmental lines, 102
  expression across domains of clinical
      science, 34
  medication, 348
  psychotherapy, empirical research on, 517
  Rorschach descriptive model and, 88
Holding/containing function, 115, 382–383. *See
    also* Residential treatment
Holographic metaphor, 529
Holonic model, 528
Homeless personality-disordered substance
    abusers, 412–413

Homeostasis, 49
Hospitalization. *See* Day treatment; Residential
    treatment
Human evolution, 29–31
Human habit system, 26–27
Humor, 449
Hypochondriacal Personality Disorder, 100,
    103
Hypomanic Personality Disorder, 100, 102
Hysteric adaptation (reactors), 195
Hysterical Personality Disorder, 98, 102

Id/ego/superego, 8, 65, 93, 94, 96, 198,
    285–287, 299
Identification, 152
Identity diffusion, syndrome of, 104
Illness. *See* Medical patients, personality-
    guided therapy for treating
Imagination, 81
Imbalanced/conflicted/deficient personality,
    79
Important persons and their internalized
    representations (IPIRs), 152, 167
Impulse control, strengthening impulse control
    (children/adolescents), 477–479
Impulsivity and affective instability (two
    underlying traits, Borderline Personality
    Disorder), 141
Infants, naturalistic observations of, 533
Injunctions, 199
Inpatient treatment. *See* Day treatment;
    Residential treatment
Integrative psychotherapy movement/models,
    62–63, 67–68
Intermittent life-cycle treatment (unified
    model), 549
Internal mediating processes, 44
International Society for the Study of
    Personality Disorders (ISSPD), 62
Interpersonal:
  assessment domains, and parallel therapies,
      38–40
  behavior, changing, 176–177
  cognitive-interpersonal cycle (diagram), 171
  effectiveness skills, 229
  models, 8, 66
  psychiatry, development of, 61
  relationships, medical patients, 427
Interpersonal-dyadic triangle (two-person
    system), 8, 536–537
Interpersonal Reconstructive Therapy (IRT),
    151–167
  gift of love (GOL), 153
  growth collaborator (Green), 153, 160
  how therapeutic challenges are
      conceptualized and managed, 164–166
  important persons and their internalized
      representations (IPIRs), 152, 167
  mechanisms of change and therapeutic
      action, 166
  range of psychopathology and personality
      disorders within scope of treatment,
      153–154
  regressive loyalist (Red), 153, 160

research and empirical support, 166–167
rules, 154
  including affect (A), behavior (B) and
    cognition (C), 161
  relating interventions to the case
    formulation, 160–161
  relating interventions to the five steps, 161
  seeking concrete illustrative detail about
    input, response, and impact on self,
    161
  supporting growth collaborator (Green)
    more than regressive loyalist (Red),
    160
  working from baseline of accurate
    empathy, 159–160
steps, 154–155
  blocking problem patterns, 163
  collaboration, 162
  enabling will to change, 163–164
  learning about your patterns, 162–163
  learning new patterns, 164
technical interventions, 161–164
theoretical components, 151–153
treatment methods and technical aspects or
  interventions, 154–155
Interpretation, 105, 287
Intimacy, avoidance of, 449
Intrapsychic assessment domains:
  intrapsychic objects, 42
  morphologic organization, 43–44
  parallel intrapsychic therapies, 44
  regulatory mechanisms, 42–43
Intrapsychic-biological triangle (individual
  system), 536
Intrapsychic restructuring:
  affective restructuring, 543
  cognitive-behavioral restructuring, 543
  cognitive restructuring, 542–543
  defensive restructuring, 540–542
  neurobiological restructuring, 544
Introjection, 152

Labeling (cognitive distortion), 170
Labels, pathological (useful *vs.* pejorative), 5,
  8–9
Learning, generalizing (telephone coaching),
  226–227
Learning theory, 224
Lexical hypothesis, 81
Libido, 96
Life-cycle treatment, intermittent, 549
Life positions/scripts, 200
Light, 447, 459
Lithium, 345–346, 349
Long-term treatment (unified model), 549
Love (attachment theory/relational matrix),
  532–533

Machine model, 50–51
Macrotreatment/microtreatment, 85
Maintenance treatment (unified model), 549
Malignant Narcissism Syndrome, 100, 103
MAOIs (monoamine oxidase inhibitors),
  342–343, 350, 351

Masochistic disorders, 34, 80, 98, 102
Maximization/minimization, 170
Medical model, diagnosis and, 130
Medical patients, personality-guided therapy
  for treating, 426–440
  clinical case example, 432–437
  coping with illness, 430–432
  health risk behaviors, 428
  mechanisms of change, 437
  multidirectional relationship between
    personality and physical health, 427–432
  somatoform disorders, 429–430
  team approach (importance of), 437–438
  therapeutic challenges, 439
Medications. *See* Pharmacotherapy
Mentalization, 468, 472–473, 475–480, 490–493
Mesosystem restructuring (MR), 547
Meta-analysis of treatment of personality
  disorders, 513–514
Metaphor strategy, 233
Methadone-maintained patients, proposed
  Stage II study, 410–411
Milieu therapy, 548
Millon Clinical Multiaxial Inventory
  (MCMI-I/II/III), 79–80, 84, 88
Millon Index of Personality Styles (MIPS), 79
Mind-body medicine, 426
Mindfulness kills, 229
Mind-reading, 170
Minorities, treatment models for, 71–72
Mixed Personality Disorder, 191
Modeling, 224
Monoamine oxidase inhibitors (MAOIs),
  342–343, 350, 351
Mood/temperament therapies, 44–45
Moral aspects of self-memory, 455–457
Morphologic organization, 43–44, 49
Motivational aspects of personality
  organization (affects/drives), 96–99
Movement through time, development of,
  448–452
Multimodal therapy, 28
Multiple family therapy (modality of
  treatment, unified model), 548

Narcissism Syndrome, Malignant, 100, 103
Narcissistic Character Disorder with
  borderline features, 453
Narcissistic Personality Disorder:
  borderline personality organization, 100
  cognitive conceptualizations/treatment, 187,
    188
  developmental line, 103
  expression across domains of clinical
    science, 34
  medication, 347–348
  psychotherapy, empirical research on, 517
  SASB model example, 152
  social factors in, 138
  subtypes, 80
  trait modification therapy, 142–143
  youngsters, 473, 481, 483
Nature *vs.* nurture, 85, 333
Negativistic Personality Disorder, 34

NEO Inventory (NEO-PI/NEO-PI-R), 81, 83–84
Neurobiological restructuring, 544
Neurobiology of personality disorders, 69, 457–459, 533–534
Neuroscience, emergence of (and study of consciousness), 63
Neuroticism, 7, 81, 82, 85
Neurotic personality organization, 8, 100–101
Neutrality, technical, 105–106
Normal personality, structural characteristics, 92–96
Novelty Seeking, 85, 88, 92

Object-centered interventions, 115
Object relations, 39, 65, 93–94, 104. *See also* Time-limited dynamic psychotherapy
Object representations, 49
Obsessive-Compulsive adaptation (responsible-workaholic), 195, 196, 201, 209–210
Obsessive-Compulsive Personality Disorder, 98, 103, 515
    adaptations, 201
    clinical recommendations, 522
    cognitive conceptualizations/treatment, 187, 188
    expression across domains of clinical science, 34
    medication, 351
Openness to Experience domain, 7, 81, 82–83, 85
Operant/instrumental conditioning, 224
Opioid antagonists, 347
Oral/anal/genital characters, 98
Organization. *See* Personality, organization
Over-generalization, 170

Panic Disorder, 351
Paradigmatic shift, 62
Paradox, entering the, 233
Paranoid adaptation (brilliant-skeptic/persisters), 195, 196, 207–208
Paranoid Personality Disorder
    borderline personality organization, 100
    cognitive conceptualizations/treatment, 187, 188
    developmental line, 103
    expression across domains of clinical science, 34
    medication, 336
    older adults, 502
    psychotherapy, empirical research on, 517
Paranoid process, close process attention method, 280, 296–298
Parents, 470, 472, 489–493
Passive Aggressive adaptation (playful-resister/rebels), 195, 196, 208–209
Passive Aggressive Personality Disorder:
    adaptations, 201
    cognitive-behavioral treatment, 188
    interpersonal reconstructive therapy and, 165
    Oppositional Disorder and, 156
    psychotherapy, empirical research on, 517

Pathogenic processes, three levels of:
    complex syndromes, 36
    personality patterns (styles/disorders), 36
    simple reactions, 36
Pathological labels (useful *vs.* pejorative), 5, 8–9
Patterns. *See* Personality, patterns
Permissiveness, 358
Persistence, 85, 92
Personality:
    classification (*see* Classification of personality)
    deficient/imbalanced/conflicted, 79
    defining, 5–6
    mutability of, 18–19
    organization:
        Axis II clusters and, 8
        borderline, 8, 69, 71, 99–100, 447
        morphologic organization, 43–44, 49
        motivational aspects of (affects/drives), 96–99
        neurotic, 8, 100–101
        normal, 92–96
        psychotic, 8, 99
    patterns:
        continuum, 37
        interpersonal reconstructive therapy and, 162–164
        maladaptive, 257–258, 261, 275, 276
        vs. personality styles/disorders/traits, 36, 93
    stability of, 18–19
    subtypes, 30–31, 80 (*see also* Classification of personality)
    systemics, 19–20, 531
    theory (*see* Theory)
    trait, 93
Personality disorder(s). *See also specific disorder:*
    assessment (*see* Psychopathologic assessment)
    characteristics, 356
    classification (*see* Classification of personality disorders)
    as construct, 5
    co-occurring conditions, 12 (*see also* Comorbidity)
    day treatment, 356–377
    diagnosis, 5, 8–9, 32–35, 130–131
    differential therapeutics, 4
    etiology, 13–20
        attachment experience, 17
        biopsychosocial model, 13–14
        chaos and complexity theory, 14–15
        computer modeling, 15
        computer network model, 15–16
        developmental personology, 19
        diathesis-stress model, 14
        factors, 16–18
        family constellation and dysfunction, 17–18
        general system theory, 14
        genetic predisposition, 16–17
        personality, mutability of, 18–19

personality systemics, 19–20, 531
sociocultural and political forces, 18
traumatic events, 17
as harmful dysfunction, 6
hospitalization (*see* Day treatment;
    Residential treatment)
impact of, 11–12
interest in, early history, 3–4
medication (*see* Pharmacotherapy)
mutual relationships (diagram), 102
pathological labels (useful *vs.* pejorative), 5,
    8–9
patient populations (*see* Children/
    adolescents, treatment of dramatic
    personality disorders in; Dual Focus
    Schema Therapy (DFST); Medical
    patients, personality-guided therapy for
    treating; Elderly, treatment of
    personality disorders in)
prevalence in contemporary society, 9–13
vs. relational disconnection, 120–132
    avoiding retreat into diagnosis/labels/
        theory, 130–131
    prevalence of sexual abuse in etiology of
        borderline patients, 126
    PTSD, 122, 127, 128, 129
    relational-cultural theory (RCT), 120–121
    relational development *vs.* personality
        development, 123–125
    relational stance, 128–130
    role of mutual empathy in therapeutic
        process, 121–123
    shame/disconnection/isolation, 123
research on (*see* Research)
social sensitivity and, 136
stigma of label, 5
as trauma disorders, 461–462
treatment models, contemporary (*see* Close
    process attention method, in
    psychoanalytic psychotherapy; Cognitive
    therapy; Dialectical behavior therapy of
    severe personality disorders; Eye
    Movement Desensitization and
    Reprocessing (EMDR); Interpersonal
    Reconstructive Therapy (IRT);
    Redecision therapy; Time-limited
    dynamic psychotherapy)
unified model of (*see* Unified model)
Personality-guided relational therapy, 529
Personality-guided therapy, 13, 27–28
Personalization, 170
Personology/psychotherapeutic approaches,
    history/trends/evolution, 58–64
    1890–1949 (early modern personology and
        psychotherapy), 58–60
    development of character analytic
        approaches, 60
    development of psychoanalysis, 59
    emergence of trait psychology as a
        dominant force in psychology, 60
    formal study of personality theory as a
        separate discipline, 60
    rise of behaviorism, 59–60

single school and dueling school phase,
    58–59
1959–1979 (later modern personology and
    psychotherapy), 60–61
    development of attachment theory, 61
    development of interpersonal psychiatry,
        61
    emergence of psychopharmacological
        treatment of major mental disorders,
        61
    emergence of system theory, 61
    rapprochement among dominant school
        phase, 60–61
1980–1999 (contemporary personology and
    psychotherapy), 62–63
    advances in psychopharmacology
        treatment, 62
    cognitive revolution, 63
    development of DSM and the emphasis on
        personality disorders, 62
    emergence of affective science, 63
    emergence of neuroscience and the study
        of consciousness, 63
    integrative movement phase, 62
    rediscovery of trauma theory, 63
    rise of the integrative psychotherapy
        movement, 62–63
2000–present (unified personology and
    psychotherapy), 63–64
    call for unified model for social and
        biological science, 64
    development of Millon's model for
        unification, 64
    Sternberg's call for unification of
        psychology, 64
    unification phase, 63–64
developmental, 19
Pharmacotherapy, 331–352
    antidepressants, 336, 343
    antipsychotic medications, 348–349
        atypical, 335, 343–344
        typical, 336, 344–345
    axiolytics, 346–347
    beta blockers, 349–350
    children/adolescents, 471–472
    Cluster A (odd/eccentric), 335–337
        Paranoid Personality Disorder, 336
        Schizoid Personality Disorder, 336
        Schizotypal Personality Disorder, 335–336
    Cluster B (dramatic/erratic), 337–350
        Antisocial Personality Disorder, 348
        Borderline Personality Disorder, 337–347
        Histrionic Personality Disorder, 348
        Narcissistic Personality Disorder, 347–348
    Cluster C (anxious/fearful), 350–351
        Avoidant Personality Disorder, 350
        Dependent Personality Disorder, 350–351
        Obsessive-Compulsive Personality
            Disorder, 351
    empirical research, 519–521, 522
        Avoidant Personality Disorder, 521
        Borderline Personality Disorder, 520
        Schizotypal Personality Disorder, 520–521

Pharmacotherapy (Continued)
  lithium and anticonvulsant mood stabilizers,
      345–346, 349
  monoamine oxidase inhibitors (MAOIs),
      342–343, 350, 351
  older adults, 502–503
  opioid antagonists, 347
  perspectives, practical/theoretical
      perspectives:
    behavioral inertia, 333–334
    heterogeneity, 332–333
    nature vs. nurture, 333
    state vs. trait (transient vs. chronic), 332
  selective serotonin reuptake inhibitors
      (SSRIs), 336, 338–342, 349
  strategies for choosing a medication:
    algorithm, affective dysregulation
        symptoms, 339
    algorithm, cognitive-perceptual symptoms,
        341
    algorithm, impulsive-behavioral dyscontrol
        symptoms, 340
    comorbidity, 334–335
    spectrum traits, 334
  theoretical relevance, 61, 62, 66
  unified model, treatment modality, 548
Philosophy/theory, 28–35
Phobias, 98
Physical health, personality and, 427–432
  coping with illness, 430–432
  health risk behaviors, 428
  somatoform disorders, 429–430
Physician, primary care (role of, with older
    adults), 500–501
"Playing It Right" strategy, 478, 482
Polarity model/schema, 8
  active-passive, 8, 30, 79, 80, 88
  changes, 79
  dialectical worldview and, 225
  DSM personality disorders and, 79, 80
  evolutionary model, 30–32
  pleasure-pain, 8, 30, 31, 79, 80, 88
  principle of, 225
  self-other, 8, 30, 79, 80, 88
  therapy modalities and, 46
Potential space, concept of, 299
Potentiated pairings, 51
Problem-solving, 226, 228
Prototypal classification of personality, 8, 31,
    32
Psychoanalysis, development of, 59
Psychoanalytic model for classification of
    personality disorders, 93–94, 99–101
  borderline personality organization, 99–100
  neurotic personality organization, 100–101
  normal personality structure, and
      temperament/character, 92–96
  psychotic personality organization, 99
  severity dimension, 99
Psychoanalytic psychotherapy. See Close
    process attention method, in
    psychoanalytic psychotherapy
Psychobiological models, 66–67

Psychodynamic models:
  ego psychology, 65, 299
  object relations, 39, 65, 93–94, 104
  self psychology, 65, 516–517
  structural-drive theory, 65
Psychodynamic therapy, 70, 104–110
  for Borderline Personality Disorder, 516
  channels, 106
  group (day treatment), 363–364
  interpretation, 105
  steps, three consecutive, 104
  tactical approaches in each hour, 107–110
  technical neutrality, 105–106
  therapeutic frame, 105
  therapeutic strategy, 104–110
  therapeutic techniques, 105–107
  transference analysis, 105, 107–110
  treatment setting, 105
Psychoeducational intervention (unified
    model, modality), 548
Psychological structure (in family system
    diagram), 69
Psychopathologic assessment, 24–53
  application of informed classification to
      therapeutic strategy, 35–36
  clinical utility of diagnostic classifications,
      24–28
  complex syndrome treatment goals, 36–45
  domain-oriented assessment (and parallel
      therapeutic modalities), 34, 38–45
    cognitive modes, 40–41
    expression of personality disorders across
        domains of clinical science, 34
    expressive behaviors, 38
    interpersonal/relational conduct, 38–40
    intrapsychic objects, 42
    mood/temperament, 44–45
    morphologic organization, 43–44
    regulatory mechanisms, 42–43
    self-image, 41–42
  from philosophy to theory, 28–35
    creation of a meaningful personologic
        diagnosis, 32–35
    evolution as a natural framework, 29–32
    synergistic integration in a personality-
        guided context, 45–53
Psychopathology, theory of, 151–153
Psychotherapy, 513–522
  dynamic (see Time-limited dynamic
      psychotherapy)
  as education, 140
  empirical research on, 513–518
  first use of word, 4
  group (day treatment), 363
  history (see Personology/psychotherapeutic
      approaches, history/trends/evolution)
  individual (unified model), 548
  integrative, 62–63, 67–68
  method (see Close process attention method,
      in psychoanalytic psychotherapy)
  psychodynamic, 104–110
  specification of, for personality disorders,
      398–399

treatment models, contemporary (*see* Close process attention method, in psychoanalytic psychotherapy; Cognitive therapy; Dialectical behavior therapy of severe personality disorders; Eye Movement Desensitization and Reprocessing (EMDR); Interpersonal Reconstructive Therapy (IRT); Redecision therapy; Time-limited dynamic psychotherapy)

Psychotic personality organization, 8, 99

PTSD, 127–129, 305, 323, 333, 373, 460–461

Punctuated equilibrium, 50

Quality-of-life interfering behaviors, 238–239

Rackets/racket analysis, 198, 203

Rational-emotive therapy, 41

Rational responses, 175

Reaction formations, 98

Reactive types, 98

Reality confrontation, 358

Reality testing, 99, 445

Recapitulation, 152

Redecision therapy, 194–219
  adaptations, six basic, 194–195, 196
  basic assumptions, 197
  clinical case example, 211–217
  process of therapeutic approach, 204–211
    brilliant-skeptic (paranoid), 207–208
    charming-manipulators (antisocial), 206–207
    combined adaptations, 210–211
    creative-daydreamer (schizoid), 206
    enthusiastic-overreactors (histrionic), 210
    playful-resister (Passive-Aggressive), 208–209
    responsible-workaholics (Obsessive-Compulsive), 209–210
  range of psychopathology and personality disorders within scope of treatment, 201
  research and empirical support, 217–219
  theoretical components, 195–201
    contact doors, 196
    Gestalt techniques, 197–198
    redecision therapy, 196–197
  transactional analysis concepts, 198–201
  treatment methods and technical aspects or interventions, 202–204

Reflective functioning, 299

Regressive loyalist (Red), 153, 160

Relapse prevention, 177–178

Relational classification of personality, 8

Relational-cultural theory (RCT), 120–125
  consideration of sociocultural/economic/political factors, 124
  emphasizing chronic disconnection instead of psychopathology, 124–125
  outcomes, 121
  PTSD and, 122
  relational development *vs.* personality development, 123–125

role of mutual empathy in therapeutic process, 121–123
  shame/disconnection/isolation, 123

Relational-dyadic restructuring, 545–546

Relational stance, 128–130

Relational-triadic restructuring/configuration, 8, 537–538, 546

Relationship(s):
  distorted perceptions of, 321
  dysregulation, 223
  maladaptive patterns of, 257–258
  self-memory and, 445

Representational mismatch, 469–471

Repression, 449

Research, 513–523
  clinical recommendations based on literature, 522–523
  difficulty of (unified model), 530
  empirical support:
    cognitive therapy, 187–190
    dialectical behavior therapy, 250–251
    Eye Movement Desensitization and Reprocessing (EMDR), 323–325
    interpersonal reconstructive therapy (IRT), 166–167
    redecision therapy, 217–219
    relational disconnection, 131–132
    time-limited dynamic psychotherapy, 274–276
    unified model of treatment, 550
  future directions, 523
  literature summary, 521–522
  psychopharmacological treatment, 519–521
    Avoidant Personality Disorder, 521
    Borderline Personality Disorder, 520
    Schizotypal Personality Disorder, 520–521
  psychotherapy for personality disorders, 513–522
    Avoidant Personality Disorder, 514–515
    Borderline Personality Disorder, 515–517
    meta-analysis of treatment of personality disorders, 513–514
    mixed Axis II samples, 517–519
    Obsessive-Compulsive Personality Disorder, 515
    relation of Axis II diagnosis to the outcome of treatment for Axis I disorders, 518–519
  theory and generation of, 73

Residential treatment, 379–396
  case illustration, 387–395
  characteristics of candidates for, 379–382
  containing function, 382–383
  effectiveness, 385–386
  phases of treatment in a psychodynamic therapeutic community, 386–387
  therapeutic community model, 383–385

Resistance, 185–186, 285–286, 356

Resister, playful (Passive Aggressive adaptation), 195, 196, 208–209

Respondent/classical conditioning, 224

Restructuring, 540
  affective, 543
  cognitive-behavioral, 543
  defensive, 540–542
  dyadic, 544–546
  dysfunctional family systems, 547
  expected-transactive, 544
  intrapsychic, 540–544
  maladaptive social systems, 547
  mesosystem (MR), 547
  neurobiological restructuring, 544
  relational dyadic, 545–546
  relational triadic, 546
  self-other, 545
  symbolic-relational, 546–547
  triadic, 546–547
Reward Dependence, 85, 86, 87, 92
Risk behaviors, health, 428
Rorschach Descriptive Model, 87–88
Rorschach Inkblot Test, 449

Sadistic Personality Disorders, 34, 80
SASB. *See* Structural Analysis of Social
  Behavior (SASB)
Schedule for Nonadaptive and Adaptive
  Personality (SNAP), 88–89
Schema(s), 41, 402–403
Schizoid adaptation (creative-daydreamer),
  195, 196, 206
Schizoid Personality Disorder:
  adaptations, 196, 201
  borderline personality organization, 100
  cognitive-behavioral treatment, 188
  developmental lines, 103
  DSM criteria, 32–33
  expression across domains of clinical
    science, 34
  heterogeneity, 332
  medication, 336
  polarity model/goals, 48, 79
  psychotherapy, empirical research on, 517
Schizophrenia, 12
Schizotypal Personality Disorder:
  adaptations, 196
  borderline personality organization, 100
  cognitive-behavioral treatment, 188
  day treatment, 369
  developmental line, 103
  expression across domains of clinical
    science, 34
  genetic influences, 93
  medication, 335–336, 520–521
  psychotherapy, empirical research on, 517
School-based *vs.* domain-based language,
  530
School phase, dominant, 58–61
Scripts, life, 200
Selective abstraction, 170
Selective serotonin reuptake inhibitors (SSRIs),
  336, 338–342, 349, 350, 351
Self:
  acts of, 262, 269
  acts of others toward, 262–263, 270

  acts of the self toward the (introject), 263, 270
  separate, 132
Self-actualizing methods/therapists, 42, 47
Self-consciousness, 82
Self-Defeating/Masochistic Personality
  Disorder, 80
Self-directedness, 86
Self-image therapies, 41–42
Self-injurious behavior (SIB), 347
Self-memory, 443–463
  aging and personality, 452–453
  description, 444–447
  development of movement through time,
    448–452
  dissociative abyss, 453–454
  driving force for survival, 445
  encapsulation of traumatic memories, 448
  gender role socialization, 459–461
  light and memory, 447
  moral aspects of, 455–457
  neurobiology of personality disorders,
    457–459
  reality testing, 445
  relationships and, 445
  sound and, 449–450
  time, space, and light, 459
  trauma and, 445–446, 448, 450–451, 460–461
Self-monitoring, 175
Self-other polarity, 8, 30, 79, 80, 88
Self-other restructuring, 545
Self psychology, 65, 516–517
Self-referencing skills, lack of, 321
Self-referral, older adults, 499
Self-regulation/dysregulation, 223, 477–479
Self-Transcendence, 86
Separation-individuation, 94
Sessions, spacing/length (unified model), 549
Setting, treatment, 4, 105, 503–504. *See also*
  Residential treatment
Seven-Factor Model (Cloninger), 85–87
Severe personality disorders, treatment models
  for, 69–70. *See also* Dialectical behavior
  therapy of severe personality disorders
Sexual abuse (DFST for depressed women with
  history of), 413–414
Short-term treatment (unified model), 549
"Should" statements, 170
Skills training, 226, 228, 229
Social factors in personality disorders, 137–139
Social Phobia, 12, 370
Social sensitivity, personality disorders and,
  136
Social structures in treatment of patients with
  personality disorders, 143–144, 547
Society for Exploration of Psychotherapy
  Integration (SEPI), 62
Society for Psychotherapy Researchers (SPR),
  62
Sociocultural factors, 18, 124, 135–144
  Antisocial Personality Disorder, 137–138
  Avoidant Personality Disorder, 138–139
  Borderline Personality Disorder, 138, 141–142
  clinical implications, 139–143

cultural differences and young adulthood, 136–137
Narcissistic Personality Disorder, 138, 142–143
personality disorders and social sensitivity, 136
social factors in personality disorders, 137–139
trait modification therapy, 141–143
treatment, and social structures, 143–144
Sociocultural-familial triangle (mesosystem), 538–539
Somatic preoccupation, older adults, 502
Somatoform disorders, 12, 429–430
Sound, and self-memory, 449–450
SSRIs (selective serotonin reuptake inhibitors), 336, 338–342, 349, 350, 351
Staff relations group, 362–363
State *vs.* trait (transient *vs.* chronic), 332
Strategic goals of therapy, 52
Structural Analysis of Social Behavior (SASB), 8, 152, 274, 275
Structural-drive theory, 65
Structural-dynamic classification of personality, 7–8
Substance abuse and personality disorders, 12, 399–402. *See also* Dual Focus Schema Therapy (DFST)
Suicidality, 110–112, 141, 238
Superego, 93, 94, 98, 285–287
Support groups, 143–144
Surface, analytic, 284–285
Symbolic-relational restructuring, 546–547
Symptom Checklist-90, 369
Synergistic integration/therapy (personality-guided context), 45–53
    domain tactics, 49
    modality selections, 51–52
    polarity goals, 46, 48–49
    potentiated pairings and catalytic sequences, 47–48
    system transactions, 49–51
Systematic eclecticism, 528
Systemic model, triadic configurations, 8
Systemics, personality, 19–20, 531
System theory, 14, 61

Team approach, 437–438, 502
Technical eclecticism, 28
Technical neutrality, 105–106
Telephone coaching (generalizing learning), 226–227
Temperament, 16, 69, 85–86, 92, 427
Temperament and Character Inventory (TCI), 86
Termination, 180–181, 266–267, 493–494
Theory, 56–74
    ability to generate relevant research, 73
    of change, 153
    clinical utility of, 72–73
    clinician as clinical theorist, 73
    contemporary theories of personality disorders and treatment, 65–73

child and adolescent models of treatment, 70–71
    cognitive-behavioral models, 66
    elderly, treatment models for, 71
    family models, 67
    integrative models, 67–68
    interpersonal models, 66
    minorities, treatment models for, 71–72
    personality disorder and severe psychiatric disturbance, 70
    psychobiological models, 66–67
    psychodynamic models, 65
    severe personality disorders, treatment models for, 69–70
    unified models, 68–69
    definition, 57
    of drives, 96
    evaluating (Rychlak's guidelines), 72
    formal study of personality theory as separate discipline, 60
    "good enough," 57
    history/trends (*see* Personology/ psychotherapeutic approaches, history/ trends/evolution)
    issue of competing theoretical models, 57–58
    from philosophy to theory, 28–35
    "poor," 57
    of psychopathology, 151–153
Therapeutic bargain, 487–489
Therapeutic community, 358, 383–385, 411–412
Therapists/analysts:
    alliance building, 178–180, 472–473
    empathy, 132, 159–160
    genuineness, 42
    motivating/enhancing skill, 227
    reactions (*see* Countertransference; Transference)
    superego function, 285–287
Therapy. *See* Psychotherapy
Therapy-interfering behaviors, 184, 238
Time-limited dynamic psychotherapy, 254–276
    acts of others toward the self, 262–263, 270
    acts of the self, 262, 269
    acts of the self toward the self (introject), 263, 270
    assumptions, five basic, 257–258
    clinical case example (sessions), 267–274
    cyclical maladaptive pattern (CMP), 261
    expectations of others' reactions, 262, 263
    formulation, 261–263
    goals, 258–260, 270
    how therapeutic challenges are conceptualized and managed, 274
    process of therapeutic approach, 261–267
    range of psychopathology and personality disorders within scope of treatment, 255–257
    research and empirical support, 274–276
    selection criteria for determining a patient's appropriateness for, 256
    strategies, 263–266
    termination, 266–267

Time-limited dynamic psychotherapy
    (*Continued*)
  treatment methods and technical aspects
      and interventions, 257–261
Time/space/light, 459
Training:
  advanced (unified model), 530
  parallel psychoanalytic, 107
Trait(s):
  domains (criteria for
      selection/development), 37
  vs. personality patterns, 36, 93
  spectrum, 334
  stability, 139–140
  vs. state (transient *vs.* chronic), 332
Trait modification therapy, 140–143
Trait psychology, emergence of (as dominant
    force in psychology), 60
Transactional analysis concepts:
  counterinjunctions, 199
  early decisions, 200
  ego states, 198
  escape hatches, 200–201
  games, 198–199
  injunctions, 199
  life positions, 200
  life scripts, 200
  rackets, 198
Transference, 104, 105, 107–110, 185, 484. *See
    also* Countertransference
Transference-focused management of affect
    storms, 112–117
Transference focused therapy (TFP), 70
Transitional space, 486–487
Trauma:
  large T *vs.* small t, 305
  personality disorders and, 17, 486
  PTSD, 127–129, 305, 323, 333, 373, 460–461
  self-memory and, 445–446, 448, 450–451,
      460–461
  theory:
    rediscovery of, 63
    unified model, 534
Triadic restructuring, 546–547
Triangle(s), 67, 435, 535–540
  of conflict, 435
  interpersonal-dyadic (two-person system),
      536–537

intrapsychic-biological (individual system),
    536
process depiction using, 535–539
relational-triadic configuration (three-person
    configurations), 537–538
sociocultural-familial (mesosystem),
    538–539
systemic model, triadic configurations, 8
True therapy, 44

Unified model, 63–64, 68–69, 528–550
  advantages/disadvantages, 529–530
  application of theory to dysfunction of the
      personality system, 539
  aspects of, 534
  avoiding "pathological" theoretical certainty,
      549
  empirical support and evidence of
      convergence, 550
  "genetic" code, reading, 539–540
  movement toward, inevitability of, 528
  restructuring:
    dyadic, 544–546
    intrapsychic, 540–544
    mesosystem, 547
    triadic, 546–547
  systemically based ecological model,
      531–534
  treatment, 540, 547–550
  triangles, using to depict process, 67, 435,
      535–540
Unified personology and psychotherapy (2000
    to present), 63–64
Unprincipled subtype, 80

Validation strategies, 232–233
VAST Project, 275
Vicious circles, 36
Victim/victimizer, 103

Wise mind, 233–234
Women (gender role socialization), 459–461

Zen, 224–225